TradeStation™ Made Easy!

Founded in 1807, John Wiley & Sons is the oldest independent publishing company in the United States. With offices in North America, Europe, Australia and Asia, Wiley is globally committed to developing and marketing print and electronic products and services for our customers' professional and personal knowledge and understanding.

The Wiley Trading series features books by traders who have survived the market's ever changing temperament and have prospered—some by reinventing systems, others by getting back to basics. Whether a novice trader, professional or somewhere in-between, these books will provide the advice and strategies needed to prosper today and well into the future.

For a list of available titles, visit our Web site at www.WileyFinance.com.

TradeStation™ Made Easy!

Using EasyLanguage™ to Build Profits with the World's Most Popular Trading Software

SUNNY J. HARRIS

WILEY

John Wiley & Sons, Inc.

Published by John Wiley & Sons, Inc., Hoboken, New Jersey.
Published simultaneously in Canada.

For general information on our other products and services or for technical support, please contact our Customer Care Department within the United States at (800) 762-2974, outside the United States at (317) 572-3993 or fax (317) 572-4002.

Wiley also publishes its books in a variety of electronic formats. Some content that appears in print may not be available in electronic books. For more information about Wiley products, visit our web site at www.wiley.com.

ISBN 978-0-471-35353-9; ISBN 978-1-118-06315-6 (ebk);
ISBN 978-1-118-06316-3 (ebk); ISBN 978-1-118-06317-0 (ebk)

Printed in the United States of America

10 9 8 7 6 5 4 3 2 1

I've been working on this book since 1996; that's 12 years now. Wow! When I first began, my daughter was pregnant with my second grandson, whose name is Sterling Kodiak Yates, now 10. This book is dedicated to Sterling and to my back-ordered grandchildren (hopefully from my son's new wife, Laurel).

The human mind, once stretched to include a single new idea, does not shrink back to its original proportions.

—Oliver Wendell Holmes

Until one is committed, there is hesitancy.

—W. H. Murray

We must never assume that which is incapable of proof.

—G. H. Lewes

Be sure of it; give me the ocular proof.

—Shakespeare

Contents

Foreword

One of the early users of TradeStation software, Sunny Harris has been studying and programming trading strategies for more than 30 years.

I have watched her progress as a researcher and trader over the years, from the time we were still offering the DOS version of SystemWriter and TradeStation was a fledgling company.

Sunny is one of the most studious and diligent people I know and gives generously in teaching others what she has learned through the school of hard knocks. Having a software background herself, and writing books that focus on helping beginners (*Trading 101—How to Trade Like a Pro*, *Trading 102—Getting Down to Business*, *Electronic Day Trading 101*, and *Getting Started in Trading*) have inevitably led to the writing of this book.

Successful traders have one thing in common: they approach trading by developing an objective strategy and then use it consistently.

TradeStation allows traders to design their own trading strategies, back-test them on years of historical data, and then computer-automate them. The power of EasyLanguage is what makes all of this possible. Therefore, by mastering EasyLanguage, you have the power to test any idea you can imagine.

Through the many examples, Sunny Harris walks you through in this book, you'll have a much better understanding of how to use EasyLanguage to create your own strategies. This book also provides you with an invaluable guide for trading strategy development that will contribute greatly to the understanding and improvement of your EasyLanguage skills.

Sunny's unique ability to blend her highly theoretical math degrees with her artistic and graphics talents makes her understanding of markets both logical and intuitive. She has been a friend of TradeStation for many years, always lending insight and advice, and as one of our beta testers she has helped create the best possible market analysis software there is today: TradeStation.

Analyzing the markets can be daunting—a task taken on by many but mastered by few. As an aid to all analysts, our software has to be ready manage incredibly difficult tasks and the most pedantic at the same time. Sunny's 20-plus years of self-taught market analysis combined with her 10 years of experience teaching others to trade has led her to write the most readable and invaluable of books about EasyLanguage.

Through the many examples in this book, you'll have a much better understanding of how to use EasyLanguage to create your own strategies. This book also provides you with an invaluable guide for trading strategy development that will contribute greatly to the understanding and improvement of your EasyLanguage skills.

The time you invest in mastering EasyLanguage will be the best investment of your trading life.

If you are a TradeStation or ProSuite user, this book is a must. If you are serious about learning to trade, read Sunny's books—the truth lies within.

I wish you a very successful trading career.

Bill Cruz
Founder and former CEO of TradeStation

Preface

This book is one of a kind. It is perhaps the only book written by a self-taught EasyLanguage speaker (programmer) who learned and helped improve EasyLanguage before there was even a TradeStation, and who is an actual trader.

I was trading beginning in 1981, when just about the only good graphics analysis package was called MasterChartist, by Roberts-Slade. The problem was, there was no testing language with which to evaluate and back-test your trading ideas. Back then we were running DOS only; or, there was no Windows yet. Testing your strategies amounted to using a rudimentary version of Excel and pencil and paper. It was tedious at best.

Along came a program by Omega Research, called SystemWriter Plus. It was a god send! At last I could rough out my ideas and test them against mounds of historical data. However, as with everything, there was a serious drawback. It only worked on daily data, not on intraday data. I was able to receive intraday data on MasterChartist but not to test it. I could draw (with a pencil) on the charts but not strategize buy and sell opportunities. With SystemWriter Plus I could print out mounds of data analysis, but the charts were rudimentary, coming out of a dot matrix printer, and only on daily data. What to do?

As necessity is the mother of invention, I decided to divide my real-time data from MasterChartist into 15-minute increments and treat it as if it were daily data over a very long period of time. I imported the fake daily data into SystemWriter. It took me 18 months to massage the data and convert it into years and years worth of 15-minute increments. (There was no CompuTrac yet either.) In order to make sense of a chart, it is necessary to demarcate dates and times along the x-axis. This took some ingenuity, and some "gerfinger-pointing." I created a ruler with tiny marks along each day to designate 15-minute increments and ignored the Monday, Tuesday, Wednesday markings on the chart itself. To find a time during any particular day, I had to measure and mark divisions with my specially marked ruler.

It worked. I was able to test intraday trading concepts and determine success or failure statistically, even without software that operated on an intraday basis. Finally, Microsoft invented Windows, and the software vendors followed suit with more and more sophisticated programs, soon allowing not only 15-minute increment data but any minute divisions and even tick-by-tick charts.

The most important component of this new and powerful tool was in running walk-back and walk-forward tests. Did my theory of making profits hold up last week, last month, and last year? It quickly became obvious that I could spot a theory that would work for the past three Fridays; but when I tried it in real time, I lost money for the next three Fridays. Why did that happen?

For several years I plugged away with spreadsheet, pencil, and lots of erasers at hand, keeping copious notes of the ideas that I tried against market data to see if there was any hope of creating a mechanical system that worked.

What did "worked" mean? That in itself is a whole 'nother problem. I realized I had two large problems: finding a system that worked and finding a set of statistics that measured success. It took me the better part of three years devoting 18 hours a day to the task to come up with a meaningful system and statistics that measured its success.

In this book I share with the reader not only what I learned through three solid and dedicated years of 18-hour research days, but what I have learned subsequently through real-time trading. I wish you the best in your efforts. But I would admonish you to read this book over and again and to spend the time doing your own research following the pattern set out herein.

And now it's 2010—and according to author Thomas Friedman, the world is flat. We are living in a flat world devoid of boundaries of language, communications, or even time constraints. We can talk with anyone, anytime, anywhere with the help of email, Skype, GoogleTalk, and tiny onboard cameras. Our computers and software are purchased over the Internet, constructed of tiny parts made in China and Taiwan, and our customer support folks are in India. When the market crashed in September 2008, it was China that bought 49% of our debt from many of our banks. No more walls. Even our cell phones are now computers that link us with the whole world: I can take your picture and send it with text to anyone, anywhere. I can make a PowerPoint presentation, put it in pdf format, and make my product demonstration to you from my cell phone or my PDA. It's endless and magnificent.

Without EasyLanguage, where would we all be? Someone had to do it. And, as luck, good fortune, and the wisdom to see and act on the opportunity would have it, the Cruz brothers and their sister (Ralph, Bill and Michelle) were the team to pick up the gauntlet and run with it. And now we trade 24-hour markets, all over the world, in a flash, with the push of a button on a TradeStation screen. The data is next to free, the software is included in the price of your having an account at TradeStation Securities, and the commissions are ridiculously low.

It's a M-U-R-I-C-A-L. (Miracle.)

TradeStation almost doesn't need a manual. It is so easy to use and so intuitive that it almost seems silly to write this book. But there is more to it than just a users' manual. Besides getting the software up and running on your computer, you need the benefit of my years and years of experience making every mistake "in the book." There is no need for you to repeat my errors, nor for you to hunt and peck your way to success. In this book I hope to lead you through the process of installing the program, using it for the first time or two, and writing your first several indicators and strategies. If you tried it on your own, from the TradeStation Users' Manual, you would probably give up before you even got to the point of trading. By design, all users' manuals are full of technical descriptions of all the program's bells and whistles from A to Z. In that order. There's no rhyme or reason to what the user needs to do first, second, and third: it's just an alphabetical reference to everything in the program.

Instead of a reference manual, however, with this tome I am writing a cookbook. Step 1, do this; step 2, do that. It is a simplistic approach, but one that will get you on the road to doing it yourself much quicker and with much more confidence. Then you can go back to the reference materials with some understanding of what to look for.

One more thing before I get on with it. I have been using TradeStation since before it was called TradeStation. I have seen the versions go from 1, to 2, all the way to 8.8 and now 9.0, which is the version I am currently using. In many ways all the versions are alike, and in many ways they differ vastly. When I first started writing this book, I thought I would give instructions for the most recent three versions of TS and compare and contrast the differences. As the years went on and the book progressed, the versions kept coming and coming and coming—faster than I could write. And that is still true. As I am putting the finishing touches on the manuscript, yet another version of TS has been released, which differs in many respects from the prior version. Never fear! This book applies to them all.

One of the biggest differences between TradeStation 2000i and TradeStation 4.0 is in the way they engage systems. TradeStation 2000i made enhancements for testing a variety of entries and exits without getting back into EasyLanguage and modifying your code. This can be a great advantage, unless you are entrenched in the methods of 4.0 and are reluctant to change. On first inspection, it would seem that TradeStation has added two steps to every attempt to employ a system, and initially that is irritating. But once you realize the tremendous advantages to mixing and matching entry and exit signals, you'll get used to it and be thankful.

After version 2000i, the company again integrated EasyLanguage with the main program. With versions 8.8 and 9.0 it has once again separated the EasyLanguage Editor from the main program and made it stand-alone. In spite of all these changes, this book will apply universally to all versions before and hereafter. Don't worry if you are reading this book years after it was first released. The concepts are applicable to whatever version of TradeStation you are using.

With version 9.0 TradeStation's EasyLanguage is a complete programming language, much like VB or C++. It has tremendous strides in extensibility for programmers. We are not going to address any of that in this easy book. that will be left for the advanced book.

Acknowledgments

Thanks to Pamela van Giessen for originally telling me I could write, and encouraging me to write my first book, *Trading 101—How to Trade Like a Pro*. I really thought that I had nothing to say.

And thanks to Bill Cruz, co-founder of TradeStation, who helped me along the way with learning EasyLanguage.

Because of all he has contributed to this industry, and to my personal learning, a great big thanks goes out to Larry Williams, who really trades for a living.

My 88-year-old, nearly blind, mother proofread this manuscript with her magnifying glass, all 733 pages of it. I'm eternally grateful for her help and her inspiration. My children and grandchildren have been patient and understanding as I sat behind my laptop while they watched TV and movies, played games, and built Lego monuments. I've been halfway participating for years during the growth of this tome. I thank them for their creativity and their love.

And most of all, I thank my partner of 21 years for her continued support and understanding and encouragement during thick and thin. She's an exceptional partner and a magnificent physician.

To those who are reading this book, I thank you also. You will grow by immeasurable bounds as you read and learn. Keep up the good work. And tell your friends.

Author's Note

Please understand that this book is intended to be educational in nature. I am not recommending that you trade, nor am I giving trading advice. Further, I am not suggesting that any of the methods presented in this book will generate a profit or will not generate losses.

Sunny J. Harris, Sunny Harris & Associates, Inc. and Sunny Harris Enterprises, Inc. accept no liability whatsoever for any loss arising from any use of this information.

This information is in no way a representation to buy or sell securities, bonds, options, or futures. Always check with your licensed financial planner or broker before buying or selling on any advice whether contained herein or elsewhere.

It should not be assumed that the methods, techniques, or indicators presented in this book will be profitable or that they will not result in losses. Past results are not necessarily indicative of future results. Examples in this book are for educational purposes only. This is not a solicitation of any offer to buy or sell.

Trading and investing are speculative and include risk of loss. Past performance is no indication of future results.

Hypothetical or simulated performance results have certain inherent limitations. Unlike an actual performance record, simulated results do not represent actual trading. Also, since the trades may not have been executed, the results may have under- or overcompensated for the impact, if any, of certain market factors, such as lack of liquidity. Simulated trading programs in general are also subject to the fact that they are designed with the benefit of hindsight. No representation is being made that any account will or is likely to achieve profits or losses similar to those shown.

Any statements of facts herein contained are derived from sources believed to be reliable but are not guaranteed as to accuracy, nor do they purport to be complete. No responsibility is assumed with respect to any such statement, nor with respect to any expression of opinion herein contained. All trade recommendations should be discussed with your broker and made at your own risk.

CHAPTER 1

Introduction to EasyLanguage

INTRODUCTION

EasyLanguage is TradeStation's proprietary command language that lets you specify your trading ideas in plain English and test them before you trade. EasyLanguage allows you to write your own trading systems for TradeStation, OptionStation, and ProSuite without having to know complicated computer programming languages.

EasyLanguage is one of the most powerful and useful features of TradeStation and with some practice, you can become an expert, even if your background in computers is limited.

That said (it's from the splash screen introduction to TradeStation software), all software comes with stumbling blocks. I have yet to open a software box and install and use the product with no problems along the way. Furthermore, TradeStation's EasyLanguage is more than just software; it's a programming language. And with the advent of the new Object-Oriented EasyLanguage with TradeStation version 9.0, it is more like C++ than any easy language. Albeit the easiest to use of the complex trading tools, it is still so full of features that it can't help but be difficult in spots. As I work with EasyLanguage I hum the old song by The Essex from 1963: "Easier Said Than Done."

The working title for the ideas presented in this book was "EasyLanguage Ain't." Neither Bill Cruz, prior co-CEO of TradeStation, nor my editor, Pamela van Giessen, liked that title. Nevertheless, the viewing public seemed to appreciate the reality of the working title. Each time I mentioned the project in a lecture I got nods of recognition from non-programming TradeStation, SuperCharts, and OptionStation users.

"EasyLanguage Ain't" was never meant to be disparaging to TradeStation, but rather a reflection of the simple truth that programming a computer, no matter how friendly the programming language, is never easy. Becoming a good coder takes study, sometimes years of study. It is the intent of this book to walk the reader through that learning process in small and simple steps that will make the process comfortable. I have recently noticed the tendency of some of my competitors to use the paraphrase "EasyLanguage Isn't," and I herewith forgive them their lack of imagination.

Computer manuals aren't meant to be read cover to cover. The TradeStation Users' Manual is no exception. *TradeStation Made Easy*! however, is intended to be read from cover to cover, with pauses along the way to try the examples. Hopefully it will be an informative and enjoyable experience for you. After reading this book, you will be more prepared to go back and use the TradeStation manuals with ease and as reference.

In *Trading 101—How to Trade Like a Pro*, I wanted to introduce the basic concepts of trading to the general public. In *Trading 102—Getting Down to Business* my hope was to introduce the concepts of system design and testing. *TradeStation Made Easy*! is intended as a procedural guide to getting comfortable with programming TradeStation's EasyLanguage.

At the same time I am writing this book I am also researching one more: *Grading the Gurus*. You will probably be interested in *Gurus* as well, since it is all about using TradeStation (and other popular software) to test the theories, strategies and technical analysis of some of the famous systems designers. The intent of the *Gurus* book is to discover both the advantages and downfalls of following other people's systems. After that I want to write a book exploring all the commonly available systems and strategies from nongurus, strategies you find published in books, their benefits and pitfalls, and maybe call it "Breaking the Rules."

We, the trading public, owe a debt of gratitude to Bill and Ralph Cruz and their crew, whose dedication to an initially narrow market has expanded that market and created tools we can all use to profitable ends. Thanks, guys; you have a great product.

During late January of 1999 I took a little trip to the Bahamas and then to Miami, where I had the pleasure of spending several days with TradeStation personnel. The purpose of my visit was to get an advance look at the impending, latest release of TradeStation, called 2000i, as part of the research for this book. For their generosity, hospitality, and help I would like to thank Loren Costantino, Gaston Sanchez, Kevin Feuerlicht, Amy Solt, Janette Perez, Bill and Ralph Cruz and the rest of the TradeStation staff. You're the greatest!

WHAT THIS BOOK IS NOT

TradeStation Made Easy is not meant as a replacement for the TradeStation manuals. This programming guide is not meant to help you learn the mechanics of setting up TradeStation or your computer, or to help you with the trials and tribulations of getting data into your computer.

This book is also not meant to teach you systems, or to give you systems that are necessarily profitable, though we may discover some along the way. We will cover the essence of programming in EasyLanguage and stick with a consistent set of data and a consistent elementary system throughout. We will not fill the book with a variety of working systems with which you can experiment; there are other books for that.

In particular, if you are looking for fancy EasyLanguage programming ideas I would suggest these sources:

- **Cynthia Kase**
  Kase and Company, Inc.
  PO Box 226 Cheyenne, WY 82003
  (505) 237-1600
  www.kaseco.com

- **Joe Krutsinger**
  PO Box 4223
  Kansas City, KS 66104
  (800) 927-1035
  www.joekrut.com

- ***Using Easy Language* by Arthur G. Putt**
  available from Ruggiero Press

- Murray Ruggiero
  Ruggiero Press
  18 Oregon Ave., East Haven, CT 06512
  1-203-564-1956

- ***TS Express* by Bill Brower**
  Inside Edge Systems, Inc.
  10 Fresenius Rd., Westport, CT 06880
  1-203-454-2754

- ***Ask Mr. EasyLanguage* by Sam Tennis**
  129 Staff Drive, NE
  Fort Walton Beach, FL 32548
  1-850-243-5105
  http://www.vista-research.com

WHAT THIS BOOK IS

This book is a guide to understanding the basics and beginning to use EasyLanguage. I offer this service because it fills a gap—no one else has dedicated their writings to the beginners. The more advanced tasks to becoming a TradeStation expert are between you and TradeStation, and perhaps a consultant to help you along the way. Bill Brower is an excellent resource for advanced techniques, but his efforts at teaching beginners are still too advanced for most novices.

By the end of this book you will be able to write simple and intermediate programs using EasyLanguage. Hopefully your programs will accurately reflect the theories you have, discover, or read about the markets.

By the end of this book you will have the confidence to open TradeStation's PowerEditor to a blank page and begin writing.

As I began this book, I put in examples for all the existing versions of TradeStation at that time. Now, many years later, I'm pruning it all down to the current version only. All references to ProSuite, 2000i, and earlier versions of TradeStation are being removed. If you need help with a previous version of TradeStation, give me a call and we'll talk about it.

A CHART IS A CHART IS A CHART

This book is not about learning to trade; it is about learning to program. Nevertheless, throughout the book we will be reviewing and using trading concepts as examples while learning to program. In learning programming concepts, it really does not matter what our underlying data is. What we will cover in this book is how to express your theories and ideas about whatever market interests you, independent of any particular market.

A chart, is a chart, is a chart. They all go up, or down, or sideways, or all three. If you were not told what instrument (stock, bond, mutual fund, commodity) was used to produce the chart in Figure 1.1, you would not be able to guess it. No, it is not the Dow. I have not given you a reference axis for time frame (X-axis), nor is there a reference axis for price (Y-axis). In spite of that absence of information, you could tell me some things about the chart. You could tell me that the second half of the chart is less volatile than the first half. You could tell me that in the beginning, price moves downward. You could tell me that after the beginning downward move, there is a period of nearly upward movement followed by downward movement. You could not tell me that in general the bias is to the upside. You could also tell me there is a mild correction (downward movement) in the last third of the chart.

(In fact, I will give a crisp new $20 bill to the first person who calls me and correctly identifies the chart in Figure 1.1.)

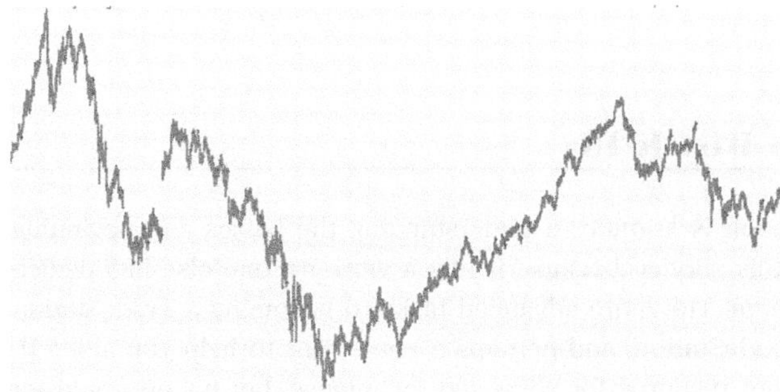

FIGURE 1.1 An Anonymous Chart

This sort of analysis is what I call "What is?" or "What is true?" I begin every investigation by repeatedly asking myself "What is true of the chart at which I am looking?" It's the "what is" that leads to rich brainstorming sessions and possibilities for analysis.

What you could not tell me is whether this is a chart of a commodity, stock, or mutual fund. You could not tell me if it is a chart of 1-minute, 5-minute, 60-minute, or daily data. And you could not tell me whether this price action happened in 1927, 1987, or 2010.

In fact, this is an example of what they mean when they say the markets are fractal. Each subset, or smaller time frame, looks like any other time frame. They all go up, they all go down, and they all go sideways. It's just another way of saying "a chart is a chart is a chart."

For the purpose of this book, the particulars of the chart do not matter; what matters is that the chart has movement and that we can describe it in programming language.

The best way I know to make this book easy to use and comprehend is to build on a simple concept from beginning to end. To this end, I will introduce a single set of data that we will use throughout. That data is available for you on my Web site: www.moneymentor.com/TSME.html. If you'd like to receive a CD of the data, just contact my office in California at 1-760-444-4174 Skype or my cell at 1-760-908-3070. I ask only that you observe Pacific Standard Time.

We will use the same chart and the same data throughout this book. We will take different perspectives, sometimes viewing daily data, sometimes weekly, sometimes intraday, but it will all be of the same vehicle. I have always wondered why authors choose a different chart to illustrate every new concept. I've wondered whether the concepts are only applicable to certain subsets of charts. As I tackle this book, I guess I am about to find out.

I will also start early in this book with a simple program to analyze the data and build on that program as we progress. That way you will be learning about the structure of EasyLanguage, not struggling with a new program every few pages. You will become intimately familiar with one set of data and one small program. We will analyze this single set of data at increasing depth, and will alter and enhance our initial program until it becomes sophisticated.

After you finish this book you can easily branch off and apply your new language to very complex concepts. You will be able to understand many of the sophisticated techniques presented in *Omega* magazine, TradeStation's manuals, *Technical Analysis of Stocks & Commodities* magazine, *Futures* magazine, *Traders' Catalog & Resource Guide*, and the various other sources and books mentioned herein.

FONTS, SYMBOLS, AND CONVENTIONS

I've used a few symbols in the book and some typefaces to separate code from text. All programming code herein is designated by using the typeface `OCRA`. All computer commands are shown in the typeface **Helvetica.** An arrow (→) means to pull down the menu and choose the next command. A mouse symbol (🖱) means to use the mouse to pull down or click to the command. Everything else is pretty much self-explanatory.

CHAPTER 2

Quick Start

In This Chapter

- Introduction
- Pseudo-Steps
- Detailed Steps
- Conclusion

INTRODUCTION

You just spent a small fortune on trading software, data, and computers and you can't even use it. Or you opened a hefty trading account with TradeStation just so you could use the software. You probably thought that getting TradeStation was the solution to all your trading problems, not the beginning of them. You just want to trade, not to become a programmer. Right? And now, with the new version, 9, it has been extended into a full-fledged programming language.

The first step I like to take with students is to show them how easy TradeStation really is to use. Because of the vast capabilities of the software, it can appear that the learning curve is insurmountably steep. Broken down into the elementary steps, however, you will find that using TradeStation is actually quite simple and straightforward. TradeStation really is the toolbox that lets you solve all your trading problems.

Just to show you how easy it can be, this Quick Start chapter will guide you through the steps of writing your first system, the associated indicator, and checking your profit or loss. I will not offer detailed explanation of the steps in this chapter. I just want you to have a template for success. Later, throughout the book, we will go over the details.

It's easy to get a computer to do something. It is not always easy to get it to do what you **want it to.** Computers will do exactly what you tell them, no more, no less. The challenge is always in putting your thoughts into clear, logical steps that mean the same thing to the computer that they mean to you.

PSEUDO-STEPS

I like to use "pseudo-code" to sketch a map for myself. Writing the pseudo-code is essentially defining your goal and making an outline. Whenever I begin a new project, no matter how large or how small, I like to have a goal and an outline of how to get there. (This especially goes for driving, since I can get lost going home from work. In fact, I have GPS and printed driving instructions from MapQuest.com when I'm going somewhere, just in case.) **Without a clearly defined goal and milestones, you won't get there!**

The pseudo-code for the process covered in this book might look something like:

1. Open TradeStation.
2. Open chart with data.
3. Open EasyLanguage PowerEditor.
4. Write indicator.
5. Put indicator on chart.
6. Write system.
7. Apply system to chart.
8. View system results.
9. If system results exceed CPC™ Index, then prepare to trade, else loop back to step 6 and continue homework.

We will go through those steps now, one at a time.

DETAILED STEPS

Step 1: Open TradeStation

Opening TradeStation is as easy as 1, 2, 3, 4, 5.

1. First, double-click the **TradeStation** icon (TradeStation 9.0) on your PC's desktop (assuming you have already installed TradeStation from CD or download). This icon will vary slightly depending on the version you are using.

2. Then fill in your name and password in the pop-up box shown in Figure 2.1.

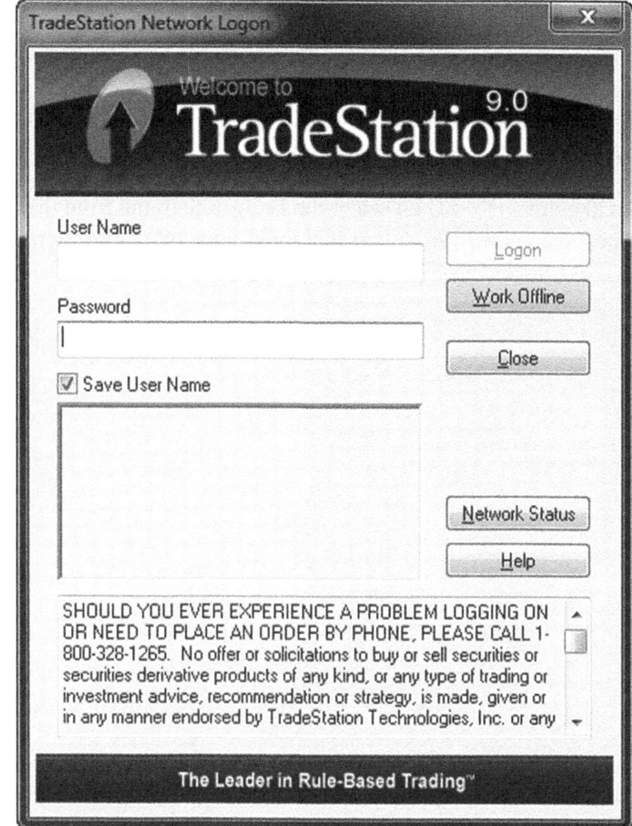

FIGURE 2.1 Login Screen

3. Now click the **Logon** button, or **Live Trading** button, or **Simulated Trading** button, to accept and open either a blank workspace, or the workspace(s) previously opened.
4. If no workspace is open, simply use the sequence **File** → **New** → **Workspace,** and create a new workspace.

Step 2: Open Chart with Data

5. Now that you have an empty workspace, you need a chart showing data. So, click on the **Chart Analysis** icon in the Vertical Toolbar on the left of your screen. It should look like 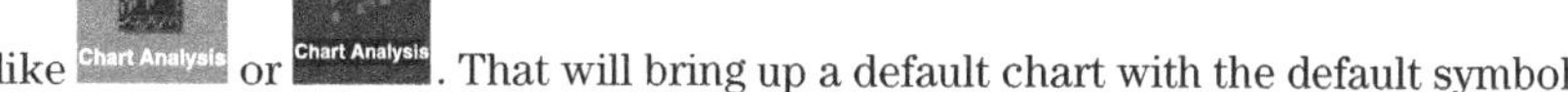 or . That will bring up a default chart with the default symbol.

That's it. You're off to the races.

Now, to stay consistent with the data in this book, let's display the symbol DIS (Disney). If you want to use the same time frame as I'm using, simply go to www.moneymentor.com/TSME/DIS.txt and download the data. From there you can import the data into TradeStation. Or, if you want to use current data, simply type the letters DIS and TradeStation will display the data it has for Disney.

By default, my version of TradeStation brings up a 5-minute chart. I want to display daily data, so I simply click on the little clock in the horizontal toolbar near the top of the screen. It looks like this: . Then select the Daily time frame from the pull-down menu.

You should now have a chart that looks something like the one in Figure 2.2.

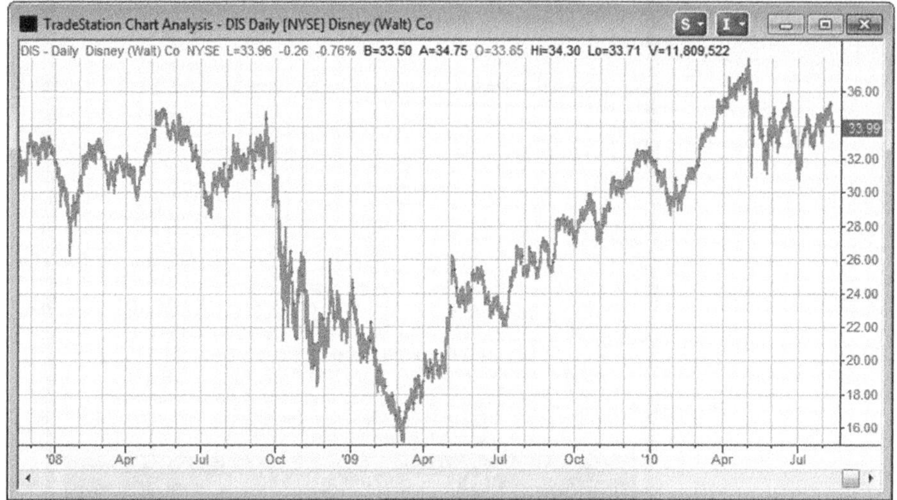

FIGURE 2.2 Your First Chart

Wasn't that easy?

If your chart shows up black, with white bars, don't worry. I'll teach you how to make it look more like mine later on.

Step 3: Crank Up the PowerEditor (Open EasyLanguage)

All we need to do now is put these pseudo-programming steps into the computer (TradeStation and EasyLanguage) code. To do this, we simply open the EasyLanguage PowerEditor and go to it. Right?

Well, not exactly. When you open a TradeStation chart, you are at a fork in the road. When you go to the EasyLanguage PowerEditor, you are at another fork in the road. You must make a choice. In the words of the famous Yogi Berra, "When you come to a fork in the road, take it." Let's look at all the forks.

If you are not already looking at the EasyLanguage PowerEditor, simply look again at the Vertical Toolbar on the left, and click on the EasyLanguage icon. It looks like this: . Or, in version 9, like this: . This will bring up a menu of choices: either **Open EasyLanguage Document,** or **New EasyLanguage Document.** The **"New..."** selection has more choices. As you can see if you hover over the selection, it will bring up lots more choices, shown in Figure 2.3.

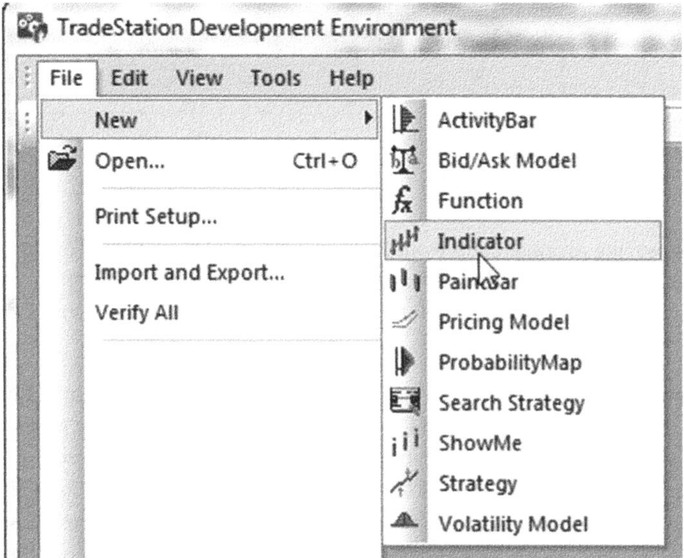

FIGURE 2.3 Menu Sequence to Start a New Indicator

For now, choose the sequence **New EasyLanguage Document → Indicator.** This will open a new blank window for you, upon which you can begin to type EasyLanguage Reserved Words, functions, variables, and general code. But before you can actually get to the blank window, you must give it a name and choose which programs it will be available to, and choose a template (or none) for the code it lays down.

It is sufficient to give it just a simple name and click **OK.** You'll get something to begin working with.

A note about naming conventions: There are already names of indicators from A to Z in TradeStation. And, over time, you will download files from TradeStation.com and from vendors. How are you going to find your documents if you name them similarly? To make finding my files easy, I always start my EasyLanguage documents (indicators, functions, strategies, etc.) by prefacing them with my initials and an underscore. For instance,

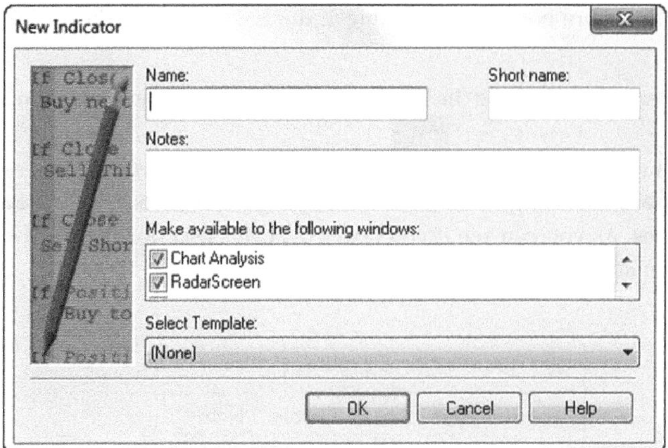

FIGURE 2.4 Naming Your Indicator

my moving average code would be named "sjh_MovingAvg." That way, all of my code ends up at the same place, and is easily identifiable. (See Figure 2.4.)

Next, we'll see how to put some code in this blank window.

Routine Types Before writing our first code sample, you must know the different types of routines available within EasyLanguage. There are several types of routines to choose from (and from time to time they add more), and they each serve a different purpose. In this book we will address only Functions, Indicators, PaintBars, ShowMes, and Signals. There are more routine flavors in EasyLanguage (EZL), but those are best left to the advanced EZL books.

Each of these routine types has its own set of requirements, as to inputs and outputs. And, each type of routine serves a unique purpose in TradeStation.

Let's briefly look at two routine types, to give you an idea of what they are and how they are distinguishable. The additional routine types will be covered more in depth in Chapter 4, Basic Use of TradeStation.

Indicator

An indicator plots data on a chart. For the moment, let's go back to the Chart Window. If you don't already have a chart window open, with DIS daily data on it, then open a chart in your TradeStation window, and put some data on it. Without data, you can't have a chart, and without a chart, you can't have an indicator.

Your chart still looks like Figure 2.5, from Figure 2.2 above.

Now click on the **Insert** menu item and pull down to **Indicator.** Click (or use the **ALT+C** control sequence). For this exercise, choose the "Mov Avg 1 line" indicator supplied with the software (as seen in Figure 2.6), and click **OK.** (See Figure 2.6.)

FIGURE 2.5 Your First Chart

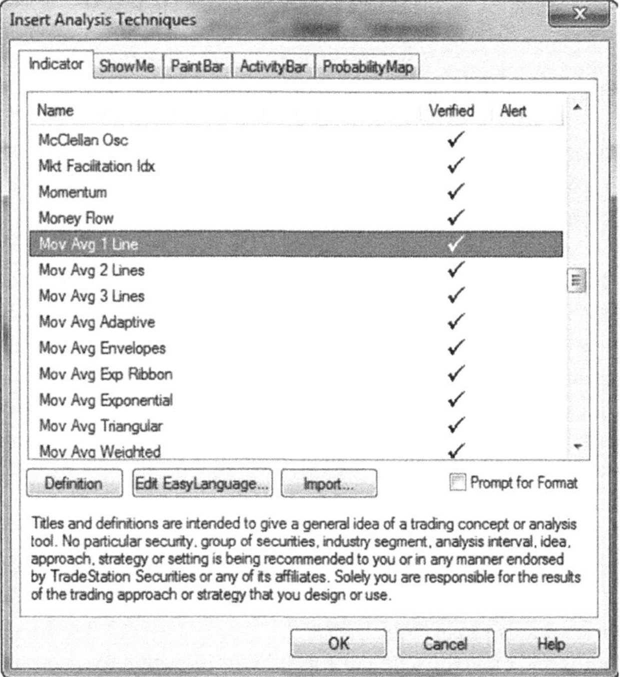

FIGURE 2.6 Pull-down Menu

Accept the default input parameters by clicking **OK** (Price = Close and Length = 9), so we can get right to the issue at hand—plotting something on a chart. My chart now looks like Figure 2.7 with the data and a smooth (thin) cyan line that sort of follows the data. **That cyan line is a plot.** Of course, in this book the cyan line is gray.

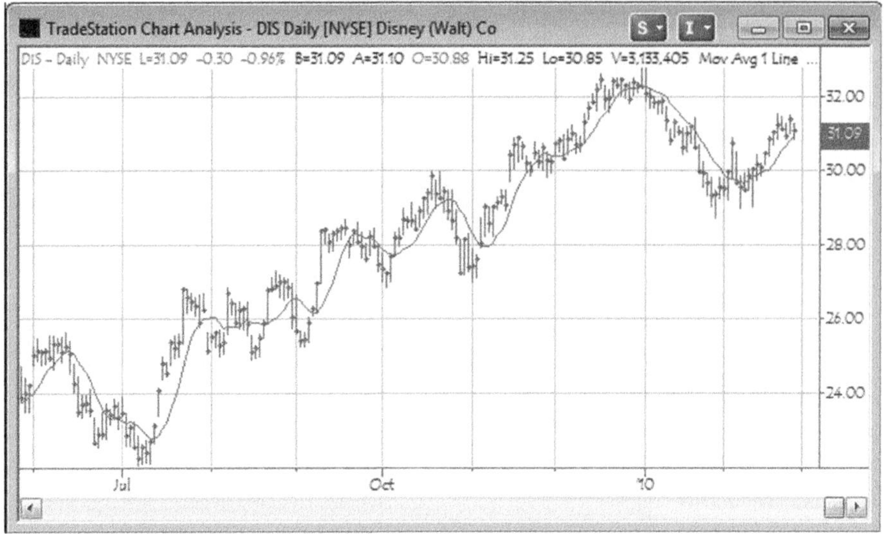

FIGURE 2.7 Chart with a Moving Average Plot

The moving average line on this chart is very difficult to see. By default, it is a thin, solid line and is a light color. We can change all of that. But, for now we are going to keep moving forward; later we'll enhance the look of the display.

Plot 1 . . . In olden times TradeStation allowed only four plots on one window. Nowadays you may have as many as 99 plots in any one indicator. You may base the plot on any of the four elements of price (open, high, low, or close), and you may calculate just about anything you can imagine to be plotted. As your coding gets more sophisticated, you can manipulate the plot by varying colors, line thickness, and other style aspects of the plot.

What about volume? That's not considered part of the data of a bar. It is an indicator, plotted by inserting an indicator called Volume.

The Plot Reserved Word has the format:

```
PlotN(Expression[,"<PlotName>"[,ForeColor[,Default[,Width]]]]);
```

- where `N` may range from 1–99
- `Expression` is the value or formula for the value to be plotted
- `PlotName` in quotes gives the plot a textual name with which you can identify it later

and the rest of the values are optional and will be discussed later.

One thing to keep in mind: While the software is versatile enough to allow 99 plots on one chart, you can't realistically distinguish more than about 7, so don't overdo putting plots on one chart.

Now let's make some changes to our simple indicator.

Step 4: Write an Indicator

Previously you looked briefly at the EasyLanguage PowerEditor. You were confronted with a blank window and not a clue as what to do.

Let's go back to that step and open the code for the simple moving average we placed on the chart in Figure 2.7. Here are the quick steps:

1. Click on the **EasyLanguage icon** and pull-down to **Open EasyLanguage Document,** from the vertical menu bar on the left of your screen.
2. Select **Indicator** from the Select Analysis Type selection box, as shown in Figure 2.8.

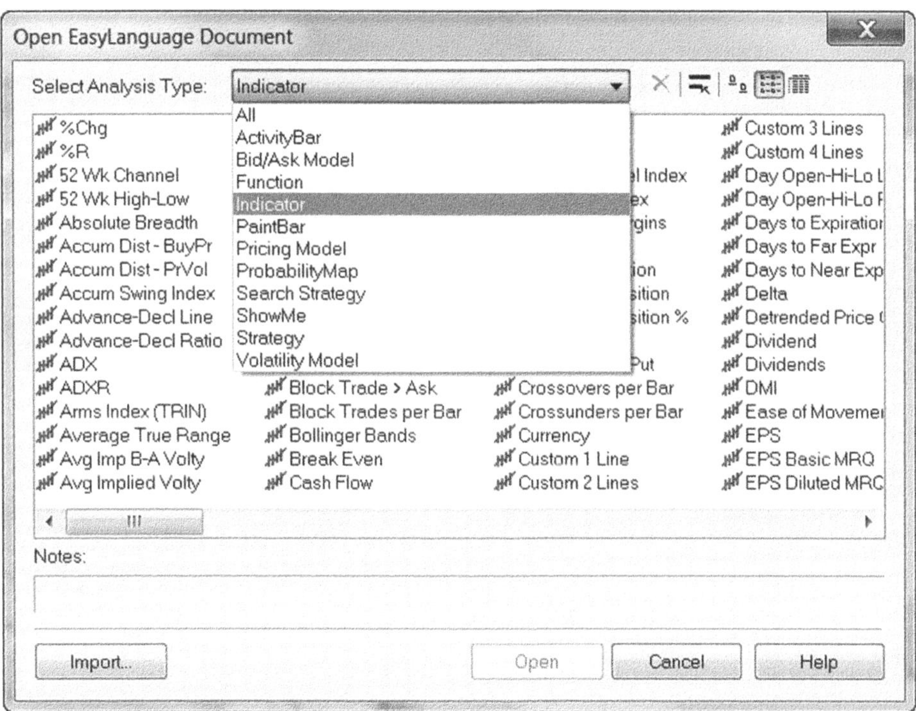

FIGURE 2.8 Open EZL Indicator

3. Scroll over and select the **Mov Avg 1 Line** indicator (see Figure 2.9) from the list of indicator names, and click **Open.**

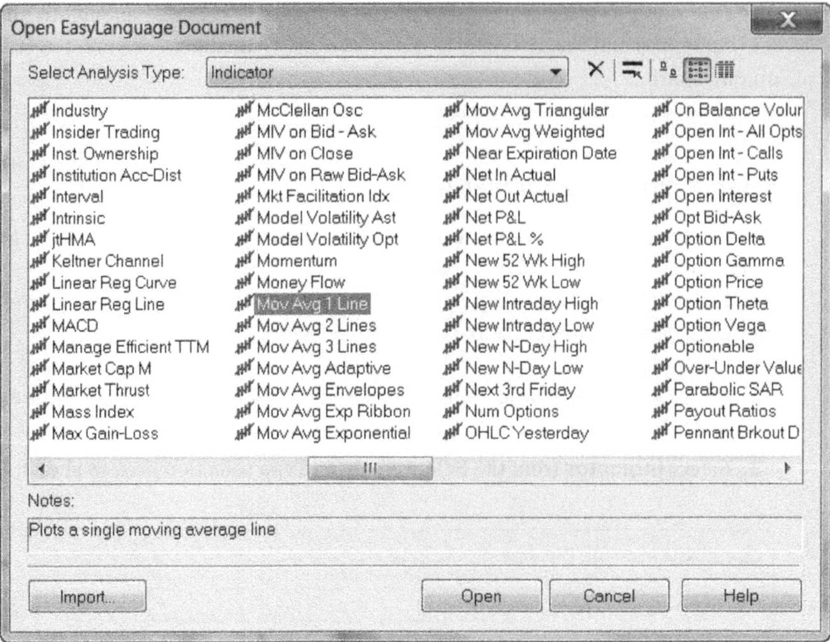

FIGURE 2.9 Select Mov Avg 1 Line

4. TradeStation will open a new window with EasyLanguage code in it. The code, which is as yet undecipherable to you, looks like that in Figure 2.10.

TradeStation Indicator - Mov Avg 1 Line

```
inputs:  Price( Close ), Length( 9 ), Displace( 0 ) ;
variables:  Avg( 0 ) ;

Avg = AverageFC( Price, Length ) ;

if Displace >= 0 or CurrentBar > AbsValue( Displace ) then
    begin
    Plot1[Displace]( Avg, "Avg" ) ;

    { Alert criteria }
    if Displace <= 0 then
        begin
        if Price crosses over Avg then
            Alert( "Price crossing over average" )
        else if Price crosses under Avg then
            Alert( "Price crossing under average" ) ;
        end ;
    end ;

{ ** Copyright (c) 2001 - 2009 TradeStation Technologies, Inc. All rights reserved. **
  ** TradeStation reserves the right to modify or overwrite this analysis technique
     with each release. ** }
```

Ln 1, Col 0 SAVEI VERIFIEI NUI

FIGURE 2.10 Your First Look at EasyLanguage Code

EasyLanguage code is composed largely of Reserved Words, arithmetic operators, variables, inputs, and comments. The most significant line of code in this EZL document is:

```
Plot1[Displace] (Avg, "Avg");
```

The "Displace" variable is optional, so let's take it out. Now the line just looks like this:

```
Plot1(Avg, "Avg");
```

Avg is the data we want plotted, one data point at a time. **"Avg"** is the name we give to the data stream to identify it. That's all there is to it. Except for one more, very important piece of information.

The **semicolon** tells EZL that our "sentence" is complete. Each complete thought, or sentence, or command (whatever you want to call it) must be terminated with a **semicolon** (;).

If you forget to terminate your sentence with the semicolon, you will get an error message from EZL. Sometimes it will say you forgot the semicolon; sometimes it will tell you that it a variable name is undefined; and sometimes it will say something else. It all just means that EZL cannot decipher your sentence until it comes to the next semicolon.

Don't worry about the rest of the code. Most of it is extraneous, and is used for more esoteric applications. The only code you need in your indicator is this:

```
inputs: Price( Close ), Length( 9 );
variables: Avg(0);
Avg = Average (Price, Length);
      Plot1( Avg, "Avg" );
```

We can simplify the code even further, if we don't yet care about variables and inputs. The most basic EZL code for a simple, one-line moving average is:

```
PLOT1(Average(C,9),"MAV1");
```

Aside: Moving Averages In every seminar[1] I teach I find that several people don't know what a moving average is. That's OK. You probably only know that sort of thing if you are a math major or engineer or scientist of some kind. For those who don't recognize this terminology, it will be explained in Chapter 5, Basic Math. Basically, just know that it is a string of numbers which are calculated by averaging together a selection of numbers and then moving forward in the list and averaging the next selection.

---

[1]My seminars are given in person and on the web, by arrangement and on occasion. The most popular seminar is called "Solving the Puzzle." Other seminars are "Advanced EasyLanguage" and "TradeStation Made Easy." All my seminars are for novice and intermediate traders.

Conventions By convention, I like to put my initials in front of the name for all routines I write. That way, when I search for my work later, it is all alphabetized under "sjh_" in a group, rather than being scattered among TS's built-in indicators or indicators I have purchased from TS solution providers. Therefore, I would likely name our new indicator "sjh_ MAV1." You may name it anything you wish.

After making the above changes to your code, go up to **File** and pull down to **Save As** (see Figure 2.11). Look carefully, because there are other Save As commands to save your workspace and your desktop as well as your EasyLanguage Document.

Select **Save EasyLanguage Document As...** and give your document a new name.

In the "Name" box type the name you have chosen for this indicator. You do not need to fill in "Short name" or "Notes" at this time. Now click **OK.**

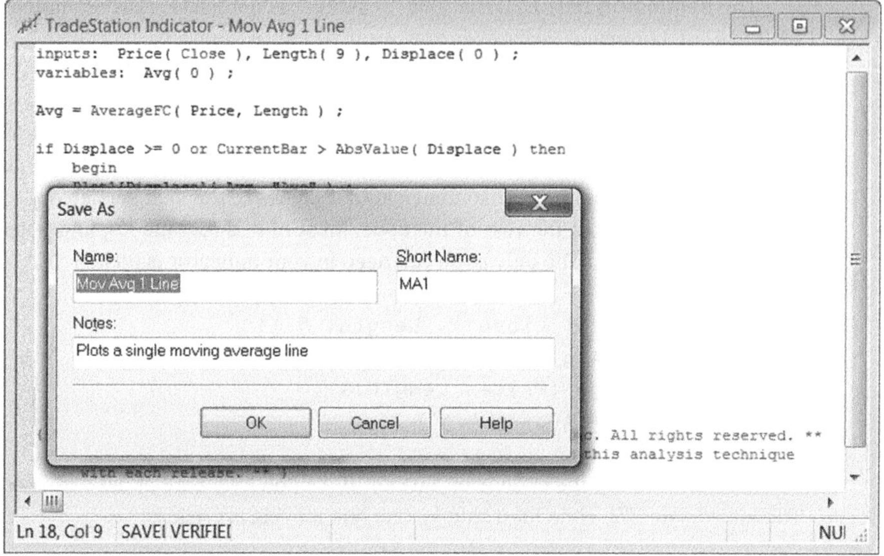

FIGURE 2.11 Mov Avg 1 Line

That's it. You did it! Later on I will explain to you what all those strange words meant. For now, I just want you to see the process from beginning to end.

The only other thing you have to do is to Verify the code. That's the next step.

Code Verification Before TradeStation will allow you to use a routine on a chart, it wants to make sure that you haven't made any blatant coding errors. Thus, the EasyLanguage PowerEditor will check the **syntax** of your code for you, so you don't spend tremendous amounts of time debugging.

To verify your code, you may either press the F3 key, click on the verify icon, or use the **File → Verify** menu sequence. If your code is syntactically correct, TS will first say "**Verifying**" and then respond with "**Verification Successful.**" Back in the way back, Easy-Language used to respond with "**Excellent!**" and it was thrilling and encouraging. Once they became a securities company, it had to get rid of that response, as it might be misconstrued as an indication that your code might be profitable. Now it's just a simple "**Verification Successful,**" not even an exclamation point.[2]

If your verify is not successful, go back and check each and every semicolon, space, and comma until your code looks just like mine and your verify gives you ". . . successful."

Now you have written an indicator with the PowerEditor.

Step 5: Putting an Indicator on the Chart

To see your new indicator, you need to put it on the chart. In the previous step we put a built-in indicator on your chart, just so you could quickly see what an indicator was. If you haven't already, take that indicator off your chart. You will do so by selecting the plot and pressing the Delete key.

When you click on the indicator on your chart, be sure to place your cursor (the point of the arrow) right on top of the indicator line. When you click, little black boxes will appear at intervals on the indicator (see Figure 2.12). This means that you have actually selected the indicator. If the little black boxes don't appear, you haven't yet clicked in exactly the right spot.

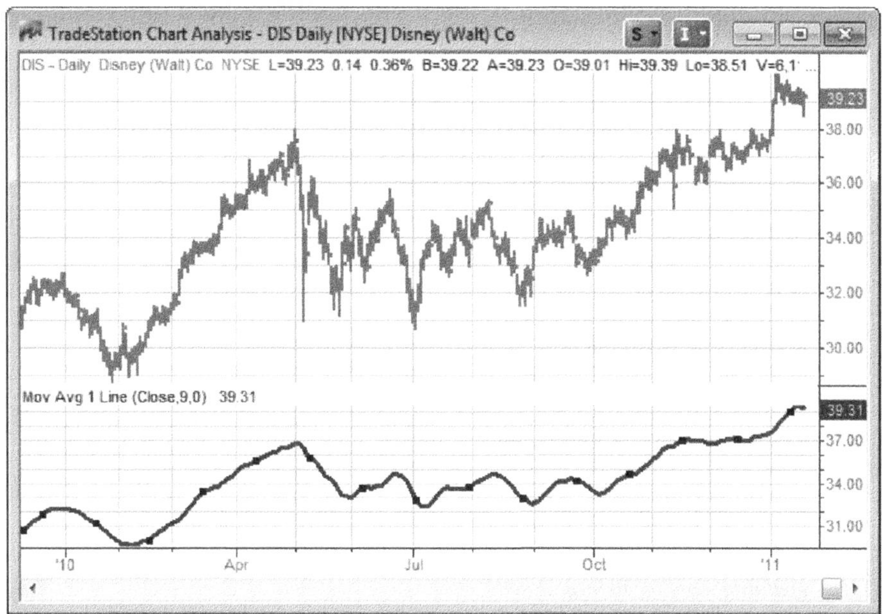

FIGURE 2.12 Chart with Built-in Indicator Selected

[2]It gets worse. With the very latest release of TradeStation, the company even has taken away the "Verification Successful." Now at the bottom of the screen, TradeStation responds blandly with "0 error(s), 0 warning(s)."

Pressing the **Delete** key while the black boxes are showing on the indicator will remove the indicator from your chart.

Now you can put your new indicator on the chart, using the Insert Indicator pull-down menu shown in Figure 2.13.

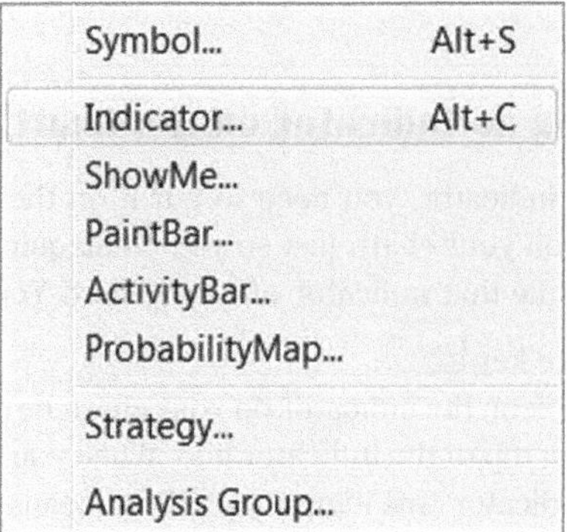

FIGURE 2.13 Insert Indicator

Go to Insert on the upper, horizontal menu bar and pull down to Indicator and click. This will bring up a list of all the indicators available to you. Select the one we just created and click on its name. This will place the indicator plot on the chart.

Experiment with taking that indicator off the chart and putting new indicators on the chart. With each indicator, take a look at "what is true" of the indicator in relationship to the movement of the underlying market. What happens to the indicator, for instance, when the market changes direction? Is there anything that you could use to pinpoint highs and lows or turning points?

Your chart window should now look like mine, shown in Figure 2.12. Again, the moving average is in subgraph two.

Step 6: Write a Strategy

A strategy could also be called a recipe, a map, a procedure, a system, or a method. **A strategy is an algorithmic approach to trading** and does not involve guessing or intuition.

A strategy, therefore, is a *set of steps that are followed precisely each time you wish to evaluate whether to buy or sell.*

In **TradeStation 4.0,** a system is created in a single routine, which examines each and every bar of your chart to see whether your buy or sell conditions are met. This routine is called a **system** in TradeStation 4.0.

In **TradeStation 2000i,** a system is called a **strategy** and can consist of one or more routines called **signals,** which are linked together to create the strategy. If you have been a user of TradeStation 4.0, at first this new mechanism will seem burdensome. However, after the first time you want to include (and separately test) multiple entry and exit possibilities, you will be thankful for the change.

In TradeStation 8 and 9, there is no system; there are only collections of strategies. When you insert a strategy on a chart, it brings you to a pop-up menu where you can select strategy components.

For the purpose of this instruction, we will address writing a system, writing a signal, and writing a strategy as the same thing, independent of the version of TS you are using.

Strategy **A strategy contains buy and/or sell commands.** We can create a strategy using our simple, one-line moving average. For starters, let's make a strategy that buys when the high price of a bar crosses above the moving average and sells when the low price of a bar crosses below the moving average. Of course, we don't yet know whether this system will make us any money; that's what TradeStation is for.

The strategy would look like this:

```
IF H Crosses Over Average(C,9) THEN BUY;
IF L Crosses Under Average(C,9) THEN SELL;
```

Again, we can get lots more sophisticated than this, but keep your pants on; this is just the Quick Start.

IMPORTANT Please note that later versions of TS have enhanced the SELL command to read SELL SHORT. If you use just the SELL without the word SHORT, you would have only one entry to buy with one exit to sell that position. For all users of the current version of TS, the strategy should look like this:

```
IF H Crosses Over Average(C,9) THEN BUY;
IF L Crosses Under Average(C,9) THEN SELL SHORT;
```

This strategy will buy and sell short, and buy and sell short with each crossing of the moving average.

To create a strategy, click on the EasyLanguage icon on the Vertical menu bar and select **New EasyLanguage Document → Strategy.**

Now's the time to use your naming convention to choose an appropriate name for your new strategy. I'm going to call mine `sjh_S_MovAvg1`, where the S is for strategy. Place your chosen name in the **Name** box and ignore the other box (see Figure 2.14).

Now click on **OK** to accept the new name, which opens a window with default strategy code in it. In this window we are going to program the new signal. You can examine the code that EZL generates to learn about writing your strategy. That's the way all programmers learn to code: by copying the code that someone before them wrote.

When you are through examining the default code, erase it by highlighting it all and pressing the **Delete** key. Now you'll have a blank window on which to write your strategy.

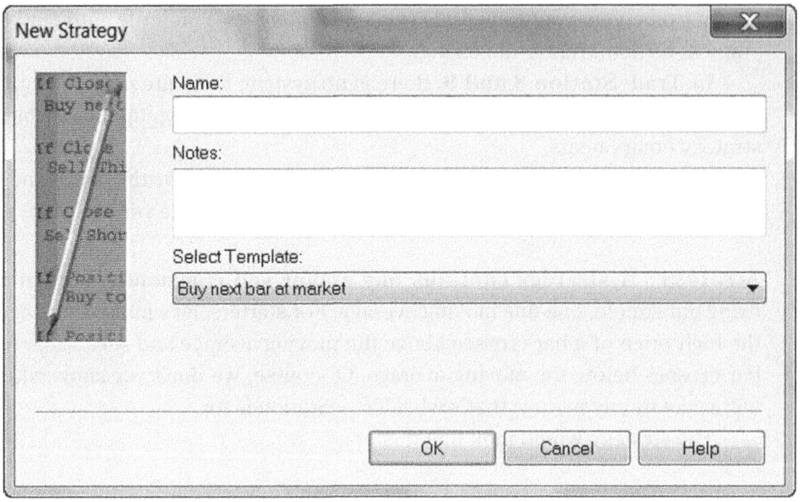

FIGURE 2.14 Naming Your New Strategy

Remember that we discussed rules for our system earlier in this chapter. Our rules are:

- Buy when the high price of a bar crosses above the moving average.
- Sell when the low price of a bar crosses below the moving average.

In the blank window, in EasyLanguage, type in the code for this signal:

```
IF H Crosses Over Average(C,9) THEN BUY;
IF L Crosses Under Average(C,9) THEN SELL SHORT;
```

Verify the code using one of the three methods discussed earlier: Press the F3 key, click on the verify icon, or use the **File → Verify** menu sequence. If you have not made any typographic errors, you should get the **Verification Successful** response from the PowerEditor.

What?! Your code doesn't verify? Well, as of TradeStation version 7, the buy and sell commands had something else added to them. To complete the strategy we must correct the structure of the buy and sell commands. To do so, highlight the buy in your code and type in "`Buy next bar at market`". To correct the sell command, type "`Sell Short next bar at market`". The other structure available to you is to buy or sell "this bar at close". TradeStation now distinguishes between selling to close a position and selling to go short.

To create your trading system, you may want a collection of several strategies. Or, maybe not. Maybe you will program all of your ideas in one strategy. Whichever you choose, just remember that it is perfectly acceptable to combine several strategies together to form a system. In these examples, we will be putting all of the code for our systems into a single strategy.

Here we go. Let's put the strategy on your chart.

Step 7: Apply the System to a Chart

From the **Insert** menu, pull downward and select **Strategy** (see Figure 2.15).

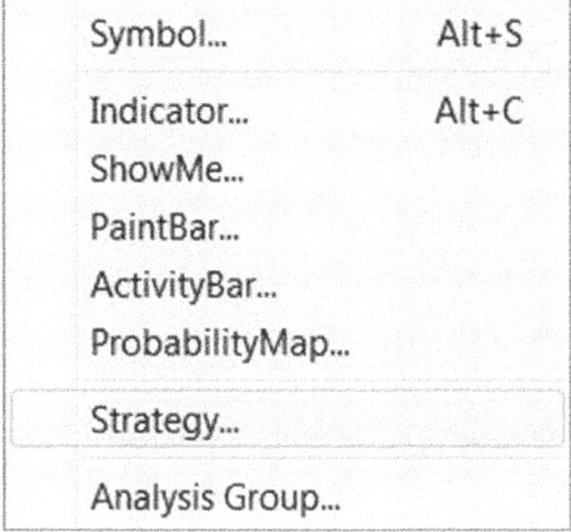

FIGURE 2.15 Insert Strategy

A pop-up window will display the names of all of your available strategies. Scroll down and select yours (remembering what you named it), and then click on the **OK** button.

To bring up the next formatting window, double-click on the name of your strategy in the **Format Analysis Techniques & Strategies** window (see Figure 2.16). This window allows you to format your strategy by selecting values for the inputs and configuring the entry and exit markers. There are no inputs in this strategy (so far), so there will be nothing to select under that tab. Click on the **Entries** tab and select color and shape for your buy arrows. Click on the **Exits** tab and you will see that there is nothing there to deal with. Go ahead and click on **Calculation** just to take a look, but for now ignore this section too. (See Figure 2.17.)

Click on **OK** to close this pop-up and then on **Close** to finalize the formatting of your strategy.

This sequence will place your strategy on the chart and mark the buys and sells with the arrows you have selected. It should look something like the chart in Figure 2.18, allowing for differences in color and shape of the arrows.

Step 8: View System Results

I don't know about you, but it seems like we've come a long way. At least I have been doing a lot of writing. Are you tired too? Stand up, sing a song, do some push-ups, we're about to get to the good stuff!

Now is the time to use the **View → Strategy Performance Report** menu sequence. With the chart with the strategy selected, use the sequence **or** press **ALT+SHIFT+P.** The resultant screen will look like the one in Figure 2.19.

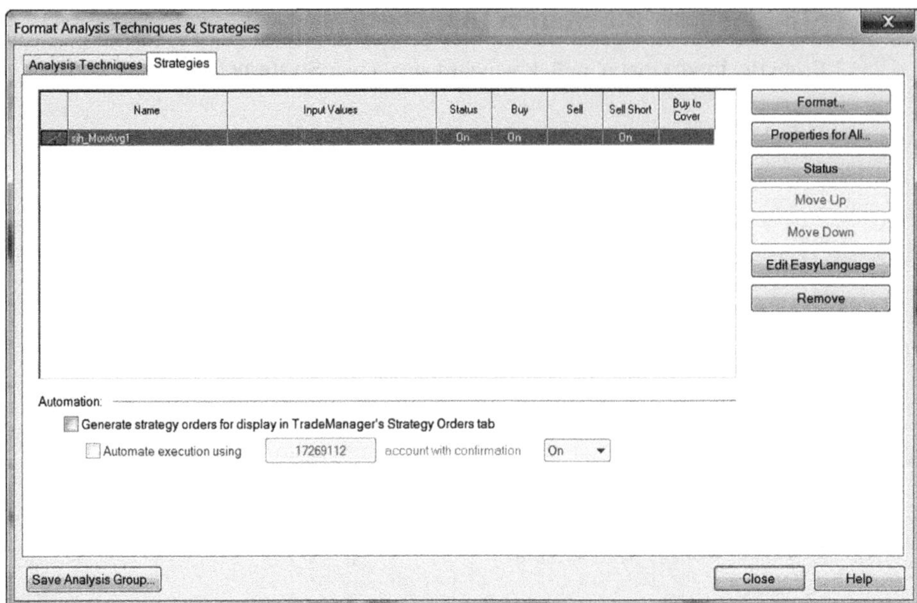

FIGURE 2.16 Format Analysis Techniques

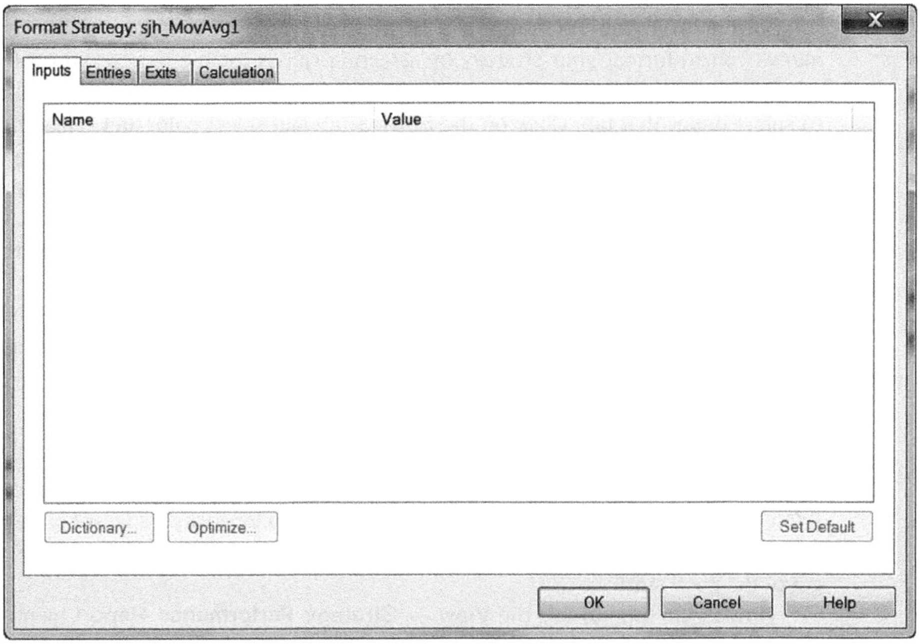

Format Strategy: sjh_MovAvg1
Inputs
Entries
Exits
Calculation
Name
Value
Dictionary...
Optimize...
Set Default
OK
Cancel
Help

FIGURE 2.17 Formatting the Strategy

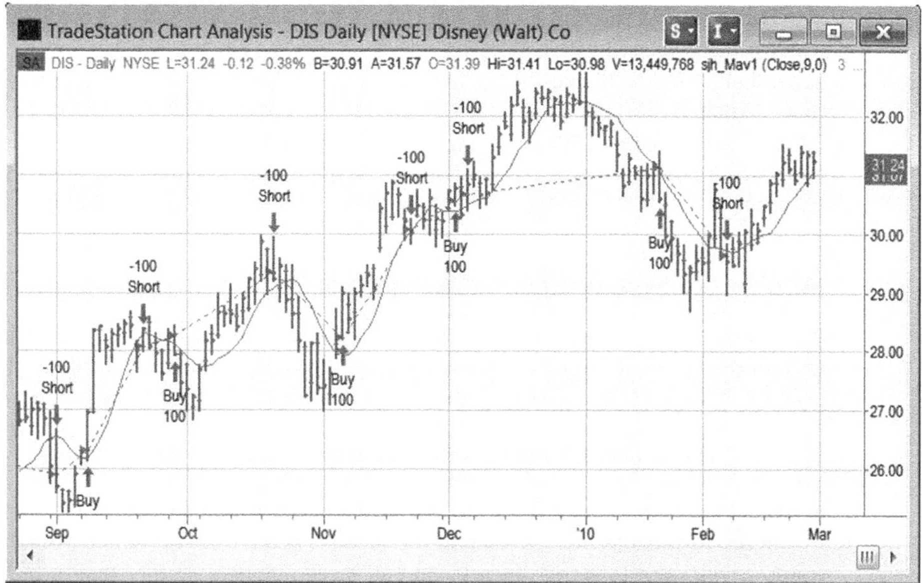

FIGURE 2.18 Strategy on the Chart

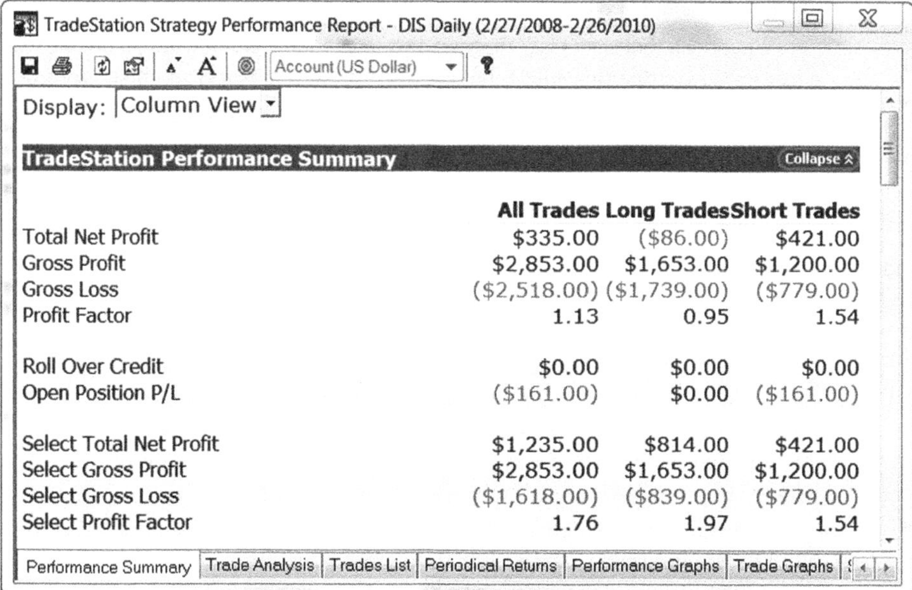

	All Trades	Long Trades	Short Trades
Total Net Profit	$335.00	($86.00)	$421.00
Gross Profit	$2,853.00	$1,653.00	$1,200.00
Gross Loss	($2,518.00)	($1,739.00)	($779.00)
Profit Factor	1.13	0.95	1.54
Roll Over Credit	$0.00	$0.00	$0.00
Open Position P/L	($161.00)	$0.00	($161.00)
Select Total Net Profit	$1,235.00	$814.00	$421.00
Select Gross Profit	$2,853.00	$1,653.00	$1,200.00
Select Gross Loss	($1,618.00)	($839.00)	($779.00)
Select Profit Factor	1.76	1.97	1.54

FIGURE 2.19 TradeStation Strategy Performance Report

This screen is the one all the work and sweat and tears comes down to. This is the window that tells it like it is. Many traders don't want to see this screen; they would rather hope, than to know the hard, cold facts. In my book, however, it's better to use logic than "into-wishing."

I'm here to tell you, it's next to impossible to find a winning strategy. The fact that this very first system of ours shows positive returns is unusual. But then, that's why I am writing the book.

Step 9: Are System Results Acceptable?

If you have read my other books (*Trading 101*, *Trading 102*, *Electronic Day Trading 101*, or *Getting Started in Trading*) or have attended any of my seminars, you already know what my **CPC™ Index** is. If not, suffice it to say, for this Quick Start, that the product of

(Percent profitable) ∗ (Ratio avg win/avg loss) ∗ (Profit factor)

needs to be greater than 1.2 for me to start being happy with the performance of a system.

In recent versions of TradeStation the stats needed are not all visible from the reduced window; you need to scroll down to find all three numbers. Rather than print the whole window in this book, I'll just tell you that in this example Percent profitable = 41.67%; Ratio avg win/avg loss = 1.47; and Profit factor = 1.13.

We can then calculate that (.4167) ∗ (1.47) ∗ (1.13) = 0.692 is not greater than 1.2. Without this calculation, you might initially conclude that the system is profitable; but with CPC, you find quickly that this strategy is not robust enough to trade.

What does that say? Only that we have some more homework to do. More specifically, a low CPC says that this single moving average system is too simplistic to produce consistent profits in the stock we have just analyzed. Later in this book we will continually ask my favorite question: "What is true?" We will examine and refine this system by asking this question again and again.

CONCLUSION

The beauty of this Quick Start is that all the steps are now outlined for you. That's really all there is to it. You have learned the basics of using TradeStation in record time.

In the chapters that follow, we will get deeper into tricks of the trade. We will learn how to write indicators and signals that are more complex. But each and every time you will start with opening TradeStation and go through to checking the system results. We will just be adding layers of sophistication to the steps.

All too often I encounter novice traders who want to execute the steps once, and give up in frustration if they haven't found the answer by then. Notice that in the last step (Are the System Results acceptable?) I did not say to give up after finding low CPCs. I said we have more homework to do. A low CPC is not yet cause for alarm, nor is it justification to declare that a system doesn't work. It is just time for more homework.

CHAPTER 3

Understanding the Process

In This Chapter

- Review
- Step 1: Observation
- Step 2: Research
- Step 3: Programming and Quality Assurance
- Step 4: Marketing and Sales
- Summary

REVIEW

It astounds me how many calls I get from aspiring "young" traders (many older than I) who have heard the success stories in the markets and want to start trading. Many of them tell me that they are having financial problems and want to trade the markets to get ahead. No one likes it when I tell him or her that it usually takes three years to become profitable. Some disregard my advice and lunge headlong into throwing money at the markets, but none of these people has ever come back to tell me of their success. Many, however, call me back to acknowledge that they now understand what I said and are looking for help in what I call "doing the homework."

The people who have returned to tell me of their eventual successes are invariably the same people who have spent months and years studying suggested materials, reading dozens if not hundreds of books on the subject, and practicing and testing strategies before ever trading them.

Every great musician has had to study the masters who came before him. And every great musician knows how to get to Carnegie Hall: practice, practice, practice.

An intelligent person will not leap into a subject as complex as trading, hoping to blaze new trails, without studying the trails that have already been tried. To understand trading, you must first study the classics. In Chapter 5, Charting Methods, we study some of the classics. In Chapter 3, however, we are going to look at the forest, not the trees. We are going to continue taking a broad look at the overall project.

As I see it, there are four essential steps to any project, whether it is creating a new business or designing a trading system:

1. Observation
2. Research
3. Programming and quality assurance (also known as manufacturing)
4. Marketing and sales

These same four steps can be translated into terminology specific to trading and system development:

1. Observation: Observe price action and ask "What is true?"
2. Research: Develop a systematic approach
3. Programming and quality assurance: Test the system before trading it and prove the system can profit
4. Marketing and Sales: Follow the system

The ingredients of these four steps are covered in depth in *Trading 101—How to Trade Like a Pro*, in *Trading 102—Getting Down to Business*, and in *Getting Started in Trading*. You may want to read (or review) those books before diving into this one, as I just might make reference to some of the material presented therein.

I recently heard someone summarize all motivational speakers: "Idea, plan, stick, stick, stick." That is about what we're doing here. The same summarizer asked how you get your first idea. That is what our step 1 is for. Careful observation generates the ideas. **Getting the right answers is only about asking the right questions.** According to Japanese business tradition, it is more important to ask the right questions than to find the right answers.

STEP 1: OBSERVATION

What Is True?

Whenever I begin a project, not just a programming project, I like to assess what I already know. I inventory my tools. I ask myself: What is true about the situation I am in? If I am going to do laundry I need to know whether I have detergent, whether I am to do dark or light clothes, whether I have the time available to complete the task, and whether I can get someone else to do it for me. When I am going to do grocery shopping I need to know the time frame for which I am buying (a day, a week, or a month), I need to have menus planned, and from those menus I need a distilled list of ingredients. And I need to know whether I can get someone else to do it for me.

When analyzing a particular market, I again ask what is true about the chart I am looking at. The questions I will pose look for direction and velocity and for whether there is any profit to be made. These things, however, I like to do for myself.

Sometimes I sit for minutes, and sometimes I sit for hours, looking at charts of the markets. I get a feel for the chart. I look at what is true. I ask myself questions about the chart. But, most of all, I look to see whether there's any money in it. One of the ways I study a chart is to find a big move and ask what came before it. What led up to the move that could have been a trigger?

What, in Figure 3.1, would have led to the big moves near the beginning of the chart? Furthermore, is this move even "big"? These are questions we will examine further as we get to more sophisticated concepts in this book.

FIGURE 3.1 A Big Move

Talking about Data

To talk about data, moves, and profits we must first discuss the ways in which TradeStation refers to data. It is time to learn a little EasyLanguage vocabulary.

Data, as transmitted by the exchange, is delivered in packets of trade-by-trade information, called tick data. Each tick has a price and an exact time (in hours, minutes, and seconds) associated with it. This information is also called time-and-sales. Rather than deal with the real-time tick data, as analysts we often compress the data into more manageable slices, called time frames, or compression. If we group all the tick data into 15-minute windows, we are creating a 15-minute time compression. Likewise, we can create any whole number time compression we would like by observing the first price of the slice (open), the last price of the slice (close), the highest price (high), and the lowest price (low) of the time slice. Each time slice is then plotted on a single bar.

Every bar on a TradeStation chart, whether it is 1-minute, 15-minute, hourly, or daily, has four basic components: Open, High, Low and Close. Those components are presented graphically in Figure 3.2.

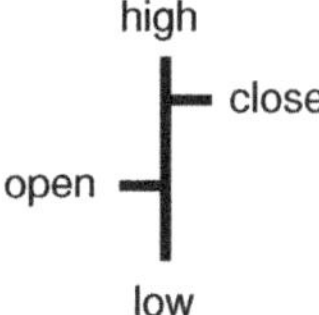

FIGURE 3.2 The Components of a Bar

The closing price (close) is the last price that is traded in the time compression of the bar. In TradeStation, all these ways of referring to that component mean the same thing:

- Close
- C
- close
- c
- cLOsE

TradeStation ignores capitalization, so don't worry whether the shift or caps-lock keys are on. Capitalization is ignored, but no spaces are allowed between the letters. Code is easier to read if you use the word "`Close`," but as you get familiar with programming EasyLanguage, you will probably relax and use just the "`C`".

The designations just shown are known as **Reserved Words.** You may not name one of your own variables `C` or `close`. TradeStation keeps those two words for internal reference purposes only, and they always mean the same, very specific, thing. Again, these are called reserved words. I have created an appendix with the most commonly used reserved words, so you can use it as a reference guide. TradeStation's manuals do not single out these terms in a convenient form, and I find myself referring to my own appendix every time I code EasyLanguage.

Rather than digress into specifics about coding and manipulating data here, I leave the rest of these conventions for later in the chapters on Charting Methods: Chapters 6 and 7. For now, I want to continue with the four steps of designing a trading system.

Show Me the Money

As part of the observation step, I want to know whether there is money to be made. That, after all, is the only goal in the business of trading. Or at least it should be. If I spend days and weeks observing a stock that only moves from 53 to 54, I am wasting my time. So, before going any further, I determine whether my time is going to be well spent in observation.

In *Trading 101—How to Trade Like a Pro* I went into lengthy explanation of why people trade with other motivations. Suffice it to say, there are folks whose main goal is to fail, or to see how smart they are, or to have a challenge, but not necessarily to make a profit. In my book there's only one reason to trade, and that's to make money.

In discovering whether there is profit to be made from a particular vehicle (stock, option, forex pair, futures contract, or mutual fund), I take these three initial steps:

- Hold the x-axis constant.
- Hold the y-axis constant.
- Mark all the significant highs and lows.

Furthermore, I take a look at all markets on the same scale, over a one-year period, and mark the ideal entries and exits from both the short and the long perspective. This convention allows me to assess a chart more quickly, since all my charts are on the same relative scale.

For instance, Figure 3.3 is a chart of "our vehicle" and some other trading vehicle. I have purposely blocked out the scales on the right side of the chart. Can you tell which one you should trade to make the most money? My instant gut reaction would be to say the top one. It seems to have lots more swings that I could catch from both the long and the short side.

FIGURE 3.3 Comparing Two Trading Vehicles without a Scale

In Figure 3.4 the price scales are back on the right side of the chart, the y-axis. It is still difficult to quickly determine which of the two stocks would net you more profit, however, because they are not on the same scale. You would have to spend some time calculating in order to draw a meaningful conclusion.

FIGURE 3.4 Comparing Two Trading Vehicles with Scales

In Figure 3.5 I have scaled both instruments to the same relative scale. By that I mean that I have manually set the price scale to range from a minimum of 20 to a maximum of 150.

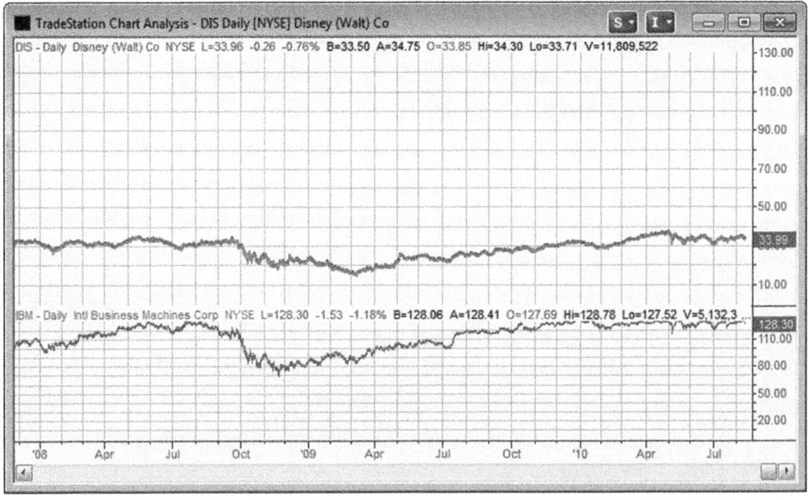

FIGURE 3.5 Comparing Two Trading Instruments with the Same Relative Scale

Notice that the top subgraph spends most of its time between 20 and 40, while the bottom subgraph runs the gamut from 80 up to 140. Now, just making a quick guess, which one do you think would provide you more trading opportunity?

Using fixed price scales, we have an entirely different view of how these two charts compare to each other. With this information, we get an entirely different perspective.

With the stipulation that charts must be on the same scale and same timeline, we get a realistic view of which vehicles are tradable. Anything else is just wishing.

Try it yourself. Using your software, bring up a chart of a single stock. (**File → New → Window → Chart Analysis** 🖱 `DIS`). Then create another new window and open a second stock in that window (**File → New → Window → Chart Analysis** 🖱 `IBM`). I chose `IBM` and `DIS` because I know that they are in different price ranges.

Use the **Arrange** tool from the upper, horizontal, menu bar, under the **Window** command (**Window → Arrange Horizontally**) to align the two charts horizontally, one above the other. (Of course, I am assuming that you have followed the instructions so far in this book and thus have only two windows on your workspace.) Notice that TradeStation scales each chart automatically, choosing the scale that will **maximize the use of the screen.**

With the automatic scaling of each of the two stocks, your workspace should make it seem that the two stocks have very similar movement and should probably be traded with the same methods. See Figure 3.6 to view TradeStation's automatic scaling.

FIGURE 3.6 Automatic Scaling

Now, if you click on the bars of the IBM chart window to select the data and then use the **Format → Symbol → Scaling** tab menu sequence, you will come to a pop-up window (Figure 3.7) where you can choose several different ways to scale your data. Way back when, it was just a matter of choosing **Screen, Entire data series,** or **User defined.** No longer. TradeStation is expansive and comprehensive in its flexibility these days.

For the purposes of this exercise, I want you to set up IBM so that the scale ranges from 70 on the low end to 130 at the top. To effect the change, look in the middle of the pop-up, under the label **Range,** and click the button marked **Fixed.** Then fill in **Min** with `70` and **Max** with `130` for the `IBM` chart.

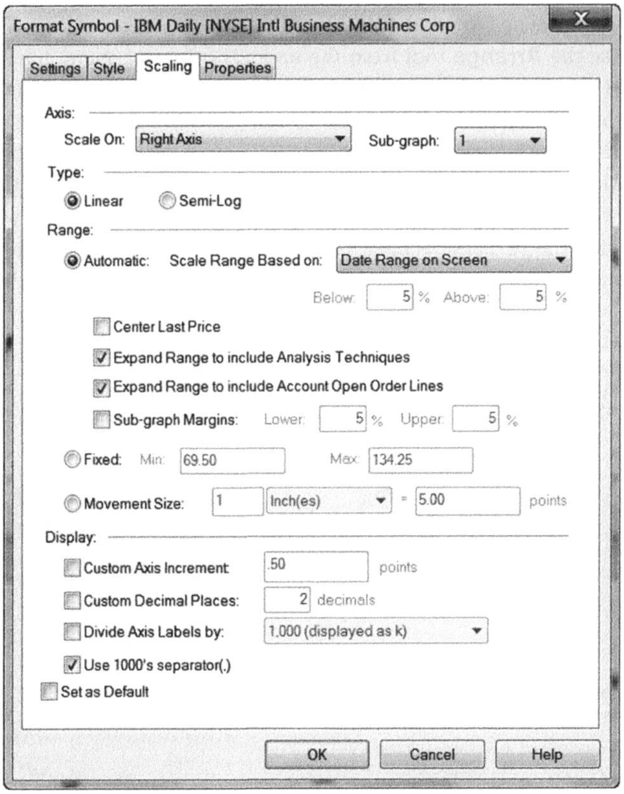

FIGURE 3.7 Scaling Your Data

Now click **OK.** Select the `DIS` chart window, and change its range to **Min** `10` and **Max** `70`. Your workspace should now look like mine in Figure 3.8.

With the charts (in fact, this should apply to every chart you study) on the same relative scale, you can now conduct a quick visual inspection and learn something. Before we interfered with TradeStation's automatic scaling, the two stocks appeared to be very similar; see Figure 3.6 again. After setting the scales so their ranges matched, point for point, it becomes

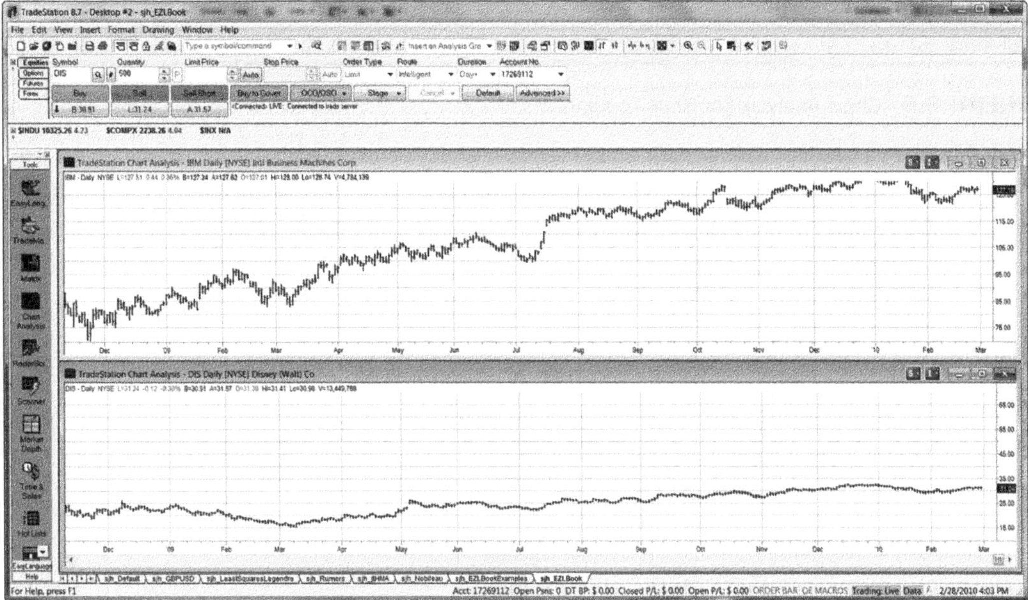

FIGURE 3.8 IBM and DIS Scaled Proportionally

immediately obvious that one stock is tradable and the other is just sitting in a flat range. See how important scaling is? This is the first blaring example of asking "What is true?"

NOTE: As a shorthand way of telling you to "use your mouse, click on a menu item, and then pull down to the desired submenu item," I use the 🖱 (mouse) and the → (arrow) symbols to denote those steps.

Using those notation conventions, here is my shorthand way of telling you the steps to creating two chart windows, with two different symbols, and scaling them proportionally.

- File → New Window → 🖱 Chart Analysis
- DIS
- File → New Window → 🖱 Chart Analysis
- IBM

Alternatively, you could simply press **CTRL+N** and click on the **Chart Analysis** icon.

Next, you'll want to change the time frame compression (interval) to Daily instead of the default time compression chosen by TradeStation (unless it was already Daily.) Doing that requires you to click on the little clock icon in the chart analysis shortcut tool bar, horizontally at the top. It is shown in Figure 3.9.

FIGURE 3.9 Chart Analysis Shortcut Toolbar

About midway over in the toolbar you will see a black-and-white image of a clock with bars behind it. If you hover your mouse over it, the word "Interval" will come up. Click on the clock and a pull-down menu will appear, from which you can pick your time frame. For this example, choose "Daily." This pull-down menu is shown in Figure 3.10.

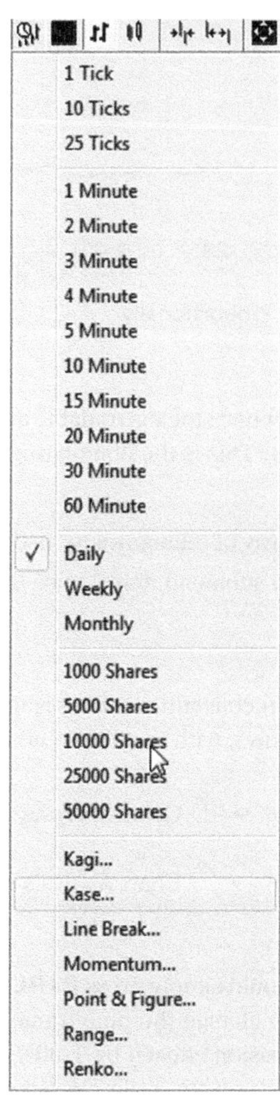

FIGURE 3.10 Intervals

Now you understand how to begin observing your chart. To conduct an investigation into "Where's the money?" you must start by comparing apples to apples; in other words, scale your charts the same.

Trading Opportunities

For the time being, let's assume that you want to trade from both the long side and the short side. The goal of trading versus investing is to make more money timing the market with long and short positions than you could through using a buy-and-hold approach.

Thus, the buy-and-hold approach is our benchmark. To know whether trading is better than investing, you need to know what the potential income of investing would be.

If we could buy IBM at 100 on January 1 and sell it at 150 on December 31, 12 months later, then the buy-and hold approach would net us 50 points per share.

For us to be happy with a trading approach, the same vehicle, IBM, should net us **more than** 50 points through trading. In fact, it should net us considerably more than buy-and-hold to make up for our commissions and the extra time we spend trading. Just how do you analyze hundreds of stocks (bonds, futures, forex, etc.) and find out whether investing or trading is better? That brings us to the next topic.

PHW™ Analysis

The backbone of all my work is a technique I call **PHW™**, for **Potential Hourly Wage,** Analysis. The first step of PHW Analysis is marking tradable highs and lows. You can learn about the technique in depth from *Trading 102—Getting Down to Business*, through my correspondence course, *Solving the Puzzle*, or in any of my seminars and lectures. Or you could join in my blog at the Money Mentor (www.moneymentor.com/blog.html) on the web. I believe it is so important to the process that I include the subject in every forum in which I speak.

As a review of the process, before tackling a trading project, we want a preview of whether trading is "worth it." Can we make more money trading than working at McDonald's for minimum wage? Can we make more money through trading than with a buy-and-hold approach? Can we make more money trading one instrument than another? Can we make more money trading in one time frame than another? To deduce this, we will perform the PHW™ analysis in three steps:

1. Mark meaningful highs and lows.
2. Calculate the maximum profit.
3. Calculate PHW (40% of the maximum).

By "meaningful highs and lows," I mean moves that you might be able to catch and moves that are wide enough to produce a profit.

Using the symbol `DIS`, the first step is to identify the meaningful highs and lows. I like to use **yellow circles** for marking the target areas. You may print out a chart if you wish and draw circles by hand, you may use TradeStation's drawing tools to create circles (ellipses), you may write an indicator to calculate the circles, or you can call my office about my EasyLanguage PHW Indicator for TradeStation.

Figure 3.11 is an illustration of "our chart" printed out and then guesstimated by hand. When I am doing a quick analysis by hand, I don't worry about the details; I just round off all the numbers so I can add quickly.

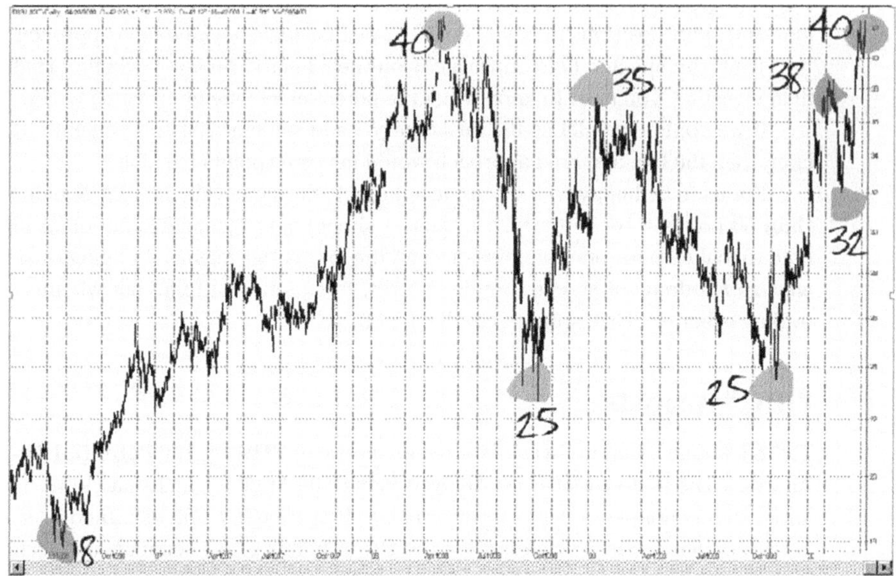

FIGURE 3.11 Yellow PHW Circles on DIS

In TradeStation there is a drawing tool for creating circles (ellipses) (see Figure 3.12). As you may have rearranged or reconfigured the toolbars, I can't tell you exactly where it is, but I can tell you that it is found under the **Drawing** menu item and is called **Ellipse.** If you hold down the Shift key while drawing an ellipse, it constrains it to a circle. The menu sequence is currently **Drawing → Ellipse.** (I say "currently" because with every version, the TradeStation folks move the menus around.)

Click once on the tool to activate it. To draw the circle, move your cursor to the right edge of the chart and then click and drag a circle. Your circle may come out more like an oval, but that's fine. It's just a way to mark significant highs and lows.

Depending on the color defaults, your circle may or may not come out yellow like mine. By default the first ellipse you draw usually comes out dark blue with a red line encircling it. If you have selected **"Remain in Drawing Mode"** from the bottom of the Drawing menu, then go back and deselect it for now. Next, click on the perimeter edge of the circle to select it. Then, to set the color defaults, right-click on the circle and underneath **"Format 'Ellipse'..."** you may choose fill colors, circle perimeter colors, styles, and weights, as in Figure 3.13.

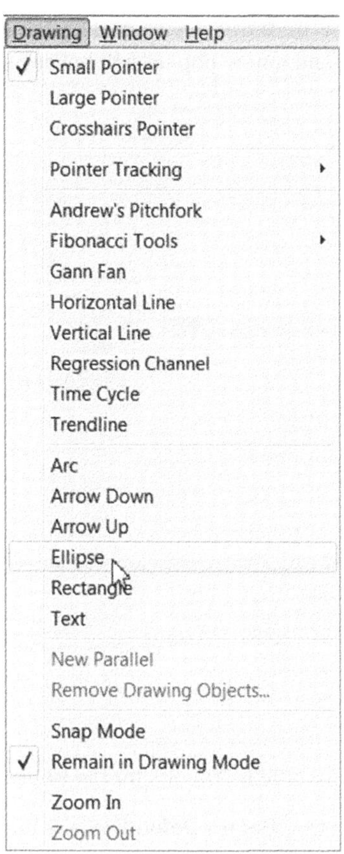

FIGURE 3.12 Drawing Menu

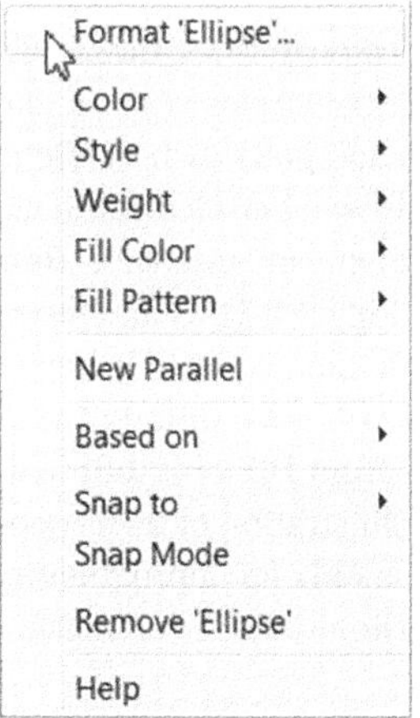

FIGURE 3.13 Format Ellipse

To choose your preferred styles and set them as defaults, click on the "**Format 'Ellipse'...**" choice and a new pop-up will appear for you to choose and set defaults (see Figure 3.14).

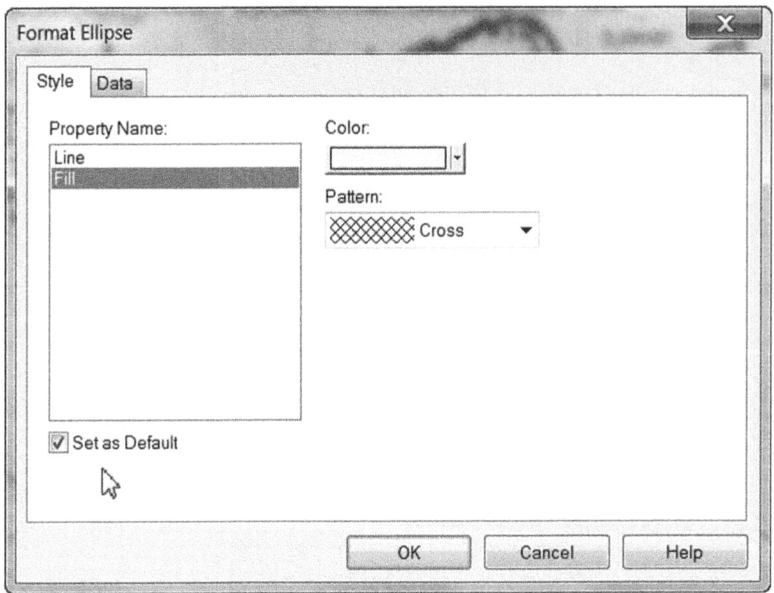

FIGURE 3.14 Setting Your Defaults for the Ellipse

Be sure to click the "**Set as Default**" check box. Then click "**OK**" to save your preferences. Now each circle you draw will be in your default color and style.

If you want to draw many circles at one sitting (which you will if you are drawing PHW circles by hand), you will quickly tire of clicking the ellipse tool to activate it followed by drawing a single circle. You can force the program to remain in drawing mode, so that you can draw multiple sequential circles without clicking the ellipse tool every time. To do this, go to the **Drawing** menu and pull down to "**Remain in Drawing Mode**". Now you can draw lots of circles. To stop drawing circles you must select a different tool, like the pointer, or go back to the Drawing menu and uncheck "**Remain in Drawing Mode**".

Using the circles in Figure 3.11 as an illustration of the process, the table in Figure 3.15 is used to calculate the maximum possible ideal profit. Clearly, if you marked different highs and lows than I did, you will get a different value for the maximum ideal profit. And if you used a different data set from DIS or a different time frame, you will certainly get different numbers. This is just an illustration of the process.

Since the outcome is only an approximation of potential, I like to use round numbers to calculate the input. The numbers for highs and lows in Figures 3.11 and 3.15 are thus approximations.

Figure 3.15 represents seven perfect trades in DIS. Let's say we were trading 100 shares at a time. We started trading at 18, so if we had bought 100 shares it would have cost $1,800.

Buy or Sell	Entry	Exit	Profit
B	18	40	22
S	25	40	15
B	25	35	10
S	35	25	10
B	25	38	13
S	38	32	6
B	32	40	8
		TOTAL	84

FIGURE 3.15 Maximum Ideal Profit Potential

By the end of the seven trades, we've made 84 points profit, on 100 shares, so that's $8,400 profit. $8,400 profit on an original investment of $1,800 is (8400/1800) 467% profit! That's Step 2: Calculate the Ideal Profit Potential. Keep in mind that you have no idea what the time frame for this example is—it could be minutes, days, or months.

Next, for Step 3, we acknowledge that we will never pick all the tops and bottoms. It doesn't happen. Over the years, my experience has suggested that a more realistic estimate is that we can capture roughly half of the available profit, more likely 40% of the available profit. We probably won't get more than that. In reality, we will likely get into most trades late and get out of most trades late. When the trade results in a large move, that is fine with us—we still have a fair amount of profit. But, when our entry is late, and the market doesn't go very far if we then also exit late, we lose money.

To compensate for this inevitable sloppiness in entries and exits, I take 40% of the maximum number (84) for a result of roughly 33 points. By experimentation and experience I have found that 40% of the ideal is usually achievable, but much more than that is just hope and wishing. Forty percent of the ideal would still represent $3,300 profit, for a 183% return in the example.

Nothing at this stage of the analysis tells us whether it is really possible to achieve this goal. All we're doing here is sketching out a goal.

The next step in your data analysis is to determine whether it is possible to find or invent **indicators** that will assist you in buying at or near the goal and selling at or near the goal.

Using PHW™ Highs and Lows

If you create an indicator (or buy mine) to mark all your PHW highs and lows and calculate the 40% goal (which my indicator prints right on the chart), you can use it as an indicator in RadarScreen to sort for stocks that have high PHWs. You can also leave the indicator on every chart, by creating a template, so that as you are doing your research, you will be reminded of your goal. PHW circles on a chart keep you alert for effective indicators as you do your research. I put PHW circles on every chart I look at, to keep me honest and to remind me where the best trades are. In Figure 3.16 you can see what my normal, default chart looks like.

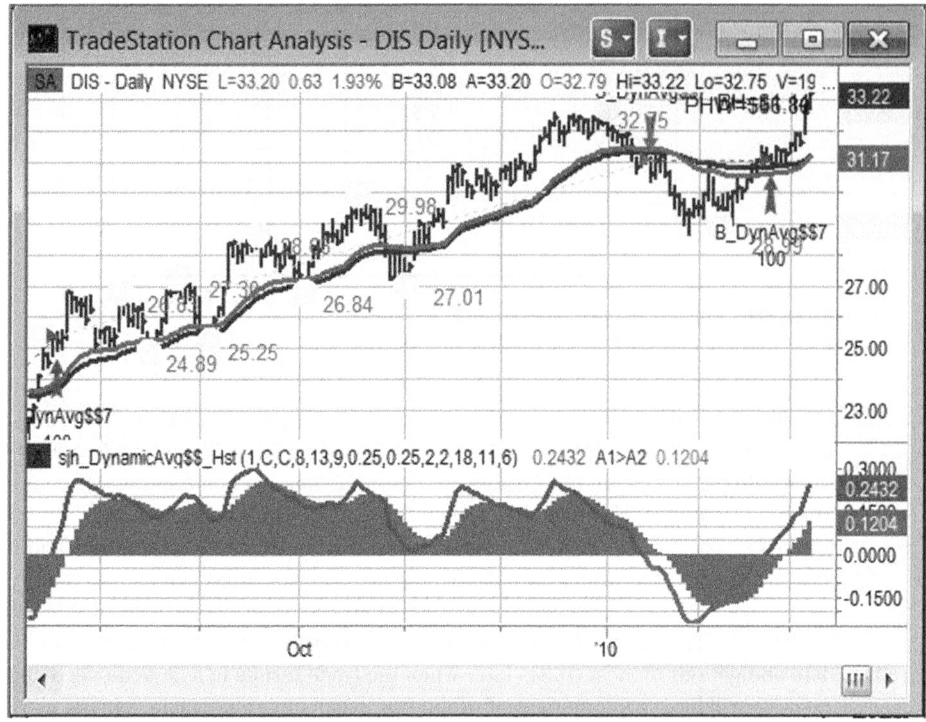

FIGURE 3.16 My Default Chart Configuration

Notice that the yellow (gray) PHW circles appear on every ideal trade's highs and lows. This is my indicator at work doing the calculations automatically, not me with a highlighter. The gold and purple smooth lines are my dynamic moving average, which smooths out false, choppy fakeouts. And the red and green line and the gray shading in the subgraph window is the dynamic moving average plotted as a histogram for easy reading of turns and exhaustion. You can also use lower highs on the histogram as a signal.

Whether you use an indicator or do it by hand, I suggest keeping the circles on every chart as you conduct your research. It keeps me on target; I hope it helps you.

STEP 2: RESEARCH

After marking the ideal trades on your chart, you need to figure out how to predictably achieve the desired results. I call this **hitting the targets.** Figure 3.11 is a chart with PHW points marked, as I see them. I have left the y-axis visible in order for you to analyze the profit potential. Figure 3.17 is another chart, this time with my indicator drawing the circles.

Notice on the right side is a legend with five items: the date range of the data, the ideal possible profit, the number of trades in that ideal calculation, the PHW analysis, and the amount of profit you would have made using a buy-and-hold approach. That gives us a

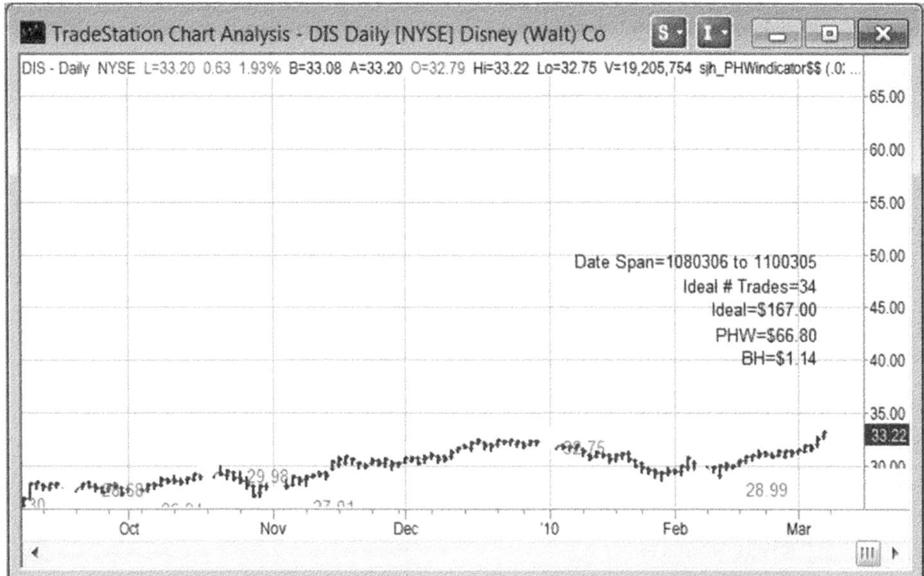

FIGURE 3.17 PHW Indicator on a Chart

consistent measuring stick for comparison. These numbers were put on the chart by the indicator, not me calculating them by hand. Convenient, huh?

The goal in this chapter is to apply indicators from the TradeStation library to find one that will approximate the target circles on the chart. Goals later on will include modifying the indicators, writing your own indicators, and purchasing systems and indicators from others. In each case, keep the PHW circles up there, for comparison and to keep you on track.

Applying Indicators

Most new market technicians, and even many experienced ones, begin the discovery process by throwing indicators on the chart and running the analysis software to see if they made money. Then they will use the **optimization utility** in the software to maximize the profit. (If you don't yet know what "optimization" is, you can read about it in *Trading 102—Getting Down to Business*, or you can hang on and we'll discuss it in Chapter 17.) I think the slam-bam approach is backward. Rather than ask the software how much is possible through brute-force optimizations, I first find out how much money can be made through pen-and-paper analysis, and then I use the software to match my ideal targets. After finding my ideal PHW, the next step I take is to apply indicators to the chart. **To reach your goal, you must first know what the goal is.**

From the TradeStation menu, pull down **Insert → Indicator** and take a look at the dozens of possibilities (see Figure 3.18). In fact, at this writing there are 101 indicators provided with the standard TradeStation installation.

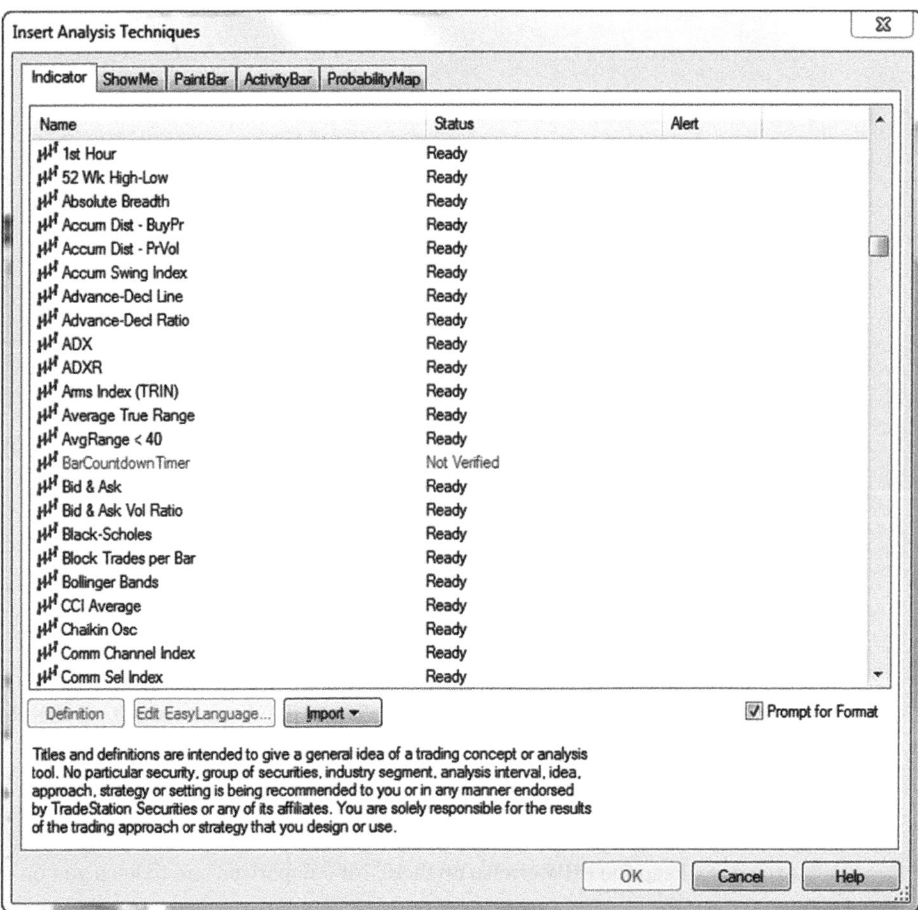

FIGURE 3.18 Dozens of Indicators

How many indicators do you need to make money? Just one good one. Or maybe one pretty good one and a good filter. This next part of our journey will show you the steps to finding that one good one.

For starters, let's select a simple moving average (MAV) crossover and accept the default settings. Here is the menu sequence:

Shorthand notation:

Insert → **Indicator** (or Alt+C) → **Mov Avg 2 Lines** → **OK**

Spelling it out:

- **Insert** → **Indicator** (or Alt+C).
- Click the **Indicator** tab.

- Scroll down to the M's and select **Mov Avg 2 Lines.**
- Click **OK.**
- Accept the default inputs by clicking **OK** again.

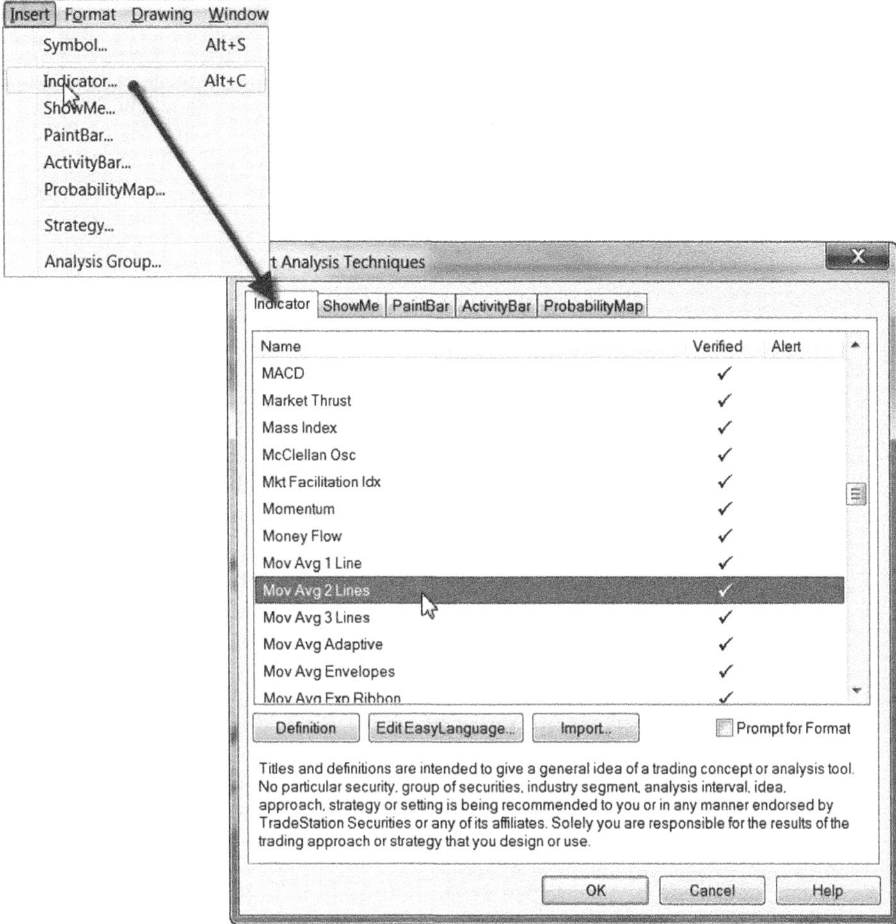

FIGURE 3.19 Inserting an Indicator

The resultant chart will look something like mine, in Figure 3.20. If you have left the original color settings in TradeStation, the chart will look like a negative of mine, with a black background and white lettering. It's a matter of personal preference, but I prefer to look at off-white paper instead of black. I find it easier on my eyes.

If you accepted all the defaults, one line will be red and one will be blue. On my chart the background is off-white and the two lines are magenta and cyan. Notice that the cyan (faster) line more closely follows the closing prices on the chart than the magenta (slower)

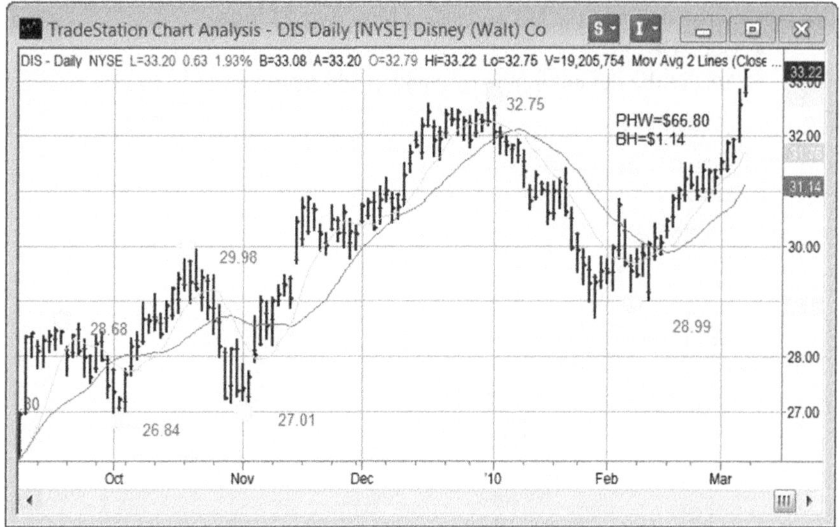

FIGURE 3.20 Off-White "Paper"

one. That is because the cyan line has 9 as the number of bars to use in calculating the moving average—we call it the shorter moving average. The magenta line is the longer moving average and uses 18 bars for its calculation.

I don't know about you, but I am compelled at this point to make some adjustments on my chart. I can hardly see the cyan and magenta lines. They seem very thin to me. Here are the steps for changing the color and thickness of the plot lines.

Changing the Styles of Your Plot

The easiest way to get to the right menu is to **right-click** on one of the plot lines and choose the first option, **Format 'Mov Avg 2 Lines...'** as in Figure 3.21.

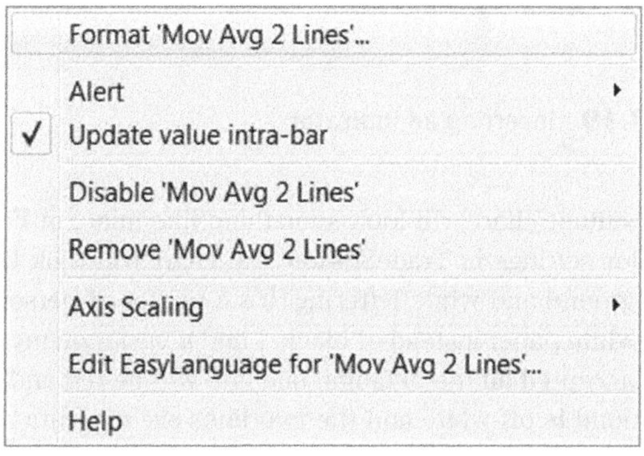

FIGURE 3.21 Changing the Style of Your Plot

That will bring you to a menu where there are seven tabs across the top: General, Inputs, Alerts, Style, Color, Scaling, and Advanced (see Figure 3.22).

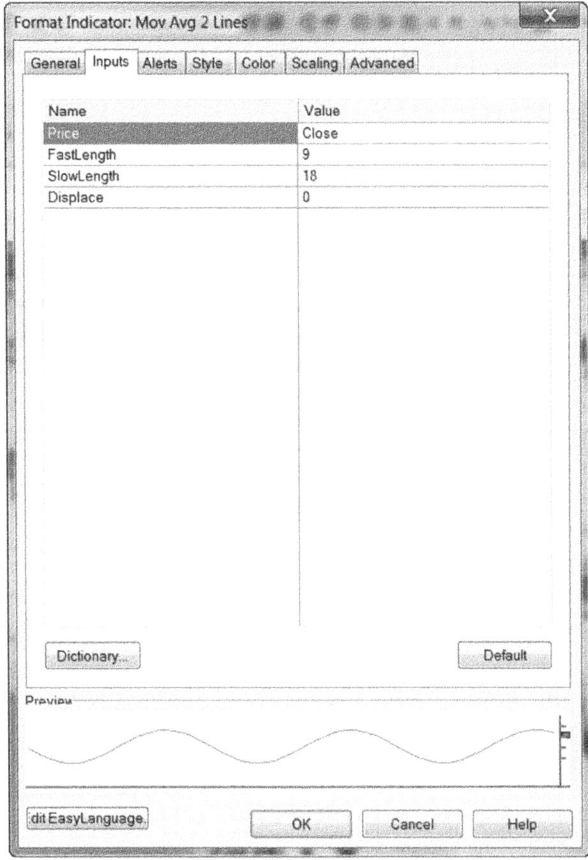

FIGURE 3.22 Format Indicator

I want you to choose the tab labeled Style, by clicking on it. From the new window (see Figure 3.23) you can see that I have labeled four items for you to look at.

1. Names of each plot (line on the chart)
2. Type of plot to draw (by default ours is a line chart)
3. Style of the line that is plotted (straight or various broken lines)
4. Weight is the thickness of the line drawn (plotted)

You may experiment with choosing different values for each plot and visually inspecting the results. Know that to change the magenta line, you would choose **SlowAvg** and to change the cyan line, you would choose the **FastAvg.** Of course, you can also click on the **Color** tab and change the colors of the lines.

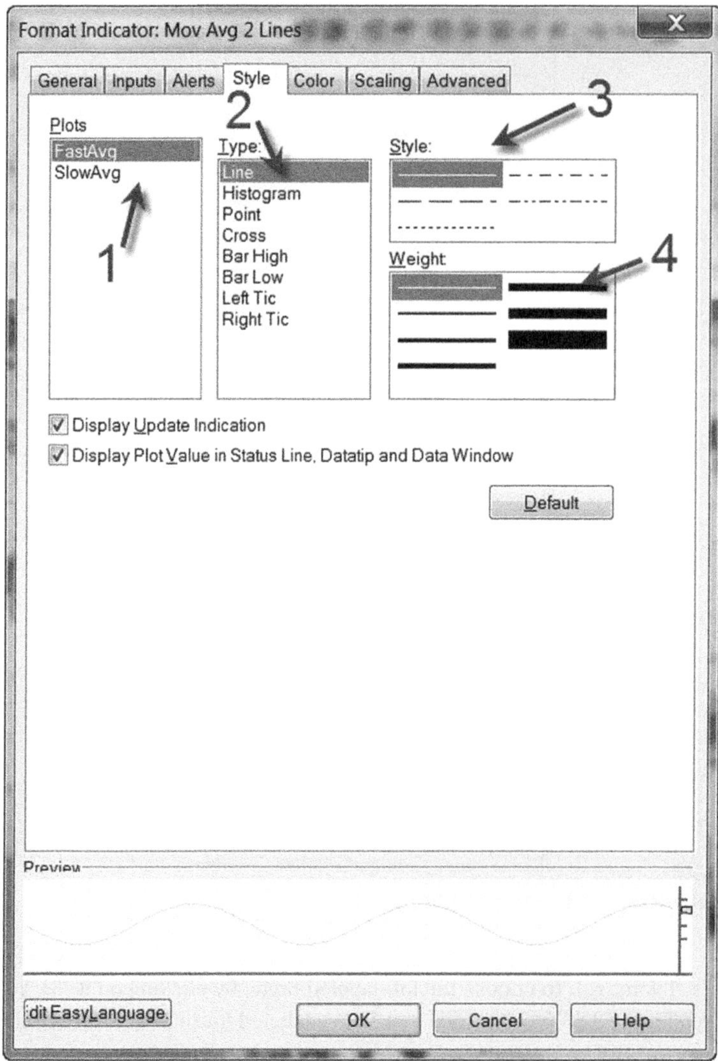

FIGURE 3.23 Changing Styles

For now, we are only going to change the thickness of the lines so we can see them more easily. Select **FastAvg,** item 1, by clicking on it and then click on item 4, **Weight,** and choose a thicker line. Then select **SlowAvg** in item 1 and click on a thicker line in item 4.

I prefer the third thickness, not too thick and not too thin. My chart now looks like Figure 3.24.

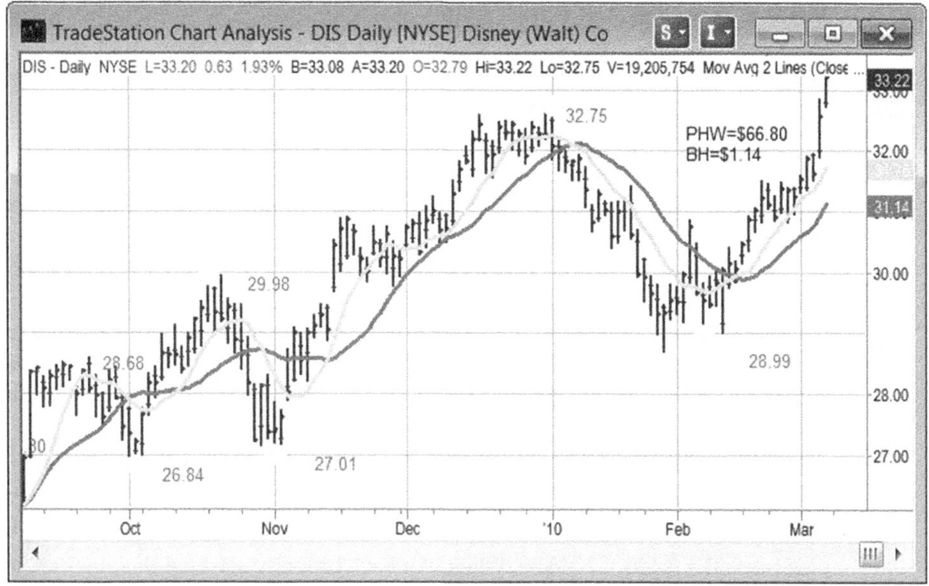

FIGURE 3.24 Chart with Thicker Plot Lines

Now that little housekeeping chore is complete and we can get back to addressing indicators in general. I leave it to you to experiment with thicknesses and dots and dashes and colors. When you begin setting these values inside EasyLanguage code, you will need to address the choices by number. These are listed in Appendix A.

More about Indicators

The theory behind a two moving average crossover trading system is to reverse your position when the two lines cross. If you were long, you would go short, and if you were short, you would go long; that's why we call it a reversal system. When the shorter moving average crosses the longer one from above, you would go short, and when the shorter moving average crosses the longer one from below, you would go long.

Compare the crossovers in Figure 3.24 to the targets we previously marked. Note that the crossovers of the two lines are not coincident with our targets. Sometimes the lines cross-over fairly close to the yellow PHW circles, but many times the crossover is much later than the ideal.

Logically, the lines cannot cross *at* the yellow PHW dot, as that would be predicting the market turn before it began. That just doesn't happen. All indicators will be lagging, that is, later than the ideal turning point. That's as good as it gets. Your job is to find time intervals and markets where there is sufficient profit in each move that taking the trade a little bit late still yields a satisfactory profit.

Moving Averages Are Late At this discovery, many new technicians would abandon the simple moving averages and go on to try the next indicator. After all, there are 101 indicators immediately available for testing, many more available for free download at TradeStation.com, and more available at a price.

Rather than abandon moving averages as ineffective, we will modify the two moving averages to more closely approximate our targets. We could experiment with longer or shorter values for the lengths (9 and 18) and we could use weighted or exponential averages instead of the simple moving average.

At this stage, we will be doing visual inspection of the chart. This is another step that many technicians avoid and yet is one that I consider crucial. To accurately determine which moving average produces the most profit, later on we will create a reversal system that executes the buys and sells on the crossovers and then study the performance data of that system. In Chapter 12, Buying and Selling, we do just that, as an exercise to writing our first system.

In these next few figures, I am going to delete the current indicator from the chart and add a new one, exploring the various moving average possibilities with you. The simplest way to delete a plot from a chart is to select it by clicking anywhere on one of the lines and then press the delete [Delete] key. When you have properly selected the plot line, it will have little black dots on it every 10 bars or so, indicating that it is selected. Pressing the [Delete] key will remove the whole indicator from the chart (i.e., both lines in this two line plot).

After having deleted the simple MAV 2 lines, go back up a few steps and insert a new indicator on your chart. To do so, use this menu sequence:

Insert → Indicator → Mov Avg Exponential → OK

With this, you will get a single line on your chart. There is no two-line exponential MAV built in to TradeStation. In order to test moving average crossovers, we need two lines. There are two ways to tackle this conundrum. You can either *write your own*, or you can *download it from me*. Figure 3.25 shows a 2-line Exponential Moving Average on one chart.

With each test of moving average crossovers you will need an indicator with two lines and a matching strategy that buys and sells on the crossovers. Indicators plot something; strategies buy and sell. It would be very nice if there were a way to combine or link them, but there is not. At least not in this version of TradeStation.

I have set these up for you at my Web site, **www.moneymentor.com.** From the main menu at moneymentor.com click on **Downloads** on the left-side column. This hyperlink will take you to a page where you can choose EasyLanguage Indicators for this exercise: XAvgCrossover, WAvgCrossover, TAvgCrossover, AAvgCrossover. Read the description associated with each type of moving average and choose the ones you want to experiment with. When you have had enough of playing with indicators, go back to the **Downloads** link, grab the `sjh_MAVTest` strategy, and play to your heart's content with optimizing moving averages. It's fun and informative. There is rough documentation on the Web site to explain the inputs, but not much more. It's up to you to experiment.

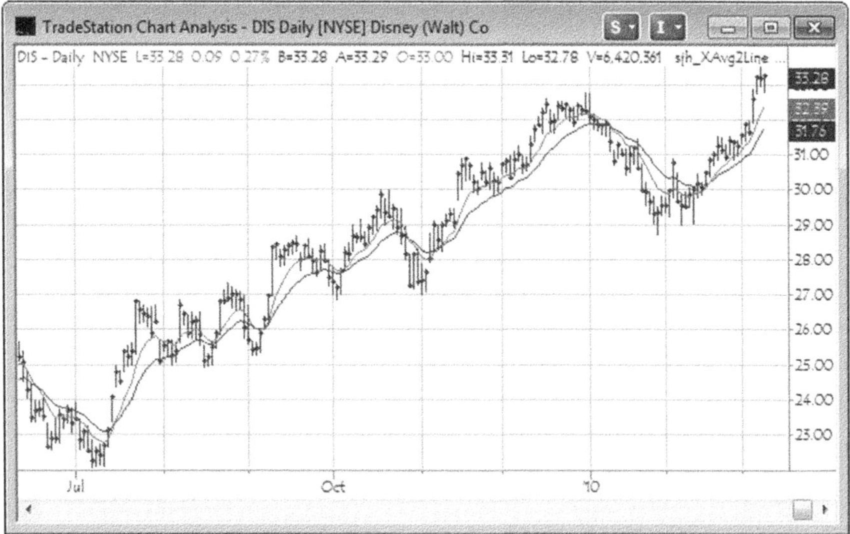

FIGURE 3.25 Exponential Moving Average

Varieties of Moving Averages Figures 3.26 through 3.32 demonstrate the variety we can achieve by making the changes in the input parameters. Figure 3.29 changes not only the inputs but the type of moving average. All of the charts were produced using TradeStation's built-in indicators. None of these is my proprietary work.

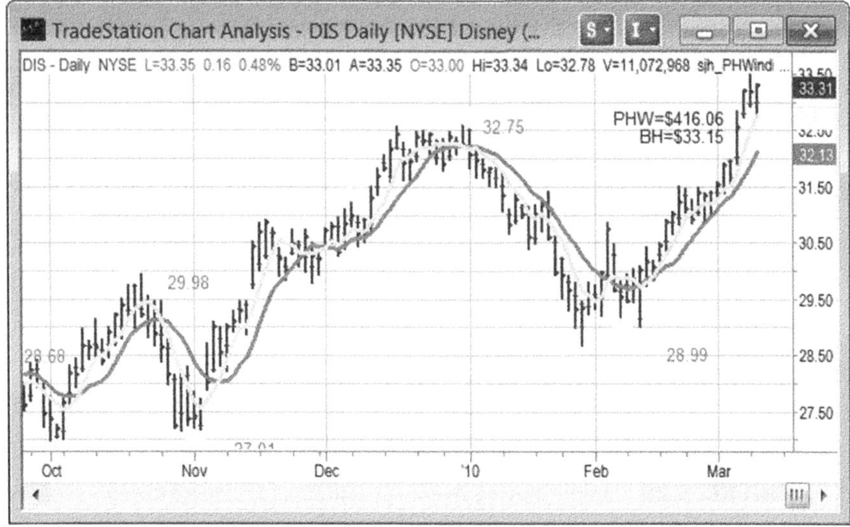

FIGURE 3.26 Simple Moving Average (Close,5,10)

FIGURE 3.27 Simple Moving Average (Close,2,5)

FIGURE 3.28 Simple Moving Average (High,2) and Simple Moving Average (Low,21)

FIGURE 3.29 Weighted Moving Average (C,9,18)

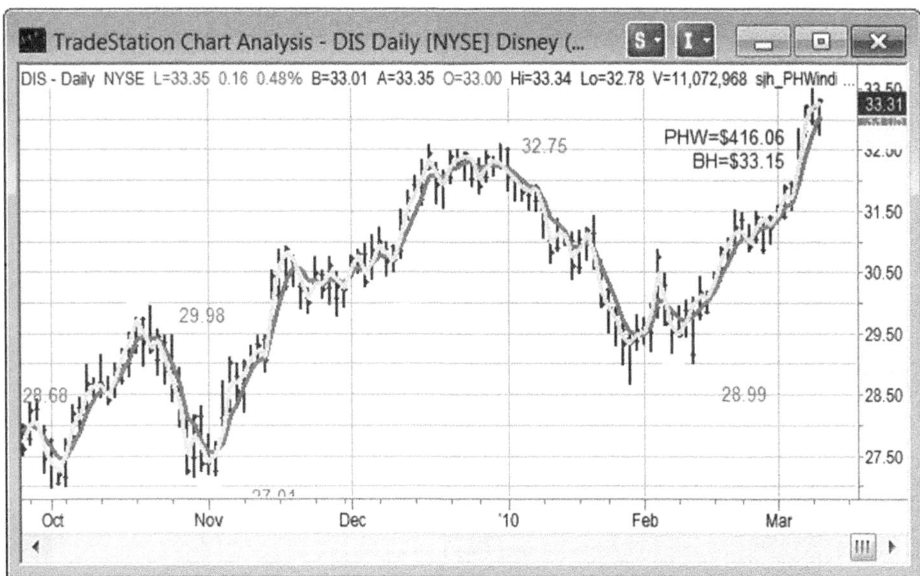

FIGURE 3.30 Weighted Moving Average (C,2,5)

FIGURE 3.31 Exponential Moving Average (Close,9,18)

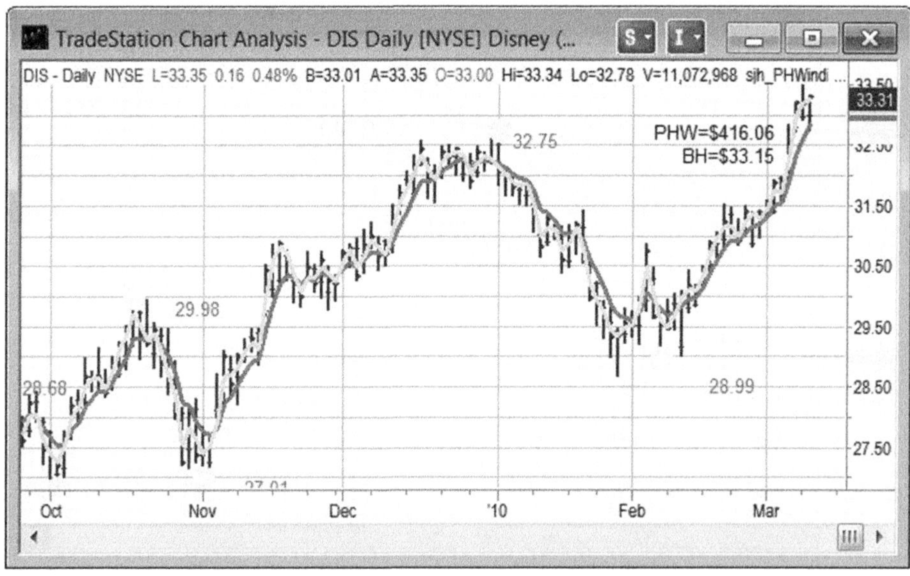

FIGURE 3.32 Exponential Moving Average (Close,2,5)

Examine the charts. What's the difference between weighted and simple? Between weighted and exponential? And there's more. There are triangular moving averages and adaptive moving averages in TradeStation. Experiment with those too.

Just to keep you on your toes, I have pulled a couple of fast ones on you in Figures 3.26 to 3.32. Look at the caption under Figures 3.29 and 3.30. Note that I have assumed you will remember that `C` is the equivalent of `Close` in TradeStation. I have also made the assumption that you will understand that the numbers in parentheses are the inputs to the indicator. It's good for you to have to think a bit.

What Is True?

Look again at Figures 3.26 through 3.32. Ask yourself: "What is true?" What is common to the seven charts? What are their differences? What happened as we shortened the length of the moving averages? What happened as we changed the type of average from simple to weighted to exponential?

One of the things I see is that as we shorten the length of the moving averages, we get more crossover signals. While it is true that we also get closer to the target circles, in the process we generate too many signals.

How can we make the best of both worlds? We want to keep the accuracy of the shorter moving averages and yet not get so many signals where we don't have yellow PHW targets.

One way is to use a second indicator as a filter, to add a condition that must also be met for us to consider it valid. We will address conditions in Chapter 9.

There are scores of indicators built into TradeStation. There are thousands more you can purchase, download, or program yourself.

The goal with indicators is not to collect the biggest pile but rather to find one or two simple and reliable indicators that work for you. Again, your goal should be to approximate the targets you have drawn.

If you come up with an indicator that appears promising but gives too many signals, don't abandon it just yet. We can filter out signals more easily than we can generate signals. More about that later.

Your Lab Book

Your search for the one or two good indicators will cover lots of territory, hopefully. If you are doing your homework and not just hoping for the holy grail to come to you, you will need to keep careful track of your attempts and your progress. Probably the easiest, and most valuable, way to keep track of your experiments is to use a spreadsheet program to record your activities. In *Trading 102* I address the use of a lab book, so I won't do it again here, but suffice it to say that now is the time for you to begin the meticulous logging of your findings.

Your lab book is your key to research success. It will show you where the successful techniques lie and will keep you from repeating experiments. Using Microsoft Excel for your book is not only convenient, it allows you to sort on any field to order your tests by best results, by variable, or by any chosen column.

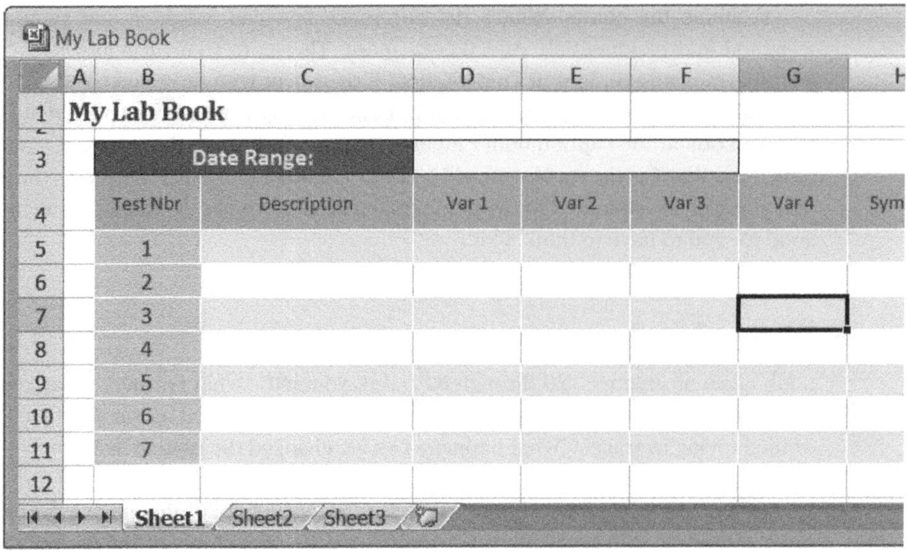

	A	B	C	D	E	F	G	H
1	My Lab Book							
3		Date Range:						
4		Test Nbr	Description	Var 1	Var 2	Var 3	Var 4	Sym
5		1						
6		2						
7		3						
8		4						
9		5						
10		6						
11		7						
12								

FIGURE 3.33 Beginning Your Lab Book

Please, please study the chapters in *Trading 102* that address record keeping, experiments, and your lab book. And if you want to use my lab book as a beginning template, the file in Figure 3.33 is available for download at www.moneymentor.com/TSME.html.

STEP 3: PROGRAMMING AND QUALITY ASSURANCE

After isolating a few choice indicators that do a good job of turning at or near the targets you've drawn, it is time to test their profit-generating potential. Thanks to TradeStation, this task is a jillion times easier than it was when I began testing and trading in the 1980s. Imagine running 1,000 tests all with pencil, paper, and calculator!

Programming your system is simply a matter of determining what events trigger buys and what events trigger sells and expressing these ideas in EasyLanguage.

EasyLanguage

EasyLanguage will tell you if it doesn't understand your expressions. In fact, it does an excellent job of isolating programming errors and helping you fixing them. It does not, however, know what you wanted to achieve. EasyLanguage can help you with your sentence structure, but it does not know the intended meaning of the sentence. Look in the appendix for a list of error codes.

To this day, as I design a new strategy for the markets, I begin the analysis by hand. I sketch a picture of my idea. I test my theory over a small sample of data to see that what I said is what I meant. I test the same ideas with pencil and paper and then test them with a spreadsheet. Then, and only then, do I test the ideas with TradeStation.

With the power of computers, it is easy to make mistakes faster. **A computer will do exactly what you tell it to,** no more and no less. In the programming phase, you need to verify that your logic is correct as well as your programming.

The more facile you are with EasyLanguage, the smoother this stage will be. Careful study of Chapter 4 and then Chapters 7 through the end of the book will assist you in becoming proficient at speaking EasyLanguage.

Attendant to the programming phase is the requirement for some heavy-duty analysis. While it may be true that *past results do not guarantee future results*, it's all we have to go on. The markets will never again behave exactly as they did yesterday, but we have no way of analyzing tomorrow. The best we can do is ask for some modicum of statistical assurance. The latest release of TradeStation goes the extra mile in providing valuable statistical tests in its Strategy Performance Reports, many of which are the product of David Stendahl and Leo Zamansky from RINA Systems.

Chapter 6, Basic EasyLanguage, is where we will get into the beginning of coding in TradeStation's proprietary language. This book will teach you the elements of programming in TradeStation's market language in a step-by-step approach. You will learn the difference among functions, indicators, and strategies. You will learn how to draw mathematical lines on a chart. You will learn how to make TradeStation buy and sell. But before we get to the basics of programming, we have to go through some basic math essential for programmers and traders.

In Chapter 18, Systems Performance, I will show you the tests I perform that allow me to feel comfortable trading a system. These tests are part of the quality assurance phase of bringing your product to market.

The entire rest of this book is devoted to **programming.** Throughout the remaining chapters you will be learning to speak EasyLanguage and to apply your programming to create trading strategies. Learning to speak any language is a matter of first memorizing the nouns. Babies spend the first two years memorizing and testing nouns. Only after they understand and are comfortable with some 200 nouns do they begin to learn adjectives and verbs. Use the appendix in this book with its reserved words to begin your memorization. There I have pulled out the most important reserved words for a QuickStudy. I have not provided a list of all the reserved words available in TradeStation, but only the ones you are likely to use in your first two years of programming EasyLanguage. When you are ready for the full and complete list, you can address that through TradeStation's EasyLanguage Dictionary, which is a little blue book icon on the toolbar.

Keep in mind at every turn to ask whether **you said what you meant.** And use your common sense. If you have done an elegant job of programming and the result doesn't look right on the chart, go back and ask elemental questions. Try the technique by hand. Ask "stupid" questions. That is what I mean by quality assurance.

STEP 4: MARKETING AND SALES

You are your market. If you are an individual trader, your product—the end result of your programming efforts—is going to be used by you. You have to convince yourself to use the product. You have to do follow-up customer service to be sure you continue to be comfortable using the product. In order to stick to the plan, you must continually market to yourself, creating and reinforcing the confidence it takes to stick to the plan.

Perhaps the **most difficult component of trading is the discipline.** You can have the best trading system in the world, and yet if you can't follow it you will be no better off than having no system at all. Also, you can be the world's most disciplined person, but if you are religiously following a bad system, you are doomed to financial failure.

Only one issue stands between you and following your system: **trust.** You must trust the system you have developed in steps 1 through 3. How does trust happen? Through experience. Your good experiences will generate trust; your bad experiences will engender doubt and skepticism.

Your neurology will not know the difference between real and imagined experiences. Both will serve to build or destroy trust. Hundreds of tests with thousands of successful trades will allow you to begin trusting your system. Knowing which statistical measures point to a robust system will engender trust. It is only through doing lots and lots of homework that you begin to trust your product.

If you know the statistics of your system backward and forward, if you know your CPC Index, if you know how many losses you might encounter in a row before seeing a winning trade (runs), then you begin to trust your system. I have trained over 1,000 traders. I have influenced tens of thousands with my books and articles. They come back to talk to me and write to me. If they all have one thing to say it is: "It's really difficult to follow a system." Everyone has this problem. Human nature is to jump in and correct the errors. Nevertheless, circumventing the system usually results in losses.

SUMMARY

In this chapter we have overviewed the four steps necessary in analysis of any scientific experiment or any entrepreneurial venture. Whether you are starting a new business of any kind, beginning your own trading business, or just coming up with a trading plan, you have to go through the same four steps.

In Chapter 18, Systems Performance, we cover the statistics of trusting your system. The single most important component of learning to trust your system is probably repetition. The testing and coding that go with creating a system, get repeated thousands of times during the process. Your neurology will accept the good results and remember to avoid the bad results. The repetition of the process creates the mental marketing that allows you to later follow your system with discipline.

As part of your marketing effort, you must keep good records. Record each and every trade in a lab book. Time stamp your trades and keep track of your profits and losses. In addition to logging each trade (whether hypothetical or real), create a summary record of monthly and quarterly results. From your monthly results, create an equity chart so you can view your results graphically.

CHAPTER 4

Basic Use of TradeStation

In This Chapter

- Introduction
- Basic Elements of TradeStation
- Older Versions of TradeStation: Read This Section
- All Versions Come Here
- Quick Start to Tailoring Your Chart and Strategy

INTRODUCTION

In this book, I am attempting to teach EasyLanguage independent of the version of TradeStation you are using. Whether you are using TradeStation 4.0 or TradeStation 2000i, the basic structure of the programming language is the same. Therefore, I will refer to the program as TradeStation (TS), without specifying the version number. In instances where there is a difference between the implementation of the two versions, I will give you examples of both and tell you which is which.

TradeStation is a software tool to help you describe and test your trading system ideas. TradeStation is not a trading system, it is a toolbox. If you want prepackaged, allegedly profitable systems right out of the box, you will need to contact TradeStation solution providers. In the appendix I provide a listing for your easy reference.

Think of TradeStation as the most sophisticated box of tools you can buy. Now you just need to learn how to use them.

BASIC ELEMENTS OF TRADESTATION

A trading system is just a map, recipe, or procedure that traders use over and over again in a methodical way. A trading system is an objective set of rules that describes when to buy and when to sell. To create a trading system with TradeStation's toolbox, you will need to learn how to assemble the elements of the puzzle to make a coherent strategy.

Once upon a time TradeStation was a program you bought (or leased) to run on your own computer, on a CD (they didn't even have DVDs yet). You installed the program, which came in three modules, and then leased a different program (by a different vendor) to supply the data. There were several data vendors to choose from and several formats for the data. There was competition among the data vendors for your attention, and correspondingly the price structure for leasing data began to go the way of all capitalistic ventures—it got cheaper. Supply and demand at work. At the same time, brokers were in competition for your commissions. And commissions got cheaper. Along came the Internet, and computing went the way of its previous incarnation and headed back to centralized mainframes. First there were mainframes, then there were personal computers, and then the personal computers grew so powerful that they became servers located in a central location, which we now use as mainframes again.

You may skip the next section if you use the current version of TradeStation on the company's computers that you access via the Internet. If you have an old version of TradeStation, say 4.0, Pro, or 2000i, you should read the next section before going on.

OLDER VERSIONS OF TRADESTATION: READ THIS SECTION

The first concept you need to grasp to use older versions of TradeStation is the distinction between the pieces and parts. We will call the pieces and parts modules. There are three separate and distinct modules within TradeStation: the part that collects the data, the part that displays the charts, and the part that allows you to write your own code. Each of these parts is a separate program, known to programmers as executables. These three parts communicate with each other seamlessly, so you may not even realize that they are separate and distinct. In fact, in recent versions of TradeStation, since it became web-based, you no longer see the data-collection module. The company has it on its server, behind the scenes. I make mention of the data-collection module for folks who still have older versions of TS.

You don't need to understand the computer structure behind executables to run a program, but you should understand that there are three separate modules you will need in order to use the full capabilities of TradeStation. To navigate fluidly through TradeStation you should be comfortable with the distinction between the parts and know when to use which one.

You can recognize that you are using different modules, because in TradeStation you will use the **Go** (or in TS 4, the **Tools**) pull-down menu from the toolbar to navigate from one module to the other. (See Figure 4.1.)

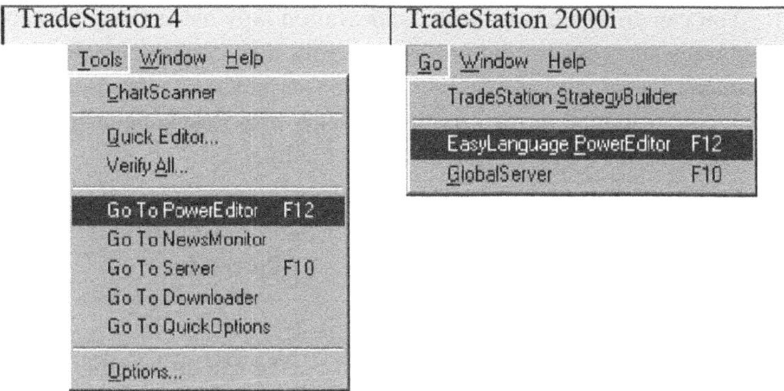

FIGURE 4.1 Go Pulldown Menu Showing All Three Modules

Let's say you have all three modules running (charting, editor, and data) and you are in the charting module, viewing charts. If you would like to write code for an indicator, you would need to be in the module that allows you to write code: the PowerEditor. To get there you would navigate as shown in Figure 4.2.

TradeStation 4	TradeStation 2000i
Tools → Go to PowerEditor	**Go → EasyLanguage PowerEditor**

FIGURE 4.2 Navigating to the PowerEditor

To use TradeStation, two executables are mandatory. A third executable is optional, and used only when you want to create your own systems and indicators. The two mandatory executables are shown in Figure 4.3.

Version	Module (Executable) Name	Purpose
TS 4	Server for {Signal}	To get data into computer.
TS 2000i	GlobalServer	To get data into computer.
>TS 8.0	not applicable	
TS 4	TradeStation	To display charts and analysis.
TS 2000i	TradeStation or ProSuite	To display charts and analysis.
>TS 8.0	TradeStation	To display charts and analysis.

FIGURE 4.3 TradeStation Mandatory Modules

You can go a long way with TradeStation only using these two elements. In fact, you could trade successfully and never write your own code: You could buy systems from programmers, known as TradeStation solution providers (TSPs). But since this book is about coding and testing your own trading systems with EasyLanguage, our focus will be on the third element, the PowerEditor, shown in Figure 4.4.

Version	Module (Executable) Name	Purpose
TS 4	TradeStation PowerEditor	To edit and modify systems, indicators, and other studies.
TS 2000i	EasyLanguage PowerEditor	To edit and modify signals, indicators, and other studies.
TS 8.0	EasyLanguage PowerEditor	To edit and modify strategies, indicators, and other studies.

FIGURE 4.4 Getting to the PowerEditor

If you accepted all the default settings when you installed TradeStation, the icons in Figure 4.4 will appear on your desktop. Starting TradeStation is as easy as double-clicking the **DataServer** or **GlobalServer** icon shown in Figure 4.3.

To Run TradeStation

There is not much to it anymore. Way back when, it was a matter of starting up the GlobalServer to bring in the data and then running TradeStation. If you wanted to create your own indicators and strategies, you needed to start the third executable in the group, the **EasyLanguage PowerEditor.** Not so any longer. Now you simply double-click the TradeStation icon on your desktop and TradeStation runs.

To Run the EasyLanguage Power Editor

Double-click the EasyLanguage icon on your desktop, shown in Figure 4.4. This action will start the program that allows you to write and modify systems, indicators, functions, and other studies. This program is called the PowerEditor. The PowerEditor is much like a word processor, say Microsoft Word. You are faced with a blank piece of paper and you get to fill it with your ideas. Just as Microsoft Word doesn't write your letter for you, EasyLanguage doesn't write your code for you. Only you know what you want to say.

If you have followed the default installation steps in your install of TradeStation, you will have some data for us to play with. If not, you will need to get data into TradeStation from the HistoryBank CD-ROM or from HistoryBank.com. Come back to this step when you are ready.

ALL VERSIONS COME HERE

No matter what version of TradeStation you are using, there are common elements to the process of starting TradeStation, opening a chart, changing the parameters, and putting a strategy on the chart. The next Quick Start takes you through the general steps common to all users.

QUICK START TO TAILORING YOUR CHART AND STRATEGY

So you will feel like we're getting somewhere fast, let's start up TradeStation and start manipulating a chart. (See Figure 4.5.)

In this Quick Start we are going to do seven things:

1. Start TradeStation.
2. Bring up a new chart.
3. Add an indicator to the chart.
4. Change the time frame of the chart.
5. Change the scale of the chart.
6. Apply a system.
7. Look at the system's performance.

FIGURE 4.5 Steps for Quick Start

Following are the detailed steps to bringing up your first chart with TradeStation.

Step 1: Start TradeStation

Double-click on the TradeStation icon on your desktop, or from the Windows Start icon click on All Programs and go to TradeStation. Say **Yes** to allow the program to make changes to your computer. Next, enter your username and password and click LiveTrading, Simulated Trading, or Work Offline. These choices determine whether you will be collecting real-time data or not, but it doesn't much matter either way for the purposes of this exercise.

If TradeStation asks you whether you want to upgrade to the latest version, just say **No** for now.

At this point you should be looking at a blank TradeStation desktop with no workspace. It will look like Figure 4.6. All the toolbars will be showing, at the top and on the left side. The best way to learn how to use any program, TradeStation included, is to start pressing buttons. You won't break it. Click on an icon or menu item and see what happens. Pull down the menus, starting with File and going all the way across. If something happens that gets you lost, or you don't understand, just close the program and start again from step 1. You can go a long way by familiarizing yourself with the commands under each menu item. That way, when you need to accomplish something, you will remember that you saw a command like that under a menu item. Soon you won't have to hunt and peck; you will remember where they are when you need them.

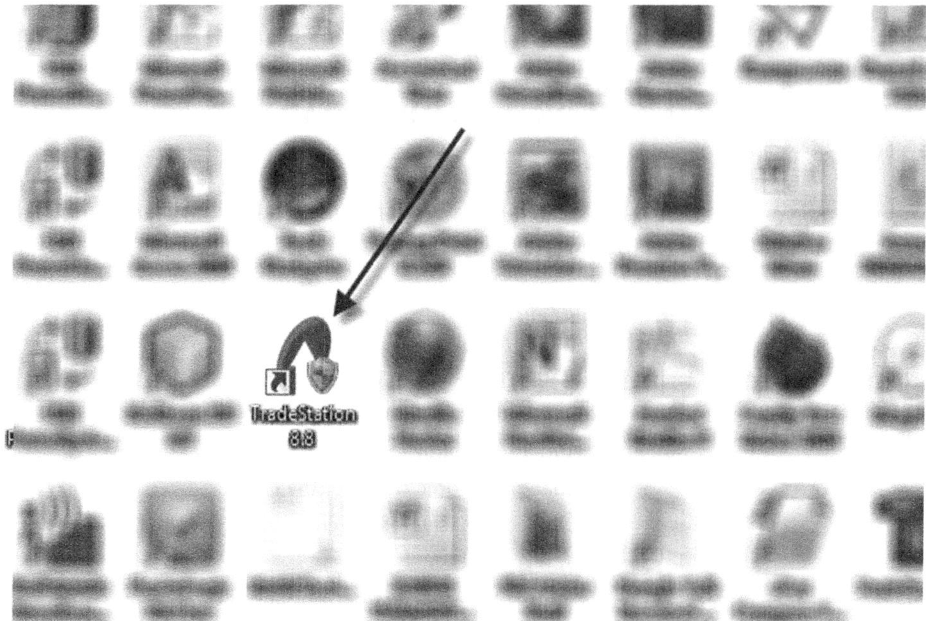

FIGURE 4.6 The TradeStation Icon on My Windows Desktop

Step 2: Bring Up a New Chart

Before you can make a trade you need to be looking at a chart of the entity you want to trade. You need to see current prices and historical prices. You need to be looking at the time frame you want to trade with and longer-term time frames for reference.

To bring a chart onto your desktop, click on the **Chart Analysis** icon on the left-side toolbar. It is the fourth item down from the top, under **Tools.** (See Figure 4.7.)

Your chart may or may not look like mine. (See Figure 4.8.) The data may be more or less compressed. The OHLC bars may not be blue and thick; they may be thin and black, or

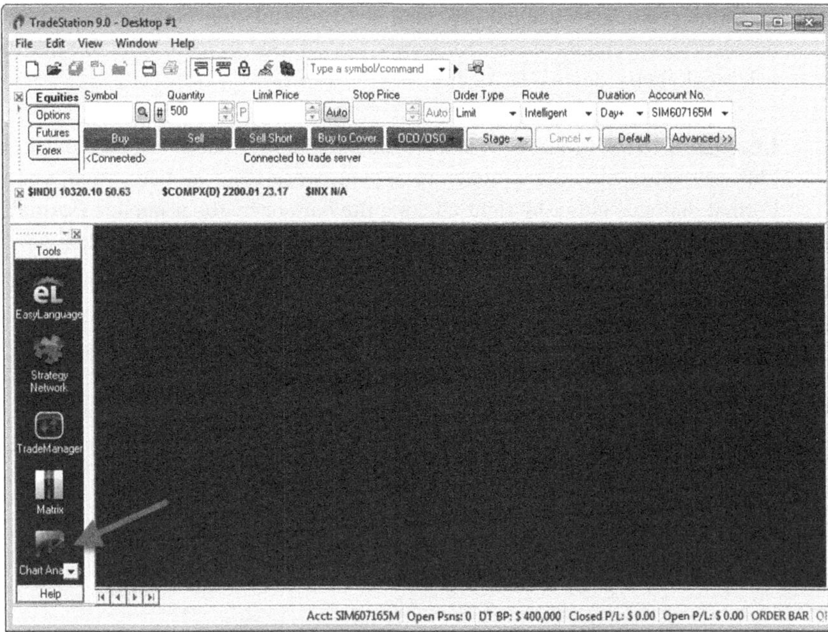

FIGURE 4.7 Click on the Chart Analysis Icon

FIGURE 4.8 A Chart on Your Workspace

something else. Your background may be black and your bars may be white. It all depends on what your defaults are set to. Now's a good time to learn how to alter the defaults. We will break Step 2 down into details.

Changing the Defaults Click on the bars of your bar chart, so the data become active. This will cause little black boxes to appear every 10 or so bars. Next, you may get to the Format dialogue either by right-clicking the bars or by the sequence **Format** → **Symbol**... Whichever you choose, you will come to the dialogue box in Figure 4.9.

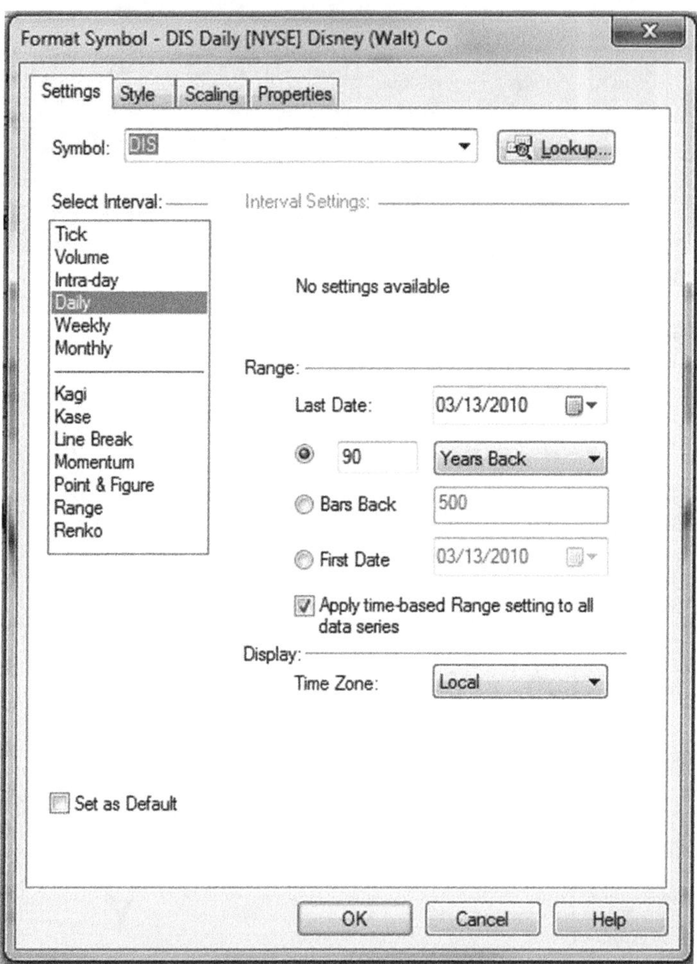

FIGURE 4.9 Format Symbol Dialogue Box

You will see that there are several choices you can make in this dialogue box. They are:

1. Settings
2. Style
3. Scaling
4. Properties

When you expand each of these selections, you have more to choose from:

1. Settings
   a. Symbol
   b. Select Interval
   c. Range
   d. Display
   e. Set as Default
2. Style
   a. Bar Type
   b. Bar Components
   c. Regular Session
   d. Outside Regular Session
   e. Same Color/Weight for All Components
   f. Display Update Indication
   g. Make Price Data Invisible
   h. Set as Default
3. Scaling
   a. Axis
   b. Type
   c. Range
   d. Display
   e. Set as Default
4. Properties
   a. Symbol
   b. Category
   c. Country
   d. Currency
   e. Session
   f. Time Zone
   g. Price Scale
   h. Min Move
   i. Big Point Value

For most of these choices, in a beginning book, we will simply accept the defaults. There are, however, several selections that we want to experiment with.

Select Interval Perhaps one of the most important considerations for what you are going to trade is time frame, or Interval. It is often the case that a daily chart of your symbol may not be tradable, while a 15-minute chart is tradable. In fact, students of mine report frequently that they have found the 13-minute chart to be quite valuable, even more than the 15-minute chart. Let's experiment now with choice 2.b, **Select Interval.** The choices under **Select Interval** are:

1. Tick
2. Volume
3. Intraday
4. Daily
5. Weekly
6. Monthly

and beneath that are:

1. Kagi
2. Kase
3. Line Break
4. Momentum
5. Point & Figure
6. Range
7. Renko

For completeness sake, I will show you through Figures 4.10a to 4.10f what each of these charts looks like. I will, however, not go into depth about the use and characteristics of each type. There are many books on each chart type that you can refer to.

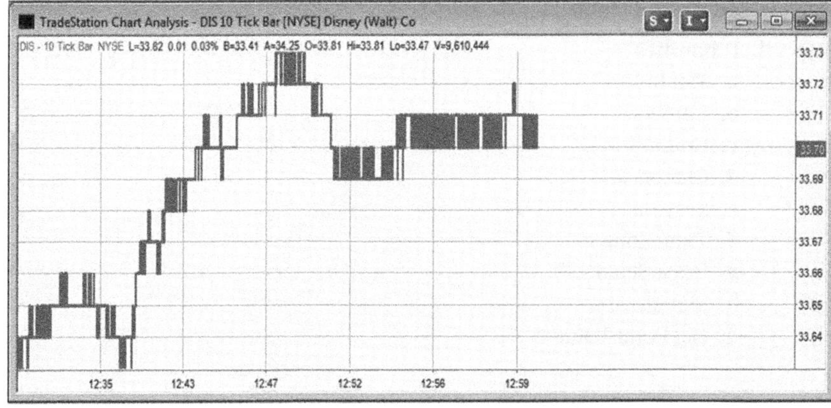

FIGURE 4.10a Tick Chart of DIS

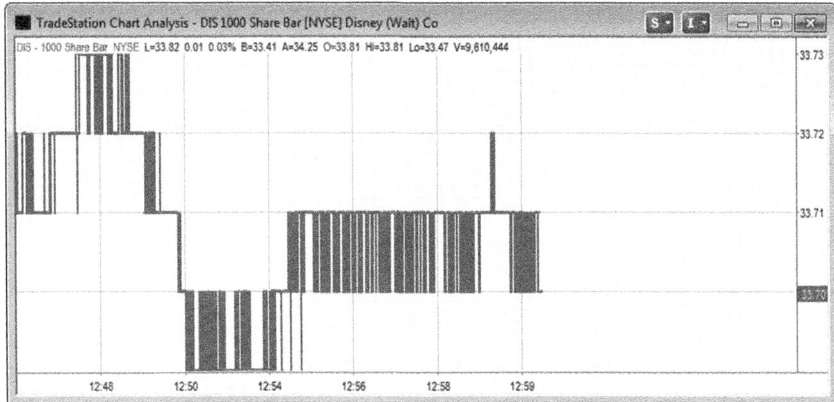

FIGURE 4.10b Volume Chart of DIS

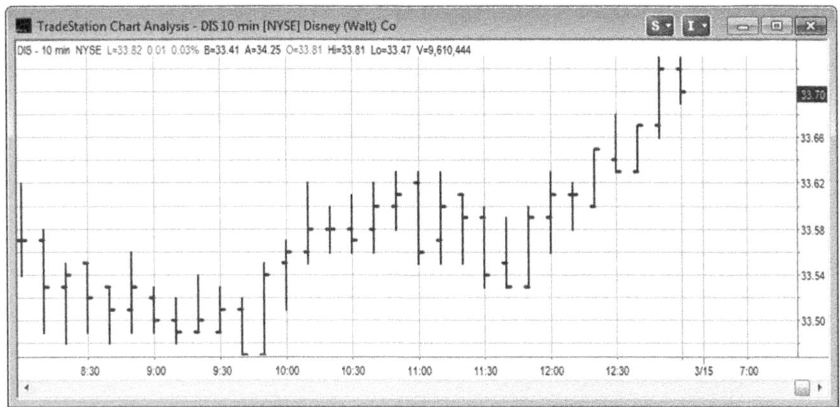

FIGURE 4.10c Intraday Chart of DIS

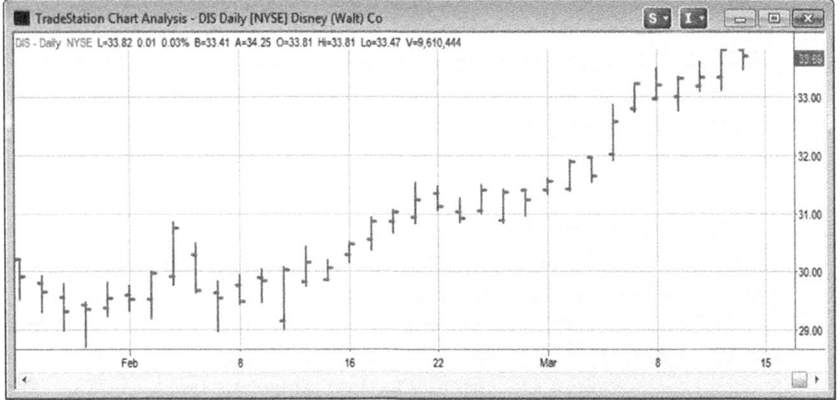

FIGURE 4.10d Daily Chart of DIS

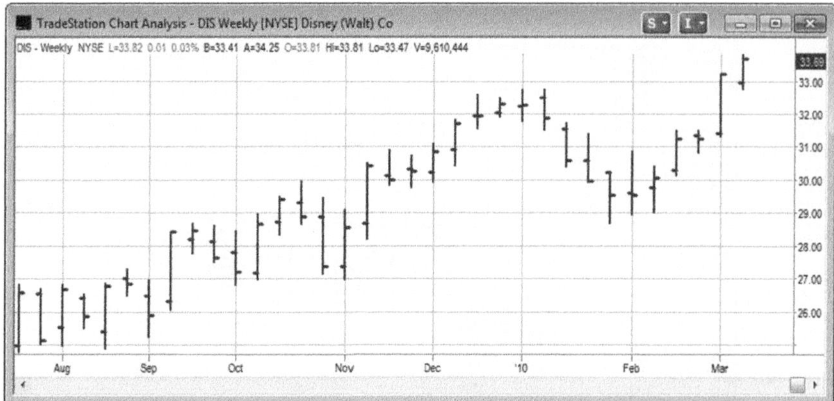

FIGURE 4.10e Weekly Chart of DIS

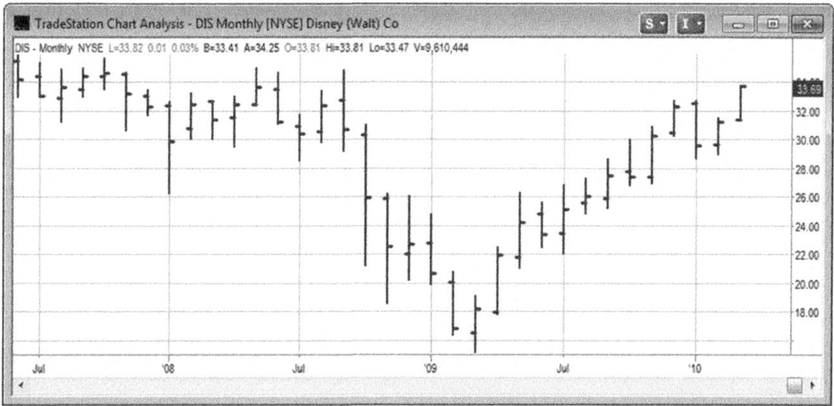

FIGURE 4.10f Monthly Chart of DIS

NOTE: It is important for you to notice that the time period covered by each of these charts is different. The time frame is listed on the top left of the chart, right after the symbol. TradeStation can display only just so many bars on a single chart. Thus, the tick chart (Figure 4.10a) will display only a day or part of a day, while the monthly chart (Figure 4.10f) displays years of data.

With each successive chart you are displaying more data in time. In these figures you have gone from micro to macro view. Turning points that were significant in the tick chart don't even show up in the daily chart.

In Figures 4.11a to 4.11g, you will get a look at the rest of the chart types that are available under **Format → Symbol → Select Interval.** They really aren't time frames, but this is where these choices are currently located. The chart types are: Kagi, Kase, Line Break, Momentum, Point & Figure, Range, and Renko.

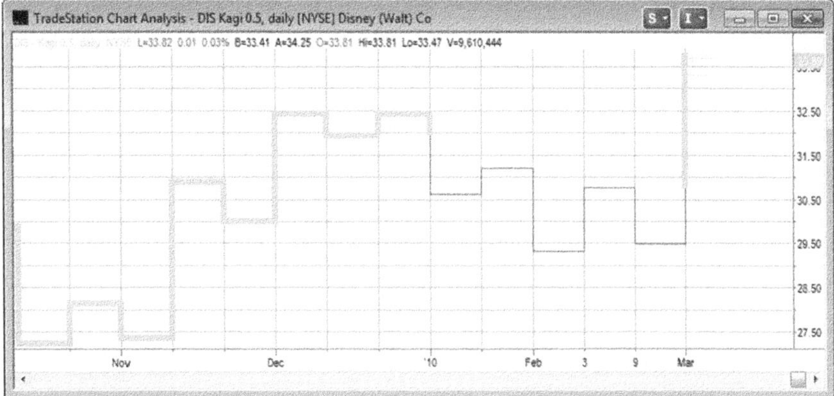

FIGURE 4.11a Kagi Chart

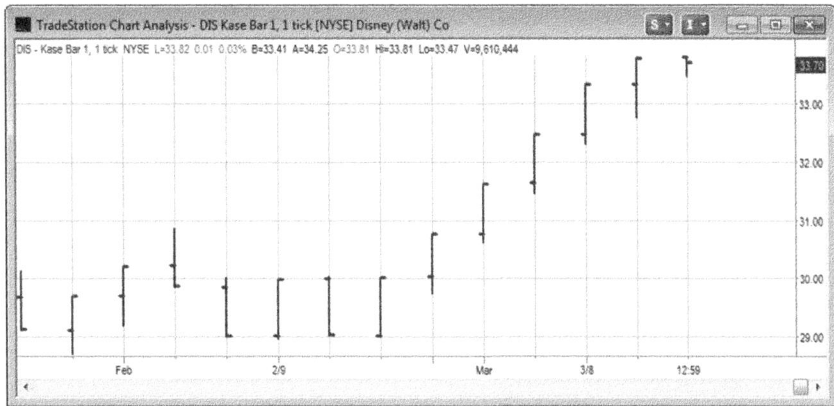

FIGURE 4.11b Kase Chart

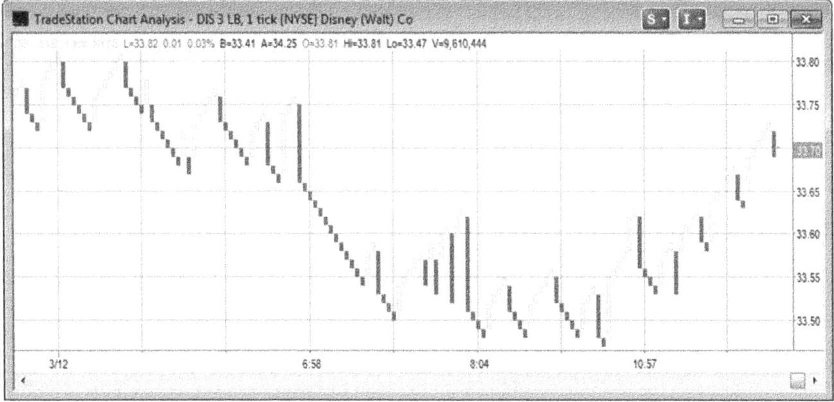

FIGURE 4.11c Line Break Chart

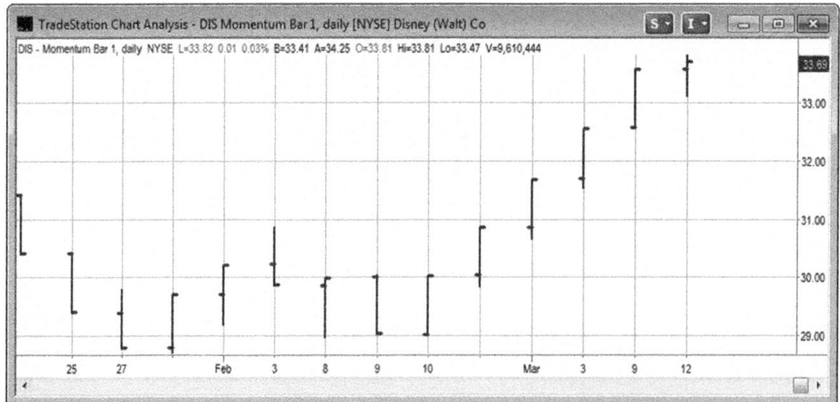

FIGURE 4.11d Momentum Chart

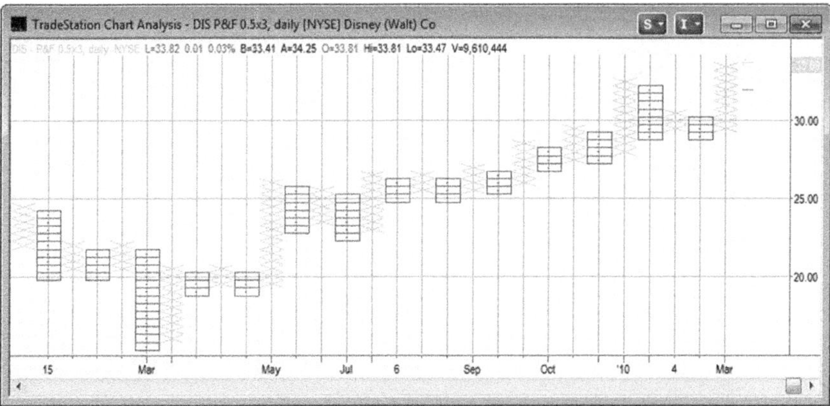

FIGURE 4.11e Point & Figure Chart

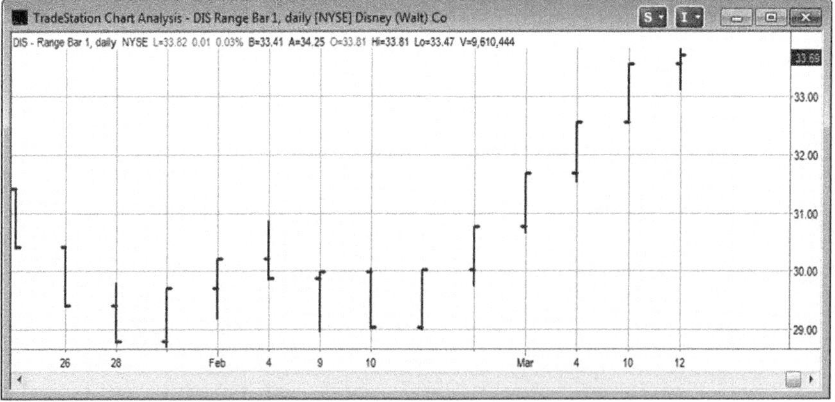

FIGURE 4.11f Range Chart

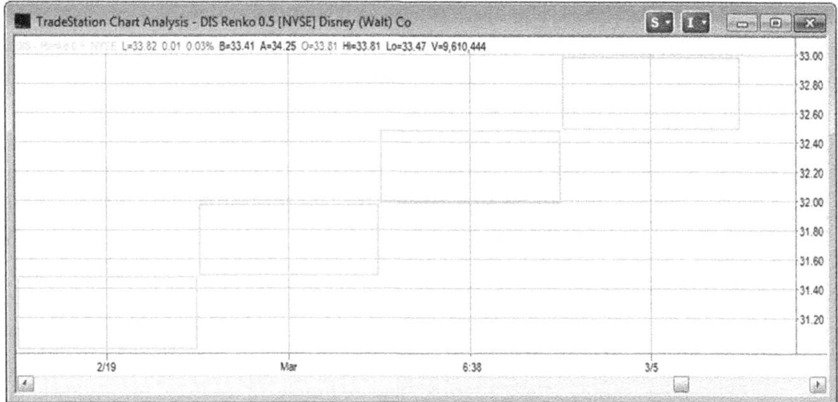

FIGURE 4.11g Renko Chart

Each of these figures represents a different way of displaying data. It's the same data: Open, High, Low, Close. That's about all there is. Analysts keep trying to come up with "the answer"—a better way of displaying the data so that they can make a killing in the markets. Study these figures and see if there is some hidden meaning you connect with. Different charts appeal to different people.

Format Range Now that we have tried every possibility for **Interval** under the **Format → Symbol** dialogue, let's play with a few more buttons. Under the same **Format → Symbol** dialogue, from Figure 4.9, take a look at the section labeled **Range** in the right part of the frame. You can choose the section of data you want to display. You can tell TradeStation what section you want in several different ways.

- **Last Date** tells TS the last date you want to see on your chart. You could, for instance, tell it you want to see the last day in 1987 by selecting the date with the calendar control button.
- In combination with Last Date, you can tell TS how many **Years Back** you want displayed. You could end at 12/31/1987, for instance, and go 90 years back. Actually, even though you ask for 90 years back, it will only give you as much data as is available in its data banks. DIS only goes back to 1/2/1968, and that's not 90 years. If your data is displayed in intraday format, the **Years Back** will change to **Days Back.**
- You can also specify how many **Bars Back** you want displayed, instead of how many Days or Years Back. **Bars Back** is useful if you are calculating something in your indicator or strategy that uses a specific number of bars. It is also helpful if you want to keep the same number of bars in each data set and don't want to calculate the dates around that count. For instance, you could evaluate 100 bars back from 12/31/2010, 100 bars back from 12/31/2000, and 100 bars back from 12/31/1990. You wouldn't have to know what those dates were to perform these calculations.
- Instead of specifying the Last Date, you can specify the **First Date** for calculation. You might want to leave October 19, 1987, out of calculations, so you could specify the First Date to be 10/22/1987.

- Last, but not least, you may choose to display your data in your **Local Time Zone** or in the Time Zone of the **Exchange** which carries your data. I prefer to use Local, because I get my data from a Chicago Exchange and from a New York Exchange, which are in two different time zones.

Format Styles Figure 4.11 shows the **Format → Symbol → Style** sequence. From this dialogue box you can select **Bar Type, Bar Components,** colors and weights for **Regular Session** and **Outside Regular Session.** Let's try a few of these buttons, starting with the **Bar Type.**

The choice **OHLC** shows all the data transmitted by the Exchange on a single bar. It displays the Open, High, Low and Close. The next choice, **HLC,** shows everything except the **Opening** price. Some Exchanges do not transmit the Open price on some symbols.

The next choice, **Candlestick,** has volumes of written information about it. Go to TradersLibrary.com, under Books, and search for candlestick. My favorite books on the subject are by Steve Nisson, arguably the U.S. expert on the subject. Figure 4.12 shows DIS in candlestick format.

FIGURE 4.12 Candlestick Chart

Just briefly, a candlestick shows the OHLC in an easy-to-read format, which lets you quickly discern where the open was in relation to the close. The **body** of the candle shows the open and the close, with the candle being **solid** if the open was higher than the close and **hollow** if the open was lower than the close. With most software, you can not only reverse this convention, you can make the body different colors, like red and green, to denote where the open was in relation to the close. The wicks, or **shadows,** of the candle, on the top and bottom of the body, pinpoint the high and the low of the bar.

For a closer view, Figure 4.13 shows a single candle with explanation. (Thanks to www.babypips.com.)

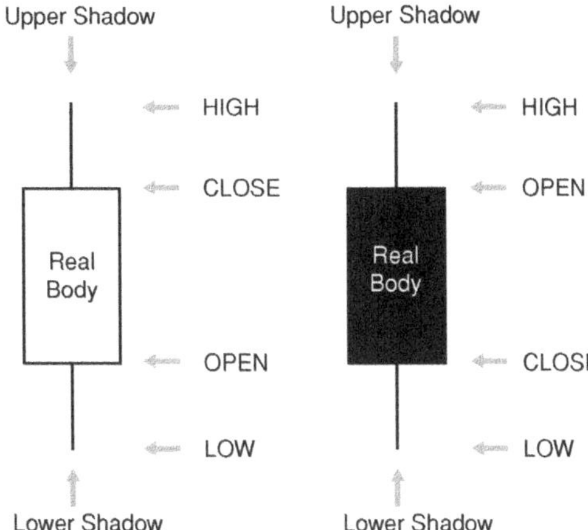

FIGURE 4.13 Single Candle

From the Web site www.babypips.com we get this summary of candlestick charting:

Candlesticks are formed using the open, high, low, and close of the chosen time period.

- *If the close is above the open, then a hollow candlestick (usually displayed as white) is drawn.*
- *If the close is below the open, then a filled candlestick (usually displayed as black) is drawn.*
- *The hollow or filled section of the candlestick is called the "real body" or body.*
- *The thin lines poking above and below the body display the high/low range and are called shadows.*
- *The top of the upper shadow is the "high".*
- *The bottom of the lower shadow is the "low."*

Long bodies indicate strong buying or selling. The longer the body is, the more intense the buying or selling pressure. . . .

Short bodies imply very little buying or selling activity. In street forex lingo, bulls mean buyers and bears mean sellers. . . .

Upper shadows signify the session high. Lower shadows signify the session low. . . .

Candlesticks with a long upper shadow, long lower shadow and small real bodies are called spinning tops. . . . The pattern indicates the indecision between the buyers and sellers.

The next choice under **Format → Symbol → Style** is candlestick with trend. (See Figure 4.14.) This configuration displays an enhancement to the standard candlestick chart. In this chart, candlestick bars are displayed with hollow/filled bodies where the bar color is used to indicate the trend direction. By default, green indicates an up trend where the current bar close is greater than the previous close; red indicates a down trend where the current bar close is less than the previous close; and gray indicates no change in close from the previous to current bar. Compare the chart in Figure 4.12 to the one in Figure 4.14.

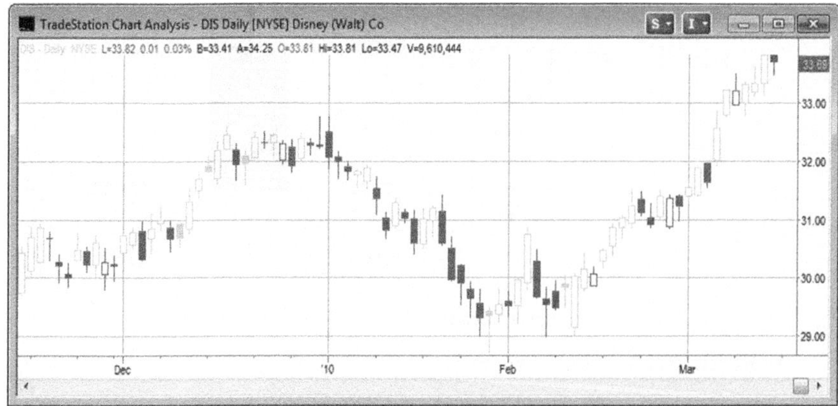

FIGURE 4.14 Candlestick with Trend

Compare the chart in Figure 4.13 to the chart in Figure 4.11. At first glance they appear to be the same. Take another look, however, and you will see that there are subtle differences, beyond the hollow candles. In the candles with trend, some of the bars that were red in Figure 4.11 turn to green. The bars in Figure 4.13 do more than those in Figure 4.11: They denote trend by comparing successive closes.

The next available selection is dot on close. Figure 4.15 shows the resultant chart. In this chart, open, high, and low are ignored and a dot is drawn at the closing price of each bar. The information available to the viewer is very limited and is similar to that of the next chart, in Figure 4.16, line on close.

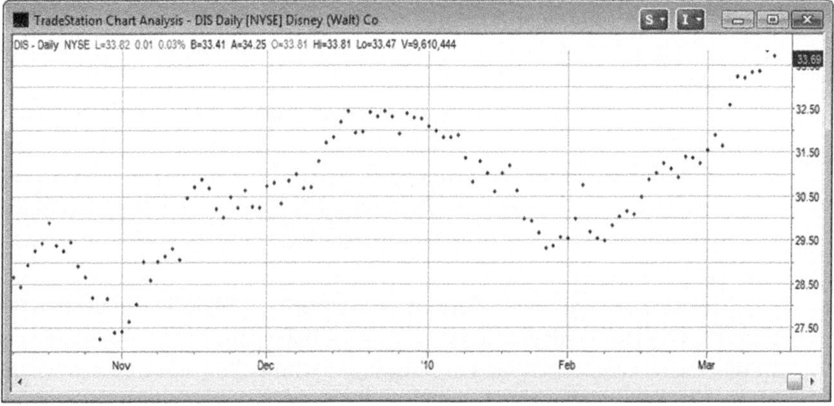

FIGURE 4.15 Dot on Close

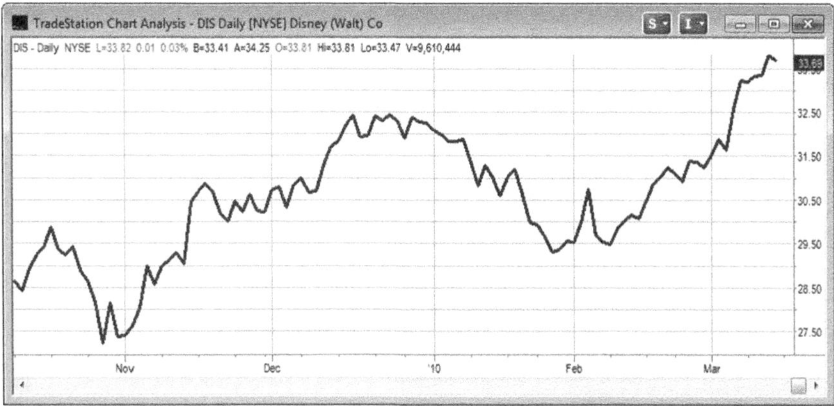

FIGURE 4.16 Line on Close

Format More Styles Having pushed every button in the **Format → Symbol → Style → Bar Type** section, let's turn our attention to **Bar Components.** First, if you are still on the **Line on Close** selection from **Bar Type,** scroll back up and click on **OHLC Bar** under **Bar Type.** We are going to change the chart so that the open is easily distinguished from the close of the day before.

The Bar Components section allows you to configure the open, high/low, and close separately. I like to have my charts so that the open and high/low are the same thickness, and the close is twice as thick. Take a look at the choices I've made in Figure 4.17.

Select OHLC Bar then under **Bar Components** click on **Open.** While on that selection go to the right and choose the second bar thickness under **Weight.** And now, before you go any further, uncheck the box labeled "Use same color/weight for all components within each bar type". This way you can make different choices in weight for the open, close, and the high/low that are a single unit. Do this maneuver again to select the second thickness for High/Low. Now all three will be of one thickness. Next, click on **Close** and choose the fourth weight for its thickness. The preview at the bottom of the window will show you how it is going to look. The close will now stick out. Last, click the checkbox labeled **Set as Default** to make all subsequent charts appear this way.

To further distinguish the open from the close, go back into the **Format** box and change the open to be the same weight but change the **color** to **red.** Now your chart will look something like mine in Figure 4.18. Now it's easy to tell what was the open and what was the close.

Format the Scale of the Data Using the menu sequence **Format → Symbol → Scaling,** we will now take a look at all the options for scaling your chart. How you *look at* the data means just about everything. Let me exaggerate the importance of this concept by showing you two different views of the Crash of 1929. The first chart will show you the data from way back then until now, all on the same **linear** scale (Figure 4.19). The second chart will have the data scaled **semi-log,** which means the y-axis will be logarithmic, while the date or x-axis

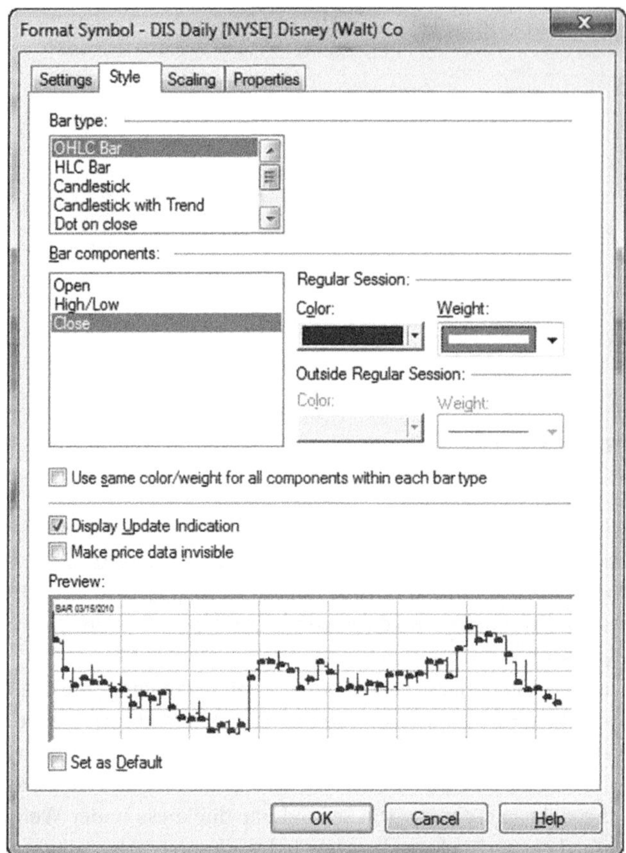

FIGURE 4.17 Bar Components Separate

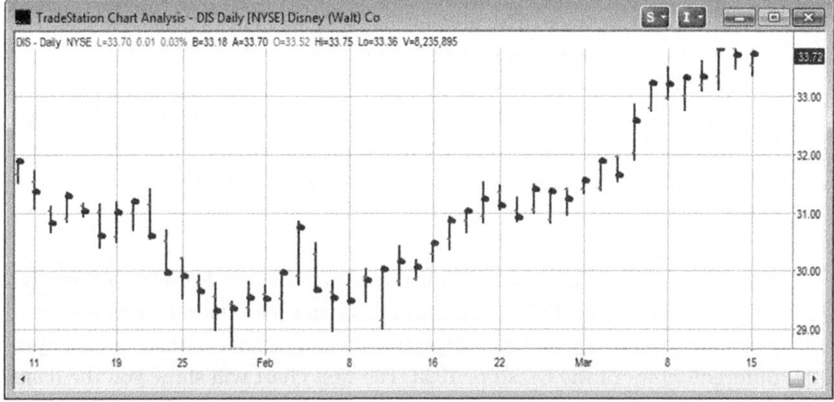

FIGURE 4.18 Red Open, Blue Close

will stay linear. I can't continue to use DIS for this illustration, as the data doesn't go back that far. But, TradeStation supplies data for the Dow Jones 30 Industrials back that far, and that symbol is $INDU. That's what we will use for this example.

The first thing to do is change the symbol by simply typing `$INDU` on the keyboard while you are on the chart. This will bring up the new data. Second, under the **Settings** on the **Format** window, change it to display the data **Monthly.** We can't go back 81 years viewing it as daily data on one screen.

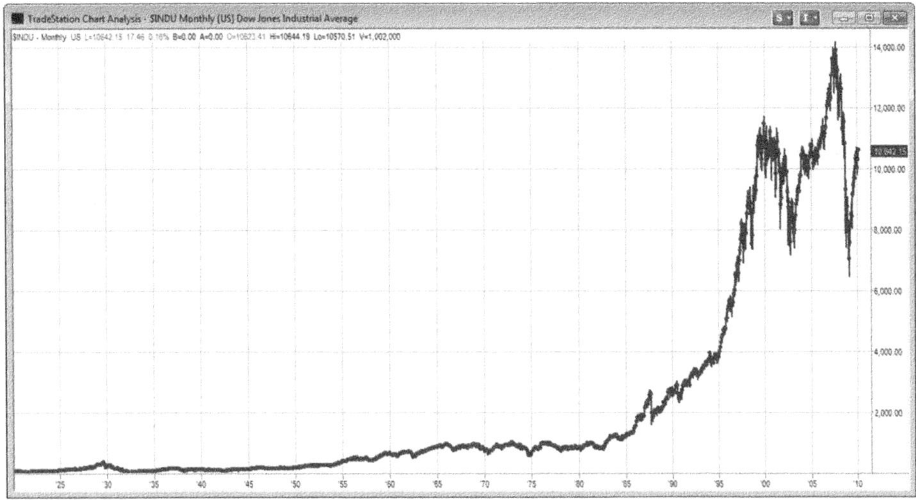

FIGURE 4.19 1929 to 2010 Linear Scale

Wow! What a difference. On Figure 4.19 the Crash of 1929 was just a tiny blip in the data on the left side. But Figure 4.20 shows its full impact as the worst crash in history. Comparing them on the semi-log scale, the Crash of 1987 appears small. That's because using semi-log causes the data to appear more in the currency of the time than in today's dollars. The TradeStation Help files say this about the subject:

Linear charts are commonly used to display recent price data (1 min, 30 min, daily) where the price movement is relatively small compared to the long term price of the symbol. When looking at prices over much longer time periods, however, it may be useful to look at data from a different perspective such as using a semi-log chart to try to give more weight to the percentage change in prices compared to just the absolute price.

To learn more about the meaning of logarithms, trust our faithful Google. An explanation is beyond the scope of this book.

From this single example you not only learned about scaling data, you learned that clicking the radio button labeled Linear makes a lot of difference from clicking the radio

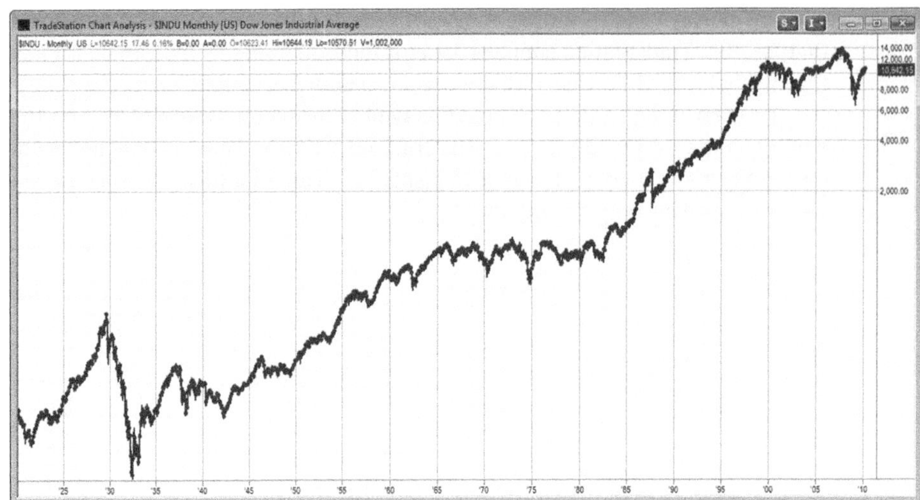

FIGURE 4.20 1929 to 2010 Semi-Log Scale

button labeled Semi-Log. When you are looking at long time periods, always consider using semi-log.

I am going back now to the DIS symbol, by typing `DIS` from my chart window. Actually, first, before doing that, I changed the scaling back to **Linear.** Don't want to lose you here.

Figure 4.21 shows the **Scaling** box, under **Format → Symbol.**

We have already explored what the ◉ **Linear** and ◉ **Semi-Log** radio buttons do, so let's move on to axis. By changing the default of **Scale On: Right Axis** to **Scale On: Left Axis,** you will move the y-axis (probably Price) to the left side of the chart. Usually it's on the right because the most recent prices (which you may be trading) appear on the right. The most recent price is the rightmost price. I don't really know why you would want it for trading, but by selecting No Axis you can remove the y-axis altogether.

Playing with the charts produced by making selections under **Sub-graph** is left to the reader. It is pretty obvious what happens if you simply try a few selections by yourself.

Next in line is the section called **Range,** shown in Figure 4.22. The default is ◉ **Automatic:** ◉ **Scale Range Based on:** and then the default selection is **Date Range on Screen.** This displays your charts as you have been seeing them in all of the examples of DIS so far. Below that choice is **Entire Date Range,** which will do just as it says and display the data on a scale that covers all of the data in the database for that symbol. DIS, for instance, goes back to 1968, where it opened at $0.16, or effectively zero. Thus, if you scale over the entire date range, the y-axis will go from zero to 45. If you had left it on the default, as you scroll back and forth across the whole date range the y-axis would change to accommodate each data range. Try it now and see what happens.

Further, under the **Scale Range Based on:** selector, you will see the last choice, **Percent Below/Above Last.** When you make that selection, it highlights the percentage above and below specification boxes, with a default of 5% for each. Use that choice for now and look at the resultant chart, shown in Figure 4.23.

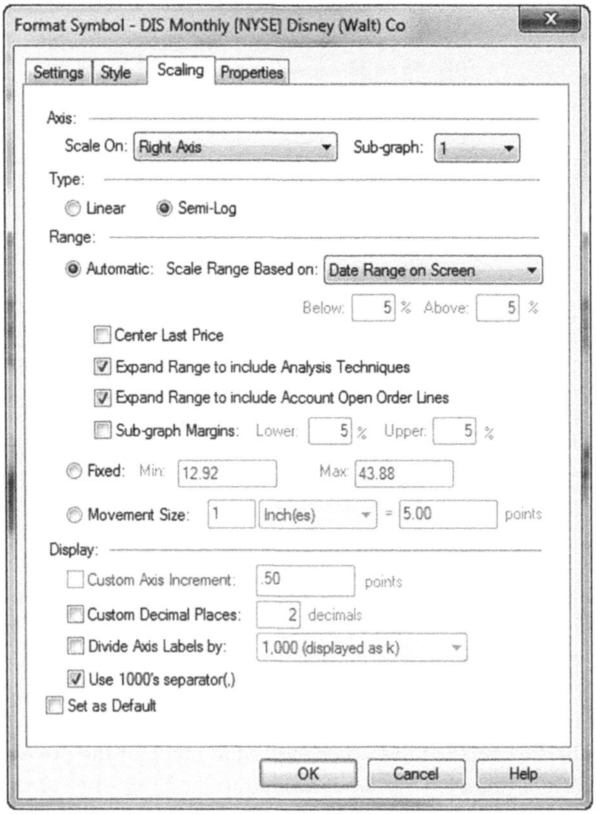

FIGURE 4.21 Format Symbol Scaling

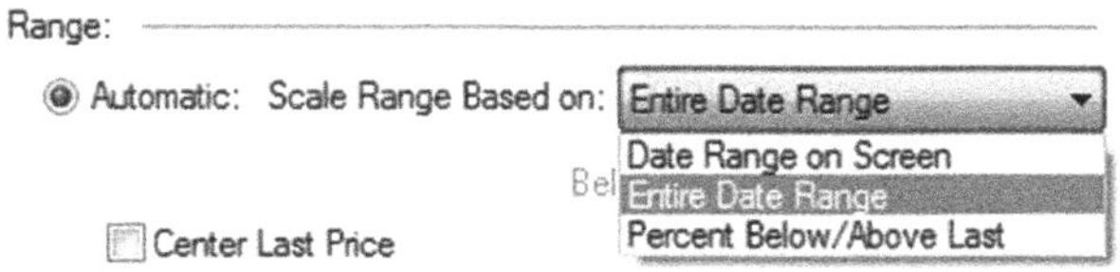

FIGURE 4.22 Entire Data Range

What a mess that is! What happened to the data?

The last price of DIS is the closing price of the most recent bar. It closed at 33.72. Five percent above 33.72 is 35.41, and 5% below 33.72 is 32.03. TradeStation makes some sophisticated calculations to round this off to nice numbers for the display and places the low on the y-axis at 32.00 and the high at 35.50. Therefore, you cannot see the highs and lows of your data because you have forced the range and it is too small. Play with those ranges a while and I'll meet you back at **Entire Date Range.**

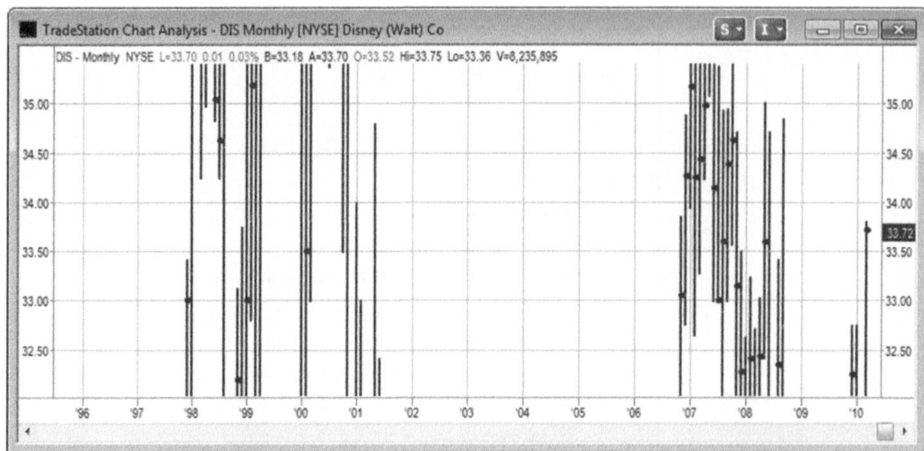

FIGURE 4.23 5% Below and Above

The last section I want to address under **Scaling Range** is **Center Last Price.** Sometimes, especially if you are making text and drawings on your chart, you might want the most recent data to appear in the center of your chart. That's when you select **Center Last Price.** I use it when I am having TS automatically place text so that I don't have to make complex calculations in my code to determine how much space I have above the last price to write something. The resultant chart will look much like Figure 4.24. While the last price on the chart is in the center of the y-axis, note that much of the price activity is in the lower half of the chart. I think it's better all around to let TS do the calculations for placing the data automatically.

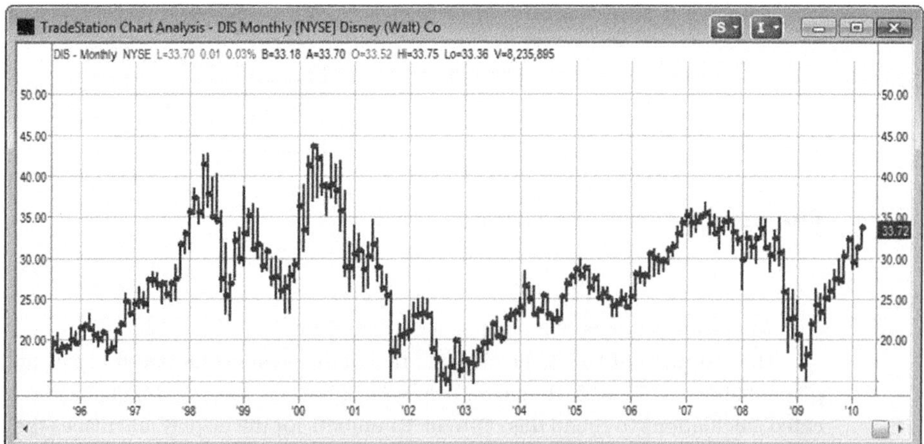

FIGURE 4.24 Center Last Price

Now you should be off to the races. We have done a lot of exploring under the **Format** box, and the rest of the experimentation in that box is left to the reader (as they used to say in my math books).

Next we will begin to put indicators on the charts and learn to manipulate the settings for the indicators.

Step 3: Add an Indicator to the Chart

In Step 4 of Chapter 2, we created a basic indicator, consisting of a single, simple moving average. Let's open that indicator now. I called mine `sjh_MAV1`. I hope you remember what you called yours.

Follow this menu sequence to open your indicator: **File → Open EasyLanguage Document → Indicator,** and then select yours from the list window. See why I wanted you to use your initials as the prefix to the name?

At this point, let's add some more basic tools to your repertoire. When you added the indicator to the chart in Chapter 2, it went into a space below the price bar chart. This area is called the **subgraph area.** If you add another indicator, it will be added below the first one and you will have a main graph (aka subgraph 1) and two subgraphs, called subgraph 2 and subgraph 3. You may have as many as 50 subgraphs in a single window, but the chart will display only 16 at a time. It gets overcrowded, however, as you put more than two or three in the same space, so don't go crazy.

Usually I prefer to see my prices and my indicators together—that is, in the same subgraph. I find the analysis easier when I can see just how close my yellow dots are to my indicators. This makes sense as long as they are both scaled on the same data. If you have your main chart scaled on data that goes from zero to 50, and your indicator is data that ranges from −100 to 100, it doesn't make much sense to put them together. This is what subgraphs are for.

To bring your indicator on top of the price chart, click on the indicator to activate it. The little black boxes will appear at intervals on the indicator. Then, **click and drag** the indicator, pulling it upward without letting go of your mouse as the cursor changes to a rectangle with squiggly lines in it. Let go of the mouse when your cursor is over the price chart and the indicator will drop into place, right on top of your price chart.

While we are at it, let's play around a bit more with the chart, to enhance its look. Figure 4.25 shows the pop-up window from which you format your indicator. Double-click (🖱 🖱) on the indicator (not the price bars) and a pop-up window will appear, with seven tabs:

1. General
2. Inputs
3. Alerts
4. Style
5. Color
6. Scaling
7. Advanced

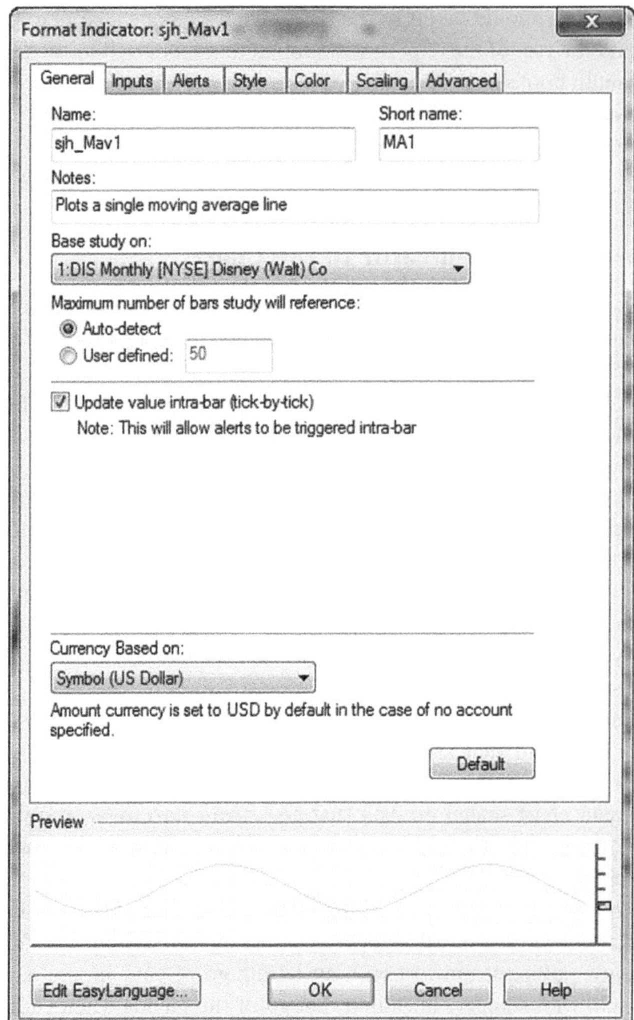

FIGURE 4.25 Format Indicator

NOTE: Another way to get to this **Format → Indicator** box is with the menu sequence **Format → Analysis Techinques → Format.**

Click on the **Style** tab, and in the **Weight** box, pull down to choose a thicker line weight, as we did in earlier chapters. There are seven thicknesses to choose from. See Figure 4.26 for a refresher. I am partial to the third weight.

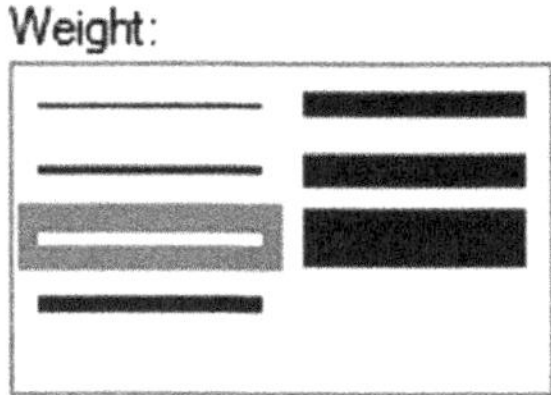

FIGURE 4.26 Changing the Line Weight

While we are changing style elements, let's change the **color** of the indicator line. Long ago I established a color scheme that I use to make charts more easily interpreted (by me). My primary indicators are usually two moving averages, and I always make the slower one green and the faster one blue.[1] That way I can glance at a chart and know instantly what I am looking at. To that end, let's change the color of this indicator to green, specifically dark green. It is the third color over from the left on the top row of color choices. (See Figure 4.27.)

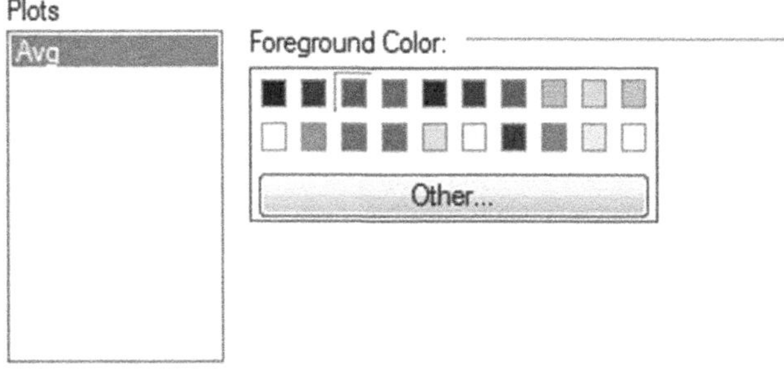

FIGURE 4.27 Color Choices

Double-click the indicator and the pop-up window will again appear. Click on the **Style** tab, and in the **Color** box, click on the **Other** button below the 20 standard color choices. These standard color choices are all listed in the appendix, along with their names and color numbers. You may pick any one you want, but I suggest you begin to standardize, so that rapid chart interpretation becomes second nature to you.

Continuing to play around in the **Format Indicator** box, let's now select the **Style** tab, as shown in Figure 4.28. We looked briefly at this box in Chapter 3. Now we will explore all the selectors important to beginning traders.

Everyone takes their cues from different alerts. I like green and blue lines for my indicators. Some folks have trouble distinguishing those colors and would prefer to have their

[1]Faster moving averages have smaller numbers for the number of bars to average. Slower moving averages have larger numbers of bars to average. Faster would mean that moving average adapts faster to changes in the market, and slower means it adapts more slowly. Sometimes these are called longer and shorter moving averages.

indicators differentiated by using dotted and dashed lines, or solid and dashed. Let's explore the choices under the **Style** tab to see what's available. (See Figure 4.28.)

The different types of line styles are:

1. Line
2. Histogram
3. Point
4. Cross
5. Bar High
6. Bar Low
7. Left Tic
8. Right Tic

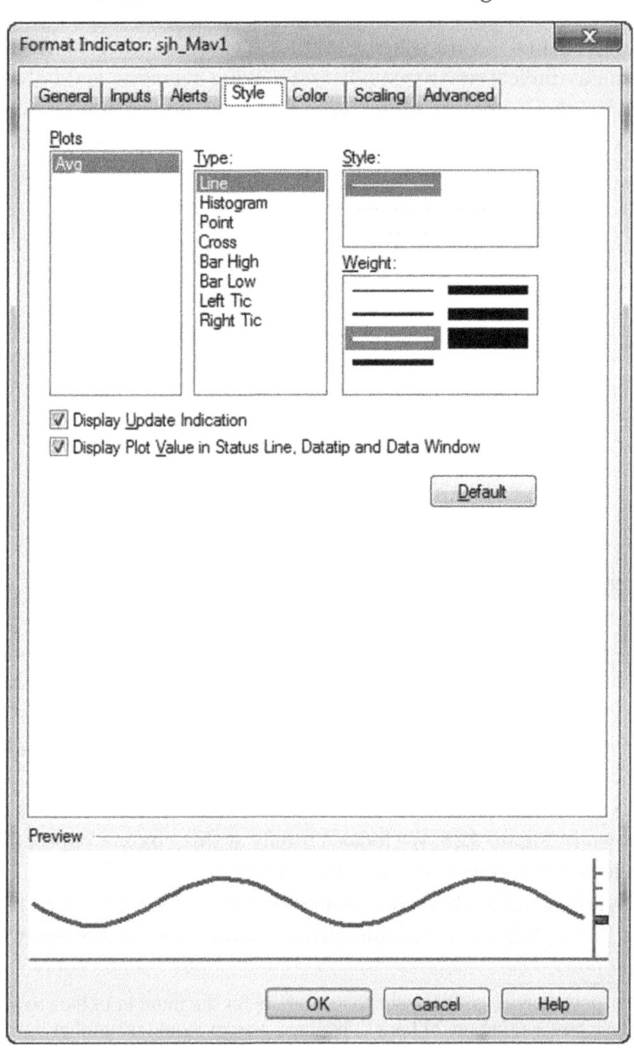

FIGURE 4.28 Format Indicator

Figures 4.29a to 4.29f will demonstrate the difference between each of these style choices. Again, we are still using the symbol DIS on daily data.

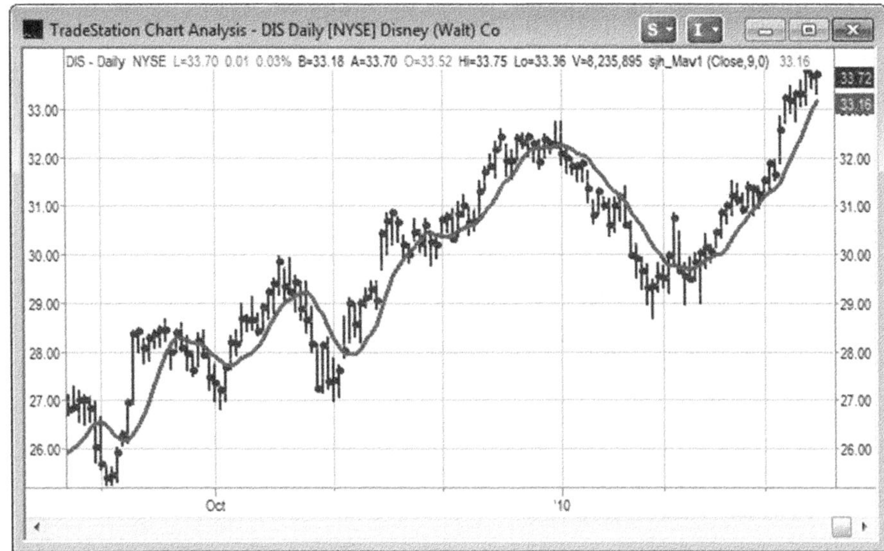

FIGURE 4.29a Line

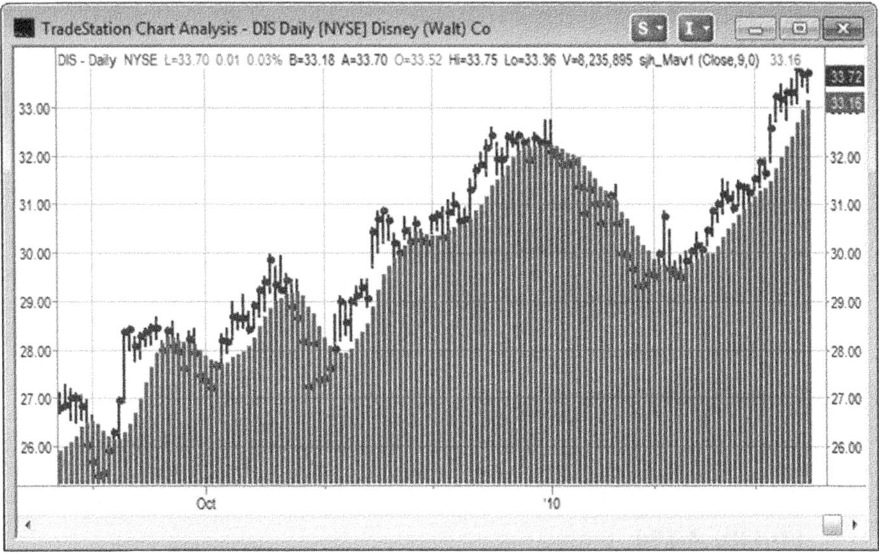

FIGURE 4.29b Histogram

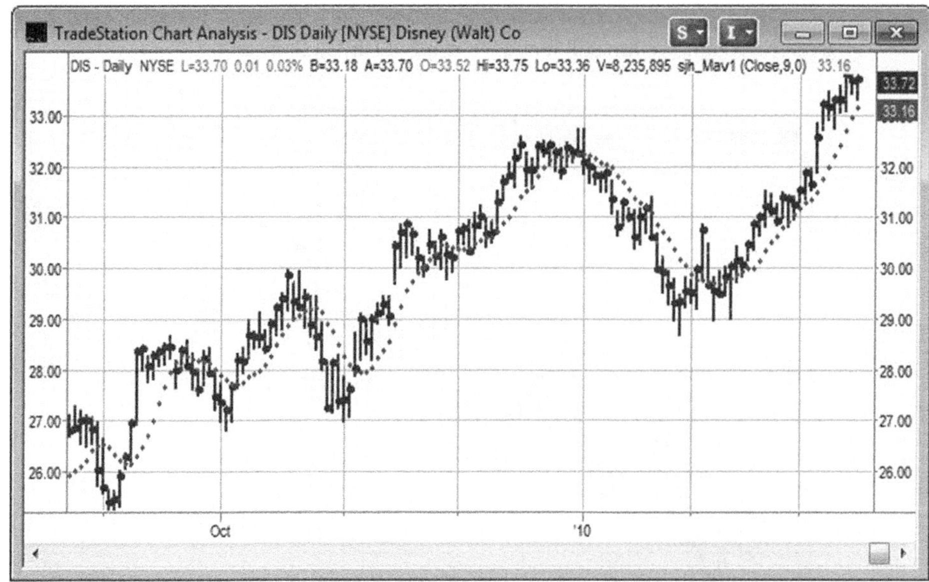

FIGURE 4.29c Point

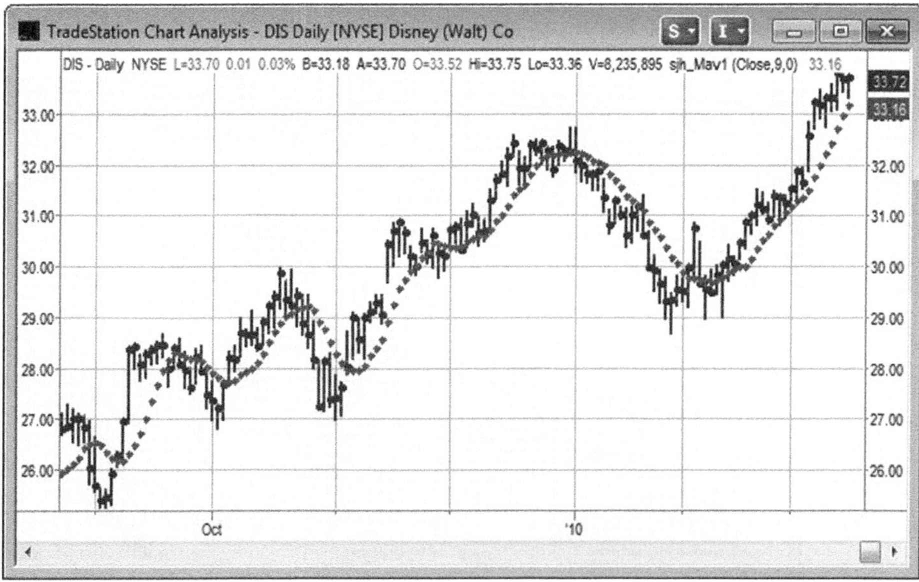

FIGURE 4.29d Cross

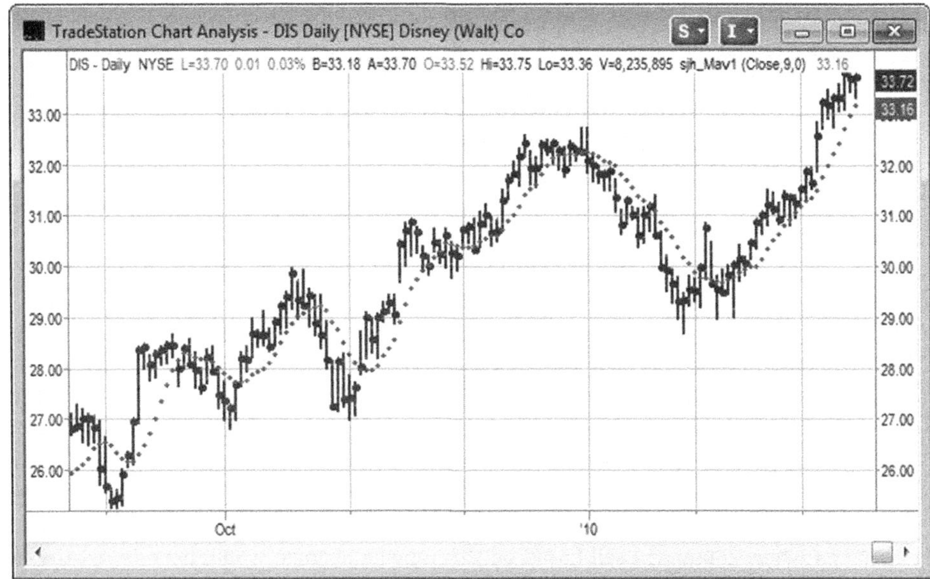

FIGURE 4.29e Left Tic

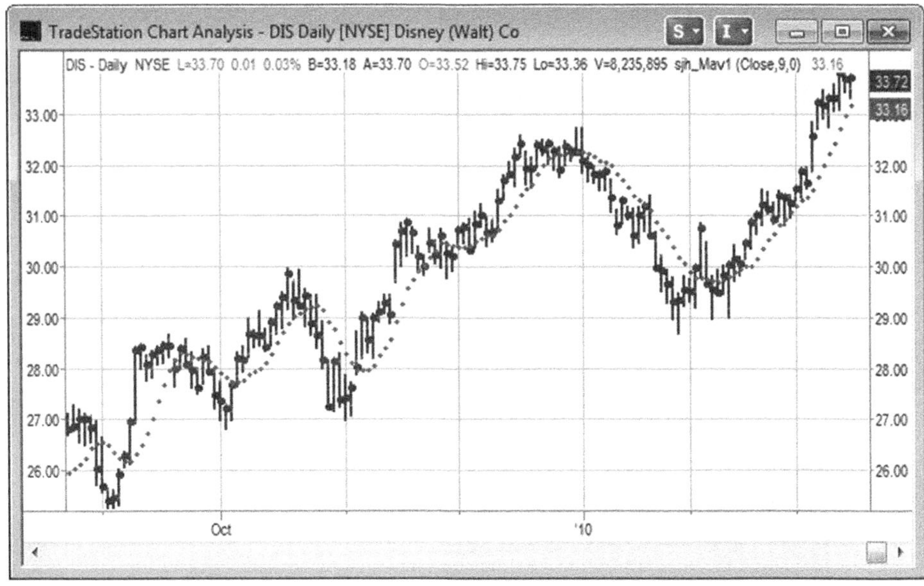

FIGURE 4.29f Right Tic

A picture is really worth 1,000 words. I couldn't have explained it well enough for you to get it but the figures above say it all. Now you know what the **Format Indicator** → **Style** → **Type** is all about.

We have thoroughly explored **Color, Style,** and **Scaling.** Next let's take a look at another tab in the **Format Indicator** box. This time click on the tab labeled **Inputs.** Under this tab we find that the default length for our moving average is set to 9. How did TradeStation know that? You told it in the code we generated in Chapter 3. One line of your code read

```
inputs: Price( Close ), Length( 9 ), Displace( 0 ) ;
```

The `9` in parentheses after the word `Length` is where TS got the default. Your default is always set by the code and then altered by you in the dialog box.

How do we know if 9 is the right value for the moving average? Wouldn't it be nice if you could automatically try every length for your moving average, say from 1 to 30, and see which is best? This poses the question, what does "best" mean? Does "best" mean it fits the data most closely, or that it makes the most profit? I think you know my answer: There is only one reason to trade, and that's to make money. So, best means that some indication of when to buy and sell based on this moving average would have to net the most profit. That's what strategies are for. Indicators can't be optimized, but strategies can. We'll get to the strategies and the optimizing a little later.

For now, just know that changing the length of the indicator changes the chart, sometimes dramatically. See Figures 4.30a to 4.30d for a few examples of different lengths.

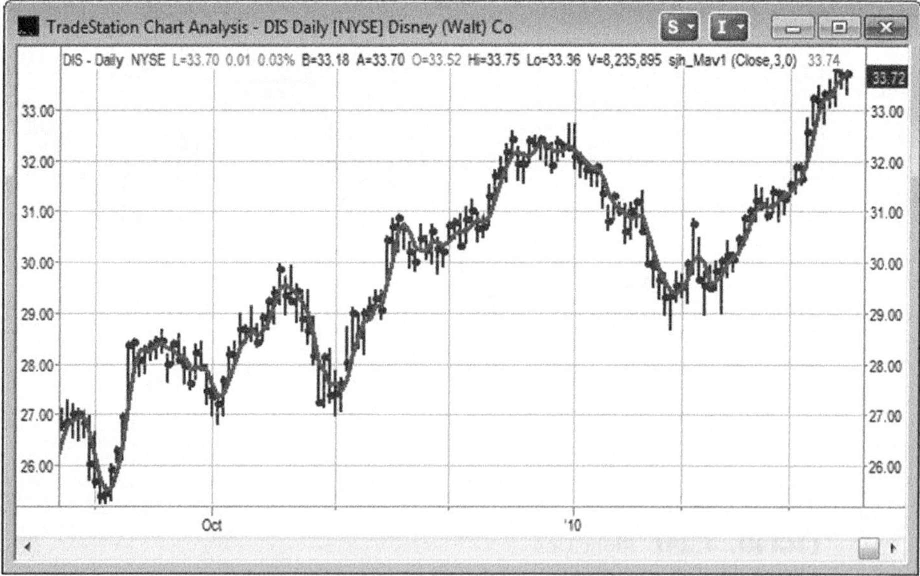

FIGURE 4.30a Length=3

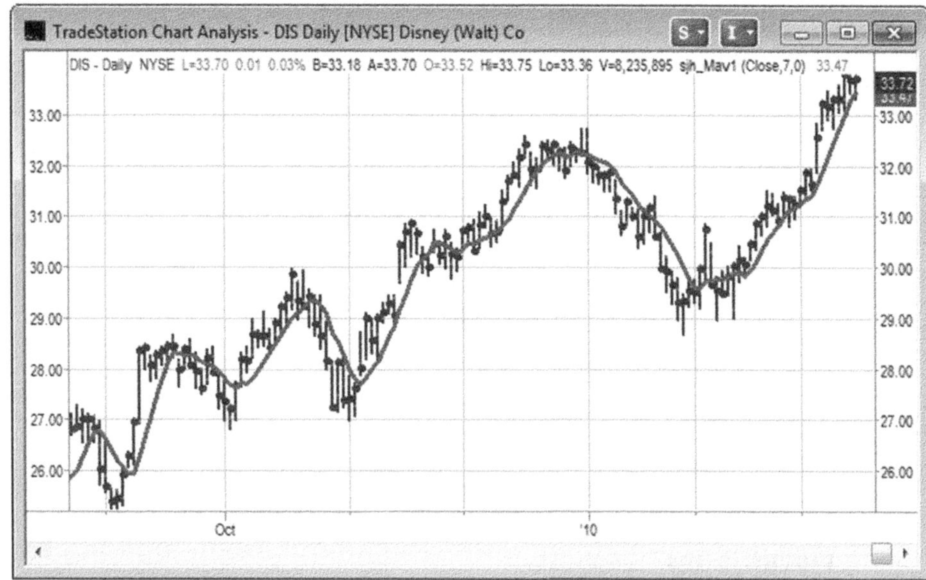

FIGURE 4.30b Length=7

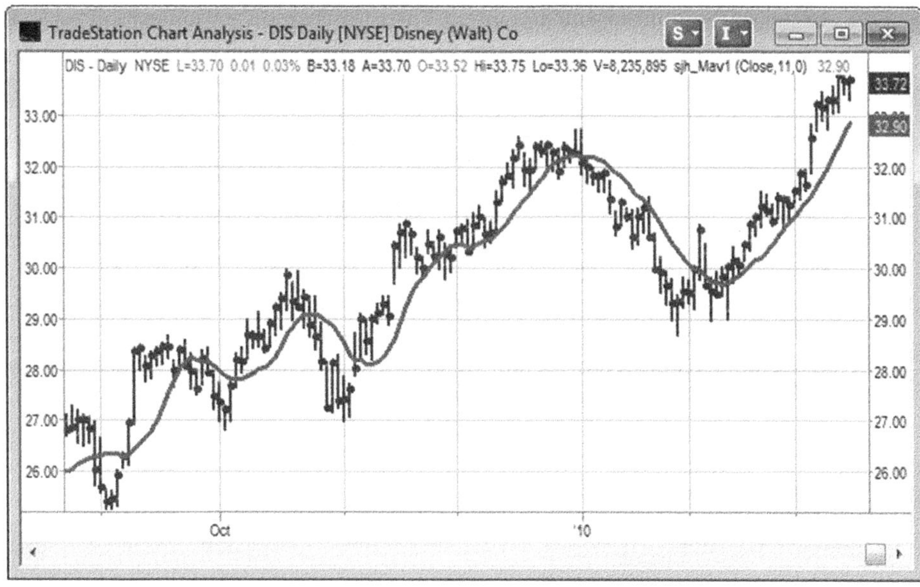

FIGURE 4.30c Length=11

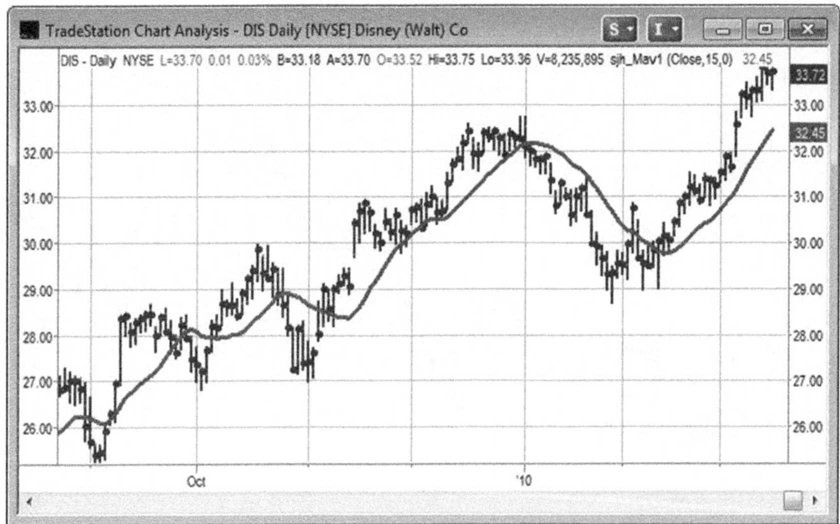

FIGURE 4.30d Length=15

In my Solving the Puzzle seminars I teach what to do with these different length averages, how to use them for trading success, along with how to program them. Sorry I don't have the time to do that kind of training in this book. But this book is about programming, not about the ultimate winning system. There are volumes and volumes of books all purporting to demonstrate winning systems. My goal with this book is to teach you how to program in TradeStation sufficiently that you can pick up one of those books and begin to code its ideas.

Of the seven tabs in the **Format → Analysis** box, we have covered Style, Inputs, Scaling, and Color. We are not going to cover the **Advanced** tab, other than to say that you should leave it on the default setting of **Auto Detect.**

The next tab we will discuss is the **Alerts** tab. You can see the available choices under this tab in Figure 4.31.

By clicking the check box next to **Enable Alert** you can turn on the alarms within TS. Within EasyLanguage you construct code to set up the alarms (Alerts); then from this tab box you call the Alerts into action. An example of Alert code that can be used in an indicator was that which was in the first indicator we wrote, before we took it all out and simplified it. That section of the code looked like this:

```
{ Alert criteria }
if Displace <= 0 then
        begin
        if Price crosses over Avg then
                Alert( "Price crossing over average" )
        else if Price crosses under Avg then
                Alert( "Price crossing under average" ) ;
        end ;
```

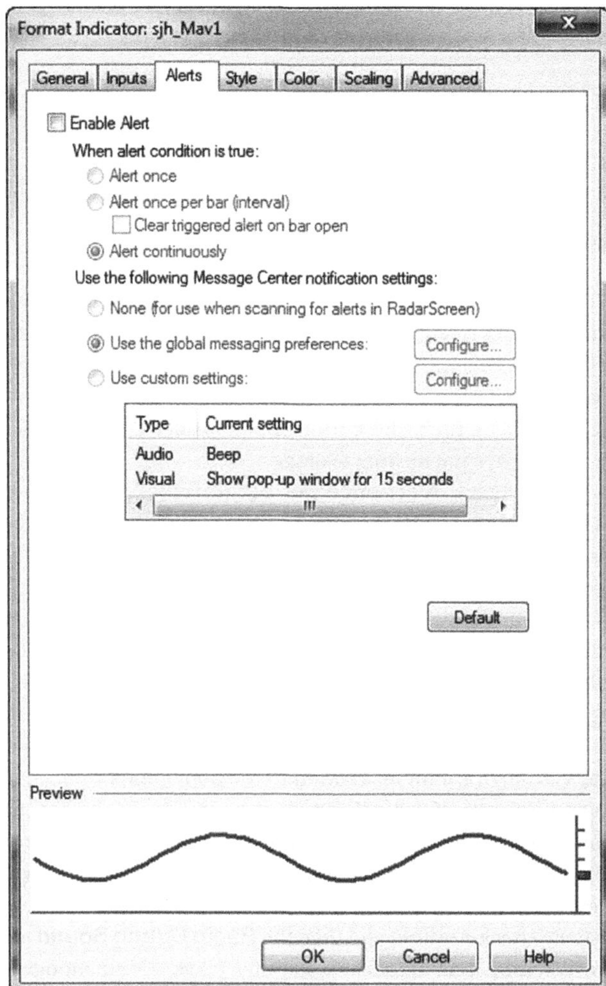

FIGURE 4.31 Format Alerts

It is not necessary to understand, or be able to program it at this point; it is sufficient to view it and note that there is a **Reserved Word** called **Alert** that is given a name in parentheses. The code says that if price goes above the moving average, the Alert will be called. And, likewise, if price goes below the moving average a differently named Alert will be called. When the Alert box pops up during trading hours, it will tell you the name given in parentheses so you will know which condition triggered the alarm. In short, if your condition happens, an alarm will pop up.

So that I could get a figure to show you the real-time Alert pop-up, I used our sjh_MAV1 on the symbol GBPUSD on a 1-minute bar chart. I enabled Alerts and as soon as the price jumped above the moving average, I got the Alert shown in Figure 4.32.

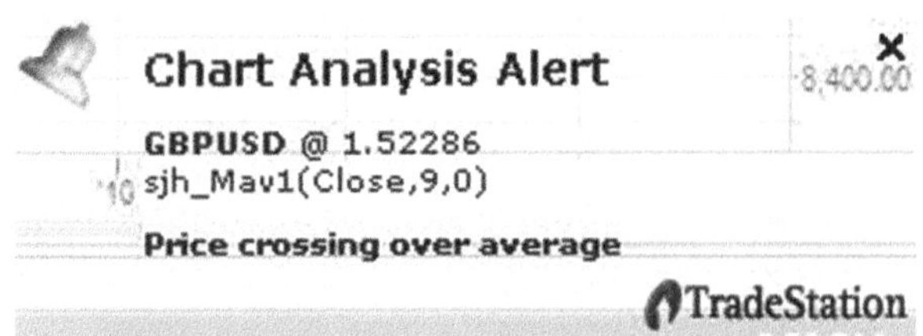

FIGURE 4.32 Alert Pop-up

This little box is triggered so that if you click on the alert, it will take you immediately to the chart that generated it. Convenient, huh? The box will pop up continually, every time price ventures over the moving average if you click the radio button labeled **Alert Continuously.** If you click the radio button labeled **Alert Once,** it will only pop up the first time price crosses above the moving average.

The other choice, **Alert once per bar (interval),** causes the alarm to appear once per bar and then not again until the next bar begins forming. If you choose **Alert Continuously,** the little box will pop up over and over and over. It gets quite annoying. That is probably not the selection I would choose.

A little farther down in the **Format Alerts** box is a section that begins with the words **Use the following Message Center notification settings.** The choices are: **None, Use the global messaging preferences,** and **Use custom settings.** By default the **Use global messaging preferences** choice is selected. Beside that choice is a button labeled **Configure.** Clicking that brings up more choices, this time whether you want the Alert to include **Audible, Visual,** or **Email** in addition to the pop-up box.

If you have selected **Alert Once,** it is nice to have TS send you an email when the condition is met. Thus, if you are automating your trading or are away from the TS screen at the time the condition is met, you will get an email warning with the words you set up in your Alert code.

I usually check **Audible** and then the **Radio Button Sound** and I select the sound called **ahooga.** When I get an alert, the computer plays a loud ahooga sound. It's obnoxious, but it certainly gets my attention. This sound is standard with your TS and is the first selection under **Configure.** (See Figure 4.33.)

Format General The last tab we will explore in the **Format Indicator** box is the first tab: **General.** Most of the default settings are everything you will ever need. One that is not immediately obvious is **Base study on.** Under this selection you can select which data to base your indicator on. This applies only if you have more than one symbol on your chart. If you have two or more symbols on your chart, this selection allows you to choose which one to base the study on. You might, for instance, have DIS and $INDU on your chart. If you have DIS in subgraph 1, TS will by default base the study on the symbol in subgraph 1. If you want to base it on the second symbol, $INDU, you will have to tell TS in this box.

The next item of importance in this box is **Maximum number of bars study will reference.** The two choices here are: **Auto-detect** and **User defined.** I always leave the default

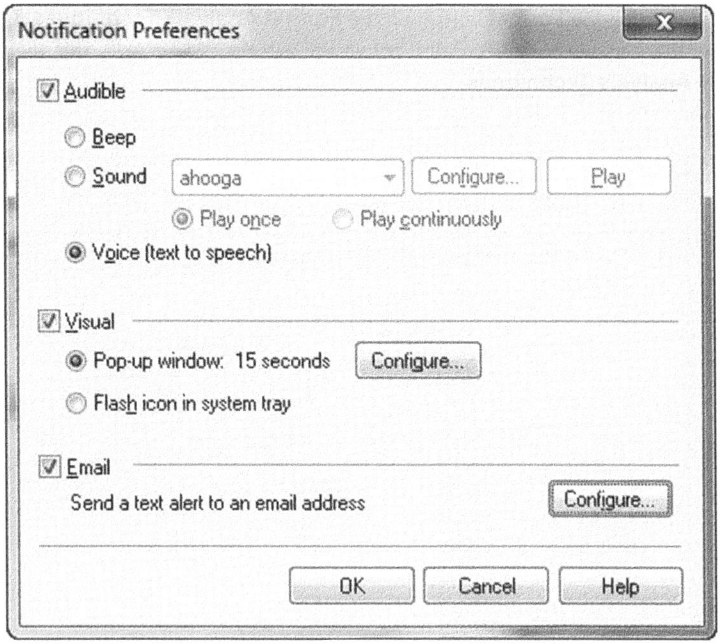

FIGURE 4.33 Notification Preferences

Auto-detect selected. **User defined** is there so that you can minimize or maximize the number of bars used at the beginning calculation of your indicator. For instance, in our moving average we currently have the length set to 9. We could, therefore, make the **User defined** set to 9 since we only need 9 bars to calculate the moving average. However, as soon as we decide to try a different average length and set the input length to 10, TS will no longer calculate the average and will generate an error message and turn the **Status** of the indicator to **Off.** That's why I let TS auto-detect the length it needs.

Update value intra-bar (tick-by-tick) is the next section in the **Format General** box. By default the check box is selected (checked) ☑. If you deselect or uncheck it, TS will alert you only after a full bar is formed. That would be one way of not getting continual alerts, but if you are a short-term trader you may want to know what is going on as the bar is forming; if so, you would want to be updated intra-bar, or tick by tick.

Last in this section is the **Currency Based on** selection. For the most part you will want your calculations done in the currency in which your trading account is denominated. Here in the United States we use dollars. Thus, whether one choses **Symbol** or **Account** for displaying the symbol DIS, it's all in dollars. This choice becomes important when you are trading, say, currencies, in a different country than your account resides. Be careful and experiment with this one to familiarize yourself if you are working cross currencies like this.

That's about it for this in-depth review of the **Format** → **Indicator** workings. There is one last thing I need to bring to your attention, though. That's the Status button, which is underneath the **Format** button on the **Format Analysis Techniques & Strategies** box. You get there as we have been all through the last many pages, by this menu sequence: **Format → Analysis Techniques.**

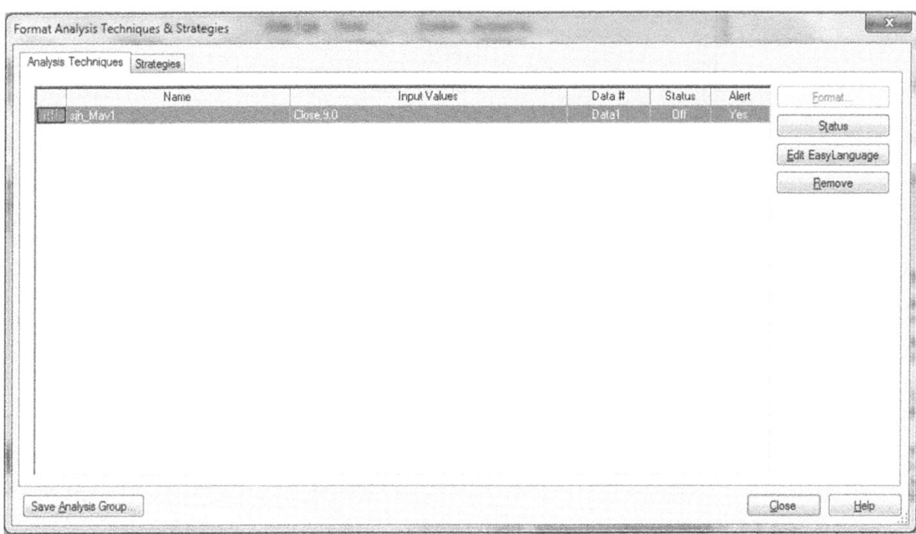

FIGURE 4.34 Status

On the upper right, under the **Format** button, is the **Status** button (see Figure 4.34). Click it and it seems like nothing happens. But if you can see underneath the box, or if your chart hangs out around the edges, you will see that the indicator that was on the chart disappears. Clicking the button again turns the indicator back on. Also notice that there are column headings in the dialogue box, one of which is labeled **Status.** Under the label the word will toggle from **On** to **Off** and back again as you click the Status button.

At last we are ready for another step.

Step 4: Change the Time Frame of the Chart

When working with students, I find that "time frame" is an ambiguous term. Often they are not sure whether I mean to change from a daily chart to a weekly chart or to change the time spanned by the chart from last year to this year.

TradeStation uses the word "compression" when referring to the frequency at which bars are sampled. A daily chart samples data from the open, high, low, and close of the day; a weekly chart samples data from the open, high, low, and close of the week.

We will stick with TradeStation's terminology for specifying 15-minute bars, 30-minute bars, daily bars, weekly bars, and so on. This is called **compression.** Sometimes you will see it referred to as time compression or data compression.

When I ask you to alter the time frame of the chart, I am referring to the time spanned by the data, for example, from 1995 to 2005. To maintain testing consistency, it is important to compare apples to apples. If you told me that one system generated $4,000 and another generated $400, I would first want to know that both comparisons were done on the same time frame. For instance, if the $4,000 system was covering 10 years and the $400 system was covering 10 days, I would probably choose the $400 system.

As a convenience (again, I like a standardized convention), I like to view a **one-year time frame on all charts.** That way, I am instantly comparing apples to apples. Let's make that change to our chart now.

Double-click somewhere **on the data** in your chart (the OHLC bars). This action will bring up the **Format Symbol** dialogue box, where you can click on the **Settings** tab (see Figure 4.35).

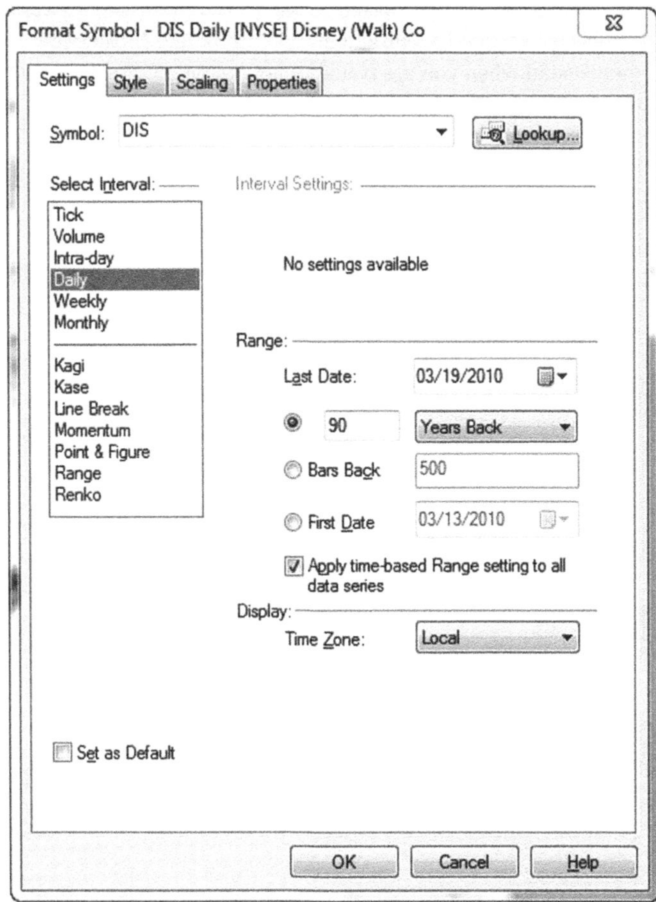

FIGURE 4.35 Data Compression and Time Frames

The last date in "our data" (DISdata) is February 26, 2010 (It might be updated by the time this book is published, but for purposes of this example we need an end date from which to work.) To display a chart of the previous year, one would simply put 365 into the "Days back" entry, right? Nope—that would be calendar days. How many trading days are there per year? Approximately 5/7ths of 365, which would be approximately 261. Let's call it 260, giving us Columbus Day off. Do that now; put 260 in the "Days back" box and your chart should look something like that in Figure 4.36.

If you will take your mouse and run your cursor over the first bar on your chart (you may have to use the "squeeze bars"[2] first to get all the bars on a single view), you will be able to read the first date on your **Data Window,** the pop-up that appears when you hold down the mouse button over a bar. Figure 4.37 shows the cursor down position over the first bar on the chart, so you can see the **Data Window.**

If your chart is short of filling up the chart space, you might like to spread out the chart so the whole sheet of paper is covered by the year under discussion. For this little trick, use the "spreaders" on the top menu bar to **increase bar spacing.** The "spreaders" and the "squeezers" are the two little icons that look like those shown in Figure 4.38. They are extremely useful when you are trying to get an overall look at some pattern and compare it to a broader look at the data.

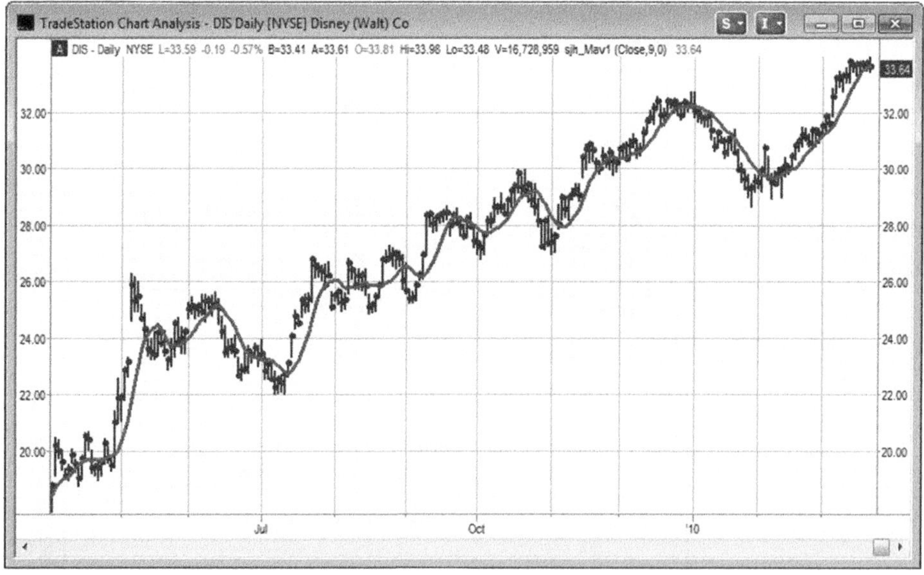

FIGURE 4.36 One Trading Year on a Daily Bar Chart

[2] I call it "squeeze bars," but it is actually the icon labeled **Decrease Bar Spacing.**

FIGURE 4.37 Data Window Showing First Bar on Chart

Remember that we want to compare apples to apples, as stated earlier. It is for this reason, in viewing and constructing charts, that I like to establish a convention of viewing all research charts on a one-year time frame, in addition to viewing them on the same y-axis scale. Conventions such as these give you, the researcher, a head start at chart analysis and thus at finding answers.

FIGURE 4.38 Squeezers and Spreaders, Increase or Decrease Bar Spacing

Step 5: Change the Scale of the Chart

In step 4 we standardized the x-axis of our chart, so that we can quickly view all charts on a one-year time frame. We put 260 bars on a chart with the **Format → Symbol → Bars Back** menu sequence.

In this next step we will standardize the y-axis, so that we can quickly review all charts for moneymaking potential. Figure 4.39 shows three different stocks using TradeStation's automatic scaling—that is, "scale to screen." At first glance, it would appear that each of these stocks provides about the same moneymaking potential.

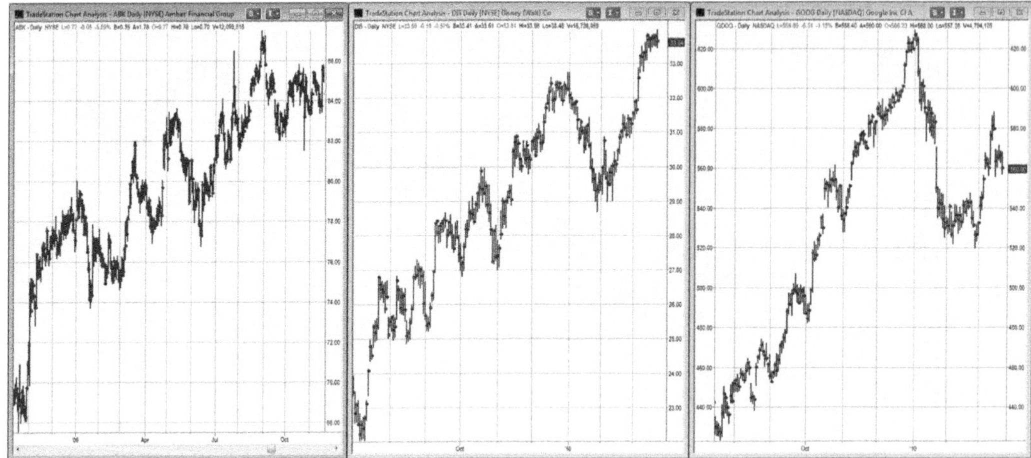

FIGURE 4.39 Three Charts with Automatic Scaling

If we now scale all three charts to the same scale, say 0 to 500, we can take an impartial view of the potential monetary rewards. Figure 4.40 shows the same three stocks on identical scales.

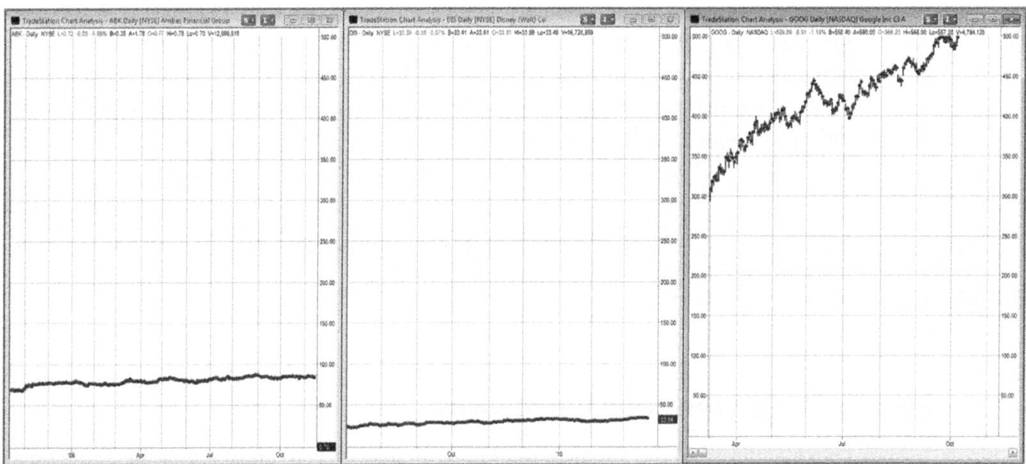

FIGURE 4.40 Three Charts Scaled from 0 to 500

Scaled on a very wide scale from 0 to 500, we still cannot determine whether one is more tradable than the other. Let's try again. This time we will evaluate the range of the data on each chart and scale the y-axes so that there are the same amount of points on each individual y-axis.

Since the first chart's data goes from 68 to 86, the second's from 22 to 34, and the third's from 300 to 565, we need to use the third chart as the common denominator. Each chart will need to range 265 points from bottom to top to match the scale of the third (see Figure 4.41). Try again, this time scaling to a 30-point range, as in Figure 4.42.

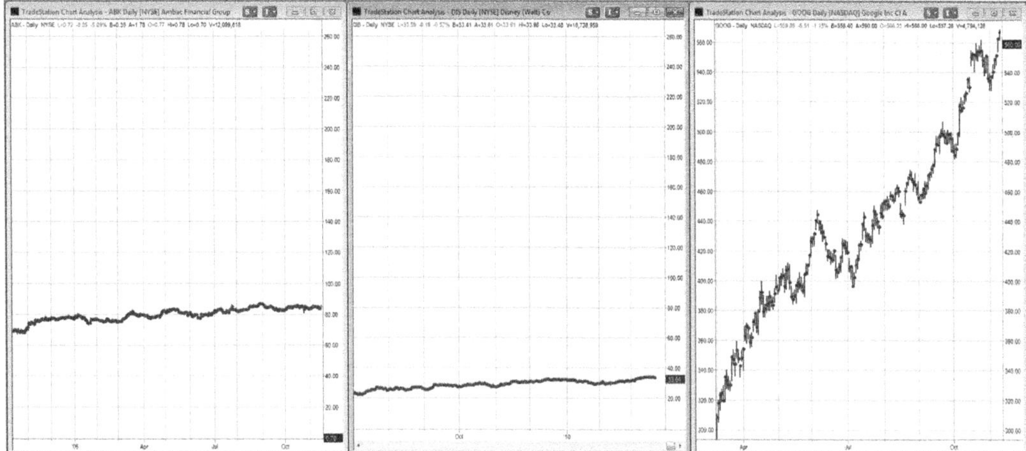

FIGURE 4.41 Three Charts Scaled with a Range of 265 Points

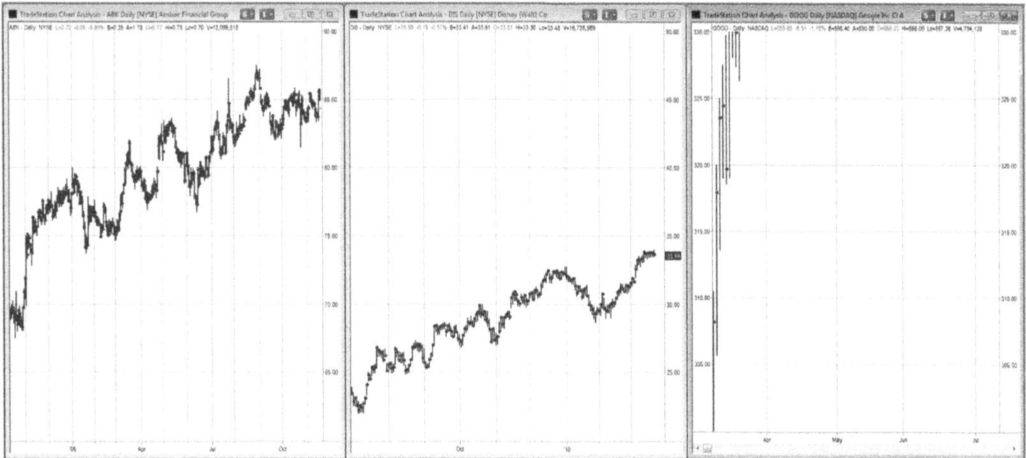

FIGURE 4.42 Three Charts Scaled with a Range of 30 Points

Now that you've seen several attempts at scaling data proportionally so that you can visually inspect each for profit potential, I want to show you two things: my PHW Indicator on the chart to automatically find profits, and how to do the scaling yourself. The next section is about scaling charts.

Scaling Your Charts for Profit Finding We did all this already, in Chapter 3, Show Me the Money, and again earlier in this chapter. In this section we are focusing on the moneymaking aspects of scaling. In Figure 4.43. we scaled three symbols several different ways in an attempt to discern which would be more tradable.

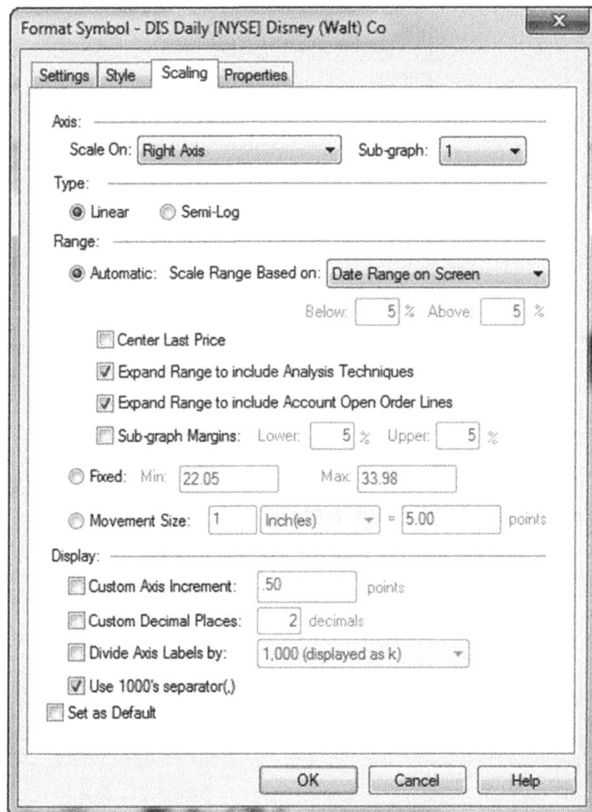

FIGURE 4.43 Scaling Dialogue Box

Now I will quickly show you how to do this scaling, and then I'll show you my indicator.

Figure 4.43 shows the dialogue box for scaling your data. You reach it with the menu sequence **Format → Symbol → Scaling.** When you enter this box, the settings will be TS's defaults or the current settings of the chart you are on, if you have already set the scaling. If you have not previously set the scaling, then the "Scale type" is set to "screen". This means that TradeStation will automatically scale the chart to fit the entire screen. We want to change that and impose our own scaling.

To do so, click on the **Fixed** radio button and input your own values for **Maximum** and **Minimum.** For this exercise I want you to use 100 for the maximum and 0 for the minimum, for the symbol DIS.

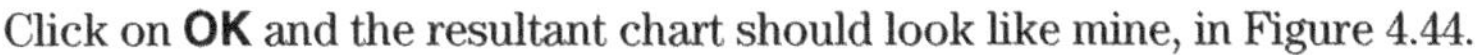

Click on **OK** and the resultant chart should look like mine, in Figure 4.44.

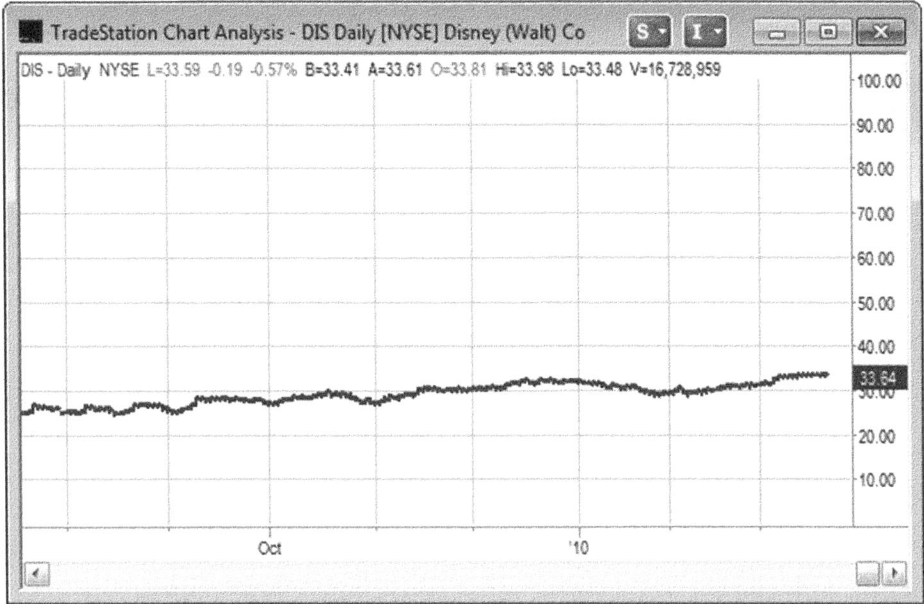

FIGURE 4.44 User-Defined Scaling on Our Chart

As a matter of personal preference, I keep most of my charts on a semi-log graph. Notice in Figure 4.43 there are two radio buttons under **Axis Type,** one for linear and one for semi-log charting. This time let's click the semi-log radio button and take another look at the chart. Oops! TS won't do it; it gives an error message. What happened? It's the nature of semi-log, which won't do zero or negative numbers. When we used **Fixed** for the scaling we entered zero for the lower range of the data. Semi-log can't handle that. If we make a tiny little change and set the lower end of the range to 0.1, it should work. The resultant chart is displayed in Figure 4.45.

Terrible! That's not what we wanted. It is worse than the first view of the data in Figure 4.43. What happened? The logarithmic scale on the y-axis gives equal significance to the lower range of the data, in the zero area. It overemphasizes the lower end of the data.

Let's try something else. This time let's use semi-log again, but set the range of the data from the lower value of 25 to an upper value of 35. In a fairly narrow price range, such as this, you won't see much difference in the linear and the semi-log scaling of the charts. But when you get charts that move from 2000 to 10,000 like the Dow, the semi-log scaling will afford you the percentage-eye view of the market. Rather than looking at how many points the Dow moved today and comparing that to points in 1988, the semi-log chart

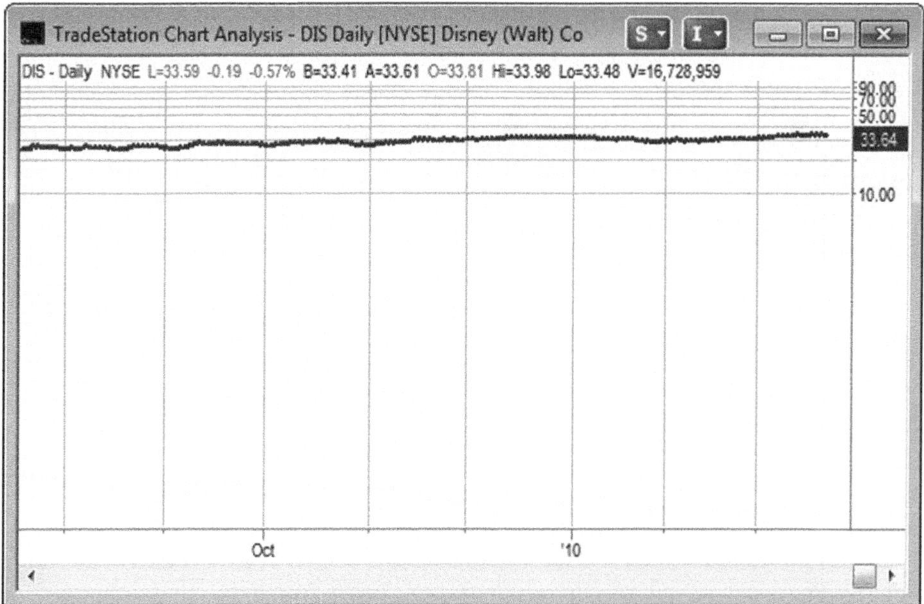

FIGURE 4.45 Semi-Log Scaling on Our Chart

givs you the perspective of "relative points," or how much is the market moving compared to itself.

Try a chart of the Dow over the last 10 years. Observe it on a linear chart and then on a semi-log chart. See which makes most sense to you. It doesn't make much difference in this time frame. The semi-log scaling really only starts making sense when you pull in data from many years ago, like bringing in the data from the 1960s.

Let's do it. Set the symbol to $INDU by clicking on the chart and simply typing `$INDU` on the keyboard. Then double-click on the price bars to bring up the **Format Symbol** dialogue box. (See Figure 4.46.) Click on the tab labeled **Settings.** Change the **Select Interval** to **Monthly.** Now change the **Range** to include the 1920s by typing `90` in the **Years Back** selection. I chose 90 because that's the maximum TS will currently allow.

Next, click the **Scaling** tab and make sure the **Linear** radio button is selected for this first exercise. We are going to compare the scaling of the Dow on linear and semi-log. The chart in Figure 4.47 shows the Dow in linear scaling. Take a look at the data in 1987; it has minimal significance compared to the current data. Take another look at the left end of the chart, in the 1970s. That end just basically looks like zero.

Now let's change the scaling to semi-log. Again, double-click on the bars to bring up the **Format Symbol** dialogue box. Leave the settings under **Settings** the same as we previously set them. The only thing we are going to change this time is to click the radio button labeled **Semi-Log.** Now view the chart in Figure 4.48, the Dow y-axis scaled logarithmically.

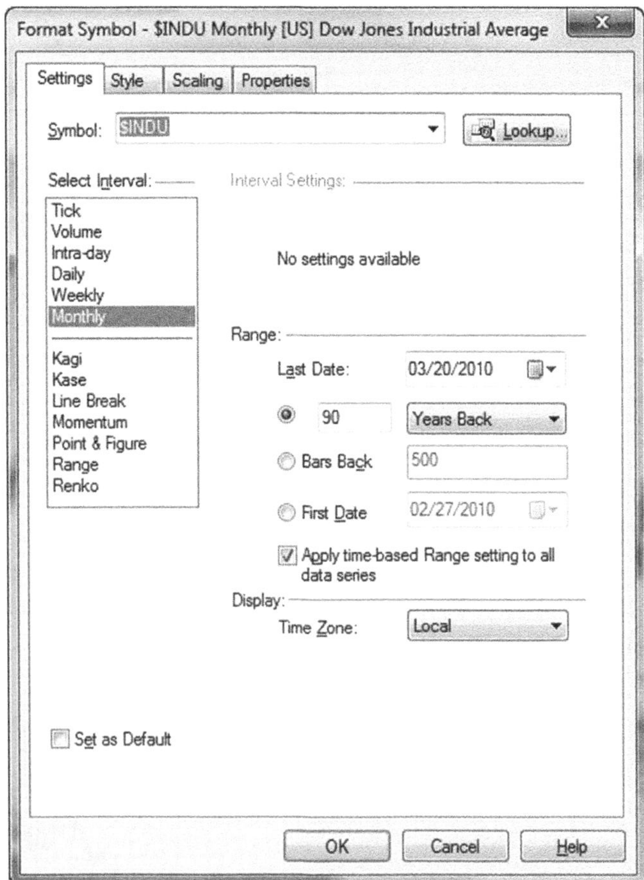

FIGURE 4.46 Format Symbol Dialogue Box

On semi-log scaling we can read and evaluate the data in the beginning of the chart. With this scaling equal significance is given to the beginning and the current data. How often will you use this scaling? Only when you are conducting research on whether to trade this vehicle, when you need to see long time ranges where data changes from very low values to very high values. Semi-log scaling allows you to view data with great disparities.

Before moving on to the next topic, let's take a quick look at another symbol that needs semi-log scaling. Any symbol that has data going back many years, that has had a wide range of prices, say 0 to more than 100, could benefit from semi-log scaling. IBM is another one of those. Figures 4.49 and 4.50 show IBM first with linear scaling and then with semi-log scaling.

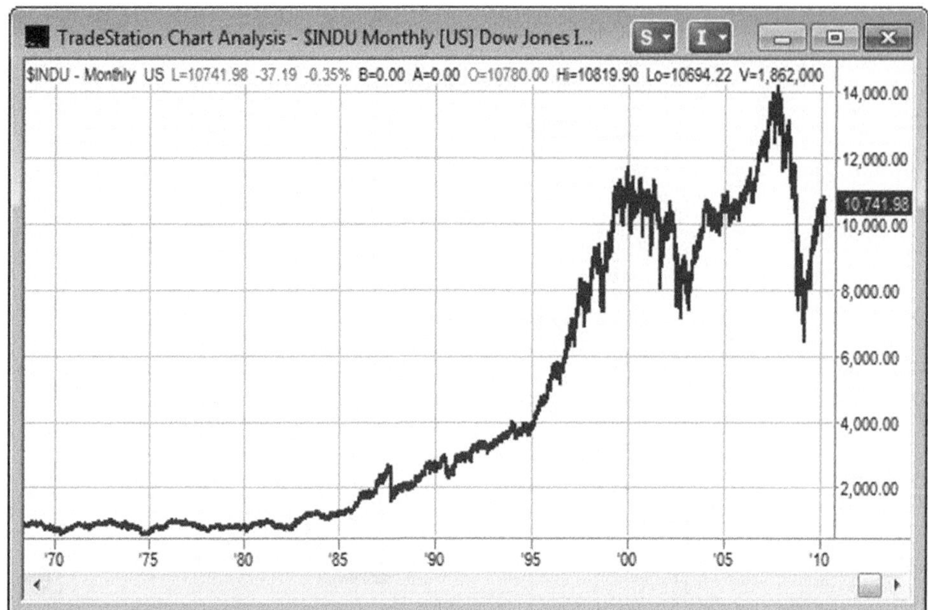

FIGURE 4.47 $INDU in Linear Scaling

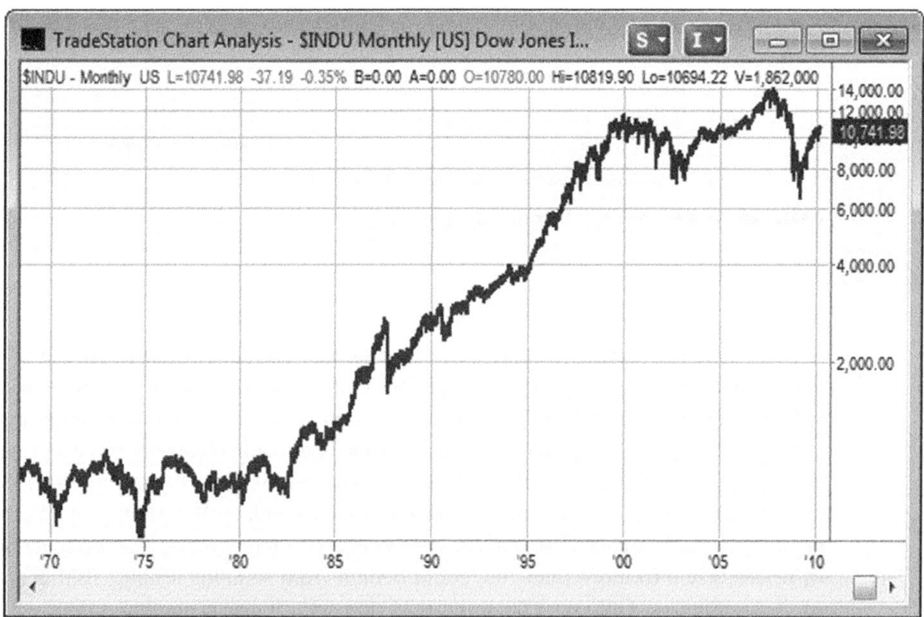

FIGURE 4.48 $INDU on Semi-Log Scaling

FIGURE 4.49 IBM on Linear Scaling

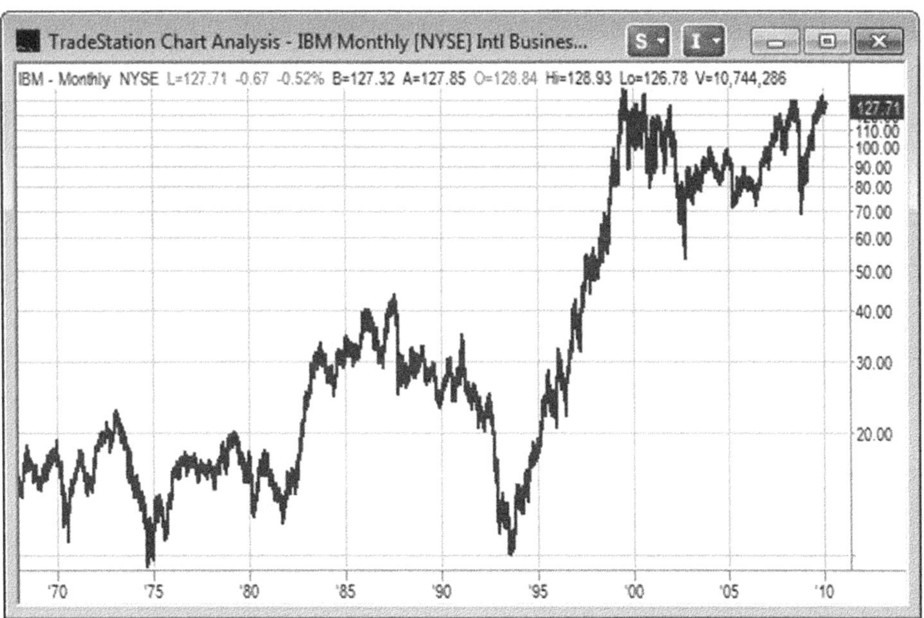

FIGURE 4.50 IBM on Semi-Log Scaling

Not a huge difference from Figure 4.49 to Figure 4.50, but it is significant. The data in the 70s through the 90s was tradable at the time, based on the currency of the time. A dollar was worth a lot more back then. The chart in Figure 4.50 demonstrates this tradability better than the chart in Figure 4.49.

The importance of semi-log scaling becomes even more obvious when drawing yellow circles around tradable highs and lows. Which brings me conveniently to the subject of my PHW Indicator.

My PHW Indicator for Finding Profits Download it from **www.moneymentor.com** under Downloads for a trial version and call me for the password. Not only does the indicator draw the ideal circles, it automatically calculates and prints out on the chart the ideal profit, the buy-and-hold profit, and the PHW profit for the active symbol.

I said earlier that I like to keep PHW circles on all charts at all times to compare my efforts to the ideal possibilities. As we move forward in this chapter, it becomes even more important, as we get to trying out systems.

Figures 4.51 and 4.52 show IBM with PHW circles on both linear and semi-log scales. These examples make it more clear as with linear scaling we can hardly distinguish

FIGURE 4.51 IBM Linear with PHW Circles

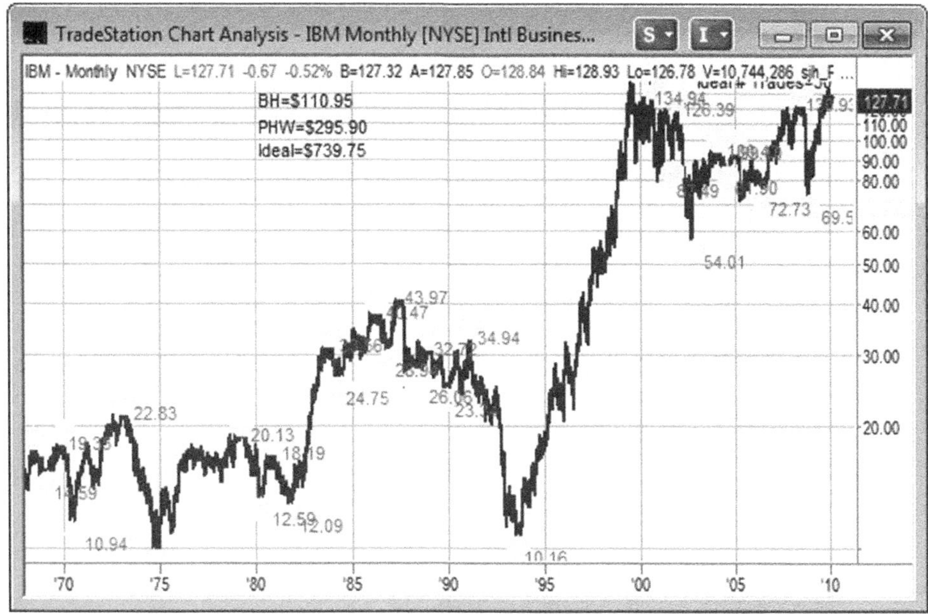

FIGURE 4.52 IBM Semi-Log with PHW Circles

the dots. They almost fall on top of each other. But with semi-log scaling they are distinguishable.

Perhaps the most important part of the PHW Indicator, even more than the yellow dots, is the text that calls out the BH (Buy-and-Hold) dollars, the Ideal profit in dollars, and the PHW profit in dollars. This indicator, when applied to a RadarScreen, is of huge significance, as you can quickly sort on all symbols to find those with the highest ideal profit. No more paging through chart after chart to find how they compare against each other for tradability.

Just to whet your appetite, Figure 4.53 is a RadarScreen of the Dow Jones 30 Industrial symbols with the PHW Indicator on it. I've double-clicked the column labeled PHW to sort with the highest profit on top and descending. We won't get into RadarScreen much in this book, so it's appropriate to give this example here. Visit the figure for a few minutes. Notice that not only does it show you the Ideal and PHW profits, it tells you the number of trades in the ideal and gives you the dates of the most recent highs (MRO_H) and lows (MRO_L). A huge amount of information on one chart.

In the figures that follow in this book, I will not always leave the PHW dots on the chart. When I am trying to illustrate some facet of an indicator or a strategy, the dots may obscure the topic at hand. When illustrating a strategy or an indicator's profitability, I will put the dots back on the chart.

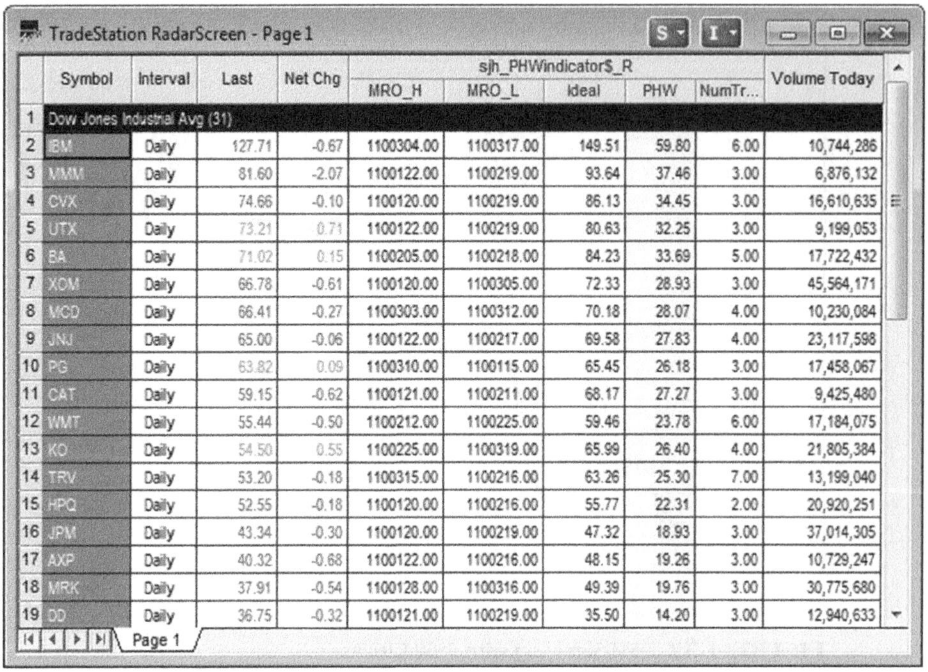

TradeStation RadarScreen - Page 1

	Symbol	Interval	Last	Net Chg	sjh_PHWindicator$_R					Volume Today
					MRO_H	MRO_L	Ideal	PHW	NumTr...	
1	Dow Jones Industrial Avg (31)									
2	IBM	Daily	127.71	-0.67	1100304.00	1100317.00	149.51	59.80	6.00	10,744,286
3	MMM	Daily	81.60	-2.07	1100122.00	1100219.00	93.64	37.46	3.00	6,876,132
4	CVX	Daily	74.66	-0.10	1100120.00	1100219.00	86.13	34.45	3.00	16,610,635
5	UTX	Daily	73.21	0.71	1100122.00	1100219.00	80.63	32.25	3.00	9,199,053
6	BA	Daily	71.02	0.15	1100205.00	1100218.00	84.23	33.69	5.00	17,722,432
7	XOM	Daily	66.78	-0.61	1100120.00	1100305.00	72.33	28.93	3.00	45,564,171
8	MCD	Daily	66.41	-0.27	1100303.00	1100312.00	70.18	28.07	4.00	10,230,084
9	JNJ	Daily	65.00	-0.06	1100122.00	1100217.00	69.58	27.83	4.00	23,117,598
10	PG	Daily	63.82	0.09	1100310.00	1100115.00	65.45	26.18	3.00	17,458,067
11	CAT	Daily	59.15	-0.62	1100121.00	1100211.00	68.17	27.27	3.00	9,425,480
12	WMT	Daily	55.44	-0.50	1100212.00	1100225.00	59.46	23.78	6.00	17,184,075
13	KO	Daily	54.50	0.55	1100225.00	1100319.00	65.99	26.40	4.00	21,805,384
14	TRV	Daily	53.20	-0.18	1100315.00	1100216.00	63.26	25.30	7.00	13,199,040
15	HPQ	Daily	52.55	-0.18	1100120.00	1100216.00	55.77	22.31	2.00	20,920,251
16	JPM	Daily	43.34	-0.30	1100120.00	1100219.00	47.32	18.93	3.00	37,014,305
17	AXP	Daily	40.32	-0.68	1100122.00	1100216.00	48.15	19.26	3.00	10,729,247
18	MRK	Daily	37.91	-0.54	1100128.00	1100316.00	49.39	19.76	3.00	30,775,680
19	DD	Daily	36.75	-0.32	1100121.00	1100219.00	35.50	14.20	3.00	12,940,633

Page 1

FIGURE 4.53 RadarScreen with PHW Indicator

Step 6: Apply a System to the Chart

Let's go back to our basic chart with our sjh_MAV1 indicator on it and begin to establish a system.

We've been through a lot. Do you remember how to set it up? Real quickly:

- Type `DIS` to bring up the symbol.
- **Format → Analysis Techniques → Format → Style.**
- Choose the third thickness under **Weight.**
- Select **Color** tab.
- Choose your favorite color.

Your chart should look like mine, in Figure 4.54. The input value for length in the moving average was set to 9 in the code we wrote, so when it is first placed on the chart it will be set to the default value of 9. Let's leave it at that value for now.

Remember, a system is just a set of rules for buying and selling. Our system should reflect both the characteristics of the indicator we just built and the rules we set out in the Quick Start in Chapter 2. When we get a little farther along we will add inputs to the indicator and inputs to the system. These values in both the indicator and in the system should stay in agreement for easy reference. It becomes very confusing when you have a system that is based on an indicator but you put a different indicator on the chart.

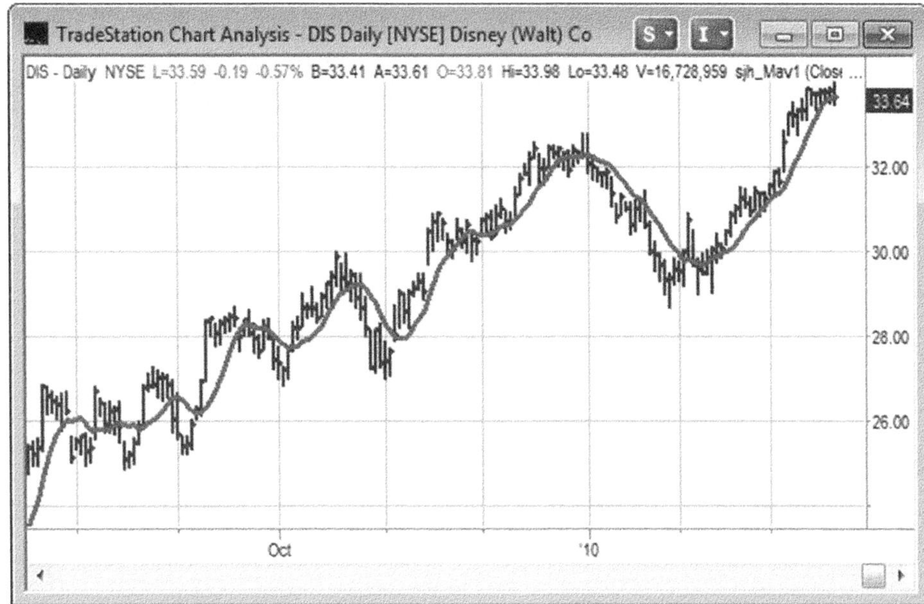

FIGURE 4.54 Back to DIS with sjh_MAV1

To write a system, we first get the rules in our mind, then get the rules on paper, then tell the rules to TradeStation. All too often I see people trying to start from the end, writing rules in TradeStation before they have thoroughly thought out what they want the rules to accomplish.

Look back to Chapter 2, Quick Start, Step 6, and review the steps to applying a system to your chart. If you did all of those steps, you should still have a strategy that uses the single moving average. I called mine sjh_S_MAV1; did you begin a testing log and enter the name of your new system into the log under the column headed **Description**?

Insert the strategy "sjh_S_MAV1" into your chart, which should currently have price bars and a moving average displayed on it.

Here are the steps: **Insert** → **Strategy** → **sjh_S_MAV1** → **Close**

For easy reference, here is the code again for the simple strategy:

```
IF H Crosses Over Average(C,9) THEN BUY next bar at market;
IF L Crosses Under Average(C,9) THEN SELL SHORT next bar at market;
```

The results of the strategy are displayed in Figure 4.55.

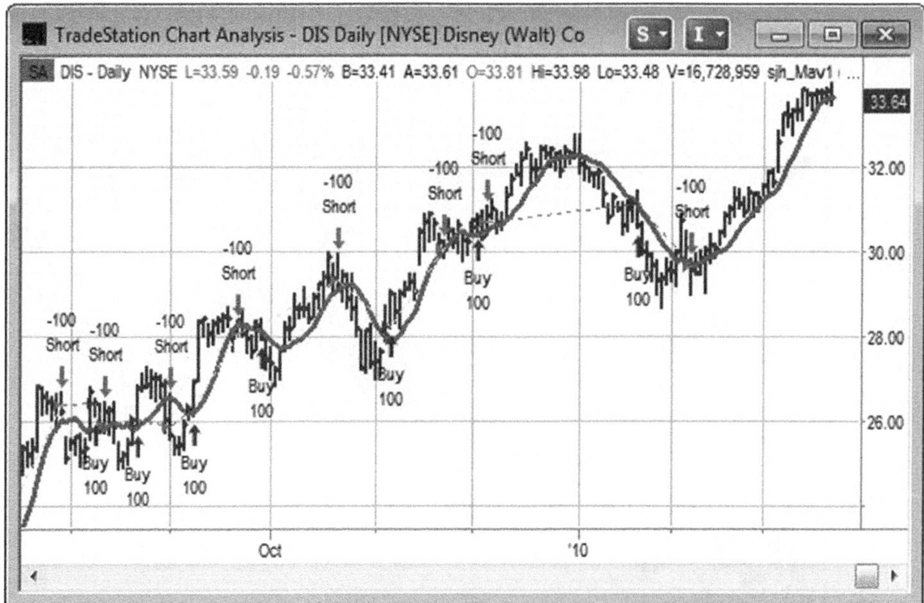

FIGURE 4.55 sjh_S_MAV1 Strategy

You will see red down arrows and blue up arrows indicating buys and sells. These are the places your system would have executed buys and sells, as the price moved above or below the moving average.

With earlier versions of TS, it is important that you check the scaling of the indicator before going further. Click on the tab labeled **Scaling.** In the box labeled **Scale type** you probably have the ◉ **Screen** radio button selected. Now select the radio button labeled **Same as Symbol,** and click **OK.** Your chart will change to more accurately reflect your system. When the high price crosses above the indicator a buy signal will be generated; when the low price crosses below the indicator a sell signal will be generated.

Current version users: The problem has been solved. The default scaling for indicators is **Same Axis as Underlying Data,** and you would have to choose **Right Axis, Left Axis,** or **None** to make the problem happen.

Changing the Strategy Format Before going further with the main purpose of a strategy, the moneymaking part, we are going to divert a little bit and make the strategy pretty. Each of us will have individual preferences about sizes, shapes, and colors. Let's look into that for a while.

Either double-click on an arrow, or use the menu sequence **Format** → **Strategies** to get to the dialogue box in Figure 4.56.

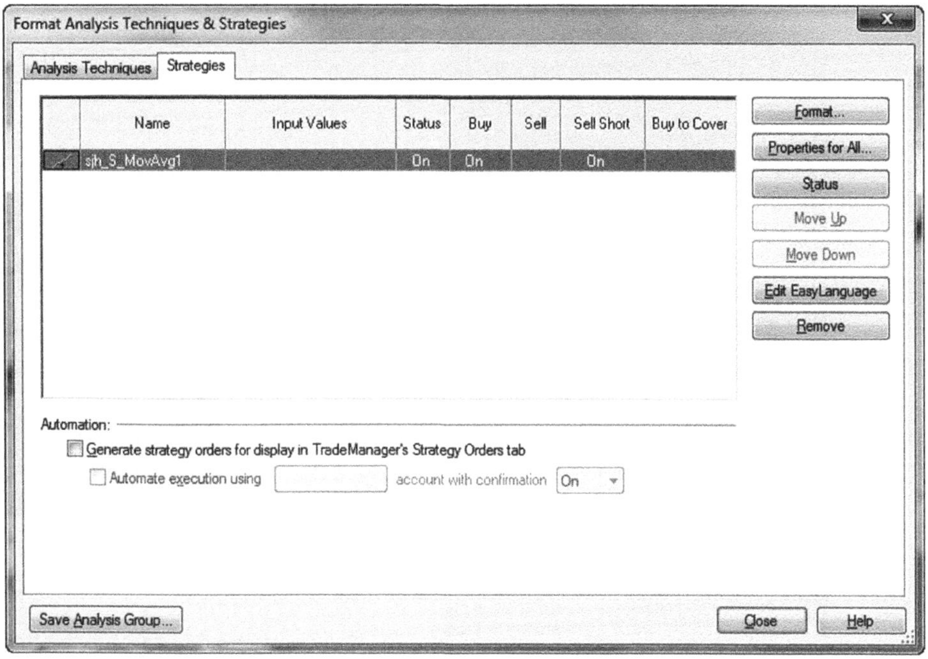

FIGURE 4.56 Format Strategies

Click on the **Format** button in the upper right corner of the window. This will bring you to a dialogue window that allows you to alter **Inputs, Entries, Exits,** and **Calculation.** At this juncture you have no inputs, but we are going to have some soon, so you need to know where this is.

Next, click on the **Entries** button. A new window will appear where you can play 'til your heart's content with arrows and ticks and colors (see Figure 4.57).

Again, I keep conventions consistent throughout my trading. Green, to me, means buy; red means sell. I don't go for the blue arrows for buys. Sorry, TradeStation. The first thing we are going to do is change the color of the arrows to match my preferences.

Click on the pull-down on the side of the **Entry Arrow Color** menu. The standard 20 Windows colors are now available, along with a button labeled **Other,** which allows you to choose from 48 standard colors or make up your own colors. Very convenient for folks who have trouble differentiating colors from thousands of combinations. I'm going for the standard dark green for the BUY arrows and the standard red for the SELL arrows. You can make those changes. There is one other color selection that should probably match the BUY and SELL arrows. It's the entry tick color. I like mine to match to arrows, but you might want them to be some other bright color.

The entry tick is a little triangular marker that shows, on the chart, exactly where the buy takes place. Without it you might think you got the best price of the bar, that is, the low

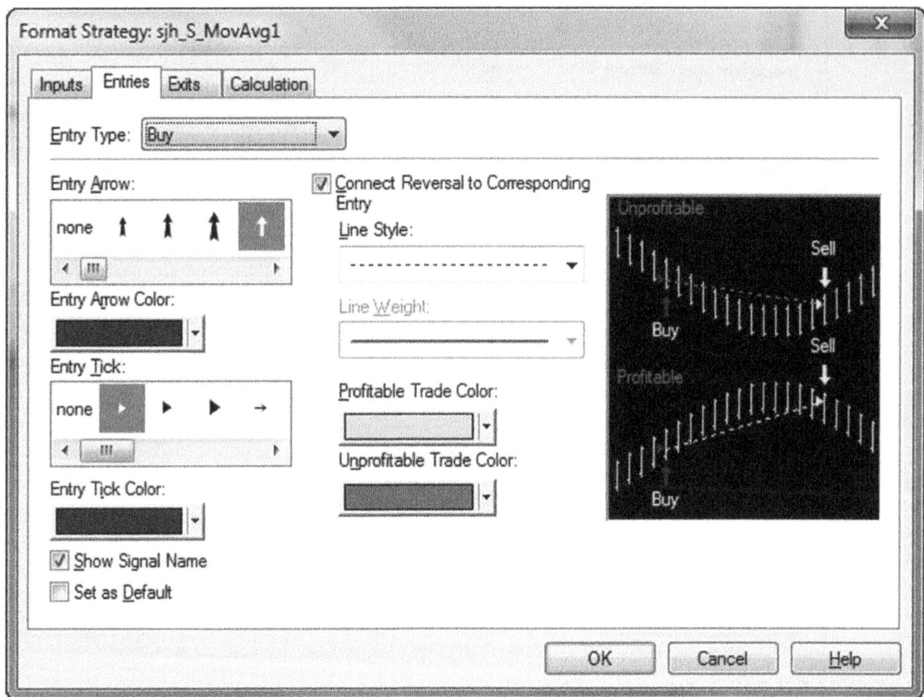

FIGURE 4.57 Format Entries

on a buy. Chances are you didn't. Chances are you bought the high of the bar, and this little triangular marker will show you that fact.

Before I show you the resultant chart, let's do one more thing. Let's change the shape of the arrows to something that would stand out more on the background of bars. We want it to look unlike the up-and-down lines of the OHLC bars. I am quite partial to the arrow that lives to the left of the default arrow. It has a nice little curve to it and flares at the bottom. It shows up quite well on a chart.

If you scroll over to the right on the arrow shapes selection box, there are even more exciting arrow shapes. Learn what's available to you, make a choice, and then stick with it so your psyche gets cued when the arrow pops up. Several of the arrow choices are illustrated in Figures 4.58 and 4.59.

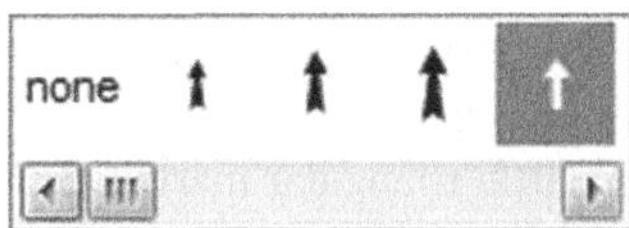

FIGURE 4.58 Arrows

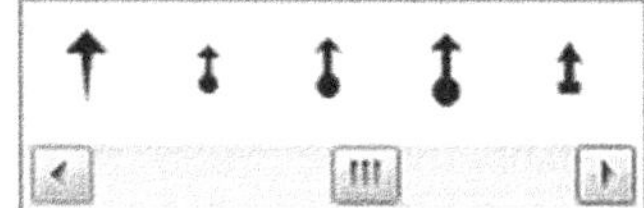

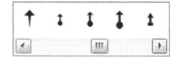

FIGURE 4.59 More Arrows

There are also more shape choices than the default triangle for the entry tick marker. Pick one that you can see easily. I like the one with a little curve to it for the same reason I like curves for the BUY and SELL arrows: It stands out from the straight lines of the OHLC bars. Shown in Figure 4.60 are several choices for the entry tick marker.

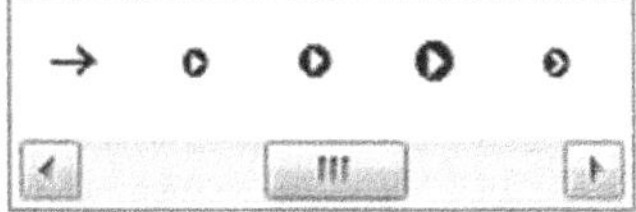

FIGURE 4.60 A Few Shapes of Entry Tick Markers

Have you made these changes? Have you picked colors for the **Entry Arrows** and for the **Entry Ticks?** Have you set the shapes for your Entry Ticks and Entry Arrows? If yes, then in the pull-down menu box labeled **Entry Type,** pull-down to reveal **Sell Short.** With this, the arrows will go the other direction, downward. The rest is the same, and you are on your own to make corresponding color and shape changes for your SELL arrows. I find that the default red works just fine for me for selling. I don't prefer the dark red, as I preferred dark green for buying.

As an aside, let me give you a quick advance tidbit. When we start programming Easy-Language you will need to know the names for the colors, or at least their color numbers, to tell them to EZL. They are found in the appendix of this book. Dark green and red are the colors I use primarily. Oh, and yellow for PHW dots.

Now that your colors and shapes are all configured, check the **Set as Default** check box in the lower left of the window to keep your selections for all future charts containing this strategy.

Following the Success of Trades There is one more item of interest in the **Format Strategy** dialogue box (Figure 4.57). In the middle of the dialogue box there is a section with **Line Style, Line Weight, Profitable Trade Color,** and **Unprofitable Trade Color.** These selections are easily turned off with the **Connect Reversal to Corresponding Entry** check box. Click it and the preview lines go away. Click it again and toggle the lines back on.

These lines connect one trade exit on one trade to the trade entry of the subsequent trade. To me they kind of clutter the chart. However, they do serve a subtle purpose: The lines have one color for winning trades and a different color for losing trades. By default the winners are connected with a tealish line (cyan) and the losers with a red line. Of course, I have my own conventions. For winners I like the cyan line, but for losers I prefer magenta.

Otherwise, the red nonprofit line can get confused with the red arrows and various indicator lines.

If you accept the default, the lines will be dotted. You cannot change the thickness of a dotted line (in this version of TS). If you want to make the lines thicker, you'll need to change them to straight lines and then change the thickness.

A chart with my preferred arrows and lines is displayed in Figure 4.61.

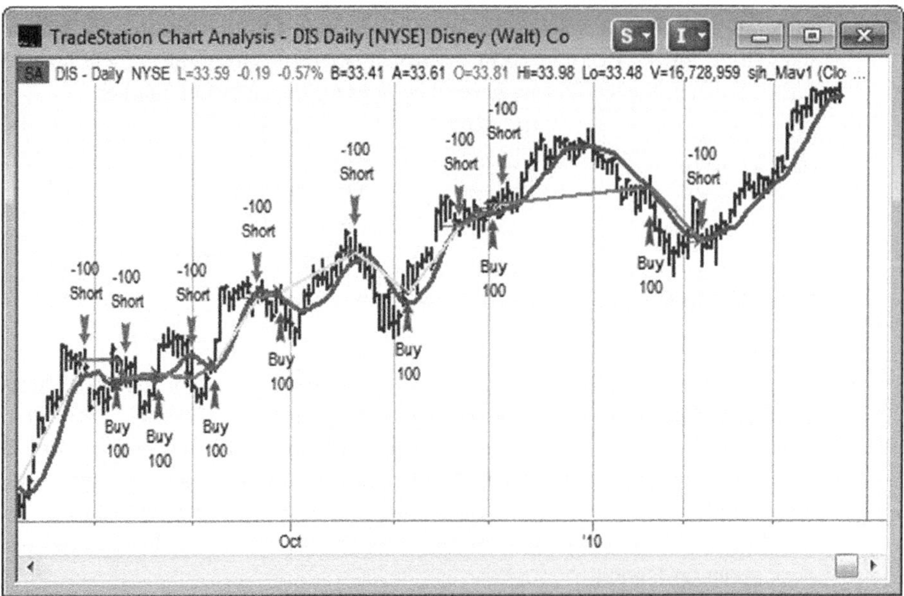

FIGURE 4.61 Configuring Arrows and Tick Markers

Now that we have all the configurations declared, it is almost time to look at the success of our first system. We have one more button to push in the **Format Strategies** dialogue box (Figure 4.56). This button is labeled **Properties for All,** and is found in the upper right of the dialogue window, right under the **Format** button. After clicking this button, the pop-up dialogue box displayed will look like Figure 4.62.

Several important selections reside in this box. In fact, one of them is a choice of much import and much debate. It is the **Commission** specification under the **Costs/Capitalization** heading. **Slippage** is likewise important and controversial. We will address these first, as they are so controversial. Many of the other numbers on this dialogue box will be ignored, and left to the reader to experiment with.

Commission and **Slippage** both have two choices associated with them: **per Trade** and **per Share/Contract.** These selections are pretty self-explanatory, so I'm not going to cover them in depth. **Per Trade** means the amount will be subtracted from the profit of the whole trade, regardless of how many shares were traded. **Per Share** means the amount will be multiplied by the number of shares before being subtracted from the profit of the whole trade.

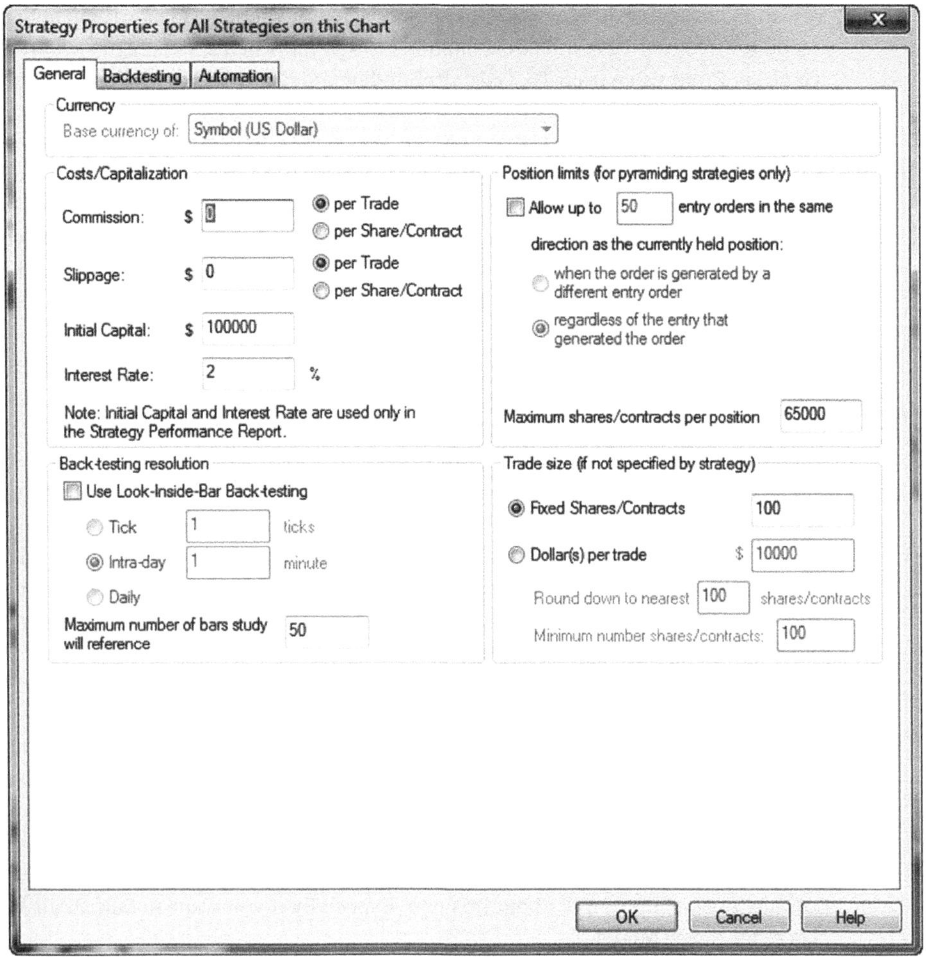

FIGURE 4.62 Properties for All

What I do want you to consider is how much your ideal system will suffer if you add even a little bit of commission and slippage. Back in the olden days, when I first began trading, commission on a futures contract was $50 per round turn (RT). Shortly after I began trading futures, commission became very competitive and dropped to $25/RT. It stayed there for a while before dropping little-by-little over the years until it came to its current low rate of $2-$10/RT.

Setting these two important numbers will likely turn your marginally profitable strategy into a losing strategy. When I first began doing trading research, I found that every strategy became unprofitable as soon as I added in commission and slippage. It became very frustrating. Over the years I came to two separate, but companion, realizations. First, while doing research, I never use a value for either commission or slippage. I leave them both set to zero. Second, I trust my CPC Index calculations to tell me when a strategy is profitable, not the Total Net Profit value from TS. Only after finding a strategy with a CPC Index of about 2.0 do I put numbers in for commission and slippage.

The word on the street, the common knowledge, is generally to set both numbers to 50. I think that's way too much. Over time, after thousands of trades, I have found that the positive slippage just about matches the negative slippage in real life. By that I mean that on one trade you will get a better fill than you expected and on the next trade your fill will be worse. They seem to pretty much average out. Commission, however, continues to eat at your profits. For this reason, it is important to determine whether your strategy is robust enough to handle commission.

Before we can take a look at an example of how commission and slippage affect the bottom line, profitability, we have to examine the performance report. But before we do that, let's finish examining the **Format → Strategies → Properties for All** dialogue box. There are a few more selections to discover.

Looking in the lower right square of the dialogue box you will see **Trade size (if not specified by strategy).** This is another important variable. By default the value 100 is set in the **Fixed Shares/Contracts** box. This means that whenever you make a trade, it will be for 100 shares of the symbol in question. If you have an account with $20,000 in it and want to trade as many shares as you can with that much money, you might want to select the second choice and tell TS you have $20,000 for the dollars per trade.

Another way to utilize this important tool is to split your account into portions and trade each vehicle (stock, EFT, or future) with the allotted portion. For instance, if you have $75,000 and are trading three different vehicles, you could split your account into three virtual portions and tell TS you want to trade $25,000 per trade. This way you would begin trading more shares as your first virtual account grows and fewer shares as your second virtual account gets smaller. If you have money management rules in place (see Ralph Vince's books), you could balance your three virtual portions as some of them grow and some don't. Call me if you want to talk about this one. Especially if you want to talk about Vince's new "Leverage Space Models."

Now's the time to move on to the really important topic: the money.

Step 7: Look at the Strategy's Performance

Back in the Quick Start of Chapter 2 we ran through this step. Let's review it again quickly. Here are the commands:

TS2000i users, use the **View → Strategy Performance Report** menu sequence. TS4.0 users, use the **View → System Report** menu sequence. Users of current versions of TS, use **View → Strategy Performance Report,** or **ALT+Shift+P.**

These sequences will bring up a window (see Figure 4.63) with an overview of the statistics related to the performance of your current system. For this exercise, I have set the Fixed Shares to 100. I am not using the wonderful feature that varies the number of contracts based on the value of the account, as it would be unlikely that you could produce the same or similar results with that large a variable in our setup.

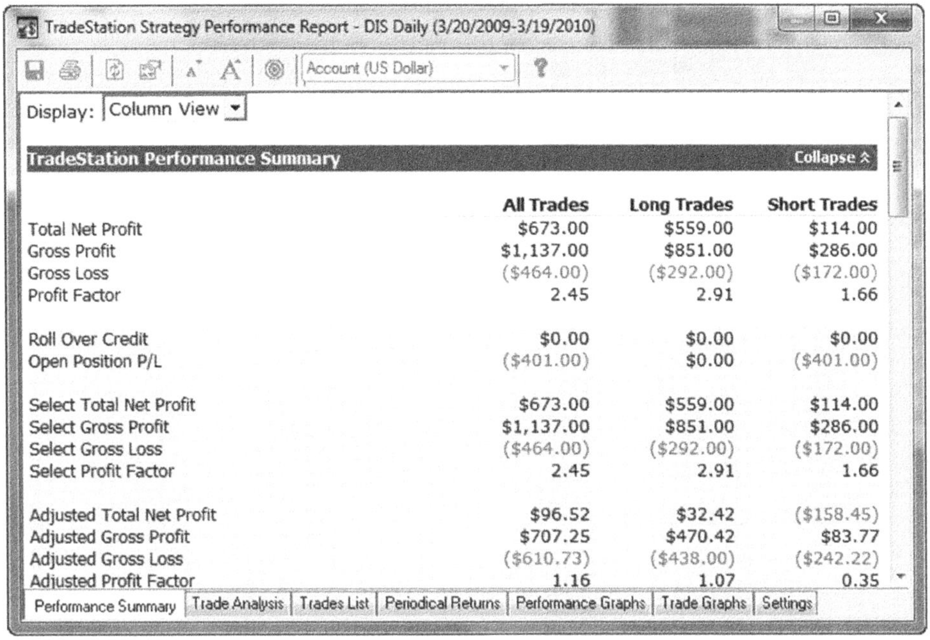

TradeStation Strategy Performance Report - DIS Daily (3/20/2009-3/19/2010)

Display: Column View

TradeStation Performance Summary Collapse

	All Trades	Long Trades	Short Trades
Total Net Profit	$673.00	$559.00	$114.00
Gross Profit	$1,137.00	$851.00	$286.00
Gross Loss	($464.00)	($292.00)	($172.00)
Profit Factor	2.45	2.91	1.66
Roll Over Credit	$0.00	$0.00	$0.00
Open Position P/L	($401.00)	$0.00	($401.00)
Select Total Net Profit	$673.00	$559.00	$114.00
Select Gross Profit	$1,137.00	$851.00	$286.00
Select Gross Loss	($464.00)	($292.00)	($172.00)
Select Profit Factor	2.45	2.91	1.66
Adjusted Total Net Profit	$96.52	$32.42	($158.45)
Adjusted Gross Profit	$707.25	$470.42	$83.77
Adjusted Gross Loss	($610.73)	($438.00)	($242.22)
Adjusted Profit Factor	1.16	1.07	0.35

Performance Summary | Trade Analysis | Trades List | Periodical Returns | Performance Graphs | Trade Graphs | Settings

FIGURE 4.63 Performance Summary without Commission or Slippage

This is hardly a winning system. We don't have any commission or slippage in the system. And there is just barely any profit. Nevertheless, it is a positive number and we can improve on this pretty easily.

Commission on the Side Let's take a brief excursion to see what effect specifying commission and slippage would have. Going in to the **Format Strategies** box by double-clicking on an arrow and then clicking the **Properties for All** button gets us to the window where we can change the commission and slippage. (See Figure 4.62.) Let's put commission up to $7 per trade, which is pretty realistic, and leave slippage alone for a minute. Going back to the **Performance Report,** we see that **Total Net Profit** has dropped and is now $421.00, as in Figure 4.64. For the next figure, let's make slippage be $5 per trade, which is about one tick per share. The resulting **Performance Report** is in Figure 4.65. You can see that we now have only $241 Total Net Profit. Pretty significant change!

We will get back to including commission and slippage in our testing in another chapter, but not for now. We are going to remove these values because they are variable, from broker to broker and from day to day. Set both values back to zero in the **Format → Analysis Techniques → Properties for All** menu sequence. Leave the other numbers at their defaults.

Back-testing Resolution The only other selection that might affect our testing is in the section labeled **Back-testing resolution.** (In the 3rd quadrant of Figure 4.62.) Let's try it to

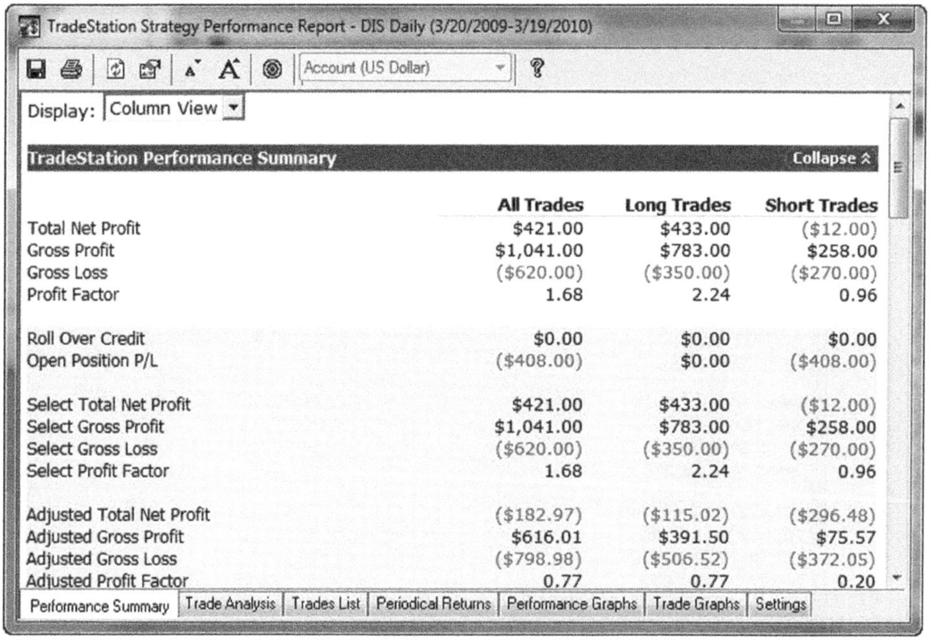

TradeStation Strategy Performance Report - DIS Daily (3/20/2009-3/19/2010)

Account (US Dollar)

Display: Column View

TradeStation Performance Summary — Collapse

	All Trades	Long Trades	Short Trades
Total Net Profit	$421.00	$433.00	($12.00)
Gross Profit	$1,041.00	$783.00	$258.00
Gross Loss	($620.00)	($350.00)	($270.00)
Profit Factor	1.68	2.24	0.96
Roll Over Credit	$0.00	$0.00	$0.00
Open Position P/L	($408.00)	$0.00	($408.00)
Select Total Net Profit	$421.00	$433.00	($12.00)
Select Gross Profit	$1,041.00	$783.00	$258.00
Select Gross Loss	($620.00)	($350.00)	($270.00)
Select Profit Factor	1.68	2.24	0.96
Adjusted Total Net Profit	($182.97)	($115.02)	($296.48)
Adjusted Gross Profit	$616.01	$391.50	$75.57
Adjusted Gross Loss	($798.98)	($506.52)	($372.05)
Adjusted Profit Factor	0.77	0.77	0.20

Performance Summary | Trade Analysis | Trades List | Periodical Returns | Performance Graphs | Trade Graphs | Settings

FIGURE 4.64 Performance Summary with $7 Commission

see what happens. Click the check box named **Use look-inside Bar Back testing** to activate it. The default on mine is set to **Intraday 1-minute.** Let's leave it there for now. Also, leave the **Maximum number of bars study will reference** set to 50, the default for most Bars Back settings.

What happened? Not much, except that an error message popped up saying: "Insufficient data for Look-Inside-Bar Back testing." Not sure what that means, it's time to do some more investigating. Looking at the bottom of the message, in the area labeled **Event Details,** the message is longer. It says: **Your strategy will begin calculating on 03/23/2009 but the data required for Look-Inside-Bar Back-testing is only available starting on 03/11/2010. Strategy calculation prior to 03/11/2010 will not use Look-Inside-Bar Back-testing.** Still cryptic. What data is required? And, why does it not start until 03/11/2010 when the data stream begins on 03/23/2009? Perhaps it is the fact that we limited the timespan to one year back. Remember we specified 260 bars back? Let's change that to allow all of the data in and see what happens.

Before doing that, however, we need to know what the Performance Report looks like over the whole span of data. So, we need to go back to **Format Symbol** → **Settings** and change **Years Back** to 90, the maximum allowable.

That changes the **Total Net Profit**. (See Figure 4.66.) We won't worry about the rest of the numbers right now; we just want this report documented so that we can compare apples to apples.

TradeStation Strategy Performance Report - DIS Daily (3/23/2009-3/19/2010)

Account (US Dollar)

Display: Column View

TradeStation Performance Summary Collapse

	All Trades	Long Trades	Short Trades
Total Net Profit	$241.00	$343.00	($102.00)
Gross Profit	$981.00	$743.00	$238.00
Gross Loss	($740.00)	($400.00)	($340.00)
Profit Factor	1.33	1.86	0.70
Roll Over Credit	$0.00	$0.00	$0.00
Open Position P/L	($413.00)	$0.00	($413.00)
Select Total Net Profit	$241.00	$343.00	($102.00)
Select Gross Profit	$981.00	$743.00	$238.00
Select Gross Loss	($740.00)	($400.00)	($340.00)
Select Profit Factor	1.33	1.86	0.70
Adjusted Total Net Profit	($373.11)	($207.39)	($398.80)
Adjusted Gross Profit	$580.51	$371.50	$69.71
Adjusted Gross Loss	($953.62)	($578.89)	($468.51)
Adjusted Profit Factor	0.61	0.64	0.15

Performance Summary | Trade Analysis | Trades List | Periodical Returns | Performance Graphs | Trade Graphs | Settings

FIGURE 4.65 Performance Summary with Both Commission and Slippage

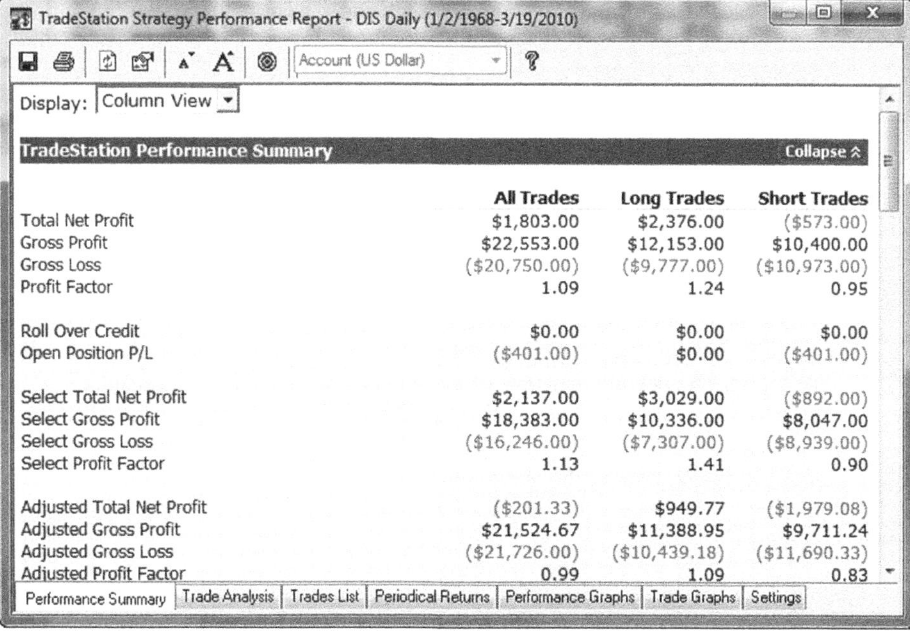

TradeStation Strategy Performance Report - DIS Daily (1/2/1968-3/19/2010)

Account (US Dollar)

Display: Column View

TradeStation Performance Summary Collapse

	All Trades	Long Trades	Short Trades
Total Net Profit	$1,803.00	$2,376.00	($573.00)
Gross Profit	$22,553.00	$12,153.00	$10,400.00
Gross Loss	($20,750.00)	($9,777.00)	($10,973.00)
Profit Factor	1.09	1.24	0.95
Roll Over Credit	$0.00	$0.00	$0.00
Open Position P/L	($401.00)	$0.00	($401.00)
Select Total Net Profit	$2,137.00	$3,029.00	($892.00)
Select Gross Profit	$18,383.00	$10,336.00	$8,047.00
Select Gross Loss	($16,246.00)	($7,307.00)	($8,939.00)
Select Profit Factor	1.13	1.41	0.90
Adjusted Total Net Profit	($201.33)	$949.77	($1,979.08)
Adjusted Gross Profit	$21,524.67	$11,388.95	$9,711.24
Adjusted Gross Loss	($21,726.00)	($10,439.18)	($11,690.33)
Adjusted Profit Factor	0.99	1.09	0.83

Performance Summary | Trade Analysis | Trades List | Periodical Returns | Performance Graphs | Trade Graphs | Settings

FIGURE 4.66 Performance Report for DIS Going Back 90 Years

Now we will change the **Back-Testing Resolution** to **Use Look-Inside-Bar Backtesting.** Check the checkbox. Again, we get the message about "Insufficient data". How can that be with 90 years of data? This time the detailed message at the bottom of the window says it will begin calculating on 01/02/1968 but the data necessary for calculation only starts on 03/11/2010. Those two statements taken together give us a clue. It seems that the "inside bar" data only begins on 03/11/2010. A quick call to the TradeStation technical support people verifies this. TradeStation saves only 10 days of look-inside-bar data. Thus, we can't benefit from checking this box when using daily data over a long period. It would, however, seem it might be beneficial when using intraday data like 5-minute bars for the last 10 days. This is something for our TradeStation wish-list.

Just to complete this discussion, without displaying all the screenshots for the exercise, when I changed the data to 5-minute TS quit giving me the error message. That was the problem. Nevertheless, it didn't make any difference to the **Total Net Profit** whether I checked **Look-Inside-Bar** or left it unchecked.

Back to the Essence of Step 7 We have examined the basics of the Strategy Performance Report. Finishing up the menu sequence **Format → Strategies → Properties for All,** there are two more tabs that we haven't looked at yet. These tabs are labeled **Backtesting** and **Automation.** These two tabs are for advanced users settings and are not addressed in this book.

Back in Chapter 2's Quick Start we created a basic strategy and examined its profits. Refresher: It made $335 **Total Net Profit.** In this section we are going to get a bit more sophisticated. This time we are going to introduce a variable that we can optimize.

NOTE Remember that when you change the value of the moving average length in the strategy, it doesn't change the value in the indicator. It would be nice to have a link to connect the indicator on the chart to the strategy on the chart, but that's not the way the current version of TS works. So, when you optimize your strategy, be sure you look up the resultant length and insert that value into the indicator.

For convenience, the code for our first, basic strategy is included in Figure 4.67. It is very simple, indeed. Just a buy and a sell; nothing more. To allow us to optimize the length of the moving average, we must change the 9 to a variable in the call to the built-in function **Average.** The default structure of the function is found in the appendix of this book. It is also to be found in the **EasyLanguage Dictionary** by clicking on the little blue book icon in the horizontal menu bar that runs along the top of your TS desktop. It is shown in Figure 4.68a, at the far right of the horizontal bar.

```
IF H Crosses Over Average(C,9) THEN BUY;
IF L Crosses Under Average(C,9) THEN SELL SHORT;
```

FIGURE 4.67 Simple Strategy Number One

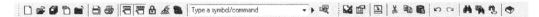

FIGURE 4.68a EasyLanguage Dictionary Icon in the Menu Bar (Early Versions) Far Right

In versions 8.0 and above, the dictionary is a pop-out over at the right side of the window and not in the menu bar. It is shown in Figure 4.68b.

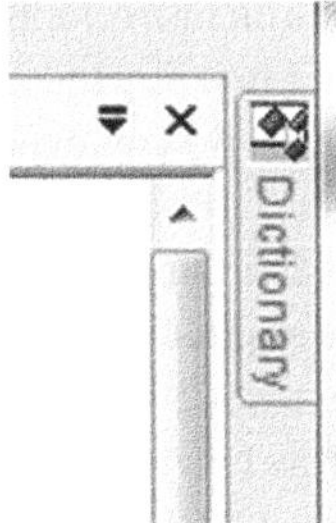

FIGURE 4.68b Dictionary Pop-out

Bring up the **EZL Dictionary** and type the word `average` in the **Search for:** box.

If the word started with "Z", TS would scroll down to the Zs in the list. Because we are asking for a word starting with "A", the list is already in the As and all we have to do is click on the word **Average** with the category **User Functions.** Then click on the **OK** button. If you want to read a full and detailed explanation of the function **Average,** before clicking on the **OK** button, click on the **Definition** button. Doing so will bring up a plethora of information about the **Average** function and its uses. Of greatest import is the syntax of the function, which is:

```
Average(Price,Length).
```

In our simple strategy shown in Figure 4.67, we have used `C` (for Close) as the **Price** and the constant `9` for **Length.** It is this Length to which we now turn our attention. By using a variable instead of a constant in our code, we can test every value imaginable without changing the code. We do this through a process called **Optimization,** outside of the EZL Editor, by specifying a range of values to try one at a time.

For instance, if we wanted to test all the values from 2 to 25 for the Length, we would tell the optimizer to test:

```
2:25:1
```

that is, "from 2 to 25 in steps of 1". Pretty simple! The starting value is 2; the ending value is 25; and we test every value by increasing the length by 1 with each subsequent test. Thus, we would be testing the values: 2, 3, 4, 5, 6, . . . , 23, 24, 25. That's 24 tests.

If we wanted just to test the even values in that range (to speed up the testing process), we would specify:

```
2:25:2.
```

This is, to my mind, the most powerful feature of TradeStation. The optimizer is invaluable to trading researchers.

Way back when, I used to do all this work by hand. I mean by hand! I had a calculator and paper. When things got a little more sophisticated I used a spreadsheet and formulas. But this was before TradeStation. I first started using the introductory product, SystemWriter, in the 1980s. It was a DOS program; do you even know what DOS is? It was so much better than a spreadsheet that I was ecstatic. I could write a little system like the one just shown and test every combination from 2 to 25 in about an hour. Huge improvement over the spreadsheet! When the strategies got more sophisticated and I was testing combinations of four variables at a time, running 1,000 or so tests, I would start up the optimization at bedtime and get the results the next morning. It was heavenly.

When running sequences of test like this, it is critical that you keep track of your results—and your inputs. This is where your lab book comes in. That's what I use the spreadsheet for these days. It is a great convenience to collect all my results in one place and be able to sort on any parameter until I find the results I want.

Let's start with our basic strategy and run some optimizations now. First, we need to have a baseline for comparison, so we will run the strategy with default parameters, no fancy stuff, and log in the results. The setup is: C, 9, one year of daily data, last date 3/21/2010, do not connect reversals, no intrabar calculations, no commission, no slippage. I get a Total Net Profit of $673.00. How about you? That's the same as back in Figure 4.63. Good. We have our baseline. To get off to the right start, we must be consistent and put the information from the Strategy Performance Report into the Lab Book spreadsheet. Do that now. Mine is in Figure 4.69.

My Lab Book

My Lab Book

Date Range: 3/23/2009-3/19/2010

Test Nbr	Description	Length	Var 2	Var 3	Var 4	Symbol	Interval	Nbr Trades	Avg Trade Net Profit	Total Net Profit	PF	P	R	CPC>1.2	Avg Time in Trade	Open Trade	Total Net w Open
1	sjh_MAV1	9				DIS	Daily	18	$ 37.39	$ 673.00	2.45	38.89%	3.50	3.33	13d9h	$(401.00)	$ 272.00
2																	
3																	
4																	
5																	
6																	
7																	
8																	

Sheet1 Sheet2 Sheet3

FIGURE 4.69 Lab Book

Next, we are going to change the code of the strategy to allow for variable lengths. Open the EasyLanguage PowerEditor by clicking the **EasyLanguage Icon** at the top of the vertical toolbar, usually on the left of your TradeStation desktop. From here choose **Open**

EasyLanguage Document and select your saved strategy (mine is sjh_S_MAV1). **HINT:** If you type "S" while looking at the list of available strategies, TS will move you over to the Ss for easier selection. Before going any further, let's save the strategy with a new name, so we don't make a bunch of mistakes and save them over our working strategy. This will also help clarify our record keeping in the Lab Book. Simply go up to **File** and pull-down to **Save EasyLanguage Document as....** I am going to name my new strategy sjh_S_MAV1_01 to distinguish it from the first one while still keeping the same idea going. I name subsequent strategies 1, 2, 3, and so on. When I start a fresh, new idea that doesn't hinge off the current one, I give it a new name altogether.

OK, it's time to change the code. Earlier I said we would introduce a variable in place of the constant. We do that by changing the 9 to **j_Length.** Why didn't I say Length? Because I start all my variables, input, and the like with my middle initial since there are very few Reserved Words that start with "j." This way I don't run the chance of trying to name something that is already one of TS's names.

After simply replacing the 9 with the word **j_Length,** the code becomes that shown in Figure 4.70.

```
IF H Crosses Over Average(C,j_Length) THEN BUY next bar at market;
IF L Crosses Under Average(C,j_Length) THEN SELL SHORT next bar at market;
```

FIGURE 4.70 Initial Code for sjh_S_MAV1_01

After making these changes yourself, press F3 to verify the code. What happens? TradeStation starts out right by saying "Verifying" but then the error message shown pops up in Figure 4.71.

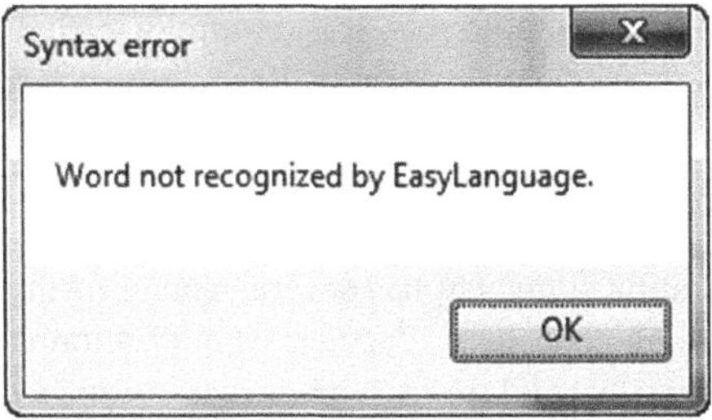

FIGURE 4.71 Error Message

How are you supposed to know which word it doesn't like? EasyLanguage will highlight the syntax error if it can. In this instance, the word **j_Length** is highlighted in black, to contrast with my white background. It is shown in Figure 4.72. Because I have been doing this for umpty-ump years, I know what it is complaining about. As a new TS programmer, you won't automatically see the error. It takes time, lots of time, to have this be second nature.

The pop-up message is not always enough information to discern the error. If you use the key combination **CTRL + SHIFT + E** or go to **View → EasyLanguage Output Bar,** TS

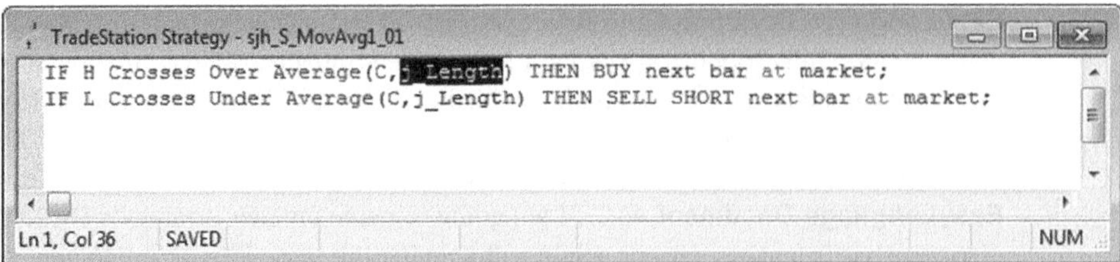

FIGURE 4.72 Syntax Error in the Code

will display more precise information related to its error message. The **Output Bar** appears at the bottom of the TS Desktop. In this case, viewing Figure 4.73, you can see that TS tells you what line(s) contains the error. In this case, we have only two lines of code and both lines contain errors.

Description	Technique	Line	Type
Word not recognized by EasyLanguage.	sjh_S_MovAvg1_01 (Strategy)	1	Error (#61)
Word not recognized by EasyLanguage.	sjh_S_MovAvg1_01 (Strategy)	2	Error (#61)

FIGURE 4.73 EasyLanguage Output Bar

Taking a look at the highlighted word in Figure 4.72 lets me know that I forgot to define the word to TradeStation. EasyLanguage knows its **Reserved Words** and built-in functions. That's all. If you make up a word (variable), you have to tell EZL what it is. In this case it is not an Input; it is a Variable. These words must be declared to EasyLanguage. There is a statement with which you do this. It is, naturally, called a **declaration statement.** In this case we are going to declare a variable. Here's how it is done:

```
VARIABLES: j_Length (0);
```

This declaration statement has several similar forms: `VAR, VARS, VARIABLE, and VARIABLES` are all equivalent. Further, capitalization is not recognized by EZL in this instance, so it is equally valid to say: `VaR, var, varIABLE,` and any other combination of lower case and caps.

The declaration statement goes in the code before the variable is used. By convention we usually place the declaration statements at the top of the code, but you don't have to. You just need to be sure a variable is defined before it is used.

The zero in parentheses gives EZL a starting value for the variable. By convention zero just means you will be calculating the real value later in the code. You could set the value in parentheses to 9 and be done with it; that is equally valid. Now that we have defined `j_Length`, try to **Verify** once again by pressing [F3]. This time it works. EZL responds with

Verification successful. The code as just discussed is presented in Figure 4.74 for your convenience.

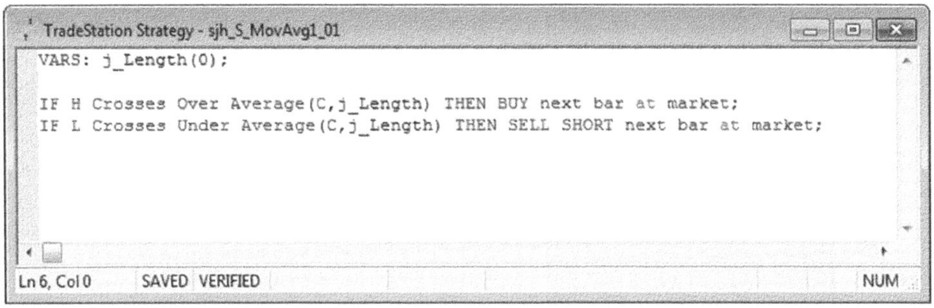

```
TradeStation Strategy - sjh_S_MovAvg1_01
VARS: j_Length(0);

IF H Crosses Over Average(C,j_Length) THEN BUY next bar at market;
IF L Crosses Under Average(C,j_Length) THEN SELL SHORT next bar at market;

Ln 6, Col 0    SAVED VERIFIED    NUM
```

FIGURE 4.74 Verified Code

Well and good. Now how do we optimize to find the best length for the moving average? We don't. While we did define j_Length to EZL in the declaration statement, we did not make it accessible from outside this routine. A variable can be used for calculations within the routine but is not communicated to other routines or to the outside world. There is another declaration statement for that purpose. It is called **Inputs.** Like the VAR statement, this one can take several forms, all equivalent. The forms for the **Input** statement are: `INPUT` and `INPUTS`. Again, capitalization doesn't matter, so you can say input or inputs or use any combination of lower case and caps.

ASIDE There are other declaration statements for defining other types of custom words to behave as variables in your routine. We won't get into them here, but for completeness sake, I list some of them here:

- ARRAY
- CONST
- NUMERIC
- STRING
- TRUEFALSE

There are other variations on these themes (i.e., more specific words like NumericSimple) but since I'm not going into them here, I won't go into them here.

Going back into the code from Figure 4.74, we need to get rid of the **Variable** statement and replace it with an **Input** statement. In the EZL PowerEditor, which you can use much like a word processor, remove the line with the `Vars` statement, and replace it with: `INPUTS: j_Length ( 0 );` In fact, all you really need to do is replace the `Vars` with `Inputs`.

Simple change, but oh so powerful. Press [F3] again, and the code should once again **Verify.** The new code is presented in Figure 4.75.

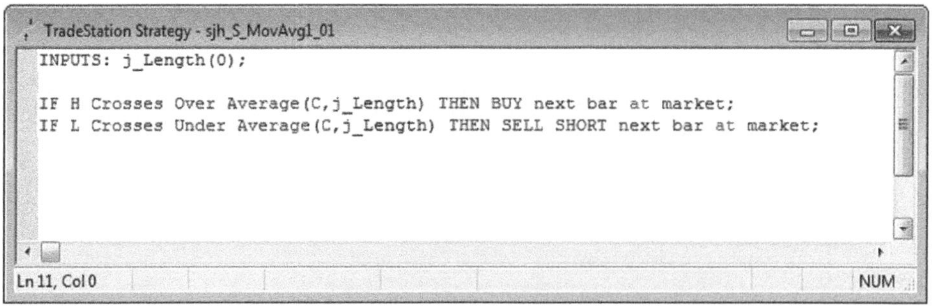

```
INPUTS: j_Length(0);

IF H Crosses Over Average(C,j_Length) THEN BUY next bar at market;
IF L Crosses Under Average(C,j_Length) THEN SELL SHORT next bar at market;
```

TradeStation Strategy - sjh_S_MovAvg1_01 — Ln 11, Col 0 — NUM

FIGURE 4.75 sjh_S_MAV1_01 Attempt 2

It doesn't seem like much happened, but in reality the change was huge. Variables are not communicated to the outside while Inputs are. If you will delete the current strategy from your chart, or create a new chart, and insert this new strategy, I'll show you something fantastic. Just click on an arrow on the chart to select the strategy and press the [Delete] key to get rid of the original strategy.

If you go to the **Format** → **Strategies** window, you will notice something new. In the **Inputs** column you will see the value 0, where previously (see Figure 4.56) there was none. On clicking **Close** to see the results, we are instead presented an error message saying: **Floating point invalid calculation.** What does that mean? Simply this, the value zero for the input causes a divide by zero to happen in our calculations and that gives a floating point overflow. The solution is to change the value quickly to 9, either by clicking **Format** and changing the input value or by changing the EZL code so that the default length is 9. Either way works. I prefer you change the code; that's what I'm going to do.

We haven't gotten very far, but we've learned a lot in the process.

Now it is time to utilize the new feature we added to our code and crank up the optimizer. It's very easy now that we have added the Input value to the code. Simply 🖱 **Format** → **Strategies** → **Format** → **Optimize** → **OK.** This sequence will tell TS to optimize the lengths using the values 5, 6, 7, 8, 9, 10, 11, 12, and 13.

Figure 4.76 shows you the zero value in the **Input Values** column. Figure 4.77 illustrates the location of the **Optimize** button in the lower left of the dialogue box (next to Dictionary). Figure 4.78 shows you how the inputs values are set to **Start, Stop** and **Increment** values.

When you press the **OK** button in the optimization parameters box, TS will show you the shorthand for the optimization paramenters as 5:13:1. I will use this shorthand notation again and again, from now on.

With these values set, it is time to let 'er rip! That's what I say each time before I run an optimization.

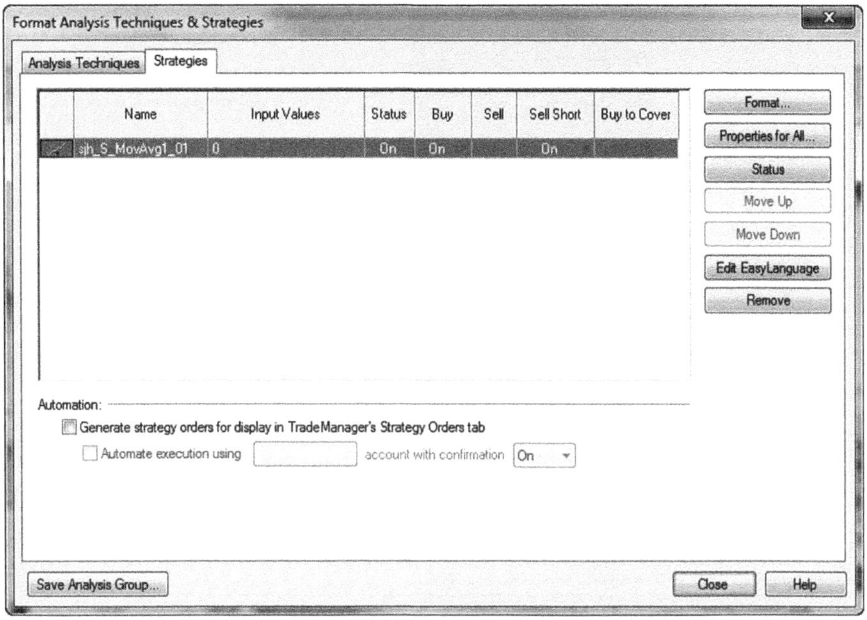

FIGURE 4.76 Format Strategies

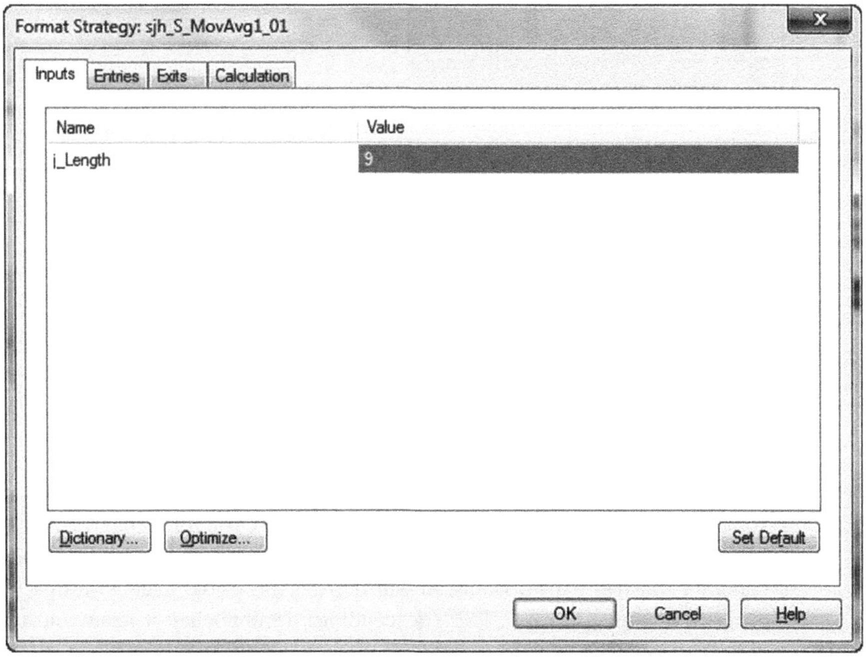

FIGURE 4.77 Optimize Button in Lower Left

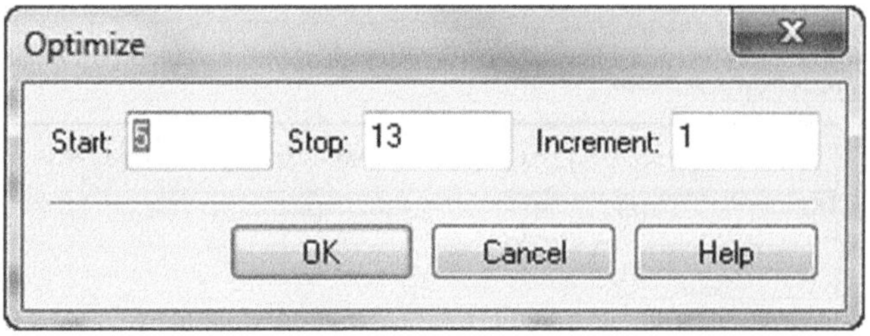

Optimize

Start: 5 Stop: 13 Increment: 1

OK Cancel Help

FIGURE 4.78 Optimize

It takes less than a second for this optimization to calculate and present the results. It almost seems as if nothing happened. But something did happen because the **Total Net Profit** value is larger. That's what optimization is all about. TNP (Total Net Profit) has gone from its previous value of $673.00 to its current value of $1,391.00—more than double the return. Now let's inspect the **Optimization Report,** which is found by **ALT+SHIFT+O** or **View → Strategy Optimization Report.** It is shown in Figure 4.79.

TradeStation Strategy Optimization Report - DIS Daily [NYSE] Disney (Walt) ...

	S_MovAvg1 j_Length	Test	All: Net Profit	All: Gross Profit	All: Gross Loss	All: Total Trades	All: % Profitable	All: Winning Trades	All: Losing Trades
1	13	9	372.00	758.00	-386.00	13	46.15	6	7
2	12	8	584.00	966.00	-382.00	15	40.00	6	8
3	11	7	722.00	1,075.00	-353.00	17	47.06	8	8
4	10	6	859.00	1,188.00	-329.00	18	50.00	9	8
5	9	5	673.00	1,137.00	-464.00	18	38.89	7	10
6	8	4	929.00	1,303.00	-374.00	16	56.25	9	7
7	7	3	1,391.00	1,650.00	-259.00	18	72.22	13	5
8	6	2	1,273.00	1,601.00	-328.00	18	77.78	14	4
9	5	1	1,197.00	1,486.00	-289.00	18	77.78	14	4

FIGURE 4.79 Our First Strategy Optimization Report

The values TS tried for j_Length are sorted in the first column, with the largest number on top (descending). When you get down to the value 7 you'll see that the row is highlighted. TS is pointing out that this value produces the highest TNP. Double-click on the label for the column **All: Net Profit.** Doing so will reorder the whole page with that column sorted in order of highest to lowest TNP (descending). Double-click it again and the ordering is changed to ascending (lowest to highest). You can double-click on any column and sort the values in ascending or descending order.

After sorting the **All: Net Profit** column descending, I always save the spreadsheet by clicking the diskette icon in the top left of the window. It is shown in Figure 4.80.

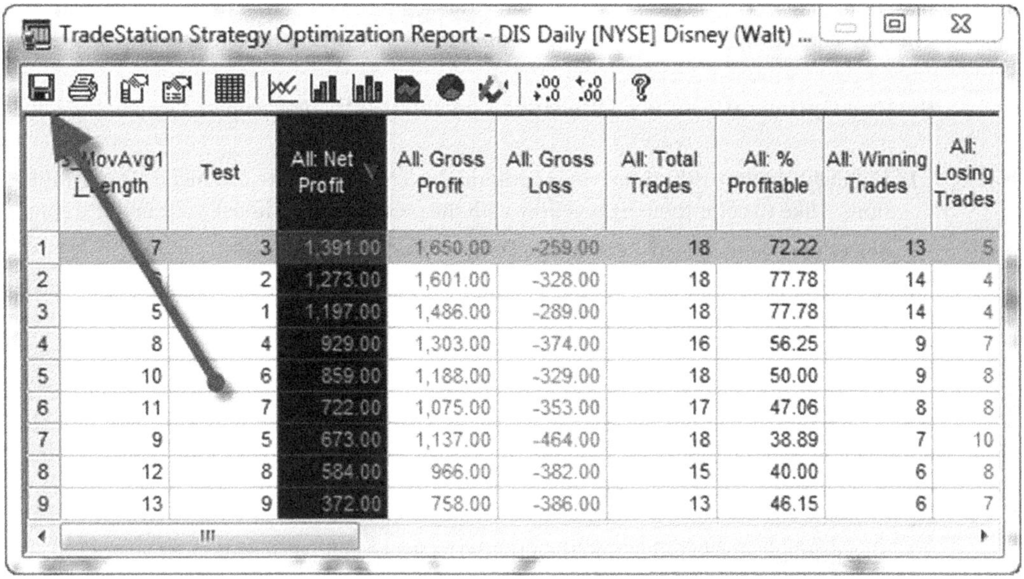

TradeStation Strategy Optimization Report - DIS Daily [NYSE] Disney (Walt) ...

	s_MovAvg1 i_Length	Test	All: Net Profit	All: Gross Profit	All: Gross Loss	All: Total Trades	All: % Profitable	All: Winning Trades	All: Losing Trades
1	7	3	1,391.00	1,650.00	-259.00	18	72.22	13	5
2	6	2	1,273.00	1,601.00	-328.00	18	77.78	14	4
3	5	1	1,197.00	1,486.00	-289.00	18	77.78	14	4
4	8	4	929.00	1,303.00	-374.00	16	56.25	9	7
5	10	6	859.00	1,188.00	-329.00	18	50.00	9	8
6	11	7	722.00	1,075.00	-353.00	17	47.06	8	8
7	9	5	673.00	1,137.00	-464.00	18	38.89	7	10
8	12	8	584.00	966.00	-382.00	15	40.00	6	8
9	13	9	372.00	758.00	-386.00	13	46.15	6	7

FIGURE 4.80 Save the Optimization Report

This action saves the information in spreadsheet (.txt) format. You need to tell Windows where to store the file and give it a name you will later recognize. Again, I have a convention. I labeled this file Op_20100322_934. The convention is Op stands for Optimization, the next field is today's date in programmer's order, and the last field is the time of day. Of course, I then put this file name in my lab book, which now looks like Figure 4.81.

The text file can be easily opened from Excel (or any other spreadsheet program) by **File → Open** and navigating (from within Excel) to the location of the file you just saved. You won't be able to see it initially; you need to switch file types to **All Files** so the .txt file will show up. Now click **Next** and then **Finish.** Your file should now be imported to Excel and

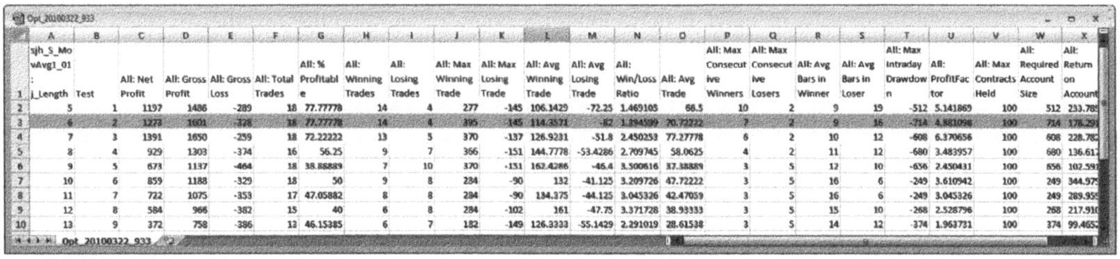

Opt_20100322_933

	A	B	C	D	E	F	G	H	I	J	K	L
1	sjh_S_MovAvg1_01: i_Length	Test	All: Net Profit	All: Gross Profit	All: Gross Loss	All: Total Trades	All: % Profitable	All: Winning Trades	All: Losing Trades	All: Max Winning Trade	All: Max Losing Trade	All: Avg Winning Trade
2	5	1	1197	1486	-289	18	77.77778	14	4	277	-145	106.1429
3	6	2	1273	1601	-328	18	77.77778	14	4	395	-145	114.3571
4	7	3	1391	1650	-259	18	72.22222	13	5	370	-137	126.9231
5	8	4	929	1303	-374	16	56.25	9	7	366	-151	144.7778
6	9	5	673	1137	-464	18	38.88889	7	10	370	-151	162.4286
7	10	6	859	1188	-329	18	50	9	8	284	-90	132
8	11	7	722	1075	-353	17	47.05882	8	8	284	-90	134.375
9	12	8	584	966	-382	15	40	6	8	284	-102	161
10	13	9	372	758	-386	13	46.15385	6	7	182	-149	126.3333

	M	N	O	P	Q	R	S	T	U	V	W	X
1	All: Avg Losing Trade	All: Win/Loss Ratio	All: Avg Trade	All: Max Consecutive Winners	All: Max Consecutive Losers	All: Avg Bars in Winner	All: Avg Bars in Loser	All: Max Intraday Drawdown	All: ProfitFactor	All: Max Contracts Held	All: Required Account Size	All: Return on Account
2	-72.25	1.469105	66.5	10	2	9	19	-512	5.141869	100	512	233.785
3	-82	1.394599	70.72222	7	2	9	16	-714	4.881098	100	714	178.29
4	-51.8	2.450253	77.27778	6	2	10	12	-608	6.370656	100	608	228.78
5	-53.4286	2.709745	58.0625	4	2	11	12	-680	3.483957	100	680	136.61
6	-46.4	3.500616	37.38889	3	5	12	10	-656	2.450431	100	656	102.59
7	-41.125	3.209726	47.72222	3	5	16	6	-249	3.610942	100	249	344.97
8	-44.125	3.045326	42.47059	3	5	16	6	-249	3.045326	100	249	289.95
9	-47.75	3.371728	38.93333	3	5	15	10	-268	2.528796	100	268	217.91
10	-55.1429	2.291019	28.61538	3	5	14	12	-374	1.963731	100	374	99.465

Opt_20100322_933

FIGURE 4.81 My Lab Book after Finding Islands and Alligators

ordered by TNP in column C. My patented, trademarked, proprietary testing methods now come into play. (Just teasing about the patent.) I teach this process in depth in my Solving the Puzzle seminars and in private consulting. I do this differently than anyone else I've seen, but I think the process is essential. I'm going to teach it to you here. For this chapter I'll just give you a quick start, but in Chapter 19, Optimization, we will go into the subject in depth.

Sorting Optimizations for Alligators and Islands™ Here are the steps:

1. Highlight the top 10% of the rows (ordered by TNP) to isolate the highest-profit situations. I like to color them light yellow with the paint bucket. Choose your favorite color.
2. Select the whole spreadsheet and go **Data → Sort → sjh_Length.**
3. Now, choosing a darker yellow, or perhaps orange, highlight the center of the widest yellow zone.

This new orange zone will be the zone of safest trading. It will be the island in the center of the alligators. It will not necessarily be the greatest profit, but it will allow you to make a mistake with the parameters and still be safe with your choice, because there are other values on either side where there is still profit. The lab book with these new values is in Figure 4.81.

This example doesn't illustrate the process as well as an optimization with hundreds of tests would. When you have hundreds of tests, there might be several zones of protection. Pick the largest zone of good results. And then pick the center of that zone. I'll show you more details in Chapter 19.

Before leaving the optimization subject for now, I want to show you one more parameter that you will want to alter and one more tidbit you should know. The tidbit is: As soon as you leave your **Optimization Report** and go to a different window different chart, or change the parameters of your chart, the **Optimization Report** will disappear. To get it back you will have to run the optimization again. So, if you want to keep it, you need to save it for Excel as I showed you earlier.

Now for the parameter change. With the chart highlighted, use the menu sequence **View → Chart Analysis Preferences .....** This will bring up the window in Figure 4.82. If it is not already active, click the **Strategy** tab. Under this tab the first section is labeled **Optimization Report Settings.** By default TS has the setting as **Keep the Highest 200 tests.** Since computers are so fast now, and have so much memory, and because Excel is also fast and can store thousands of cells, it is no longer a concern to keep the number of tests saved at a minimum. I like to keep the best 999 tests. If you want to set the optimization so that you won't have to reorder the tests by TNP, the third selection is **Default sort field.** You can change this so that TS keeps the tests ordered by TNP. Choose **All: Net Profit.** That gives you one less step to perform when you are in research mode. The rest of this window can be left at default settings.

Let's take a look at the **Performance Report** for the best test now. Remember that the setting for j_Length of 7 was the most profitable test. However, the island in the alligators was at the 6 setting, so that's what we are going to use for our report. Using the sequence

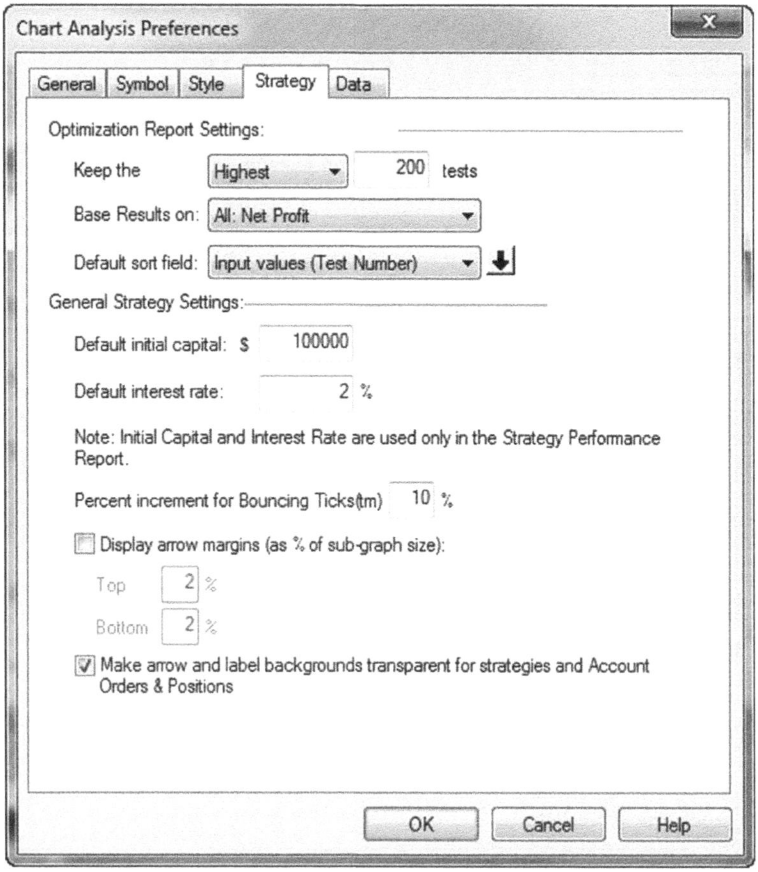

Chart Analysis Preferences

General | Symbol | Style | Strategy | Data

Optimization Report Settings:

Keep the Highest 200 tests

Base Results on: All: Net Profit

Default sort field: Input values (Test Number)

General Strategy Settings:

Default initial capital: $ 100000

Default interest rate: 2 %

Note: Initial Capital and Interest Rate are used only in the Strategy Performance Report.

Percent increment for Bouncing Ticks(tm) 10 %

Display arrow margins (as % of sub-graph size):

Top 2 %

Bottom 2 %

Make arrow and label backgrounds transparent for strategies and Account Orders & Positions

OK Cancel Help

FIGURE 4.82 Save the Best Tests

Format → **Strategies** → **Format,** set `j_Length` to 6. Now the **Performance Report,** which was still visible, changes to show TNP of $1,273.00. Figure 4.83 shows you the first part of my **Performance Report.**

By default TS shows you the **Expand**ed report. Clicking on **Collapse** in the upper right corner will give you the report in Figure 4.84. What's the difference? you say. The collapsed report is the original configuration from older versions of TS; the expanded report has many more statistics, originally designed by RINA Systems. I like the collapsed report because I can more easily see the three numbers that are so critical to my system testing: PF, P, and R.[3] Recall that these three numbers multiplied together are my CPC Index, which is the key to my trading. It is the single most important number I use to compare systems to each other. For this strategy the CPC Index is $(4.88 * 0.7778 * 1.39) = 5.28$, which is well above the 1.2 requirement. My Lab Book now looks like Figure 4.85.

[3]PF=Profit Factor; P=Percentage Profitable; R=Ratio Avg. Win:Avg. Loss.

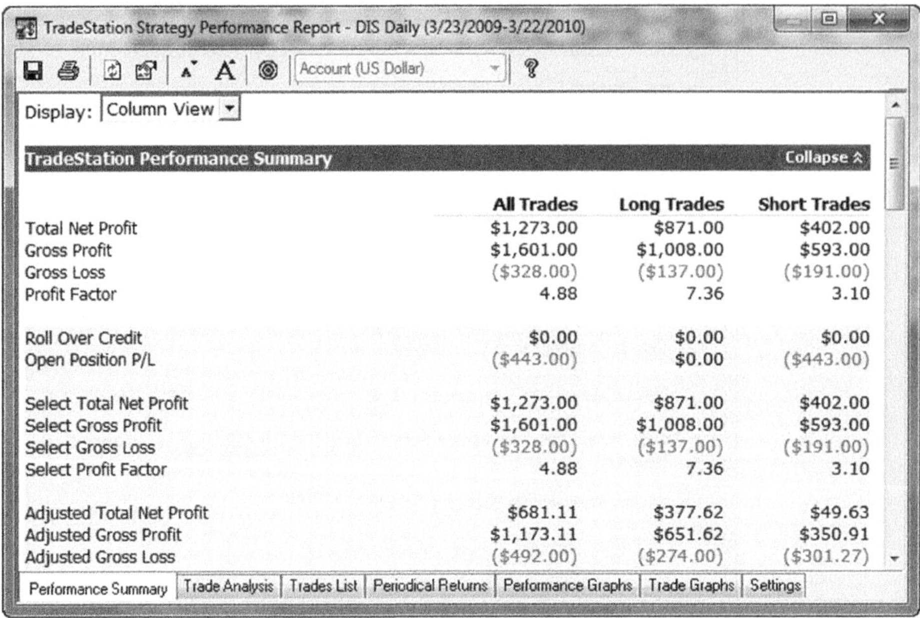

TradeStation Strategy Performance Report - DIS Daily (3/23/2009-3/22/2010)

Account (US Dollar)

Display: Column View

TradeStation Performance Summary — Collapse

	All Trades	Long Trades	Short Trades
Total Net Profit	$1,273.00	$871.00	$402.00
Gross Profit	$1,601.00	$1,008.00	$593.00
Gross Loss	($328.00)	($137.00)	($191.00)
Profit Factor	4.88	7.36	3.10
Roll Over Credit	$0.00	$0.00	$0.00
Open Position P/L	($443.00)	$0.00	($443.00)
Select Total Net Profit	$1,273.00	$871.00	$402.00
Select Gross Profit	$1,601.00	$1,008.00	$593.00
Select Gross Loss	($328.00)	($137.00)	($191.00)
Select Profit Factor	4.88	7.36	3.10
Adjusted Total Net Profit	$681.11	$377.62	$49.63
Adjusted Gross Profit	$1,173.11	$651.62	$350.91
Adjusted Gross Loss	($492.00)	($274.00)	($301.27)

Performance Summary | Trade Analysis | Trades List | Periodical Returns | Performance Graphs | Trade Graphs | Settings

FIGURE 4.83 Strategy Performance Report

TradeStation Strategy Performance Report - DIS Daily (3/23/2009-3/22/2010)

Account (US Dollar)

Display: Column View

TradeStation Performance Summary — Expand

	All Trades	Long Trades	Short Trades
Total Net Profit	$1,273.00	$871.00	$402.00
Gross Profit	$1,601.00	$1,008.00	$593.00
Gross Loss	($328.00)	($137.00)	($191.00)
Profit Factor	4.88	7.36	3.10
Total Number of Trades	18	9	9
Percent Profitable	77.78%	88.89%	66.67%
Winning Trades	14	8	6
Losing Trades	4	1	3
Even Trades	0	0	0
Avg. Trade Net Profit	$70.72	$96.78	$44.67
Avg. Winning Trade	$114.36	$126.00	$98.83
Avg. Losing Trade	($82.00)	($137.00)	($63.67)
Ratio Avg. Win:Avg. Loss	1.39	0.92	1.55
Largest Winning Trade	$395.00	$395.00	$175.00

Performance Summary | Trade Analysis | Trades List | Periodical Returns | Performance Graphs | Trade Graphs | Settings

FIGURE 4.84 Collapsed Strategy Performance Report

My Lab Book

Date Range: 3/23/2009-3/19/2010

Test Nbr	Description	Length	Var 2	Var 3	Var 4	Symbol	Interval	Nbr Trades	Avg Trade Net Profit	Total Net Profit	PF	P	R	CPC>1.2	Avg Time in Trade	Open Trade	Total Net w Open	FileName
1	sjh_MAV1_01 best	7				DIS	Daily											
2	sjh_MAV1	9				DIS	Daily	18	$ 37.39	$ 673.00	2.45	38.89%	3.50	3.33	13d9h	$(401.00)	$ 272.00	
3	sjh_MAV1_01	5:13:1				DIS	Daily	Optimization										Op_20100322_933
4	sjh_MAV_01 best	6				DIS	Daily	18	$ 70.72	$1,273.00	4.88	77.78%	1.39	5.28	13d10h	$(443.00)	$ 830.00	
5																		
6																		
7																		
8																		

FIGURE 4.85 My Lab Book Expanded

Notice in the Lab Book that there are two numbers not on the collapsed report and one number not apparent on either report: **Open Position P/L** and **Avg Time in Trade.** You will find **Avg Time in Trades** by clicking on the tab at the bottom of the **Performance Report** window labeled **Trade Analysis.**

You might decide to add many more columns to your lab book than I have here. It's better to have too many, as you can always delete them, but you don't want to go back and repeat all the tests just to get more statistics.

More about the Performance Report Let's take a look at some of the other statistics on the Performance Summary. Notice that while we have a high percentage of winning trades (Percentage Profitable 77.78% on my summary), we still only make $830 after counting in the Open Trade. Remember that this is a full year for the time frame. That's not a lot of money to make in a year. It is also important to bring your attention to the fact that you have been "trading" 100 shares at a time with this system. The number of shares is printed over the arrows on your chart. You can change this parameter in the **Properties for All** box. So, a high Percentage Profitable does not guarantee immense success. Certainly bigger wins than losses would help, though that isn't the final answer either. And even though my CPC Index was quite high, we still only made a small profit. Forging ahead, we will experiment with other systems in the near future.

We will soon learn the EasyLanguage for closing the last trade, so that it will be included in the Performance Summary statistics rather than being added in the lab book. Further, take a look at the average winning trade and the average losing trade. What about that disparity? Shouldn't your average win be at least twice as large as your average loss? This process is part of the exercise I call "asking what is true."

Let's look again at the chart with the system on it. And this time I will include the PHW dots on the chart so we can see how well we are doing compared to the ideal. Take a look at the chart in Figure 4.86.

Can you now begin to diagnose some changes that would improve your performance? What about the most obvious losers? Aren't we missing the trades that trend? In other words, we are short for the run-up in December 2009 and short for the run-up in February 2010. What caused that?

We will refine and eliminate these problems as we get farther into the book and learn more EasyLanguage. For now, I want you thinking about the questions, not just the answers.

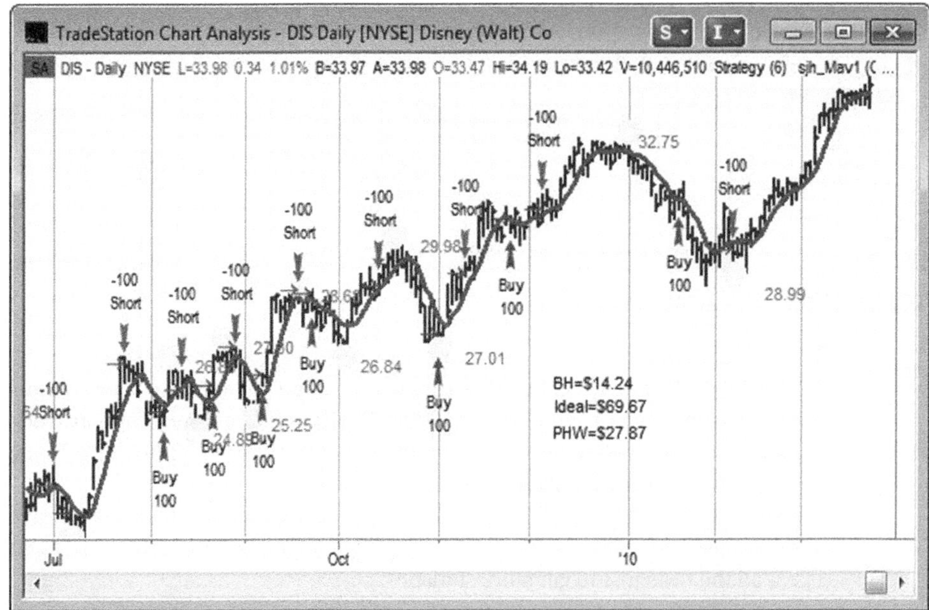

FIGURE 4.86 Strategy on Chart

In the meantime, it is time to go over some essential mathematics. I assume you know the basics, but there are a few twists and turns necessary to our EasyLanguage programming. If you think you already know it, just skip to Chapter 6. If you are not sure, browse through Chapter 5 rather than skipping it. If you are pretty sure you don't know it, study.

CHAPTER 5

Basic Math

In This Chapter

- Introduction
- Adding and Subtracting
- Multiplying and Dividing
- Decimals and Fractions
- Absolute Value
- Percentages
- Ratios and Proportions
- Exponentiation (Powers) and Logarithms
- Linear and Semi-Log Scaling
- Relational Operators
- Averages

INTRODUCTION

I assume you already know how to do basic math. But, do you know how to program it? Do you know how to program it in EasyLanguage? If you already feel comfortable with basic programming, skip this chapter. If not, let's go over a few a basic mathematical concepts as they relate to EasyLanguage.

ADDING AND SUBTRACTING

The mathematical laws governing addition and subtraction are:

Zero Factor

1. For every real number a, a*0 = 0.
2. If ab = 0, then either a = 0 or b = 0.

Laws for Negatives

1. $-(a) = a$
2. $(-a)(-b) = ab$
3. $-ab = (-a)b = a(-b) = -(-a)(-b)$
4. $(-1)a = -a$

Addition

1. $a+b = b+a$
2. $a-a = 0$
3. $(a+b)+c = a+(b+c)$

Subtraction

1. $a - b = a + (-b)$

You can do your adding and subtracting in any order you wish on paper or in your head. You need to do your adding and subtracting after the equal sign in programming. For instance, on the back of an envelope you might write `C + H + L / 3 = Target`. While you can figure this out, in programming and in EasyLanguage, this statement would not be recognized. Programming statements like this are called **assignment statements** and must follow the mold of assignment statements. The variable to which you are assigning a value must be to the left of the equal sign and must be the only thing on that side of the equal sign. The statement must follow the convention and read `Target = C + H + L / 3`.

In short, all arithmetic operations will be putting the results of the stuff on the right of the equal sign into the value on the left of the equal sign. Whether you name the variable yourself in **declaration statements** or use EasyLanguage's **built-in variable names,** you will always be putting the result of your calculation into the variable name. Think of it as an old-fashioned post office box, the pigeonhole kind. When you place new mail into the slot, it pushes all the old mail out the back. The old contents of the box are replaced by the new contents.

Thus, if you have a variable named **counter,** each time you execute the statement "counter=counter+1;" you are adding the value 1 to the existing value of **counter** and getting rid of the old value.

EXAMPLES

```
Target = (C + H + L) / 3;
Value1 = C + C[1] + C[2] + C[3] + C[4]; {sum of past 5 closes}
Value1 = H - L; {range of this bar}
Value1 = Value1 + 1; {add 1 to the previous Value1}
Counter = Counter + 1; {same}
LEntry = Highest(H,5) + 1 tick;
SEntry = Lowest(L,5) - 1 tick;
Value1 = C[0] - C[10]; {10 day momentum}
TrueRange = TrueHigh - TrueLow ;
```

MULTIPLYING AND DIVIDING

Multiplication and division in programming are really no different from adding and subtracting. Keep all your calculations on the right side of the equal sign and you'll be OK.

One word to the wise: Use parentheses to clearly define your intent. We will go over the use of parentheses in Chapter 6. For now, remember that more is better.

In the examples, which would be the average of the three prices, close, high, and low? The answer is `Target = (C + H + L) / 3`. The other expression, `Target = C + H + L / 3`, only divides the low by 3. It would be much better to use parentheses to say `Target=(C+H)+(L/3)` if that were what you meant. The intent would be clear then.

Let's say we are looking for the average of today's closing price and today's opening price in the market. Which expression would correctly give us that average?

```
CLOSE + OPEN / 2
```

or

```
(CLOSE + OPEN) / 2
```

The first expression would not be the average of the two. It would be read as "the sum of the close and half the open."

EXAMPLE

```
Avg = (C + C[1] + C[2] + C[3] + C[4])/5; {5 bar moving average}
```

A common formula that uses addition, subtraction, and division is Welles Wilder's RSI:

```
RSI = 100 – 100/(100+(average upcloses/average downcloses)
```

DECIMALS AND FRACTIONS

The mathematical laws for quotients are:

1. −a/b = −a/b = a/−b = −(−a/−ab)
2. −a/−b = a/b
3. a/b = c/d if and only if ad = bc.
4. a/b = ka/kb for k any nonzero real number.

There are practice problems for these rules later in this section.

Trading can involve huge numbers and tiny numbers—both extremes. For instance, the US T-Bond contract trades in 32nds. The fraction 1/32 translated to decimals is 0.03125. A single bond contract has a value of $1,000. Thus, a one-point move (1/32) on the bond is worth (1/32) * (1,000) = $31.25.

Figure 5.1 shows fraction-to-decimal equivalents in 32nds. While bond and stock prices are quoted in fractions (some in 1/8ths and some in 1/16ths), if you are programming or using a spreadsheet to calculate your profits and losses, you will want to turn these numbers into decimals, so you can relate to them in dollars and cents.

Fraction	Decimal Equivalent	Reduced Fraction
1/32	0.03125	
2/32	0.0625	1/16
3/32	0.09375	
4/32	0.125	1/8
5/32	0.15625	
6/32	0.1875	3/16
7/32	0.21875	
8/32	0.25	1/4
9/32	0.28125	
10/32	0.3125	5/16
11/32	0.34375	
12/32	0.375	3/8
13/32	0.40625	
14/32	0.4375	7/16
15/32	0.46875	
16/32	0.5	1/2
17/32	0.53125	
18/32	0.5625	9/16
19/32	0.59375	
20/32	0.625	5/8
21/32	0.65625	
22/32	0.6875	11/16
23/32	0.71875	
24/32	0.75	3/4
25/32	0.78125	
26/32	0.8125	13/16
27/32	0.84375	
28/32	0.875	7/8
29/32	0.90625	
30/32	0.9375	15/16
31/32	0.96875	
32/32	1	1

FIGURE 5.1 Fractions to Decimals

While working with fractions, whether through multiplication or division, sometimes we end up with a number that has been calculated that is not a perfect fraction. For instance, if we calculated the number 100.3732 through whatever means and needed to convert it to a fraction for trading purposes, what would that fraction be? Hard to tell. In fact, it would take some fancy programming to calculate the nearest fraction. For that reason, TS has just such a function available for us. It is called **Round2Fraction.** This function returns the decimal value rounded to the nearest fraction in the price scale.

EXAMPLE

```
Value1 = Round2Fraction(100.3732);
```

would cause Value1 to contain the decimal number 100.375, which is the decimal equivalent of 100 3/8. The Round2Fraction function is always based on the price scale for the symbol type being evaluated.

Decimals are numbers represented by whole numbers on the left of the decimal and the fractional portion on the right of the decimal. The number 13.4, for instance, is the same as 13 and 4/10ths. Do you remember how to reduce the fractional portion? The idea is that 4 and 10 can both be divided by 2 to make a more compact fraction, 2/5ths. To change this mixed number to a decimal number, we divide 10 by 4 to get the decimal 0.4 and add it to the whole number to get 13.4.

Here's a few practice problems to work on. The answers are found at the end of this chapter.

PRACTICE

1a. 16/20	1b. 4/12	1c. 9/42
2a. 9/54	2b. 14/21	2c. 15/36
3a. 4/8	3b. 8/16	3c. 12/48
4a. 3/33	4b. 4/36	4c. 12/12
5a. 10/42	5b. 14/48	5c. 9/18

ABSOLUTE VALUE

Sometimes we need to know the size of a number without its sign. We don't care about whether it is negative or positive, we just want the number part. That is called **absolute value.**

It is designated in mathematics by placing vertical lines, called pipes by programmers, on either side of the number. If we wanted to specify the absolute value of the number −7.5, it would be written |−7.5|. TradeStation doesn't have pipes in its Reserved Words list, so there is a function called **AbsValue** that returns the positive value of any number put in its argument.

EXAMPLES

```
AbsValue(-27.82) returns a value of 27.82
AbsValue(134.9) returns a value of 134.9
```

It always returns a positive value, regardless of the sign of the input. If we wanted to assign the absolute value of a number to the value Value1, in EasyLanguage we would write:

```
Value1 = AbsValue(number);
```

PERCENTAGES

If you are interested in futures trading or if you have a large equity account and want to trade it on margin, you'll want to know about percentages.

If your equity account is backed by another account or by a cash instrument, your broker may let you use that cash value to leverage your equity account. You should be able to figure percentages if you use margin for your equity account.

"Cent" in French (I don't know Latin) means 100. "Percentage," then, means "per 100." Anything divided by 100 is a percentage. For example, 50% is 50/100ths of the whole.

If the stock price goes up to $25 (and we'll ignore commission for this exercise), what percentage profit have you made on your investment? We figure this on the cash outlay, not on the total account value. Thus, you would have made a $5 profit per share on 1,000 shares with a $10,000 investment.

That's (5 * 1,000)/10,000 = 5,000/10,000 = 5/10 = 1/2 or 50%. Wow!

Let's say that you determine that the annual chart of a stock (or futures contract, or mutual fund, or any other trading instrument) could yield 100 points of movement in a year's time trading from both the short and the long sides. Assuming that each point is worth $1 and that you are trading 100 shares of the instrument, what is the value of 40% of the total movement for the year?

Well, the full movement would yield ($1 * 100) * 100 = $10,000. So, 40% of that would be $10,000 * 0.40 =$4,000.

Percentages can also be expressed as fractions. For example, 40% is equivalent to 40/100. You may use whichever form appeals to you more. If you are at all uncomfortable with decimals, percentages, and fractions, you would do well to study a Schaums Outline on basic mathematics and carry around a small calculator in the meantime.

TS provides an EZL function to calculate the percent change in price of the current bar over the price length bars ago. It is called **PercentChange** and has this syntax:

```
PercentChange(Price, Length)
```

PercentChange returns a numeric value containing the percent change in price of the current bar over the price length bars ago. The input **Price** specifies which bar value (price, function, or formula) to be considered. **Length** sets the number of bars to be considered.

EXAMPLE

```
PercentChange(Close, 14)
```

If the result of the example just above returns a value of 0.35, there was a 35% increase in the closing price of the current bar compared to the closing price of 14 bars ago.

PercentChange takes the difference in between the current value of **Price** and the Price specified by **Length** bars ago and then divides the result by the **Price** of **Length** bars ago.

EXAMPLE

```
PercentChange(High, 25);
```

returns a value of −0.15, indicating that there was a 15% decrease in the High price of the current bar compared to the High price of 25 bars ago.

EXAMPLE

You could use the **PercentChange** function to alert you when the closing price has increased 10% from the closing price of 10 bars ago by using the following syntax:

```
Value1 = PercentChange(Close, 10);
Plot1(Value1, "PctChange");
If Value1 >= .10 Then Alert;
```

To work with some more percentages, let's take a look at a **Performance Summary** output from TradeStation, in Figure 5.2. In the second column of the figure, you'll see "Percent profitable 77.78%". The way this number is calculated is:

```
Percent Profitable Trades = (Number of winning trades)/
(Total # of trades)
```

So, in this case:

```
Percent Profitable Trades = 14/4 = 77.78%.
```

RATIOS AND PROPORTIONS

Formally, a ratio is the comparison by division of two quantities expressed in the same units. That just means that first of all, you can't compare apples and oranges. Second, it means that you divide one number by the other to get a ratio. Why bother, when you could just have easily stayed with percentages? Sometimes ratios present the information to you more visually. For instance, if you have a system where the ratio of wins to losses is 4, you know right away that on average each win will be four times as large as each loss. Sure, you could have said you had a system where each win was 400% of each loss, but it just doesn't ring as intuitively.

Symbolically we represent this concept as 4:1, which is equivalent to 4/1. You'll often see a ratio written as a fraction, even though that is not precise.

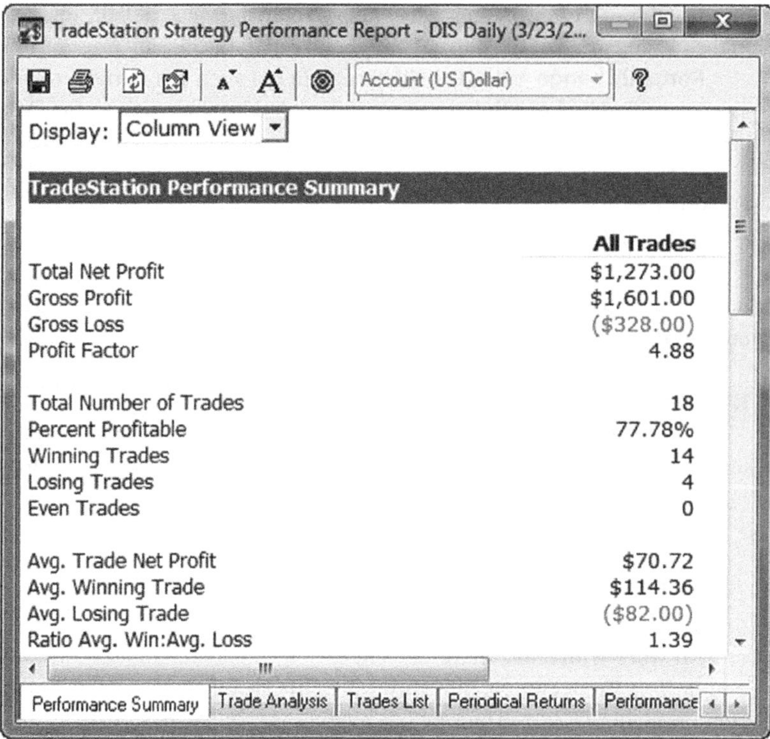

FIGURE 5.2 Strategy Performance Report

Let's take another look at a **Performance Summary** output from TradeStation in Figure 5.3. It is the same window, only this time I have exposed more of it.

What is the ratio of the average number of bars in winning trades to the average number of bars in losing trades? There are 8.79 bars in the average winning trade and 15.75 bars in the average losing trade. Thus, the ratio is 8.79:15.75 = .5581, or 56%, or approximately 1:2. That's scary. We like to hang on to winning trades and get out of losers quickly, and this system is doing just the opposite. There is no such ratio on the **Performance Summary,** so you need to be able to do that for yourself.

As a reminder, when you divide 8.79 by 15.75, your calculator will display 0.5581; how did I get a percentage out of that? A percentage is a number expressed as a fractional value, where the denominator (the bottom number) is always 100. So, 0.5581 is the same as 55.81/100. Mathematicians agree to the assumption of the number always being divided by 100, so we express it as 55.81%, or rounded off to 56%.

Here's an EasyLanguage function for you that uses ratios. It's called **Extreme Price Ratio.** If you'll plot it on a chart you will see that extremes are usually found at turning points in price activity. The code in the example assigns the output of the function to **Value1** and then plots the simple ratio of extreme prices for the trailing 10 bars. It measures the

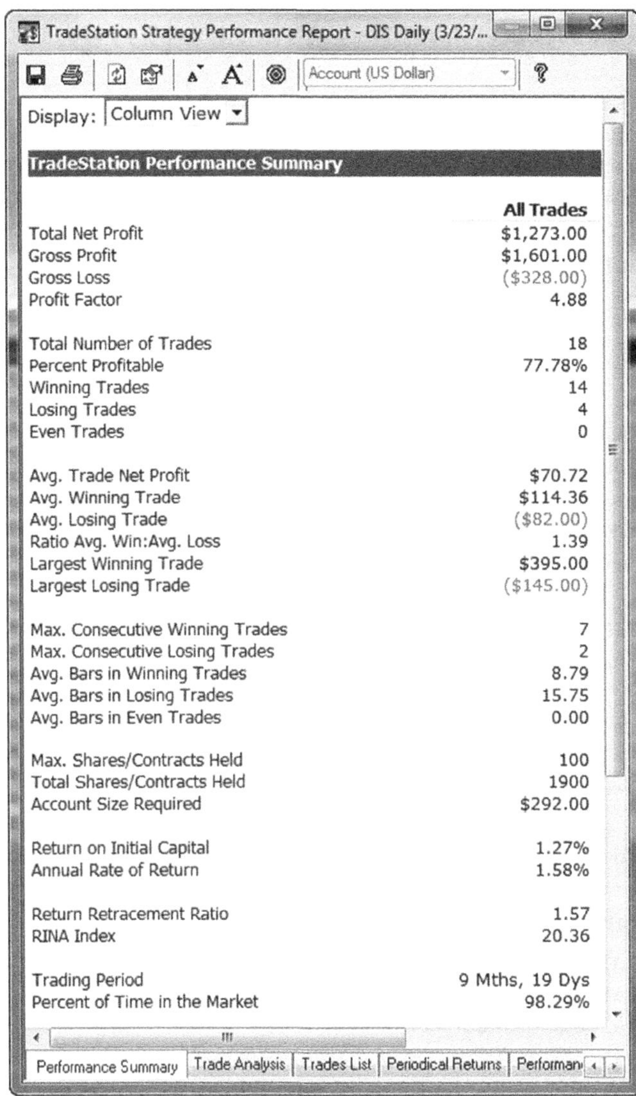

TradeStation Strategy Performance Report - DIS Daily (3/23/...

Display: Column View

TradeStation Performance Summary

	All Trades
Total Net Profit	$1,273.00
Gross Profit	$1,601.00
Gross Loss	($328.00)
Profit Factor	4.88
Total Number of Trades	18
Percent Profitable	77.78%
Winning Trades	14
Losing Trades	4
Even Trades	0
Avg. Trade Net Profit	$70.72
Avg. Winning Trade	$114.36
Avg. Losing Trade	($82.00)
Ratio Avg. Win:Avg. Loss	1.39
Largest Winning Trade	$395.00
Largest Losing Trade	($145.00)
Max. Consecutive Winning Trades	7
Max. Consecutive Losing Trades	2
Avg. Bars in Winning Trades	8.79
Avg. Bars in Losing Trades	15.75
Avg. Bars in Even Trades	0.00
Max. Shares/Contracts Held	100
Total Shares/Contracts Held	1900
Account Size Required	$292.00
Return on Initial Capital	1.27%
Annual Rate of Return	1.58%
Return Retracement Ratio	1.57
RINA Index	20.36
Trading Period	9 Mths, 19 Dys
Percent of Time in the Market	98.29%

Performance Summary | Trade Analysis | Trades List | Periodical Returns | Performan...

FIGURE 5.3 Extended Strategy Performance Report

ratio of the extreme prices for a specified number of bars. The extreme prices used are the Highest High and Lowest Low over that many bars.

EXAMPLE

```
Value1 = ExtremePriceRatio(10, FALSE);
Plot1(Value1, ``EPR'');
```

EXPONENTIATION (POWERS) AND LOGARITHMS

You are already familiar with exponents. You know what a square is, right? The square of something is that thing multiplied by itself; it is that thing raised to the power 2. The 2 is the exponent. In math we write the exponent smaller, above and to the right of the number we are raising to a power.

EXAMPLES

$2^2 = 4 \quad (2 \times 2)$

$3^2 = 9 \quad (3 \times 3)$

$4^2 = 16 \quad (4 \times 4)$

In programming we cannot write this little number above another. We use a simplified notation to express the power. In spreadsheets like Excel, whenever you see a caret (^), that means we are specifying an exponent. Some other programming languages use two asterisks to mean exponentiation (**). EasyLanguage has two built-in functions to achieve exponentiation: **Square** and **Power.**

EXAMPLES

This is how we would write the examples just shown in programming notation:

```
2^2 = 4
3^2 = 9
4^2 = 16
```

To square a number in EasyLanguage, you use a built-in function called **Square.**

EXAMPLES

```
Value1 = Square(2); {Value1 = 2**2 = 4}
Value1 = Square(3); {Value1 = 3**2 = 9}
Value1 = Square(4); {Value1= 4**2 = 16}
```

To raise numbers to values other than 2, you use the **Power** function. For instance, the number 2 raised to the power 3 ("2 cubed") is written:

2^3 in math

```
2^3            in programming
Power(2,3)     in EasyLanguage
```

A logarithm is the inverse of an exponent. For instance, the log of 4 base 2 is 2. That is, the power to which 2 must be raised to get 4 is 2. The easiest way to think of it is to ask the question "How many of one number do we multiply to get another number?" For instance, how many 2s need to be multiplied to get 8? The answer is 3. We need to multiply 3 of the 2s to get 8. So the logarithm is 3.

I know that can be pretty confusing if you are not a mathematician, physicist, or engineer, but you don't really need to understand the theory to be able to do it in EasyLanguage. First you need to know that EasyLanguage assumes the base is e (the natural logarithm, not base 10, the number base we are all accustomed to). And second, you might pick up a copy of *Practical Algebra: A Self-Teaching Guide* by Peter Selby in the bookstore to brush up on some algebra. Note also that a log can be calculated only for positive numbers, so keep your inputs to this function positive, that is, greater than zero. To access the log base 10, that we are all accustomed to, you must use the Reserved Word LogXY and specify the input X to be 10.

EXAMPLES

- The $\log_{10}(4) = 0.602$. Working backward, $10^{0.602} = 4$.
- The $\log_{10}(16) = 1.204$. Working backward, $10^{1.204} = 16$.
- The $\log_{10}(100) = 2$. Working backward, $10^2 = 100$.

LINEAR AND SEMI-LOG SCALING

Linear scaling produces a scale with equally spaced segments on the y-axis, similar to those on a thermometer. A move from 30 to 40 is given the same amount of space on the scale as a move from 100 to 110. You can tell at a glance whether the chart is linearly scaled by determining whether the tick marks on the y-axis are equally spaced.

Figure 5.4 shows the Dow Jones 30 Industrial Average ($INDU) on a linear scale. Note that the tick marks (and scale numbers) on the y-axis are equally spaced. There is the same

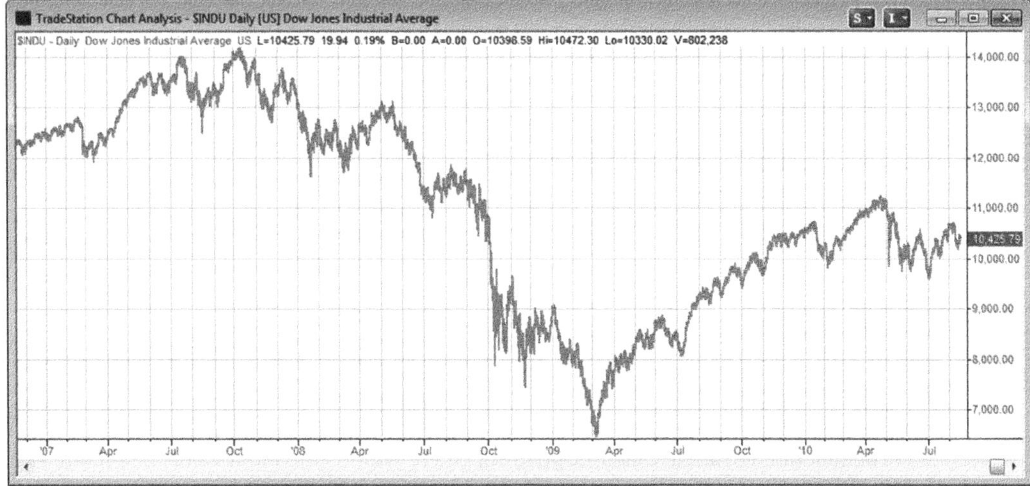

FIGURE 5.4 Linear Scaling on the DJI 30

amount of space between 7000 and 8000 on the bottom of the scale as there is between 10000 and 11000 at the top of the scale.

To produce this chart, I used the entire data range of 25000 bars back, squeezed the bars together to reduce bar spacing, and chose the radio button "**entire data series**" for scale type.

True logarithmic scaling is not often used in the stock market, because it scales both the x and y axes logarithmically. We don't want the x-axis, which is usually the date axis, to be shown logarithmically. Therefore, when we use log scaling, we isolate it to the y-axis only. That is called **semi-log** scaling. Semi-log scaling produces a scale that is weighted toward the percent of change in a chart. For example, a move from 30 to 40, which is a 33% increase, is given more space on the scale than a move from 100 to 110, which is a 10% increase, even though both arithmetic differences were just 10 points.

The same data displayed in semi-log fashion looks like the one in Figure 5.5. Notice that the chart data is all squeezed up near the top now, leaving large amounts of white space at the bottom of the chart.

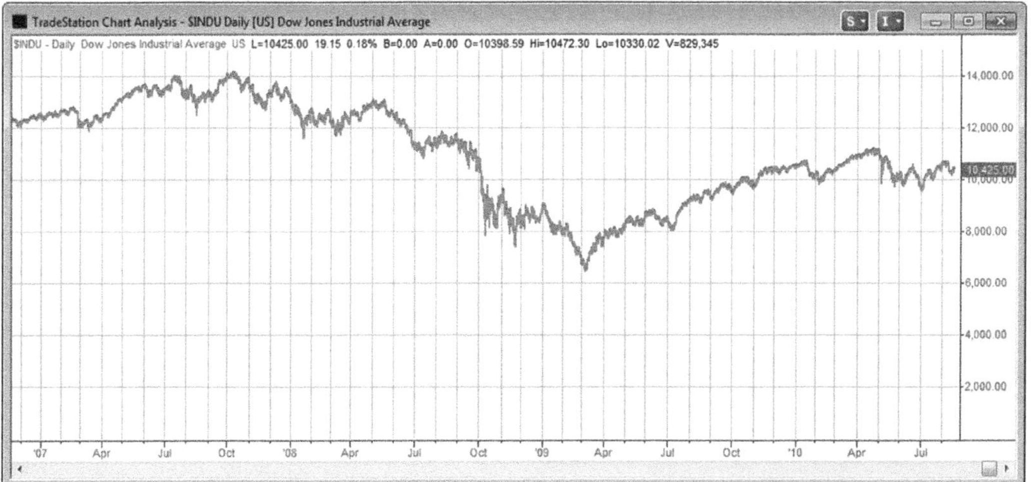

FIGURE 5.5 Semi-log Scaling on the DJI 30

What happened? Each successive move of 1,000 points gets less significance on the y-axis scale. This view gives you the opportunity to compare moves apple to apple. On this type scale, how does the crash of 1929 compare to the crash of 1987? We addressed that in an earlier chapter.

Of course, EasyLanguage has a function to take logarithms for you. You don't have to understand more than the fact that the scaling changes over time as price increases significantly.

The function in EZL is called **Log(Num),** where **Num** is the input value, a numeric expression to be used in the calculation. This function uses a base **e** system, not base 10. Remember that logs can be calculated only for positive numbers. This would be a good place to use the **AbsValue** function.

EXAMPLES

```
Log(4.5) returns a value of 1.5041
Log(172) returns a value of 5.1475
```

RELATIONAL OPERATORS

Relational operators establish the comparative value of two sides of an operation.

With the operator =, both sides of the equation are balanced. They are equal.

The other operators listed in Figure 5.6 are for comparing **inequalities.** With inequalities, both sides of the operation are **not equal.**

Operator	Meaning
=	Equal to
<>	Not equal to
<	Less than
<=	Less than or equal to
>	Greater than
>=	Greater than or equal to

FIGURE 5.6 Mathematical Operators

In math class they would have you draw graphs of inequalities, showing the universe of numbers that would satisfy the statement. We don't really care about that. What we want to know is whether one side is bigger than the other side or whether they are equal.

In programming we really only care whether the statement is **true** or **false.** We want EasyLanguage to gather the prices we are examining and let us know how they compare to previous prices or other calculated values. For instance, we might want to know whether the close of today is higher or lower than the close of yesterday.

TradeStation evaluates your expression and returns a true or false value.

These concepts will be easier to grasp with some concrete evidence. Let's work again with the data for DIS (available on my website). The first five bars of our data are presented in Figure 5.7.

Date	Open	High	Low	Close	Volume
09/30/88	16.219	16.344	15.781	16.219	4996400
10/07/88	16.219	16.375	15.844	16.375	6146000
10/14/88	16.375	16.688	16.250	16.531	6458000
10/21/88	16.531	16.875	16.281	16.844	6218800
10/28/88	16.844	17.094	16.563	16.563	4540000

FIGURE 5.7 First Five Bars of DIS

Keep in mind that the current bar (the most recent bar) for this exercise is the last bar, or the bar for the date 10/28/88. Figure 5.8 shows a few expressions for you to evaluate with the data in Figure 5.7. See if you come up with the same answers that TradeStation and I do.

Expression	Value
H = H[1]	False
H > H[1]	True
H >= H[1]	True
Close > Open	False
H < H[2]	False
H > H[2]	True
V < 0.9*V[1]	True

FIGURE 5.8 Evaluating Expressions

The way you will see these expressions used is generally in **IF. . .THEN** statements. An IF. . .THEN statement is to be read as

```
IF (something is true) THEN (consequence)
```

The consequence is usually an action like BUY or SELL but can just as easily be the beginning of another IF. . . THEN statement. The "something is true" part is the **condition** you are examining, which can be as simple or as complex as you wish.

EXAMPLES

```
IF High = High[1] THEN BUY;
IF High > High[1] THEN Condition1=True;
IF Close > Open THEN UpBar=True;
IF Close < Open THEN Value2=Close;
```

EasyLanguage provides another pair of operators that are useful for comparing prices, such as moving averages that cross each other. Personally I am not fond of these comparison words, but you should be aware of their existence. Right after I explain how these operators are used, I will tell you why I don't use them.

At first glance at Figure 5.9, it would seem that **Crosses Over** is equivalent to **Greater Than;** wrong. Crosses Over is more powerful than Greater Than. Crosses Over includes the condition that it just happened from the last bar to this bar. Crosses Over is a very stringent condition and is true only at the **exact crossing point.**

If you are only looking for the exact crossover point of an indicator, then Crosses Over (and Crosses Under) are the comparisons to use. You could use these comparisons with

Operator	Meaning	Value
Crosses Over or Crosses Above	X crosses over Y	True when X is greater than Y on the current bar after being less than or equal to Y on the previous bar.

Operator	Meaning	Value
Crosses Under or Crosses Below	X crosses under Y	True when X is less than Y on the current bar after being greater than or equal to Y on the previous bar.

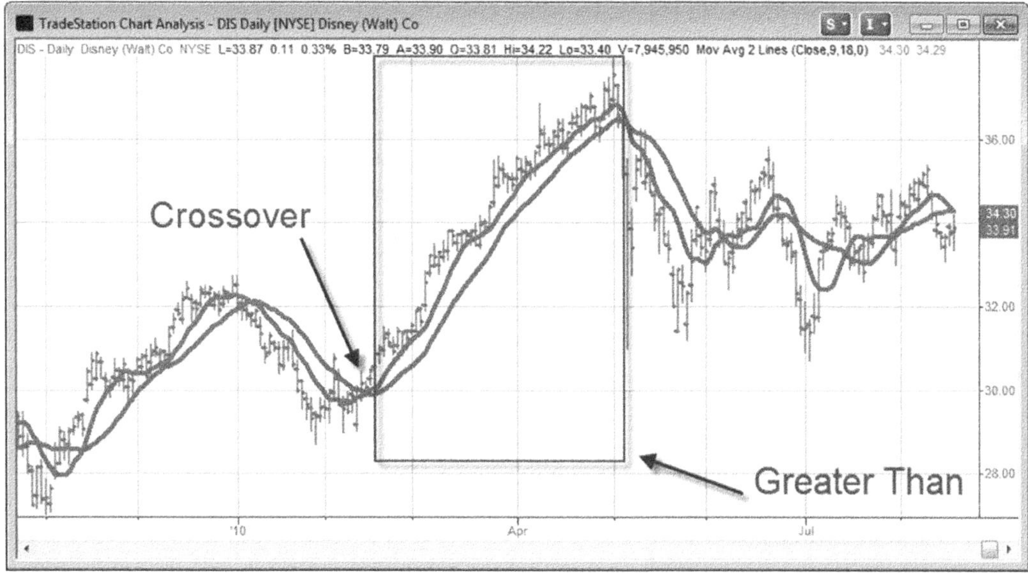

FIGURE 5.9 Crossover vs. Greater Than

moving averages or MACD, for instance. However, if you were to add a condition, like requiring the ADX to signify trending, or requiring that the day be Friday, or that the time be later than noon, then both would have to occur on exactly the same bar for your Crosses Over or Crosses Under condition to be true.

Often I am looking for something like the MACD to signal a setup for a trade and the ADX to confirm it. In that case, the ADX might turn (increase in value) several bars after the MACD crossed. The crosses over and under comparisons, combined with the ADX rising, would then be false. The condition I was looking for would have happened and yet my code would not have detected it, because it did not happen at exactly the same moment in time. Nevertheless, the computer would have done exactly what I asked it to.

EXAMPLE

```
INPUTS: j_Length(9);
IF H Crosses Over Average(C,j_Length) THEN BUY next bar at market;
IF L Crosses Under Average(C,j_Length) THEN SELL SHORT next bar at
market;
```

Recognize the code in the last example? It's the code we generated in Chapter 3. Back then you didn't understand what it meant, but now you do. What would happen to the code if you changed Crosses Over to Greater Than? Try it and see. It is an important exercise, and you will need to know the answer in later chapters. (This exercise is left to the reader.)

This next example is straight from the EasyLanguage library. This is the code for the long entry portion of the MACD strategy:

EXAMPLE

```
inputs: FastLength(12), SlowLength(26), MACDLength(9) ;
variables: MyMACD(0), MACDAvg(0), MACDDiff(0) ;
MyMACD = MACD(Close, FastLength, SlowLength) ;
MACDAvg = XAverage(MyMACD, MACDLength) ;
MACDDiff = MyMACD - MACDAvg ;
if CurrentBar > 2 and MACDDiff crosses over 0 then
      Buy ("MacdLE") next bar at market ;
```

AVERAGES

The average, or the mean, of a set of values is calculated by adding together all the values and then dividing by the number of values in your set. For instance, given the values in Figure 5.10, the sum is 82.532 and there are five values. Thus, the average would be calculated as: 82.532/5 = 16.506.

	Close
	16.219
	16.375
	16.531
	16.844
	16.563
Sum	82.532
Average	16.506

FIGURE 5.10 Averaging Data

In mathematical notation this would look like:

$$\frac{1}{5}\sum_{i=1}^{5} Close_i$$

An average of "n" numbers, as in an n-period moving average for instance, would be the sum of all n numbers divided by n.

$$\frac{1}{n}\sum\nolimits_{i=1}^{n} Close_i$$

When we discuss EasyLanguage's treatment of moving averages, in Chapter 12, you may want to refer back to this section.

Moving averages are perhaps the most well-known technical indicators and certainly one of the easier to calculate. With each new data point the moving average is calculated anew using the most recent "n" numbers (five in Figure 5.10), and the new value is plotted on the chart. The average smooths out the curve, with the curve more closely approximating the data with small n and becoming a loose approximation as n gets larger. Figure 5.11 shows a 5-period moving average of closing prices, while Figure 5.12 shows a 20-period moving average of closing prices.

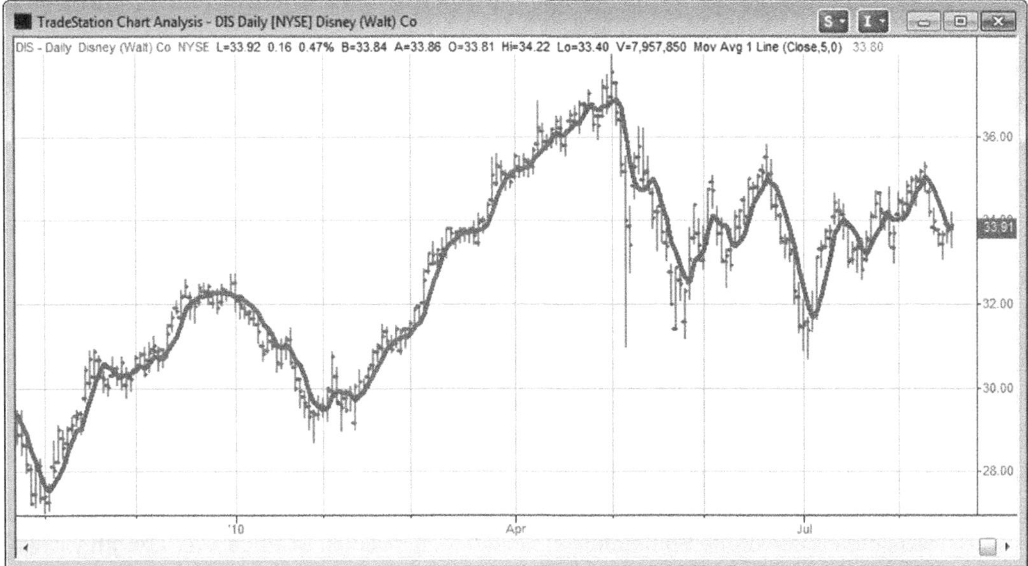

FIGURE 5.11 5-Bar Moving Average

EXAMPLE

```
inputs: Length( numericsimple ) ;
AvgTrueRange = Average( TrueRange, Length ) ;
```

The code in this example is from the EasyLanguage function **AvgTrueRange.** You can see how EZL assigns the function its value as the last line in the code. On the right side

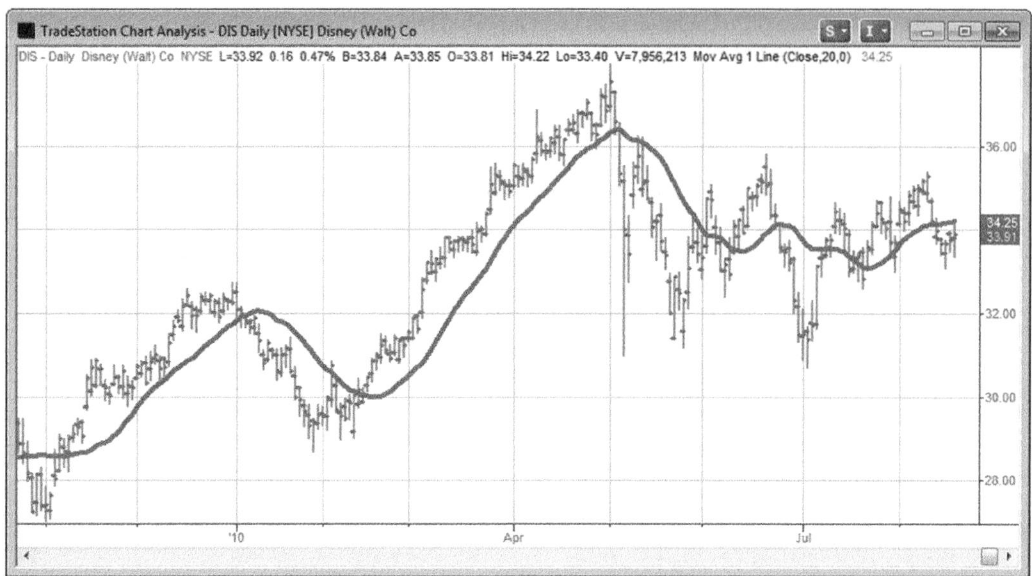

FIGURE 5.12 20-Bar Moving Average

of the equal sign you'll see the **Average** function at work, averaging the value TrueRange over Length number of bars. Let's look further into this and visit the code for the **Average** function.

EXAMPLE

```
inputs: Price( numericseries ), Length( numericsimple ) ;
Average = Summation( Price, Length ) / Length ;
```

In this example we are getting closer and closer to the investigation. **Average** is assigned the value of the **Summation** function's manipulation of **Price** over **Length** values, then divided by **Length.** Let's go one more step and see what the **Summation** function says.

EXAMPLE

```
Sum = 0;
for Value1 = 0 to Length - 1
      begin
             Sum = Sum + Price[Value1] ;
      end;
 Summation = Sum ;
```

At last we get to the meat of the issue. The **Summation** function shows us where the addition over "n" number of values takes place. It is here that the addition part of the averaging takes place. This function reads "for n number of times add Price onto Sum."

ANSWERS

1a. 4/5	1b. 1/3	1c. 3/14
2a. 1/6	2b. 2/3	2c. 5/12
3a. 1/2	3b. 1/2	3c. 1/4
4a. 1/11	4b. 1/9	4c. 1/1
5a. 5/21	5b. 7/24	5c. 1/2

CHAPTER 6

Basic EasyLanguage

In This Chapter

- Introduction
- Skeletons (Templates)
- Writing Your Own
- Charting Your Indicator
- Summary

INTRODUCTION

What Is EasyLanguage?

EasyLanguage is a trademark of TradeStation; it is a software product name. The EasyLanguage product can be thought of as a specialized word processor, or editor, that allows you to draw (plot) indicators and to specify and test trading strategies.

Like any software program, EasyLanguage has a set of conventions or rules you must follow to get the program to work. The rules are called the program's **syntax.** The same is true of the language you speak, whether it is English, Spanish, or Hungarian. To be understood, you must use sentence syntax that the person to whom you are speaking understands.

TradeStation has done a remarkable job of both making the rules easy to understand and learn, in addition to providing the power and complexity that an advanced programmer might need. Also, like any software program, there are commands you must memorize before you can operate the software.

EasyLanguage is comprised of simple words, operators, and punctuation that allow you to specify your trading rules or instructions.

After you type your EasyLanguage code into the editor, EasyLanguage will verify that your syntax is correct, according to its internal rules. Getting the editor to perform this task is called "**verifying**" your code. When you verify your code, EasyLanguage checks for spelling and grammar errors. (Programmers call this "compiling" your code.)

Before you can apply a trading strategy or place an indicator on a chart, your code must be verified. Verifying the code does not guarantee that your system will make money, or even do what you want it to do; it only checks the code for spelling and grammatical errors. And, of course, that's all it can and should do. When we begin to verify EasyLanguage code, you will become accustomed to the command sequence **File → Verify** or to using the F3 key to make EasyLanguage perform the verification.

EasyLanguage Basics

As in any language, we have stop signals, connectors, modifiers, and words with special meanings. This is true in EasyLanguage as well. You must learn the meanings of EasyLanguage's special signals, connectors, and modifiers before a "sentence" will make any sense to you.

EXAMPLE

```
IF Close of Today > Close[1] THEN Buy; {Buy upward move}
```

Do you understand that sentence without any interpretation? Let's take apart the EasyLanguage sentence:

- Capitalization is for your edification only and doesn't matter to EasyLanguage.
- Spaces are important in that they break up words, but extra spaces won't bother EasyLanguage
- "{" and "}" bracket comment words that EasyLanguage ignores. These comments make it easier for you to remember your code and thoughts about it later on. They also make it easier for someone else to understand your code.
- The semicolon ";" ends the sentence. Every sentence must have an ending.
- "[" and "]" are the way EasyLanguage refers to an event that happened before now. [0] means the current bar, [1] means "one bar ago," [5] means "five bars ago."
- The symbol ">," as in math, means "greater than." (Refer back to Chapter 5, or take my correspondence course if you need further help.) Greater than or equal is specified using the symbols >= together.
- "Close" is the EasyLanguage Reserved Word that refers to the closing price of the bar under investigation. "Close" can be abbreviated as "C" for EasyLanguage if you wish.
- "of Today" is another way to say just "Close" or "C" or "C[0]", all referring to the closing price of the current bar under investigation.
- The IF. . .THEN construct we referred to in the previous chapter is present in this example. Notice that "Close of Today > Close[1]" is the "something is true" part, also called the condition. After the word "THEN" comes the consequence, which in this case is "Buy".
- Buy what? And at what price? Those items are inferred by the software unless you specify otherwise, which we learn to do in the next chapter. In the default interpretation, it means Buy one share/contract of the symbol on the chart.

Type the sentence from the example into your EasyLanguage PowerEditor. To do that, you might need to refer back to Chapter 4, Basic Use of TradeStation to get started. If you already are familiar with opening, closing, and locating the various TradeStation modules, jump ahead. Otherwise:

- Start TradeStation.
- Start the EasyLanguage PowerEditor by clicking the EasyLanguage icon.
- Select **New EasyLanguage Document.**
- Select **Strategy.**
- Give your indicator a name (something like sjh_Test) and click on **OK,** as shown in Figure 6.1.

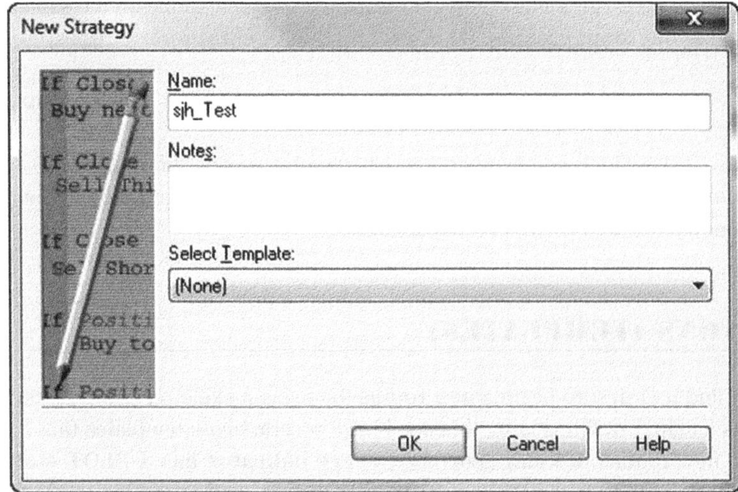

FIGURE 6.1 Naming Your New Strategy

Now you will have a blank page to work with in the PowerEditor. Start typing away, typing just the code from the sample on the previous page. The cursor should be blinking at you in the upper left corner of the blank page. This is where you start typing.

When you have finished typing the code, exactly as I had it in the example on the previous page, press the F3 key or use the menu sequence **File → Verify** to see if EasyLanguage understood your code. If so, it will respond **Verification successful.** If not, it will help you find the error.

In this example, I led you straight into an error. I did so to illustrate a point, of course. In older versions of TradeStation the code you entered was sufficient. But the current version of TS requires you to say more than just "Buy" to be clear about what you mean. Every Buy or Sell command has to be followed by "This Bar" or "Next Bar on Open." Why? Beats me! EasyLanguage will tell you what it wants you to enter after the Buy or Sell command, so why doesn't it just assume it and put it there itself? I truly don't know.

As we get into the next chapters, you will learn more EasyLanguage coding, but at this point, you have already programmed the essentials of a strategy. Whether it works (read: "makes money") is an enormous field of endeavor that is addressed in my seminars or in private consulting, but is not the subject of this book.

One other piece of information you just learned by copying this example: how to make comments. A comment in your code is a section that is ignored by EZL[1] It is just there for your edification, either for readers or to help you remember what you meant to do when you come back to this code a year later.

Comments can take two forms, either inline or block. If you make a block comment, you do so by placing your text in between curly braces. You start with { and end with }. Block comments can be a word, a sentence, or paragraphs in length. The comment in 6.1 is: {`Buy upward move`}. The other way to make a comment is to put two slashes and then your text. This is called an inline comment because it is usually done on the same line as your code. It takes this form:

```
IF Close of Today > Close[1] THEN Buy; // Buy upward move
```

I use block comments when I have a lot to say about a section of code; I use inline comments to document a single line of code. Whichever you use, be generous with your comments. You will appreciate it later.

SKELETONS (TEMPLATES)

I find it easiest to begin a new routine by using a skeleton or template. Then programming is a matter of filling in the blanks. I have several blank templates that I use when beginning a new routine. If I may generalize, **every indicator has a PLOT statement, every system/strategy has a BUY or SELL statement, and every function ends by assigning a value to the function.**

Within these routines, you may or may not have variables that use names you need to declare; you may or may not have conditions that use names you need to declare; and you may or may not have input values to the routine. In my templates, I leave space for these items, designated by "xx" in the code. To me, this just means there is a blank space here that needs to be filled. Using the **Find** function of the text editor allows me to search for "xx" anytime I want to.

INDICATOR TEMPLATE

```
{INDICATOR NAME AND PURPOSE: xxx}
INPUTS: xx;
VARIABLES: xx;
Condition1 = xx;
IF Condition1 THEN BEGIN
```

[1]I use EZL and EasyLanguage interchangably. By both I mean the TradeStation EasyLanguage editor.

```
        Value1 = xx;
        xx;
END;
Plot1(Value1,"Value1");
```

STRATEGY TEMPLATE

```
{STRATEGY NAME AND PURPOSE: xxx}
INPUTS: xx;
VARIABLES: xx;
Condition1 = xx;
Condition2 = xx;
IF Condition1 THEN BEGIN
        BUY xx THIS BAR;
IF Condition2 THEN BEGIN
        SELL xx THIS BAR;
END;
```

FUNCTION TEMPLATE

```
{FUNCTION NAME AND PURPOSE: xxx}
INPUTS: xx;
VARIABLES: xx;
Condition1 = xx;
Value1 = xx;
IF Condition1 THEN BEGIN
        xx;
        xx;
END;
xxx=Value1;
```

At this point, you do not yet know what inputs, variables, and conditions are. In the next chapter we will be getting into the details of the mechanics and rules of writing EasyLanguage. For now, just trust that templates are enormously helpful.

In fact, it might be a good idea to create and save these templates now. You may copy and paste them each from my Web site (www.moneymentor.com/TSME.html) or you may type them in exactly as shown. Whichever way you choose, you must first open the EasyLanguage PowerEditor. If you haven't yet mastered how to open the EasyLanguage PowerEditor, flip back to Chapter 2, Step 3, and follow those steps. Then come back here.

As you open the PowerEditor, you must select which type of routine you wish to write. The three we are concerned about in this book are indicators, functions, and strategies. (Strategies used to be called Signals, where a System was a collection of Signals; forgive me in advance if I slip and use one of these other words.) To create your first indicator template, click on the menu choice "Indicator", as shown in Figure 6.2. Next, a pop-up box will ask you to name your indicator. Pick something easy and at the same time meaningful. Mine is named `sjh_Ind_Templ` as an abbreviation for "indicator template," and of course, I put my initials at the front of the name.

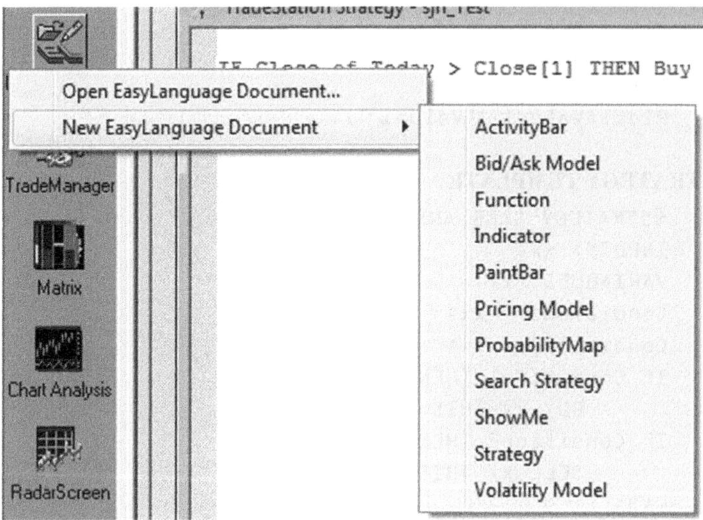

FIGURE 6.2 New Indicator

This is exactly as we did for the example on page 158 and Figure 6.1, only this time you are writing an indicator, not a signal. Go ahead; put all three types of templates in there.

WRITING YOUR OWN

The way programmers learn to code is:

- By apprenticeship
- By trial and error
- By taking classes
- By copying and modifying code that already works

The last method is probably the most commonly used technique. That's what we are going to do—copy success. To this end, we will open and modify one of the EZL indicators included with TradeStation.

Open the Moving Average Indicator

If you haven't already, click on the EasyLanguage icon and this time choose Open Easy-Language Document. With this selection a pop-up will appear listing the myriad of routines available in the EZL library. The button at the top of the box can be changed back and forth between all the routine types: ActivityBar, Bid/Ask Model, **Function, Indicator,** PaintBar, Pricing Model, ProbabilityMap, Search Strategy, ShowMe, **Strategy,** and Volatility Model. Again, we are only concerned with three: Function, Indicator, and Strategy. For this exercise, choose Indicator and let's look at what's available. See Figure 6.3 for a snippet of available indicators.

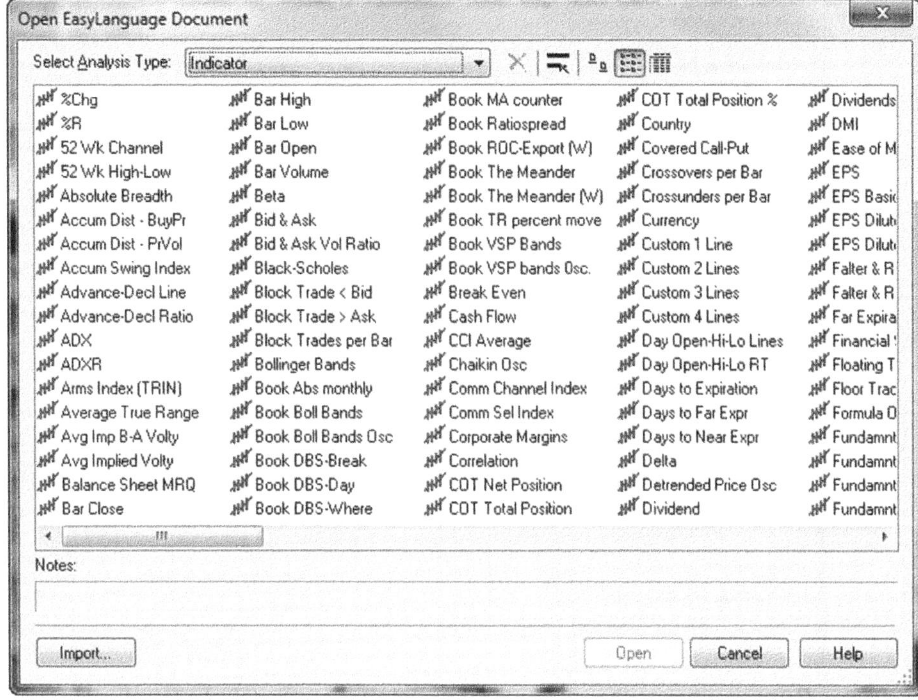

FIGURE 6.3 First Pane of Available Indicators

Now confronted with a long list of options, both from the drop-down menu items and the associated list for each of those choices:

- Choose Indicator from the drop-down menu box at the top left of the box, as in Figure 6.3.
- Scroll down to **Mov Avg 1 line** and click on it (Figure 6.4).
- Click the **Open** button near the bottom of the frame, and EasyLanguage will open a page with approximately 18 lines of code, as in Figure 6.5.

WOW! Lots of confusing code. I can hear you hoping that you are not expected to understand this, and some of you swearing that you will never be able to understand it.

Before you do anything else, save this code with a different name. If you forget and just save it, you will overwrite TS's code, whether you make any mistakes or not. Since we're just beginning, let's not overwrite TS's code; let's call this indicator `sjh_MAV1`, for simplicity. To accomplish this task, you will use the **File** → **Save As** menu sequence.

Not to worry, we are going to get rid of most of the code and simplify. TradeStation put most of this code in here to allow for an option (Displace) that we are not even going to use in this book. For our current purposes, novice programming, we don't need it.

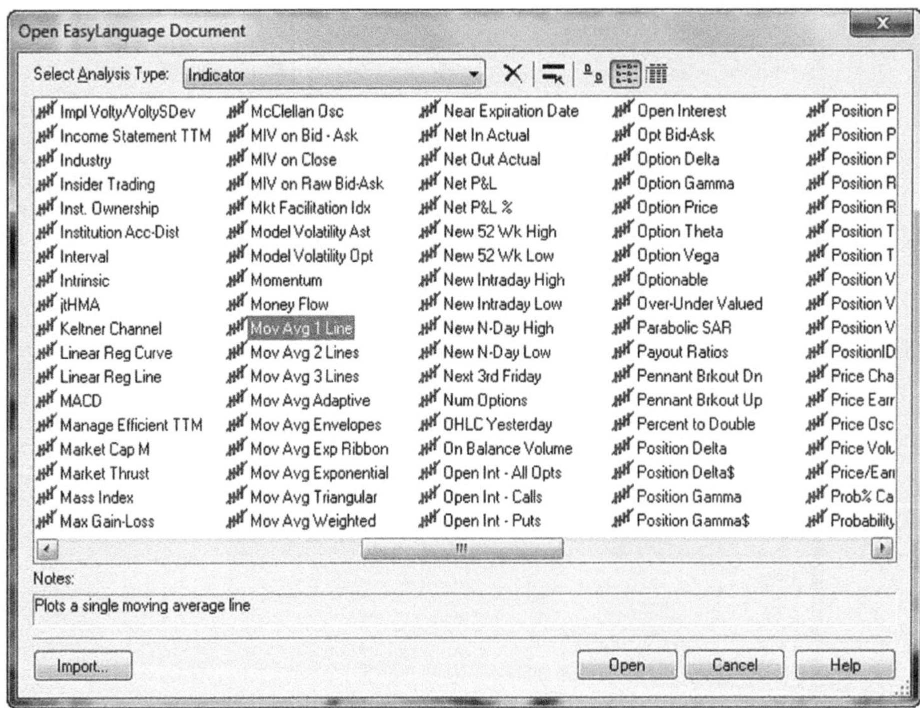

FIGURE 6.4 Select Mov Avg 1 Line

```
TradeStation Indicator - Mov Avg 1 Line
inputs:  Price( Close ), Length( 9 ), Displace( 0 ) ;
variables:  Avg( 0 ) ;

Avg = AverageFC( Price, Length ) ;

if Displace >= 0 or CurrentBar > AbsValue( Displace ) then
    begin
    Plot1[Displace]( Avg, "Avg" ) ;

    { Alert criteria }
    if Displace <= 0 then
        begin
        if Price crosses over Avg then
            Alert( "Price crossing over average" )
        else if Price crosses under Avg then
            Alert( "Price crossing under average" ) ;
        end ;
    end ;


{ ** Copyright (c) 2001 - 2009 TradeStation Technologies, Inc. All rights reserved. **
  ** TradeStation reserves the right to modify or overwrite this analysis technique
    with each release. ** }
Ln 23, Col 28    SAVED VERIFIED    NUM
```

FIGURE 6.5 EZL Code for Mov Avg 1 Line

Anything between curly braces { } in EasyLanguage is a comment. A comment is just for your understanding or to jog your memory later. So, first thing I want you to do is remove the last three lines of code.

With your mouse, highlight everything from the first { through and including the last }. Now press the Delete key [Delete] on your keyboard. That should erase everything you highlighted and the copyright notice should be gone.

See why I didn't want you to overwrite TS's code? What if you erased the wrong lines?

Now highlight the line that begins with { `Alert criteria` } and scrub[2] downward all the way through the second `end ;`. When you have successfully highlighted it, press the [Delete] key and get rid of the Alert criteria.

Next, remove the lines that read

```
if Displace >= 0 or CurrentBar > AbsValue( Displace ) then
      begin
```

leaving the `Plot1[Displace]( Avg, ''Avg'' );` in place. Place your cursor after the semicolon in that statement and highlight everything else on the page. Press the Delete key [Delete] and remove all of that code.

Your Indicator should now read as shown in Figure 6.6.

```
inputs: Price( Close ), Length( 9 ), Displace( 0 ) ;
variables: Avg( 0 );
Avg = AverageFC( Price, Length ) ;
      Plot1[Displace]( Avg, ''Avg'' ) ;
```

FIGURE 6.6 Your Revised Indicator

Isn't that much simpler? Let's see if it verifies. Press [F3]. If you get **Verification successful** then your typing skills are great; otherwise go back and check every little comma and space in your code to see that it matches the code in Figure 6.6.

We are going to simplify it one more time before finishing. There is no need for the `Displace` references for our current purposes. Follow these steps:

- Remove `[Displace]` from the Plot1 statement.
- Remove `, Displace( 0 )` from the inputs statement.
- Press [F3] to verify again.

Now your code should look like Figure 6.7 and it should verify. Again, if it doesn't, check every comma and semicolon, every paren, and all spelling.

[2]"Scrub" is the word I use to mean click the left mouse button and move the mouse downward to highlight the designated items.

```
inputs: Price( Close ), Length( 9 ) ;
variables: Avg( 0 ) ;
Avg = AverageFC( Price, Length ) ;
      Plot1( Avg, "Avg" ) ;
```

FIGURE 6.7 The Final Indicator

CHARTING YOUR INDICATOR

Now would be a good time to put your new indicator on a chart. Do you remember all the steps? Look back at Chapters 2 and 3, or use these steps as reminders:

1. Run TradeStation.
2. Click **Chart Analysis** to bring up a new chart window.
3. Input the symbol `DIS`.

This sequence should result in a chart of Disney Holding Co in your workspace. Now it is time to put your indicator on the chart.

4. From the Menu Bar on the top, click on **Insert** and pull down to **Indicator.**
5. Select your indicator. Mine is named `sjh_MAV1`.
6. Click **OK.**

The resultant chart should look like mine in Figure 6.8.

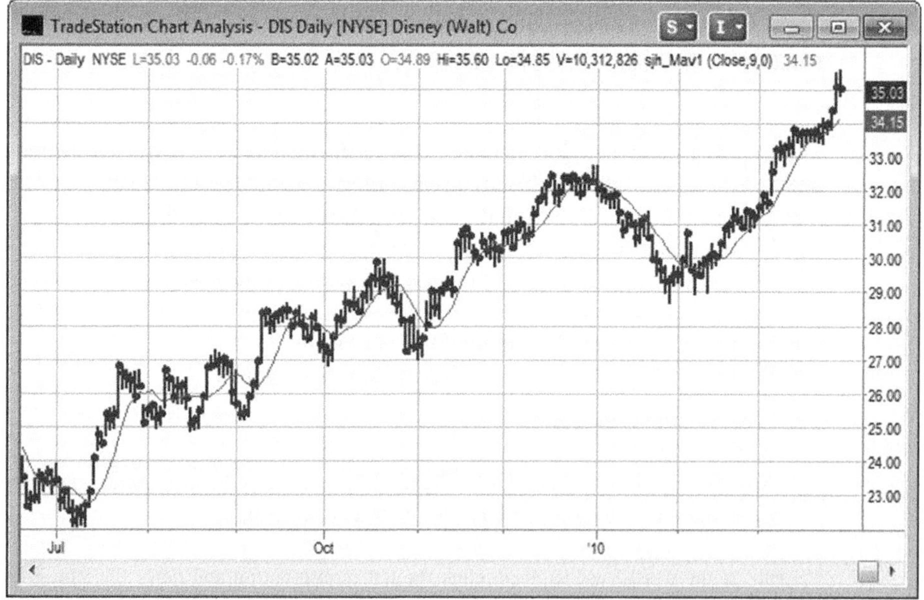

FIGURE 6.8 sjh_MAV1 Indicator

Again, as previously, the line is too skinny to be seen well. And I don't like the default color. We can change this as we did before with **Format** → **Analysis Techniques** → **Format** → **Style** or this time we can make permanent changes by writing the style options into the EasyLanguage code.

To find out what sort of Reserved Words are available for changing styles, click on the little blue book on the top menu bar, at the far right. It looks like . This action will bring up a window that looks like Figure 6.9. In the **Search for**: bar, type in `set`. We are going to set the color and weight of Plot1.

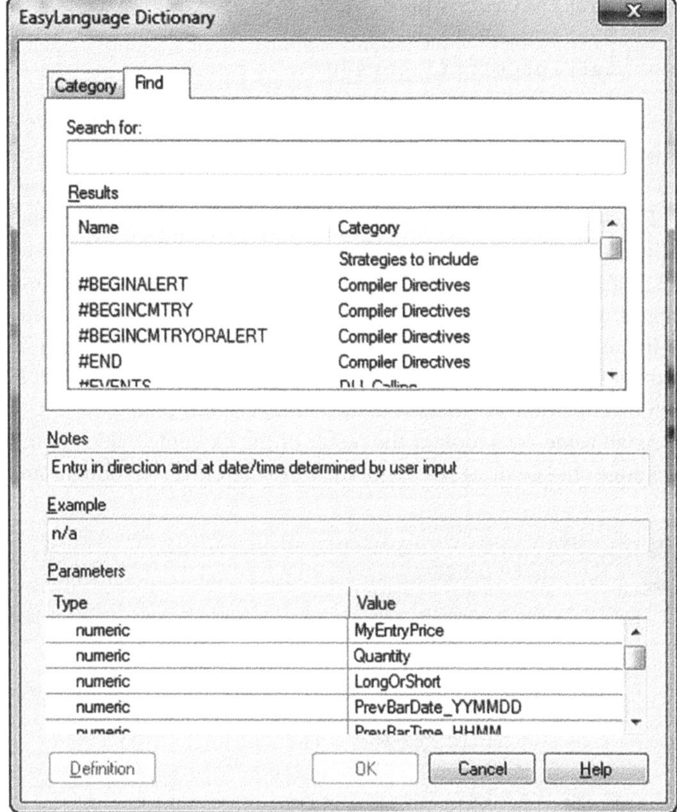

FIGURE 6.9 EasyLanguage Dictionary

First we are going to select **SetPlotColor** and after that come back to this window and select **SetPlotWidth.** Before clicking **OK,** click on the **Definition** button and read the information about what this Reserved Word can do. Don't worry if you don't understand all the computerese at first. Programmers write the manuals and they speak a special language. In short, the information in the dictionary says, and I quote:

This reserved word is used to change the color of a particular plot in a price chart or grid.

```
SetPlotColor(Number, Color);
```

Number is a number from 1 to 99 representing the number of the plot to modify. **Color** is the EasyLanguage color to be used for the plot.

EXAMPLE

The next EasyLanguage statements change the color of the plot to Blue when the RSI Indicator is over 75 and Green when it is under 25.

```
Plot1(RSI(Close, 9), "RSI");
If Plot1 > 75 Then
   SetPlotColor(1, Blue);
If Plot1 < 25 Then
   SetPlotColor(1, Green);
```

Notice that the initial Plot1 statement resets the plot color to the indicator's default color setting each time the EasyLanguage code is run on each bar. This means that the indicator plots the default color unless the RSI value is "greater than 75 or less than 25".

This tells us the syntax of the Reserved Word in the second line; that is, we specify the function and as inputs we give it the number of the plot (e.g., 1 in our case), and the color we want (e.g., dark green). Remember that you can find the main color names in the appendix of this book, and a wide selection of color specifications on my Web site.

In the next line the dictionary tells us that we can have plot numbers 1 through 99, which we knew from an earlier chapter. In our code we specify them as Plot1, Plot2, . . . , Plot99, but in this function we just give it the number of our plot.

As an aside, let's look at the result of the example, which is in Figure 6.10. The example changes the color of the RSI Indicator when it is overbought and underbought. It is for

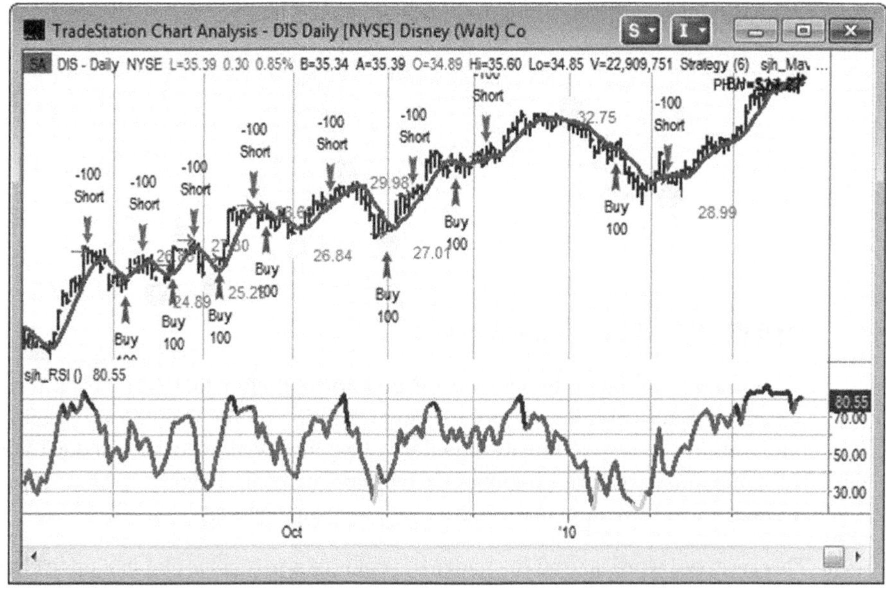

FIGURE 6.10 RSI Using SetPlotColor

convenience of interpretation. I hope they print this book in color. If I end up publishing it myself on the Internet you'll be able to see color; if the publisher prints it in black and white, however, you won't be able to see that RSI is blue at the tops and green at the bottoms.

We want to do this to our `sjh_MAV1` indicator by setting the color to dark green so we don't have to do it each time with the Format command. After the `Plot1` statement in `sjh_MAV1` put the following code, and don't forget the semicolon:

```
SetPlotColor ( 1, DarkGreen ) ;
```

FIGURE 6.11 SetPlotColor Statement

Now that you see how to use **SetPlotColor,** we will move on to the next style change and investigate **SetPlotWidth.** Going back to the EasyLanguage Dictionary is the best and easiest way to learn the nouns you need to memorize and their associated syntax and meaning. Looking up **Set** again, we find **SetPlotWidth** and select it. Clicking on **Definition** brings up the full explanation where we can see that the syntax for this one is:

```
SetPlotWidth(Number, Width);
```

That means that we need to insert this code into `sjh_MAV1` after the **SetPlotColor** statement as follows:

```
SetPlotWidth(1, 3);
```

This tells TradeStation that Plot1 should have the third width selected. Let's see what the plot looks like now, in Figure 6.12.

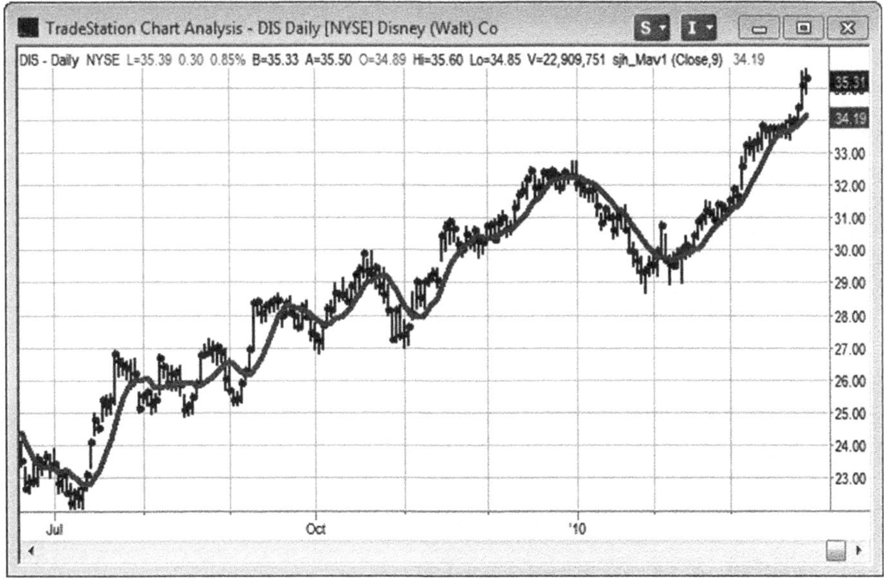

FIGURE 6.12 sjh_MAV1 Indicator with Permanent Style Changes

At last! We now have something cool. In the EasyLanguage Dictionary, ignore the other two SetPlot... Reserved Words: **SetPlotType** and **SetPlotBGColor.** They are for RadarScreen.

To complete these exercises, I include the code for the current state of our indicator in Figure 6.13. This is what mine looks like at this point.

```
inputs: Price( Close ), Length( 9 ) ;
variables: Avg( 0 ) ;
Avg = AverageFC( Price, Length ) ;
Plot1 ( Avg, "Avg" ) ;
SetPlotColor(1, DarkGreen);
SetPlotWidth(1, 3);
```

FIGURE 6.13 sjh_MAV1

Just so you can see what else can be done with the **SetPlotWidth,** I present here the code from the EasyLanguage Dictionary under the **SetPlotWidth** explanation:

```
Plot1(Momentum(Close, 10), "Momentum");
If Plot1 > 0 Then SetPlotWidth(1, 4);
If Plot1 < 0 Then SetPlotWidth(1, 1);
```

Figure 6.14 is the resulting chart. Here the width of the plot line gets thicker when momentum is greater than zero, showing that the market has started moving. I like to show the code examples from the EasyLanguage Dictionary; they come up with some pretty cool stuff.

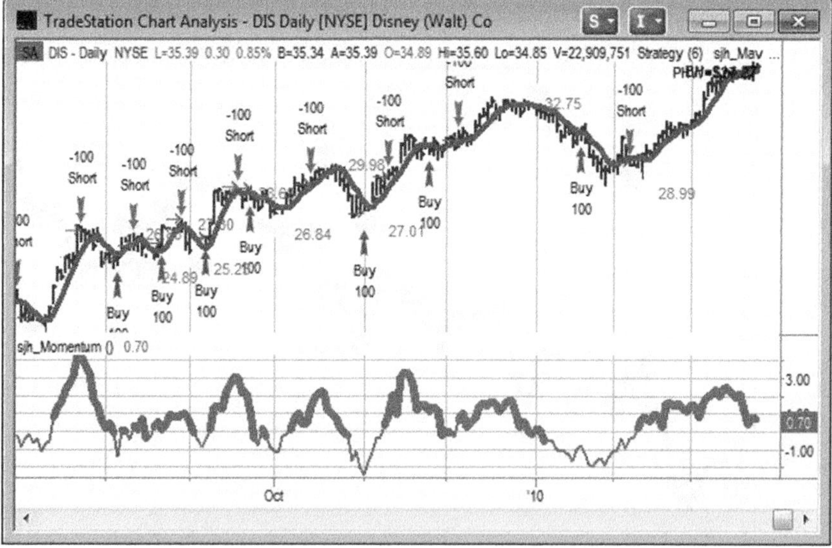

FIGURE 6.14 SetPlotWidth with Momentum

SUMMARY

We've been through it now, a couple of times. You probably understand how to get started, how to put a chart in the Workspace, and how to put an indicator on the chart. You've even written your own indicator and made some pretty fancy modifications to it. You have also created a strategy, added it to your chart, and analyzed the results.

Next we are going to get down to the nitty gritty of programming EasyLanguage. We will get into some details and structure of the language. It will be slow going for the next chapter, as we delve into rules and regulations necessary for the following chapters where your programming will become more sophisticated.

CHAPTER 7

Programming Conventions

In This Chapter

INTRODUCTION

You may find this chapter repetitious. In fact, you may find the whole book repetitious. It is, in that I am building on a concept as we go, getting more and more complex with each subsequent chapter. I started you out with a Quick Start so you could begin using TradeStation right away (unlike other books that make you read the topics in the current chapter first). Now, because of this, we are going over territory we have already covered. Here goes.

A computer will do exactly what you tell it to do. No more and no less. You want to say exactly what you mean to a computer. Your grammar must be precise.

When I was growing up, my parents stressed education and proper English. I grew up in Appalachia, where not everyone spoke proper English, and my dad wanted us to appreciate the power of the spoken word. We always had to structure our sentences correctly if we didn't want to be reprimanded. "I found a pen lost by a woman filled with green ink" was the sample sentence we heard whenever we used improper structure. Just as that sentence is ambiguous, programming sentences are often ambiguous.

To avoid ambiguity in programming, systems designers implemented conventions a long time ago that would provide consistent interpretation of programming sentences. In this chapter, we will review some of those conventions and I will introduce some of the conventions I use to make my own programming easy for me to read.

ORDER DEPENDENCIES AND THE LIBERAL USE OF PARENTHESES

In the shorthand notation we use in mathematics and programming, it is important that we not be ambiguous. When several operations take place in a statement, they are evaluated according to a well-defined hierarchy so that the results are always predictable.

When evaluating mathematical statements, we use the **next order of precedence.** If two or more operators are of the same level of precedence, the operations are executed left to right. Here is the order of precedence:

- parentheses: (and)
- exponentiation: **
- multiplication and division: * and /
- addition and subtraction: + and –
- less than, greater than, equal, less than or equal, greater than or equal, not equal < , >, =, <=, >=, <>
- AND
- OR

We will discuss AND and OR in Chapter 9, when we review symbolic logic. For now, let's just investigate the arithmetic operators.

I am making the assumption that you are familiar with and understand the operators just listed. If you have a question about any of them, any seventh-grade algebra text will give you a good review.

From your early mathematics training, I am sure you remember hearing the words "commutative" and "associative." Most people don't remember what they mean, but that's okay.

Suffice it to say that 3 * 5 is the same as 5 * 3 and 3 + 5 is the same as 5 + 3. However, 3 * (5 + 3) is not the same as (3 * 5) + 3.

EXAMPLES

1. 3 * (5 + 3) = 24
2. (3 * 5) + 3 = 18
3. 7 * (6 / 3) = 14
4. (7 * 6) / 3 = 14
5. 3**2 = 9
6. 3 + 3**2 = 12
7. (3 + 3) **2 = 36

Looking at the next equation, our job is to evaluate the expression and come up with a value for X.

```
X = 3 + 4 * 5
```

This equation could be ambiguous the way it is written. You and I might come up with different answers. Did you say X equals 23 or X equals 35?

We can use parentheses to make our equation clear, so that you and I both get the same answer for X. Here's how:

```
X = (3 + 4) * 5 = 35
```

or

```
X = 3 + (4 * 5) = 23
```

If no parentheses are present, the computer still has a consistent and unambiguous method of interpretation. The computer will follow the order of precedence set out as shown. With that in mind, the computer's interpretation of our equation would be: first do the multiplication and division, yielding 4 * 5 = 20 as the first operation, and then do the addition and subtractions, yielding 20 + 3 for the answer 23.

You are better off with too many parentheses than too few, assuming, of course, that you have equal numbers of right and left parentheses.

TAKE IT SLOWLY—ONE STEP AT A TIME

While nothing in EasyLanguage precludes your writing pages and pages of code before you verify, I would suggest you verify frequently. I verify each line or two of code as I write it.

With the advent of the enhanced 2000i PowerEditor, EasyLanguage evaluates the code and colorizes it as you type. (Microsoft Word checks your sentences for grammar and spelling as you type.) If you are still using TradeStation 4.0, your code will not be evaluated until you verify, and there is no colorizing along the way.

When you press F3 or go to **File → Verify,** the PowerEditor evaluates the entire routine for errors and performs the additional step of saving your work automatically. Sometimes you will have errors in your code and want to save it anyway, with the errors. In this case, press Control + S or go to **File → Save.**

PUNCTUATION

In math we generally make the assumption that the end of a line is the end of the equation. In programming we cannot make this assumption as we sometimes have code that is quite long. While some use run-on sentences in English, proper grammar dictates that you use a terminator at the end of each sentence to indicate that the thought is complete. Likewise with EasyLanguage—we need a terminator.

When you have completed a line of EZL code, you will use the semicolon (;) to signal the end of the statement. Use of the semicolon permits you to make your code "pretty" by employing several lines for a single statement.

As you develop your own templates and styles for coding, you will select structures that are pleasing to you and easy for you to read. I like to separate statements into parts across several lines. For instance, I might write:

```
IF condition1
   and condition2
   and condition3
THEN BUY next bar at market;
```

That way the consequence, or the action, stands alone and is easy for me to see. I also like to capitalize certain words, in particular Reserved Words, to make them stand out and distinguish them from variables and inputs I have created. Notice that I have capitalized "if", "then", and "buy" in the statement. It makes it easier for me to key in on the important parts of the sentence.

SKIP WORDS

EZL needs only a select set of commands to interpret your meaning. To provide for easier reading, EZL also allows you to utilize a set of reserved words that it ignores when processing your code. They are called **Skip Words.** You may use these words if you wish, but they are solely for your own edification and entertainment. Figure 7.1 is a list of EZL Skip Words.

a	by	of	the
an	does	on	was
at	from	place	
based	is	than	

FIGURE 7.1 Skip Words

EXAMPLES
These EasyLanguage statements are all equivalent:

```
If C > H[1] then buy next bar market;
IF C[0] > H[1] THEN BUY next bar at market;
If the Close > the High of 1 Bar Ago then buy on the next bar at
   the market;
```

Note also that capitalization is used by the author to make statements more readable but is ignored by EasyLanguage.

ALL ABOUT BARS

In Chapter 3, in the section Talking about Data, we discussed the components of a bar. They are Open, High, Low, and Close, abbreviated O, H, L, and C. Each of these is loosely referred to as Price. When a formula or function calls for Price, you select one of these components as input. Usually we use Close as the price to measure against things like moving averages or MACD or RSI, but not always.

Data Intervals

The data on your chart is displayed in small sections called intervals. The charts you are accustomed to seeing are usually in intervals of daily bars. That is, each bar represents the price activity of a whole day. Investors like daily bars, or even weekly or monthly bars. Traders often like intraday bars, such as 60-minute or 15-minute bars.

TradeStation refers to these bars as data interval, bar interval, and data compression. Each of these terms refers to the same thing, what I often call the time frame of the chart. These time intervals can be as infrequent as monthly bars, in TradeStation, or as frequent as tick bars. Tick bars represent every trade that takes place on the Exchange. Figure 7.2 shows the various Data Intervals available in TradeStation.

There is another data compression available in TradeStation, which compresses the data received into the number of shares traded. This interval isn't time-based; it depends on

Non–Time-Based Intervals:

- Tick Bars: values can range from 1 to 4095.
- Volume Bars: values can range from 1 to 500,000,000.

Time-Based Intervals:

- Intra-day Minute Bars: values can range from 1 to the number of minutes in the trading day.
- Daily, Weekly, or Monthly Bars: no interval setting is required

FIGURE 7.2 Data Intervals

a certain number of shares being traded before a bar is formed. Data can be compressed into 1000, 5000, 10000, 25000, and 50000 shares.

BarType

When data is compressed into intervals, the resultant bar has a type associated with it. This is a name, or a number, given to the data compression. There is an EasyLanguage function called **BarType** that will return one of the values shown next, so you can make decisions based on the returned value.

BarType returns a numeric value that represents the bar interval type of the chart:

0 = TickBar
1 = Intraday
2 = Daily
3 = Weekly
4 = Monthly
5 = Point & Figure
6 = (reserved)
7 = (reserved)
8 = Kagi
9 = Kase
10 = Line Break
11 = Momentum
12 = Range
13 = Renko

There is another function in EZL that will tell you what BarType your data is. That function is called DataCompression. It has no arguments (inputs) and its output is a number, where:

0 = TickBar
1 = Intraday
2 = Daily

3 = Weekly
4 = Monthly
5 = Point & Figure

This function is retained for backward compatibility with older versions of TS. Here's a line of code from one of my indicators, a real live use of the DataCompression function:

```
IF DataCompression >=2 THEN j_Time=0; {--Data Compression:
   0 for tick,
1 for intra-day, 2 for dly, 3 for wkly, 4 for mnthly, 5 for P&F --}
```

While that code still works, it is not the currently recommended usage. TS changes EasyLanguage from time to time, adding and subtracting Reserved Words, but for the most part the company is very good about maintaining backward compatibility.

BarInterval

The **BarInterval** function returns a number which is the interval setting from the **Format Symbol** dialog. So, if you have 13-minute bars on your chart, **BarInterval** will return the value 13. Here's a really valuable snippet of code that you probably will use regularly:

```
CalcTime(Sess1EndTime, -BarInterval)
```

This snippet returns the time of the last bar before the close of the trading session for an intraday time-based chart. **Sess1EndTime** is a function that returns the ending time of the first session (day session) of the symbol on your chart; **CalcTime** is a function that adds and subtracts minutes from a reference time. The reference time is a numeric value in 24-hour military time format: HHMM (Hour Hour Minute Minute). For example, 2:45 pm would be 1445. This function takes care of the problem of adding and subtracting a 10-based number from a 60-minute-based time.[1] The **-BarInterval** input to the **CalcTime** function subtracts the minute equivalent of one bar on the chart in question. If you are on a 15-minute bar chart, this function would tell you the time of the last bar before the close. That's really helpful if you, for instance, want to evaluate your moving average right before the close and exit your trade without holding overnight.

Bar Number

Each bar in a TradeStation chart is numbered, beginning with the first bar on the chart and ending with the current bar being formed. While they are numbered this way, we don't refer to them by number. I wouldn't, for instance, ask for bar number 354 in a chart, because as each subsequent bar forms the numbering changes dynamically. However, we can refer

[1]For instance, adding 15 minutes to 1445 would result in 1460, not 1500 which is what you want. The CalcTime function takes care of this problem.

easily to "this bar," meaning the one being formed, or the current bar. We call the current bar bar 0, and its notation is `C` or `C[0]`. Take a look at Figure 7.3 to see how bars are numbered.

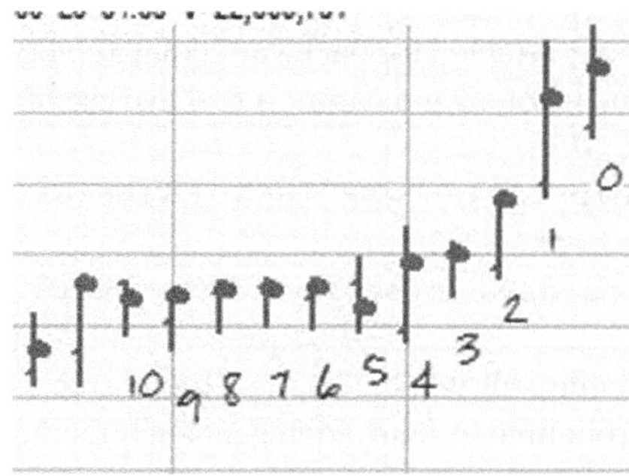

FIGURE 7.3 Bar Numbering

In EasyLanguage you will often refer to a bar by "how many bars ago" it happened. For instance, in momentum studies you will want to measure "this bar's" close against the close of "10 bars ago." EasyLanguage has a notation to make it easy to refer backward. When you want to refer to a price that happened 10 bars ago, you put square brackets around the "number of bars ago" after the price you are referring to.

Let's look at the **Momentum** function code in Figure 7.4.

```
inputs: Price( numericseries ), Length( numericsimple ) ;
Momentum = Price - Price[Length] ;
```

FIGURE 7.4 Momentum Function

The first line declares the inputs to be `Price` and `Length`. The second line sets the value of the function `Momentum` to `Price minus ''Price length bars ago.''` If, for instance, the `Lengthinput` had been `10`, the equation would read:

```
Momentum = Price - Price[10];
```

There is another way to do it in EasyLanguage, it's just not as succinct. You may use the statement `Close of 1 Bar Ago` to mean the same thing as `Close[1]`. Yet another example of bars ago is:

```
Average(Close, 10) of 1 Bar Ago
```

which returns the Average of the last 10 close prices as calculated on the previous bar. That one is pretty tricky.

CurrentBar

To specify times within EZL you need to know the format used in the computer. If you put dates in a spreadsheet in the format 01012010 for January 1, 2010 and 01012009 for January 1, 2009 and then try to sort them, they don't become ordered the way you would think. Try it with the numbers in the next table. Sorting results in all the Januarys together and all the Februarys together.

01012010
02012010
01012009
02012009
01012008
02012008

To alleviate this problem, TradeStation specifies dates with the year first, followed by the month and day. To specify the date March 21, 1989, one would write 890321. When Y2K came along and all the computer programs had to be modified, TradeStation simply changed the 99 to 100 and solved the dilemma. Thus, today's date, March 27, 2010, would be written as 1100327.

The current bar is always the last bar on the chart. It is the bar that is still forming. However, if you want to reference how many bars ago something happened, say how many bars ago a signal was given or how many bars ago the moving averages crossed, you would use the EZL function **CurrentBar,** which is different from the current bar.

In the section titled Bar Number, Figure 7.3 showed you the count back from the current bar, bar 0. However, I also told you that each bar gets a number beginning with the first bar on the chart. I know this is a little confusing, but sometimes you want to reference bars from bar number 1, to determine how long ago a particular condition occurred.

You can use the function **CurrentBar** to determine this:

```
If Condition1 then
   Value1 = CurrentBar;
If CurrentBar > Value1 then
   Value2 = CurrentBar - Value1;
```

Value2 would then hold the number of bars ago Condition1 occurred.

MaxBarsBack

Since one of the primary purposes of EZL is to compare current prices to past prices, we need to take a quick look at how TradeStation does this. If I write a piece of code that refers to today's price and the price five days ago (e.g., to find momentum) I need to know what the price was five days ago.

EasyLanguage evaluates your code beginning with the very first bar of information. So, if I examine the close of the very first bar and ask for the close of five bars ago, I am out of luck. There is no bar "five bars ago" yet. It is only when the sixth bar is in place that I can make the calculation.

TradeStation gives us a way to tell it how many bars back we look in our code. That way EasyLanguage grabs the number of bars it needs to make your calculations before it performs the first calculation. This setting is called **MaxBarsBack.**

You can allow TradeStation to calculate the MaxBarsBack setting automatically by clicking the "Auto-Detect" radio button as shown in Figure 7.5.

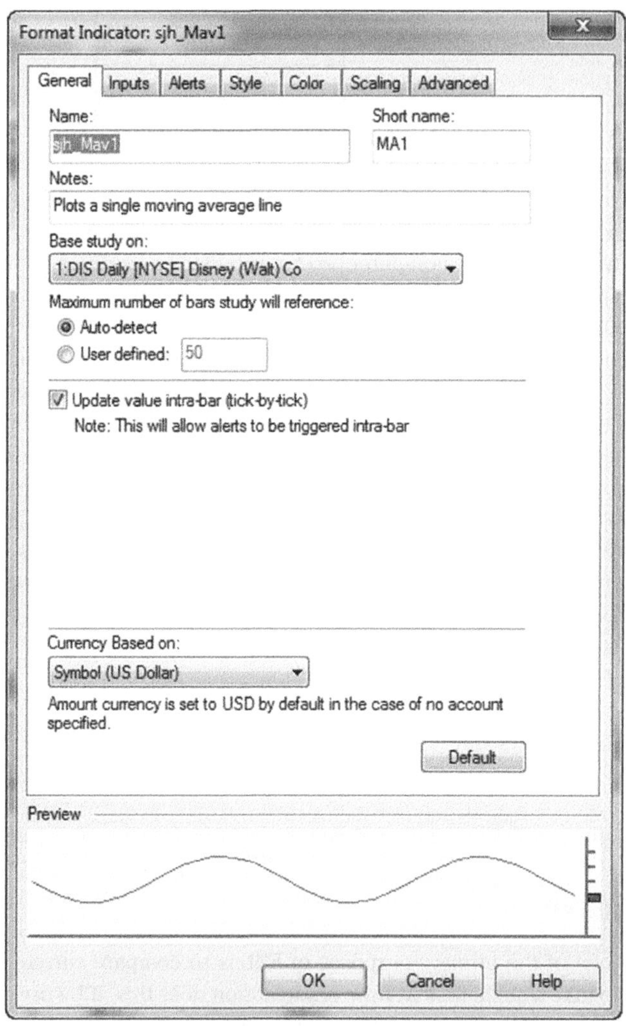

FIGURE 7.5 Auto Detect MaxBarsBack

Or you can specify the setting yourself, using the "User specified" setting.

Why, you ask, would we need both? Why not just have TradeStation calculate how many bars it needs automatically? Good question.

When TradeStation automatically calculates MaxBarsBack, it always gathers the exact number of bars it needs for the routine it is working on. So, when testing a 10-bar moving average, TradeStation will not calculate until the 11th bar. When testing a 20-bar moving average, TradeStation will not calculate until the 21st bar.

The problem arises when you want to compare the profit from one trading system to another trading system. If you had 100 bars total in the sample you are studying and used the last 90 in one test and the last 80 in another test, you could very well be comparing apples and oranges. There might have been trades in the first system test that won't appear in the second test. If those missing trades were all winners, the first test will look more profitable; if those missing trades were all losers, the first test will look less profitable.

To balance the experiments and compare like sets of trades, you can set MaxBarsBack to the same number for each test. Setting MaxBarsBack to 20, in this example, will cause each test to begin calculating profit/loss on the 21st bar.

Take a look at the chart in Figure 7.6. This chart shows the beginning of our data and the moving average we've been working on. Notice that the green moving average doesn't begin until the 10th bar. That's what I'm talking about.

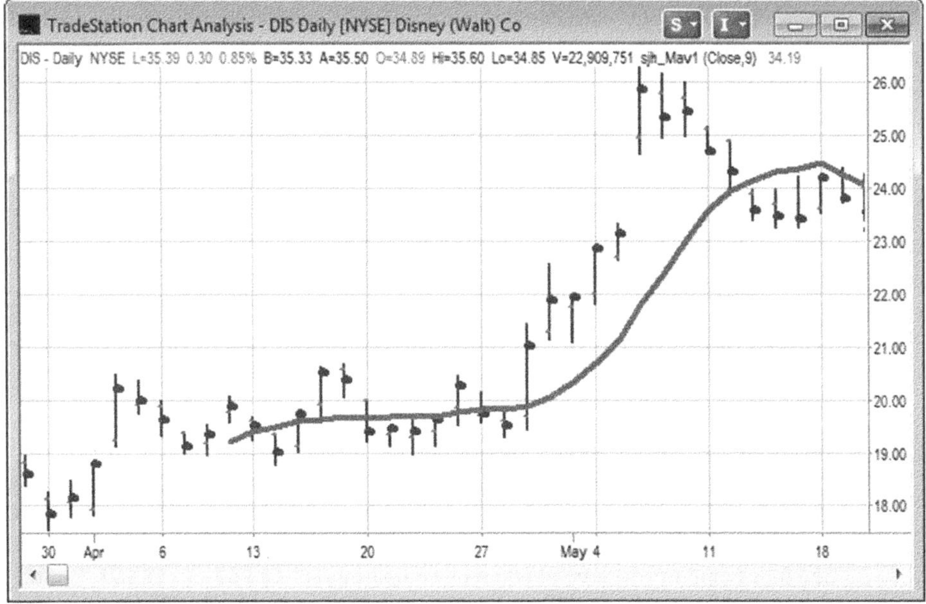

FIGURE 7.6 MaxBarsBack

Now that you know what MaxBarsBack is, I'm going to be more accurate with one statement. I previously said that bar number 1, for the BarNumber function, is the first bar on the chart. Actually, it is the first bar after MaxBarsBack have passed. It is the first bar available for calculating. Yes, it's confusing, but you will always refer to these bars relative to each other or relative to some event like a moving average crossing, so don't worry, it all works out.

INPUTS AND VARIABLES

Inputs

You are allowed to pass information to your code. These pieces of information are called "inputs" and are specified when you make reference to the routine. For ease of understanding, I will call functions, indicators, activitybars, signals, and systems "routines" when making a general reference to them.

The inputs to the moving average indicator are "price" and "length". You would specify them as:

```
Average(C,9)
```

which says that the price you want to average is the closing price and the length of the average should be 9 bars.

If you wanted to write a routine that tested yesterday's close against the close of two days ago, you could "hard-code" that information, as in Figure 7.7, or you could think ahead to the future and plan for comparing yesterday's close against the close three days ago, as in Figure 7.8.

```
IF C[1] > C[2] THEN…
```

FIGURE 7.7 Variables Hard Coded

```
INPUTS: N1(1), N2(2);
IF C[N1] > C[N2] THEN ...
```

FIGURE 7.8 Variables as Inputs

In Figure 7.8, you would want to pass two inputs to your routine: a `1` to specify yesterday and a `2` to specify the day before that. With inputs you have allowed yourself the flexibility of specifying any two days you wish to examine. For instance, you could put `55` and `56` as the inputs and the code would then be comparing `IF C[55] > C[56] THEN...`

Inputs are especially valuable when you want to find the optimum value for something in your routine. Let's say, for instance, you want to know what length moving average gives you the most profit. You could hard-code the length of your first attempt and change the code for each subsequent trial. Or you could let the length be an input to the routine and not change the code again.

In Chapter 9 we will thoroughly examine inputs.

Variables

Variables are used to **store values** that you will use and change in your routine. Variables help make your code easier to read and understand. A variable is often used to change values at different stages in the routine.

You might use a variable to count events as they happen, like the number of times yesterday's high is greater than today's high. You might use a variable as a switch, turning it off and on as a flag. You might use a variable to accumulate numbers, like summing closing prices so you could calculate an average.

EasyLanguage provides 100 default variable names **Value0** through **Value99,** or you can create your own and name them as you wish, as long as you don't use a Reserved Word or Skip Word.

EasyLanguage also provides a set of 100 conditional (true/false) variables, named **Condition0** through **Condition99.** You may use these built-in names or you may create your own.

Variable names and types are "declared" in the first few lines of your EasyLanguage code. You would tell EZL that you are going to create a variable of your own using a declaration statement like this:

```
Variables: j_Value1(0), j_Value2(9):
```

In Chapter 8 we will thoroughly examine variables.

STATEMENTS

In programming, a sentence is called a **statement.** In statements we can compare, declare, calculate, act, and operate. Some statements are **assignment** statements. They assign a value to a variable. Some statements are **declaration** statements. They set up the structure to be used later in the routine.

A statement can take several forms. See Figure 7.9 for examples.

```
Y = X + 2;
Value1= High - Low;
Variable: BarRange(0);
Input: Length1(10), Length2(20);
Print("Moving Average = ",Average(C,10));
Plot1(Volume,"Volume");
```

FIGURE 7.9 Examples of Statements

None of these statements needs to mean anything to you yet. Just accept the terminology. More on statements in Chapter 8.

COMMAND STRUCTURE

Just like any language, EasyLanguage understands a certain sentence structure. Incorrectly specify the sentence and EasyLanguage will get confused. The structure of the sentence, or command, is called the **syntax.** Each command in EasyLanguage has a similar structure. Commands have descriptive names and most have input values. Functions and indicators are examples of commands.

Commands have the following basic structure:

```
EZLCommand (input1, input2, ... inputi)[offset];
```

An example of an EZL command would be: `Average(C,9)`. Here the EZL command is "Average", input1 is `C` (or `Close`), and input2 is the value `9`. To denote the average of two days ago you would use the offset value as `Average(C,9)[2]`.

PROGRAM STRUCTURE

Beginning with ProSuite 2000i, not much needs to be said about Program structure. The PowerEditor, since version 2000i, pretty much does it for you. Nevertheless, you should decide on a consistent structure and maintain it. Your code will be much easier for you to read and understand if you stick with a structure.

My structural approach is fairly simple:

- Capitalize reserved words.
- Place the condition (IF) and consequence (THEN) on separate lines so I can more easily find them.
- Indent each BEGIN . . . END group together for clarity.

My code tends to look like the code shown in Figure 7.10.

```
IF O*C*H*L > 0  {No zero values to mess up the calcs}
THEN BEGIN
   IF C<>0
              THEN Value1=AbsValue((H-L)/C);
   IF C<>0
              THEN Value2=AbsValue((C-O)/C);
   IF Value2<>0
              THEN Value3=Value1/Value2;
END;
```

FIGURE 7.10 Looking for Narrow Ranges

One of the things that holds true of the market, year after year, is that it tends to move—one way or the other. It doesn't stay still for long. I like to look for narrow trading ranges, with the thought that the market will ultimately break out of the range. The code in Figure 7.10 is one way of looking for narrow ranges.

FLOW

EZL reads any chart from left to right, one bar at a time. When your EasyLanguage code is applied to a chart, each bar of the chart is analyzed, one at a time, from left to right.

As each single bar is being analyzed, it is called the "current" bar. The current bar is numbered 0 (zero). Thus, the close of the current bar could be referred to as `Close[0]`, or `C`, or `C[0]`.

Refer back to Chapter 3 for more information on this subject.

COMMENTS

Right after you create your second indicator, function, or system, you will forget the meaning of some of the code you wrote in the first indicator, function, or system (routine). To facilitate your understanding of your code in the future, to make it easier to code in the first place, and to allow others to read your code, you need to liberally document its purpose and structure.

Comments are for documenting your code. Anything placed between two curly braces, {}, will not be read by the EZL compiler. A comment in your EZL code might look like this:

```
{--This is a comment that explains the following line of code--}
```

Comments may be placed within the line of code or on a separate line—it doesn't matter to EZL. EZL will ignore your comments altogether. The other form comments can take is using two forward slashes followed by your comment. These are called inline comments. Do not let the inline comment wrap over to the next line. Keep it to one line only. They look like this:

```
Value1 = 2 * Value2; //This is the inline comment
```

Different strokes for different folks; everyone comes up with their own preferred way of structuring their code and their comments. My code doesn't look like that of my programmers'. Michael Scott, one of my programmers, liberally comments with slashes:

```
///////////////////////////
//DESCRIPTION OF STRATEGY
///////////////////////////

////////////////////////////////////////
```

```
///////////////////////////
//Notes on some variables:
///////////////////////////

//PositionQuantity:The input value which specifies the quantity
      of the position to be taken.

/////////////////////////////////////
// Inputs that act as parameters.
/////////////////////////////////////

//Strategy inputs.
inputs: PositionQuantity(1), ManualEntry(true);

///////////////////////////////
//Specific strategy variables.
///////////////////////////////
vars: MACDDiffLowerFrame(0), MACDDiffUpperFrame(0),
      MACDLowerWaitOnCross(0), MACDUpperWaitOnCross(0),
      AlertSignal(0), MACDLowerCross(0),
MACDUpperInitialSign(0), ExecutedTrade(0), MACDLowerInitialSign(0);
```

This next block of code is from the book *New Trading Systems and Methods* by Perry Kaufman. His code doesn't have comments in it, but it is indented consistently and very "prettily."

```
For Missing = 2 To Vacuum Begin
      FillDay = JulianToDate(DateToJulian(Date[1]) + (Missing-1));
      If DayOfWeek(FillDay) > 0 and DayOfWeek(FillDay) < 6 Then Begin
        TradeStr2 = NumToStr(FillDay, 0)+ ",," + NumToStr(MarketPosition, 0)
      + ","
             + NumToStr(RiskValue, 2)+"," +NumToStr(PosProfit[1],2)
      +","+"0"+New Line;
             FileAppend(FName, TradeStr2);
          End;
End;
```

Last, but not least, my own code uses blocks of {} comments mixed with // comments. My indentation is based on placement of IFs and THENs.

```
IF jNums<>0 THEN BEGIN {--plot text showing numbers of H & L of
pennant--}
       Value55=Text_New(Date, Time, H[jHBar],NumToStr(H[jHBar],2));
       Text_SetColor(Value55, Black); //set text to black
```

```
        Text_SetStyle(Value55, 1, 1); // placement of text
{--Horiz: 0 Right,1 Left, 2 Centered; Vert: 0 Beneath, 1 Above, 2
Centered--}
        Value56=Text_New(Date, Time, L[jLBar], NumToStr(L[jLBar],2));
        Text_SetStyle(Value56, 1, 0); // place text right and beneath
        Text_SetColor(Value56, Black); // set text to black
END;
```

VERIFYING YOUR CODE

Before TradeStation can understand the code you have written in EasyLanguage, you must allow TradeStation to check the code for syntax errors. To achieve this, simply mouse up to the menu bar, select **Tools → Verify.** Alternately you may simply press the F3 function key.

If EasyLanguage likes the syntax of your code it will respond with **Verification successful.** It used to respond with **Excellent!** which made me smile every time. Now that the company is also a brokerage firm, it can't do anything that looks like it is telling you that your code might be profitable.

If EasyLanguage cannot interpret your code due to syntax errors, it will respond with an error message, as shown in Figure 7.11. It also pops up a window that tells you what line of code is bad.

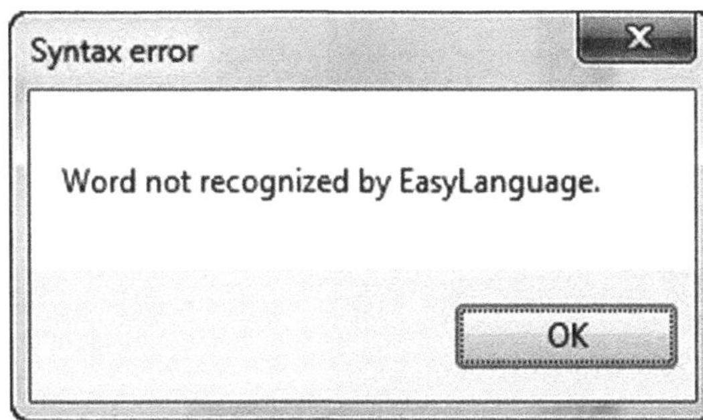

FIGURE 7.11 Verification Error

If there are errors in your code, you will need to click **OK** and correct your errors.

Verifying does not check your code for fitness for purpose. EasyLanguage has no way to know whether your routine will produce profits in any given market. Verifying your code is like running a spell-checker in your word processor. Your spell-checker doesn't guarantee that your letter will achieve the desired results.

Once the verification process is completed, you can view any verification errors in the **EasyLanguage Output Bar,** under the **Verify** tab. If you can't see this bar, use this sequence: **CTRL+SHIFT+E** or **View → EasyLanguage Output Bar.**

Verifying an analysis technique simultaneously saves the analysis technique. If you want to save the routine without verifying it, simply **File → Save EasyLanguage Document.**

HINT : Rather than writing multiple lines of code and then verifying, save yourself some headaches by verifying each line as you write it. Verifying often saves you the confusion of debugging complex routines.

ERROR HANDLING

Most errors in your EasyLanguage programming will appear on your monitor as syntax errors right after an attempt to verify your code.

"Word not recognized by EasyLanguage" usually means that you have probably

- Made a typing mistake.
- Used a variable or input name without declaring it.
- Spelled a reserved word incorrectly.

With experience and practice, you will learn to quickly recognize your errors. One of my common typing errors is I misspell the Reserved Word "condition" as "conditon" when typing quickly. EasyLanguage catches me every time.

Another TradeStation error occurs while your routine is running. This type error is called a "runtime error".

Runtime errors can occur if you incorrectly define the maximum number of bars back (MaxBarsBack) an indicator needs to reference. The reason for the runtime error is displayed in Figure 7.12.

A runtime error automatically disables the indicator by turning its status to **Off.**

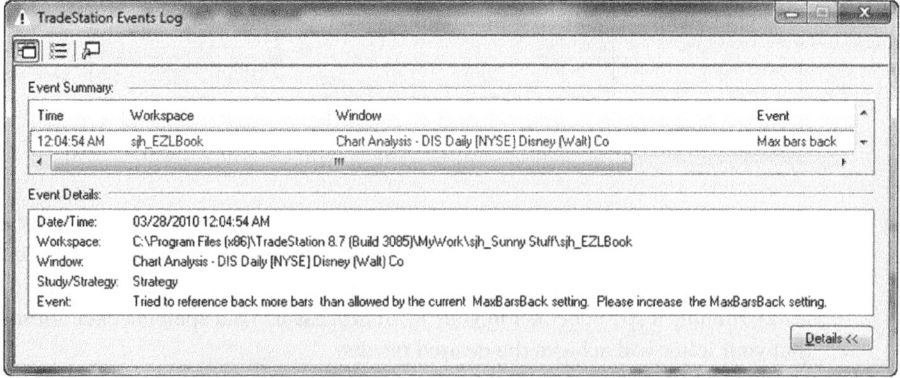

FIGURE 7.12 Dialogue Box

To correct a runtime error, you must modify the **MaxBarsBack** number to be greater than or equal to the number of bars the indicator will reference, or set it to **Auto-Detect.** After correcting the settings, you must then turn the indicator status back **On,** using the **Format → Analysis Techniques** window (Figure 7.13).

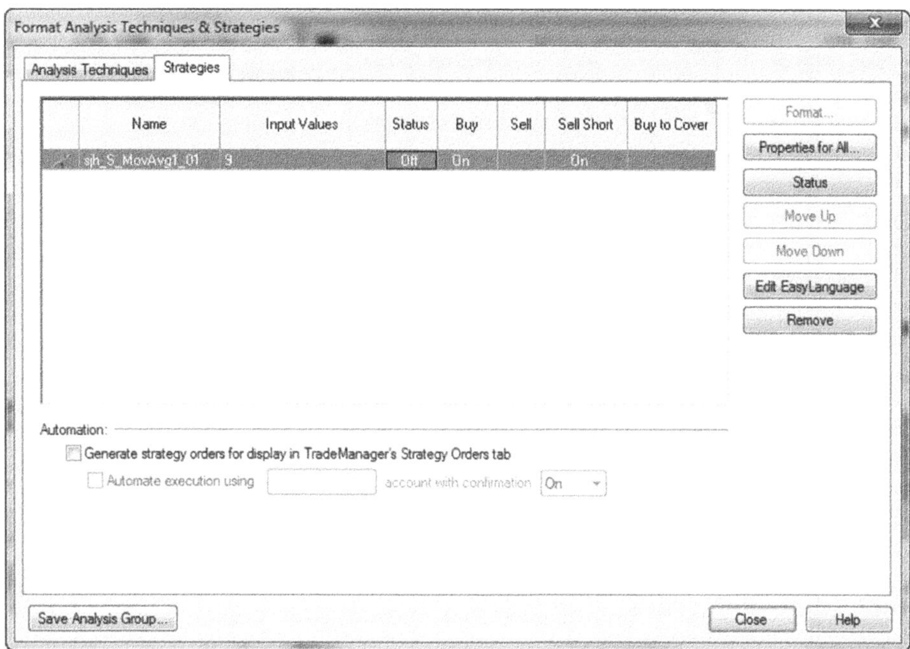

FIGURE 7.13 Turning the Strategy Back On

Click on the **Status** button, and the indicator status will toggle from **Off** to **On.** Then click on the **Properties for All** button and change the MaxBarsBack setting. (See Figure 7.14.)

DEBUGGING TRICKS

One Step at a Time

Probably the single most important rule of thumb in programming and debugging is to take one step at a time. Verify each and every line as you enter it. This trick will save you a lot of time and effort in the long run. It is a lot easier to fix an error in a single line of code than in 30 lines where errors could be interlinked. Furthermore, the more lines you enter, the more interlinked they become and the more confused the Editor is when it finds a syntax error.

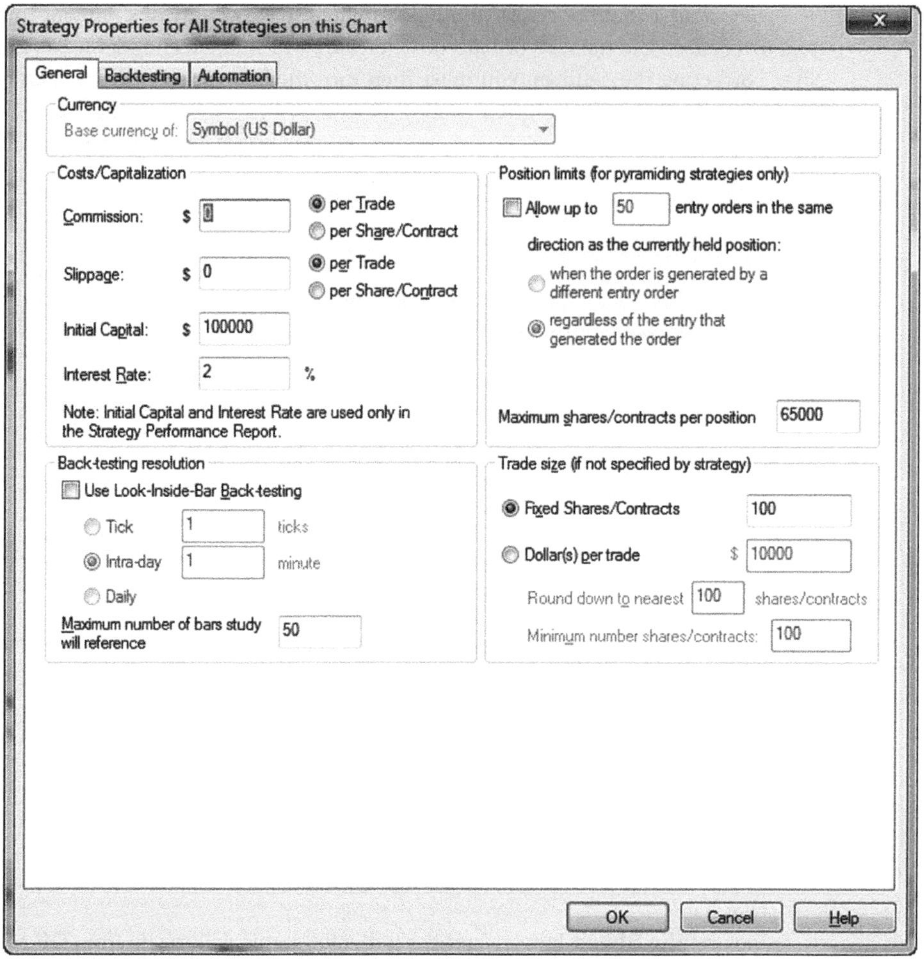

FIGURE 7.14 Setting MaxBarsBack

Print

EasyLanguage can catch your syntax errors, but it cannot catch your logic errors. If you said `X > Y` when you meant `X < Y`, EasyLanguage would have no way to read your mind.

If what you think you said is not what you meant to say, often you can find the logic error by printing the results of each calculation or statement as it would be encountered by TradeStation. Debugging your logic then becomes a matter of reading your **Print Log** (TS 4.0) or **Message Log** (2000i), **Print Log** in all later versions of TS, until version 8.8 when it becomes the **Output** bar, one line at a time and comparing the actual output to your expected output.

The full format of the **Print** statement is:

```
Print([where],"text",information[formatting]);
```

The parameters in the print statement are:

where	the optional destination of your print statements (Print Log, File, or Printer)
"text"	the alphanumeric information to print
information[formatting]	the variables to print and their formatting

If no "where" is specified, the output will be sent to the **Print Log.**

To send information to a specified file instead of the **Print Log,** specify the file and path as the first parameter. Enclose the file name and path in quotation marks. To send the information to the default printer, include the word Printer as the first parameter.

EXAMPLES

```
Print(Printer, Date, Time, Close); // sends the date, time, and
        closing price of the current bar to the default printer

Print(File("c:\data\mydata.txt"), Date, Time, Close); // sends
the same information to an ASCII file called mydata.txt on the C:
drive in the data folder
```

You can format the numeric expressions displayed using the Print Reserved Word. To do so, use the following syntax:

```
Print(Value1:N:M);
```

`Value1` is any numeric expression, `N` is the minimum number of integers to use, and `M` is the number of decimals to use. If the numeric expression being sent to the **Print Log** has more integers than what is specified by `N`, the **Print** statement uses as many digits as necessary, and the decimal values are rounded to the nearest value. For example, assume `Value1` is equal to 3.14159 and we have written this statement:

```
Print(Value1:1:4);
```

The numeric expression displayed in the **Print Log** would be 3.1416. The first parameter after the colon tells EZL how many numbers are to appear on the left of the decimal while the parameter after the second colon tells EZL how many numbers are to appear on the right of the decimal.

As another example, to format the closing prices, you can use this statement:

```
Print(ELDateToString(Date), Time, Close:0:4);
```

The parameters may be any valid string expression, numeric series, or numeric expression separated by commas. To output to a file or printer, use the File and Printer statements respectively with the Print statement.

EXAMPLES

If you wanted to send the date, time, and close information to the Print Log (Output log or Message Log) when you applied an analysis technique, you could use this syntax:

```
Print(Date, Time, Close);
Print(Date [n:m], Time [n:m], Close [n:m]);
```

To send the same information to an ASCII file named file.txt, you could use this syntax:

```
Print(File("c:\file.txt"),Date, Time, Close);
```

To send the same information to the printer, you could use this syntax:

```
Print(Printer, Date, Time, Close);
```

The formatting, in square brackets, is optional; that's why it is in square brackets. You may specify it if you want or allow TS to use the default formatting.

Formatting is specified between colons, telling TS how many characters to display and how many decimal places to display. Figure 7.15 illustrates the outputs from various formatting options.

Item	Output without Formatting	Formatting	Output
Date	980403.00	Date:6:0	980403
Time	1600.00	Time:4:0	1600
Close	105.63	Close:8:5	105.63000

FIGURE 7.15 Formatting Options

To view the Message Log in TS2000i, you must add a window to your workspace. Use the **File → New → Message Log** menu sequence to add a **Message Log** window to your workspace. Viewing the Print Log in TS4.0 is simply **File → New Window → Print Log.** In the current versions of TS, view the **Print Log** by this menu sequence: **View → EasyLanguage Output Bar.**

You must include a Print statement within the EasyLanguage of your analysis technique to send a message to the **Print Log** or the **Message Log.** For more information, see Print Statements in Chapter 8.

One more thing before I leave the **Print** statement. You can format your output using quotes and spaces. In the earlier examples, we output the date, time, and closing price of the current bar. Using the Print statements, the output would look like what is shown in Figure 7.16.

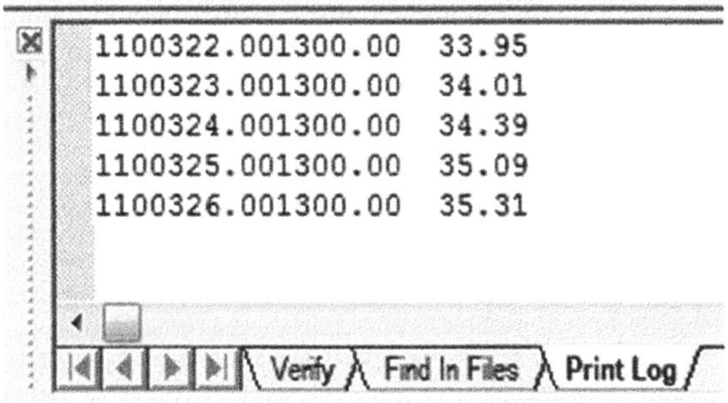
1100322.001300.00 33.95
1100323.001300.00 34.01
1100324.001300.00 34.39
1100325.001300.00 35.09
1100326.001300.00 35.31
Verify
Find In Files
Print Log

FIGURE 7.16 Unformatted Print Log

That's not very pretty. It is difficult to visually separate the date from the time, and neither is recognizable in its current form. Using the optional information formatting, we can separate the date from the time with a space and get rid of the trailing zeros. The new Print statement would look like:

```
Print(Date:7:0, " ", Time:4:0, " ", Close);
```

and the output in the Print Log changes to Figure 7.17.

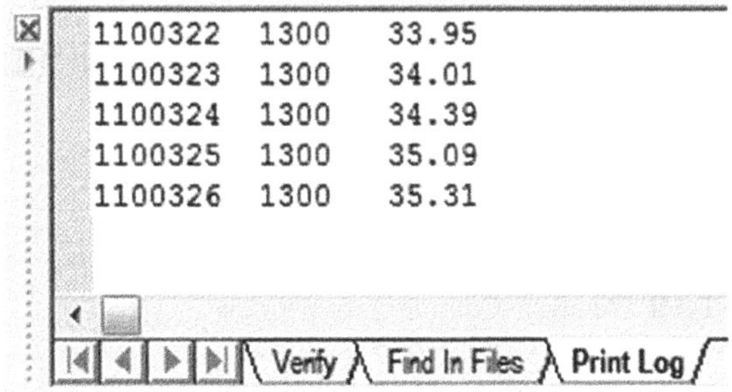
1100322 1300 33.95
1100323 1300 34.01
1100324 1300 34.39
1100325 1300 35.09
1100326 1300 35.31
Verify
Find In Files
Print Log

FIGURE 7.17 Formatted Print Statement

Expert Commentary

Expert Commentary sends expressions to the Analysis Commentary window for the selected bar. Ordinarily you would expect Expert Commentary to contain sage advice from a noted authority about the indicator in play. However, using Expert Commentary is a neat trick for your own debugging.

In your EZL code you write **Commentary** statements. If Analysis Commentary is turned on (**View → Analysis Commentary**), when you click on a bar on your chart the Commentary window pops up and displays the text and values you specified in your Commentary statements. (See Figure 7.18.)

With Analysis Commentary on, you can use the cursor to view your parameters one bar at a time. You can move backward and forward over the chart, displaying any bar and its associated commentary at will. It is a great debugging tool.

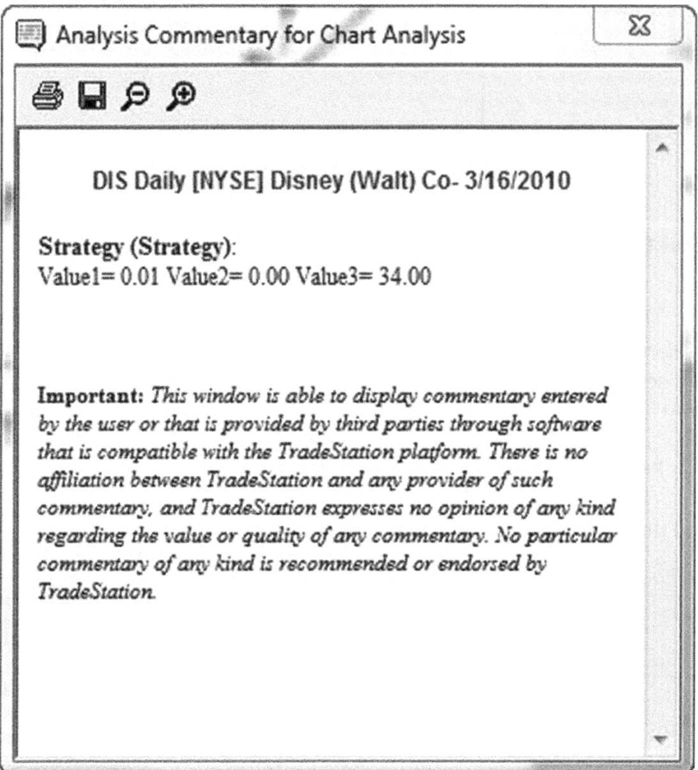

FIGURE 7.18 Analysis Commentary Window

Using the same code from an earlier example, I have inserted Commentary statements after each variable calculation. The commentary will be visible in the Analysis Commentary window.

```
IF O*C*H*L>0
        THEN BEGIN
               IF C<>0
                     THEN Value1=AbsValue((H-L)/C);
                     Commentary("Value1= ",Value1, " ");
```

```
                IF C<>0
                     THEN Value2=AbsValue((C-O)/C);
                     Commentary("Value2= ",Value2, " ");
                IF Value2<>0 THEN Value3=Value1/Value2;
                     Commentary("Value3= ",Value3);
          END;
```

BREAKPOINT

This command is a compiler directive; when placed in your EasyLanguage code, it automatically opens the Debugger window when encountered as the study calculates.

The format of the statement is: **BreakPoint("BreakPointNameID");** *where* **BreakPointNameID** is a string expression or string variable.

Each occurrence of BreakPoint must be named. The name parameter may be specified as a string expression, following the keyword. A string variable can also be used as the name or in combination with a literal string value, such as: `BreakPoint("BreakID"+ GetSymbolName)`.

While the Debugger is open, activity in all TradeStation windows is halted. No data, alerts, or strategy orders will be generated. Any window, including Chart Analysis, in open workspaces will not update until the Debugger is closed. The Debugger is intended for use in a development environment. Debugging should not take place while trading or using strategy automation.

EXAMPLES

```
For Counter = 0 to Length - 1 Begin
Sum = Sum + Close[Counter]; BreakPoint("Break at Sum");
```

CHAPTER 8

Statements

In This Chapter

- Introduction
- Declaration Statements
- Variables
- Inputs
- Assignment Statements
- Data Manipulation
- Print Statements
- IF. . .THEN Statements
- Plot Statements
- Further Reading and Reference

INTRODUCTION

A **statement** is a way of assigning a value to something. In statements we can compare, declare, calculate, act, and operate. Some statements are **assignment statements.** They assign a value to a variable. Some statements are **declaration statements.** They set up the structure to be used later in the routine.

EasyLanguage statements are instructions, such as **If . . . Then** statements, **Plot** statements, **Arrays,** and so on, used to create analysis techniques in the EasyLanguage PowerEditor.

When programming we must follow the conventions of the language we're using, so the computer understands what we mean.

On paper we understand both X=Y+1 and Y+1=X to mean the same thing. The computer needs you to be more structured than that. A computer statement needs to have one variable on the left side of the equal sign, to which will be assigned the value calculated on the right-hand side. In other words, X=Y+1 is okay and the other structure is not.

A statement can take several forms. Statements look like:

```
Y = X + 2;
Value1= High - Low;
Variable: BarRange(0);
Input: Length1(10), Length2(20);
Print("Moving Average = ",Average(C,10));
Plot1(Volume,"Volume");
```

We will use statements in later chapters to perform actions and calculations. In this chapter, we will go over their structure.

DECLARATION STATEMENTS

EasyLanguage has provided 200 variable names that you may use without any declaration statements. These variables are called **Value0, Value1, Value2,**. . . through **Value99** and **Condition0, Condition1,** . . . through **Condition99.** When I am doing a quick program that has only a few variables in it, I use these default variable names.

When things get more complex, it would be difficult to remember the meaning of all these "vanilla" variables. You would find yourself eventually asking "What did I mean by Value67?" For these situations, EasyLanguage lets you create your own variables.

The two basic rules about these variables are:

1. You cannot name them any of the Reserved Words.
2. You must tell EasyLanguage the names of the variables before you use them.

VARIABLES

A variable is an alias—a name you assign a formula to so that you can reference the alias instead of the formula. In EasyLanguage, you can think of variables as **storage containers** that hold a value. This value can be a number, true/false condition, or a string of text.

The words "**Variable**", "**Variables**", "**Var**", and "**Vars**" are all synonymous and may be used to set up the variables you will use in your routine. When you set up your variables, you "declare" them.

Typical variable declaration statements would look like:

```
VARIABLES: Length1(0), Length2(0), Counter(0);
VARS: j_Length1(0), j_Length2(9);
```

In addition to the basic rules, there are three more specific rules about declaring variables.

1. A variable name can contain up to 20 alphanumeric characters including the period (.) and the underscore (_).
2. A variable name cannot start with a number or a period (.) .
3. The **default value** of a variable is declared by a number in parentheses after its name.

EXAMPLE

```
VARIABLES: Countup(0), Countdown(10);
{declares the variables Countup and Countdown and initializes
       their values to zero and ten, respectively}
```

EXAMPLE

```
VARS: MADiff(0), XMADiff(0);
{declares the variables MADiff and XMADiff, initializing the
       values of both to zero}
MADiff=Average(C,100) - Average(C,50);
XMADiff=XAverage(C,100) - XAverage(C,50);
```

EXAMPLE

```
VARIABLE: Switch(true);
{declares the condition (true/false) variable Switch to true}
IF Close>Open THEN Switch=False ELSE Switch=True;
```

INPUTS

An input is like a variable, except that inputs are **passed into your routine from outside of the routine.** Inputs must be declared in declaration statements, just like variables.

The **INPUT** statement takes the following form:

```
INPUTS: Length1(0), Length2(0);
```

In addition to the basic rules, there are four more specific rules about declaring inputs.

1. An input name can contain up to 20 alphanumeric characters including the period (.) and the underscore (_).
2. An input name cannot start with a number or a period (.).

3. Inputs are constants that cannot start a statement.
4. The **default value** of an input is declared by a number in parentheses after the input name.

Inputs are used in calculations within your routine. For example, the MACD compares two moving averages, a fast moving average with a slow moving average. Typically the default inputs for the MACD are 12 and 26. Because these numbers are inputs to the routine, they may be changed before charting and before strategy testing.

The ability to quickly change the input values, external to the routine, allows you to perform sophisticated **optimizations,** and to try a variety of input values on the fly. That's what optimization (in TradeStation) means: trying a variety of input values external to the routine automatically. Instead of trying the input values 1, 2, 3, 4, 5, and 6, you would simply specify to try "1:6:1," which means start at 1 and go to 6 in increments of 1. Isn't that easy?

Figure 8.1 is an illustration of the following sequence. This sequence is used to modify a strategy's inputs. This is a shorthand notation to get you up and running. To modify a strategy's inputs:

1. Use the **Format →Analysis Technique** menu sequence.
2. Click the strategy whose inputs you want to modify, and click **Format.**
3. Click the **Inputs** tab.
4. Click the input you want to edit, and click **Edit.**
5. Type the new input value or expression in the **Expression** box.
6. To modify the inputs using EasyLanguage, click **Dictionary.** For more information, see Working with the EasyLanguage Dictionary.
7. To optimize the input, select the **Optimize** check box. For more information on optimizing a system's inputs, refer to Optimizing Your Trading Systems.
8. When the input has been modified, click **OK.**

EXAMPLE

```
Input: Price(Close), Length(10);
{declares the constants Price and Length, initializing the val-
ues to the
        Close of the bar and ten, respectively}
```

EXAMPLE

```
Input: FastMA(12), SlowMA(26);
{declares the constants FastMA and SlowMA, initializing the val-
ues to
       twelve and twenty-six, respectively}
```

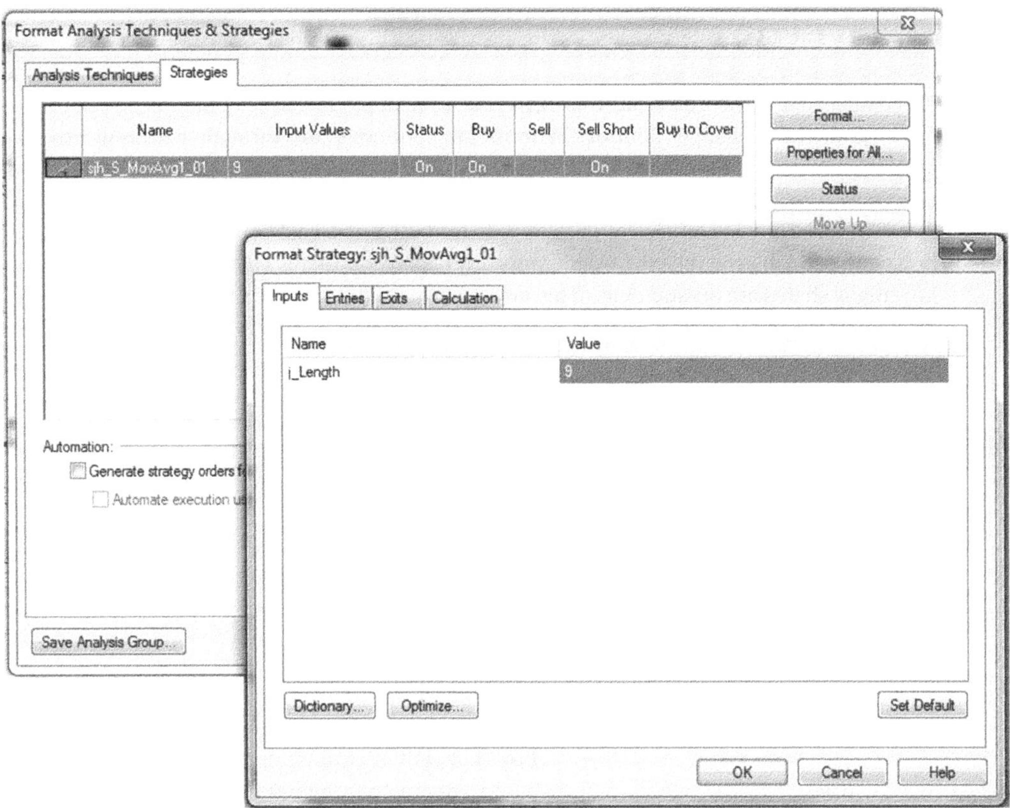

FIGURE 8.1 Formatting Inputs

ASSIGNMENT STATEMENTS

The assignment statement assigns a value to a variable; it replaces the variable with calculations or an expression. An assignment statement is of the form "something = something else".

Assignment statements place the variable on the left side of the equal sign (=) and the replacement expression on the right.

EXAMPLE

```
VARS: OvrBotSold(0);
OvrBotSold=(High-Open)+(Close-Low)/2*Range;
```

EXAMPLE

```
Vars: Top(0), Bottom(0);
Top=Average(High, 20);
Bottom=Average(Low, 20);
```

DATA MANIPULATION

Remember that market data has four basic components to it. These components are transmitted from the exchange (floor or electronic) to your computer through various electronic networks, including the Internet. The four basic components of any time-compression bar are: Open, High, Low and Close. In addition to these four data elements, each trade has a size. The size (number of shares or contracts traded) gets translated into Volume. In addition, at the end of each day, the Open Interest for each contract is calculated, to let us know how many shares are outstanding. (This information cannot be used on bars of shorter compression than daily.)

PRINT STATEMENTS

The full format of the **Print** statement is:

```
Print([where],"text",information[formatting]);
```

The parameters in the print statement are:

where	the optional destination of your print statements (Print Log, File, or Printer)
"text"	the alphanumeric information to print
information [formatting]	the variables or print and their formatting

If no "where" is specified, the output will be sent to the **Print Log** by default.

The parameters may be any valid string expression, numeric series, or numeric expression separated by commas.

By default the information from a **Print** statement is sent to the Print Log in TS 4.0 and to the Debug Window in ProSuite 2000i, which in the latest builds of TS is called the **EasyLanguage Output Bar** under the **Print tab.**

To output to a file or printer, use the **File** and **Print** statements respectively with the Print statement.

The **Print** statement was discussed pretty completely in Chapter 7 under Debugging. The format is again provided here for convenience.

EXAMPLE

If you wanted to send the date, time, and close information to the Print Log or Message Log when you applied an analysis technique, you could use this syntax:

```
Print(Date, Time, Close);
```

To send the same information to an ASCII file named file.txt, you could use this syntax:

```
Print(File("c:\file.txt"),Date, Time, Close);
```

To send the same information to the printer, you could use this syntax:

```
Print(Printer, Date, Time, Close);
```

Formatting in the Print Statement

The formatting, in square brackets, [and], is optional; don't confuse these square brackets with the square brackets that mean "bars ago". In this case the formatting just means that you may specify it if you want, or allow TS to use the default formatting.

Decimal Places

Formatting your information, especially data such as date or time, makes reading your output easier. The default format for EasyLanguage is to give each number two places after the decimal. For an illustrative example, let's say that the date is September 20, 1999, the time is 10:00 am, and the closing price is 92 1/16th. Thus, the date September 20, 2010, would be printed as 1100920.00.

In fact, the result of the print statement

```
Print(Date, Time, Close);
```

would be

```
1100920.001000.0092.11
```

It is not very readable, is it? I prefer my dates to look like 1100920. In order to achieve this, we can use the optional formatting to tell EasyLanguage we want six places to the left of the decimal and no places to the right of the decimal, as such:

```
Print(Date:6:0, Time, Close);
```

The printout then becomes

```
11009201000.0092.11
```

Still unreadable because there is no space between the date and the time. Let's put some spaces in. Likewise with the time information, I prefer to display 10:00 a.m. as 1000, rather than 1000.00. So, again I would format the print statement, this time as

```
Print(Date:6:0, " ", Time:4:0," ", Close);
```

And this time the printout then becomes

```
1100920 1000 92.11
```

The closing price, however, is another matter. Stock prices are sometimes quoted in 64ths. In that case, I would like to see all the decimal places, namely 1/64th is 0.015625. Since the default for the print statement is two decimal places, our closing price has been truncated. Thus, for closing prices I want to specify six places after the decimal. Now the print statement changes form again, to:

```
Print(Date:6:0, " ", Time:4:0," ", Close:4:6);
```

And my output takes the form:

```
1100920 1000 92.105625
```

Labels for Readability

You might want your print output to call out the various fields, so you can interpret them at a glance. Using the optional "information" part of the Print statement takes care of this. Let's use some **literals** or **string information** to make our report a little prettier. A literal (aka **string** or **text**) is enclosed in quotes and will be printed exactly as you typed it in.

For instance, if I change the print statement to

```
Print("Date=",Date:6:0, " ", Time:4:0," ", Close:4:6);
```

my output takes the form:

```
Date=1100920 1000 92.105625
```

That's better, but the time and closing price also need labels. This time we add more literals to distinguish each field. Note that I have moved the space into the labels, as a space before the label word.

```
Print("Date= ",Date:6:0, " Time= " Time:4:0, " Close= ",
Close:4:6);
```

And my output now becomes

```
Date= 1100920 Time= 1000 Close= 92.105625
```

Play with the formatting and the use of literals. You can create any kind of report you can imagine.

IF...THEN STATEMENTS

The **IF . . . THEN** statement uses **conditions** and **consequences** to cause an action to happen or not happen, depending on the value of the condition.

If the condition is **true** the consequence happens. If the condition is **false** the consequence does not happen. **IF . . . THEN** statements take this form:

```
IF condition THEN consequence;
```

Conditions can be complex or simple. Conditions can contain other conditions.

EXAMPLE

```
IF High = High[1] THEN BUY at market;
IF High > High[1] THEN Condition1 = True;
IF Close > Open THEN UpBar = True;
IF CurrentBar > Value1
      THEN Value2 = CurrentBar - BarNumber;
```

Conditions in an **IF . . . THEN** statement often use relational operators, covered in Chapter 5, Basic Math.

PLOT STATEMENTS

The **Plot statement** tells TradeStation that you want to plot something on your chart. TradeStation then plots the value of the expression you have specified. Plot statements are valid in **indicators only.** You may not use the plot statement in a strategy or function.

The general format of the Plot statement is

```
PlotN(value,text)
```

where `value` is the expression you wish plotted and `text` is a word or phase that will appear in your legend.

You are allowed to use as many as 99 Plot statements in one indicator, and the Plot statements are numbered Plot1, Plot2, Plot3, . . . , Plot99.

Beginning with TS2000i the Plot statement has additional, optional inputs with which you may specify foreground color, background color, and the width of the line you will be applying.

The full Plot statement, with optional inputs, looks like this:

```
PlotN(Expression[,"<PlotName>"[,ForeColor[,Default[,
Width]]]]);
where
```

`N` is a number from 1 to 99 specifying the plot number

`Expression` is the value to be plotted (can be a function or calculation)

`PlotName` is the text name given to the plot
`ForeColor` corresponds to the numeric value or EasyLanguage reserved word corresponding to the foreground color you want to assign to a plot
`Width` is a numeric expression representing the plot's width when applying the indicator to a chart
`Default` is a placeholder reserved for future use

EXAMPLE

If you wanted to plot a variable, say Value1, on a chart with default values for color and width, you could use this syntax:

```
Plot1(Value1, "Value1");
```

or

```
Plot1(Value1, "Value1", Default, Default, Default);
```

If you wanted to play a variable, Value1, on a chart in blue with a line thickness of 3, you could use this syntax:

```
Plot2(Value1, "Value1", Blue, Default, 3);
```

EXAMPLE

The MACD indicator could be specified as:

```
Input: FastMA(12),SlowMA(26),MacdMA(9);
Plot1(MACD(C,FastMA,SlowMA),"MACD",blue,2);
Plot2(XAverage(MACD(C,FastMA,SlowMA),MacdMA),"MACDAvg",
DarkGreen,2);
```

FURTHER READING AND REFERENCE

For more practice in programming conventions, I recommend the following books. Study them and try to program the examples.

Introduction to Symbolic Logic by Karl J. Smith. Out of print but possibly available at your local library or through Amazon.com's out-of-print locator.

Symbolic Logic by Irving M. Copi.

EasyLanguage Essentials: Programmers Guide by TradeStation and available for free in .pdf at its Web site.

CHAPTER 9

Ifs, Ands, and Buts

In This Chapter

INTRODUCTION

Possibly the most important concept to grasp in learning EasyLanguage is the **IF . . . THEN** statement. You really need to be good at this one. The only way to be really good at it is to be proficient at symbolic logic. That's what this chapter is about. We examined the **IF . . . THEN** structure as one of the statement types in Chapter 8, but this chapter will go further into the use of the statement as it concerns the trader.

SYMBOLIC LOGIC

If you use the Internet to search for information, you probably have used symbolic logic. You might not have realized it, however. If I wanted to find information about economic indicators and bonds on the Internet, I might say:

```
SEARCH FOR: economic AND indicators AND bonds
```

Probably the result of this search would yield thousands of matches. Many of the matches would not be what I am looking for. For instance, the search would probably yield "bail bonds"—hopefully not something I am looking for.

To tell the search engine not to give us bail bonds as a match, we could perform this search:

```
SEARCH FOR: (economic AND indicators AND bonds) AND NOT bail
```

Using AND as the operator doesn't present much in the way of difficult logic. Two other concepts, OR and NOT, raise the bar just a bit higher. These three operators are called Boolean operators, after George Boole. Boolean algebra is the algebra of logic.

TRUTH TABLES

For a statement containing expressions separated by **AND**s to be true, **all of the expressions must be true.** For a statement containing expressions separated by **OR**s to be true, **at least one of the expressions must be true.**

If I say "Sunny is 6 feet tall AND has red hair," the statement is true, because both expressions are true. If I say "Sunny is 6 feet tall AND has green hair," the statement is false, because both expressions must be true, and I do not have green hair. If I say "Sunny is 5 feet tall OR has red hair," the expression is again true, because one of the expressions is true: I have red hair. OR is a less stringent operator than AND.

A quick and easy way to evaluate conditional statements is by looking up the answer in a "truth table," as seen in Figures 9.1 and 9.2.

	OPERATOR		RESULT
T	AND	T	T
T	AND	F	F
F	AND	T	F
F	AND	F	F

FIGURE 9.1 AND Truth Table

	OPERATOR		RESULT
T	OR	T	T
T	OR	F	T
F	OR	T	T
F	OR	F	F

FIGURE 9.2 OR Truth Table

EXAMPLE

Again using the data from DIS, presented (in part) here for convenience, let's evaluate some conditional statements using the truth tables. Don't forget that C and C[0] refer to the most recent bar, the bar of "now". So, C would be on the date 10/14/88 in Figure 9.3.

Date	Open	High	Low	Close	Volume
09/30/88	16.219	16.344	15.781	16.219	4996400
10/07/88	16.219	16.375	15.844	16.375	6146000
10/14/88	16.375	16.688	16.250	16.531	6458000

FIGURE 9.3 Three Weeks of DIS

Cover up the right-hand column (Evaluation) in Figure 9.4 and try to calculate the answers yourself. See if you come up with the same answers as I do.

	Condition	Evaluation
1.	C > H[1]	T
2.	High = High of 1 Bar Ago	F
3.	H > H[1] AND H[1] > H[2]	T
4.	O[1] < C[1] OR O < C	T

FIGURE 9.4 Evaluating Conditions

To drill yourself on these issues, use the **ExpertCommentary** statement to see your conditional statement evaluated bar by bar.

DECISIONS (CONDITIONS)

IF. . .THEN

If "something" happens, then we will do "consequence" is the focus of this chapter. More specifically, it is the "something" we will tackle here. The "something" is called a condition.

In Chapter 8 we talked about the form of the statement itself, from a syntax perspective. In the first part of this chapter we have been talking about conditions from a symbolic logic perspective. Conditions always evaluate to True or False.

If it is raining outside, then we will take the umbrella. The condition in this sentence is "it is raining outside." The consequence is what we do if the condition is true—the "something else." By default, there is an implied second consequence in the sentence. The implied part is what happens if the condition is false. In this case, the implied consequence is we don't take the umbrella.

If we wanted to be very precise in our statement, with no assumptions as to what is implied, we would write:

```
IF (it is raining outside) THEN (we will take the
        umbrella) ELSE (we will not take the umbrella);
```

Statements like that are called **IF . . . THEN . . . ELSE** statements. In the example, the ELSE is redundant, since it is assumed to be NOT the first consequence.

A NOT truth table is pretty simple. (See Figure 9.5.) IF the statement is true, NOT the statement is false. In symbolic logic notation you will often see the tilde (~) symbol or the prime (') symbol used to denote NOT. For instance, you might see ~T=F, or you might see T=F'.

p	NOTp
T	F
F	F

FIGURE 9.5 Truth Tables

We are still waiting for the NOT logic to be installed in EasyLanguage. The word NOT is reserved but is not used yet. This is one of those areas we have to work around, but it is nevertheless important for you to understand.

The work-around is obvious. When you want to say "it is not the case that the high is greater than the open", symbolically ~(High > Open), you would simply look for the value of High > Open to be false.

IF. . .THEN. . .ELSE

The **IF . . . THEN . . . ELSE** structure in EasyLanguage is used when the second consequence is not just the reverse of the first consequence. For instance, if I wanted to take my umbrella when it was raining outside but wanted to stay indoors if it was not raining outside (humor me, I'm Irish), then I would need to employ the ELSE structure. A statement like that would be written

```
IF (it is raining outside) THEN (we will take the umbrella)
        ELSE (stay indoors);
```

IF. . .THEN. . .ELSE statements become enormously useful when combined with the **BEGIN** structure, which we will discuss in Chapter 10.

EXAMPLE

This example is charted for you in Figure 9.6, below.

```
IF Close < Open
        THEN SELL at (Close - 1 point) or lower
        ELSE BUY at market;
```

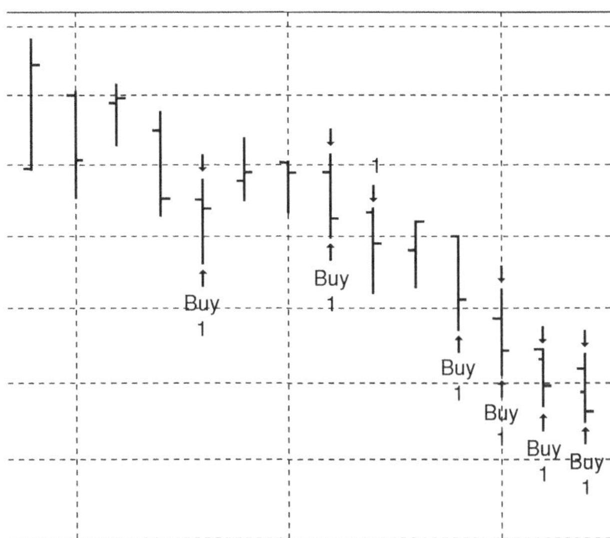

FIGURE 9.6 Example Charted

Notice, as always, I prefer the liberal use of parentheses to avoid confusion. OK, this is a nonsense example, and of course it loses money if you test it. That's not the point; remember, this book is about learning to program.

REAL-LIFE EXAMPLE

While beginning this book I exchanged the following emails with a new contact. Her problem will serve as a good example for this chapter.

From: Maryfisch@aol.com
Sent: Thursday, August 19, 1999 6:11am

Dear Sunny:

I am a recent user of TradeStation and have a lot of trouble using EasyLanguage. Are there any Internet newsgroups that you know of that would entertain basic as well as advanced questions?

Also, I've been searching for a reference book beyond what is included with TradeStation. Any ideas? I think TradeStation can be useful, but find I am wasting a lot of time trying to figure out how to code what I consider very simple ideas. Any information would be greatly appreciated.

By the way, your two books sit on my desk constantly and are beginning to show the wear and tear of constant use! Thanks; hope you have more books in the pipeline.

From: sunny@moneymentor.com
Sent: Thursday, August 19, 1999

Nice to hear from you, Mary.

Thanks for your kind words. Yes, the pipeline is full. I just completed *Electronic Day Trading 101* which was to be released October 22, 1999 at Barnes & Noble and all other major bookstores.

I'm about 3/4 through with *EasyLanguage Step-by-Step* which probably is exactly what you want.

Wanna help me?

Tell me the questions you have, and I'll answer them for you, and in the book.

Thanks,
Sunny

From: Maryfisch@aol.com
Sent: August 24, 1999 4:31 am

I would like to be able to enter on the same bar that confirms a signal. For example, conditions 1, 2, and 3 are met but I only want to enter on tomorrow's open if it is below today's close. Seems from reading the *ELA Users Guide* that it is not possible, but that can't be, can it?

From: sunny@moneymentor.com
Sent: August 24, 1999 8:16 am

Mary,
Try this. Let me know if it does what you want.

```
Condition1=H>H[1];
Condition2=H[1]>H[2];
IF Condition1 AND Condition2
            THEN BUY tomorrow C - (1 point) STOP;
```

From: Maryfisch@aol.com
Sent: August 31, 1999 6:31 am

Sunny,

Thanks so much for your help. It worked, it worked!! Amazing how something so basic is not covered in the *TS EasyLanguage User's Guide*. In writing your book, don't hesitate to get very basic. I think that TS is almost too powerful; I'm sure there is a lot it can do that many people don't realize. I consider myself pretty computer literate but I get easily bogged down trying to figure out pretty elementary things in TS. Used to do a lot of Excel/handtesting but it's just not that efficient.

Anyway, thanks again. I have many more questions but am currently on vacation so will be back to you when I return. Thanks for taking the time to help me.

Mary Fischer

What Happened?

What did I do with Mary Fischer's word problem? I read the paragraph twice. Then I slowly broke it down into components. When I thought I understood the components I began to sketch out pseudo-steps on my yellow pad of paper. Only after I analyzed the pseudo-steps to see if I was doing what she wanted did I begin to put code into TradeStation.

Why can't Mary readily solve this problem? Probably because she doesn't know how to examine tomorrow's open, decide on whether it is lower than today's close, and then enter on a price that is already past. Once the open happens, it is history and you can't go back and execute a trade at a historical price.

So, we need to set up an order that buys instantly if the opening price is any amount below today's close. Those type orders are called stop orders. That is, I will have a stop in place before the open, so that if the stop is hit the order instantly becomes a market order. That's about as close as we can get.

To learn more about the different types of orders you can place with EasyLanguage, refer to Chapter 13, Buying and Selling.

The smallest move that can be made by a trading vehicle (stock, bond, commodity. . .) is a point or a tick. In TradeStation a point is defined as **the minimal interval value a symbol can move.**

Now the only problem is how to write Mary's example in EasyLanguage. Again, to me the most important statement for Mary is the IF. . .THEN structure. IF (Mary's problem happens) THEN BUY (at Mary's entry). Take a look at the code in the email. That's what she wanted.

MORE ABOUT IF AND IF . . . THEN . . . ELSE

In order to use an If. . . Then. . . Else statement, a Begin. . . End statement must follow Then, as in the example below.

EXAMPLE

```
IF Condition1 THEN
 {Your Code Goes Here};
```

If is used here to start the **If . . . Then** statement. The `Your Code Goes Here` code will be executed if `Condition1` returns a value of **True.** If `Condition1` is **False,** the `Your Code Goes Here` code will not be executed.

EXAMPLE

```
If Condition1 And Condition2 Then Begin
   {Your Code Line1}
   {Your Code Line2, etc.}
End
Else Begin
   {Your Code Line3}
   {Your Code Line4, etc.}
End;
```

Notice the placement of the semicolon in the example above. It doesn't come until the end of the sequence. However, not shown in this example is your code, which will likely contain semicolons of its own. Don't get them confused or your code won't verify.

If is used in the preceding example to start the **If . . . Then . . . Else** statement. The `Line1` and `Line2` code will be executed if `Condition1` and `Condition2` return a value of **True.** If `Condition1 or Condition2` is **False,** the `Line3` and `Line4` code will be executed.

EXAMPLE

Figure 9.7 presents a beautiful section of code from the EasyLanguage Library. The strategy is named _**HistoricalEntry.**

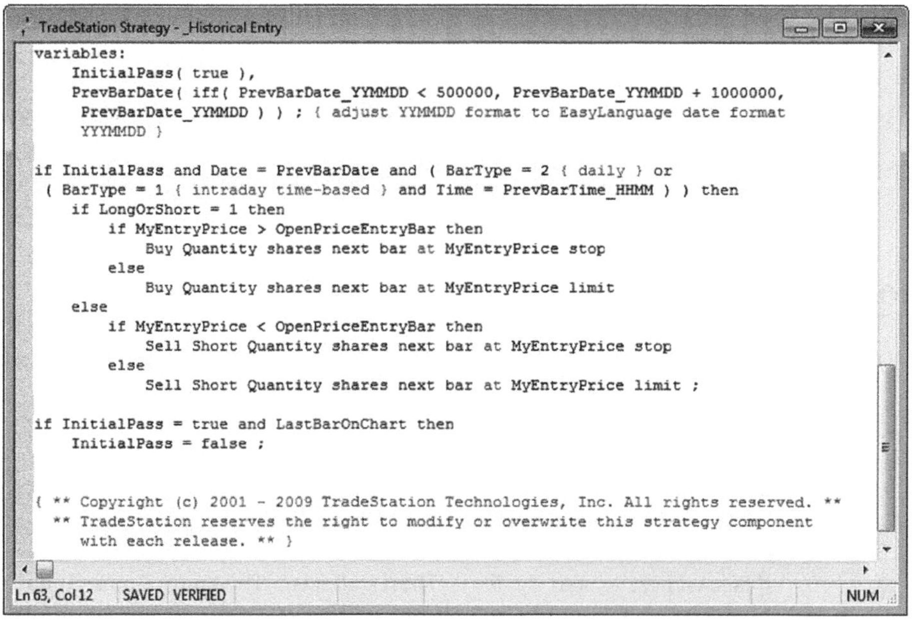

TradeStation Strategy - _Historical Entry

```
variables:
    InitialPass( true ),
    PrevBarDate( iff( PrevBarDate_YYMMDD < 500000, PrevBarDate_YYMMDD + 1000000,
     PrevBarDate_YYMMDD ) ) ; { adjust YYMMDD format to EasyLanguage date format
     YYYMMDD }

if InitialPass and Date = PrevBarDate and ( BarType = 2 { daily } or
 ( BarType = 1 { intraday time-based } and Time = PrevBarTime_HHMM ) ) then
    if LongOrShort = 1 then
        if MyEntryPrice > OpenPriceEntryBar then
            Buy Quantity shares next bar at MyEntryPrice stop
        else
            Buy Quantity shares next bar at MyEntryPrice limit
    else
        if MyEntryPrice < OpenPriceEntryBar then
            Sell Short Quantity shares next bar at MyEntryPrice stop
        else
            Sell Short Quantity shares next bar at MyEntryPrice limit ;

if InitialPass = true and LastBarOnChart then
    InitialPass = false ;


{ ** Copyright (c) 2001 - 2009 TradeStation Technologies, Inc. All rights reserved. **
  ** TradeStation reserves the right to modify or overwrite this strategy component
     with each release. ** }
```

Ln 63, Col 12 SAVED VERIFIED NUM

FIGURE 9.7 Code from _**HistoricalEntry**

IFF

There is another EasyLanguage function to deal with Boolean Algebra **True** and **False** values. It works much like the **IF** statement in Excel and other spreadsheet programs. It is called **IFF,** which in mathematics means **If and Only If.**

The **IFF** function is used to conditionally return one of two specified numeric values. You pass the function three inputs: the condition to test, the value you want returned if the test is true, and the value you want returned if the test is false. Its syntax is:

```
IFF(Test, TrueVal, FalseVal)
```

where

Test	Specifies a conditional expression to check (such as Close > Open)
TrueVal	Sets a numeric value to return if Test expression is true
FalseVal	Sets a numeric value to return if Test expression is false

The function returns the numeric value of TrueVal if Test is true and the numeric value of FalseVal if Test is false.

EXAMPLE

Assigns to Value1 the number `-1` if `Close>Open` is true or the number `-1` if `Close>Open` is false.

```
Value1 = IFF(Close>Open,1,-1);
```

By using the **IFF** function, you are able to evaluate one or more conditions in the Test input expression, returning one numeric value if Test is true and returning another numeric value if Test is false. It avoids lengthy setups of **If**. . .**Then**. . .**Else** conditions for just this sort of binary situation.

FURTHER READING AND REFERENCE

For more practice in symbolic logic, I recommend the following books. Study them and try to program the examples.

Introduction to Symbolic Logic by Karl J. Smith. Out of print, but possibly available at your local library or through Amazon.com's out-of-print locator.

Symbolic Logic by Irving M. Copi.

Mathematics and Plausible Reasoning by George Polya.

An Introduction to Symbolic Logic by Susanne Katherina Langer.

Introduction to Symbolic Logic and Its Applications by Rudolf Carnap.

CHAPTER 10

Begin and End (Block Statements)

In This Chapter

- Introduction
- Block Statements
- Nested Block Statements
- Working on Our Strategy

INTRODUCTION

This chapter and the next both cover intermediate EasyLanguage structures. These structures, **BEGIN . . . END** and **LOOPS,** are powerful tools and take you into the next level of programming. Both structures are simply a way of saying "do this until I say stop."

When you become comfortable with these two structures you will find yourself using them frequently.

BLOCK STATEMENTS

A Block statement is simply an IF {condition} THEN {consequence} structure in which we want more than one consequence based on the same IF.

Just as it sounds, a block statement is a group of statements that act together as a block. Programmers often indent the block of statements together for easy reading.

The form of a block statement looks like Figure 10.1.

```
IF {Condition} THEN BEGIN
        {the block of code goes here}
END;
```

FIGURE 10.1 Block Statement

You, of course, will supply the {`Condition`} and {`the block of code goes here`} part. When I am testing strategies to see whether they work, I like to compare apples to apples statistically. One tool for getting there is to close the last trade of each system, so there is never an open trade on the performance report. The open trades don't get counted in the statistics.

The code for closing the final trade is best accomplished in a **block** statement, as in Figure 10.2.

```
IF LastBarOnChart AND MarketPosition<>0 THEN BEGIN
   IF MarketPosition=+1 THEN ExitLong;
   IF MarketPosition=-1 THEN ExitShort;
END;
```

FIGURE 10.2 Close Last Trade

Block statements make your code more efficient and easier to read. Let me show you, in Figure 10.3, how this code would look without a block statement.

```
IF LastBarOnChart AND MarketPosition<>0 AND MarketPosition=1 THEN ExitLong;
IF LastBarOnChart AND MarketPosition<>0 AND MarketPosition=-1 THEN ExitShort;
```

FIGURE 10.3 Without the Block

That's not so bad, because there are only two lines of code in the block. Notice that the computer has to evaluate the expression "IF LastBarOnChart" twice, however. That slows down the computer just a little bit. When you get large blocks of code, containing 10 or 20 statements, the duplication of IF statements becomes cumbersome and inefficient, actually slowing your computer down quite a bit.

Figure 10.4 shows a block of code I use frequently in my own work. What? you say. That's not code. It does nothing. You are right, and you are wrong; it does two things. When I first begin to program a block statement, I copy and paste this into place so I don't forget the "END;" statement. Otherwise it is too easy to get 5 or 10 lines of code down and forget the **END;** especially when you are programming nested blocks (blocks within blocks).

```
IF Length1 < Length2 THEN BEGIN
        xx
END;
```

FIGURE 10.4 Block Template

When I am working on an idea and want to leave a placeholder, I use "xx". I use the "xx" to keep me from having writer's block; I just put in "xx" and keep going. Furthermore, the "xx" allows me to be certain I have the semicolon and the END in the right place before the coding gets more complex. I then come back and fill in the code where the "xx" is, removing it and filling in the blank.

Why else do I use the block of code in Figure 10.4 frequently? Because when using the optimization feature of system testing, TradeStation considers the combination (9,18) valid, as well as the combination (18,9). If I am testing for a moving average crossover, I only want to evaluate combinations where the shorter moving average crosses over the longer moving average. The block of code in Figure 10.4 eliminates the erroneous combinations. The block of code will not execute unless the lengths are in the "right" order. With this code in place, it is much easier to evaluate optimization reports.

The block statement always starts with an **IF . . . THEN** statement. The purpose of the block statement is to use a certain block of code only when "something" happens. To determine whether the something has happened, we use the **IF . . . THEN** statement.

Remember, there is an assumption with the **IF. . .THEN** statement. The assumption is about the **ELSE** clause. IF "something" is true THEN EasyLanguage will do the block, ELSE EasyLanguage will not do the block.

The block statement can save you numerous steps. When your task has several steps you want to perform if the condition is true, structuring the steps as a block allows you to state the **IF. . .THEN** part only once.

For instance, the code in Figures 10.5 and 10.6 would produce the same results.

```
IF Length1<Length2 THEN Value1=ADX(9);
IF Length1<Length2 THEN Value2=Value2+1;
IF Length1<Length2 THEN Value3=Value2/Value1;
```

FIGURE 10.5 Without the Block

```
IF Length1<Length2 THEN BEGIN
   Value1=ADX(9);
   Value2=Value2+1;
   Value3=Value2/Value1;
END;
```

FIGURE 10.6 With the Block

Which do you think is prettier? Which do you think is more efficient in the computer?

Writing the code in a block makes it easier to understand, and also reduces the work your computer must do. Block statements work to make your code less confusing. Blocks are particularly useful when you want to evaluate additional conditions.

Let's examine a routine from Arthur Putt's *Using EasyLanguage* (see Figure 10.7). On page 17, he gives a routine that plots support and resistance based on standard floor trader formulas. You might find the code useful, and it is a clear example of using block statements.

```
VARS: pHigh(0), pLow(99999), Pivot(0), Support(0), pC(0), Resist(0);
IF Time=Sess1StartTime+BarInterval THEN BEGIN
  pHigh=High;
  pLow=Low;
END;

IF High>pHigh THEN pHigh=High;
IF Low<pLow THEN pLow=Low;

IF Time=Sess1EndTime THEN BEGIN
  PC=Close;
  Pivot=(pHigh+pLow+pC)/3;
  Support=(Pivot*2)-pHigh;
  Resist=(Pivot*2)-pLow;
END;

Plot1(Support[1],"Support");
Plot2(Resist[1],"Resistance");
```

FIGURE 10.7 From Arthur Putt's *Using EasyLanguage*

Notice that Putt uses the **IF . . . THEN** statement four times in this small amount of code. Of those four times, he constructs two blocks of **IF . . . THEN . . . BEGIN** code. Figure 10.8 is a chart of Putt's coded indicator.

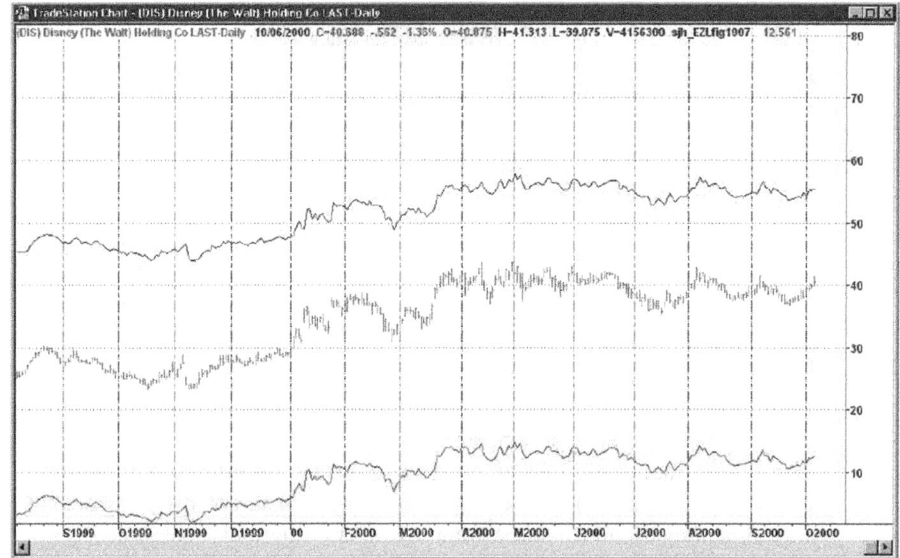

FIGURE 10.8 Putt's Support and Resistance Indicator

Contact Murray Ruggiero (see Appendix H) if you would like to have this code (and lots more) on disk or CD.

NESTED BLOCK STATEMENTS

You may place block statements within block statements. These blocks within blocks are called "nested blocks." Nested blocks allow you to evaluate additional conditional statements. You might think of nested blocks as "if something and if something more and if something even more, then. . ."

Nested blocks make your code look pretty if you indent them properly, as you should for readability. (See Figure 10.9.)

```
IF Length1 < Length2 THEN BEGIN
   IF ADX(9)>ADX(9)[1] THEN BEGIN
      IF Average(C,Length1)>Average(C,Length2) THEN BEGIN
         BUY 5 shares at Market;
      END;
   END;
END;
```

FIGURE 10.9 Nested Blocks

In each case, if the condition is true, TradeStation will run the block of code, down to the END statement; if the condition is false, TradeStation will skip down to the END statement, ignoring the block of code, and continue onward.

In Figure 10.9 we are first asking whether the shorter length input is actually shorter than the longer one (for cases in which we might be running an optimization). The second IF tests to see if the **Average Directional Movement Index** (**ADX**) is rising from yesterday to today, or from the previous bar to the current bar in the case of other than daily data.

The third IF block asks whether one moving average is greater than another moving average, based on the inputs `Length1` and `Length2`.

Nested all the way inside these three blocks is the single line of code that does the buying. It gets executed **only if all** the conditions preceding it are true.

Else Statements

- **ELSE** is an optional part of the **IF . . . THEN** structure. If **ELSE** is not specified, it is assumed to be the negation of the consequence.
- **ELSE** is used to execute a section of code based on a condition that has returned a value of **False.**
- **ELSE** can be used only following an **IF . . . THEN** statement.

Just as in setting up **IF . . . THEN** block statements, I like to use a template wherever possible. Templates 1 and 2 are the two templates I use for creating **IF . . . THEN . . . ELSE** blocks. At this level of complexity, your code can get confusing and you can have difficulty getting it to verify. Use templates wherever you can.

TEMPLATE 1

```
IF Condition1 THEN
   {Your Code Line1}
      ELSE
         BEGIN
      {Your Code Line2}
               END;
```

ELSE is used here to begin the code that will be executed if `Condition1` returns a value of **False.** No semicolon should be used after the single line of code following **THEN.**

TEMPLATE 2

```
IF Condition1 AND Condition2 THEN
        BEGIN
        {Your Code Line1};
        {Your Code Line2, etc.};
END
ELSE
              BEGIN
              {Your Code Line3};
              {Your Code Line4, etc.};
              END;
```

ELSE is used here to begin the block of code that will be executed if either `Condition1` or `Condition2` returns a value of **False.** In other words, the stringent **AND** condition is not met. No semicolon should be used after the word **END** preceding the **ELSE** statement.

EXAMPLE

```
IF Close > H[1] THEN
   BUY
ELSE BEGIN
   IF C < L[1] THEN
      SELL SHORT;
END;
```

If the current closing price breaks above yesterday's high, then buy the breakout; otherwise, if the current closing price breaks below yesterday's low, then go short.

The chart of this little strategy is displayed in Figure 10.10. The Strategy Performance Report associated with this strategy is in Figure 10.11. It's not much, but it illustrates the use of blocks. And, hey, it's not negative!

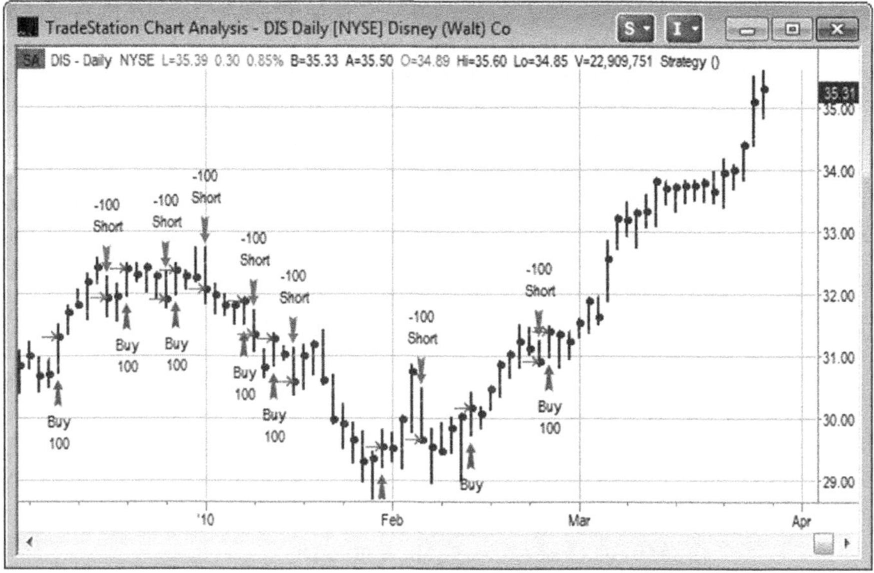

FIGURE 10.10 Strategy

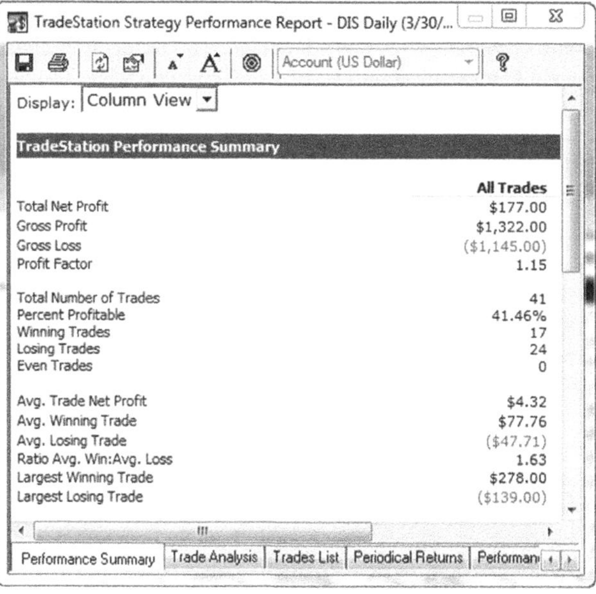
TradeStation Strategy Performance Report - DIS Daily (3/30/...

Account (US Dollar)

Display: Column View

TradeStation Performance Summary

	All Trades
Total Net Profit	$177.00
Gross Profit	$1,322.00
Gross Loss	($1,145.00)
Profit Factor	1.15
Total Number of Trades	41
Percent Profitable	41.46%
Winning Trades	17
Losing Trades	24
Even Trades	0
Avg. Trade Net Profit	$4.32
Avg. Winning Trade	$77.76
Avg. Losing Trade	($47.71)
Ratio Avg. Win:Avg. Loss	1.63
Largest Winning Trade	$278.00
Largest Losing Trade	($139.00)

Performance Summary | Trade Analysis | Trades List | Periodical Returns | Performan

FIGURE 10.11 Strategy Performance Report

EXAMPLE

Some people think there is a bias toward Mondays and Fridays being volatile trading days. More specifically, they say that if the market begins to move on a Monday, it will move fast and that you should only buy on a Friday if the market proves itself.

What does that mean? That's up to interpretation and also to historical testing, which will develop robust numbers for the ranges to examine. For the meantime, we will assume that if the market moves more than x% of yesterday's range on a Monday, we will be willing to buy, but in order to be buyers on Friday, we require y% of the range to be broken.

NOTE: For declared variables and inputs, I often put my middle initial (j) as the first letter of the variable's name followed by the underline character (_). I use this convention to avoid any conflict with EasyLanguage's reserved words.

```
INPUTS: j_X(100), j_Y(200);
IF DayOfWeek(Date) = 1 THEN BEGIN
   Value1 = j_X*(H[1] - L[1])+ C[1];
   IF Close > Value1 THEN BUY this bar;
       END;
IF DayOfWeek(Date) = 5 THEN BEGIN
   Value1 = j_Y*(H[1] - L[1])+ C[1];
   IF Close > Value1 THEN BUY this bar;
END;
```

Again, this example is not to show you the world's most successful strategy but to teach you to program with EasyLanguage. The associated chart and Performance Report are shown in Figures 10.11 and 10.12. They give you a basis to build from.

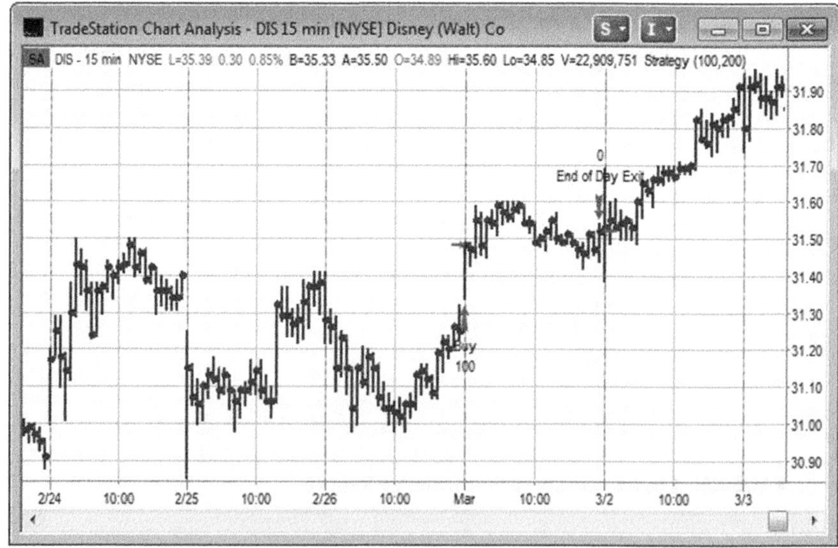

FIGURE 10.12 Trade on Mondays or Fridays

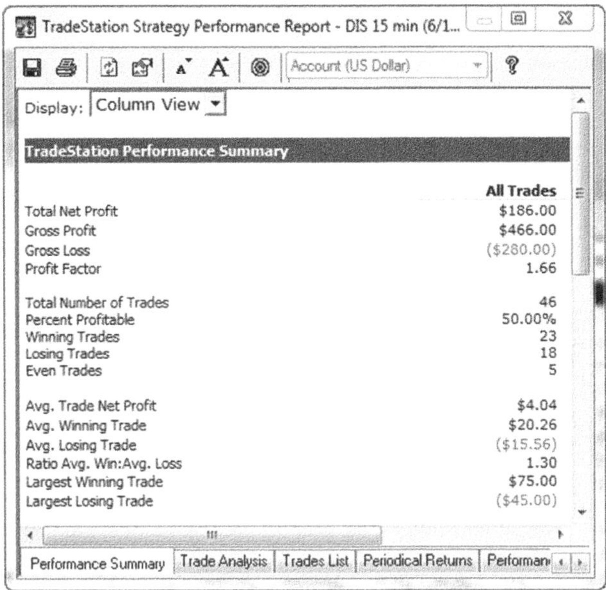

FIGURE 10.13 Mondays or Fridays Performance Report

WORKING ON OUR STRATEGY

Let's take a break here and get back to work on the little strategy we started umpteen chapters ago. We had started a simple moving average indicator and accompanying strategy where buys and sells were initiated when the closing price crossed over the moving average. Now I want to change the condition that price moves over the moving average and instead have two moving averages crossing each other. This is called a **Moving Average Crossover** strategy. We previously had $1,273.00 Total Net Profit in the Strategy Performance Report. Let's see what happens as we refine the strategy.

For the life of me, I don't know why, but now that a week has passed since I wrote Chapter 3, the Strategy Performance Report gives a different Net Profit. No, it's not the addition of the days, because I've gone in to the settings and requested the same starting and ending dates and for a single year back. I do know that data gets corrected from the original transmissions as the Exchanges clean the data, so perhaps that's it. In any case, the TNP now shown in the Strategy Performance Report for the exact same code and parameters is $1,238.00. This kind of thing happens all the time in testing and trading, so get used to it. It is very difficult to compare apples to apples and conduct clear and concise research. My advice—just do the best you can and keep good logs; nothing will be the same when you start trading with real money anyway.

I'll display the chart again in Figure 10.14 and the Performance Report in Figure 10.15. The input parameter, j_ Length, is set to 6, MaxBarsBack = 50, and the data ranges from 3/23/2009 to 3/22/2010.

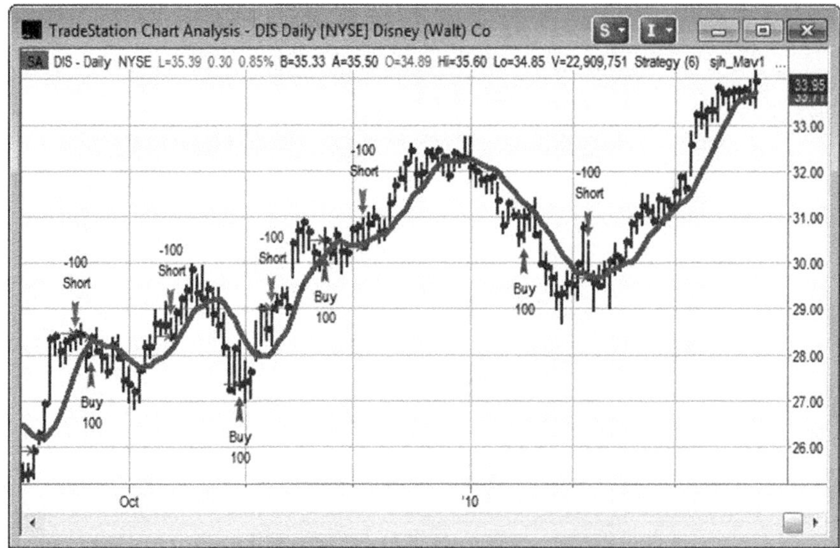

FIGURE 10.14 Our MAV1 Indicator with Strategy

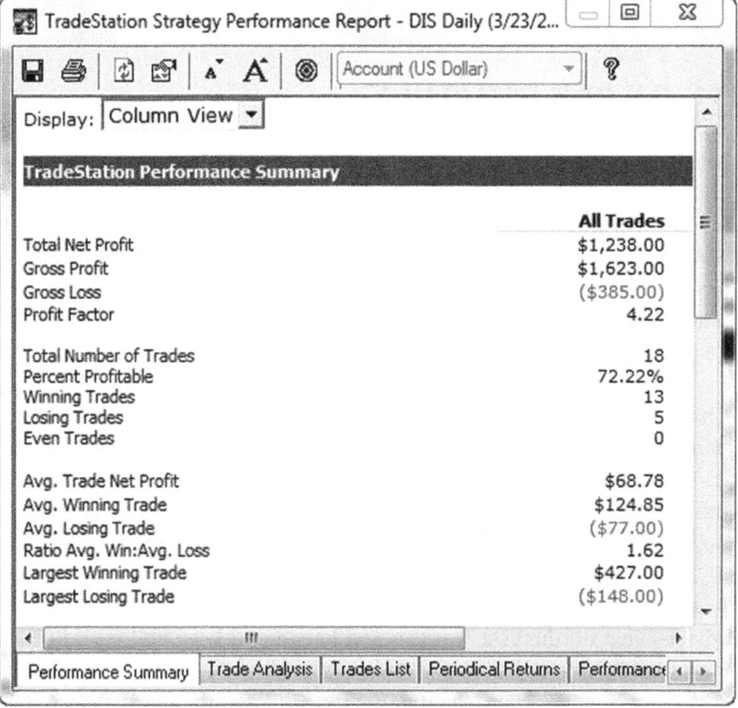

	All Trades
Total Net Profit	$1,238.00
Gross Profit	$1,623.00
Gross Loss	($385.00)
Profit Factor	4.22
Total Number of Trades	18
Percent Profitable	72.22%
Winning Trades	13
Losing Trades	5
Even Trades	0
Avg. Trade Net Profit	$68.78
Avg. Winning Trade	$124.85
Avg. Losing Trade	($77.00)
Ratio Avg. Win:Avg. Loss	1.62
Largest Winning Trade	$427.00
Largest Losing Trade	($148.00)

FIGURE 10.15 Strategy Performance Report

We are now going to change this single moving average with price crossover to a dual moving average strategy where prices don't cross-over, but rather the signal is taken from the moving averages crossing each other.

Our code will now look like that shown in Figure 10.16.

```
inputs:
   Price( Close ),
   FastLength( 9 ),
   SlowLength( 18 ) ;
variables:
   FastAvg( 0 ),
   SlowAvg( 0 ) ;
FastAvg = Average( Price, FastLength ) ;
SlowAvg = Average( Price, SlowLength ) ;
Plot1( FastAvg, "FastAvg", DarkGreen, default, 3 ) ;
Plot2( SlowAvg, "SlowAvg", Blue, default, 3) ;
```

FIGURE 10.16 Code for sjh_MAV2

Did you follow along? It's not really much of a surprise; we've gone over all these concepts. For this new routine we have added a second average and a second Plot statement. In the Plot statements we have used the long notation to specify the color and thickness. That's all.

Figure 10.17 presents the chart.

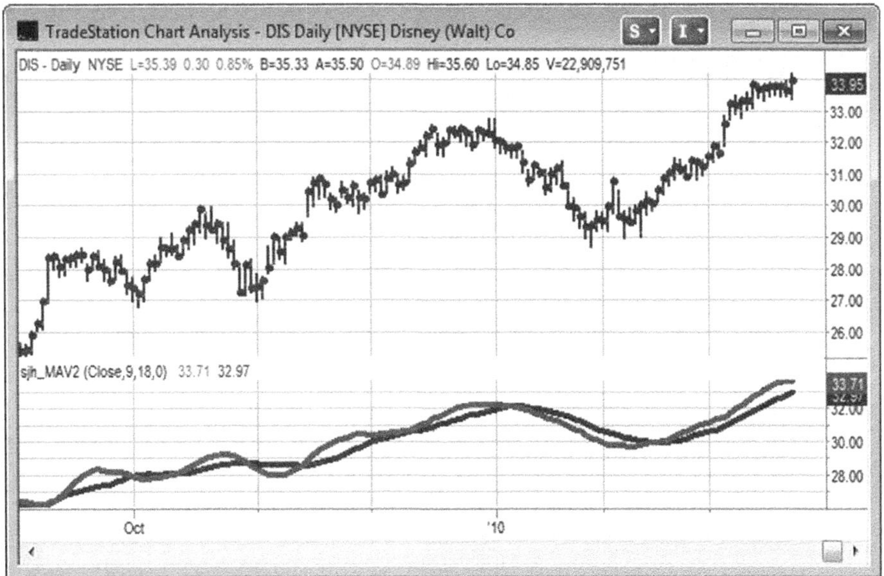

FIGURE 10.17 sjh_MAV2

Looks like there's a little problem here. The dual moving average indicator is in subgraph2 beneath the price bars. I like to have them on top of each other to make the crossover signals more apparent. To fix this, simply grab the moving averages, by clicking your mouse and not letting go, and drag them up to the subgraph with the blue bars on it. Now your chart should look like mine in Figure 10.18.

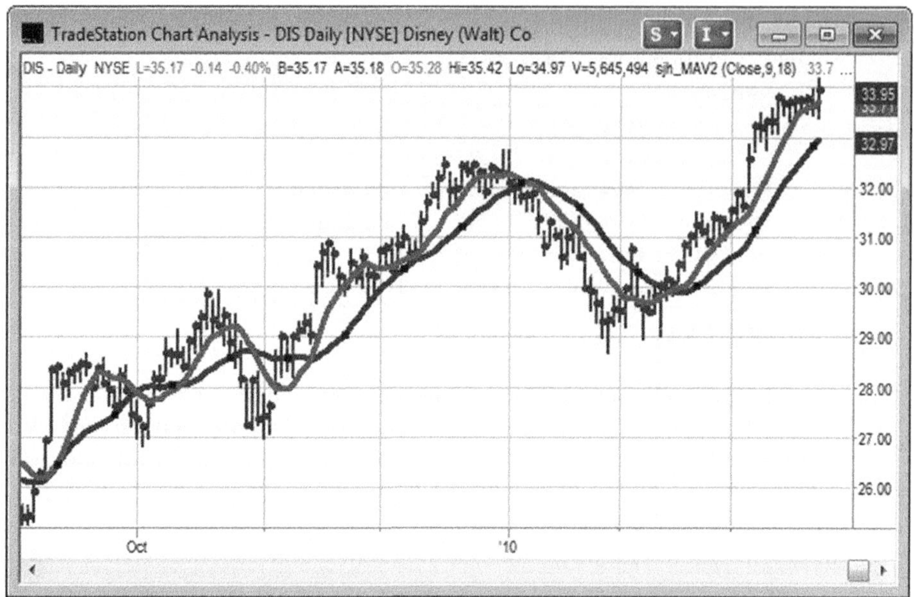

FIGURE 10.18 Moving Averages in Subgraph1

That blue moving average line is a little hard to see over the blue price bars. Let's use the fancy color specifications available in TradeStation and change the blue line to teal, my favorite color. The RGB value for teal is (0,153,144). We specify it like this:

```
Plot2(SlowAvg, "SlowAvg", RGB(0,153,144), default, 3);
```

I'm not going to show you the chart, as it's just a color change and this book may not end up being printed in color anyway. What I am going to show you instead is a small table of RGB color values. (See Figure 10.19.) To view the large table, in color, go to my Web site (www.moneymentor.com/TSME.html) and click on the link for a page of color values.

Creating the New Strategy

Creating a strategy from an indicator is almost as easy as cut-and-paste. Basically you will change the Plot statements to orders.

R - 000 G - 204 B - 000	R - 051 G - 255 B - 051	R - 102 G - 000 B - 102	R - 153 G - 051 B - 153	R - 204 G - 102 B - 204	R - 255 G - 153 B - 255
00FF00 R - 000 G - 255 B - 000	330033 R - 051 G - 000 B - 051	663366 R - 102 G - 051 B - 102	996699 R - 153 G - 102 B - 153	CC99CC R - 204 G - 153 B - 204	FFCCFF R - 255 G - 204 B - 255
00FF33 R - 000 G - 255 B - 051	330066 R - 051 G - 000 B - 102	663399 R - 102 G - 051 B - 153	9966CC R - 153 G - 102 B - 204	CC99FF R - 204 G - 153 B - 255	FFCC00 R - 255 G - 204 B - 000
00FF66 R - 000 G - 255 B - 102	330099 R - 051 G - 000 B - 153	6633CC R - 102 G - 051 B - 204	9966FF R - 153 G - 102 B - 255	CC9900 R - 204 G - 153 B - 000	FFCC33 R - 255 G - 204 B - 051
00FF99 R - 000 G - 255 B - 153	3300CC R - 051 G - 000 B - 204	6633FF R - 102 G - 051 B - 255	996600 R - 153 G - 102 B - 000	CC9933 R - 204 G - 153 B - 051	FFCC66 R - 255 G - 204 B - 102
00FFCC R - 000 G - 255 B - 204	3300FF R - 051 G - 000 B - 255	663300 R - 102 G - 051 B - 000	996633 R - 153 G - 102 B - 051	CC9966 R - 204 G - 153 B - 102	FFCC99 R - 255 G - 204 B - 153

FIGURE 10.19 Small Sampling of RGB Color Values

Click on the EasyLanguage icon, in the vertical menu bar at the left of your TS Desktop, and select **New EasyLanguage Document → Strategy.** This will open a new, hopefully blank, strategy document for you. If it is not blank, simply select all the code on the page by scrubbing it (click and drag) and press the Delete key.

Next, go to the indicator we have been working on (I named mine `sjh_MAV2`) and copy all the code from that document by scrubbing it and pressing **CTRL+C.** Then go back to the empty strategy and press **CTRL+V** for paste. All of the code should drop into place. Now save it by pressing **CTRL+S** and name it something like `sjh_S_MAV2Crossover`.

Now delete both Plot statements and replace them with the next code, which will place orders.

```
IF FastAvg > SlowAvg THEN BUY this bar;
IF FastAvg < SlowAvg THEN SELL SHORT this bar;
```

Did you remember to press F3 to verify the code? If not, do so now. Mine responded with **Verification successful.** How about yours?

The next step is to go back to the chart in question and insert the strategy. Using the menu sequence **Insert → Strategy,** select the strategy you have named something like `sjh_S_MAV2Crossover`. Press **OK** and it will instantly show up on your chart complete with buy and sell arrows. Do you remember how to change them to more readable colors and shapes? If not, double-click on an arrow to bring up the **Format** dialog box, select the **Strategies** tab, and click on **Format.** From here, select the **Entries** tab and change both Buy and Sell Short symbols and colors. Remember to check the **Default** box for both Buys and Sells so you won't have to change these selections every time you use this strategy.

My chart now looks like Figure 10.20.

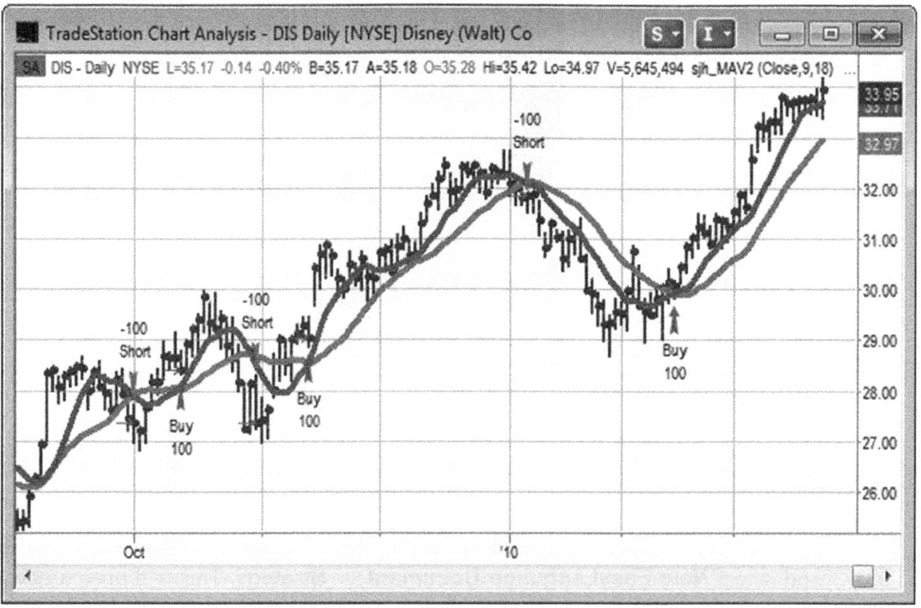

FIGURE 10.20 New Strategy on the Chart

The buys and sells now echo the movement of the market much better than the first strategy did. Yeah! Let's see what the Performance Report looks like to see if we really did any better. Take a look at Figure 10.21.

Being sure to activate the chart with the strategy, by clicking anywhere on the chart, go up to **View** and pull-down to **Strategy Performance Report,** or alternately press **ALT+SHIFT+P.**

Wow! It's worse. What happened? Compare the chart from Chapter 4, Figure 4.86, to Figure 10.20 and note the placement of the buy and sell arrows. Which strategy seems to capture the turns in the market better? Which one buys when the market is moving up and sells while the market is moving down? All in all, the new one looks better to me. But the original strategy looks better for those short-duration, choppy periods.

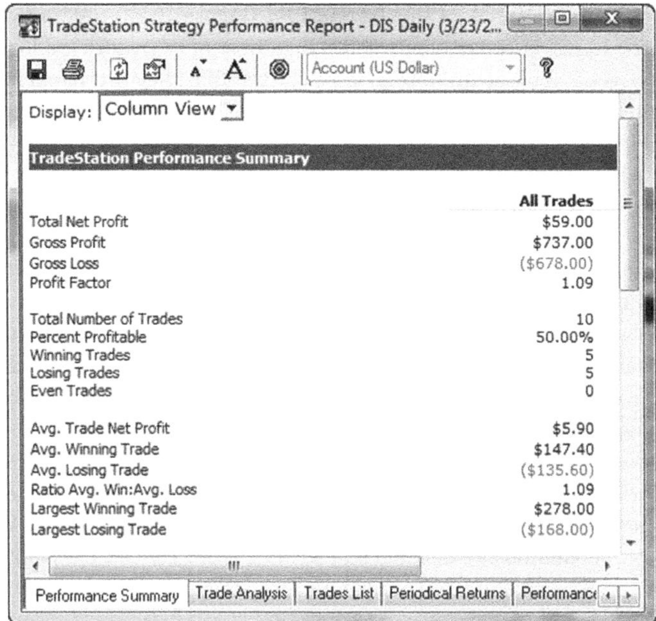

TradeStation Strategy Performance Report - DIS Daily (3/23/2...

Display: Column View

TradeStation Performance Summary

	All Trades
Total Net Profit	$59.00
Gross Profit	$737.00
Gross Loss	($678.00)
Profit Factor	1.09
Total Number of Trades	10
Percent Profitable	50.00%
Winning Trades	5
Losing Trades	5
Even Trades	0
Avg. Trade Net Profit	$5.90
Avg. Winning Trade	$147.40
Avg. Losing Trade	($135.60)
Ratio Avg. Win:Avg. Loss	1.09
Largest Winning Trade	$278.00
Largest Losing Trade	($168.00)

Performance Summary | Trade Analysis | Trades List | Periodical Returns | Performanc

FIGURE 10.21 Strategy Performance Report

TradeStation Strategy Performance Report - DIS Daily (3/23/2009-3/22/2010)

Account (US Dollar)

TradeStation Trades List

Page 1 of 1 Find <None>

#	Type	Date/Time	Signal	Price	Roll Over USD/Lot	Shares/Ctrts Profit	Net Profit Cum Net Profit
1	Buy	06/03/09	Buy	$25.08	$0.00	100	($136.00)
	Sell	06/18/09	Short	$23.72		($136.00)	($136.00)
2	Sell Short	06/18/09	Short	$23.72	$0.00	100	($165.00)
	Buy to Cover	07/20/09	Buy	$25.37		($165.00)	($301.00)
3	Buy	07/20/09	Buy	$25.37	$0.00	100	$53.00
	Sell	08/11/09	Short	$25.90		$53.00	($248.00)
4	Sell Short	08/11/09	Short	$25.90	$0.00	100	$42.00
	Buy to Cover	08/19/09	Buy	$25.48		$42.00	($206.00)
5	Buy	08/19/09	Buy	$25.48	$0.00	100	$188.00
	Sell	10/01/09	Short	$27.36		$188.00	($18.00)
6	Sell Short	10/01/09	Short	$27.36	$0.00	100	($105.00)
	Buy to Cover	10/13/09	Buy	$28.41		($105.00)	($123.00)
7	Buy	10/13/09	Buy	$28.41	$0.00	100	($104.00)
	Sell	10/30/09	Short	$27.37		($104.00)	($227.00)
8	Sell Short	10/30/09	Short	$27.37	$0.00	100	($168.00)
	Buy to Cover	11/12/09	Buy	$29.05		($168.00)	($395.00)
9	Buy	11/12/09	Buy	$29.05	$0.00	100	$278.00
	Sell	01/07/10	Short	$31.83		$278.00	($117.00)
10	Sell Short	01/07/10	Short	$31.83	$0.00	100	$176.00
	Buy to Cover	02/12/10	Buy	$30.07		$176.00	$59.00
11	Buy	02/12/10	Buy	$30.07		100	n/a
	Sell	open	n/a	$33.95		n/a	n/a

Performance Summary | Trade Analysis | Trades List | Periodical Returns | Performance Graphs | Trade Graphs | Settings

FIGURE 10.22 Trades List

If you take a look at the **Trades List** (Figure 10.22) tab on the **Performance Report** (Figure 10.22), however, you will see that most of the trades are losers. That's the problem. And if you'll look at the losers, you will see that they are happening when the market is choppy, the move isn't very long, and by the time the strategy takes the trade, the move is already over.

What can we do about that? Let's try an indicator called ADX. This is Welles Wilder's Average Directional Movement Index. He wrote about it in 1978, in a book called *New Concepts in Technical Trading Systems*. It's not new anymore, but the value of the indicator still stands. It is great for letting us know when the market is trending and when it is moving sideways.

The way it works is: When ADX is rising, the market is trending; when ADX is falling, the market is not trending. It does not tell you the direction of the trend, but it does tell you a binary answer: trending or not trending. That could be very valuable for this little strategy of ours. Let's see.

We are going to ask our strategy to take trades only when ADX says trending. Hopefully that will keep us out of the choppy, nonproductive trades. The way we discover this is to ask that "ADX of this bar is greater than ADX of the previous bar". We could ask for a more stringent condition and demand that ADX be rising for two bars, but we may not need to do that. Let's try one bar of confirmation first. Remember, this time we are trying to beat the $59 TNP.

We want to set up a condition to test whether ADX is rising; let's call it Condition1. We will be asking whether the ADX of now is greater than the ADX of one bar ago. The ADX function requires a single input parameter, Length, and this time I want to make it an input so we can optimize it; let's call it j_ADXLength. Three things need to be changed in our previous code to make these things happen: (1) We create the additional input; (2) we create

```
inputs:
        Price( Close ),
        FastLength( 9 ),
        SlowLength( 18 ),
        j_ADXLength (9) ;

variables:
        FastAvg( 0 ),
        SlowAvg( 0 ) ;

FastAvg = Average( Price, FastLength ) ;
SlowAvg = Average( Price, SlowLength ) ;

Condition1 = ADX(j_ADXLength) > ADX(j_ADXLength)[1];

IF FastAvg > SlowAvg AND Condition1 THEN BUY this bar;
IF FastAvg < SlowAvg AND Condition1 THEN SELL SHORT this bar;
```

FIGURE 10.23 Code for Dual Moving Average Strategy with ADX Condition

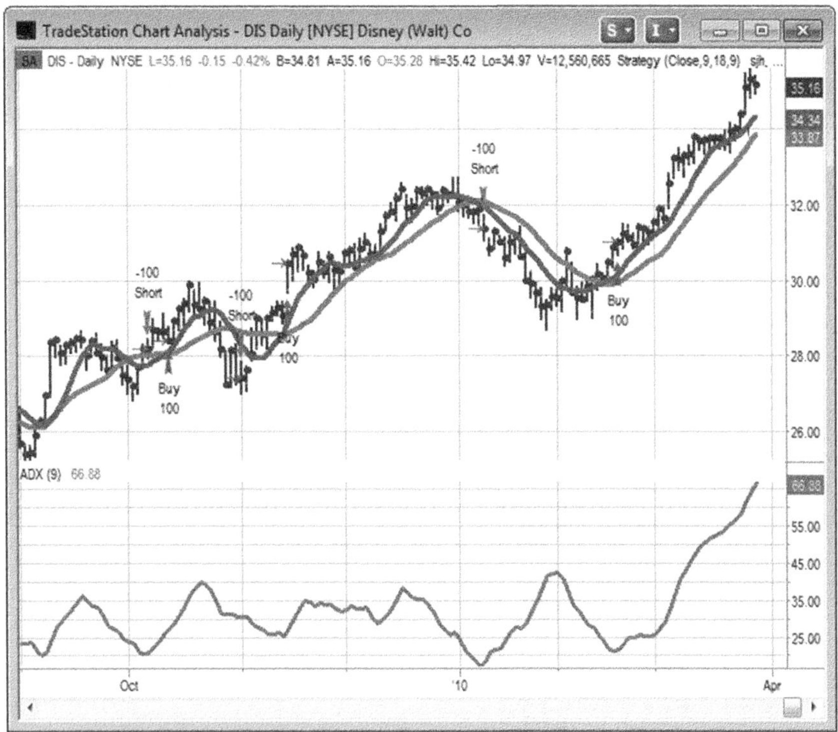

FIGURE 10.24 Chart of the New Strategy

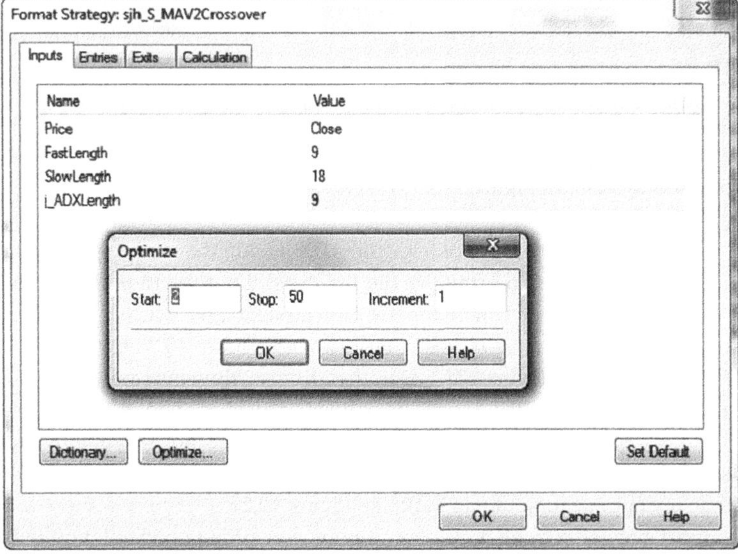

FIGURE 10.25 Running the Optimization

TradeStation Strategy Optimization Report - DIS Daily [NYSE] Disney (Walt) Co

	MAV2Cros _ADXLengtl	Test	All: Net Profit	All: Gross Profit	All: Gross Loss	All: Total Trades	All: % Profitable	All: Winning Trades	All: Losing Trades	All: Max Winning Trade	All: Max Losing Trade	All: Avg Winning Trade	All: Avg Losing Trade	All: Win/Loss Ratio	All: Avg Trade	All: Max Consecutive Winners	All: Max Consecutive Losers	All: Avg Bars in Winner	All: Avg Bars in Loser	All: Max Intraday Drawdown
1	32	31	267.00	356.00	-89.00	4	50.00	2	2	330.00	-58.00	178.00	-44.50	4.00	66.75	2	2	31	15	-305.00
2	33	32	267.00	356.00	-89.00	4	50.00	2	2	330.00	-58.00	178.00	-44.50	4.00	66.75	2	2	31	15	-305.00
3	34	33	267.00	356.00	-89.00	4	50.00	2	2	330.00	-58.00	178.00	-44.50	4.00	66.75	2	2	31	15	-305.00
4	35	34	267.00	356.00	-89.00	4	50.00	2	2	330.00	-58.00	178.00	-44.50	4.00	66.75	2	2	31	15	-305.00
5	36	35	267.00	356.00	-89.00	4	50.00	2	2	330.00	-58.00	178.00	-44.50	4.00	66.75	2	2	31	15	-305.00
6	37	36	267.00	356.00	-89.00	4	50.00	2	2	330.00	-58.00	178.00	-44.50	4.00	66.75	2	2	31	15	-305.00
7	38	37	267.00	356.00	-89.00	4	50.00	2	2	330.00	-58.00	178.00	-44.50	4.00	66.75	2	2	31	15	-305.00
8	39	38	267.00	356.00	-89.00	4	50.00	2	2	330.00	-58.00	178.00	-44.50	4.00	66.75	2	2	31	15	-305.00
9	41	40	267.00	356.00	-89.00	4	50.00	2	2	330.00	-58.00	178.00	-44.50	4.00	66.75	2	2	31	15	-305.00
10	42	41	267.00	356.00	-89.00	4	50.00	2	2	330.00	-58.00	178.00	-44.50	4.00	66.75	2	2	31	15	-305.00
11	43	42	267.00	356.00	-89.00	4	50.00	2	2	330.00	-58.00	178.00	-44.50	4.00	66.75	2	2	31	15	-305.00
12	45	44	267.00	356.00	-89.00	4	50.00	2	2	330.00	-58.00	178.00	-44.50	4.00	66.75	2	2	31	15	-305.00
13	46	45	267.00	356.00	-89.00	4	50.00	2	2	330.00	-58.00	178.00	-44.50	4.00	66.75	2	2	31	15	-305.00
14	47	46	267.00	356.00	-89.00	4	50.00	2	2	330.00	-58.00	178.00	-44.50	4.00	66.75	2	2	31	15	-305.00
15	44	43	261.00	350.00	-89.00	4	50.00	2	2	327.00	-58.00	175.00	-44.50	3.93	65.25	2	2	31	15	-305.00
16	48	47	261.00	350.00	-89.00	4	50.00	2	2	327.00	-58.00	175.00	-44.50	3.93	65.25	2	2	31	15	-305.00
17	40	39	261.00	350.00	-89.00	4	50.00	2	2	327.00	-58.00	175.00	-44.50	3.93	65.25	2	2	31	15	-305.00
18	50	49	211.00	327.00	-116.00	4	25.00	1	3	327.00	-58.00	327.00	-38.67	8.46	52.75	1	2	60	11	-305.00
19	49	48	211.00	327.00	-116.00	4	25.00	1	3	327.00	-58.00	327.00	-38.67	8.46	52.75	1	2	60	11	-305.00
20	30	29	108.00	450.00	-342.00	6	50.00	3	3	330.00	-253.00	150.00	-114.00	1.32	18.00	3	2	45	17	-305.00
21	31	30	108.00	450.00	-342.00	6	50.00	3	3	330.00	-253.00	150.00	-114.00	1.32	18.00	3	2	45	17	-305.00
22	11	10	31.00	473.00	-442.00	8	50.00	4	4	280.00	-165.00	118.25	-110.50	1.07	3.88	2	2	37	9	-351.00
23	10	9	31.00	473.00	-442.00	8	50.00	4	4	280.00	-165.00	118.25	-110.50	1.07	3.88	2	2	37	9	-351.00
24	29	28	-128.00	444.00	-572.00	8	37.50	3	5	330.00	-256.00	148.00	-114.40	1.29	-16.00	3	3	28	21	-516.00
25	13	12	-253.00	406.00	-659.00	8	37.50	3	5	280.00	-253.00	135.33	-131.80	1.03	-31.63	1	2	40	13	-527.00
26	14	13	-289.00	406.00	-695.00	8	37.50	3	5	280.00	-271.00	135.33	-139.00	0.97	-36.13	1	2	40	13	-563.00
27	12	11	-289.00	406.00	-695.00	8	37.50	3	5	280.00	-271.00	135.33	-139.00	0.97	-36.13	1	2	40	13	-563.00
28	15	14	-333.00	384.00	-717.00	8	37.50	3	5	280.00	-271.00	128.00	-143.40	0.89	-41.63	1	2	41	12	-563.00
29	25	24	-334.00	352.00	-686.00	8	25.00	2	6	281.00	-222.00	176.00	-114.33	1.54	-41.75	1	3	39	19	-465.00
30	26	25	-336.00	351.00	-687.00	8	25.00	2	6	280.00	-222.00	175.50	-114.50	1.53	-42.00	1	3	39	19	-465.00
31	24	23	-344.00	357.00	-701.00	8	25.00	2	6	298.00	-196.00	178.50	-116.83	1.53	-43.00	1	3	37	20	-425.00
32	21	20	-354.00	352.00	-706.00	8	25.00	2	6	281.00	-196.00	176.00	-117.67	1.50	-44.25	1	3	39	19	-413.00
33	22	21	-354.00	352.00	-706.00	8	25.00	2	6	281.00	-196.00	176.00	-117.67	1.50	-44.25	1	3	39	19	-413.00
34	23	22	-354.00	352.00	-706.00	8	25.00	2	6	281.00	-196.00	176.00	-117.67	1.50	-44.25	1	3	39	19	-413.00
35	28	27	-370.00	368.00	-738.00	8	25.00	2	6	280.00	-256.00	184.00	-123.00	1.50	-46.25	1	3	40	19	-516.00
36	27	26	-370.00	368.00	-738.00	8	25.00	2	6	280.00	-256.00	184.00	-123.00	1.50	-46.25	1	3	40	19	-516.00
37	16	15	-398.00	384.00	-782.00	8	37.50	3	5	280.00	-271.00	128.00	-156.40	0.82	-49.75	1	2	41	14	-563.00
38	3	2	-443.00	471.00	-914.00	10	40.00	4	6	147.00	-303.00	117.75	-152.33	0.77	-44.30	2	3	29	11	-782.00
39	18	17	-478.00	368.00	-846.00	8	25.00	2	6	280.00	-249.00	184.00	-141.00	1.30	-59.75	1	3	40	19	-519.00
40	17	16	-522.00	368.00	-890.00	8	25.00	2	6	280.00	-271.00	184.00	-148.33	1.24	-65.25	1	3	40	19	-563.00
41	9	8	-536.00	406.00	-942.00	8	37.50	3	5	280.00	-303.00	135.33	-188.40	0.72	-67.00	2	3	41	12	-726.00
42	20	19	-556.00	351.00	-907.00	8	25.00	2	6	280.00	-271.00	175.50	-151.17	1.16	-69.50	1	3	39	19	-589.00
43	19	18	-556.00	351.00	-907.00	8	25.00	2	6	280.00	-271.00	175.50	-151.17	1.16	-69.50	1	3	39	19	-589.00
44	2	1	-655.00	471.00	-1,126.00	10	40.00	4	6	147.00	-303.00	117.75	-187.67	0.63	-65.50	2	3	29	11	-994.00
45	5	4	-685.00	332.00	-1,017.00	10	30.00	3	7	139.00	-307.00	110.67	-145.29	0.76	-68.50	2	4	31	13	-1,024.00
46	7	6	-716.00	293.00	-1,009.00	10	30.00	3	7	139.00	-303.00	97.67	-144.14	0.68	-71.60	2	4	31	13	-1,016.00
47	6	5	-716.00	293.00	-1,009.00	10	30.00	3	7	139.00	-303.00	97.67	-144.14	0.68	-71.60	2	4	31	13	-1,016.00
48	4	3	-777.00	332.00	-1,109.00	10	30.00	3	7	139.00	-303.00	110.67	-158.43	0.70	-77.70	2	4	31	13	-1,116.00
49	8	7	-840.00	184.00	-1,024.00	10	30.00	3	7	92.00	-303.00	61.33	-146.29	0.42	-84.00	2	4	32	13	-1,046.00

FIGURE 10.26 Optimization Report

the condition; and (3) we change the buy and sell statements to include the condition. Take a look at the code in Figure 10.23. In Figure 10.24 you can see the chart showing the ADX and the next system. In Figure 10.25 you can see the windows where we set up the optimization parameters.

With the default input of 9 for the ADX length, the strategy lost $536 this time.

Now's the time to bring out the big guns. It is time to optimize the length input to the ADX function and see what happens. I am going to give it a very wide berth and let the length range from 2 to 50, just to see what happens. Figure 10.26 shows the Optimization Report from this run. The highest TNP is in the top row, showing that any j_ADXLength between 32 and 47 yields the highest return. Still, it isn't much; it's only $267.00.

Let's try one more thing before we learn some more coding techniques: let's optimize on all three input parameters. We will see if some combination of lengths works better. This time my optimization inputs look like Figure 10.27.

That is going to be 3,249 tests. Surely something good will pop out at us after this run. That reminds me of an email I got from a new trader today. He said "man, this is no easy business!" That's putting it mildly.

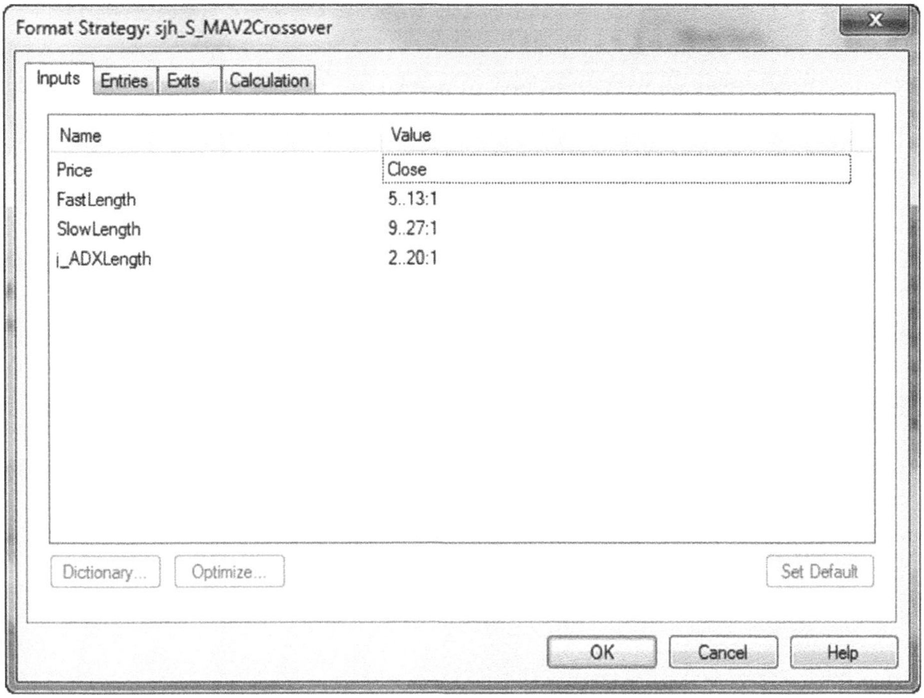

FIGURE 10.27 Let 'er Rip

A quick inspection of the new Optimization Report shows me that I need to teach you something else right quick. Take a look at Figure 10.28 and you will see that the best profit is in the area where the lengths of the moving averages is upside down; that is, when FastLength is greater than SlowLength. That may be fine for small, choppy periods, but in trends we will be in the opposite direction to the trend, going short for long runs up and long for long runs down. That will never do.

To restrict the lengths of the moving averages we will insert this code with a `Begin...End` block:

```
IF FastLength < SlowLength THEN BEGIN
```

with the `END`; at the bottom of the code.

The code now looks like Figure 10.28.

Now when we optimize we won't get any backward parameters. Trying again, we are still running 3,249 tests, but many of them will get rejected by the code we just inserted. The tests are beginning to take longer to process in the computer because of the IFs, which slow down all computers.

The results this time are a TNP of $504.00, with FastLength=11, SlowLength=12, and j_ADXLength=3. The corresponding chart is in Figure 10.29. I had to go in and choose thin

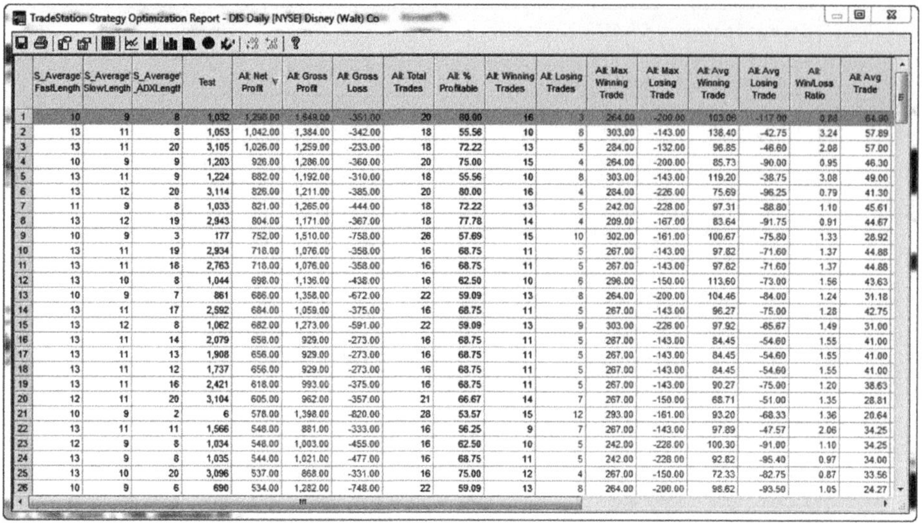

TradeStation Strategy Optimization Report - DIS Daily [NYSE] Disney (Walt) Co

	S_Average FastLength	S_Average SlowLength	S_Average _ADXLengt	Test	All: Net Profit	All: Gross Profit	All: Gross Loss	All: Total Trades	All: % Profitable	All: Winning Trades	All: Losing Trades	All: Max Winning Trade	All: Max Losing Trade	All: Avg Winning Trade	All: Avg Losing Trade	All: Win/Loss Ratio	All: Avg Trade
1	10	9	8	1,032	1,298.00	1,649.00	-351.00	20	80.00	16	3	264.00	-200.00	103.06	-117.00	0.88	64.90
2	13	11	8	1,053	1,042.00	1,384.00	-342.00	18	55.56	10	8	303.00	-143.00	138.40	-42.75	3.24	57.89
3	13	11	20	3,105	1,026.00	1,259.00	-233.00	18	72.22	13	5	284.00	-132.00	96.85	-46.60	2.08	57.00
4	10	9	9	1,203	926.00	1,286.00	-360.00	20	75.00	15	4	264.00	-200.00	85.73	-90.00	0.95	46.30
5	13	11	9	1,224	882.00	1,192.00	-310.00	18	55.56	10	8	303.00	-143.00	119.20	-38.75	3.08	49.00
6	13	12	20	3,114	826.00	1,211.00	-385.00	20	80.00	16	4	284.00	-226.00	75.69	-96.25	0.79	41.30
7	11	9	8	1,033	821.00	1,265.00	-444.00	18	72.22	13	5	242.00	-228.00	97.31	-88.80	1.10	45.61
8	13	12	19	2,943	804.00	1,171.00	-367.00	18	77.78	14	4	209.00	-167.00	83.64	-91.75	0.91	44.67
9	10	9	3	177	752.00	1,510.00	-758.00	26	57.69	15	10	302.00	-161.00	100.67	-75.80	1.33	28.92
10	13	11	19	2,934	718.00	1,076.00	-358.00	16	68.75	11	5	267.00	-143.00	97.82	-71.60	1.37	44.88
11	13	11	18	2,763	718.00	1,076.00	-358.00	16	68.75	11	5	267.00	-143.00	97.82	-71.60	1.37	44.88
12	13	10	8	1,044	698.00	1,136.00	-438.00	16	62.50	10	6	296.00	-150.00	113.60	-73.00	1.56	43.63
13	10	9	7	861	686.00	1,358.00	-672.00	22	59.09	13	8	264.00	-200.00	104.46	-84.00	1.24	31.18
14	13	11	17	2,592	684.00	1,059.00	-375.00	16	68.75	11	5	267.00	-143.00	96.27	-75.00	1.28	42.75
15	13	12	8	1,062	682.00	1,273.00	-591.00	22	59.09	13	9	303.00	-226.00	97.92	-65.67	1.49	31.00
16	13	11	14	2,079	656.00	929.00	-273.00	16	68.75	11	5	267.00	-143.00	84.45	-54.60	1.55	41.00
17	13	11	13	1,908	656.00	929.00	-273.00	16	68.75	11	5	267.00	-143.00	84.45	-54.60	1.55	41.00
18	13	11	12	1,737	656.00	929.00	-273.00	16	68.75	11	5	267.00	-143.00	84.45	-54.60	1.55	41.00
19	13	11	16	2,421	618.00	993.00	-375.00	16	68.75	11	5	267.00	-143.00	90.27	-75.00	1.20	38.63
20	12	11	20	3,104	605.00	962.00	-357.00	21	66.67	14	7	267.00	-150.00	68.71	-51.00	1.35	28.81
21	10	9	2	6	578.00	1,398.00	-820.00	28	53.57	15	12	293.00	-161.00	93.20	-68.33	1.36	20.64
22	13	11	11	1,566	548.00	881.00	-333.00	16	56.25	9	7	267.00	-143.00	97.89	-47.57	2.06	34.25
23	12	9	8	1,034	548.00	1,003.00	-455.00	16	62.50	10	5	242.00	-228.00	100.30	-91.00	1.10	34.25
24	13	9	8	1,035	544.00	1,021.00	-477.00	16	68.75	11	5	242.00	-228.00	92.82	-95.40	0.97	34.00
25	13	10	20	3,096	537.00	868.00	-331.00	16	75.00	12	4	267.00	-150.00	72.33	-82.75	0.87	33.56
26	10	9	6	690	534.00	1,282.00	-748.00	22	59.09	13	8	264.00	-200.00	98.62	-93.50	1.05	24.27

FIGURE 10.28 Optimizing All Three Parameters

```
inputs:
        Price( Close ),
        FastLength( 9 ),
        SlowLength( 18 ),
        j_ADXLength (9) ;

variables:
        FastAvg( 0 ),
        SlowAvg( 0 ) ;

IF FastLength < SlowLength THEN BEGIN

FastAvg = Average( Price, FastLength ) ;
SlowAvg = Average( Price, SlowLength ) ;

Condition1 = ADX(j_ADXLength) > ADX(j_ADXLength)[1];

IF FastAvg > SlowAvg AND Condition1 THEN BUY this bar;
IF FastAvg < SlowAvg AND Condition1 THEN SELL SHORT this bar;

END;
```

FIGURE 10.29 Code with Begin...End Block

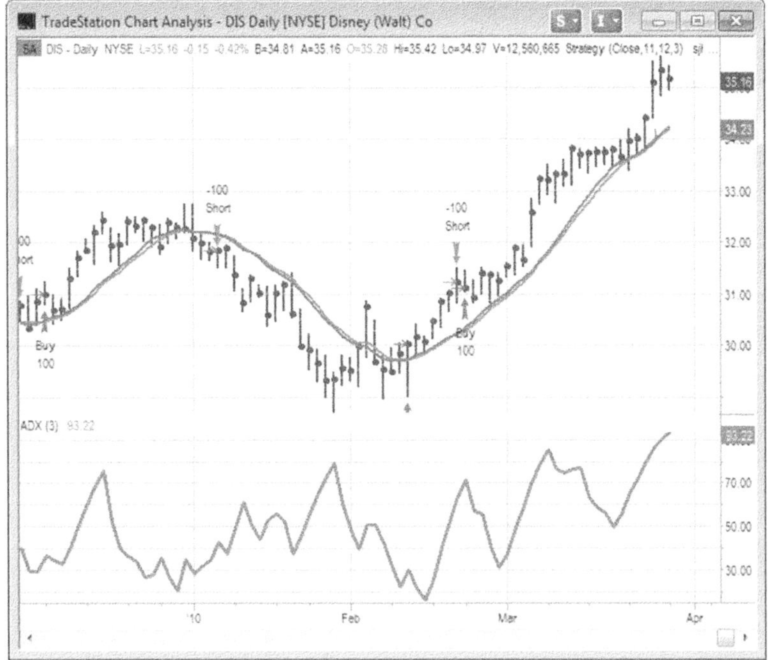

FIGURE 10.30 11, 12, 3 Inputs

lines for the moving averages in order to see the separation. When the lines were thick they just plotted over each other.

So much for that. It must be getting frustrating for you. No winning system, so far. Let me tell you, that's the way it is. I did this kind of research for three years, eight hours a day, seven days a week before I found my first real winning system. I am still using that system to this day, and I developed it in 1986. It is so robust that it has continued to work over all types of markets, over many years. I can't show you the code (it's proprietary), but in Chapter 3 I showed you some charts of it.

For now, we must get back to learning some more coding techniques. Eventually we will code a strategy that works. You'll see; just stick around. You've got to learn the basics. It's like football; it's all about the basics.

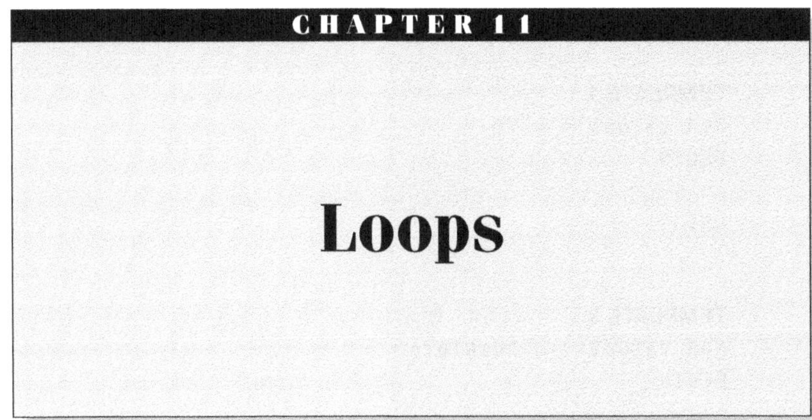

CHAPTER 11

Loops

In This Chapter

- ➤ Introduction
- ➤ For
- ➤ While

INTRODUCTION

A **loop is just as it sounds; it goes around and around until you tell it to stop.** A loop defines a group of instructions that will continue executing until a condition is met. The condition being met will cause the loop to stop.

A **FOR** loop will execute a predefined number of times. The predefined number of times is the condition. A **WHILE** loop will continue to execute while (as long as) the condition is true.

Loops allow you to calculate something over a range of values, such as from 1 to 10. Or to take action only while a condition is met, such as: while it is the month of October, only take short trades. Loops allow you to calculate averages, and summations and even count backward.

As your programming skills become more proficient, you will find yourself discovering more and more uses for loops.

FOR

TEMPLATE 1

```
FOR Value1 = m TO n
BEGIN
...
END;
```

TEMPLATE 2

```
FOR Value1 = m DOWNTO n
BEGIN
...
END;
```

The **FOR** command always appears with a **BEGIN**... **END** block and is sometimes referred to as a **FOR**... **BEGIN** command. The **FOR** command is always followed by a set of variables that define the starting and ending number of steps to execute the loop. This structure is pretty complex until you get accustomed to it; then it will become second nature, so don't start worrying yet. Templates for these concepts are shown above. You will specify m and n, and provide code for your task in place of the ... s.

FOR is always followed by a variable name (`Value1` in Figure 11.1). The command tells the computer to perform a set of actions a specified number of times. The variable counts the number of times as it steps through the loop. Each time it reaches the **END** statement, it increments (in Template 1) or decrements (in Template 2) the variable until it reaches the ending value specified in the command.

To illustrate the looping concept, let us evaluate the statement in Figure 11.1, step by step.

```
Value2=0;
FOR Value1=1 TO 3
BEGIN
  Value2=Value2+1;
END;
```

FIGURE 11.1 A Simple Loop

The computer will do the actions in the **BEGIN**... **END** block with `Value1` set to `1`. When it reaches the END statement, it will loop back up to the top and set `Value1` to `2` (it incremented `Value1` by `1`) and do the actions in the **BEGIN**... **END** block again, this time with Value1 set to 2. When it reaches the `END` statement, it will loop back up to the top and set Value1 to 3 and do the actions in the **BEGIN**... **END** block again, this time with Value1 set to 3. This time, when the computer reaches the **END** statement, it looks at Value1, and sees that it is already at 3 (the ending value specified in the **FOR** statement); it will stop this block and go on to the next line of code, keeping the values most recently determined. Value2 will have the ending value of 3.

The starting value for the variable does not have to be 1; you can start the loop at 4, or 7, or any integer you choose. In fact, you can start the loop at 0. EasyLanguage assumes that you will always be incrementing (or decrementing) by 1, however. For instance, if you wanted to investigate market action during the last month of the year, you could increment from 330 through 365, counting and analyzing the days, one day at a time.

EXAMPLE

This example calculates an average of closing values from the current bar back nine bars—that's ten samples. Before starting, however, it zeros out any old data from Value2, to be safe. The computer will run through the loop until Value1 reaches 9, accumulating the sum of the previous Value2 and the Close of Value1 Bars Ago. It will finish that evaluation and then stop the loop at the END; statement. After completion of the loop, the computer evaluates Value3=Value2/10, which averages the accumulated sum collected in the FOR loop.

```
Value2=0;
FOR Value1 = 0 TO 9
BEGIN
Value2=Value2 + C[Value1];
END;
Value3=Value2/10;
```

EXAMPLE

A generalized example of the use of the **FOR** loop is found in the EasyLanguage built-in function **Average.** You're on your own to study this code.

```
INPUTS: Price(NumericSeries), Length(NumericSimple);
VARIABLES: Sum(0), Counter(0);
Sum=0;
FOR Counter=0 TO (Length-1) BEGIN
Sum=Sum + Price[Counter];
END;
IF Length > 0 THEN
        Average = Sum / Length
        ELSE
        Average=0;
```

WHILE

TEMPLATE 1

```
WHILE (something is true)
BEGIN
...
END;
```

EXAMPLE

In the first example we used the **FOR** statement to calculate an average by specifying the beginning and ending values for the loop. In this example we will specify only the ending value using the **WHILE** statement and let the loop run as long as (while) the statement is true.

```
WHILE Value1 < 10
BEGIN
        Value1=Value1+1;
        Value2=Value2 + C[Value1];
END;
Value3=Value2/10;
```

FOR and **WHILE** are similar statements; they are both used for looping. The difference is in the **FOR** loop you specify the start and end, and in the **WHILE** loop you keep doing it until the condition is no longer true.

EXAMPLE

If you believe that October is a month to avoid trading altogether, you could surround your system's code with a **WHILE** loop that allows everything to happen except when it is October.

```
Condition1 = Month(Date)<>10;
WHILE Condition1
BEGIN
        {your code for buy and sell strategies goes here}
END;
```

How did I know that there was a built-in function called **Month** in EasyLanguage? And what does it do? Whenever I have an idea I would like to try in EasyLanguage, I think of the name or topic area I'm interested in, and then under the **Tools** menu pull down to **EasyLanguage Dictionary.** Since, in this example, I am worried about the month of October, I clicked on the `Find` tab and entered `Month` into the **Search for**: bar. (See Figure 11.2.) Scrolling through the results leads me to a **Date and Time function** named **Month.** Then clicking on the **Definition** button at the bottom of the screen tells me the full definition of the function under question. If this was not what I was looking for, I would close the box and continue searching and looking at definitions.

FIGURE 11.2 Searching for the Word Month

Here's another example for you, this time from Perry Kaufman's *New Trading Systems and Methods*, possibly the world's most definitive book on trading indicators and systems. Perry is a good friend and has graciously allowed me to share some of his code with you here.

This code calculates the geometric mean. The geometric mean, in mathematics, is a type of mean or average that indicates the central tendency or typical value of a set of numbers. It is similar to the arithmetic mean, which is what most people think of with the word "average," except that instead of adding the set of numbers and then dividing the sum by the count of numbers in the set, n, the numbers are multiplied and then the nth root of the resulting product is taken.

Calculating the geometric mean of two numbers, say 2 and 8, is just the square root of their product, which equals 4; that is, $2\sqrt{2} \times 8 = 4$. As another example, the geometric mean of three numbers 1, $^1/_2$, $^1/_4$ is the cube root of their product (1/8), which is 1/2; that is, $3\sqrt{1} \times {^1/_2} \times {^1/_4} = {^1/_2}$.

```
inputs: price(numericseries), length(numericsimple);
vars: product(0), ix(0);
product = 1;
for ix = 0 to length - 1 begin
       product = product * price[ix];
       end;
TSMGeometricMean = power(product,1/length);
```

Perry is a careful and meticulous programmer, and I think his code is beautiful.

CHAPTER 12

Analysis Techniques

In This Chapter

- Introduction
- Using Strategies
- Writing Your Own Systems, Strategies, and Signals
- Altering TradeStation's Strategies
- Evaluating Strategies
- Built-in Indicators
- Writing Indicators
- ShowMe
- PaintBars
- Functions

INTRODUCTION

I know you want to hurry up and get to the money part. We're almost there. This is the chapter that brings you to the buying and selling part. I started to write this chapter in linear order, moving through indicators and showmes and ending with systems. I have changed my mind. I am going to start you with systems and subsequently move into the tools you can use to make understanding and employing systems easier (functions, indicators, showme, and paintbar). So, the first thing we will do is throw a system/strategy onto a chart. We've already done that in earlier chapters, but we are going to take that strategy and get more complex in this chapter.

First, though, we will practice with the MACD.

USING STRATEGIES

You know what a trading system is. But you don't yet know what a TradeStation system is. A trading system is an objective set of rules that describes when to buy and when to sell. A TradeStation strategy is also a collection of strategies. Way back when, a TradeStation strategy was a collection of signals processed through the SystemBuilder to form a unit of order-dependent signals called a system. Nowadays you just keep adding strategies to a chart to form a system.

There are two strategies in TradeStation that comprise the MACD system; they are MACDLE and MACDSE, which stand for MACDLongEntry and MACDShortEntry. To form a system of them, you just put them both on a single chart and they will together generate buys and sells. Remembering that we don't ever modify original TradeStation code, please save the MACDLE as sjh_S_MACD. After saving, open MACDSE and copy the lower portion of the code into your newly saved strategy, combing the long entry with the short entry code. It should look like Figure 12.1.

```
inputs: FastLength(12), SlowLength(26), MACDLength(9);
variables: MyMACD(0), MACDAvg(0), MACDDiff(0);
MyMACD = MACD(Close, FastLength, SlowLength);
MACDAvg = XAverage(MyMACD, MACDLength);
MACDDiff = MyMACD - MACDAvg;
if CurrentBar > 2 and MACDDiff crosses over 0 then
      Buy (''macdLE'') next bar at market;
if CurrentBar > 2 and MACDDiff crosses under 0 then
      Sell Short (''macdSE'') next bar at market;
```

FIGURE 12.1 MACD Strategy Combination

Verify this code and using **Insert → Strategy,** choose the `sjh_S_MACD` to insert it on your chart of `DIS`. Once again you will have to go through the process of **Format**ting the arrows, shapes and colors. You know how to do that now by yourself. Go ahead.

The resulting chart will look something like Figure 12.2.

Notice the up-arrows denoting buy signals and the down-arrows denoting sell signals. Let's insert the MACD indicator on the chart to see how the crossovers look compared to the indicator crossovers. (See Figure 12.3.)

This time you can't drag the MACD indicator on top of the price bars unless you choose a different axis scaling. MACD is not the same scale as the underlying price data. Make sure when you drag the indicator upward that you tell TradeStation to scale it on the left axis. Bringing them together makes the foibles of the strategy apparent, as you can see the whipsaw at the left of this chart very clearly. Isn't there something we can do about this? Yes, glad you asked. That brings me to our next subject. As soon as I talk about writing your own strategies, I'll show you what we do about whipsaws and choppy periods.

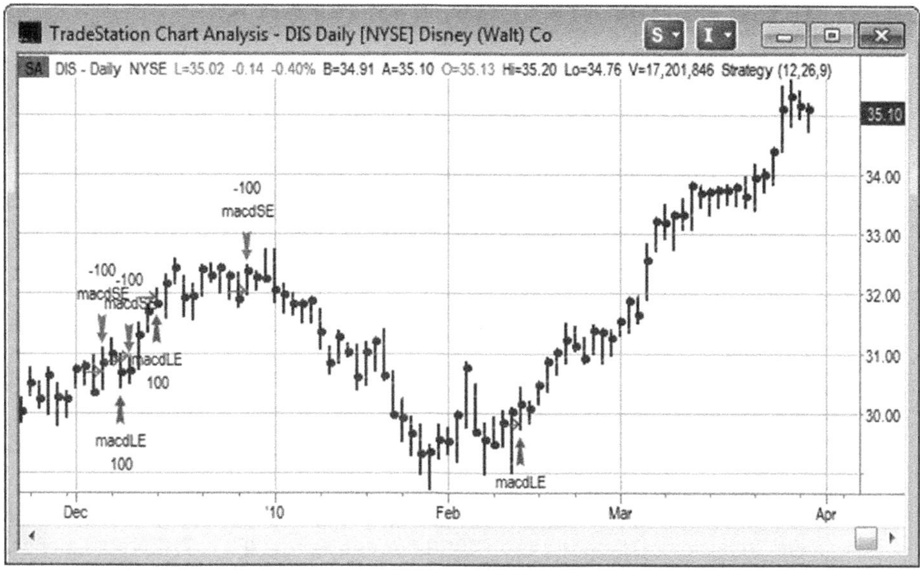

FIGURE 12.2 MACD Strategy

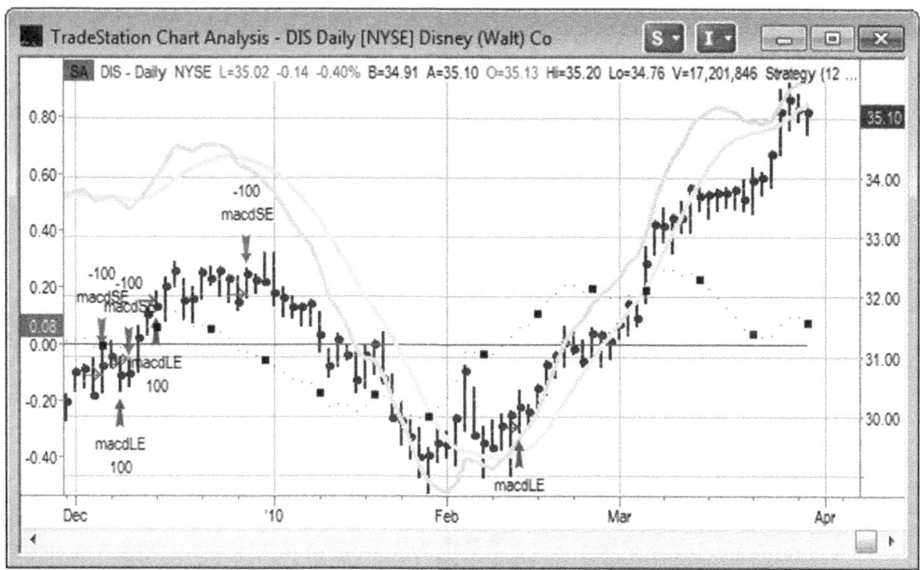

FIGURE 12.3 MACD Indicator

WRITING YOUR OWN SYSTEMS, STRATEGIES, AND SIGNALS

Steps to creating your own strategy (aka recipe):

- Open TradeStation from your Windows desktop.
- Click on the **EasyLanguage icon** in the left vertical menu bar.
- Select **New EasyLanguage Document → Strategy.**
- Name your strategy.

The steps illustrated in this "write your own" section get you to a blank piece of paper. Then what?

That brings us to the part where I said you would be better off if you memorize lots of nouns. If you have not yet familiarized yourself with the wealth of available TradeStation functions, go now to Appendix C, Built-in Functions and Indicators, and spend some time there. Then come back to this chapter.

The easiest place to begin coding a system or signal is with the **IF . . . THEN** statement. Remember, `IF condition THEN consequence`. **IF . . . THEN** statements are used in signals, strategies, and systems, and look like:

- `IF (MACD crosses above) THEN buy;`
- `IF (MACD crosses below) THEN sell;`
- `IF (stochastics turns down from above 80) THEN sell;`
- `IF (stochastics turns up from below 20) THEN buy;`
- `IF CCIAvg crosses over OverSold then BUY this bar;`

You can begin by specifying your condition in loose terms and working toward the exacting language of programming. The conditions in the parentheses are loosely specified and are not in EasyLanguage code.

Use the recipe above whenever you want to build your own strategy. In fact, keep it in mind for the prior example of copying and pasting the MACD code from TradeStation's to your own.

After you have put down the conditions of your strategy, it is time to put down the declaration statements and assignment statements. The declarations for the MACD strategy are:

```
inputs: FastLength(12), SlowLength(26), MACDLength(9);
variables: MyMACD(0), MACDAvg(0), MACDDiff(0);
```

There is really no need to specify the variables and inputs before you lay down your conditions, as you might not know what you want or need just yet. After you use FastLength, for instance, then you know you need to declare it.

It is a good idea to use TradeStation's built-in indicators as a jumping-off point for creating strategies. Put the indicators on your chart, one at a time, one after the other until you can't bear to look at another indicator. Learn what they do. Visualize how the indicator relates to the important turning points in the market. Draw the yellow PHW circles on your chart, either by hand or using the ellipse tool. Keep the circles there throughout your examination of indicators. Better yet, call me and get a one-week trial of my PHW Indicator, or purchase it and have it done for you automatically.

Once you know what a variety of indicators do, you can turn them into strategies using a few IF. . .THEN statements and by changing PLOT and ALERT statements to buys and sells. Most of the TradeStation indicators have ALERTS in them that can readily become your buy and sell statements. They already have the conditions set up and everything.

ALTERING TRADESTATION'S STRATEGIES

Getting back to the MACD system we created, we are now going to alter it so that we can attempt to eliminate some of the whipsaw conditions from our trading. In Chapter 5 I mentioned that sometimes I might be looking for ADX to confirm a signal before I would take it (i.e., ADX would need to be rising). In Chapter 10 I showed you how to write the condition for ADX rising. Let's now bring that condition into play in the MACD strategy. Change your code to match that shown in Figure 12.4.

```
inputs: FastLength(12), SlowLength(26), MACDLength(9);
variables: MyMACD(0), MACDAvg(0), MACDDiff(0);
MyMACD = MACD(Close, FastLength, SlowLength);
MACDAvg = XAverage(MyMACD, MACDLength);
MACDDiff = MyMACD - MACDAvg;
Condition1 = ADX(9) > ADX(9)[1];
if CurrentBar > 2 and Condition1 and MACDDiff crosses over 0 then
   Buy (``macdLE'') next bar at market;
if CurrentBar > 2 and Condition1 and MACDDiff crosses under 0 then
      Sell Short (``macdSE'') next bar at market;
```

FIGURE 12.4 MACD and ADX Crossover

To save space in the printing of this strategy, I eliminated the blank lines, which were there to make the code prettier. You can see how I have added the ADX condition to ensure that ADX is rising before taking the trade. There's a problem with this. We discussed it in Chapter 2 and again in Chapter 4. It is the "crosses" part of each order statement. Crosses is a very stringent condition meaning "only exactly when it crosses, not after." That is why, if you'll insert this strategy on your `DIS` chart and check for arrows, there is only one. It only happens once that the ADX is rising at exactly the same time as the crossover.

In order to fix this predicament, we must change the crosses conditions to inequalities. For the Buy signal we want the greater than condition, and for the Sell signal we want the less than condition. Change your code to look like mine in Figure 12.5.

Now you will see there are more arrows on the chart, showing up at each turn and cross of the MACD, but only where the ADX is also rising. It should look like the chart in

```
inputs: FastLength(12), SlowLength(26), MACDLength(9);
variables: MyMACD(0), MACDAvg(0), MACDDiff(0);
MyMACD = MACD(Close, FastLength, SlowLength);
MACDAvg = XAverage(MyMACD, MACDLength);
MACDDiff = MyMACD - MACDAvg;
Condition1 = ADX(9) > ADX(9)[1];
if CurrentBar > 2 and Condition1 and MACDDiff > 0 then
      Buy (''macdLE'') next bar at market;
if CurrentBar > 2 and Condition1 and MACDDiff < 0 then
      Sell Short (''macdSE'') next bar at market;
```

FIGURE 12.5 MACD and ADX Inequality

Figure 12.6. Go back and compare the chart in Figure 12.6 to the chart in Figure 12.3. Notice that there are fewer arrows in the choppy part at the left of the chart. Yeah! That's what we were aiming for.

Nevertheless, this little system doesn't make any money either. Where are the good systems? This one loses $126 in my testing. Now is the time to change the input to the ADX

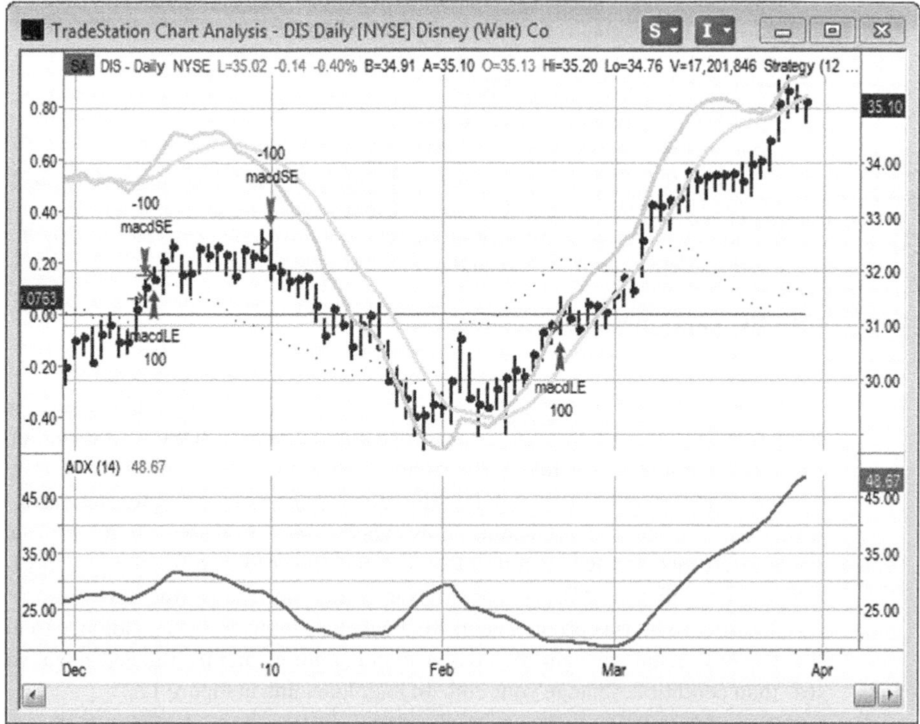

FIGURE 12.6 MACD with ADX Inequality

function to a variable, so we can optimize for better results, and run the optimizer. Can you do that alone? All you have to do is create and declare another input, say jADXLen, and change the 9 in the ADX to the name of the input. See if you can do it yourself. Verify and then go to Format to change the inputs to optimize them. I just accepted the defaults at each optimization setting and it ran 14,742 tests. Finally we are getting somewhere. This time the optimal settings produce a profit of \$1,514.00. A bit better.

One more alteration. Let's close the open trade at the end of the chart. That way it will be counted in the Performance Report, win or loss. I have a strategy (used to be called a signal, because it was to add to other strategies) called `sjh_CloseLastTrade` that does just exactly that: It closes the last trade on the chart.

The code, presented in Figure 12.7, looks to see if this is the last bar on the chart (a TradeStation function) and then, if the current market position is long, it sells and if the current market position is short, it buys. This closes the last trade.

```
IF LastBarOnChart THEN BEGIN
       IF MarketPosition(0) = 1 THEN Sell This Bar;
       IF MarketPosition(0) =-1 THEN Buy This Bar;
END;
```

FIGURE 12.7 CloseLastTrade

You don't have to do anything special, like change the code of the MACD strategy, to add this strategy to your chart. Simply **Insert → Strategy** and it will take care of itself. Doing so changes the TNP of my test to \$1,535.00, a little bit more profit. Actually, though, we have greatly improved this system. If you'll take a look at the TNP of the original MACD with crossover and no ADX, it was <\$7,529.00>. Now we are up to \$1,535.00. That is an improvement of \$9,064.00! Now if we could just get into serious profit territory. Nevertheless, the placement of trades on the chart is looking good. We have eliminated most of the whipsaw with the ADX conditions.

Now we are going to add one more set of conditions to try to make further improvements. This time we will ask that the RSI not be overbought for buys and not be oversold for sells. No need to take trades that are almost over.

To accomplish this task, we want to set up a condition for RSI being above a threshold, say 75, and another condition for RSI being too low, say below 25. We will declare inputs so we can optimize these conditions. The conditions are shown in Figure 12.8.

```
Condition2 = RSI(C,jRSI)<jR75;
Condition3 = RSI(C,jRSI)>jR25;
```

FIGURE 12.8 RSI Conditions

We also need the inputs statement altered to include these:

```
jRSI(9), jR25(25), jR75(75)
```

Next, we again go through the process of testing the default parameters against the same dates, followed by optimizing to find the best set of parameters. Running the test first with the same inputs as the last test to see if there is any improvement shows that, yes, indeed, we have again bested the former results. The results from this first test show $1759.00 TNP, an improvement of $224.00. Every little bit helps. Running the test with the default inputs, the values set as defaults in the input statements, yields a TNP of $363.00. Next, setting up a broad optimization wants to run 12,737,088 tests. Not a good idea. That many tests could take days. Not to worry, however, TradeStation stops us and says it can only run 10 million tests at a time. Luckily for us, there is yet another option. TradeStation can run a genetic algorithm and choose the best tests to run by itself. Underneath the **Method: Exhaustive** button is the **Genetic** choice. By choosing **Genetic,** TradeStation now tells us it is going to run approximately 10,000 tests. Let's see what happens.

I'm back, but not with good news. The massive tests against this RSI alteration did not yield an improvement in TNP. We'll have to try something else. This is how it is with testing—back and forth, some improvement, no improvement.

This time I am going to try something else. I am going to change the MACD, which is often slow anyway, to XAverage. It's an easy change in that we simply need to change the MACDs to XAverages. We can get rid of one of the inputs and all of the variables. Your new code should look like the code in Figure 12.9.

```
inputs: FastLength(12), SlowLength(26),
   jLen(9), jRSI(9), jR25(25), jR75(75);
Condition1 = ADX(jLen) > ADX(jLen)[1];
Condition2 = RSI(C,jRSI)<jR75; Condition3 = RSI(C,jRSI)>jR25;
if CurrentBar > 2 and Condition1 and Condition2 and
   XAverage(C,FastLength) > XAverage(C,SlowLength) then
      Buy (''XAv'') next bar at market;
if CurrentBar > 2 and Condition1 and Condition3 and
   XAverage(C,FastLength) < XAverage(C,SlowLength) then
      Sell Short (''XAvSE'') next bar at market;
```

FIGURE 12.9 XAverage Strategy Code

Later on I will share with you the code I used for testing all the averages at once, but not yet. It's fun to be able to compare all of the averages to each other through optimization. In the meantime, let's test the code from Figure 12.9.

With the default inputs, the new strategy makes a very small profit. Next I'll optimize the input parameters and see what happens.

That doesn't do it either. There is a lot more we will do to this code, but it is time we get away from testing and back to learning TradeStation and EasyLanguage. Let's get to the next topic.

EVALUATING STRATEGIES

In Chapter 2 we addressed PHW Analysis. Now is the time for you to begin using the results of that analysis. PHW is your goal; Buy and Hold is your benchmark. **You are looking for a trading system that is better than Buy and Hold and approaches the profits of PHW.**

In the strategy we have been testing, the Buy and Hold equals $35.11 while the PHW equals $416.06. This is *per share*. In our trading strategy we have been accepting the default of 100 shares per trade. Thus, we need to multiply the PHW numbers by 100 for comparison values. Buy and Hold on 100 shares would be $3,511.00, and PHW on 100 shares would be $41,606.00. Those are both huge compared to the results we have been getting. It is encouraging, however, to know that there is that much possibility on our chart. We'll work on that more later.

To take a quick look at our profit status, use the menu sequence: **View → Strategy Performance Report** or use the keyboard equivalents **ALT+SHIFT+P.** A small view of the report appears in Figure 12.10. To work on this next section, however, you need to have the full view of the report open and available to you. To get the full report you will need to click on the Expand selector in the blue bar, in the upper right of the report. The full version is shown in Figure 12.11. The best performance (optimization) of the MACD we coded was $1,759.00 TNP; the best performance of the XAverage was $923.00. I am choosing to work with the MACD with ADX and RSI because it was the best, and I like to work with the best. I am by nature a very optimistic person, but trading is such a difficult business, I prefer to keep a positive outlook.

The PHW yellow dots, and the words associated with Buy and Hold, Date Range, Ideal Number of Trades, Ideal Profit, and PHW Potential are written on the chart automatically by my indicator. Probably the easiest way to get to the PHW calculations, if you didn't yet purchase my indicator, is to add an indicator called Zig-Zag to your chart and use its peaks and valleys as your targets. Use a `strength` of `1` and a `wavepercent` of `20` as your inputs to give attainable targets.

You know how to calculate Buy and Hold: It's the last price on the chart minus the first price on the chart. The ideal number of trades is found simply by counting the pivots the chart makes that are significant enough to trade. The ideal profit is found by adding up the profit if you caught each of the highs and lows of each pivot. The PHW is 40% of the ideal profit. Without PHW you don't know what to aim for; you don't know whether your system is really any good or not.

The second measure of a system's success is my CPC Index. To evaluate the CPC Index we multiply p*PF*R to get a single number that I use to compare all trading systems. These numbers are found on the Performance Report in Figure 12.11. `PF` is **Profit Factor,** on the fourth line of the report. `P` is **Percent Profitable,** which is about halfway down the report. And `R` is the **Ratio of Average Win to Average Loss,** which is just a little farther down the page. Remember that the product of these three numbers needs to be 1.2 or greater. That's the summary measure of your trading system.

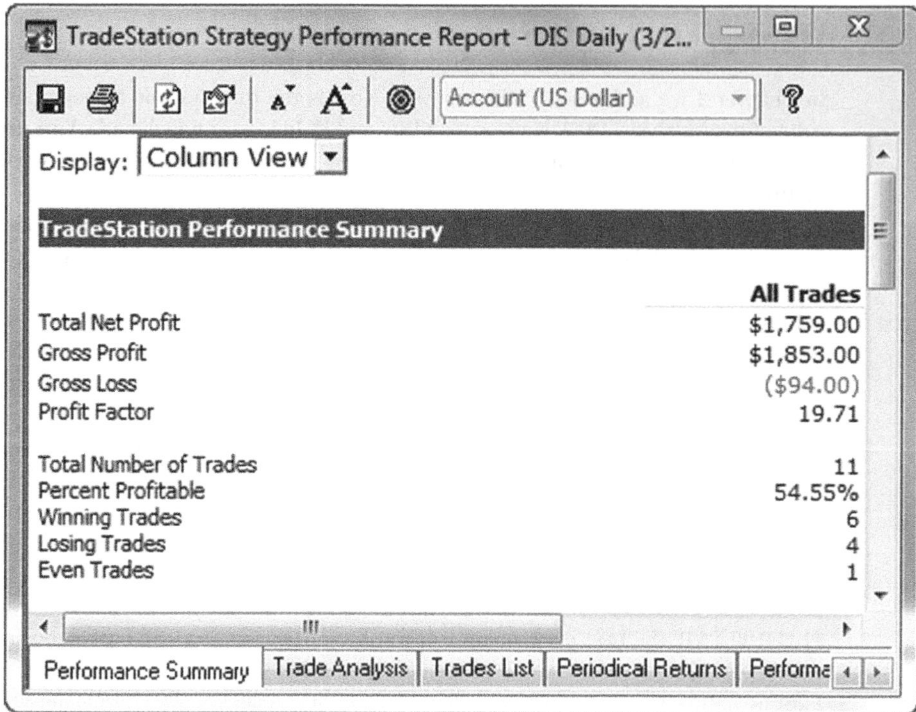

FIGURE 12.10 Strategy Performance Report

Examining the Strategy Performance Report

The **Total Net Profit** (TNP) of any strategy is how much profit it made over the period of the test. It is important to know whether the time period is a week, a month, a year, or 90 years, in order to say whether your TNP is big or small. Recall that in my testing I insist on testing everything against a single year's worth of data.

The second statistic in Figure 12.10 or 12.11 is **Gross Profit.** This is the amount of profit made by only the successful trades. Likewise, **Gross Loss** is the sum of the losses of all the losing trades. It is important that the ratio of your wins to your losses be about or above 2. The next line in the report is **Profit Factor** (PF in my formula). The Profit Factor is the ratio I just mentioned, Gross Profit/Gross Loss.

On the sixth line of the report is a statistic named **Open Position P/L.** For most of my work I use the signal `sjh_CloseLastTrade` to close that open position so it will be calculated in with all the other trades. Generally, therefore, my open position P/L will be zero.

The next statistic of import is about a third of the way down, to **Total Number of Trades.** This is just what it seems: the total number of trades that were taken. It is important that this not be just one or two, or even three. If you have very few trades, the statistics don't really carry much meaning.

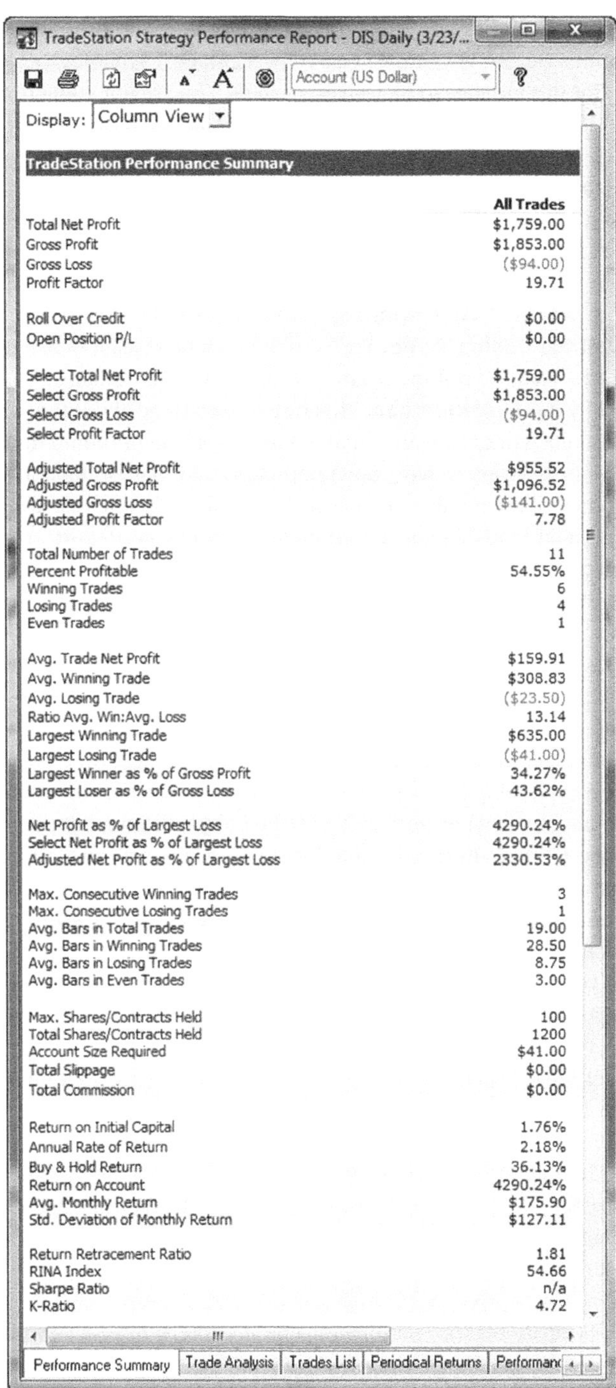

TradeStation Strategy Performance Report - DIS Daily (3/23/...

Account (US Dollar)

Display: Column View

TradeStation Performance Summary

	All Trades
Total Net Profit	$1,759.00
Gross Profit	$1,853.00
Gross Loss	($94.00)
Profit Factor	19.71
Roll Over Credit	$0.00
Open Position P/L	$0.00
Select Total Net Profit	$1,759.00
Select Gross Profit	$1,853.00
Select Gross Loss	($94.00)
Select Profit Factor	19.71
Adjusted Total Net Profit	$955.52
Adjusted Gross Profit	$1,096.52
Adjusted Gross Loss	($141.00)
Adjusted Profit Factor	7.78
Total Number of Trades	11
Percent Profitable	54.55%
Winning Trades	6
Losing Trades	4
Even Trades	1
Avg. Trade Net Profit	$159.91
Avg. Winning Trade	$308.83
Avg. Losing Trade	($23.50)
Ratio Avg. Win:Avg. Loss	13.14
Largest Winning Trade	$635.00
Largest Losing Trade	($41.00)
Largest Winner as % of Gross Profit	34.27%
Largest Loser as % of Gross Loss	43.62%
Net Profit as % of Largest Loss	4290.24%
Select Net Profit as % of Largest Loss	4290.24%
Adjusted Net Profit as % of Largest Loss	2330.53%
Max. Consecutive Winning Trades	3
Max. Consecutive Losing Trades	1
Avg. Bars in Total Trades	19.00
Avg. Bars in Winning Trades	28.50
Avg. Bars in Losing Trades	8.75
Avg. Bars in Even Trades	3.00
Max. Shares/Contracts Held	100
Total Shares/Contracts Held	1200
Account Size Required	$41.00
Total Slippage	$0.00
Total Commission	$0.00
Return on Initial Capital	1.76%
Annual Rate of Return	2.18%
Buy & Hold Return	36.13%
Return on Account	4290.24%
Avg. Monthly Return	$175.90
Std. Deviation of Monthly Return	$127.11
Return Retracement Ratio	1.81
RINA Index	54.66
Sharpe Ratio	n/a
K-Ratio	4.72

Performance Summary | Trade Analysis | Trades List | Periodical Returns | Performanc

FIGURE 12.11 Full Strategy Performance Report

Percent profitable, P for my formula, is the ratio of the number of winning trades to total number of trades, expressed as a percentage. Psychologically you need (more than you know) for this number to be well above 50%. You are not going to feel comfortable trading a system that loses as often as it wins, even if the size of losses is small compared to wins. If your percent profitable is small you will find yourself cheating on the system in short order. **Even trades** is the number of trades that close at zero profit.

Avg. Trade Net Profit is next. This number is **Total Net Profit / Total Number of Trades.** It is the average trade size. Of course, you want this number to be large enough to yield profit after you subtract commission and slippage.

The next item, **Avg. Winning Trade,** needs to be large compared to the following number, **Average Losing Trade.** You want wins to be at least twice the size of the losers.

Ratio Avg. Win/Avg. Loss is R in my CPC formula. It is simply the **Average Win** divided by the **Average Loss.** This ratio needs to be about 2 or above also. The reason the CPC formula works so well is that, while it is a rule of thumb to have R and PF at or above 2, it is not necessary to have them both above 2 if one of them is much larger. That's where the product of the numbers comes in. Two times 2 is 4, but so is 1.5 times 2.67.

The next statistics on the Strategy Performance Report are **Largest Winning Trade** and **Largest Losing Trade.** Some theorists say to remove these both from your analysis, as though they didn't happen. Some say to remove the largest win and leave the largest loss. And yet others even say to remove the largest win and double the largest loss.

I just accept it as it comes, with no modification. The one thing I do want to be careful of is that the largest win not be most of the profit. If that was the case, you could probably guarantee you would never see that serendipitous profit in real life.

The **Largest Winner as % of Gross Profit** displays how much of the **Gross Profit** was won by the single largest profitable completed trade, looking across all profitable trades, during the specified period. Same with the **Largest Loss,** but compared to the Gross Losses.

Max. Consecutive Winning Trades just tells you how many wins in a row happen in the best run. You want this number to be large. Everyone likes a winning streak. Likewise, you want the next number, **Max. Consecutive Losing Trades,** to be small. On our report it was only 1. Fantastic. Only one loss in a row. If you'll look at the top of the Performance Report you will see a **blue target** in the menu bar area. That target links to RINA Technologies software, if it is on your computer. Of course, you have to buy it; it is not free. If you haven't bought it, the target takes you nowhere. It is an amazingly powerful statistical analysis package that is made up of several components and that fits seamlessly with TradeStation. In fact, much of the current Strategy Performance Report statistics originally came from the RINA people, and Leo Zamansky. Check them out at **www.RINAFinancial.com.** Their addition to the power of TradeStation is well worth the investment. Portfolio Maestro, the RINA product I use, is incredible. It performs statistical analysis and portfolio combinations that are so complete in their scope that it doesn't seem possible a computer could do it. This is straight from the RINA Web site:

> *Evaluating trading performance is necessary to understand its strengths and weaknesses, to know the risks and rewards and to find out what changes to make in the trading method to achieve higher returns and if possible with less risk. We use our*

> *proprietary performance analysis tools, including PortfolioStream and others to analyze your trading performance and generate a report. We also describe what strategies would have generated higher return and lower risk in the past based on the historical data.*

The next to last set of numbers I want to review in the Performance Report are: **Avg. Bars in Total Trades, Avg. Bars in Winning Trades, Avg. Bars in Losing Trades,** and **Avg. Bars in Even Trades.** These should be pretty self-explanatory by now. For each trade they count the number of bars (whether day bars or minute bars, or any other kind of bars), add them all up, and divide by the number of trades. The one thing I do want to say about them is that you want your losses to be over quickly and your wins to last a long time. The old adage is: Cut your losses and let your wins run. Again the two-to-one rule applies; your winning streak should last twice as long as your losing streak, if for no other reason than you won't be able to stand it psychologically.

Trading versus Investing

Why do we want to trade when the buy and hold approach to investing works over the long term? The advantage of trading is that you can use your profits to increase your position on subsequent trades. As you build up profits, you can begin to increase the number of shares you purchase. Using a simple compounding approach and spending the profits of each trade to increase the number of shares on the next trade makes a dramatic increase in profits. One of the authorities on the subject of money management is a good friend named Ralph Vince. His books are the definitive works on the mathematics of money management, as far as I'm concerned. He's brilliant. And, Vince is an Italian descendant of Leonardo da Vinci; that should tell you something. His books are highly mathematical but important to the field of compounding. In short, if you trade too many shares as you increase your "bet size" you will end up in ruin. This is a critical concept. There is one, and only one, number that is the fraction of your portfolio size to use to increase the number of shares you trade. If you don't know this number, you will bet too much and end up with nothing, or less. This fraction is called *optimal-f* by Mr. Vince.[1]

Being a mathematician myself, his work intrigues me. I found a flaw in his calculations and pointed it out to him, once upon a time. He was very gracious and appreciative, and knew of the flaw. I then created a spreadsheet that calculates the fraction based on my revision of his work, and I renamed it *Ultimate-F* with his blessing. With this spreadsheet, you start out trading 1 unit (say 100 shares) and you increase the unit size as your equity grows and decrease the unit size as you have losses. You need more trades in the list than are created by our little example to begin compounding. Compounding properly with the correctly calculated Ultimate-F can quickly change your profits exponentially. The single most important fact, however, about compounding is that you must first have a winning system. **No amount of compounding can improve a losing system.** You must have a positive mathematical expectation to begin compounding.

---

[1]At the time of this writing, Ralph Vince has had some 400 winning trades in a row with no losses.

RINA software (the one I use is called Portfolio Maestro) has extensive compounding routines in it, including optimal-f techniques. With Portfolio Maestro you can exercise various compounding techniques to discover the best combination for your strategy.

We will thoroughly investigate buying and selling in Chapter 13.

BUILT-IN INDICATORS

At this writing there are more than 200 indicators that come with the standard, vanilla TradeStation release. This is not the book to help you learn those indicators. *Technical Analysis A to Z* by Stephen Achelis (founder of MetaStock and Equis International) is a great place to start learning about indicators and their purposes. *TradeStation Made Easy!* is about learning to program with EasyLanguage. Nevertheless, Appendix D in this book is devoted to the built-in indicators and functions. Explanations of their purpose is included, but no fitness for purpose or suggestion of profitability is implied.

WRITING INDICATORS

An indicator is just what its name implies—it indicates something. The quick rule of thumb is that *an indicator contains a plot statement.* Generally we place indicators on price charts. An indicator is a graphical representation of some pattern or formula. Hopefully, an indicator shows some type of market activity that we can then interpret for profit. There are very few predictive (or leading) indicators; most are lagging indicators. There are a few neural networks (I represent two) and Elliott Wave techniques that purport to tell you where the market is going rather than where it has been. But, for the most part, indicators are based on price history, which is lagging.

There are a multitude of indicators prepackaged with TradeStation and conveniently listed in Appendix G of this book. TradeStation has provided not only the most commonly used indicators but many others as well.

When you become familiar with the indicators that are built-in, you will want to start writing your own variations. Case in point, the dual exponential moving average indicator is not built-in. There is a dual simple moving average (Mov Avg 2 lines) and a single exponential moving average (Mov Avg Exponential) but no dual exponential moving average. Therefore, we will write it here for the exercise.

Without a doubt, the easiest way to write code is to copy code that is pretty close to what you want and modify it to suit your purpose. That's how we all get started as programmers. That said, let's open the EasyLanguage indicator Mov Avg 2 lines and modify it. Remember to do a **Save As . . .** so you don't overwrite the TradeStation code.

Indicators and systems, or signals, or strategies, are very nearly the same, as far as your coding is concerned. The basic difference between the two is that indicators have plot statements in them, to show the indicator on your chart, and strategies have buy and sell statements but no plot statements. I've always wondered why I essentially have to write the same code twice, once for the indicator and once for the system. But ours is not to reason why, ours is just to make use of this great toolbox and profit heavily.

Remember when writing an indicator that it is as simple as variables, conditions, and plot statements.

Following is the code for the standard, built-in dual moving average indicator:

```
Input: Price(Close), Length1(9), Length2(18);
IF CurrentBar >1 Then Begin
       Plot1(Average(Price, Length1), "SimpAvg1");
       Plot2(Average(Price, Length2), "SimpAvg2");
       End;
```

Altering this code for our purposes is as simple as changing the function "Average" to "XAverage". How did I know that? Appendix D lists all available choices. So I don't get confused later, when I view my indicator on a chart, it would be best to change the PlotName from "SimpAvg" to something more descriptive, like "XAvg". The code for our new indicator becomes:

```
Input: Price(Close), Length1(9), Length2(18);
IF CurrentBar >1 Then Begin
       Plot1(XAverage(Price, Length1), "XAvg1");
       Plot2(XAverage(Price, Length2), "XAvg2");
       End;
```

What now? Check your code for syntax by verifying it. You should get **Verification successful.**

To apply your new indicator to your chart, see Figure 12.12, simply open a chart and input the symbol DIS by typing it on the keyboard. Then the menu sequence **Insert** → **Indicator** or **ALT+C** will open the dialog box where you can choose the new indicator. Select it and click **OK** to put it on the chart. Next, select the indicator and drag it up to Subgraph 1 so it will be overlaid on the price bars. Once again those skinny lines! Since I never remember the sequence to the inputs of the plot statement, let's review it here:

```
PlotN(Expression[,"<PlotName>"[,ForeColor[,Default[,Width]]]]);
```

OK, let's go back into the PowerEditor and change both of our plot statements to read:

```
Plot1(XAverage(Price, Length1), "XAvg",DarkGreen,Default,3);
Plot2(XAverage(Price, Length2), "XAvg2",RGB(255,155,153),
     Default,3);
```

where I chose to use the RGB function and the numbers to get a salmon-colored line this time.

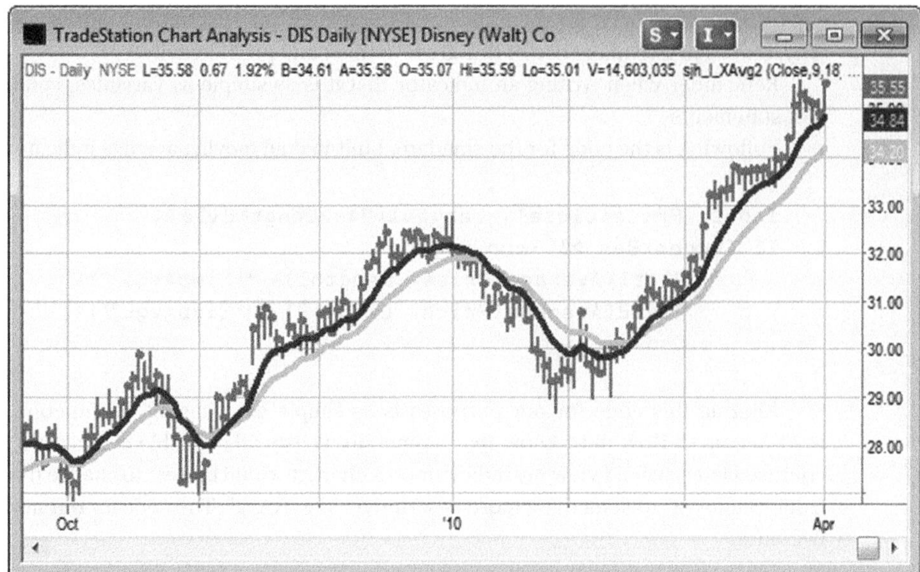

FIGURE 12.12 Dual Exponential Moving Average

An Arthur Putt Indicator

I am going to stay with the indicator subject a while longer. This is an important tool for you, and one you will use often, if you feel comfortable with the process. So, let's get you comfortable.

The example in Figure 12.13 is from *Using EasyLanguage* by Arthur G. Putt, with the kind permission of Murray Ruggiero.

```
{Open-Close Trend Indicator}
INPUTS: Length(11);
VARS: Trend(0);
Value1=Summation(Close,Length);
Value2=Summation(Open,Length);
Trend=Value1-Value2;
Plot1(Trend,''Trend'');
Plot2(0,''Zero'');
```

FIGURE 12.13 Code from Arthur Putt

The effect of this indicator is similar to an advance-decline line. In it the closes are summed and the opens are summed over length `Length` period. Then the sum of opens is subtracted from the sum of closes. Theoretically, the indicator should peak as the market

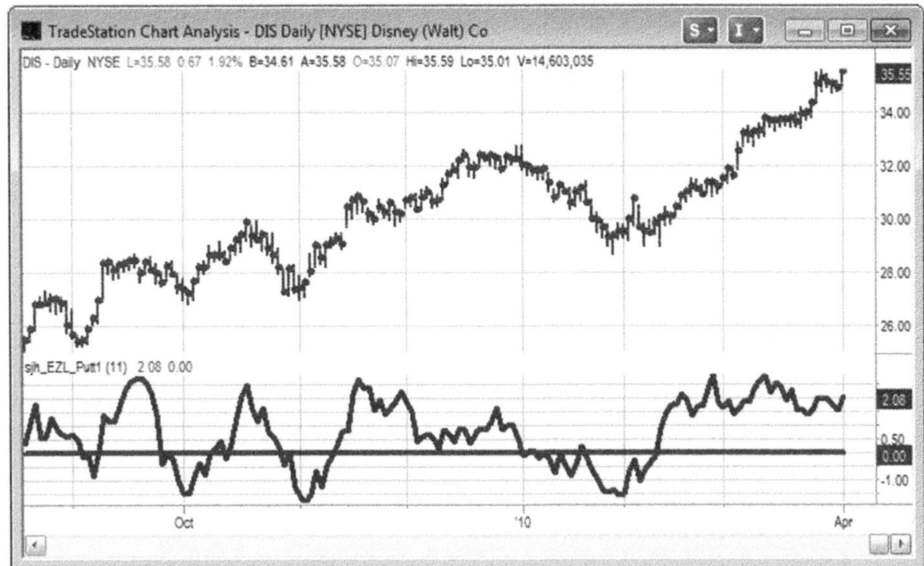

FIGURE 12.14 Chart with Indicator from Arthur Putt

is topping out, and bars are not constructed of higher closes than opens. Take a look at the chart in Figure 12.14. It's pretty valuable stuff.

While you may be able to visually determine the trend of the market, you need to teach TradeStation to identify trends. There are twice as many definitions of trends as there are market technicians, and they're all right. Again, all we care about is finding a simple way to make money consistently.

So, let's look at a simple definition of trend: If the closes tend to be above the opens, the trend is up; if the closes tend to be below the opens, the trend is down. What does "tend to" mean? We must define it. Let's say that we add up the last several closes in one variable and add up the last several opens in another variable. We compare the values to see which is greater. If the sum of the closes is greater than the sum of the opens, we will say we have an up trend.

We are still left with an open question: What is "several"? How about letting "several" be an input? That way we can test the input through optimization and find the number or numbers that best serve our purpose. Putt names the input `Length`.

To add up the last several closes we could use the brute force method or we could use a little finesse in our coding.

The brute force method might look something like this:

```
IF Length=2 THEN Value1=C+C[1];
IF Length=3 THEN Value1=C+C[1]+C[2];
IF Length=4 THEN Value1=C+C[1]+C[2]+C[3];
```

. . . etc.

But how would I know when to stop? How would I know what you might give me as an input? What if I stopped at 100 and you gave me 101 as the input? The brute force method definitely has its limitations.

Another method, with a bit more sophistication, would be to use a loop and stop when the input length was exceeded. That method might look something like this:

```
Value1=0;
For Value99= 1 to Length
         BEGIN
         Value1=Value1 + C[Value99-1];
         END;
```

That's prettier, definitely. But those who have read Appendix C know that there is already a function in EasyLanguage that will perform this task in one simple statement. It is the **Summation** function. The form of the **Summation** function is:

```
Summation (Price, Length)
```

where Price Specifies which price of the asset of interest is to be used
Length Specifies the number of trailing bars to consider

The **Summation** function returns a numeric value containing the **sum of the last Length occurrences of Price.**

Using this built-in function, we give it our input variable, `Length`, as its input variable length, and tell it that we want the **Price** to be `Close` in one case and `Open` in the other.

To decide whether we have a trend, and even what direction the trend is, we could use a logical variable and look for a true/false answer like this:

```
IF Value1 > Value2 THEN Condition1=true;
IF Value1 < Value2 THEN Condition1=false;
```

But doing so would not allow us to use the answer effectively for a chart. Since we are working on an indicator with a chart as the result, we should look at having the answer we calculate be a value we can plot. That's where Putt uses the variable `Trend`.

```
Trend=Value1-Value2;
```

The value of `Trend` will show us whether we have an uptrend, a downtrend, or a sideways market. If the closes are strongly greater than the opens, `Value1-Value2` will be a large number. If the closes are a lot less than the opens, `Value1-Value2` will be a negative number. Not only that, but the value of `Trend` seems to peak out at about 2.75 most of the time. We could measure that and use it for a signal in a trading strategy.

The final remaining task is to plot our indicator on the chart. This is done with the plot statement. Putt has chosen to use two plot statements, one to plot the indicator and one to plot a zero line. The result of this effort was illustrated in Figure 12.14.

I know I belabored that one, but I wanted you to see the thought process as well as the final code. When we get back to buying and selling in Chapter 13, we'll see what happens if we turn this into a strategy.

Writing Text with an Indicator

Sometimes you might want to plot something other than a line or curve. There are times you will want to plot words or numbers. You have already seen an example of this happening. My PHW Indicator has an input variable for plotting the numbers. It is actually an off/on switch with which I can decide to turn the number off or on. When they are turned on the chart looks like Figure 12.15.

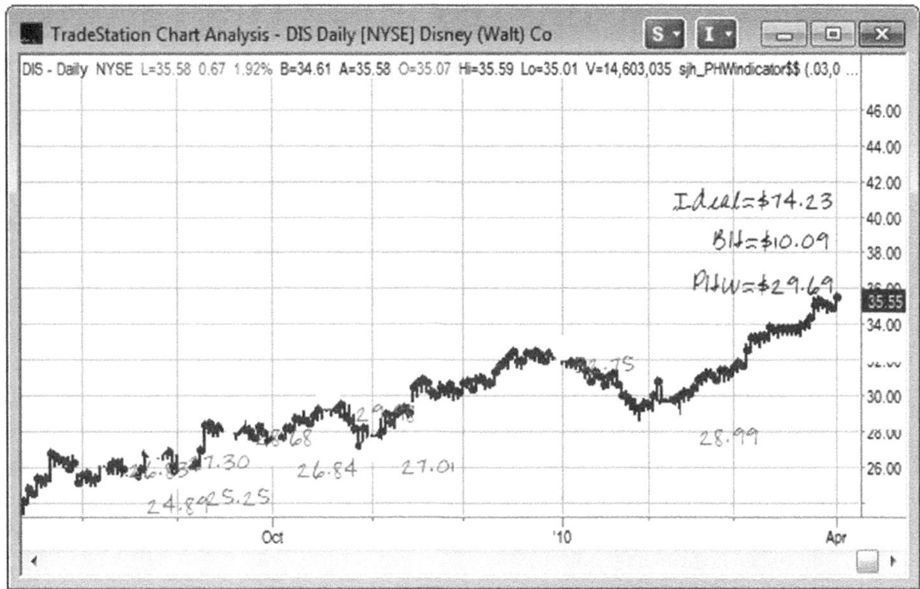

FIGURE 12.15 Writing Text on a Chart

In this figure I have turned on the text for telling me what the Ideal, Buy and Hold, and PHW values are. Also turned on are the ideal buy and sell points with the values at each point. The basic commands for writing text through an indicator are listed next. TradeStation has provided many more sophisticated text commands, but these few are essential and will get you started.

- Text_New
- Text_SetColor
- Text_SetLocation
- Text_SetStyle

These commands are in the EasyLanguage Dictionary under the subject Text Drawing. The way they work is simply to add the specified text string at the specified bar and price value. The command is actually a function, and as such it returns a value that corresponds to the ID number of the text object added to the chart. If you want to modify the text object in any way, it is very important that you capture and keep this number; the ID number is the only way of referencing a specific text object. The command looks like this:

```
Value1 = Text_New(BarDate, BarTime, Price, "MyText");
```

where **BarDate** and **BarTime** Numeric expressions corresponding to the date and time, respectively, for the bar on which you want to anchor the text object.

Price A numeric expression representing the price value at which to anchor the text object.

MyText The text string expression to add to the price chart. Value1 is any numeric variable or array and holds the ID number for the new text object.

Text objects are added to the chart using the default color and vertical and horizontal alignment of the charting application. Any of these properties can be changed using other Text-related reserved words.

NOTE: If the text cannot be drawn successfully, an error code is returned in the value of the function. When any drawing object error occurs, no additional operations will be performed on any drawing objects by the trading strategy, analysis technique, or function that generated the error. The error codes are listed in the TS help files.

For example, the next statements add a text string "Key" to a price chart every time there is a key reversal pattern:

```
Variable: ID(-1);
If Low < Low[1] AND Close > Close[1] Then
   ID = Text_New(Date, Time, Low, "Key");
```

The chart associated with this code appears in Figure 12.16.

If you are wondering why it looks like I wrote on the chart, many years ago I had my handwriting digitized and turned into a font. I use that font as the default in TradeStation.

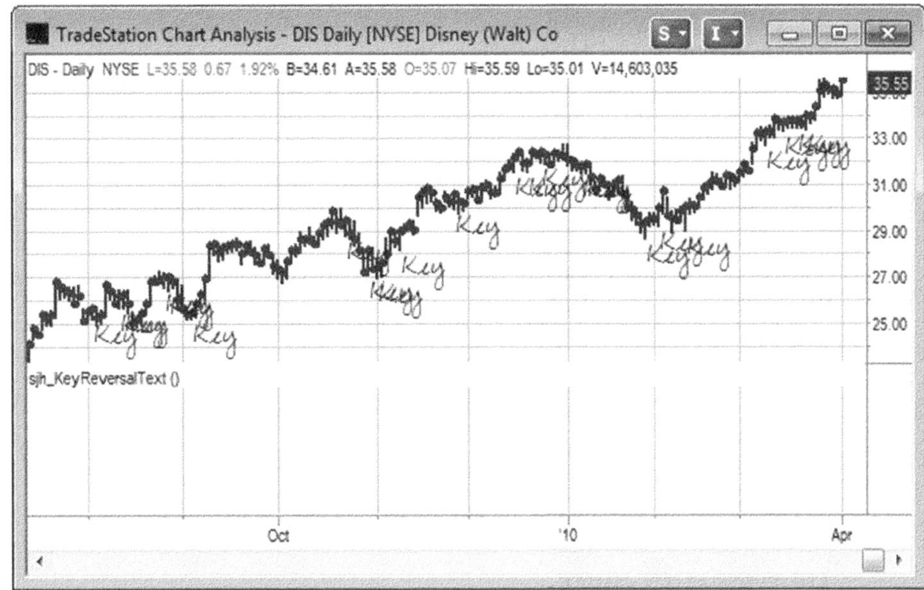

FIGURE 12.16 Key Reversals

To change the color of the text, you would use the Text_SetColor command. It's easy, nothing you don't already understand. It is simply a matter of referring to the text you just plotted, using its ID number, and then specifying the color you want. Again, you can use the RGB(000,000,000) specification to get any color under the rainbow.

```
Value1 = Text_SetColor(ID, Red);
```

As for positioning the text at a location other than the simple date, time, and price values of a bar, there are lots of computational ways to refer to other bars in the past. To set a location for the text, guess what the command would be. You're right! SetLocation. Well, almost. It is `Text_SetLocation`. It takes the form:

```
Value1 = Text_SetLocation(Text_ID, BarDate, BarTime, Price);
```

where

Text_ID A numeric expression representing the ID number of the text object to modify.

BarDate and **BarTime** Numeric expressions representing the new EasyLanguage date and time, respectively, at which to anchor the text object.

Price The new price value at which to anchor the text object.

`Value1` is any numeric variable or array. You must assign the text object Reserved Word to a numeric variable or array so that you can determine whether the Reserved Word performed its operation successfully. If an invalid ID number is used, the Reserved Word will return a value of -2 and no additional operations will be performed on any text objects by the trading strategy, analysis technique, or function that generated the error. For a list of error codes, see the EasyLanguage Error Codes in Appendix J and in the EasyLanguage Dictionary (the little blue book icon in the EasyLanguage PowerEditor).

It is recommended that you change the location of the text object rather than delete the text object and draw a new one. Relocating an existing object is faster and generates fewer ID numbers to keep track of.

EXAMPLE

This example moves the text object with the identification number 2 to January 14, 1999, 3:00 pm, at a price location of 150.

```
Text_SetLocation(2, 990114, 1500, 150.00);
```

ADDITIONAL EXAMPLE

The next statement is done only once, on the first bar after MaxBarsBack. This statement creates a new text object containing the symbol and places it above the first bar after Max BarsBack. The second statement is done on every bar (or tick) and changes the location of the text so that it always displays above the last visible bar of the chart:

```
If BarNumber = 1
      Then Value1 = Text_New(Date, Time, High + Range*.25,
                             GetSymbolName);
Value2 = Text_SetLocation(Value1, Date, Time, High + Range*.25);
```

More Indicators: Tom DeMark's Projected Ranges

Tom DeMark has based his projections of tomorrow's price ranges on the positioning of today's opening price relative to yesterday's closing price. If today's open is greater than the previous close, the projections are biased upward; if lower than the close, they are biased downward. The next indicator, from *New Trading Systems and Methods* by Perry Kaufman, uses the separate functions to plot the projected high and low of the range.

```
{TSMDeMark Projected Ranges, pp. 383-384
   Copyright 1998-2004, PJ Kaufman. All rights reserved }
      vars: TSMhigh(0), TSMlow(0);
      TSMhigh = TSM_DeMarkrangehigh(open,high,low,close);
      TSMlow = TSM_DeMarkrangelow(open,high,low,close);
      plot1(TSMhigh,"TSMhigh");
      plot2(TSMlow,"TSMlow");
```

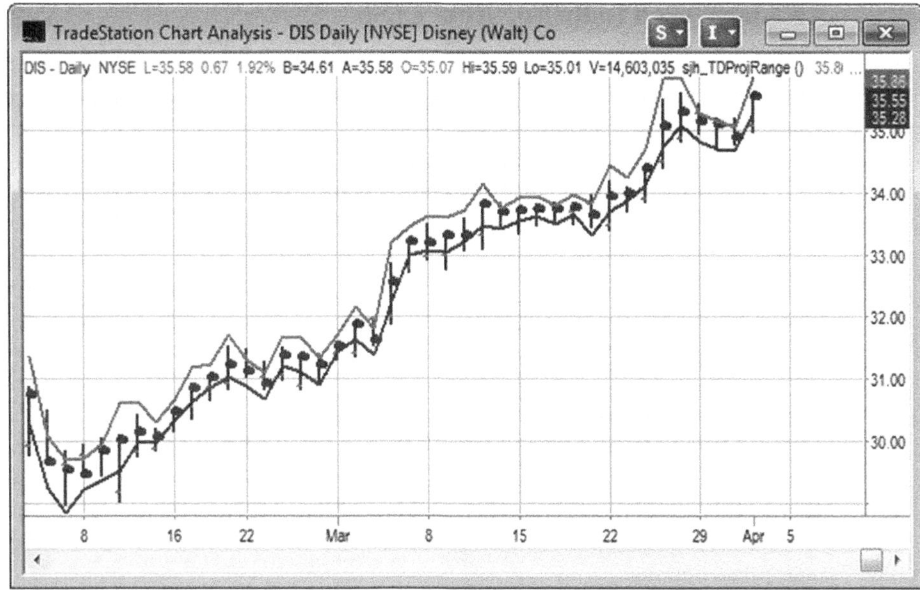

FIGURE 12.17 Tom DeMark Projected Ranges

The functions referenced in the code are supplied here, and illustrated in Figure 12.17.

```
// Range Low Function
inputs: popen(numeric), phigh(numeric), plow(numeric), pclose(numeric);
vars: avg(0);
if pclose < popen then
      TSM_DeMarkrangelow = (phigh + pclose + 2 * plow) / 2 - phigh
         else if pclose > popen then
      TSM_DeMarkrangelow = (2 * phigh + plow + pclose) / 2 - phigh
         else
      TSM_DeMarkrangelow = (phigh + plow + 2 * pclose) / 2 - phigh;
// Range High Function
inputs: popen(numeric), phigh(numeric), plow(numeric), pclose(numeric);
vars: avg(0);
if pclose < popen then
      TSM_DeMarkrangehigh = (phigh + pclose + 2 * plow) / 2 - plow
         else if pclose > popen then
      TSM_DeMarkrangehigh = (2 * phigh + plow + pclose) / 2 - plow
         else
      TSM_DeMarkrangehigh = (phigh + plow + 2 * pclose) / 2 - plow;
```

A RadarScreen Indicator from ELSI

The following RadarScreen indicator, written originally by the corporate TradeStation group called EasyLanguage Study Issues, shows how to use an indicator in RadarScreen to highlight stocks that are meeting certain criteria. We are going to take a look at that indicator right after I tell you a bit about RadarScreen.

RadarScreen is like a spreadsheet rather than a piece of graph paper. Rather than drawing a chart with a moving line and price bars, RadarScreen forms a table of numbers associated with each symbol. When you open RadarScreen, it is blank, except for the column headings. You can either type in the symbols you want to study, or you can insert a preformed list of symbols. I usually insert the Nasdaq 100 to start with, or maybe the S&P 500 if I feel like looking at that many symbols.

Inserting a symbol list into RadarScreen is as easy as right-clicking the first cell and choosing **Insert Symbol List.** After you put the symbols in the window, you will see that several default fields have filled in: **Symbol, Interval, Last, Net Chg, Net % Chg, Bid, Ask, High, Low,** and **Volume.** To insert an indicator, right-click on any one of these fields, or click to the right of them all and choose **Insert Analysis Technique.** Choose the indicator you want to add and press the **Add** button. You can then move it up or down with the appropriate buttons.

```
INPUT:PRICE(HIGH), LENGTH(0),MORETHAN(0),LESSTHAN(0),
VFLOOR(1.5),VCEILING(VOLUME * .5);
IF PRICE > AVERAGE(CLOSE,LENGTH) AND
      CLOSE >= MORETHAN AND CLOSE <= LESSTHAN AND
            VOLUME >= AVERAGE(VOLUME,LENGTH) * VFLOOR
            OR VOLUME <AVERAGE(VOLUME,LENGTH) *
            VCEILING THEN BEGIN
                  PLOT1(HIGH,"HIGH");
                  PLOT2(LOW,"LOW");
         END;
```

Inserting this indicator in a RadarScreen window will plot the highs and lows only when they meet the criteria. The resulting window is shown in Figure 12.18. Notice in the rightmost columns that only a few of the cells have numbers in them. Those are the ones that meet or exceed the criteria.

Just as an aside, I personally don't like the looks of the code just given. It is in all caps and I think it is difficult to read. My style is to capitalize Reserved Words and leave my variables in lower case. What are your thoughts?

One more type indicator and then we will move on. This next one is from the book *Street Smarts: High Probability Short-Term Trading Strategies* by Linda Bradford Raschke and Laurence A. Connors. The indicator is called `/\ ch5 20bar h/1`, which deciphered means: /\ is the prefix that identifies all of Linda's code (just like `sjh_` is the prefix for mine); `ch5` means Chapter 5 in the book, and it looks back 20 bars for highs and lows. The code is in Figure 12.19 and the chart produced by the code is in Figure 12.20. Her code is written by

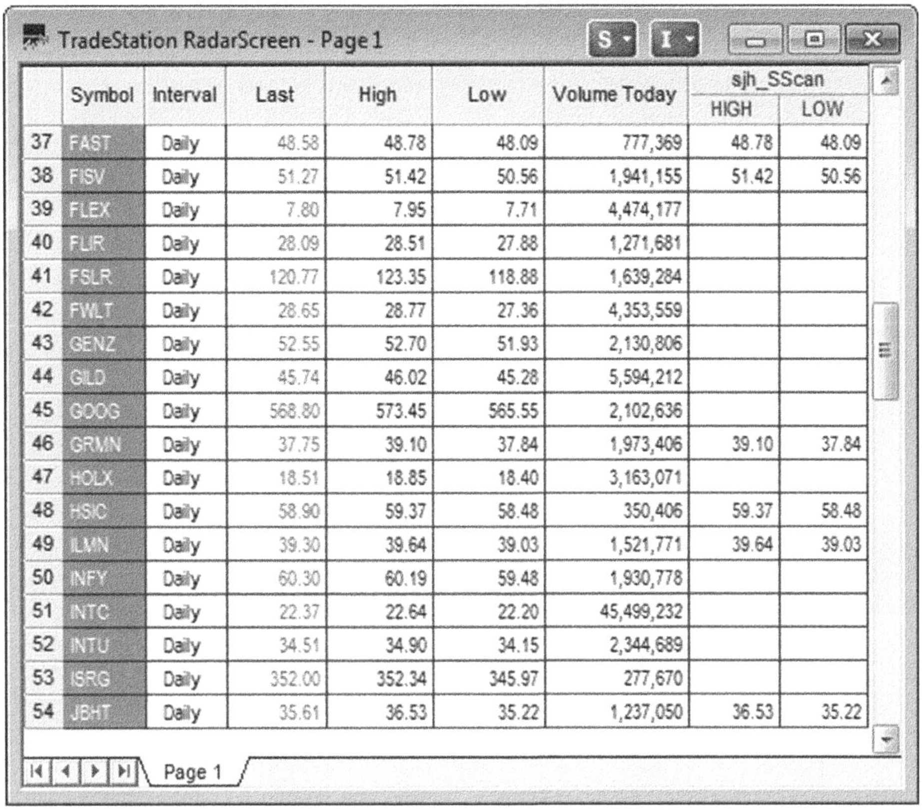

TradeStation RadarScreen - Page 1

	Symbol	Interval	Last	High	Low	Volume Today	sjh_SScan	
							HIGH	LOW
37	FAST	Daily	48.58	48.78	48.09	777,369	48.78	48.09
38	FISV	Daily	51.27	51.42	50.56	1,941,155	51.42	50.56
39	FLEX	Daily	7.80	7.95	7.71	4,474,177		
40	FLIR	Daily	28.09	28.51	27.88	1,271,681		
41	FSLR	Daily	120.77	123.35	118.88	1,639,284		
42	FWLT	Daily	28.65	28.77	27.36	4,353,559		
43	GENZ	Daily	52.55	52.70	51.93	2,130,806		
44	GILD	Daily	45.74	46.02	45.28	5,594,212		
45	GOOG	Daily	568.80	573.45	565.55	2,102,636		
46	GRMN	Daily	37.75	39.10	37.84	1,973,406	39.10	37.84
47	HOLX	Daily	18.51	18.85	18.40	3,163,071		
48	HSIC	Daily	58.90	59.37	58.48	350,406	59.37	58.48
49	ILMN	Daily	39.30	39.64	39.03	1,521,771	39.64	39.03
50	INFY	Daily	60.30	60.19	59.48	1,930,778		
51	INTC	Daily	22.37	22.64	22.20	45,499,232		
52	INTU	Daily	34.51	34.90	34.15	2,344,689		
53	ISRG	Daily	352.00	352.34	345.97	277,670		
54	JBHT	Daily	35.61	36.53	35.22	1,237,050	36.53	35.22

Page 1

FIGURE 12.18 RadarScreen Indicator

the EasyLanguage expert Richard Saidenberg, who is an amazing programmer. Note that he also uses all caps in his code.

This code counts up to `Prev` and then plots a point at the highest high of the last `Length` number of bars. If the current high is the same as the highest high, the code resets the counter to zero and starts counting again. The effect of this code is to put a point above and below the bars at support and resistance areas. Looking at the chart, you can see that when price breaks out of the resistance, it tends to move decisively. Those moves could be good short-term trades. In Chapter 13 we will take a look at Raschke's associated strategy to see how to trade with stops. For now, it is time to move on to another type of indicator: **ShowMe**.

SHOWME

The **ShowMe** study is a great tool for locating specific criteria. Much like the indicator we just looked at, the ShowMe study places a marker at each bar that meets your criteria. The

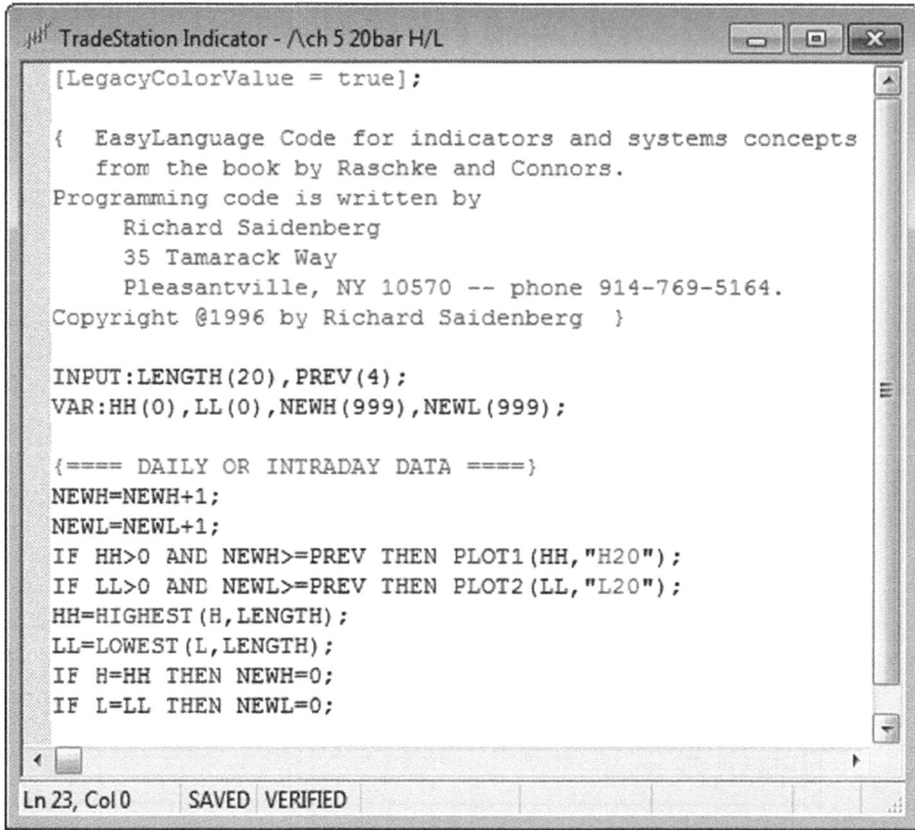
TradeStation Indicator - /\ch 5 20bar H/L

```
[LegacyColorValue = true];

{  EasyLanguage Code for indicators and systems concepts
   from the book by Raschke and Connors.
Programming code is written by
     Richard Saidenberg
     35 Tamarack Way
     Pleasantville, NY 10570 -- phone 914-769-5164.
Copyright @1996 by Richard Saidenberg  }

INPUT:LENGTH(20),PREV(4);
VAR:HH(0),LL(0),NEWH(999),NEWL(999);

{==== DAILY OR INTRADAY DATA ====}
NEWH=NEWH+1;
NEWL=NEWL+1;
IF HH>0 AND NEWH>=PREV THEN PLOT1(HH,"H20");
IF LL>0 AND NEWL>=PREV THEN PLOT2(LL,"L20");
HH=HIGHEST(H,LENGTH);
LL=LOWEST(L,LENGTH);
IF H=HH THEN NEWH=0;
IF L=LL THEN NEWL=0;
```

Ln 23, Col 0
SAVED
VERIFIED

FIGURE 12.19 /\ch5 20 Bar h/l Code

ShowMe draws a marker at the price you specify in the **Plot** statement. You can change the plot style and color of your ShowMe using tabbed items in the **Properties** dialog box.

For instance, if you would like to find every bar that is higher than the three bars to either side, a great way to do that would be to put a red dot over those bars. Having done so, visual investigation of your chart is simple.

That one is easy to see without a red dot, I hear you say. Well, how about some of the complex Larry Williams or Joe Ross patterns like `‘‘...close up X days after a day with a close lower than the previous day but greater than today’s open.’’` Patterns like this are easier to see with a red dot, believe me.

The **ShowMe** study is based on the **IF . . . THEN . . . ELSE** structure. **IF** the pattern we're looking for happens, **THEN** plot a red dot, **else** forget the red dot.

A **Key Reversal** day is a formation that is often said to have forecasting power. It is a weaker form of an **island reversal.** You may study these and many other technical analysis

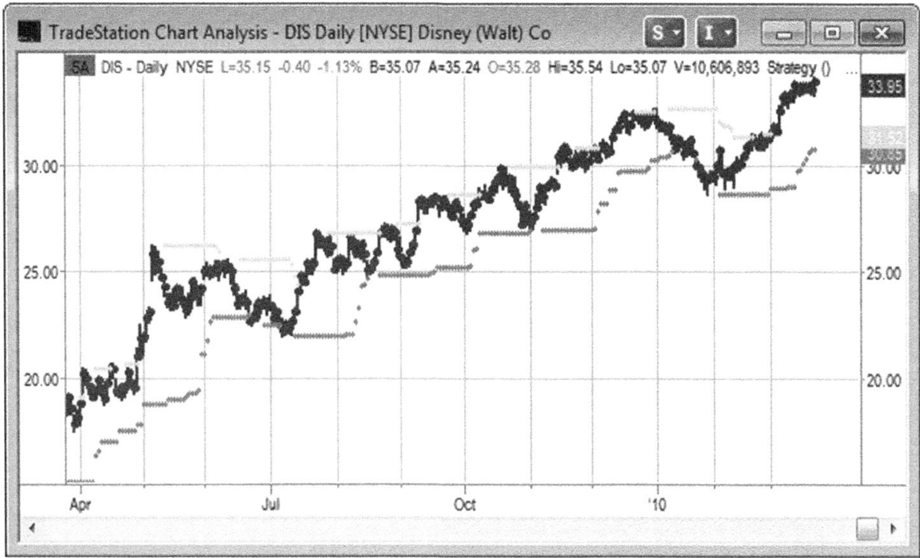

FIGURE 12.20 /\ch5 20 Bar h/l Chart

patterns in any of the standard texts mentioned in the bibliography. The TradeStation **Key Reversal Down ShowMe** marks the high of any bar whose high is higher than the previous bar's high and whose close is lower than the previous bar's close. A Key Reversal Down pattern can signify the end of an uptrend when confirmed by increases in trading volume. The code for this type ShowMe is shown in Figure 12.21.

```
Input: Length(10);
       IF CurrentBar > 1 and High > Highest(High,Length)[1] THEN
       Plot1(High,''BrkOut High'');
```

FIGURE 12.21 Key Reversal Down ShowMe

Applying the ShowMe to the chart clearly isolates the bars meeting the condition, as seen in Figure 12.22. Every time a Key Reversal Down happens, the ShowMe places a red dot above the high of the bar. Notice how often the market reverses direction, or at least stalls, immediately after the red dot.

Writing a ShowMe is just like writing an indicator, except that TradeStation is not plotting a continuous line. Instead, the ShowMe plots only when the condition is true.

The testing component of your business is perhaps the most important. Visual inspection of the chart looks promising, but putting the strategy on the chart and running

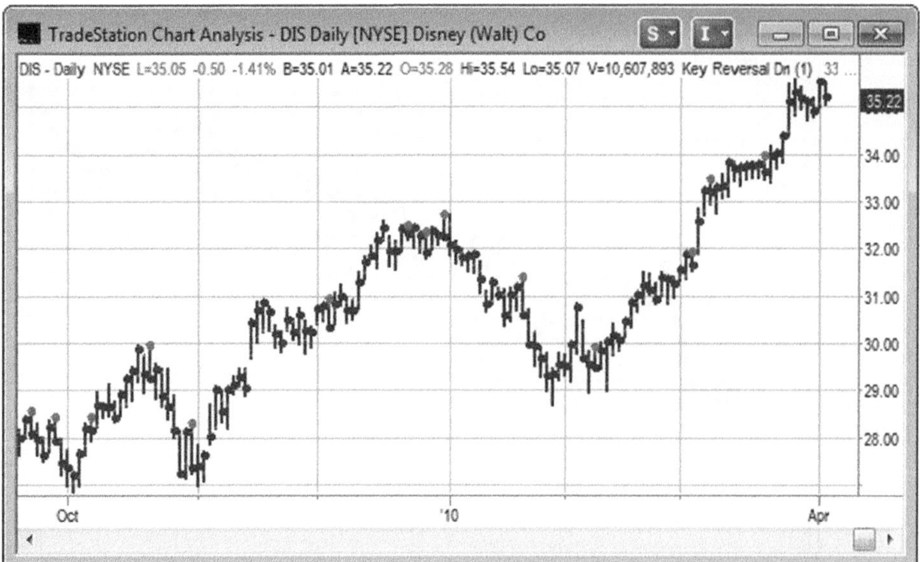

FIGURE 12.22 Key Reversal Down Chart

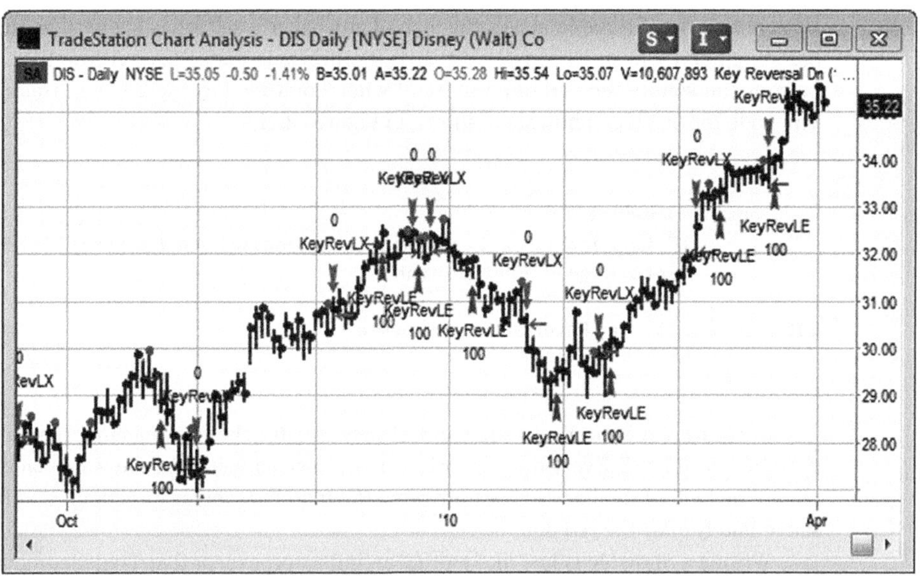

FIGURE 12.23 Key Reversal Strategy

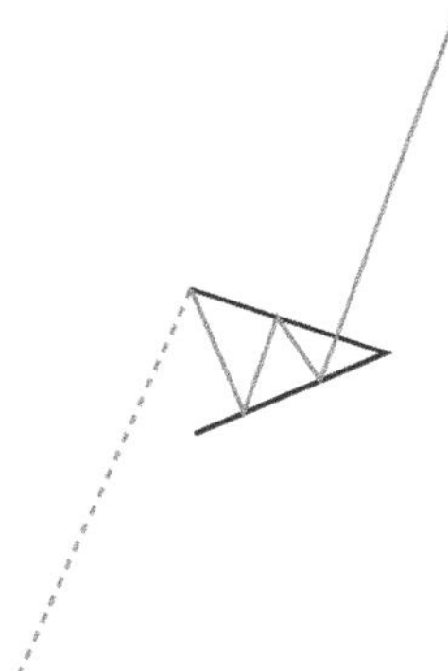

FIGURE 12.24 Pennant Formation

optimizations and analyzing spreadsheets tells the truth about the chart. The strategy for this ShowMe is:

```
inputs: Length(1);
if High > Highest(High, Length)[1] and Close < Close[1] then
      Sell Short ("KeyRevSE") next bar at market;
```

Running this with just the defaults produces a TNP of negative $558 for a one-year period. The chart for the strategy is in Figure 12.23. Just because the first pass fails, it doesn't mean this is a doomed strategy. With refinement and testing it is possible that this could become a working strategy. But we are not going to do that here; this section is about ShowMes.

ShowMe Pennant Formations

One of the many built-in ShowMe indicators provided with the standard version of TradeStation is called **PennantBrkout.** A pennant formation in what was previously an uptrend is considered a bullish signal, indicating that the current uptrend may continue. A pennant formation follows a steep or nearly vertical rise in price and consists of two converging trendlines that form a narrow, tapering flag shape. The pennant shape generally appears as a horizontal shape rather than one with a downtrend or uptrend. Apart from its shape, the pennant is similar in all respects to the flag. The pennant is also similar to the Symmetrical triangle or wedge continuation patterns; however, the pennant is typically shorter in duration. The formation is pictured in Figure 12.24.

The TradeStation code for this Pennant ShowMe is too long to present here, so I leave it to you to open the code in the EasyLanguage PowerEditor and study it on your own.

Martin Pring states in his book, *Technical Analysis Explained*, as the pennant develops, the volume tends to decrease. "A pennant is in effect a very small triangle. If anything, volume tends to contract even more during the formation of a pennant than during that of a flag." As with flags, when the pennant completes you will often observe a sharp spike in volume. In *Technical Analysis of the Financial Markets*, John J. Murphy says that pennants and flags are relatively short term and should be completed within one to three weeks. He also notes that, by comparison, the bullish patterns take longer to develop than the related bearish patterns.

Sunny's Pennant Indicator

This one is not a ShowMe. While we are on the subject of pennants, however, I thought I would show you my own Pennant Indicator. This code draws an n bar pennant, where n is an integer that I have set to 4 as default. With it one can not only draw the pennants but can instruct the indicator to draw the horizontal lines that form the breakout lines from the pennants and can have it draw the values of the high and low comprising the pennant. Mine draws more pennants than the TS indicator. I don't know if that's good or bad, but it makes a pretty sturdy strategy.

The code for my indicator is not only too lengthy to present here, but it is proprietary, so I'm not going to reveal it. I'll give you a hint, though, in case you want to try to program it yourself. All you have to do is look for n bars with lower highs and higher lows on each successive bar.

Figure 12.25 shows my pennant indicator at work. The way I trade with it is to take trades at breakouts and use stops at the lower edge of the pennants.

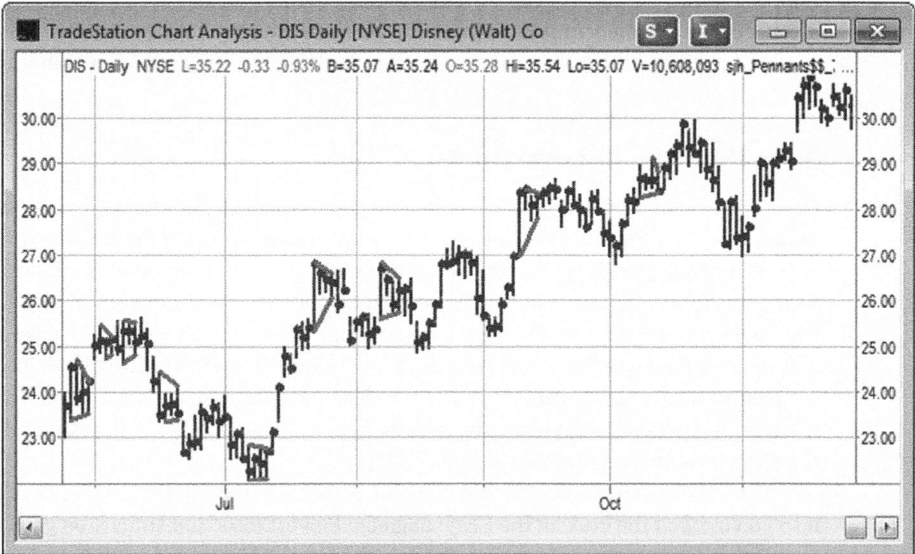

FIGURE 12.25 Sunny's Pennant Indicator

PAINTBARS

The **PaintBar** study paints the bar a different color from the rest, based on your condition. PaintBars make it easy to visually identify a series of bars that share a common characteristic. The default EasyLanguage PaintBar template is shown in Figure 12.26. You can begin with this template to construct your own code.

The PaintBar study is used to illuminate a condition. This condition might be anything that you have calculated prior to the plot statements or passed into the routine as an input.

```
IF Condition1 THEN BEGIN
      Plot1(High, ``Top of Bar'');
      Plot2(Low, ``Bottom of Bar'');
END;
```

FIGURE 12.26 Original PaintBar Template

You would use the **ShowMe** study when your condition is *infrequent* and use the **PaintBar** study when you expect the condition to occur *frequently*. The ShowMe study would place far too many dots on the chart for it to be useful information, if the condition occurred frequently.

The PaintBar study uses a **pair of plot statements** to change the color or style of a bar. The first plot statement tells where to start painting the bar and the second plot statement tells where to stop painting. Typically you would start painting the bar at the low and stop painting at the high. But there are times when you might want to paint just the top or bottom half of the bar, or any portion of it between specified values.

The modern versions of TS have replaced this pair of plot statements concept with a special plot statement called **PlotPaintBar.**

The command can be stated as **PlotPaintBar** or abbreviated as **PlotPB.** The full format, with options, is:

```
PlotPB(BarHigh, BarLow [, BarOpen [, BarClose [, ``<PlotName>``[,
ForeColor[, Default[, Width]]]]]]);
```

where

BarHigh, BarLow, BarOpen and **BarClose**	Numeric expressions representing the high, low, open, and closing prices for the bar to be drawn by the PaintBar study.
<**PlotName**>	The name of the plot.
ForeColor	An EasyLanguage color used for the plot (also referred to as PlotColor).
Default	(reserved for future use)
Width	A numeric value representing the width of the plot.

You can also specify only two of the bar parameters instead of the four: BarHigh, BarLow, BarOpen or BarClose. However, you must specify either two or four of the bar parameters, and not three.

EasyLanguage will automatically append a number from 1 to 4 to each of the four plot statements represented by the statement, in order to identify each plot name individually. If the maximum number of characters for the PlotName is used, the last character in the string will be dropped and replaced with the appropriate number for each plot. If the PlotName parameter is not included, the plots will be assigned the generic plot names Plot1, Plot2, Plot3, or Plot4.

You can use the **Plot** Reserved Word described previously to write a PaintBar study; however, it is recommended that you use the **PlotPaintBar** or **PlotPB** Reserved Word instead.

As with the regular plot statements, you can use the **Displace** option when applying the analysis technique to a chart, to displace the plot to the right or left of the underlying prices. For example:

```
Plot[-5](Average(C,9));
```

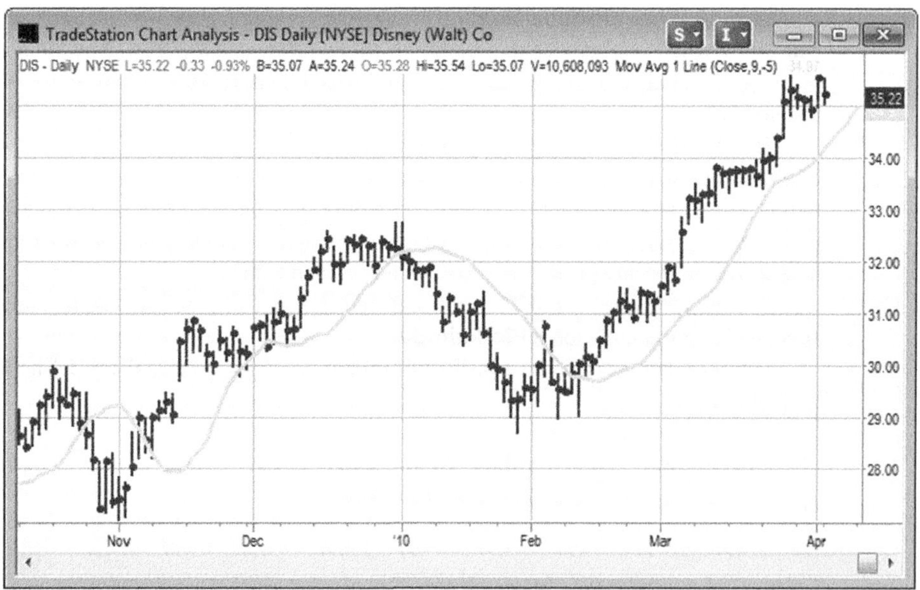

FIGURE 12.27 Displaced Plot

would calculate the plot value using the current bar, but draw it on the chart 5 bars ahead. The negative number for `displacement` was used to draw the plot ahead of the current bar. To draw the plot before the current bar, use a positive number for `displace`.

We haven't looked at this feature of EasyLanguage yet. Now is the time. I have been to numerous conferences where at least one speaker touted the predictive qualities of using a

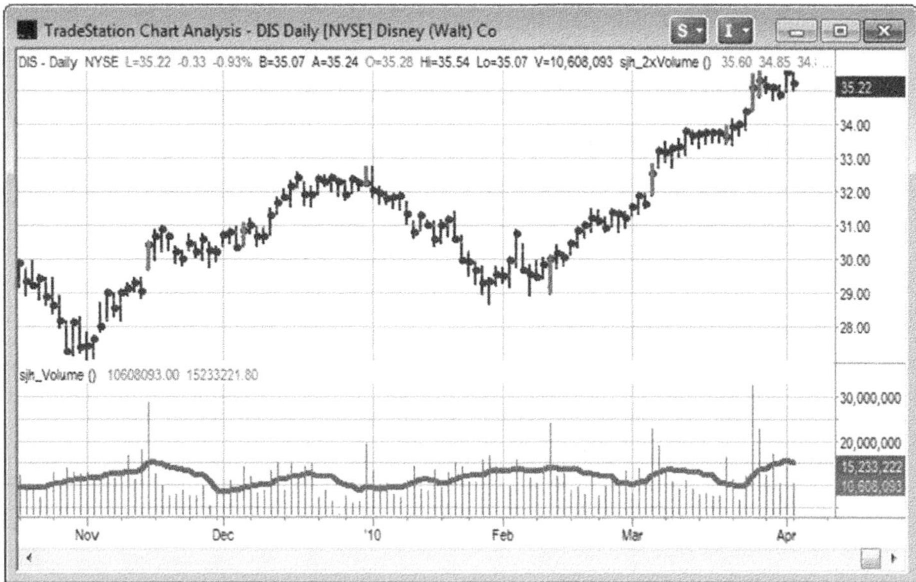

FIGURE 12.28 PaintBar 1.5x Volume

displaced indicator. I personally have not experimented enough with displacements to state either positively or negatively regarding the subject. Nevertheless, you should know how to do it. And if you find it works as a leading indicator, give me a call and let's talk. In the example, the speakers I have heard say to displace your moving average forward and then simply trade the move above or below the average. Let me know what you find out.

NOTES

The parameter `Default` currently has no effect. However, a value for the parameter is required in order to specify a width (the subsequent parameter), as discussed in the example. `Default` is just a placeholder currently.

EXAMPLE

The next instructions can be used in order to paint red, thick bars when they have 50% more volume than the 10-bar average.

```
If Volume > 1.5 * Average(Volume, 10) Then
      PlotPB(High, Low, Open, Close, "AvgVol", Red,
default, 2);
```

The chart for this example is shown here in Figure 12.28. Note that **Volume** is not a bar component (which it probably should be) but is treated as an indicator in TS. For this example, I copied the volume indicator to `sjh_Volume` and altered the code to include `Plot2(Average(Volume,10),''AvgVol'');` That way you could readily see the volume bars that exceeded the average. I suppose I could have gone the extra step and made another average that was 50% above the first average, but I generously leave that exercise to the reader.

ADDITIONAL EXAMPLE

The next instructions paint the area between the two plots of the **Bollinger Bands Indicator** when the 14-bar **ADx** value is lower than 25 (Figure 12.29):

```
Variables: Top(0), Bottom(0);
Top = BollingerBand(Close, 14, 2);
Bottom = BollingerBand(Close, 14, -2);
If ADX(14) < 25 Then
      PlotPaintBar(Top, Bottom, "Area", Blue);
```

In this example, notice that although we omitted the `BarOpen` and `BarClose` parameters, we were still able to specify the name and color of the plot.

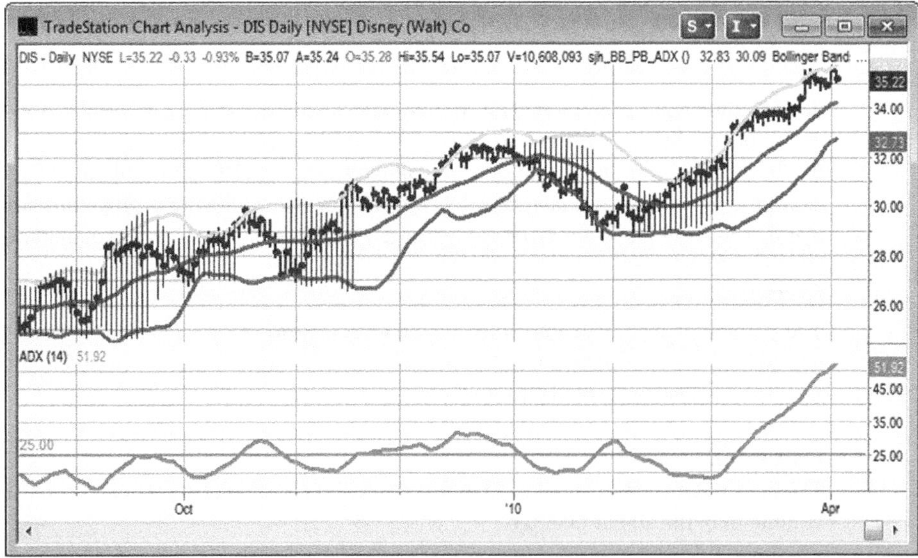

FIGURE 12.29 ADX < 25, Bollinger Bands

One More PaintBar Study

One more exercise and then we will move on down in the hierarchy of routine types. This next example shows bars that are painted only when RSI shows overbought or oversold

(Figure 12.31). The oversold bars are painted SpringGreen[2] and the overbought bars are painted red. This color scheme allows one to very quickly discern buy and sell opportunities visually. The RSI Indicator is plotted in SubGraph1 so you can compare the painted bars to the associated RSI values. The code for the chart in Figure 12.31 is shown in Figure 12.30.

```
IF RSI(C,9)>70
   THEN PlotPB(High, Low, Open, Close, ``OverBot'', red, default, 2);
IF RSI(C,9)<30
   THEN PlotPB(High, Low, Open, Close, ``OverSld'', RGB(0,255,127),
default,2);
```

FIGURE 12.30 Code for RSI PaintBar Study

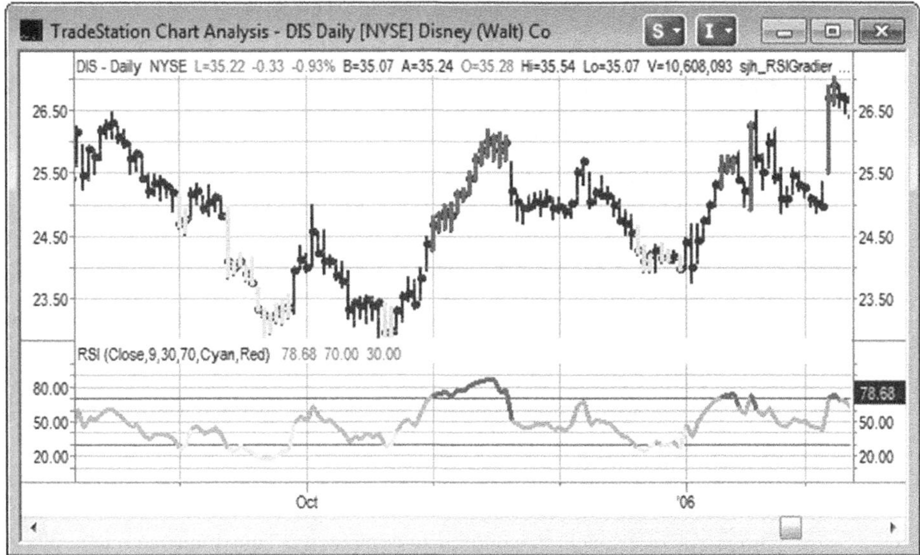

FIGURE 12.31 RSI PaintBar

FUNCTIONS

We have gone from the top downward, and we are now near the bottom of the ladder, to the basis of all the other routine types: functions. We began with strategies and moved to

[2]SpringGreen is an official color name in Windows. To view all 500 color names, go to www.moneymentor.com/Reference.html and click on Color Palette. There you will also find associated RGB and Hex values.

indicators and then into specialized types of indicators. We come now to functions, the building blocks of all other routines. A function is simply a reusable piece of code. If I've said that once I've said it 2,000 times as I have taught traders all over the world to use EasyLanguage. It makes sense when said that way. To define it officially and precisely only confuses those new to programming languages.

A function performs a task and returns a value to the routine that called it. If, for instance, you wanted to add four numbers (say, Open, High, Low and Close) and divide them by 4, you could write the code for that every time you needed it, or you could write it once and then refer to it whenever you needed the calculation done. That would be "calling a function." The return value of the function would be the result of the calculation.

If we called this function **AddParts,** then rather than writing the formula again and again, we would simply write something like:

```
Value1 = AddParts;
```

We could get more sophisticated and use input values to the function, specified in parentheses and then used in the calculation. That way the function would have some flexibility and not always have to add the same four numbers. It might look like:

```
// function AddParts
INPUTS: Price1(Open), Price2(High), Price3(Low), Price4(Close);
AddParts = (Price1 + Price2 + Price3 + Price4) /4;
```

Notice that the last line of code in the function assigns the value of the calculation to a variable whose name is the name of the function. That is the "return" value. It is the value that goes back to the original calling routine. Even if you don't want to send a value back, you must use this assignment statement and at least give it a dummy value, say zero or 1. Function names may not contain any spaces or any nonalphanumeric characters other than the underscore (_). A function can refer to another function or functions. Functions may be nested.

Functions save space; they minimize complexity. They improve readability and reduce errors. For now just know that with coding, it is time efficient both from the coder's standpoint and from the computer's standpoint to reuse code instead of repeating it.

We will get more specific and delve deeper into functions in Chapter 14, but before that, we are going to do a little buying and selling. The next chapter will teach you the basics and intermediates of buying and selling. The advanced issues of buying and selling are left to another book: *Advanced EasyLanguage*. Rather seems like an oxymoron, doesn't it?

If you want me to write *Advanced EasyLanguage*, send me an email at sunny@moneymentor.com. If there are enough responses I'll talk to my publisher about it.

As long as I'm soliciting, I'm also thinking about writing one that analyzes every indicator included with TradeStation to see what is profitable. I thought I'd also include public domain indicators and indicators from the TradeStation Forum. Let me know if you want me to write this one too.

CHAPTER 13

Buying and Selling

In This Chapter

- Introduction
- Entries
- Order Names
- Exits

INTRODUCTION

A strategy (aka system) is a collection of strategies, where a strategy is a collection of buy and sell orders along with their corresponding exits. In this chapter we will investigate the types of buy and sell orders you may specify in EasyLanguage to create strategies. An "Advanced EasyLanguage" manuscript is the place to cover combining strategies together to form systems. In this chapter, we will only address putting buy and sell orders together to form a single strategy.

Buy low; sell high. That's all there is to it. Everything else is about defining and recognizing "high" and "low."

Trading is planning followed by action. Buying and selling are the actions that make or lose money in trading. Remember that it's all on paper until you close your trade. You don't lose money if your paper profit is reduced; you lose money only when a closed trade is unprofitable. In other words, don't count your chickens until they are hatched.

Buying and selling need to be timed properly to result in a meaningful profit. Buying high, followed by selling low, doesn't get you anywhere.

All the efforts you are putting into your research are to discover what is high and what is low. The previous chapters are to assist you in discovering what is high and what is low. This chapter is to help you enter the proper orders with the correct terminology.

ENTRIES

Buying and selling at the market is perhaps the simplest concept to grasp. So, let's start there. Two of the order actions initiate an entry: **Buy** and **Sell Short.** The order actions **Sell** and **Buy to Cover** are for exiting a position.

Strategy orders are generated on the bar close event and *placed in the market* based on the order action. For example:

```
Buy this bar on close;
```

When this order is generated, the following actions are taken:

- A Buy arrow is placed on the current bar at the close tick mark.
- If the order is generated on an intraday bar and not the last bar on the chart, the order is sent directly into the market as a market order.
- If the order is generated on an intraday bar and it is the last bar on the chart, or it is a daily, weekly, or monthly chart, then the order is sent directly to the after-hours market as a Day+ limit order at the price at the close of the bar. If it is not filled in the after-hours session, then the order will be placed as a limit order on the open of the next trading day.

There are many ways to place an order to buy or sell something, but all orders consist of a few crucial elements, as shown in Figure 13.1.

Element	Meaning
Action	Buy, buy to cover, sell, sell short
Quantity	How many shares or contracts to buy or sell?
Item	What you want to buy or sell?
Order Type	Market/Limit, etc.
Condition	Under what condition will you buy or sell?
When	When should this order be placed?

FIGURE 13.1 Buy and Sell Orders

An **order** in TradeStation looks like:

```
Buy ("{Order Name}") {Number of shares/contracts} Contracts
{Order Action};
SellShort("{Order Name}") {Number of shares/contracts}
Contracts {Order Action};
```

These are the default forms of the statements. You may be more specific by adding Reserved Words to restrict or clarify your intent. Or you may be more casual, letting TradeStation assume some of your intent. The only mandatory word in the sentence is "buy" or "sell". Recall from Chapter 4 that there are Skip Words in EasyLanguage that are ignored by the processor but that make your code easier to read. They are shown again in Figure 13.2.

a	by	of	the
an	does	on	was
at	from	place	
based	is	than	

FIGURE 13.2 Skip Words

ORDER NAMES

When using multiple long entries within a strategy, it is helpful to label each entry order with a different name. By naming entry orders, you can easily identify all positions, both on the chart and in the Strategy Performance Report under the Trades tab. Also, naming the entry orders allows you to **tie an exit to a particular entry order.** For more details, see the definition of the Sell statement in the Exits section below.

To name a long entry order, include a descriptive name in quotation marks and within parentheses after **Buy.** For example:

```
Buy (``Entry1'') next bar at open;
```

The "order name" is optional and specified in parentheses. The order name is plotted above the sell arrows and below the buy arrows on your chart, for easy identification. If you use only one buy and one sell order in your system, you don't need to use the order name, but then you will only see `Buy` or `Sell` with no strategy name. However, when your system becomes more complex and incorporates several buy or sell signals, you will want to differentiate between them. For instance, you might have one buy order that takes advantage of trending markets and one that you use only in choppy markets. You would then want to see on your chart which order type was used. These two orders would look like Buy("Trendy"); and Buy("Choppy").

Figure 13.3 shows multiple strategies identified on a chart. Just for illustration, I have included our MACD, the Key Reversal, and my proprietary Solar09 strategies on this chart.

EXAMPLES

These are examples of entry statements:

- `Buy(``Support'') 5 contracts next bar at Low Limit;`
- `Sell Short(``BreakOut'') 500 Shares next bar MidPrice or Lower;`
- `Buy (``My Entry'') 100 shares next bar at open;`

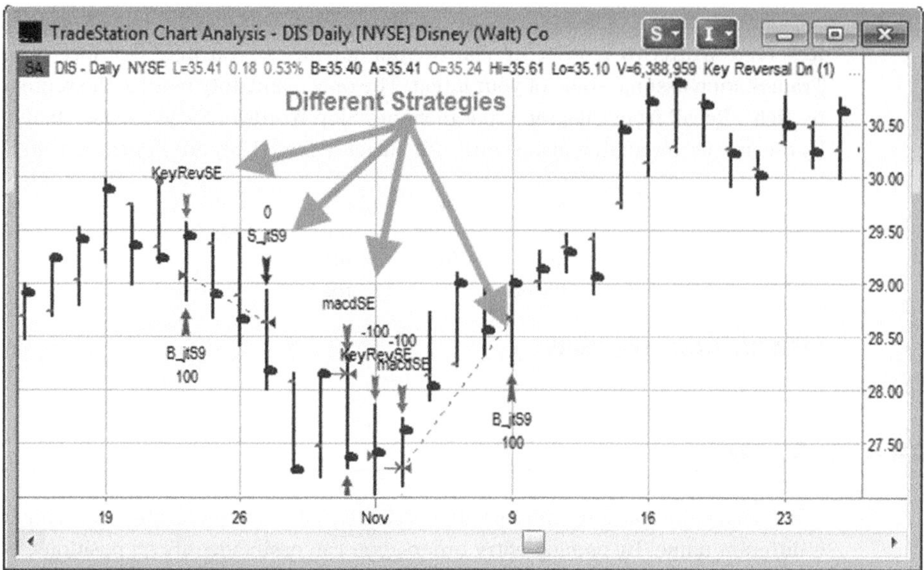

FIGURE 13.3 Order Names on a Chart

- `Buy 5 contracts next bar at 100.50 limit;`
- `Buy Value1 shares next bar at 100.50 limit;`
- `SellShort (''My Entry'') 200 Shares Next Bar at Market;`
- `SellShort 5 Contracts This Bar on Close;`
- `SellShort Value1 Shares Next Bar at Market;`

The **Buy** order is used to establish a long position. If there is already an existing open short position, an order to cover the short position is sent first. Once the short position is closed, the **Buy** order is sent to establish the long position. A **SellShort** order is used to establish a short position. If you already have an existing open long position, the order closes the long and establishes a short position.

The **Item** you want to buy or sell is governed by the symbol on the chart upon which you place the strategy. If your chart is of `DIS` and you place the strategy on this chart, you will buy and sell `DIS`. If your chart displays the symbol `ESM10`, you will trade the E-Mini.

When placing an order in TradeStation, you must specify one of the five different **order actions** with your Buy or Sell (or Buy to Cover or Sell Short) order. They are:

. . . this bar on close;
. . . next bar at open;
. . . next bar at market;
. . . next bar at `yourprice` **Stop;**
. . . next bar at `yourprice` **Limit;**

The default form of the order statement next asks you to specify the **number of contracts** you are buying or selling. With futures you buy contracts; with stocks you are buying shares. If you do not put a number in this place, TradeStation will assume either 1 or the default number of contracts you have specified in the **General** tab, under **Format → Analysis Techniques → Properties for All.** I generally leave this value set to 100, a round lot.

Strategy orders are generated on the **bar close event** and *placed in the market*[1] based on the order action. For example:

```
Buy this bar on close;
```

When this order is generated, these actions are taken:

- A Buy arrow is placed on the current bar at the close tick mark.
- If the order is generated on an intraday bar and not the last bar on the chart, the order is sent directly into the market as a market order.
- If the order is generated on an intraday bar and it is the last bar on the chart, or it is a daily, weekly, or monthly chart, then the order is sent directly to the after-hours market as a Day+ limit order at the price at the close of the bar. If it is not filled in the after-hours session, then the order will be placed as a limit order on the open of the next trading day.

In Figure 13.4, you can readily see the little tick markers that show the buy and sell being executed at the open of the next day.

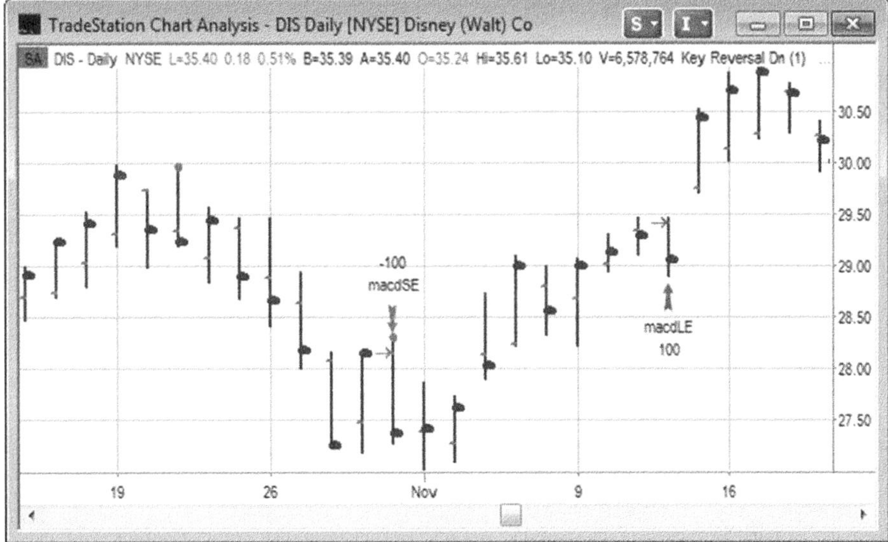

FIGURE 13.4 Buy and Sell Arrows with Entry Markers

[1]That is, given to the floor trader, or entered into the computer system that actually executes trades.

As you become more specific with your orders, you may use the more complete form of the order statement:

{action} {quantity} {item} {order type} {condition} {when}

You will use EasyLanguage Reserved Words to fill in the blanks or let TradeStation make its assumptions where you don't explicitly state them.

EXAMPLE

Action	Qty	Item	Order Type	Condition	When
Buy	3	March S&P	Market		

FIGURE 13.5 "Buy 3 March S&Ps Market"

The assumptions with this order are that I have no "conditions" and my "when" is now.

It's rather like the journalist's worksheet: who, what, where, when, why, and how. Orders placed with your broker take the form "Joe, this is Sunny. Buy 3 March S&P at the market, day order." In this short, cryptic sentence I've told my broker all five crucial elements. The action is "buy," the quantity is "3," the item is the "March S&P 500 futures contract," the condition is understood to be "at the going market price," and when is "before the close of today's trading session."

The actions listed above are presented in Figure 13.5, with the elements corresponding to each action. Think of Figure 13.5 as a pull-down menu, with the selections listed in the figure.

The full list of all possible actions and combinations is below in Figure 13.6. You won't use most of these actions for a long time to come, but at least you will have a reference to come back to when you want to know what they are. When I buy or sell something at the market, I am asking my broker or floor trader to place the order at the current price and take whatever price he gets as a bid. The risk of this type order is that the market could be trading at 101.5 when you placed your call and have run up to 102, or more, before the order gets filled. Market orders sometimes experience considerable slippage.

The advantage to a market order is that you are not trying to tell the market where to go. When you place an order at a specific price you are hoping the market will come to you. And it may not. In a fast-moving market, that 102 fill could look pretty good by the end of the day, if the market never again saw 101.5. Placing a market order is like throwing up your hands and saying "just buy it now, whatever you get."

In EasyLanguage, writing an order to buy at the market is definitely easy. It looks like this:

```
BUY;
```

The remainder of the crucial elements that specify the trade are assumed by TradeStation.

Actually, I exaggerated just a bit. EZL used to be that simple, but since TS became a brokerage house the structure of the simplest buy order command is: `BUY this bar;` I don't

Instruction	Choices
Order Name	• Limit • Market • LimitIfTouched • MarketIfTouched • StopMarket • StopLimit • TrailingStop
Frequency Once	• Once • OncePerBar • EndOfBar • Always
Account	as a string
Action	• Buy • Sell • SellShort • BuyToCover • BuyToOpen • BuyToClose • SellToOpen • SellToClose
Symbol Category	• Equity • Future • EquityOption • FutureOption
MySymbol	as a string
Quantity	as a number
Duration	• Day • Day+ • GTC • GTC+ • GTD • GTD+ • IOC • FOK • OPG • 1Min • 3Min • 5Min

FIGURE 13.6 Order Configurations

Instruction	Choices
GTDDate	mm/dd/yy
Route	• Intelligent • ARCX • BTRD • NSDQ • SuperDot • AMEX • Box • CBOE • ISE • NYSE • Arca • PHLX
AllOrNone	"True" or "False"
BuyMinusSellPlus	"True" or "False"
Discretionary	number, 0=not discretionary
ECNSweep	"True" or "False"
IfTouched	number, 0=not if touched
LimitPrice	"True" or "False"
NonDisplay	"True" or "False"
Peg	False, Best, Mid
ShowOnly	number, 0=not show only
StopPrice	number
TrailingAmount	number, 0=not using trailing amount
TrailingType	If Peg is not being used, this must be set to " ". Set to string "MinMove" if trailing amount is to be specified as a number of minimum moves. Enter "Pts" if trailing amount is to be specified in points. Enter "Pct" if trailing amount is to be specified as a percentage amount.

FIGURE 13.6 *(Continued)*

know why you must specify `this bar;` if you don't the EZL compiler will tell you that you must say `this bar`, so why can't it assume it? Whatever the reason, that is the current command structure.

Unless you specify otherwise, TradeStation assumes you want to buy one contract of whatever item you have in your chart, **at the market,** and the order is **good until canceled.** TradeStation fills all market orders at the open of the next bar.

Now that I have mentioned another input (at the open of the next bar) for "**when**", let's get to enumerating all the possibilities. The earliest order entry that can be generated with TradeStation is for the close of the current bar. Orders can be generated for (when) as shown in Figure 13.7.

```
This Bar
Next Bar
Close of current bar
On the close
Open of next bar
Open of tomorrow
Tomorrow
Today on the close
```

FIGURE 13.7 "**When**" Orders May Be Placed

The words "today" and "tomorrow" are held over for compatibility with previous versions of TradeStation but actually mean "the next bar." If you are trading with intraday data, the word "tomorrow" will still just mean "the next bar," so be careful.

Order Types

Orders may be placed not only at the market but also at specified limits or stops. The available basic **order types** in TradeStation are shown in Figure 13.8.

Closing	placed and filled on the close of the current trading bar
Market	placed and filled at the open of the next bar
Stop	placed at the open of the next bar; filled if and when condition is met
Limit	placed at the open of the next bar; filled if and when condition is met

FIGURE 13.8 Order Types

It is easy to understand how TradeStation interprets **Closing** and **Market** orders. Closing orders are filled on the currently trading bar, at the **closing price of that bar.** Market orders are filled at the **open of the next bar.** Frequently these two prices in your data will be the same. Sometimes, in fast-moving or illiquid markets, you will find a gap between the close of one bar and the open of the next. In real life, however, the market order will experience slippage and will likely not be filled at the price of the open of the next bar, but rather at a price that happens seconds (or even minutes) later. In fact, in real-life trading, in my own experience, sometimes the markets move so fast that the order doesn't get filled for long periods of time. Usually, then, they call the order Not Held, which means the broker can't be held to filling at the market price. That's when the markets are scary and exciting.

Stops and Limits **Stop** orders and **Limit** orders are a little more difficult to conceptualize.

With a **stop** order you are asking your broker to go to the market when a certain price is hit. Thus, the statement

```
BUY at 101.5 on a Stop;
```

will take a long position on the next bar at 101.5 or anything higher.

Stop orders can be useful if you are looking to take a position on a breakout. Let's say, for instance, that the market has been trading in a narrow channel and we want to buy when it breaks above that channel. A stop order above the high of the channel would be the way to place that order.

With a **limit** order, you are asking your broker to pay no more than a certain price. Thus, the statement

```
BUY at 101.5 Limit;
```

will take a long position on the next bar only if the broker can get you the price of 101.5 or lower.

Limit orders attempt to get a "good price" for the item you want to buy. You might place a limit order within a channel, looking to get a price between the high of the channel and the low. For some reason you have decided that anything above that price would be too much to pay. Personally, I never use limit orders. My feeling is that I cannot tell the market where to go or influence its movement in any way. I don't know what a good price is, because I don't know where prices will go tomorrow or next week. A stock that looked expensive at 150 could go to 300; witness the surge in Internet stocks during the dot-com boom. A limit order would have completely kept me out of the 150-point rise because I had an opinion about "expensive."

EXITS

You may want your buy signals to close your sell signals, and your sell signals to close your buy signals. This type of system is called a **reversal system.** With a reversal system you do not need to specify exits, as they just naturally happen as part of the process. Buys are closed by sells and sells are closed by buys. Usually, moving average strategies are reversal systems. When the moving average crosses upward you buy; when it crosses downward you sell. If, however, you want to exit on conditions that you specify or calculate, which may happen prior to the reversal, you will want to use Sell and BuyToCover commands to get out of your Buy and Sell Short positions.

Way back when, for you users of TS 2000i and earlier, there were two commands that worked well for exiting longs and shorts. The commands were ExitLong and ExitShort. They made a lot of sense, but they are gone in the current versions of TS. I include examples of their use only for users of older versions.

EXAMPLE

```
ExitLong 10 contracts on close;
```

{generates an order to exit 10 contracts from a long position at the Close of the current bar}

EXAMPLE

```
ExitShort from entry (“Choppy”) next bar at 175 Stop;
```

{generates an order to exit the long position “Choppy” on the next bar at a price of 175 or lower}

Sell and SellShort

The Sell order is used to close a long position. The order specifications are defined by parameters in the Sell statement. A **SellShort** order is used to open a short position. The space doesn't matter with this command: you can say **SellShort** or **Sell Short.** They are equivalent. As with buys, the **sell** and **sellshort** orders take the following form:

{action} {quantity} {item} {order type} {condition} {when}

where		
	Action	Either Sell or SellShort.
	Quantity	How many shares or contracts to sell.
	Item	What you want to sell.
	Order	Type One of: closing, market, stop or limit.
	Condition	Under which you will sell, i.e., “at High + 1 point”.
	When	When this order should be placed, i.e., “this bar,” “next bar”.

Exit orders do not pyramid. Once the exit criteria are met and the exit order is filled, the order is ignored for that position until the position is modified (i.e., more shares/contracts are bought or a new long position is established).

```
Sell [(“Order Name”)] [from entry (“Entry Name”)]
[Number of Shares [Total]]
[Execution Method];
```

Only the word Sell and the Order Action are required by the order syntax rules. For example:

```
Sell this bar on close;
```

or

```
Buy next bar at 45 stop;
```

If no other parameters are specified, the default value for the Order Name is "Sell", and all long contracts will be exited from the position.

Each portion of the statement, Order Name, Number of Shares, from entry and Execution Method are described next.

Order Name Again

When using multiple exits within a strategy, it is helpful to label each exit order with a different name. This enables you to identify these exit orders in both the price chart and the Strategy Performance Report. To assign an exit order a name, specify a name in quotation marks and within parentheses immediately after the word Sell.

EXAMPLE

```
Sell ("My Exit") This Bar on Close;
```

This instruction closes the entire long position, and the order is labeled My Exit.

Tying an Exit to an Entry

It is possible to tie an exit instruction to a specific entry. This can be achieved only if you named the long entry, and the long entry is in the same strategy as the exit order. Consider the next strategy:

```
Buy ("MyBuy") 10 Shares Next Bar at Market;
Buy 20 Shares Next Bar at High + 1 Point Stop;
Sell From Entry ("MyBuy") Next Bar at High + 3 Points Stop;
```

In this example, the strategy may buy 30 shares total; your long position is 30 shares. However, the Sell instruction closes out only the 10 shares bought using the MyBuy entry order. It ignores any other order and does not close out the other 20 shares. Therefore, this strategy leaves you long 20 shares.

You can also close part of an entry order. For example, if your entry, which you named "MyBuy", buys 10 shares, you can specify that you want to exit from entry "MyBuy" but only close out 5 shares, not the entire 10:

```
Sell From Entry ("MyBuy") 5 Shares Next Bar at High + 3 Points Stop;
```

IMPORTANT: The entry name is case sensitive. Be sure to use consistent capitalization. Also, it is important to remember that exit orders do not pyramid; therefore, if an exit does not close out an entire position, you will need another exit order (or reversal order) in order to close out the position.

Number of Shares/Contracts

To specify how many shares/contracts to close out, use a numeric expression followed by the word "Shares" or "Contracts" after the trading verb Sell.

```
Sell 100 Shares This Bar on Close;
Sell From Entry ("MovAvg") 10 Shares Next Bar at High + 1 Point
Stop;
```

NOTE: The words "Shares" and "Contracts" are synonymous.

If you do not specify the number of shares or contracts in the Sell instruction, the exit order closes out the whole long position, rendering your position flat.

When you specify the number of shares/contracts, the Sell instruction exits the specified number of shares/contracts from every open entry.

Therefore, if the strategy allows for pyramiding and has bought 500 shares twice (for a total of 1,000 shares), and an order to Sell 100 Shares is placed by the strategy, the instruction will exit a total of 200 shares: 100 shares from each of the two entries.

However, if you want to exit a total of 100 shares, you can use the word **Total** in the Sell instruction. Using the word "Total" instructs the Strategy to exit 100 shares from the first open entry (first in, first out). For example:

```
Sell 100 Shares Total This Bar on Close;
Sell From Entry ("MovAvg") 10 Shares Total Next Bar at High +
1 Point Stop;
```

Order Action

Just as in buy Orders, you must specify one of the five different order actions with your Sell order.

. . . this bar on close;
. . . next bar at open;
. . . next bar at market;
. . . next bar at `yourprice` **Stop;**
. . . next bar at `yourprice` **Limit;**

The execution method **this bar on close** is provided for back-testing purposes only; it enables you to back-test "market at close" orders, which you cannot automate using TradeStation. Since all orders are evaluated and executed at the end of each bar, TradeStation reads and issues the **this bar on close** order once the bar has closed (e.g., once the daily trading session has ended). TradeStation fills the order using the close of the current bar, but you have to place an order at market to be executed on the next bar. This invariably introduces slippage.

The execution method **Sell next bar at price Limit** instructs TradeStation to exit a long position at the first opportunity, at the specified price or higher. The execution method **Sell next bar at price Stop** instructs TradeStation to exit a long position at the first opportunity, at the specified price or lower.

By default, a strategy stop or limit order will be considered filled at the stop or limit price if that price falls within the range of the bar on which the order is active. In real-life, fast market action could pass you by and you might not get filled. TradeStation has no way to simulate that possibility; it simply "fills" if the price was seen in the bar. When automating a strategy, the user has the option of selecting whether to mark strategy orders as filled based on price activity or when the TradeManager reports that the order was actually filled in the market.

Tying the Exit Price to the Bar of Entry

When specifying the execution method, you can vary stop and limit orders by using **At$** instead of the skip word "at". Using `At$` forces the strategy to refer to the value the numerical expression price had on the bar where the entry order was generated. Consider this:

```
Sell From Entry ("MyBuy") Next Bar At$ Low - 1 Point Stop;
```

This statement places an order to exit the long position at one point lower than the low of the bar where the order to establish the long position was generated. For example, if an order to **Buy next bar** is generated today, the prices referenced will be today's, not tomorrow's. Even though the order was placed and filled tomorrow, it was generated today, and so that is the bar referenced.

To use the At$ Reserved Word, you must name the entry order, and the Sell instruction must refer to that specific entry order.

As another example, if the maximum risk you will tolerate for a position is 5 points under the closing price of the bar on which you generated the entry order, you can use this statement:

```
Sell From Entry ("MyBuy") Next Bar At$ Close - 5 Points Stop;
```

This is a valuable technique that allows you to refer easily to the prices of the bar on which the entry order was generated.

EXAMPLE

This statement exits all contracts/shares of your open long position at the close of the current bar. Your position will be flat.

```
Sell This Bar on Close;
```

MORE EXAMPLES

The next instruction exits all contracts/shares opened by `Entry#1` at the open of the next bar; the exit order is named `LongExit`.

```
Sell ("LongExit") From Entry ("Entry#1") Next Bar at Market;
```

The next statement places an order to close 5 contracts/shares in total, at the low of the current bar minus 1 point, or anything lower. This order is active throughout the next bar (until filled or canceled).

```
Sell 5 Contracts Total Next Bar at Low - 1 Point Stop;
```

The next instruction places an order to exit 100 shares from every entry at the high plus the range[2] of the current bar or anything higher. This order is active throughout the next bar (until filled or canceled) and will be named `HighExit`.

```
Sell ("HighExit") 100 Shares Next Bar at High + Range Limit;
```

The next statement allows you to monitor your risk by placing an exit order 5 points below the closing price of the bar that generated the long entry order:

```
Sell From Entry ("MyBuy") Next Bar At$ Close - 5 Points Stop;
```

SetExitOnClose

SetExitOnClose is a built-in stop Reserved Word used to place an order to exit all shares or contracts in all positions on the close of the last bar of the trading session on an intraday chart. It is similar to my function **sjh_ CloseLastTrade,** except that it is only for intraday charts and it closes out at the end of every trading session.

For historical simulations, **SetExitOnClose** generates a market order on the bar close event of the last intraday bar for each day in the chart. When used in an automated strategy placing real-world orders, **SetExitOnClose** generates a limit order into the postmarket trading session (if one exists); otherwise a market order is generated for the open of the next regular session day.

In Chapter 16 I will show you how to exit a few minutes before the end of the trading session, so you don't have to wait for the open of the next day to close your positions. This is valuable since there are frequently gaps, either for you or against you, on the open of the next day.

SetExitOnClose by default uses the closing session time specified by the custom session settings of the chart.

[2]Remember that **Range** is a built-in function that calculates the difference between the **High** and the **Low.**

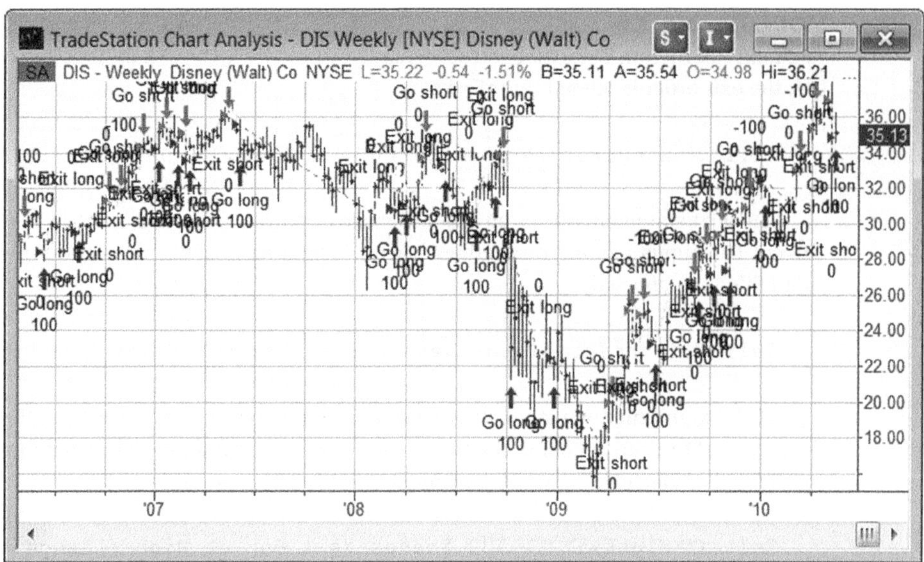

FIGURE 13.9 Gold Digger

SetExitOnClose can only be used in a Strategy; it doesn't make sense in an indicator or function.

EXAMPLES

EXAMPLE: THOMAS STRIDSMAN

This code is a snippet from the book *Trading Systems That Work* by Thomas Stridsman, downloadable on the Internet. This code shows clean and clear examples of opening a trade with a Buy and exiting it with a Sell followed by opening a short with SellShort and closing it with a BuyToCover. The chart in Figure 13.9 illustrates the code in this example.

```
Condition1 = CloseM(1) > C and CloseW(1) > C and C[1] > C;
Condition2 = CloseM(2) < CloseM(1) and CloseM(1) < C and CloseW(2)
     < CloseW(1) and CloseW(1) < C and C[2] < C[1] and C[1] < C;
If Condition1 = True Then
     Buy (‘‘Go long’’) Next Bar at open;
If C[2] < C[1] and C[1] < C Then
     Sell (‘‘Exit long’’) This Bar at close;
If Condition2 = True Then
     Sell Short (‘‘Go short’’) Next Bar at open;
If C[1] > C Then
     Buy to Cover (‘‘Exit short’’) This Bar at close;
```

EXAMPLE: LINDA RASCHKE'S TURTLE SOUP

With kind permission from Linda Raschke, the following is a real-life example of buys and sells using stops.

This strategy is presented in her book with Larry Connors, *Street Smarts: High Probability Short-Term Trading Strategies*, and is called Turtle Soup in reference to the famous Turtle Traders. The chart output by the code in Figure 13.10 is shown in Figure 13.12. Notice that the code in Figure 13.10 refers to a function called TURTLESOUPPLUS1, which has two inputs. The code for this function is presented in Figure 13.11.

Turtle Traders came about from the question: Are traders born or can they be taught to be great traders? Wall Street trader Richard Dennis, who quickly learned how to trade after starting as a runner at the Chicago Mercantile Exchange in 1966 at age 17, had made a reported $200 million by 1983. To settle an argument with fellow trader William Eckhardt about whether trading ability was innate or could be taught, he put an ad in the *Wall Street Journal* offering to teach candidates how to trade in two weeks, and then backed them with his own money. Of the thousands of people who applied, 23 turtles were accepted. Their trading made $100 million for Dennis, leading some to become highly successful traders in their own right. Why were they called turtles? The story goes that the two men were in Singapore, at a turtle farm, when they made the wager that Dennis could train traders "like they raise turtles in Singapore." Essentially, the turtles were taught to be trend-followers who used breakout patterns. This example is an extension of the turtle theory.

```
Input: LENGTH(20),PREV(4),ENTRYADD(10 POINTS);
IF TURTLESOUPPLUS1(LENGTH,PREV)=1
      Then Buy Next Bar LOWEST(L,LENGTH)[1]+ENTRYADD Stop;
IF MARKETPOSITION=1 Then Sell Next Bar LOWEST(L,LENGTH) Stop;
IF TURTLESOUPPLUS1(LENGTH,PREV)=-1
      Then Sell Short Next Bar HIGHEST(H,LENGTH)[1]-ENTRYADD Stop;
IF MARKETPOSITION=-1 Then Buy to Cover Next Bar HIGHEST(H,LENGTH)
Stop;
```

FIGURE 13.10 Raschke and Connors Turtle Soup +1 Strategy

Raschke and Connors believed that the turtle-style trading could be profitable when traded on a large basket of markets and that its success was dependent on capturing significant trends. To trade this type of system, you must be committed to the concept and willing to hold on when the going gets tough. The aim of Turtle Soup is to profit from false breakouts. When the trend is strong, the reversal will not be long. However, sometimes reversals can be quite profitable. It is a typical swing trading pattern, working well in volatile markets.

The rules for buys are:

- Today, you must have a new 20-day low and the previous 20-day low has to be at least four days earlier.
- After the new low has occurred, place an entry buy-stop 5 to 10 ticks above the previous 20-day low.
- The stop-loss is 1 tick under today's low.

```
//TurtleSoup+1 Function:
INPUT:LENGTH(NUMERICSIMPLE),PREV(NUMERICSIMPLE);
VAR:HH(0),LL(0),NEWH(999),NEWL(999),TS1(0);
TS1=0;
NEWH=NEWH+1;
NEWL=NEWL+1;
IF HH[1]>0 AND NEWH[1]>=PREV AND C>HH[1] THEN TS1=-1;
IF LL[1]>0 AND NEWL[1]>=PREV AND C<LL[1] THEN TS1=1;
HH=HIGHEST(H,LENGTH);
LL=LOWEST(L,LENGTH);
IF H=HH THEN NEWH=0;
IF L=LL THEN NEWL=0;
TURTLESOUPPLUS1=TS1;
```

FIGURE 13.11 TurtleSoupPlus1 Function

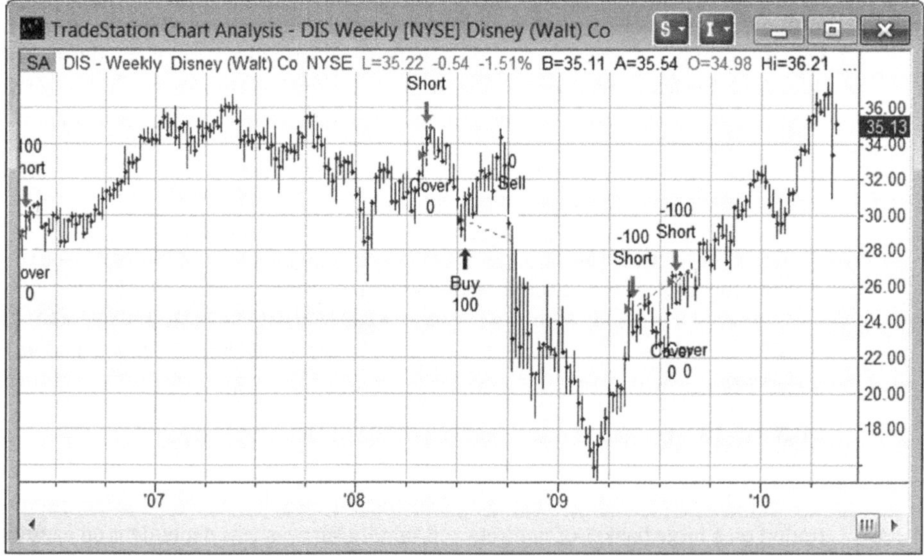

FIGURE 13.12 TurtleSoupPlusOne Chart

They suggest using a trailing stop for a trade that might last a few hours or even a few days.

Raschke and Connors named all their code, as I do, with a prefix to distinguish theirs from mine. They use the characters "/\" as a prefix to all their routines. This one is named "/\ ch 5 Turtle Soup +1." The code for all the routines in their book is available and well worth the investment.

The reason I have included this strategy here is to show you buy and sell orders using stops.

To learn more about Raschke, go to **www.lbrgroup.com.** Don't go to lbr.com, it is just a halfhearted attempt to capture folks looking for Raschke. Sign up for a free trial of her work; it's very informative. To learn more about turtles, go to **www.turtletrader.com,** the site of Michael Covel, who provides a wealth of valuable information about turtle traders and trading.

EXAMPLE: LIMITS

Using the Reserved Word `limit` in an order tells TS a condition for the buy or sell. Limit orders can be executed only on the **next** bar. Limit can be read as "this price or better," meaning **lower** for a long entry and short exit, **higher** for a short entry and long exit. Limit orders always require a reference price. (See the various examples in Figure 13.13.)

```
Buy next bar at Value1 Limit; // Goes long on the next bar at a
price of Value1 or lower

Buy next bar at 75 Limit; // Generates an order to enter a long
position on the next bar at a price of 75 or lower

SellShort next bar at 75 Limit; // Generates an order to enter a
short position on the next bar at a price of 75 or higher.

Sell next bar at 75 Limit; // Generates an order to exit a long
position on the next bar at a price of 75 or higher.
```

FIGURE 13.13 Using Limits

EXAMPLE: BUYS AND SELLS FROM BILL BROWER

This next example is from the book *Learning by Example* by William Brower of Inside Edge Systems. On page 22 he defines two functions that calculate the high and low of yesterday on an intraday basis. You'll want to keep this code, as it is very useful in many other applications. Bill uses these functions in a strategy starting on page 101. Credit for the strategy is given to Levon Patanyan. This strategy is designed for use on the S&P 500 intraday data.

To conserve printing space, I have taken the blank lines out of his code in Figure 13.14. You'll have to buy the book to see what the pretty code looks like. You can get this book and view all of his other products at **www.insideedge.net.** If you simply look up Bill Brower in Google, you will get someone's Facebook page and numerous other random links to other Bill Browers, but not the one you want. It's not our Bill Brower. Either use the link given above or search for Inside Edge Systems.

```
inputs: Percent(15), Longshort(0), noEntryafterTime(1430),
      ExitEndOfDayTime(1500), Proftarget(1500);
Vars: OT(0), Hy(0),Ly(0), LEVal(0), sEVal(0), mpos(0),
OK2Enter(false);
if currentsession(0)<>currentsession(0)[1] then OT = Open;
Hy = IES_HYstrday;
Ly = IES_LYstrday;
mpos = marketposition;
LEVal = OT+ .01*Percent*(Hy-Ly);
sEVal = OT- .01*Percent*(Hy-Ly);
if T < noEntryafterTime then begin
      if mpos < 1 and Longshort > -1
         and c < LEVal then Buy(``PctRng LE'') next bar LEVal stop;
   if mpos> -1 and Longshort < 1
         and c > sEVal then SellShort(``PctRng sE'') next bar
         sEVal stop;
end;
Buytocover(``le sx'') next bar LEVal stop;
Sell(``se lx'') next bar sEVal stop;
if T>=ExitEndOfDayTime then begin
      Sell(``EOD lx'') next bar market;
      BuyToCover(``EOD sx'') next bar market;
end;
SetProfitTarget(proftarget);
```

FIGURE 13.14 Strategy from Bill Brower

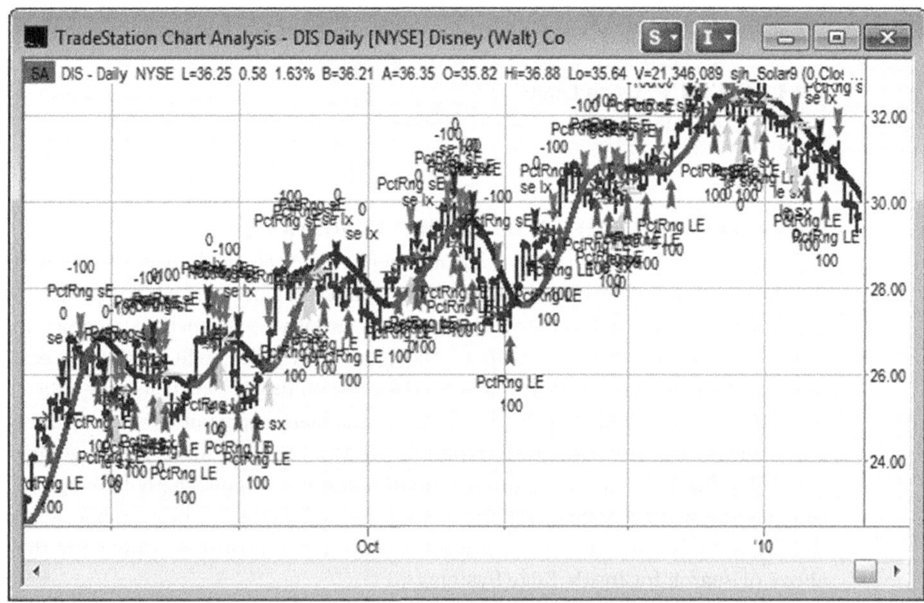

FIGURE 13.15 Levon Strategy

I will let you discover the meaning of the code by purchasing and reading *Learning by Example*. Bill explains it very well. What I want you to see is the chart of the results, which is in Figure 13.15.

There are tons of buys and sells, primarily because this strategy was intended for intraday data and for the S&P 500. Taking a look at the TNP on the Strategy Performance Report (Figure 13.16) shows us that this strategy produces a small loss of <$408.00>. I would expect a much greater loss with so many intraday trades on a daily chart. Remember that I conduct all my tests on the same one-year of data, so that we are working with apples in all cases, not apples and oranges.

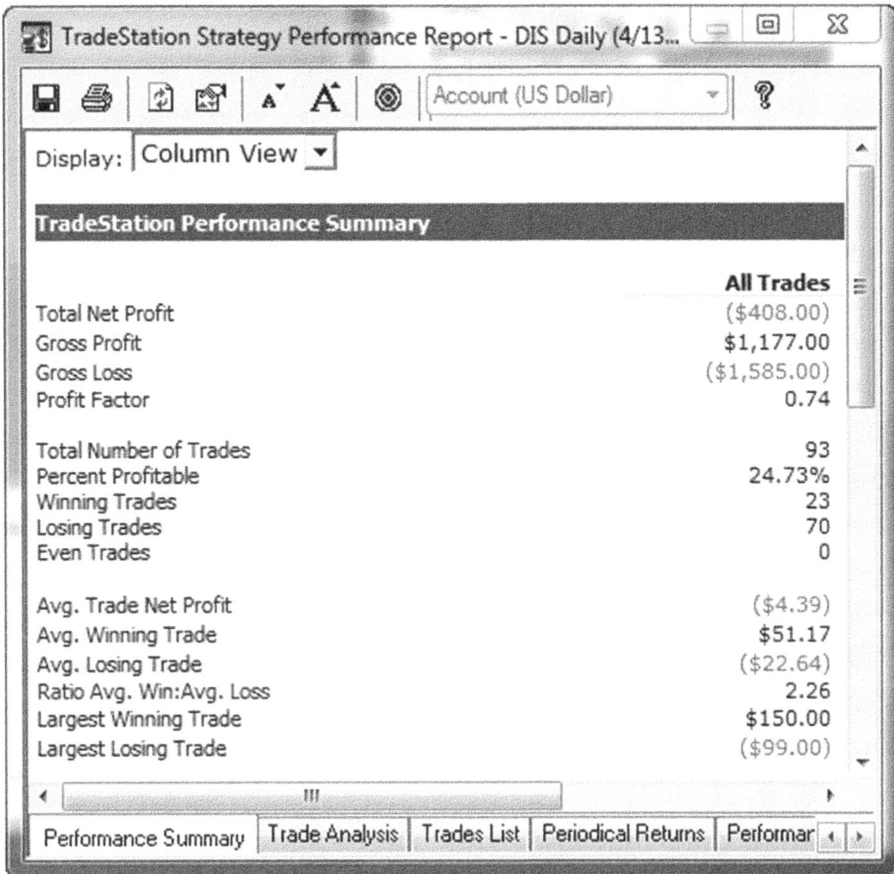

FIGURE 13.16 Strategy Performance Report for Levon

Let's change the data from daily to intraday, 15-minute data (see Figure 13.17). Again, it will be necessary to change the symbol attributes to make sure it is selecting one year of data. It would behoove you to click **Default** while you are changing the attributes,

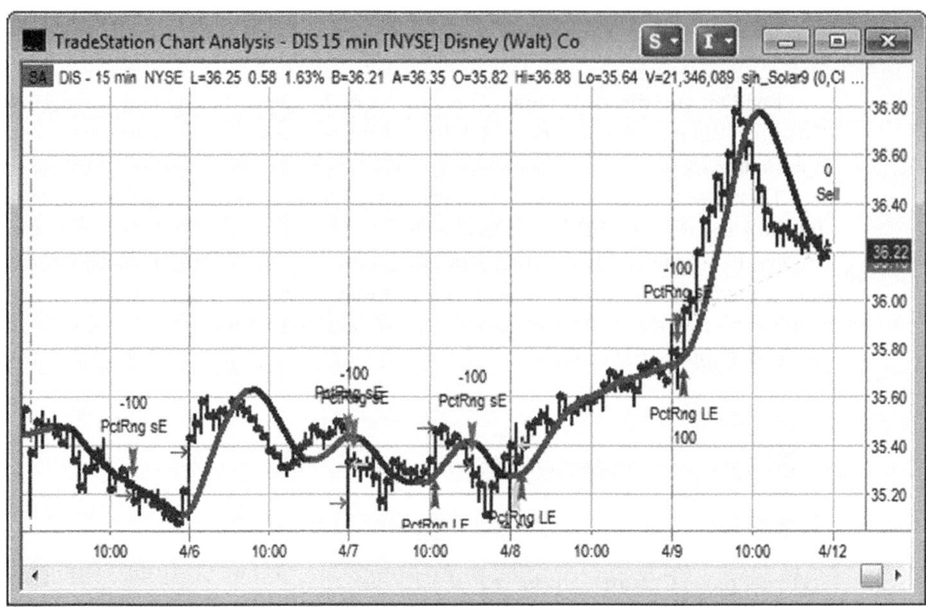

FIGURE 13.17 15-Minute Data on Levon Strategy

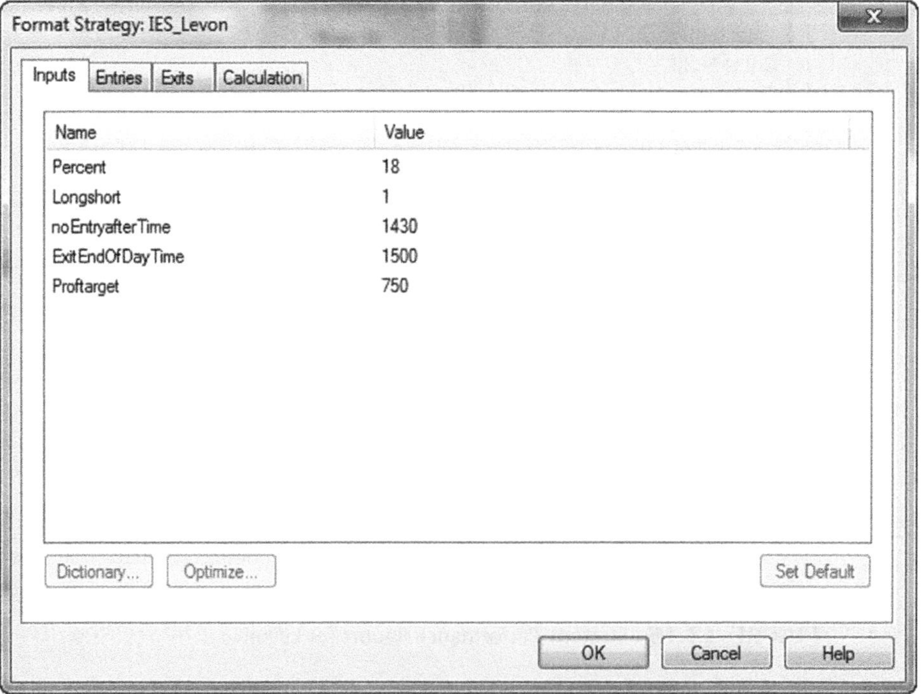

FIGURE 13.18 Inputs for 1-Minute Levon Strategy

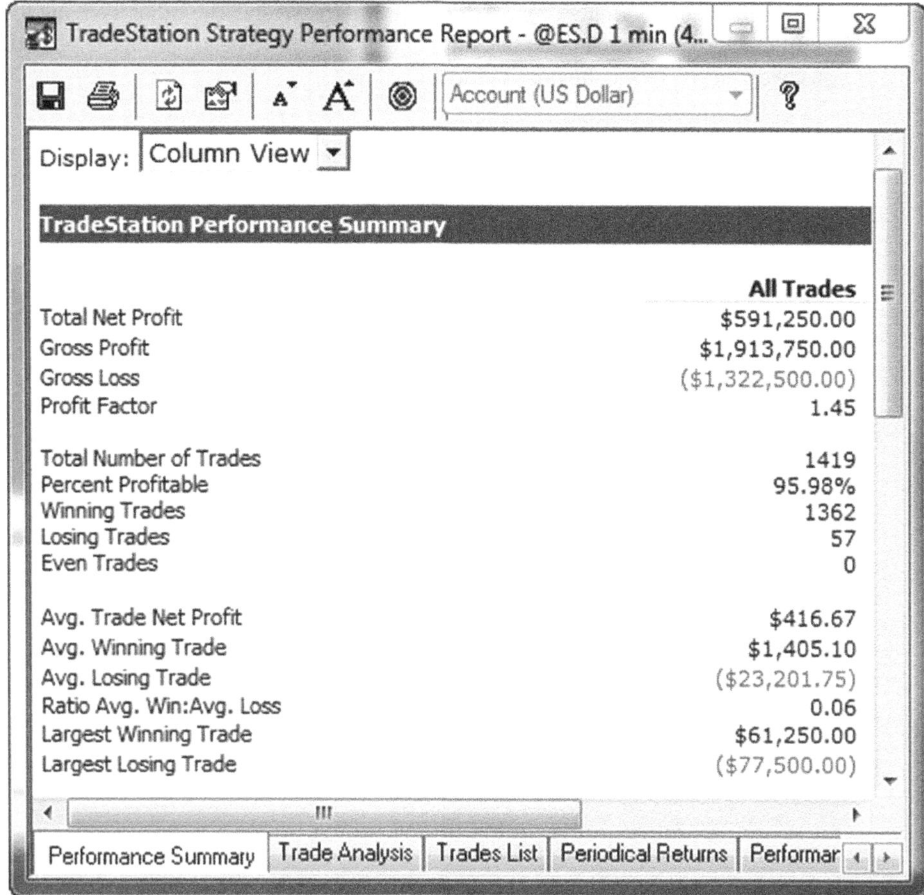

FIGURE 13.19 Optimized Results for Levon Strategy

so that in the future all 15-minute charts will contain one year of data. In addition, I added my CloseLastTrade strategy to the chart, so that TS would close the open trade and count it in the statistics. Making these changes to the chart brings us a small positive net profit of $300; the chart is in Figure 13.17.

Just so you can be thrilled and excited by the possibilities, after a few strategic optimizations I am able to show you a profitable scenario with this strategy. It turns out that the default inputs are not the best in all situations. Further, I have switched to one-minute data for this exercise. The inputs used for the TNP of $591,250 are shown in Figure 13.18. The Strategy Performance report for those inputs is shown in Figure 13.19.

Does this mean that this is the system you should use and start trading with now? Does this mean you too can make $500,000 dollars in one year? No, definitely not. You haven't tested it. You haven't gotten familiar with all its nuances and configuration possibilities. You have to make it yours first, by playing with it extensively. The other systems presented in this book also hold great potential, but none of them have been optimized as I did this one. I just wanted you to see the possibilities.

A Few More Examples of Buys and Sells

- `Buy(''Support'') 5 contracts next bar at Low Limit;`
- `Buy to Cover (''Profit'') 10 contracts next bar at MidPrice stop;`
- `Sell (''Profit'') 10 contracts next bar at MidPrice stop;`
- `Sell Short(''BreakOut'') 500 Shares next bar MidPrice or Lower;`
- `Buy (''My Entry'') 100 shares next bar at open;`
- `Buy 5 contracts next bar at 100.50 limit;`
- `Buy Value1 shares next bar at 100.50 limit;`
- `SellShort (''My Entry'') 200 Shares Next Bar at Market;`
- `SellShort 5 Contracts This Bar on Close;`
- `SellShort Value1 Shares Next Bar at Market;`

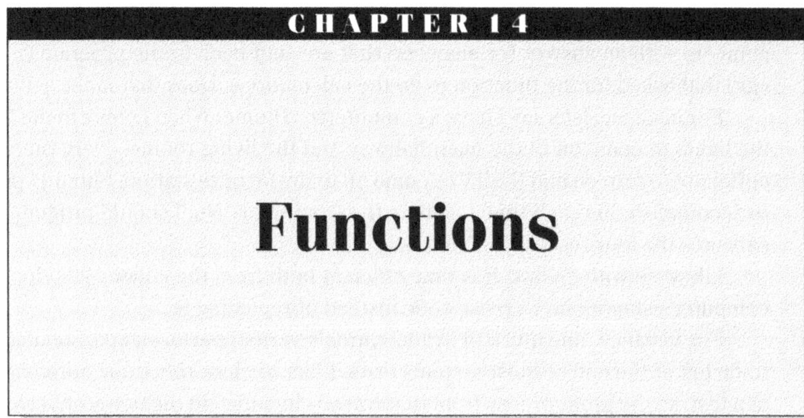

CHAPTER 14

Functions

In This Chapter

- What Is a Function?
- Structure of a Function
- Template for a Function
- Examples of Functions

WHAT IS A FUNCTION?

We have gone from the top downward, and we are now at the bottom of the ladder, to the basis of all the other routine types: **functions.** We began with strategies and moved to indicators and then into specialized types of indicators. We come now to functions, the building blocks of all other routines. A function is simply a **reusable piece of code.** If I've said that once I've said it 2,000 times as I have taught traders all over the world to use EasyLanguage. It makes sense when said that way. To define it officially and precisely only confuses those new to programming languages.

A function is a reusable piece of code. There, that's 2,001. In addition, a function **returns a value** or values to the code that initiated (or called) it. A function appears in purple in EasyLanguage code. Generally, one would assign the value of a function to a variable, in a statement like this:

```
Value1 = Average(C,20);
```

where Average is a built-in function that calculates the average of 20 numbers, in this case closes.

A function performs underlying statements, calculations, and EasyLanguage code to come up with an answer (or answers) that are sent back to the program (indicator or strategy) that asked for the function to do the calculations. Does that make sense?

For instance, let's say I have a computerized home. When I come in the front door I want the lights to come on in the main hallway and the living room—every time. I also want the coffeepot to turn on and the TV to come on to my favorite station. Should I push four buttons to accomplish this each time I walk in the front door? No, I should program one button that executes the four repeatable functions.

Likewise with coding; it is time efficient both from the coder's standpoint and from the computer's standpoint to reuse code instead of repeating it.

For instance, one quirk of TradeStation's system performance calculations is the open trade left at the end of most systems tests. I like to close this trade automatically at the end of a test, so the profit or loss from that trade is included in the net profit calculations. A little function called **CloseLastTrade** can solve that problem. At the end of all my experimental systems I simply include a line of code that looks like this:

```
Value99=CloseLastTrade;
```

A function performs a task and returns a value(s) to the routine that called it. If, for instance, you wanted to add four numbers (say, Open, High, Low and Close) and divide them by 4 to come up with the Typical Price, you could write the code for that each and every time you needed it, or you could write it once and then refer to it whenever you needed the calculation done. That would be "calling a function." The return value of the function would be the result of the calculation.

If we called this function **AddParts,** then rather than writing the formula again and again, we would simply write something like:

```
Value1 = AddParts;
```

We could get more sophisticated and use input values to the function, specified in parentheses and then used in the calculation. That way the function would have some flexibility and not always have to add the same four numbers. It might look like:

```
// function AddParts
INPUTS: Price1(Open), Price2(High), Price3(Low), Price4(Close);
AddParts = (Price1 + Price2 + Price3 + Price4) /4;
```

Notice that the last line of code in the function assigns the value of the calculation to a variable whose name is the name of the function. That is the "return" value. It is the value that goes back to the original calling routine. Even if you don't want to send a value back, you must use this assignment statement and at least give it a dummy value, say zero or 1. Function names may not contain any spaces or any nonalphanumeric characters other than the underscore (_).

A function can refer to another function or functions. They may be nested. And most functions are simple functions, with a single return value.

Functions save space; they minimize complexity. They improve readability and reduce errors.

You will want to create a collection of your favorite functions, so that you can use them over and over as you create and test systems. I'll give you a few of my favorites in this chapter.

STRUCTURE OF A FUNCTION

A **simple function** is the most common type of function. It stores only its current value. Unlike series functions, simple functions do not store historical values of themselves and therefore do not require much memory to perform their calculations. However, a simple function still can refer to other historical bar prices (such as High, Volume, etc.).

The **Function Properties → General** tab is used to set the function storage and execution method to Series, Simple, or Auto-Detect. When in doubt, select Auto-Detect and the compiler will select the most appropriate storage method for the function.

EXAMPLE

This one-line function returns an average of Volume for the most recent 10 bars.

```
VolTotal = Average(Volume,10);
```

EasyLanguage functions allow, but do not require, inputs though they do require outputs. A function could be as simple as calculating the difference between the Open and the Close. The function would have, as its output, the value of the difference.

Let's name this function OCDIFF. The code for this function could be as simple as:

```
OCDIFF=O-C;
```

To use this function, you would place it in your strategy or indicator code wherever it was needed, as a substitution for the code (Open-Close). For instance:

```
Value1=AbsValue(Open-Close);
```

in your indicator could be replaced with

```
Value1=AbsValue(OCDIFF);
```

In this case we are using two functions. `OCDiff` is the function we built, and `AbsValue` is an EasyLanguage built-in function.

The next two figures show the use of TradeStation's built-in function **AverageFC.** The FC just stands for "Fast Calculation." In Figure 14.1 the function AverageFC is called to calculate the average in the indicator. In Figure 14.2 the same function is called from a strategy, again to calculate the average. The function makes it easy to calculate the same thing over and over without having to write the same code multiple times.

TradeStation Indicator - Mov Avg 2 Lines

```
inputs:
    Price( Close ),
    FastLength( 9 ),
    SlowLength( 18 ),
    Displace( 0 ) ;

variables:
    FastAvg( 0 ),
    SlowAvg( 0 ) ;

FastAvg = AverageFC( Price, FastLength ) ;
SlowAvg = AverageFC( Price, SlowLength ) ;

if Displace >= 0 or CurrentBar > AbsValue( Displace ) then
    begin
    Plot1[Displace]( FastAvg, "FastAvg" ) ;
    Plot2[Displace]( SlowAvg, "SlowAvg" ) ;

    { Alert criteria }
    if Displace <= 0 then
        begin
        if FastAvg crosses over SlowAvg then
            Alert( "Bullish alert" )
        else if FastAvg crosses under SlowAvg then
            Alert( "Bearish alert" ) ;
        end ;
    end ;
```

Ln 14, Col 47 SAVED VERIFIED

FIGURE 14.1 Indicator Using Function

Figure 14.3 shows the code for the **AverageFC** function. It is simple code, of only a few lines, that makes a call to another function: **SummationFC.** It is the Summation function that does all the calculations, seen in Figure 14.4. Notice the elegant use of the **for** loop in this function. Figure 14.5 shows the plain vanilla **Summation** function, so you can compare it to the FC version. The FC version does the loop only one time, for CurrentBar=1, the first bar on the chart. For all subsequent bars, the sum is found by adding the new price and subtracting out the `Length`-th price ago. That is much faster to calculate than doing the loop over and again for each bar. The FC function does one calculation while the simple function does Length number of calculations.

Whenever you are going to do a calculation both in an indicator and a strategy (which is most of the time), you should create a function to do the calculations in both places. If you don't use a function, you will need to repeat the code in both places.

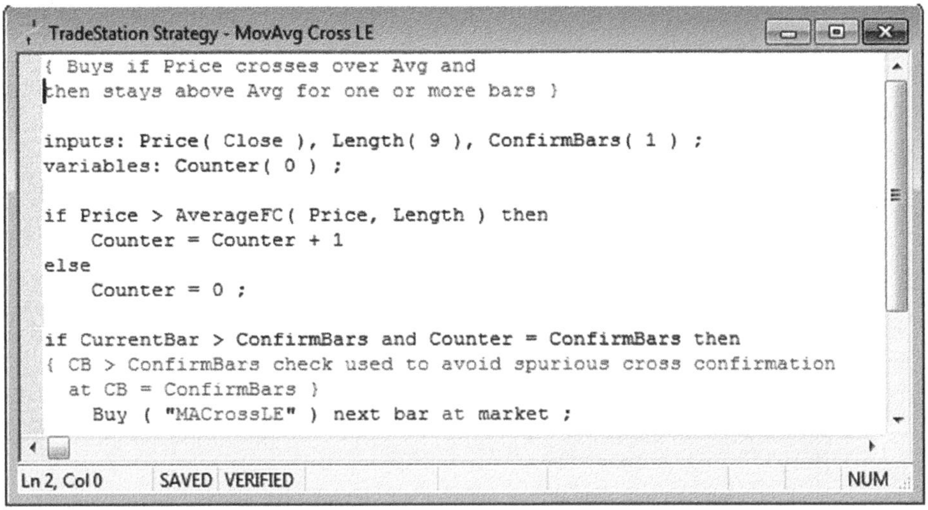

TradeStation Strategy - MovAvg Cross LE

```
{ Buys if Price crosses over Avg and
then stays above Avg for one or more bars }

inputs: Price( Close ), Length( 9 ), ConfirmBars( 1 ) ;
variables: Counter( 0 ) ;

if Price > AverageFC( Price, Length ) then
    Counter = Counter + 1
else
    Counter = 0 ;

if CurrentBar > ConfirmBars and Counter = ConfirmBars then
{ CB > ConfirmBars check used to avoid spurious cross confirmation
  at CB = ConfirmBars }
    Buy ( "MACrossLE" ) next bar at market ;
```

Ln 2, Col 0 SAVED VERIFIED NUM

FIGURE 14.2 Strategy Using Function

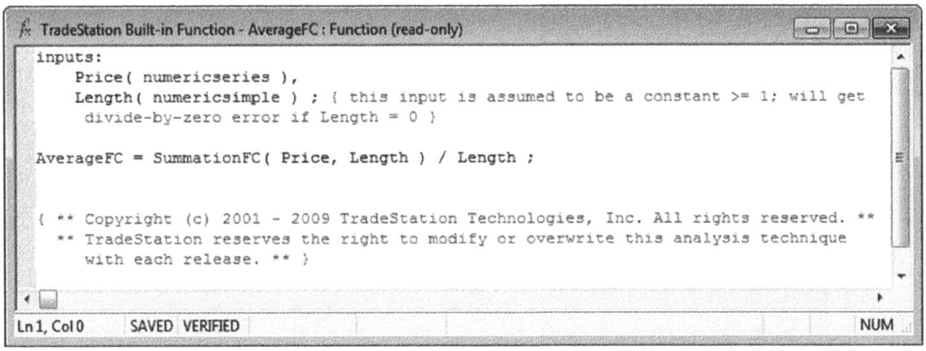

TradeStation Built-in Function - AverageFC : Function (read-only)

```
inputs:
    Price( numericseries ),
    Length( numericsimple ) ; { this input is assumed to be a constant >= 1; will get
     divide-by-zero error if Length = 0 }

AverageFC = SummationFC( Price, Length ) / Length ;


{ ** Copyright (c) 2001 - 2009 TradeStation Technologies, Inc. All rights reserved. **
  ** TradeStation reserves the right to modify or overwrite this analysis technique
     with each release. ** }
```

Ln 1, Col 0 SAVED VERIFIED NUM

FIGURE 14.3 AverageFC Function

TEMPLATE FOR A FUNCTION

```
INPUTS: input01(type), input02(type), ...;
Value1=...;
Value2=...;
Condition1=...;
Condition2=...;
FNAME=...;
```

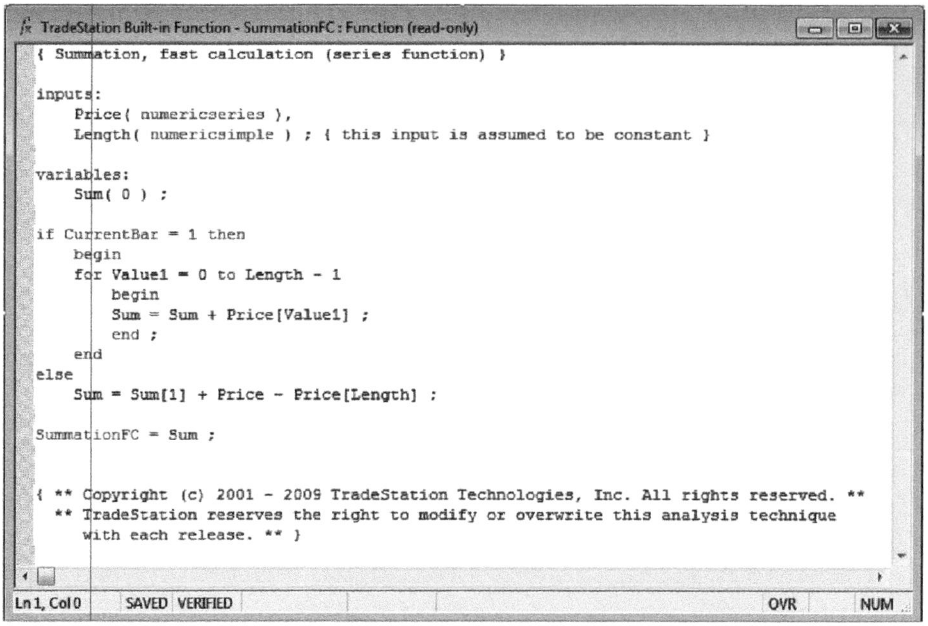

TradeStation Built-in Function - SummationFC : Function (read-only)

```
{ Summation, fast calculation (series function) }

inputs:
    Price( numericseries ),
    Length( numericsimple ) ; { this input is assumed to be constant }

variables:
    Sum( 0 ) ;

if CurrentBar = 1 then
    begin
    for Value1 = 0 to Length - 1
        begin
        Sum = Sum + Price[Value1] ;
        end ;
    end
else
    Sum = Sum[1] + Price - Price[Length] ;

SummationFC = Sum ;


{ ** Copyright (c) 2001 - 2009 TradeStation Technologies, Inc. All rights reserved. **
  ** TradeStation reserves the right to modify or overwrite this analysis technique
     with each release. ** }
```

Ln 1, Col 0 SAVED VERIFIED OVR NUM

FIGURE 14.4 SummationFC Function

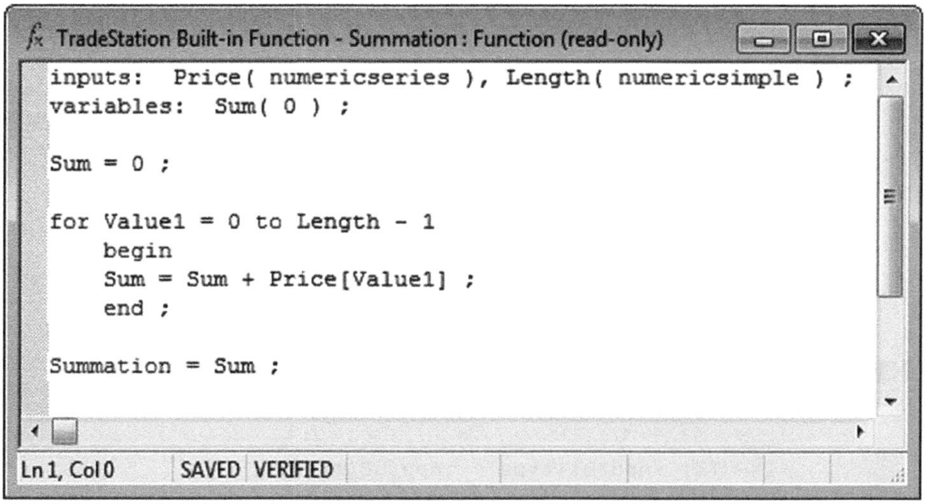

TradeStation Built-in Function - Summation : Function (read-only)

```
inputs:  Price( numericseries ), Length( numericsimple ) ;
variables:  Sum( 0 ) ;

Sum = 0 ;

for Value1 = 0 to Length - 1
    begin
    Sum = Sum + Price[Value1] ;
    end ;

Summation = Sum ;
```

Ln 1, Col 0 SAVED VERIFIED

FIGURE 14.5 Summation Function

`INPUTS`, the first line of the template, are a little different from the `Inputs` statement used in indicators and strategies. Inputs in indicators and strategies specify the default values within the parentheses. Inputs is a declaration statement. For instance, we would say

```
INPUTS: Length (9);
```

to specify that the default value of Length is 9 in an indicator. However, in a function, we do not specify default values in the declaration, rather we tell EZL what type of number the input is. The choices are: **Numeric, True/False,** or **String.** More specifically, there are these declarations:

- **Numeric** is used for inputs that can be either NumericSimple or NumericSeries.
- **NumericSimple** is a simple numeric with no historic values.
- **NumericSeries** is used for inputs whose values can be referred to historically.
- **NumericArray** is used when it expects a value passed by an array.
- **NumericRef** defines the data type of the input to a function that expects a number passed by reference.
- **TrueFalse** input will be a true/false expression.
- **TrueFalseSimple** is Simple Text without history.
- **TrueFalseSeries** defines an input as a true-false value with history.
- **TrueFalseArray** is used to define an input that expects a true-false expression passed by value for each array element.
- **TrueFalseRef** allows the code to pass a TrueFalse variable so it can be modified by the function.
- **String** defines an input as a text simple expression without history available.
- **StringSimple** defines an input as a Simple Text expression without history available.
- **StringSeries** is used to define an input as a text series expression with history.
- **StringArray** defines the data type of an input to a function that expects a text string passed by value for each array element.
- **StringRef** defines the data type of an input to a function that accepts a text string value passed by reference.

You will most probably never use most of these declarations. The basic declarations are enough for most applications. You will probably see, and use, only these declarations:

```
INPUTS: variable(numeric);
INPUTS: variable(truefalse);
INPUTS: variable(string);
```

If you design your code this way, TS will assume that you want history with your calculations and will therefore assume you mean series types.

I hear you asking, "What do you mean by history?" History is the ability to reference bars preceding the current bar. You specify which bar you want by placing square brackets around the number of bars back you want. For instance,

```
Value1 = Close - Close[3];
```

would be a reference to the `close of now minus the close of 3 bars ago.` The bars ago part is the history. Without a series you would not be able to refer to bars that went before. If you want to be able to make calculations based on a previous value of your function, it would be best to choose the type with series after its name.

EXAMPLES OF FUNCTIONS

EXAMPLE

```
{Function Name: LastBarOnChart}
IF Date=LastCalcDate THEN LastBarOnChart=true ELSE
LastBarOnChart=False;
LastBarOnChart = Date=LastCalcDate and Time=LastCalcTime;
```

EXAMPLE

```
{Function Name: sjh_TypicalPrice}
INPUTS: j_HowMany(numeric), j_Price1(numeric), j_Price2(numeric),
j-
       Price3(numeric), j_Price4(numeric);
       Value1 = j_Price1 + j_Price2 + j_Price3 + j_Price4;
       Value2 = Value1/j_HowMany;
PRINT(“Value2= ”, Value2);
sjh_TypicalPrice = Value2;
```

This function divides the (Open + High) by 2, or the (Open + High + Low) by 3, or the (Open + High + Low + Close) by 4, depending on your inputs. This brings up a programming tip that I have assumed you inherently knew. When a variable is not defined, its value is zero. In this example, if you don't pass one of the price names (open, high, low, or close) in through the inputs, then that value will be zero. Thus, when you add all four together and divide by 2 it is the same as (O+H)/2. Because of the versatility of this function, you could send the close twice and divide by 2 or send all four parameters in any order.

EXAMPLE

```
inputs:
Price(numericseries),
Length(numericsimple); // will get divide-by-zero error if
Length = 0
Average = Summation(Price, Length) / Length;
```

This is an elegant solution to the averaging equation. Rather than add up all the prices one at a time, this function calls upon the **Summation** function to do the adding. Here the first function asks the **Summation** function to add up Length number of prices and divide them by Length. Like all functions, the last statement in the code is always the assignment of a value to the name of the function.

EXAMPLE

```
Value1=GetBackgroundColor;
IF Value1=1 OR Value1=9 OR Value1=11 OR Value1=14
THEN sjh_SetColor=8
ELSE sjh_SetColor=1;
```

This is one of mine. When coding for other people, I don't know what color the background of their chart is. If I assume their charts are white with black text and I write or plot in black, invariably they will be using black as their background color and the plot won't show up. Black on black is hard to see. Likewise, if I assume they have a black background and I write or plot in white or yellow, I will find them using a white background and white or yellow won't show up for them. I've had this happen in real life. My client was complaining bitterly that my indicator didn't draw anything. It took me a long time over the phone to figure out that his background was the same color as my plot.

The purpose of this function is to assess the color of the background and the set plots to a contrasting color. The color numbers in EasyLanguage can be found in the help files or in Appendix A of this book. Black is 1 and white is 8. See if you can figure out the rest of the combinations. The code in the example above is one of those functions you will want to keep in your back pocket. It comes in very handy.

- 1 Black Tool_Black
- 2 Blue Tool_Blue
- 3 Cyan Tool_Cyan
- 4 Green Tool_Green
- 5 Magenta Tool_Magenta
- 6 Red Tool_Red
- 7 Yellow Tool_Yellow
- 8 White Tool_White
- 9 DarkBlue Tool_DarkBlue
- 10 DarkCyan Tool_DarkCyan
- 11 DarkGreen Tool_DarkGreen
- 12 DarkMagenta Tool_DarkMagenta
- 13 DarkRed Tool_DarkRed
- 14 DarkBrown Tool_DarkBrown
- 15 DarkGray Tool_DarkGray
- 16 LightGray Tool_LightGray

Built-in Functions

EasyLanguage provides some 375 functions built into the TradeStation program. They are there so you don't have to reinvent the wheel. The built-in functions cover everything from A to Z, literally. TS has covered almost everything you can imagine with the functions it supplies with the program. There are functions to handle date and time calculations, such as changing dates and times to numbers with which you can calculate, or text you can display or manipulate, such as manipulating text and making just about every kind of mathematical calculation.

Built-in functions are listed in Appendix G of this book, with explanations. Only the basic functions are provided in this book for beginners. To view the complete list of built-in functions, refer to the TS help files or to the TradeStation eBook *EasyLanguage Essentials*, available on the TS Web site.

Functions are as simple as:

```
Range = High - Low;
```

`Range` is the name of the function, and as the last line of the routine (which in this example is the only line of code) the function name is assigned the value of the calculation `High` minus `Low`. It is as simple as that.

Another built-in function is called `TypicalPrice` and reads:

```
Variables: OneThird(1 / 3);
TypicalPrice = (High + Low + Close) * OneThird;
```

This is a very commonly used calculation and is simply calculated as shown. The code supplied in TS provides the value one-third as a variable, so that the division is calculated only once, instead of each time the function is called. If, for instance, you were using TypicalPrice to construct a trading system that estimated tomorrow's price based on today's typical price, you wouldn't want to perform the division with each tick of the market. It would slow down your computer appreciably. That is a great illustration of the value of functions.

Here is another commonly used built-in function:

```
inputs: Price(numericseries), Length(numericsimple);
{will get divide-by-zero error if Length = 0}
Average = Summation(Price, Length) / Length;
```

Notice that this function is of the series type. That is, it stores all the historical values it calculates so you can refer to previous values at any time you wish. `Average(C,10)[5]` would mean: calculate the 10-bar average of closes, 5 bars ago.

In Appendix G I have listed many of the more commonly used functions, along with their explanations and usage. Here, however, is a short list of frequently used functions that are built in to TradeStation:

- AccumDist
- AdaptiveMovAvg
- ADX
- ArmsIndex
- Average
- AvgTrueRange
- BarNumber

- BollingerBand
- C_Doji
- C_Hammer_HangingMan
- CalcDate
- CalcTime
- CCI
- ChaikinOsc
- CloseD, CloseM, CloseW, CloseY
- Combination
- Correlation
- CountIF
- Cum
- DailyLosers, DailyWinners
- DaysToExpiration
- DirMovement
- Divergence
- DMI
- FastD, FastK
- HarmonicMean
- HighD, Highm, HighW, HighY
- Highest
- IFF
- KeltnerChannel
- LastBarOnChart
- LinearReg, LinearRegAngle, LinearRegSlope
- LowD, LowW, LowM, LowY
- Lowest
- MACD
- McClellanOsc
- Median
- Momentum
- OBV (OnBalanceVolume)
- OpenD, OpenM, OpenW, OpenY
- Parabolic
- Pennant
- Pivot
- Range
- RateOfChange
- RSI
- SlowD, SlowK
- StandardDev
- Stochastic
- Summation
- SwingHigh, SwingLow

- many Text Functions
- many TrendLine functions (starting with "TL")
- TRIX
- TrueHigh, TrueLow, TrueRange
- TypicalPrice
- UlcerIndex
- UltimateOscillator
- Volatility
- VolumeOsc
- WAverage
- XAverage

This list makes it easy for you to remember that you have seen a function name that might suit your purpose. There are many, many more. Read the help files, the back of the TS Users' Manual, or a free pdf book named *EL_ FunctionsAndReservedWords_Ref*, available at the TS Web site.

There is a whole 'nother set of things that look like functions but that are called Reserved Words. I listed some in a previous chapter. They are listed in full in Appendix B of this book. They act like functions, but they are mathematical operations that are included for ease of use and completeness. For instance, **AbsValue** is not a function, it is a Reserved Word. You would know this only if you read Appendix B. You could write a function that would perform this calculation, but you don't need to; it is already included in EZL.

User Functions

A function call is an EasyLanguage word (appearing in purple in EZL code) that returns a value (or multiple values) after evaluating underlying EasyLanguage statements within the function. The function's statements can be used to calculate mathematical formulas, make logical evaluations, or perform any other EasyLanguage action.

When creating a function of your own, you must specify the method used to store values returned by the function.

There are three methods of calculating functions:

1. Simple
2. Series
3. Auto-Detect

And there are three types of functions:

1. Series
2. Multiple Output
3. Wrapper

A **simple** function only stores the most recent value it has calculated. Simple functions do not store historical values and therefore do not require much memory to perform their calculations. With a simple function, one cannot refer to the function[1], meaning one bar ago. A simple function refers only to the current bar, and no "bars ago." A simple function can be thought of as a constant, for instance, the number 20, but not as a variable.

Series functions can store previous as well as current values. Because series functions store more information, they also require more memory to perform their calculation. With series functions, just as with numeric series variables, you can refer to the previous bar and the bar before that and all n bars back.

If you do not know the function's storage type, select **Auto-detect** and the function storage type is automatically determined by EasyLanguage algorithms. If you choose this option, TS allocates the maximum amount of memory needed to perform the calculations.

Writing Your Own

While there are hundreds of built-in functions in TradeStation, there are times when you will want to have a function that does something not covered in the myriad of functions already available for you.

Let's say, just for example, that you didn't know that there was an Average function built in to TS and that you wanted to find the average of 20 closes, to calculate a moving average. You could perform the arithmetic this way:

```
Value1 = (Close + Close[1] + Close[2] + Close[3] + Close[4] + Close[5] +
      Close[6] + Close[7] + Close[8] + Close[9] + Close[10] + Close[11] +
      Close[12] + Close[13] + Close[14] + Close[15] + Close[16] + Close[17] +
      Close[18] + Close[19]) /20;
```

If, however had you read Appendix G or the functions reference, you would know there was an **Average** function built-in, which would make the job as simple as:

```
Value1 = Average (C,20);
```

If you wanted to use the average in a strategy or an indicator and wanted to reference the value 20 as a variable instead of as a constant, you could do it this way:

```
Inputs: Price(C), Length(20);
Value1 = Average (Price, Length);
```

Series Function

A series function automatically stores its own previous values and executes on every bar (even if used within a conditional statement). To the end user, a series function is no different than a simple function. They are used and called the same way. The only real difference is that the end user can refer to prior values of a series function.

The built-in function **Average,** shown in Figure 14.6, is a good example of a series function. The inputs to a function specify the type of function it is. In this function Price is set to be numericseries, so that we can refer to previous values of the function.

```
inputs:
   Price(numericseries),
   Length(numericsimple); {will get divide-by-zero error if Length = 0}
   Average = Summation(Price, Length) / Length;
```

FIGURE 14.6 Built-in Average Function

Using a series function, you would be able to refer to the Average of five bars ago, like this:

```
Value1 = Average (C,20)[5];
```

The 5 in square brackets means "five bars ago."

If you had specified `Price(numericsimple)`, there would be no historical values available to you.

Multiple-Output Function

Some built-in functions need to return **more than a single value** and do this by using one or more output parameters within the parameter list. A multiple-output function has two types of parameters (or inputs)—input parameters and **input-output** parameters. Built-in multiple-output functions typically preface the parameter name with an 'o' to indicate that it is an output parameter used to return a value. These are also known as input-output parameters because they are declared within a function as a '**ref**' type of input (i.e., NumericRef, TrueFalseRef, etc.) which allows it to output a value, by reference, to a variable in the Easy-Language code calling the function.

The values of the input parameters are passed into the multiple-output function but not modified by the function. The values of the input-output parameters are passed into the multiple-output function and modified by it, and the modified values are then inherited by—or output to—the calling routine.

The input-output parameters are often used for output purposes only, and the incoming values are ignored. The value of a multiple-output function is that the outputs are in addition to the function return—it has multiple outputs. In multiple-output functions, the function return is generally used to return an error code, though sometimes the return may simply be a dummy value.

For example, the built-in function in Figure 14.8 looks for the second highest `Close` over the last 30 bars. The first four parameters are inputs used to specify

1. What price to find
2. Over how many bars
3. Which occurrence (1st, 2nd, etc.)
4. Look for the highest or lowest

The fifth and sixth parameters are outputs.

The function uses one output parameter to return the second highest `Close` to the variable `Value2` and a second output parameter to return the number of bars ago it occurred to the variable `Value3`. The function assignment itself returns the status of the search (1 if successful or -1 if an error occurred) to `Value1`.

The inputs to the multiple output function (MOF) itself look like those shown in Figure 14.7.

```
inputs:
   Price(numericseries),
   Length(numericsimple),
   N (numericsimple), {Length >= N > 0}
   HiLo(numericsimple),
      {pass in 1 for NthHighest(Bar), -1 for NthLowest(Bar)}
   oExtremeVal(numericref),
   oExtremeBar(numericref);
```

FIGURE 14.7 MOF NthExtreme

To use a multiple-output function (MOF), you set a variable to the function output (line 2 of Figure 14.8) and other variables to the other outputs, which are located in parentheses in the function call. The function can be used as shown in Figure 14.8.

```
Var: oExtremeVal(0), oExtremeBar(0);
Value1 = NthExtreme(Close, 30, 2, 1, oExtremeVal, oExtremeBar);
Value2 = oExtremeVal;
Value3 = oExtremeBar;
```

FIGURE 14.8 Multiple Output Function Usage

Remember that the input-output values usually start with the letter o, to distinguish them from other variables, but this convention is not mandatory.

EXAMPLE

The built-in function **DirMovement** is an example of a multiple-output function. The code for the function is lengthy, but I want to show you how it is used. Listed here are the inputs to the DirMovement function:

```
inputs:
     PriceH(numericseries),
     PriceL(numericseries),
     PriceC(numericseries),
     Length(numericsimple), {this input assumed to be a constant
        >= 1}
     oDMIPlus(numericref),
     oDMIMinus(numericref),
     oDMI(numericref),
     oADX(numericref),
     oADXR(numericref),
     oVolty(numericref);
```

At the end of the code for this function, the input-output values are set as follows:

```
oADX = oADX[1] + SF * (oDMI - oADX[1]);
oADXR = (oADX + oADX[Length - 1]) * .5;
```

and the return value for the function is set like this:

```
DirMovement = 1; {function return always 1, not used; only outputs
used}
```

Notice that this last value is simply a dummy, since it is always set to 1. All functions must return a value, even if it is a dummy.

Wrapper Function

When looking at the EasyLanguage code for a built-in function, you may find the term "wrapper function." This refers to a single-return function that references a multiple output function to obtain the return value. Calling a single-return wrapper function helps make your EasyLanguage code simpler by avoiding the need to set up output parameters or understand multiple-output functions. For example, the **ADX** function returns the average directional movement index value that is one of several output parameters of the **DirMovement** function.

A wrapper function wraps itself around a multiple-output function. A wrapper function is a single-return function. It provides a way for the user to avoid using multiple-output functions, which can be difficult to understand. A wrapper function is an alternate pathway to the functionality of a multiple-output function.

In wrapper functions, the input/output parameters are declared as local variables and generally initialized to zero. They are passed through to the multiple-output function without further modification. After the call, the wrapper function picks out the single output of interest and assigns it as the return of the wrapper function.

EXAMPLE

The built-in function **ADX** is a single-return wrapper function that calls the multiple-output function DirMovement. The key part of the code in the ADX function is:

```
Value1 = DirMovement(H,L,C,Length,oDMIPlus,oDMIMinus,oDMI,oADX,
         oADXR,oVolty);
ADX = oADX;
```

Notice all the input-output parameters starting with the letter o. These values are sent to the DirMovement function and sent back by the DirMovement function. One of the input-output values, `oADX`, is then set to the value of the ADX function, which is returned by that function.

CHAPTER 15

Tricky Math

In This Chapter

- Introduction
- Sign of a Number
- Rounding, Truncating, and Integer Arithmetic
- Minima and Maxima

INTRODUCTION

In *Trading 101—How to Trade Like a Pro*, on page 126, I posed the following pattern recognition problem: *What is the next number in the series 1 11 21 1211 111221?*

I had seen this stumper problem several times, but had never discovered the answer. I put it in the book in hopes that someone would call me. I did get several calls from readers wanting to know the answer, but only two people offered the solution. Thanks to Kevin Zietsoff, who emailed me, and to a stranger on an airplane ride, who also emailed me, here is the solution:

Answer: 2211111211

Solution: You start with the first three in the sequence, as the seed. Separate the digits in the middle, placing half on one side and half on the other. Exchange the two sides so right becomes left and left becomes right. Insert the previous at the end of the separated halves.

So, 21 becomes 2 | 1. Exchanging them gives 1 | 2. Place the 11 at the end, giving 1211. Likewise, splitting 1211 gives 12 | 11; exchanging them gives 11 | 12; placing the previous number at the end (the 21) gives 111221. The final answer is then given by splitting 111221

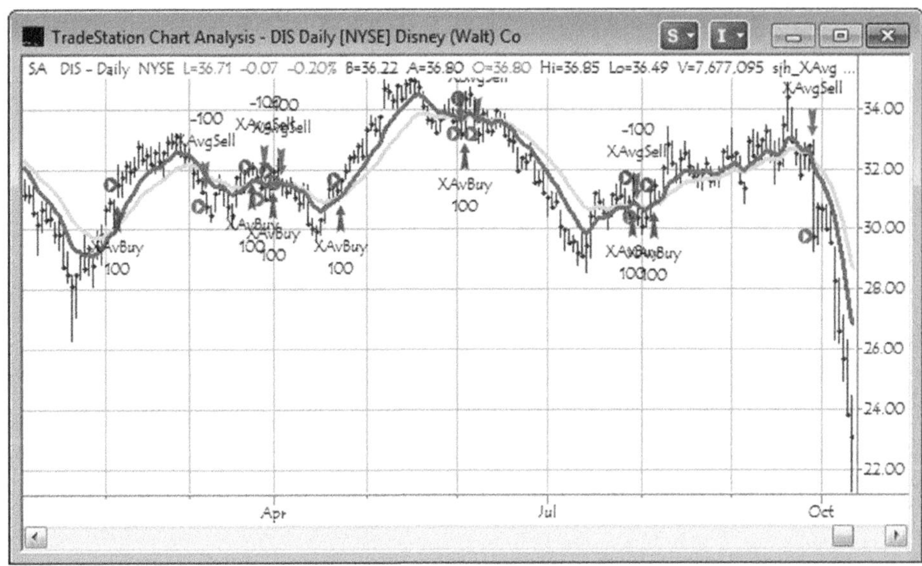

FIGURE 15.1 XAverage Crossover

to give 111 | 221; exchanging the halves gives 221 | 111; inserting the previous number gives 2211111211.

The answer is given here as a courtesy to my readers, as a thanks to Mr. Zietsoff and the unknown traveling companion, and to illustrate the tricky kinds of math one can use in solving problems. We won't get into anything so complex, but we will examine some useful techniques in this chapter.

I give you this example to remind you of my favorite question: "What is true?" Whenever we are programming, and especially when we are trying to determine what about a chart will make money, we must ask that question over and over again. In this chapter I will show you some math you can use to improve your trading.

Take a good look at the chart in Figure 15.1. What is true? With respect to what makes and what loses money, what is true? The chart has a dual exponential moving average on it, along with a simple strategy that buys and sells on crossovers. That's it. I have deliberately chosen a period of time (again this chart is DIS, as it has been throughout the book) when the market goes sideways for a time so you could see the whipsaws in the indicator. Look at the spot just left of middle in the chart and you will see an area where, as the market goes sideways, the moving average goes back and forth across itself.

The goal with this strategy would be to minimize the crossovers and yet catch the trends. One way to do this would be to use several sets of **IF** statements to confirm whether price was moving higher. Another way would be to measure the slope of the moving average itself and deny any signals when the slope was essentially flat. Later in this chapter we will take a look at what **slope** actually means mathematically. For now, however, we are going to look at a couple of elegant methods of reducing whipsaw.

The code for the strategy on the chart above is listed in Figure 15.2. We will begin to modify that code with some tricky math in the next section.

```
inputs:
       Price(Close),
       FastLength(9),
       SlowLength(18),
       Displace(0);
variables:
       FastAvg(0),
       SlowAvg(0);
FastAvg = XAverage(Price, FastLength);
SlowAvg = XAverage(Price, SlowLength);
IF (FastAvg crosses over SlowAvg) THEN
       BUY (''XAvgBuy'') next bar at market;
IF (FastAvg crosses under SlowAvg) THEN
       SELL SHORT (''XAvgSell'') next bar at market;
```

FIGURE 15.2 XAverage Crossover Strategy

In order to compare the success of our upcoming changes to the system, we need to know what our baseline is.

Using **View→Strategy Performance Report,** or **Alt + Shift + P,** bring up the Performance Report and take a look at the TNP. On my data, the Total Net Profit for this first test is <$2,959.00>, a small but significant loss. Take a look at Figure 15.3.

I am not going to use every mathematical function in this chapter in our sample strategy. Nevertheless, it is important that you know these functions exist. If you don't know that they exist, you won't think of them when a situation comes up where one of these functions would solve a problem.

SIGN OF A NUMBER

AbsValue (num)

Returns the absolute value of **num.,** where (num) is a numeric expression. The absolute value of a number is the positive part of the number, regardless of its sign. Thus, AbsValue (−5.2) would be 5.2 and AbsValue(5.2) would also be 5.2. In math books you would see it written |−5.2|, where the pipe character (or straight line) designates to take the absolute value.

EXAMPLE

`AbsValue(-27.54)` returns a value of 27.54.
returns a value of 132.5.

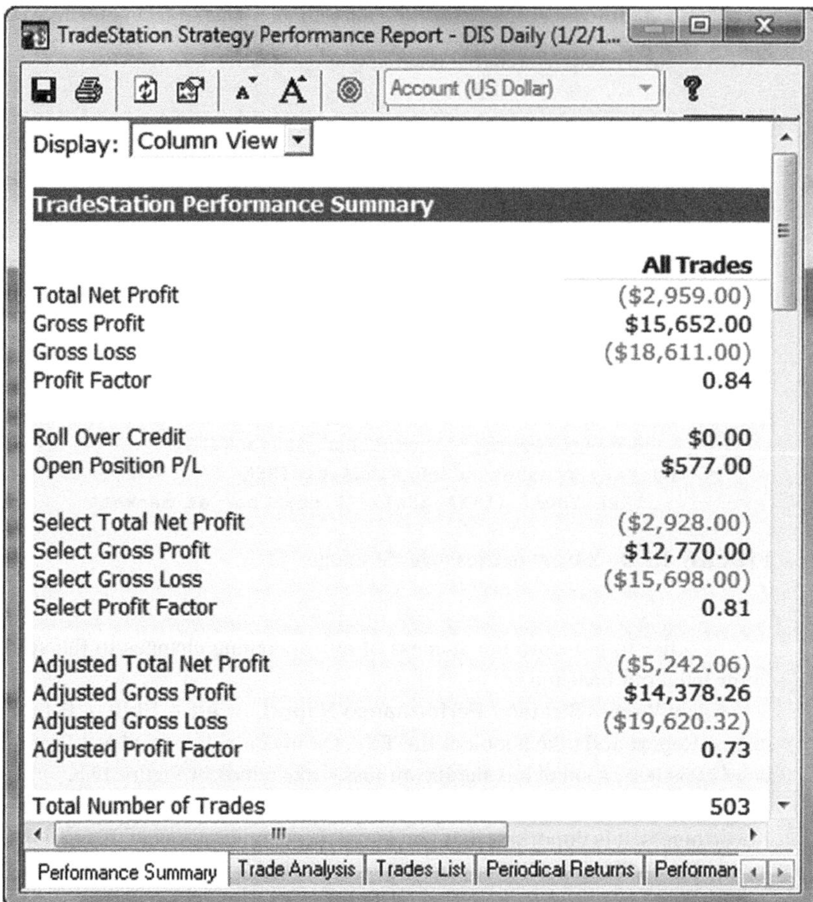

FIGURE 15.3 Strategy Performance Report

POS(num)

Is essentially the same as **AbsValue** but easier for some to understand. **POS** returns the positive value of `num`, where num is any numeric expression to be used in the calculation.

EXAMPLES

`Pos(-5)` returns 5.
`Pos(350)` returns 350.

There is also a `Neg` function. It returns the negative value of any value sent to it. It does not negate the number sent to it. That is an important difference. `(-)(-)(9)` would be `+9`, but `Neg(-9)` returns −9.

Neg(num)

Returns the absolute negative value of the number specified.

EXAMPLES
Neg(27) returns −27.
Neg(−19) returns a value of −19.

ROUNDING, TRUNCATING, AND INTEGER ARITHMETIC

Three tools of basic mathematics that can be of value to us in trading research are presented next.

Rounding

Round(num, prec)

Returns `num` rounded to `prec` decimal places (precision). When you round off a number, you remove numbers after the decimal point to the precision specified.

`Num` is a numeric expression to be used in the calculation, and `prec` is a numeric expression representing the number of decimal places to keep.

EXAMPLES
`Round(1142.3215, 2)` returns a value of 1142.32.
`Round(19.5687, 3)` returns a value of 19.569.

Exercise

In Figure 15.1 we looked at a chart that had too much precision. The indicator line jerked back and forth with each small turn of the market data. Let's use the function **Round** to take away some of the precision and see what happens. Change the part of our code (from Figure 15.2) that computes the slow and fast averages. The result should look like:

```
FastAvg = Round(XAverage(Price, FastLength),2);
SlowAvg = Round(XAverage(Price, SlowLength),2);
```

Next, I want you to experiment with different values for the precision. Try 2, then 1, then 0 and compare the results in the Performance Report.

Well, that wasn't so successful. First I tried `Round(XAverage(Price, FastLength),2)` (precision of 2) and then precision of `1` and last precision of `0`. The first two made the TNP worse, while the final test with precision of 0 made it a tiny bit better, with TNP = <$2,939.00>. Not real successful. But it did make for an interesting chart. Look at the chart in Figure 15.4 to see the effect of rounding on the indicator.

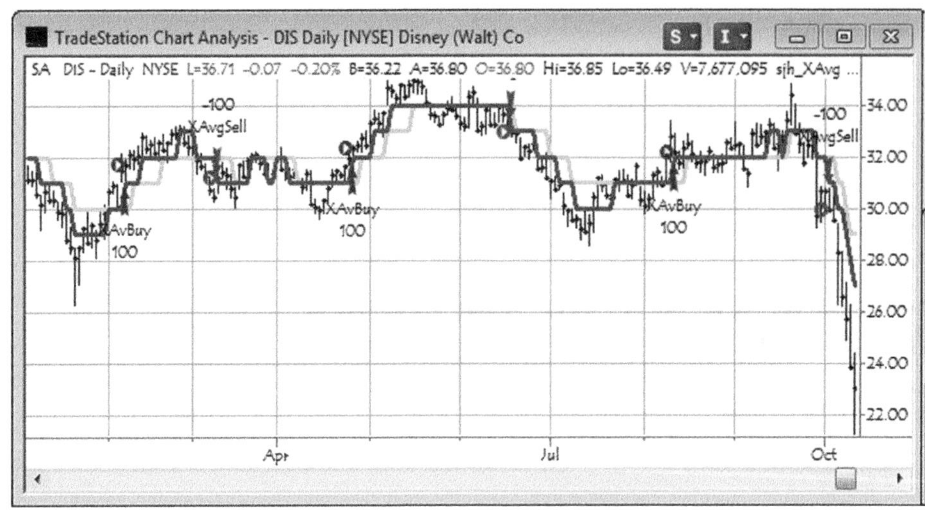

FIGURE 15.4 Round(num,0)

By reducing the precision of the exponential average in the indicator we have effectively created a step function. The nice part of this exercise is that we have reduced the crossovers left of center in the chart. Compare the chart in Figure 15.4 to the chart in Figure 15.1. This is where you need to have years of experience to tell you when not to give up. Just because the first pass with the default settings didn't give us a nice TNP doesn't mean we are done.

After running an optimization on this new indicator and strategy, we find that we can increase the TNP to $5,080.00. As they say in the math books, this exercise is left to the reader.

Truncating

FracPortion(num)

Returns the fractional portion of the specified `num`, where `num` is a numeric expression to be used in the calculation.

EXAMPLES

`FracPortion(4.5)` returns a value of 0.5.
`FracPortion(-1.72)` returns a value of -0.72.

Integer Arithmetic

IntPortion(num)

`IntPortion(1.56) = 1` returns the integer portion of the specified number, where `num` is a numeric expression representing the number for which you want the integer portion.

EXAMPLES

`IntPortion(4.5)` returns a value of 4.

`IntPortion(-1.72)` returns a value of −1.

Exercise

This function is one that we want to try in our code. Alter the average calculations this way:

```
FastAvg = IntPortion(XAverage(Price, FastLength));
SlowAvg = IntPortion(XAverage(Price, SlowLength));
```

Having done this, it is time to perform the same exercise of optimizing the strategy to see whether this code change makes a positive change or not.

This time the results are much better. The TNP for the best test is $4,971.00.

Why would I say this is better than the previous result of $5,080.00? Did you view, or save, the Optimization Report? Did you notice that in the best test of the **Round** function that the `SlowAvg` was longer than the `FastAvg`? That would produce a countertrend system, going short near the bottom and long near the top. That's great only in choppy periods. It is much better to have the SlowAvg be slower than the FastAvg. In the IntPortion test, the best test has a SlowAvg of 12 while the FastAvg is 14. That way you would be catching trends by buying low and selling high.

Always remember this exercise when you are on your own doing testing. Don't give up just because the first test doesn't work, and don't make assumptions. The best TNP is not always the best result.

Modulo Arithmetic

Mod(n,m)

Where n is the numerator and m is the divisor.

The **mod** function divides two numbers and returns the remainder.

EXAMPLES

Mod(27, 5) returns a value of 2.

Mod(457, 9) returns a value of 7.

The **mod** function is useful in determining whether two numbers divide evenly or how close they are to dividing evenly. In mathematics we write `7 mod 3` to find the remainder of 7 divided by 3.

We use mod 12 arithmetic every day when looking at our clocks. If we add 8 hours to 6 p.m. we would get 14 o'clock. But that's not right. However, 14 mod 12 is 2, which is the right answer.

MINIMA AND MAXIMA

Floor(num)

Returns the highest integer less than the specified (`num`). `Floor`, and its companion function `Ceiling`, are helpful in setting or determining support and resistance. Support and resistance often lies at whole numbers, or at powers of ten. Support and resistance also often lies at Fibonacci numbers and squares (Gann numbers). `Floor` and `Ceiling` are functions you could use in pursuit of support and resistance levels.

EXAMPLES

`Floor(41.5)` returns a value of 41.
`Floor(-1.72)` returns a value of −2.

Ceiling(num)

Returns the lowest integer greater than the specified (num).

EXAMPLES

`Ceiling(4.5)` returns a value of 5.
`Ceiling(-1.72)` returns a value of −1.

Ceiling and Floor, in mathematics, are known as LUB and GLB: Least Upper Bound and Greatest Lower Bound and are studied in a course called Boundary Value Problems in the study of Real Analysis.

MaxList(Num1, Num2, Num3, . . . , NumN, etc)

Returns the highest value of the specified inputs, where `Num1`, `Num2`, `Num3` and `NumN` are numeric expressions representing values to be used in the calculation.

EXAMPLES

`MaxList(75, 72, 56, 145, 47)` returns a value of 145.
`MaxList(28, 167, 198, 24, 35, 19)` returns a value of 198.

MinList (Num1, Num2, . . . , NumN etc)

Returns the lowest value of the specified inputs, where `Num1`, `Num2`, `Num3` and `NumN` are numeric expressions representing values to be used in the calculation.

EXAMPLES

`MinList(35, 72, 88, 122, 15, 57)` returns a value of 15.
`MinList(17, 57, 2, 198, 34, 65, 19)` returns a value of 2.

CHAPTER 16

TradeStation Tricks

In This Chapter

- Introduction
- Tricks within TradeStation
- Tips and Tricks from Bill Brower
- Eight Ball Strategy from TradeStation.com
- Tips and Tricks from Larry Williams
- Tips and Tricks from TradeStation STAD
- Tips and Tricks from Samuel K. Tennis
- Tips and Tricks from *EasyLanguage Home Study Course*
- Tips and Tricks from Glen Larson (of Genesis Financial Technologies)
- Tips and Tricks from Arthur G. Putt
- Tips and Tricks from the TradeStation Newsletter
- FileAppend
- Summary

INTRODUCTION

As in any profession, the best tricks are to be learned from the veterans. Those who have been using TradeStation and programming for years know the shortcuts. My intent with this book was to provide a beginners' how-to guide, not a collection of advanced tools, as in the other books about EasyLanguage. Thus, I have devoted this single chapter to advanced techniques.

There are many TradeStation solution providers, most of whom I have listed in Appendix H, who can assist you with EasyLanguage. There are several publications and groups devoted to the study of EasyLanguage. When I am looking to solve a tricky problem, I turn to one of these sources:

- Bill Brower
- Chuck LeBeau
- Murray Ruggiero
- Linda Raschke
- Perry Kaufman
- TradeStation STAD
- Arthur Putt

In this chapter I will reference some of these publications, with the kind permission of the authors, giving you some of their tricks. If you have questions about these routines or would like more tricks, please feel free to contact the authors.

TRICKS WITHIN TRADESTATION

It is often desirable to anchor the price of the entry bar. For instance, you might want to enter long only if price gets higher than the high of the bar on which the signal was given.

To this end, TS has given us the reserved word **AT$.** Used in trading strategies to anchor exit prices to the bar where the entry order was placed, **AT$** must be used in conjunction with an entry order that has an assigned label.

EXAMPLE

The next order buys when the 10-bar moving average crosses over the 20-bar moving average, placing a stop loss order 1 point under the low of the bar where the cross-over occurred by appending **AT$** to the **Sell** statement.

```
If Average(Close, 10) Crosses Over Average(Close, 20) THEN
      BUY (“MA Cross Over”) next bar at market;
SELL next bar from entry(“MA Cross Over”) AT$ Low - 1 point stop;
```

ADDITIONAL EXAMPLE

Sometimes I like to step away from my computer, after a long, hard morning of watching the screen. The next statements play the sound file Thatsabuy.wav when there is a key reversal pattern on the last bar of the chart: If you turn the volume all the way up on your computer and integrate this code, you will get an audible signal when the condition is true.

```
Condition1 = (PlaySound("c:\sounds\Thatsabuy.wav"));
If LastBarOnChart AND Low < Low[1] AND Close > High[1] Then
    Condition1 = true;
```

ONE MORE EXAMPLE

This code plays a blip sound when the market ticks up and a bong sound when the market ticks down. I like to have it on during the day so I can hear the activity in the market. It gets real staccato when the market is moving fast.

```
IF Time<>Time[1] THEN BEGIN
        IF C>C[1] THEN
        Condition1=PlaySound("C:\Sounds\Blip.wav")
        ELSE
        Condition1=PlaySound("C:\Sounds\Bonk.wav") ;
END;
```

TIPS AND TRICKS FROM BILL BROWER

TS Express. . .
published by Inside Edge Systems
10 Fresenius Rd., Westport, CT 06880
1-203-454-2754, fax 1-203-221-9195
1000mileman@mindspring.com

Triggers versus Switches

Often in your programming you will want a switch to be turned on if something is true, so you can evaluate that switch at various junctures in your code. If something happens you set the switch to true, and as long as the switch is true you continue merrily along. For instance, if there is no train coming (the switch is false), we leave the guardrail up and traffic continues to cross the tracks. When we sense a train is nearby, we set the switch to true and immediately bring the guardrail down, stopping all traffic. When the train is no longer nearby, we again set the switch to false, the guardrail goes up and traffic continues.

How does this apply to trading? Perhaps you want to trade only when the market is trending, and you want to stand aside when the market is choppy. Maybe you want to take trades only during certain time intervals (like in the first and last hour of trading), or as long as the advance-decline line is above a predetermined value.

Bill Brower gives us an important tip in the January/February 1994 issue of *TS Express*.... He goes into depth explaining the difference between triggers and switches, so I will pick out only his most salient points. To read the full explanation, give Bill a call, and tell him I sent you.

Do you know the difference between these two bits of code?

```
1. Condition1 = <something> = <something else>;
2. IF <something> = <something else> THEN Condition1=true;
```

The difference is significant.

The first bit of code is true if <something> is equal to <somethingelse>. Otherwise Condition1 is set to false. At the completion of every bar, TradeStation runs through the first bit of code and always resets Condition1 to true or to false. The system can then immediately react to changes in the state of Condition1. This I call a trigger.

The second bit of code is evaluated only at the conclusion of every bar. This is because if `<something>` is not equal to `<something else>` then the second half of the `IF...THEN...` statement is never evaluated. That means **Condition1** will remain in whatever state it is forever until one of two things happens. First, when `<something>` equals `<something else>` then **Condition1** is obviously set to true. Second, another bit of code elsewhere in the program could reset Condition1 to false. In fact, you must have another statement that evaluates another set of events to reset the Condition1 to false or your Condition1 statement will remain true forever.

Because the second bit of code changes state only when a singular event occurs and remains in the same state until it is reset, I refer to it as a switch.

That is Bill Brower's tip, summarized and distilled. Thank you, Bill.

MACDDiffForward

This next trick was a stumper for me in the beginning years of my trading. I initially used the MACD for trading and was totally mechanical in the approach, except for the last bar of the day. On the last bar of the day, you don't know whether the MACD will cross over until seconds after the market is closed. But the catch 22 is you can't trade after the market is closed. I therefore used an educated guess to place trades on that last bar. Sometimes it worked, sometimes it didn't. When it didn't work it was because the price didn't actually close where I guessed it might, and the MACD therefore didn't crossover.

The solution to this problem would be to enter an MOC (market on close) order at a price that would cause the MACD to cross over. If the price doesn't get hit, your trade doesn't happen.

The code for this indicator is in *TS Express*... November/December 1998 and is shown in Figure 16.1, below.

```
INPUTS: Price(C), Len1(12), Len2(26), Len3(9), NextDiff(0);
VARS: XAve1(0), XAve2(0), F1(0), F2(0), F3(0), MACDVal1(0), MACDVal2(0),
      MACDDiff(0), NextPrice(0), String1('''');
IF Len1+1 <>0 AND Len2+1<>0
THEN BEGIN
      IF CurrentBar <=1
      THEN BEGIN
      F1=2/(Len1+1);
      XAve1=Price;
      F2=2/(Len2+1);
      XAve2=Price;
      F3=2/(Len3+1);
      MACDVal1=0;
      MACDVal2=0;
      MACDDiff=0;
      END
      ELSE BEGIN
      XAve1=F1*Price+(1-F1)*XAve1[1];
      XAve2=F2*Price+(1-F2)*XAve2[1];
      MACDVal1=XAve1-XAve2;
      MACDVal2=F3*MACDVal1 + (1-F3)*MACDVal2[1];
      MACDDiff=MACDVal1 - MACDVal2;
      END;
END;
PLOT1(MACDDiff,''Diff'');
NextPrice=(NextDiff/(1-F3)+MACDVal2-(1-F1)*XAve1 +(1-F2)*XAve2)/(F1-F2);
IF AtCommentaryBar THEN BEGIN
      String1=''For MACDDiff of '' +numtostr(NextDiff,4)+ '' on the next
bar,
            price must be ''+ numtostr(NextPrice,4)+newline;
      Commentary(String1);
END;
```

FIGURE 16.1 Commentary Code by Bill Brower

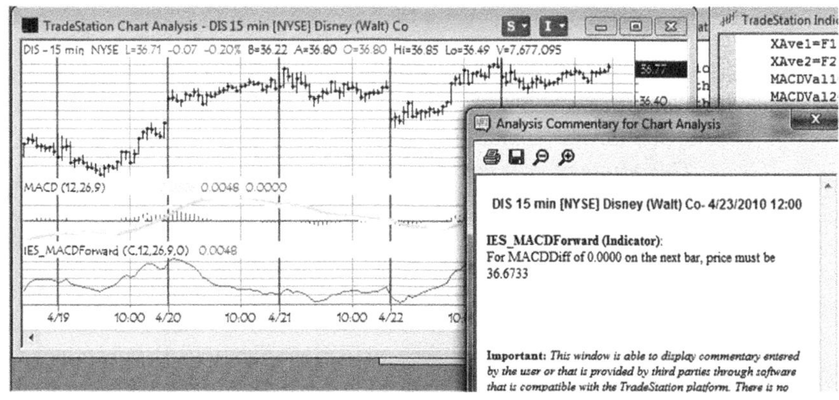

FIGURE 16.2 Commentary Pop-Up Window

The resulting window in TradeStation will look something like the chart in Figure 16.2. Caveat emptor: You must have commentary turned on for this window to pop up. You do that by the menu sequence **View → Analysis Commentary.**

EIGHT BALL FROM THE TRADESTATION USERS' FORUM

TradeStation.com/support
TradeStation Securities, Inc.
TradeStation Building
8050 SW 10th St., Ste. 2000
Plantation, FL 33324
(800) 556-2022
www.tradestation.com/Discussions/Main.aspx

The Eight Ball has been in the public domain for as many years as I can remember. I don't know why it is called Eight Ball, unless it has something to do with billiards that I don't know about. You can download the code for this strategy from TradeStation.com on the Users' Forum. Just log in and start searching with the title run together with no spaces: "eightball".

This is the explanation from the TradeStation Forum Web site:

The eightball strategy employs two exponential moving averages and a volatility trigger to enter the market. It identifies the long-term and short-term trends using the moving averages, and the volatility trigger is used to find a strong move off the opening price of the bar in the direction of the anticipated trend. The strategy will look for the slope of the averages to determine the long and short direction of the trends. If both averages are sloping in the same direction,the strategy considers the market in the setup phase.

The actual entry occurs when a market moves off its opening price by a specified multiple of its **Average True Range.** *So if both averages are rising and the market has a strong move off its open so it reaches a value greater than the 10 bar ATR, then a long position is established.*

This strategy is intended to find and capture profits out of longer, momentum based market moves, so it is best be used with trailing stops like the "Trailing Stop LX", and "Trailing Stop SX" or the "Parabolic Trailing LX" and the "Parabolic Trailing SX" strategy components.

This strategy didn't work very well on DIS (see Figure 16.4), but I found a better example in the E-Mini S&P 500 contract. The E-Mini results are displayed in Figure 16.5.

```
Inputs: Length1(40), Length2(8), Trigger(1);
Variables: ATR(0), Avg1(0), Avg2(0);

ATR = AvgTrueRange(10);
Avg1 = XAverage(Close, Length1);
Avg2 = XAverage(Close, Length2);

Condition1 = Avg1 > Avg1[1] AND Avg2 < Avg2[1];
Condition2 = Avg1 < Avg1[1] AND Avg2 > Avg2[1];

{Long Entry}
If Condition1 Then
   Buy (``Long Entry'') Next Bar at Open Tomorrow + Trigger * ATR Stop;
{Short Entry}
If Condition2 Then
   Sell Short (``Short Entry'') Next Bar at Open Tomorrow - Trigger * ATR
   Stop;
```

FIGURE 16.3 Eight Ball Code

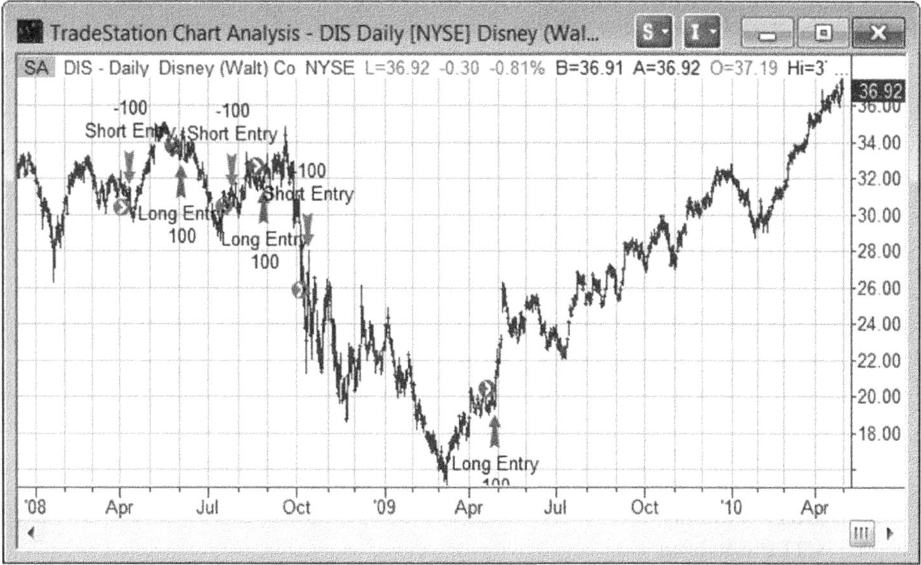

FIGURE 16.4 Eight Ball Chart

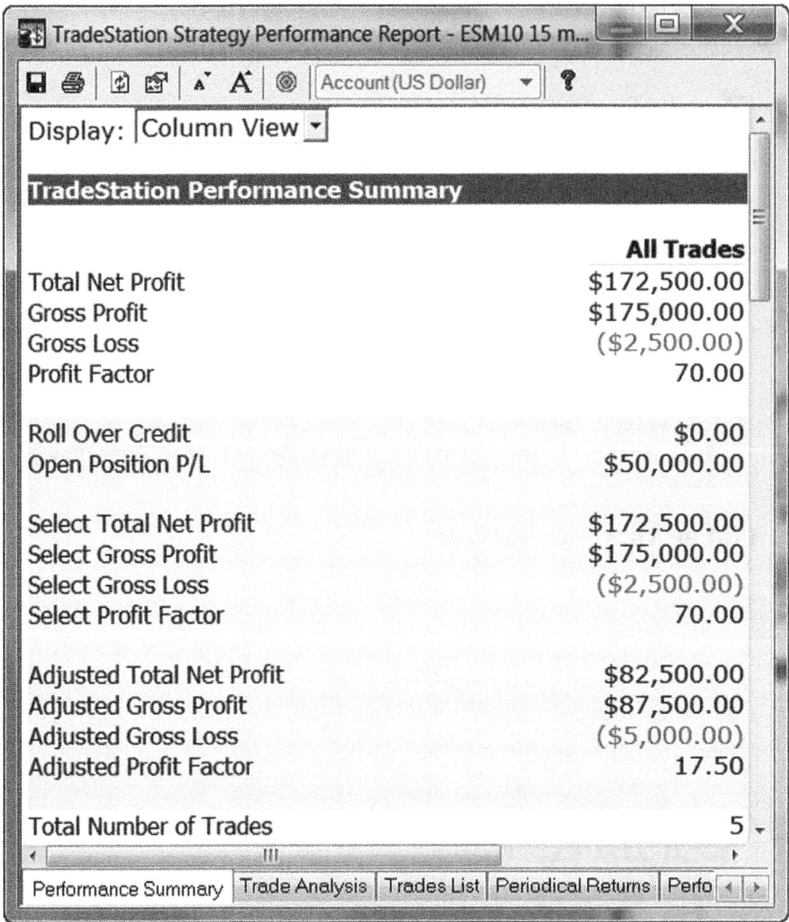

FIGURE 16.5 Eight Ball Performance Report

TIPS AND TRICKS FROM LARRY WILLIAMS

Larry Williams
CTI Publishing
5027 Anchors Way
Christianstead
St. Croix, US V. I. come 00820
1-800-800-8333
www.ireallytrade.com

The world-renowned veteran trader Mr. Larry Williams is not only the father of actress Michelle Williams, he is the father of several other successful children and the prolific author of hundreds of tradable strategies. He is a genius at spotting patterns in the markets and capturing the essence of what is true. You can read about Williams and his systems at length in my next book, *Grading the Gurus*.

Larry Williams has had many good trades but says his best have been his five children; Dr. Jason Williams, a psychiatrist at Johns Hopkins; daughter Kelly, who helps psychologically abused young women; his daughter Sara, a school principal; daughter Paige, who has her master's from Columbia; and of course the daughter everyone is aware of, Academy Award nominee actress Michelle Williams of *Brokeback Mountain* fame.

These days you're more apt to find Larry on the beaches of St. Croix in the Virgin Islands than at investment seminars as he is semiretired, enjoying the privacy of his own personal trading far from the maddening crowds. He continues to be prolific with market research and ideas, which have been covered in the leading industry magazines or freely given on his Web site.

Figure 16.6 is a simple strategy of his from years ago that is still as viable as it was back then. I have modified his code slightly to provide inputs where he had constants, to allow for optimization. You can easily spot my inputs; they all start with "j". This is from *The Definitive Guide to Futures Trading* by Larry Williams, p. 197.

```
Inputs: j_VarA(110), j_VarB(290);
Buy Tomorrow at Open of Tomorrow + (Range * (j_VarA/100)) Stop;
Sell Tomorrow at Open of Tomorrow - (Range*(j_VarB/100)) Stop;
```

FIGURE 16.6 Larry Williams's 3000 Dollar System

To show you how well this one works, I am varying a bit from my policy. Rather than show you this strategy on `DIS`, I'm switching to the `E-Mini`. For today's contract, the symbol is `ESM10`. Figure 16.7 shows the chart with arrows at buys and sells. Figure 16.8 presents the Performance Report.

This strategy can be improved by structuring similar code allowing for short positions. That exercise is left to the reader.

TIPS AND TRICKS FROM TRADESTATION STAD

Once upon a time, way back when, when TradeStation was called Omega Research, and when it used to have a group called System Trading and Development Club, it put out a booklet once a month or so. This booklet was about 100 pages in length and was chock full of tips and tricks and beautiful EasyLanguage code.

One concept that is frequently referred to in the media and in the literature is called the Keltner Channel. A chart showing the Keltner Channel is in Figure 16.9. The code for this indicator is in STAD4.

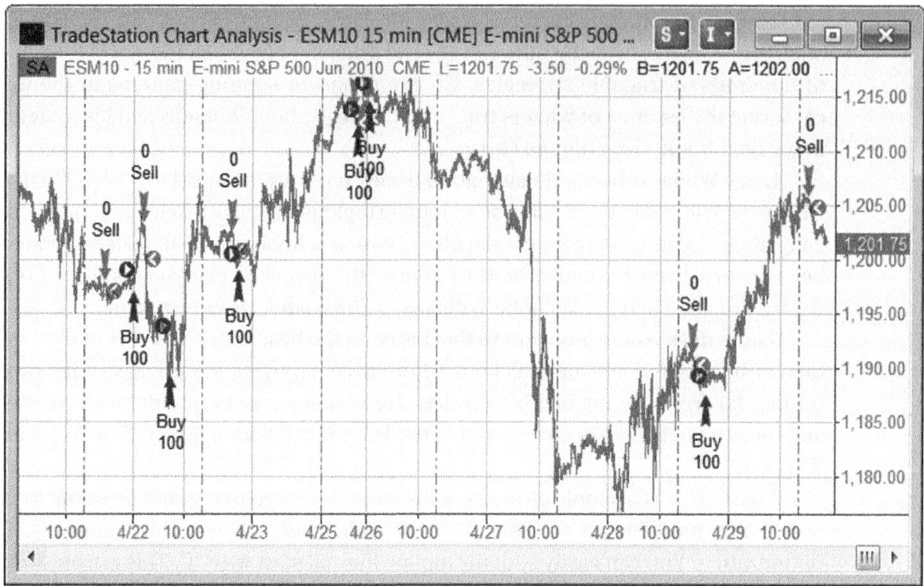

FIGURE 16.7 Chart of Larry Williams's 3000 Dollar System

Wikipedia offers the following:

Keltner channel is a technical analysis indicator showing a central moving average line plus channel lines at a distance above and below. The indicator is named after Chester W. Keltner (1909–1998), who described it in his 1960 book How To Make Money in Commodities. *But this name was applied only by those who heard about it from him, Keltner called it the Ten-Day Moving Average Trading Rule and indeed made no claim to any originality for the idea.*

In Keltner's description the centre line is a 10-day simple moving average of typical price, where typical price each day is the average of high, low and close.

The lines above and below are drawn a distance from that centre line, a distance which is the simple moving average of the past 10 days' trading ranges (i.e., range high to low on each day).

The trading strategy is to regard a close above the upper line as a strong bullish signal, or a close below the lower line as strong bearish sentiment, and buy or sell with the trend accordingly, but perhaps with other indicators to confirm.

The origin of this idea is uncertain. Keltner was a Chicago grain trader and perhaps it was common knowledge among traders of the day. Or in the 1930s as a young man Keltner worked for Ralph Ainsworth (1884–1965) backtesting trading systems submitted when Ainsworth offered a substantial prize for a winning strategy, so it could have been among those. But ideas of channels with fixed widths go back to the earliest days of charting, so perhaps applying some averaging is not an enormous leap in any case.

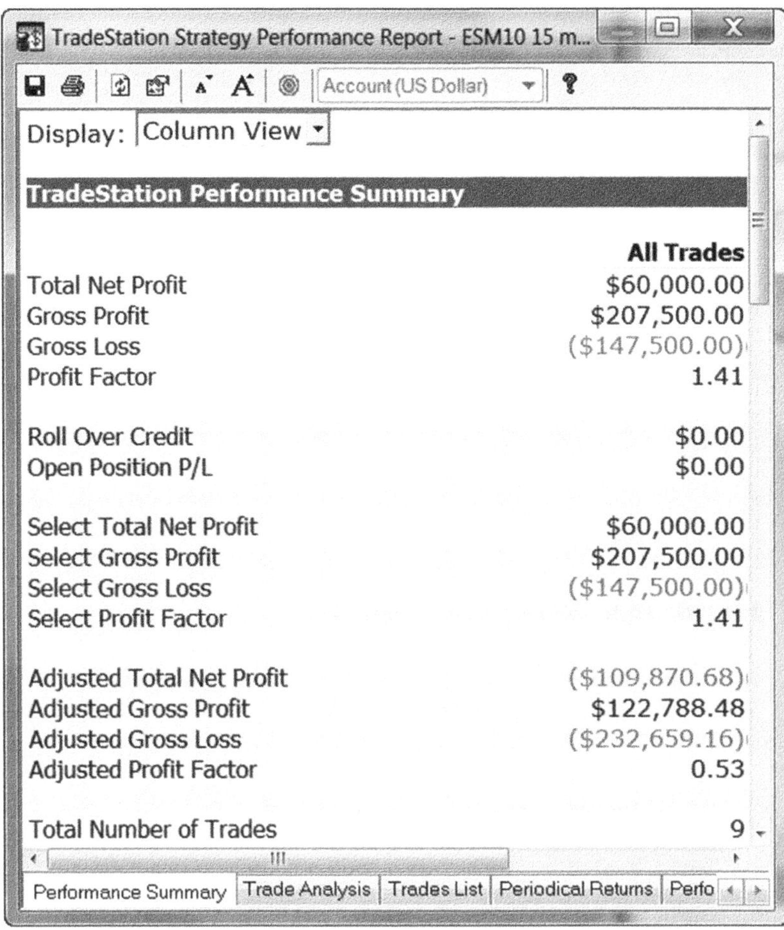

FIGURE 16.8 Performance Report on Larry Williams's System

Here is the code for the indicator, from STAD4:

```
Inputs: Price(Close), Length(10), Const(.8);
Plot1(Average(Price, Length), "CentLine");
Plot2(KeltnerChannel( Price, Length, Const ), "Upper");
Plot3(KeltnerChannel(Price, Length, -Const), "Lower");
```

And here is the function referenced in the last code:

```
Input: Price( NumericSeries ), Length( NumericSimple ),
       Factor( NumericSimple );
KeltnerChannel = Average( Price, Length ) + AvgTrueRange(Length)
* Factor;
```

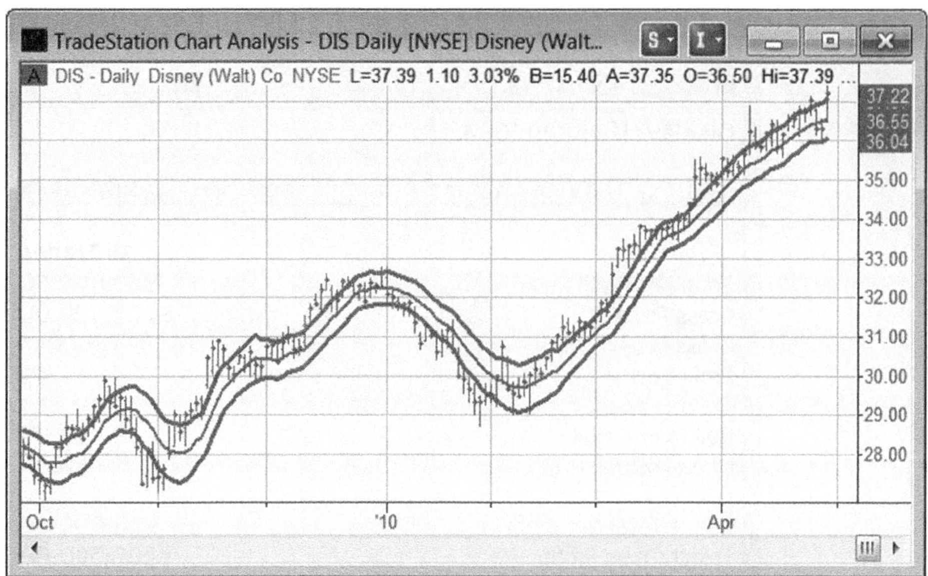

FIGURE 16.9 Keltner Channel Indicator

Figure 16.10 shows the code for the strategy, and Figure 16.11 shows the strategy at work.

```
[IntrabarOrderGeneration = false]
inputs: Price( Close ), Length( 20 ), NumATRs( 1.5 ) ;
vars: Avg( 0 ), Shift( 0 ), UpperBand( 0 ), Setup( false ),
CrossingHigh( 0 ) ;

Avg = AverageFC( Price, Length ) ;
Shift = NumATRs * AvgTrueRange( Length ) ;
UpperBand = Avg + Shift ;

if CurrentBar > 1 and Price crosses over UpperBand then
      begin
      SetUp = true ;
      CrossingHigh = High ;
      end
else if Setup and ( Price < Avg or High >= CrossingHigh + 1 point )
      then Setup = false ;

if Setup then
      Buy ( ``KltChLE'' ) next bar at CrossingHigh + 1 point stop
```

FIGURE 16.10 Keltner Channel Strategy Code

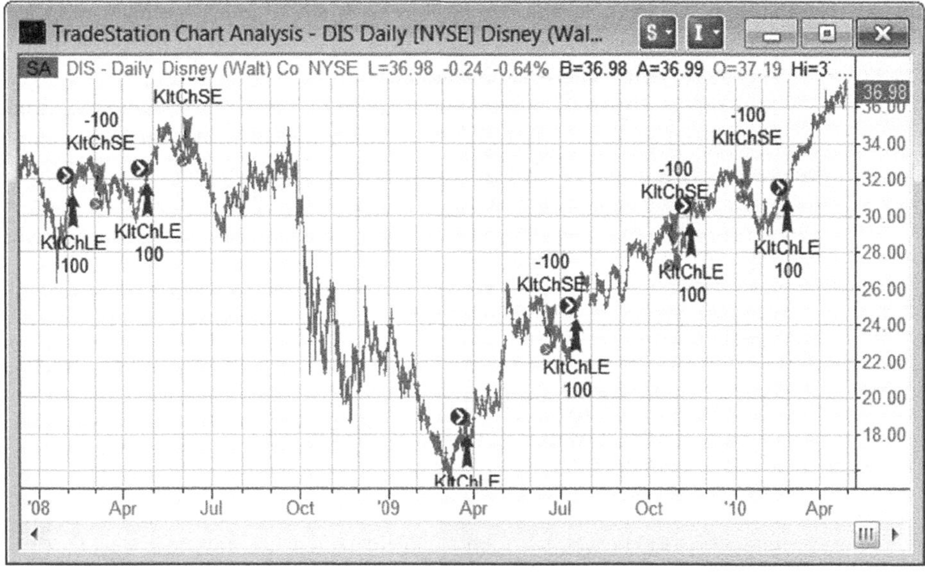

FIGURE 16.11 Keltner Channel Strategy at Work

TIPS AND TRICKS FROM SAMUEL K. TENNIS

Vista Research
129 Staff Dr. NE
Ft. Walton Beach, FL 32548
(850) 243-5105 . fax (850) 301-2884
www.vista-research.com
sktennis@vista-research.com

Sam Tennis was one of the originators of `EasyLanguage`. He used to work for Omega Research before it became TradeStation Securities and before he went out on his own. He has been known in the trading community as "Mr. EasyLanguage," because he originated it and because he speaks it like a native. Anything you want to know about EasyLanguage, you ask Mr. EasyLanguage.

In 1999 Sam published his book, *Ask Mr. EasyLanguage*. It is fantastic. It has only one shortcoming, and that is it goes from the very basic to intermediate concepts in just a few pages. That's okay; that's what *TradeStation Made Easy* is for. You've got to buy the book. It is fun to read and jam-packed with tricks only Sam could come up with. Most of the questions you would never find answers for anywhere else are in *Ask Mr. EasyLanguage*.

The example I have chosen for TSME is helpful in controlling the number of contracts in your entry and exit signals. You don't always want to trade 100 shares with every vehicle, in every environment, with every portfolio. Sometimes you might like to base the number of contracts you trade on the size of your portfolio. In fact, you might want to be able to increase and decrease the number of contracts/shares based on the profit or loss from the previous trade. That's where Sam comes in.

The code in Figure 16.12 begins on page 95 of *Ask Mr. EasyLanguage.* I had to make some modifications to get it to work. First, the Reserved Word ExitLong no longer exists in the current versions of TS. Second, Sam used "nCntrs" in one place and "nContracts" in another. I made them match as nCntrs. Last, the **AT$** needed a **"from entry"** to tie it together. Other than that, it is a very useful snippet of code. Here is his code, as modified by me:

```
INPUTS: Equity(100000), lePrice(0);
VARS: nCntrs(01);

If (Margin > 00) THEN BEGIN
nCntrs = (NetProfit + Equity) / Margin;
nCntrs = MaxList(nCntrs, 01);
END;

BUY(``le.#1'') nCntrs contracts next bar at lePrice stop;

SELL(``lx.PTarget'')
      CurrentContracts * 0.50 contracts next bar
      at EntryPrice + (2500 * BigPointValue) stop ;

SELL(``lxPanicStop'') from entry (``le.#1'')
      CurrentContracts * 0.50 contracts next bar
      AT$ Lowest(Low, 03) stop;
```

FIGURE 16.12 Sam Tennis's Code

I can't really show you a picture of this one at work. Its effect is to modify not the strategy but the number of contracts traded by your strategy. In **Format → Strategies** simply add this strategy to the list of strategies in your system. You will want to tinker with this code to find the optimum parameters for inputs. Have fun!

TIPS AND TRICKS FROM *EASYLANGUAGE HOME STUDY COURSE*

TradeStation Securities, Inc.
TradeStation Building
8050 SW 10th St., Ste. 2000
Plantation, FL 33324
(800) 556-2022
www.tradestation.com

TradeStation has written several great books elucidating the use of TradeStation software and EasyLanguage. Since the company is the originators, it should know whereof it speaks. This trick is taken from the Home Study Course, beginning on page 79. The code is for a ShowMe study, not an indicator. It draws a dot on each bar that is "that day of the week." In the inputs you specify which day you want to see, and the code plops a dot down on every day of that flavor. For instance, you might want to see every Friday so you can ask "What is true?" with the picture in front of you highlighting Fridays. The code is shown in Figure 16.13.

```
Input: DoW(Wednesday);
If DayOfWeek(Date) = DoW then
   Plot1(Close, ''DoW'');
```

FIGURE 16.13 Day of Week

This is the company's explanation:

Now let's examine the EasyLanguage code you have typed. The If...then statement uses the DayofWeek reserved word to return the day of the week for each bar on the chart. More specifically, DayofWeek returns a value for each bar on the chart based on the date for that bar. The returned value corresponds to a specific day of the week:

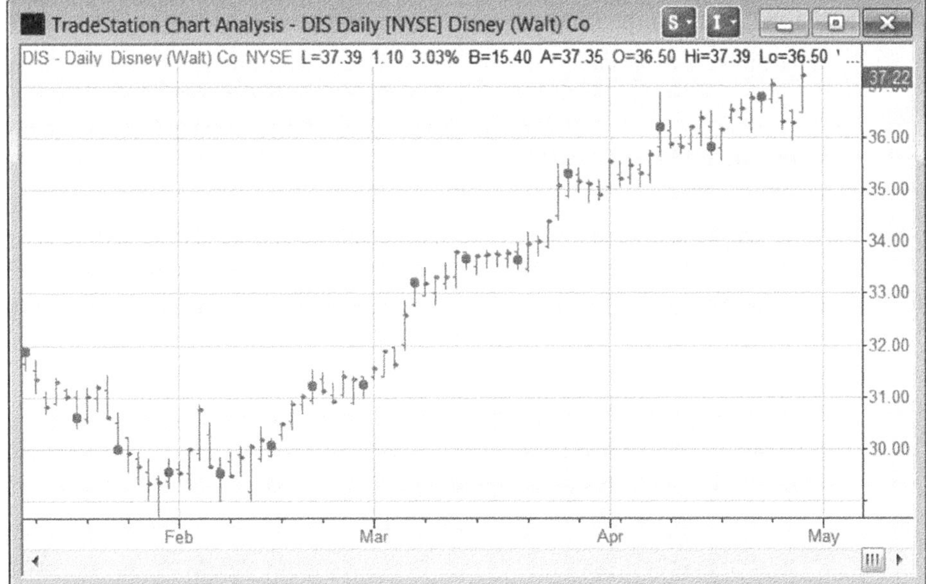

FIGURE 16.14 ShowMe Fridays

0 = Sunday
1 = Monday
2 = Tuesday
3 = Wednesday
4 = Thursday
5 = Friday
6 = Saturday

For those bars that reurn the value 3, which is equal to Wednesday, TradeStation marks the bars with a ShowMe."

The chart of DIS with Fridays highlighted appears in Figure 16.14.

TIPS AND TRICKS FROM GLEN LARSON (OF GENESIS FINANCIAL TECHNOLOGIES)

Genesis Financial Technologies Inc.
4775 Centennial Blvd., Ste. 150
Colorado Springs, CO80919
(800) 808.3282
www.genesisft.com

This code was given to me years ago by my friend Glen Larson, founder of Genesis Financial, when it was still just a data house using TradeStation. Genesis developed into much more. Give the company a call and say I sent you, after you check out the Web site.

The code in Figure 16.15 is much prettier on a wider page. Just copy the code and paste it into your new EZL Strategy. It is available for you on my Web site at **www.money mentor.com/TSME/TipsGM.html.**

```
// Buy New Highs
INPUTS:
buybase(15), { the number of bars between the last and current high bar: to
   detect new high }
sellbase(4), { the number of bars between lows: used to determine stop
   exits}
h_factor(0.5), { in determining a new high, the high must greater than last
   high by ``h_factor'' }
s_fctor1(2), { in determing an exit stop, lowest low of ``sellbase'' must be
   exceeded by s_factor }
s_fctor2(0.90), { second exit stop is triggered if the price drops 25% below
   the all-time high }
```

FIGURE 16.15 Tips by Glen Larson

```
v_factor(1.05), { new high is also determined by volume: volume must be >
than
   avg * v_factor }
v_length(30), { average length (in bars) of volume moving average }
hi_len(20);    { highest high of ``h_len'' bars ago }
VARIABLES:     lasthigh(0), lasthighbar(0), sellstop(0);
{detect a new high}
IF(high>(highest(high,hi_len)[1]+h_factor)) AND volume>(v_factor*average
(v, v_
   length)[1] )
THEN
BEGIN
   lasthigh=high;
   lasthighbar=barnumber;
   condition1=TRUE;
END
ELSE
   condition1=FALSE;
{buy breakout if condition1 is true and previous buy was more than
``buybase'' bars ago }
IF condition1=TRUE AND lasthighbar-lasthighbar[1] > buybase
THEN
BUY(``GL_Buy'') tomorrow on the open;
{ selling rules for exiting long positions }
sellstop = s_fctor2 * lasthigh;
SELL(GL_S1'') currentcontracts shares tomorrow at lowest (low, sellbase)-s_
   fctor1 stop;
SELL(``GL_S2'') currentcontracts shares tomorrow at sellstop stop;
```

FIGURE 16.15 *(Continued)*

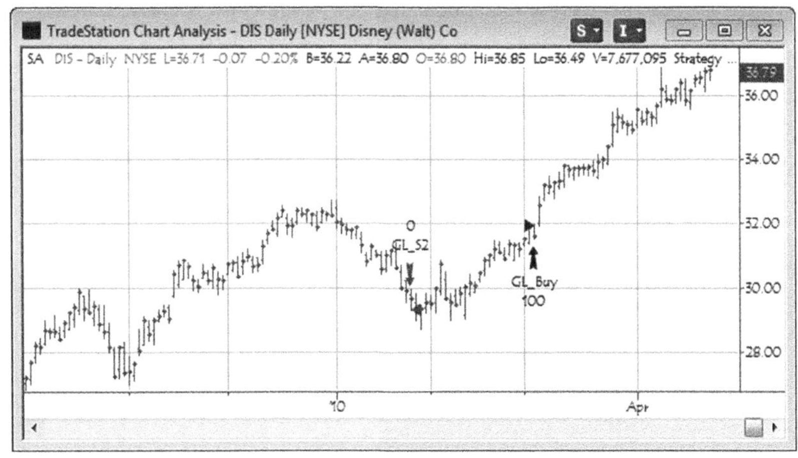

FIGURE 16.16 Chart from Glen Larson: Buy New Highs

Just run an extensive optimization on this one to find the best variable inputs. If you will let TradeStation choose the upper and lower limits of the optimization parameters, it does a good job. Then let 'er rip.

The chart to accompany this code is in Figure 16.16.

TIPS AND TRICKS FROM ARTHUR G. PUTT

TradersStudio, Inc. (Ruggiero Press)
1204 Main St. #280
Branford, CT 06405
(866) 550-0550
www.tradersstudio.com
murray@tradersstudio.com

The strategy in Figure 16.17 from *Using EasyLanguage 2000i* was supplied generously by Murray Ruggiero, publisher of Putt's book. All the code in UEL2000 is for an older version of TradeStation and had to be adapted to work in the current version.

```
{Arthur G Putt, Trend Following 1.02 }
INPUTS: Len(32), MMstop(450), PO(900);
VARS: MA(0);
MA = Average(Close,Len);
//Entry Signals
IF Close > MA AND LowestBar(Low,3) = 0 THEN
      BUY(``TrendLE'') next bar at High + 1 Point Stop;
IF Close < MA AND HighestBar(High,3) = 0 THEN
      SellShort(``TrendSE'') next bar at Low - 1 Point Stop;
//Exit Routines
      //Profit Objective
IF MarketPosition=1 THEN Sell(``TrendLPO'') next bar at
      EntryPrice + (PO/BigPointValue) Limit;
IF MarketPosition = -1 THEN BuyToCover(``TrendSPO'') next bar at
      EntryPrice - (PO/BigPointValue) Limit;
   //Stop Loss
IF MarketPosition = 1 THEN Sell(``TrendLX'') next bar at
      EntryPrice - (MMSTOP/BigPointValue) Stop;
IF MarketPosition = -1 THEN BuyToCover(``TrendSX'') next bar at
      EntryPrice + (MMSTOP/BigPointValue) Stop;
   //End of Day Exit
IF Time>= CalcTime(Sess1EndTime, - BarInterval) THEN
BEGIN
      Sell(``EOD LX'') next bar at Market;
      BuyToCover(``EOD SX'') next bar at Market;
      END;
```

FIGURE 16.17 Strategy from Arthur G. Putt

Another Trick from Arthur G. Putt

Ever wonder how to prevent trades late in the trading day? In *Using EasyLanguage 2000* Putt says:

Any good trading strategy could theoretically generate trades on the last bar of the day. If you are a day trader and want your trades open long enough to build up a profit, you might not want to take a trade late in the day. Using your own trading strategy, just before the IF statements that tell TradeStation to buy and sell add this code:

```
IF Time <= LasTrade THEN BEGIN
```

and don't forget, every IF. . .THEN BEGIN statement must be completed with an END statement. Put the END statement after the last IF for the entry sell. The variable LasTrade needs to be added to the VARS section and set to a default value of 0. An input needs to be added to the INPUT section to allow the number of minutes to add or subtract from a given time. Add the following to the INPUT section: `Minutes(30)`.

Add the following to the VARS section: `LasTrade(0)`.

Remember to separate the inputs and variables with a comma. Also add the following to your code:

```
LasTrade = CalcTime(Sess1EndTime,-minutes);
```

The chart in Figure 16.18 displays the result of the code from Figure 16.17. For more instruction on how this works, be sure to pick up a copy of *Using EasyLanguage 2000.*

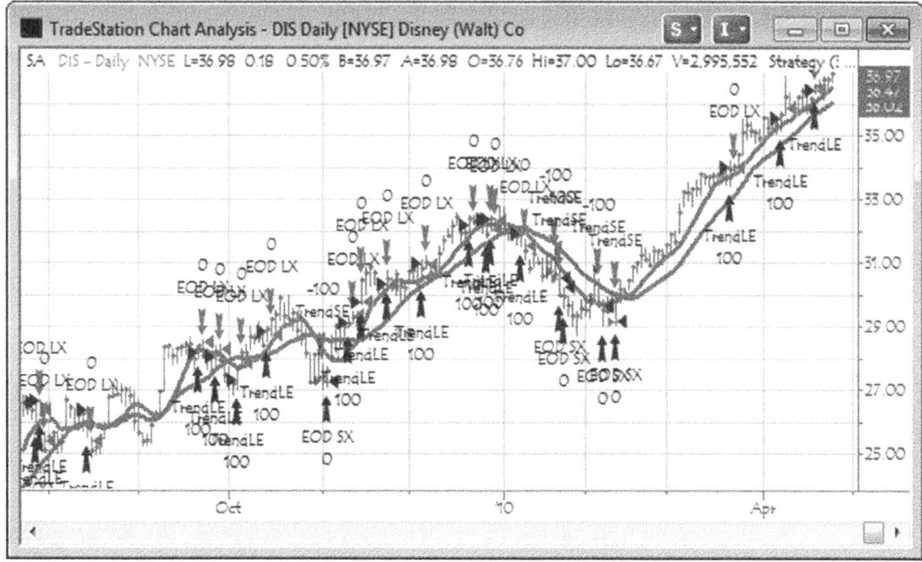

FIGURE 16.18 Chart of Arthur Putt's Trend-Following Strategy

Murray Ruggiero has some copies left, and a search of the internet can also locate copies. It is self-published; not an Amazon-type book.

TIPS AND TRICKS FROM THE TRADESTATION NEWSLETTER

TradeStation Securities, Inc.
TradeStation Building
8050 SW 10th St., Ste. 2000
Plantation, FL 33324
(800) 556-2022 or (954) 652-7000
www.tradestation.com

Determining Uptrends and Downtrends Using RadarScreen

There are many ways of determining if something is in an uptrend or a downtrend as the day progresses. It can easily be visualized when looking at an intraday bar chart in TradeStation. The human mind is superb at finding the underlying order in a relatively chaotic image. However, the human mind has a harder time creating a picture based on a series of numbers.

If you have RadarScreen and are looking at a series of stocks, for example, and if they are all updating tick by tick, it can become quite a show. It would be nice to be able to determine what the overall trend of each stock is with just a glance as the day progresses. One can draw a mental picture by looking at the open, high, low, and last, but the difficulty of doing that increases with the number of stocks and the rapidity of the ticks.

This is a very simple, but very efficient, study that allows the RadarScreen user to know the overall direction of a security without having to look at open, high, low, and last. We call it `IntraDay_Pointer`.

First, create a **function** in your EasyLanguage PowerEditor called **Q_MedianPrice_Day** with this code:

```
Q_MedianPrice_Day = (Q_High + Q_Low) / 2;
```

Next, create an indicator called `IntrDay_Pointer` with the code shown in Figure 16.19.

Once this is done, apply the indicator to your RadarScreen, sort the column to which it is assigned (by double-clicking on the column label), and watch it separate all securities in an overall uptrend from all securities in an overall downtrend. The RadarScreen in Figure 16.20 shows what you'll get.

```
Input: BGColor(White),UpColor(Blue),DwnColor(Red);
value1 = (Q_Last + Q_MedianPrice_Day) / 2;
value2 = value1 - Q_Open;
Plot1(value2,''IDP'');
If GetPlotBGColor(1) <> BGColor then
      SetPlotBGColor(1,BGColor);
If value2 > 0 then
      SetPlotColor(1,UpColor);
If value2 < 0 then
      SetPlotColor(1,DwnColor);
```

FIGURE 16.19 IntraDay Pointer

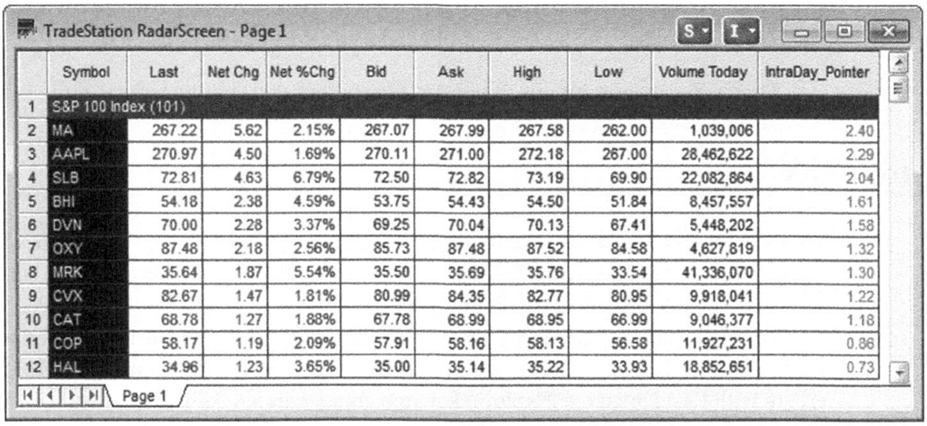

TradeStation RadarScreen - Page 1

	Symbol	Last	Net Chg	Net %Chg	Bid	Ask	High	Low	Volume Today	IntraDay_Pointer
1	S&P 100 Index (101)									
2	MA	267.22	5.62	2.15%	267.07	267.99	267.58	262.00	1,039,006	2.40
3	AAPL	270.97	4.50	1.69%	270.11	271.00	272.18	267.00	28,462,622	2.29
4	SLB	72.81	4.63	6.79%	72.50	72.82	73.19	69.90	22,082,864	2.04
5	BHI	54.18	2.38	4.59%	53.75	54.43	54.50	51.84	8,457,557	1.61
6	DVN	70.00	2.28	3.37%	69.25	70.04	70.13	67.41	5,448,202	1.58
7	OXY	87.48	2.18	2.56%	85.73	87.48	87.52	84.58	4,627,819	1.32
8	MRK	35.64	1.87	5.54%	35.50	35.69	35.76	33.54	41,336,070	1.30
9	CVX	82.67	1.47	1.81%	80.99	84.35	82.77	80.95	9,918,041	1.22
10	CAT	68.78	1.27	1.88%	67.78	68.99	68.95	66.99	9,046,377	1.18
11	COP	58.17	1.19	2.09%	57.91	58.16	58.13	56.58	11,927,231	0.86
12	HAL	34.96	1.23	3.65%	35.00	35.14	35.22	33.93	18,852,651	0.73

Page 1

FIGURE 16.20 RadarScreen IntraDay Pointer

FILEAPPEND

One last trick, before we move on. This command sends information to an existing ASCII file, whose name is specified in the inputs, and it adds the information to the bottom (or end) of the file, without overwriting the previously saved data. This tool can be incredibly powerful if, for instance, you want to analyze information about your trading in a spreadsheet. You can write all kinds of information, from your indicator or strategy, into a text file and then import it into Excel. You can write the results of calculations into the file, or information as each trade is closed or opened. You could gather statistics into the file or write debugging information. You could even create a data file with this command.

When using `FileAppend`, every field must be a string. Therefore, when numeric data is to be saved to the file, it must be converted to string data by using the `NumToStr` command. (See Appendix B.)

EXAMPLE

```
INPUTS: jLength(10);
FileAppend("C:\Temp\DIS.txt" , NumToStr(Date,0) + ","
+ NumToStr (Close,2) + "," + NumToStr(LinearRegAngle
(C,jLength),2 ) + NewLine) ;
```

The `FileAppend` command will open a new file if the filename specified does not exists.

Note that the `FileAppend` command could potentially keep writing and writing to this file ad infinitum for as long as the indicator containing the command is open and active. It could easily consume lots of hard disk drive space. To this end, there is a companion command in EasyLanguage called `FileDelete`. This command will get rid of the existing file, if it exists. You can accomplish this by using the next logic, before you begin writing:

```
IF BarNumber = 1 THEN FileDelete("C:\Temp\DIS.txt");
```

Then you can save off any important files before you run the indicator the next time.

SUMMARY

That's it for the tips and tricks for this book. This book is to get you started. Most of the other books about EasyLanguage move very quickly from the basics to very sophisticated concepts. My book is meant to fill that gap.

There are lots of wonderful works by other authors to which I will refer you for advanced concepts. This chapter was just to give you a taste of the variety clever people can create with EasyLanguage. Explore. Let your mind wander. And keep notes.

Here is the list of works you should read:

- *Ask Mr. EasyLanguage* by Sam Tennis
- *EasyLanguage Essentials* available in pdf from TradeStation.com
- *EasyLanguage Functions & Reserved Words Reference* available in pdf from TradeStation.com
- *Mastering EasyLanguage for Strategies Home Study Course* by TradeStation Technologies
- *EasyLanguage Learning by Example* by William Brower
- *TradeStation Trading Techniques* by Linda Raschke
- *Getting Started with TradeStation EasyLanguage* by TradeStation Technologies
- *Using EasyLanguage* by Arthur G. Putt

And by all means, don't forget to join the EasyLanguage Forum on www.tradestation.com.

CHAPTER 17

Optimization

In This Chapter

- Introduction
- What Is Optimization?
- How Much Is Enough?
- When to Optimize
- Run the Optimization
- Changing the Optimization Criteria
- Working with the Optimization Report
- Curiouser and Curiouser
- Conclusion

Optimization is not the enemy—abuse of optimization is.

—*Ralph Vince*, Portfolio Management Formulas

Curve fitting is right when it is used correctly, it's only wrong when it's used incorrectly.

—*Joe Ross*, Trading by the Book

INTRODUCTION

This chapter wasn't in the original manuscript for this book. But as I am finally finishing the book, I am also working on a strategy for a client and am making in-depth use of the optimization feature of TradeStation, and I realize I cannot leave it out. Optimization is perhaps the single most powerful feature of TradeStation and the thing that first set it apart from all other trading software.

Optimization is the process of fine-tuning an already profitable trading system. It is not a method for making the computer find you a profitable trading system!

You want to optimize your trading system only after you've built it, thoroughly tested it, and deemed it to be a sound system that you want to trade. Many novice system traders use optimization too early in the system development process; they try to use it to build a system. Again, optimization is not a way to build a system; it is the way to put the finishing touches on an already successful system.

WHAT IS OPTIMIZATION?

According to the dictionary, *optimization is the process of finding the best or most favorable conditions or parameters.* In system testing, usually the most favorable conditions are represented by the largest net profit. There are circumstances under which you would not consider the greatest net profit to be the best system. For instance, you might reject a system that has 1000 trades per month and a huge net profit in favor of a system that trades 30 times per month and makes a large, but not the largest, net profit. As you optimize the parameters in your system, you look for variables that produce the greatest net profit over the longest period of time.

Curve-fitting is the process of developing complicated rules that map known conditions. If you optimize a moving average to loosely fit market conditions from 1982 to 1997, you might do pretty well trading in the future. But if you optimize it so that it very closely fits the market from 1982 to the present, and you add conditions that match current and past events, you have curve-fitted the data. A curve-fitted system often does not behave well (profitably) into the future.

How much data do you need to use for testing before you can be sure of the replicability of the results? And furthermore, is there a way to keep from curve-fitting the data?

HOW MUCH IS ENOUGH?

I like to see at least 100 trades from a system before I am willing to trade it with real money. Most often you will hear the number 30 tossed around, but I am not personally comfortable with so few examples.

To test a system over a set of data that produces only 30 trades would generate a very nice model that would work well over that specific set of historical data. But as the markets fluctuate and the mood changes from bull, to bear, to sideways and back again, the model with 30 trades would probably prove to be only accurate over that subset of data for which you initially developed it. Not only do I like to see 100 trades before I believe a system works, I like the data to include up moves, down moves and sideways moves.

Often I am asked what time period the 100 trades should cover. My response is: as much time as it takes to get 100 trades. If your system generates 100 trades per year, you need a year's worth of data. If it generates 100 trades in 10 years, you need 10 years' worth of data.

WHEN TO OPTIMIZE

When you write the signals in your system, you use criteria to generate the buy, sell, and exit orders. For example, let's say you are developing a system that will take advantage of trends, and you are using two moving averages in combination with a strength indicator such as the `ADX`. You're comfortable after thoroughly testing your system on some markets that your signals are solid, and you're catching the big moves while limiting your losses in the markets' sideways modes. You'd be comfortable trading the system as is. **Now you're ready to optimize.**

By optimizing, you'll make sure that you're using the optimal moving average lengths and/or the optimal number of bars when calculating ADX. You're not trying to find new techniques to capture market moves; what you're trying to do is fine-tune techniques that you've already decided you are going to use.

To find the optimal values, you'll apply your system to a chart (to the market or markets you plan to trade) and then test a series of values for the `inputs` in your system. The optimization process involves testing various input values (or combination of input values) in a system to see if using different values would provide better results. By default, TradeStation looks for the best net profit, but you can change this criteria, as discussed in the section called Changing the Optimization Criteria, later in this chapter.

NOTE: You can optimize only values that are defined as `inputs`. If a value is written into the signal directly and not by means of an input, you cannot optimize that value. If a value is specified within the routine as a variable, you cannot optimize that value. You can optimize inputs only.

Optimization involves testing a range of values for the inputs of a system. You apply the system to a chart and then specify a range of values, and increments of values, to be tested for one or more of the system's inputs. When you run the optimization, each value in that range is tested against the system, one bar at a time.

If you optimize multiple inputs (e.g., you optimize the lengths for two different moving averages, say `LENGTH1` and `LENGTH2`), then each value in your range for `LENGTH1` is tested in combination with each value in your range of `LENGTH2`. The range and increments of values you specify determine the number of tests to be performed. The more values that must be tested, the more tests that must be run, and the longer the optimization will take.

The number of tests your optimization will perform is calculated as the **product of each of the number of tests** for each input. If I test `Length1` from 8 to 12, that's 5 tests; testing `Length2` from 15 to 20 is 6 more tests; the product of $5 \times 6 = 30$ total tests.

Let's say we're optimizing our trending system and want to test different combinations of the two moving averages. For LENGTH1, which is the fast-moving average, our default value is 9. We may want to test the values 6, 9, and 12. For LENGTH2, the slow-moving average, our default value is 18. We may want to test the values of 18, 21, and 24.

The optimization would then perform nine tests (three inputs by three inputs, or $3 \times 3 = 9$):

LENGTH1 tested with LENGTH2:

6 bars with 18 bars; 6 bars with 21 bars; and 6 bars with 24 bars;
9 bars with 18 bars; 9 bars with 21 bars; and 9 bars with 24 bars;
12 bars with 18 bars; 12 bars with 21 bars; and 12 bars with 24 bars,
for a total of nine tests.

When the optimization process is done, TradeStation generates a detailed **Optimization Report** that contains the results of each value (or combination of values) tested. The **Optimization Report** lists the results in tabular format, like a spreadsheet. In fact, you can easily export the results to **Excel.** In addition, it provides several built-in graphs and allows you to create two custom graphs. TradeStation also automatically applies the set of values that creates the best results to the chart (although you can apply any of the results to the chart, as discussed in *Applying Different Test Results to Your System*).

TradeStation's Strategy Performance Report judges the results based on best total net profit (TNP) (by default; you can change it), but the Optimization Report lists the resulting net profit along with several other fields, as discussed in the section called *Working with the Optimization Report* later in the chapter.

NOTE: Once you run the optimization and you review the report, you should look at the Strategy Performance Report to further analyze the results obtained by the optimization. The Optimization Report contains the same fields as the Summary section of the System Report.

An optimization can take seconds, minutes, or hours depending on the number of tests being run. To reduce the time required for testing, you can either reduce the number of different values being tested for each input or reduce the number of inputs being optimized at one time. However, TradeStation's No-Wait Optimization allows you to optimize a system in the background as you continue working on other projects, allowing you to continue working on something else while a lengthy optimization takes place.

What Do You Want to Do?

In Chapter 4, Basic Use of TradeStation, we used the optimization features of TS without going into much explanation. In this chapter we will discuss the concepts in depth.

When I first began trading, there was no firm and fixed procedure for backtesting and forward-testing your ideas to determine what would work and what would fail. In fact, there was barely any system testing at all back then. There were just a couple of strategy development platforms, but nothing really to do any optimizations with. Then along came a DOS program called SystemWriter, the Omega Research predecessor to TradeStation. With SystemWriter you could develop systems on daily bars, but nothing on intraday bars, where you would want to do your trading. It wasn't long until SystemWriter became TradeStation, available for the Windows environment. With TradeStation we could do serious system testing and optimization.

Still, there was no theory of testing, so I developed my own. I still use this theory of testing today on any system I am considering trading. It is critical that you perform your tests in this manner to ensure success. If you cheat on the methods you will end up with a curve-fitted strategy that won't work into the future.

The key to my approach was to test a subset of the data—I decided to use the middle third—when constructing my ideas and testing their efficacy. Having found something that is acceptable, I then tested on the first third of the data, which would be back-testing, and on the last third, which would be forward-testing (since your "system" has not yet seen that data.)

My approach, in summary, is consistent every time I encounter a new idea:

- Break your data into thirds.
- Set up the optimization.
- Run the optimization (let 'er rip) on the middle third.
- Change the optimization criteria.
- Work with the Optimization Report.
- Save results to spreadsheet.
- Cluster your results and find alligators.
- Calculate your performance statistics.
- Verify findings on other thirds.

Testing Your Data by Thirds

The key to successful system generation is to start your research using only a portion of the available data. If you create a strategy that perfectly fits the whole set of available data, there is a high likelihood that it will be curve-fitted and therefore not work into the future. If you limit your testing and idea generation to a subset of your data, then test it over the whole set of data (and get good results), then and only then can you be confident that your strategy might work in the future. At no time do you go back and fit the results to the other parts of your data.

After completing the entire research process for that limited set of data, engage in "back-testing" and "forward testing." Divide your data into thirds, testing the middle third first as you generate theories and systems. See Figure 17.1.

If you were to use the nine years of data from 1987 through 1995 for testing, the data from 1987 through the end of 1989 would be historical data to your new system. Thus, any testing you do on data that happened before the period you've proven is "back-testing." Likewise, the data that comes after 1992 (which you didn't even peek at) is future data to the

1987	1988	1989	1990	1991	1992	1993	1994	1995
	II			Data Set I			III	

FIGURE 17.1 Nine Years of Data Divided into Thirds

system. In effect, you are running a blind trial that could not have been curve-fit, because you didn't have the data as part of the initial design.

If your system performs reasonably well (within your expectations) over the backward test and the forward test, you just might have a tradable system. But don't trade it yet, there's more to find out.

Set Up the Optimization

Let's say we were investigating a simple moving average crossover system and wanted to test every possible combination from 3 to 30. That means we want to test every moving average crossover from (3,3), (3,4), (3,5), (3,6) . . . (3,30), etc. all the way to (30,3), (30,4), (30,5) . . . , (29,30), (30,30).

The code in Figure 17.2 is just that sort of strategy.

```
INPUTS: jL1(9), jL2(18);
   If Average(C,jL1) crosses over Average(C,jL2) THEN BUY this bar on
   close;
   If Average(C,jL1) crosses under Average(C,jL2) THEN SELL Short this
   bar on close;
```

FIGURE 17.2 Code for Simple Moving Average System

To set up the test we would first set up a chart with the indicator(s) on it. There is an indicator called **Moving Avg 2 Lines** built into TradeStation. Choose that one. Next, set the color and thickness of the lines so you can easily see them. Your chart should look like mine in Figure 17.3. Remember, as we go through this process, that when you find optimal results for your strategy, they will not port over to your indicator on the chart. The optimal results for your strategy will have to be entered by hand into the values for the indicator, so you can properly see how your results relate to the moving averages.

Next, either double-click on an arrow to bring up the format box, or use the menu sequence **Format → Analysis Techniques→Strategies.** This will bring up the window in Figure 17.4, where you can change your length parameters.

Next, either double-click on the **Input Values** themselves, or click on **Format** to bring up the **Format Strategy** dialogue box. It usually opens on **Entries** (see Figure 17.5), so click on the **Inputs** tab so we can alter the inputs (see Figure 17.6).

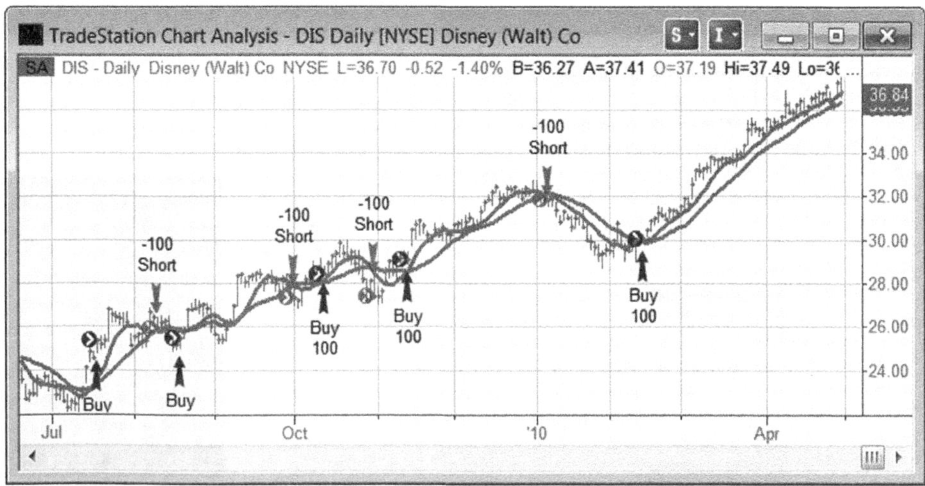

FIGURE 17.3 Two Moving Average Crossovers

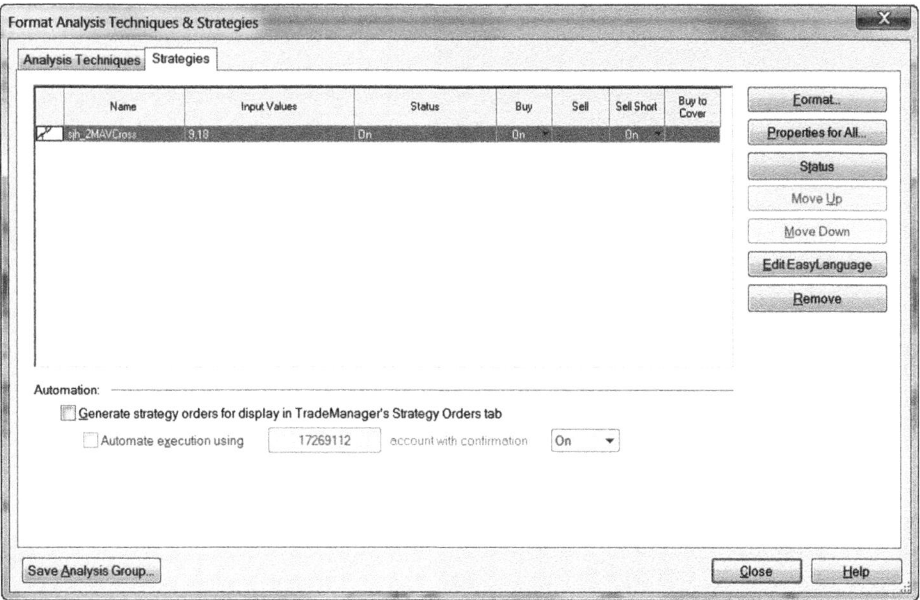

FIGURE 17.4 Optimizing Window in TradeStation

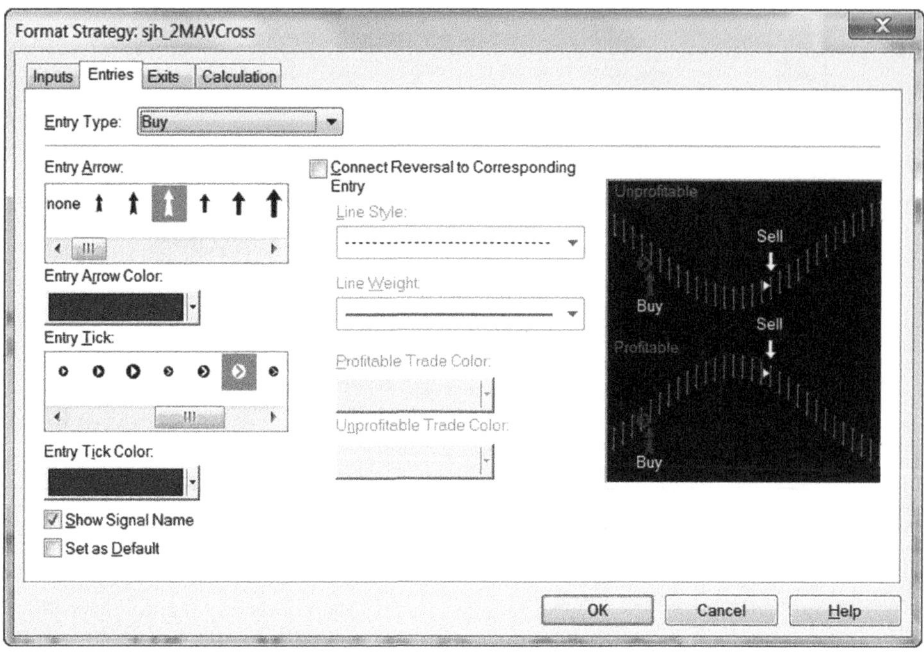

FIGURE 17.5 Format Strategy

Format Strategy: sjh_2MAVCross

Inputs | Entries | Exits | Calculation

Name	Value
jL1	9
jL2	18

Dictionary... Optimize... Set Default

OK Cancel Help

FIGURE 17.6 Change Inputs

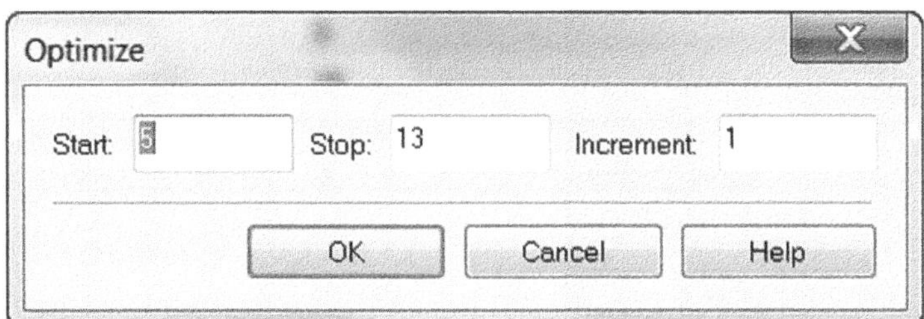

FIGURE 17.7 Optimize Inputs Dialog Box

Now click on the **Optimize** button (lower left) to bring up the little dialogue box where you can alter the input parameters. It is shown in Figure 17.7. Generally, TradeStation fills in default values that are pretty good. Sometimes, especially when the values are decimal numbers, you will have to change the defaults, but usually you can just accept the values supplied by TS. You might want to broaden the range some, but I'm going to accept the values TS chose for now. Just click **OK** to accept the parameters for `jL1` and then highlight the second input value, `jL2`. Again, click **Optimize** to bring up the dialogue box and accept or change the range of values. Click **OK** to accept both sets of values for your inputs.

Now that both input values have a range of values over which to test, it is time to run the first optimization.

RUN THE OPTIMIZATION

After having set up a range of values over which to optimize the input values, it's time to click the **Optimize** button (1) on the **Format Analysis Techniques & Strategies** dialogue box. It is shown in Figure 17.8. Depending on how many tests are to be run, you will have to wait seconds or even hours for your results. I call this part "Let 'er Rip!" This is the fun and exciting part.

While you are waiting for your tests to complete, you can view a status window that looks like the one in Figure 17.9. As the tests run, the **Current test number** will increase with each test, so you can see how far along you are. This doesn't matter much in short tests but is good when you are running thousands of tests. You can also view **Estimated time to completion,** which will let you know if there is time for a trip to the bathroom or the kitchen before your tests are ready to view. These numbers click away like an odometer on a long trip. The last number on this window that I watch for entertainment while the tests are running is **All: Net Profit.** I don't know why I don't just walk away while the tests are running, but there is a certain satisfaction in watching the **All: Net Profit** go from a negative number to a positive number to a large positive number. It's kind of like Christmas with the anticipation.

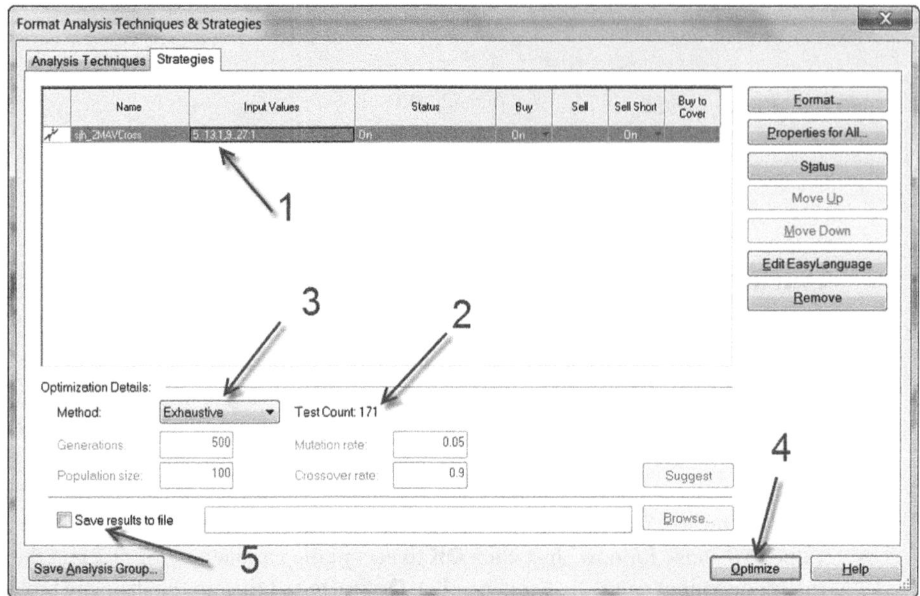

FIGURE 17.8 Format Analysis Techniques & Strategies Dialogue Box

TradeStation Chart Analysis - DIS Daily [NYSE] Disney (Walt) Co

Abort Optimization #3

Status	In progress	**Chart Settings**	
Tests		Chart	'DIS Daily [NYSE] Disney (Walt) Co'
Current test	1	Strategy	'Strategy'
Total tests	171		
Time		**Report Settings**	
Total elapsed time	0 sec	Show	Highest 200 tests
Estimated time to completion	Estimating /	Based on	All: Net Profit
Current Best Values			
All: Net Profit	-10181		
sjh_2MAVCross: jL1	5		
sjh_2MAVCross: jL2	9		

FIGURE 17.9 Optimizing Status

Before Leaving This Dialogue Box

Let me point out a couple things that you will want to use later on. I've numbered these items on the chart in Figure 17.8 for easy reference.

Item 1 we've already discussed. Double-clicking this item takes you to the dialogue box where you can input the optimization ranges.

Item 2 shows the number of tests you propose to run. Remember that it is calculated as the product of the number of tests of each parameter. In this case it will be $9 \times 19 = 171$. When you get more sophisticated and optimize many parameters, this number will get very large.

Midway down on the left side (3), under the words **Optimization Details,** there is a pull-down that shows **Exhaustive** by default. Normally, **Exhaustive** will be the choice you will want. But sometimes your number of tests will be so large that TradeStation can't run them all at once. TradeStation will only run 10,000,000 tests at a time. If you try to run too many tests, you will get a pop-up window that tells you how many tests you are trying to run and how many are allowed, and "Please reduce the number of tests by optimizing fewer inputs or by reducing the optimization range for each input." You can do that, but it is laborious to go back in and change everything. Instead, you can click on **Exhaustive** and change it to **Genetic,** which will run approximately 10,000 tests on the default settings.

Here's what the TradeStation help file (F1) says about the Genetic testing algorithm:

From Method, select Genetic to use an optimization method based on an evolutionary algorithm. Genetic optimizations are preferable when the exhaustive method is too time consuming or processing intensive. Running optimizations in shorter times will also allow you to select wider range of parameters in your strategy optimizations. Genetic optimizations do not calculate all possible strategy parameter combinations but will use an algorithm based on natural selection that will arrive to an answer that is statistically significant.

- *Gene One of the strategy parameters to be optimized.*
- *Chromosome A combination of linked genes, that is, a combination of possible strategy parameter values.*
- *Fitness Optimization criterion. By default, the optimization criterion is Net Profit, but can be changed in TradeStation by going to Chart Analysis Preferences.*
- *Generations Number of iterations that the genetic algorithm will run until it arrives to the strongest population.*
- *Population size Group of chromosomes that will be subject to the genetic selection process. After the specified generations, the outstanding population group is understood as being of improved fitness thanks to the natural selection of the genetic algorithm.*
- *Mutation rate Random rate of modification of the genes in chromosomes after each generation.*
- *Crossover rate A rate that specifies how close the replacement genes in chromosomes are picked after each generation.*

In general terms, the genetic optimization method goes through the following steps:

- *An initial population of chromosomes (combination of strategy parameters values) is randomly chosen.*
- *The fitness criterion is used to identify the best specimens.*
- *Weakest chromosomes are discarded.*

- *Mutation and Crossover is used to find new chromosomes to replace the "weak" ones.*
- *The replacement chromosomes are put in the population, defining the next generation.*
- *Return to step 2 for fitness evaluation until the last generation is concluded.*
- *Find chromosome with best fitness in the final population.*
  The final chromosome contains the optimized strategy parameter values.

I must say, I don't know what all that means. Perhaps you will. Or perhaps not, and that's okay too. The only thing you really need to know about Genetic testing is that it chooses a subset of the original number of tests to be run so that you can get an overview of the broad spectrum without running all the tests.

Item 4 is the **Optimize** button. We have already discussed it. That is the button you click when you are ready to let 'er rip.

Item 5 is for saving the results of the optimization to a file. If you'll start with just typing "test" into the box, TradeStation will do the rest by assigning the default location and file type. If you want to take control of the location of the file, just click on **Browse** and choose your own location.

The resulting file is a `.txt` file with comma delimiters, which contains all the results of each optimization. To use the file and to sort the results by different criteria, open it with your spreadsheet program (mine is Excel). Just start up Excel, ask it to open the `test.txt` file, and tell it that the file is comma delimited. Your spreadsheet should look like the one in Figure 17.10.

You can do the same thing, if you forget to save your results at this level, after the optimization completes. After running the optimization you can **View → Optimization Report,** click on the **diskette icon,** and save the results to file.

CHANGING THE OPTIMIZATION CRITERIA

In the TradeStation help files [F1] (**F1**), this section says that if you want to rank your optimization by something other than the default criterion, which is **Net Profit,** you must change it in **View → Chart Analysis Preferences before running the optimization.** That's not quite true. It is mostly true, but there is an exception.

By going to **View → Chart Analysis Preferences** (see Figure 17.11), you can click on the **Strategy** tab to bring up the selectors for criteria for your Optimization Report. Generally we want to see the **Highest Net Profit,** and that is the default setting. But you can change it to Highest or Lowest and can make 22 selections for criteria as shown in Figure 17.13.

There are times when **Net Profit** is not what you are interested in. Notice right beside the **Highest/Lowest** selector, there is a box that is set to **200 tests.** By default you will always save the best 200 tests of whatever flavor you chose. For my purposes, which you'll see shortly, I prefer to save the best 900 tests. Yes, that takes more processing time and

	A	B	C	D	E	F	G	H	I	J	K	L	M
1	sjh_2MAV	sjh_2MAV	Test	All: Net Pr	All: Gross	All: Gross	All: Total T	All: % Prof	All: Winnin	All: Losing	All: Max W	All: Max Lc	All: Avg Wi
2	10	9	6	4703	36050	-31347	1872	49.46581	926	822	669	-763	38.93089
3	12	10	17	4267	30976	-26709	1304	53.91104	703	538	594	-986	44.06259
4	12	9	8	4226	28459	-24233	1122	55.88235	627	442	662	-925	45.38915
5	11	9	7	3669	31904	-28235	1394	51.72166	721	585	669	-894	44.24965
6	12	11	26	3122	33607	-30485	1694	50.53129	856	728	594	-1014	39.26051
7	11	10	16	3101	35335	-32234	1768	51.35747	908	719	594	-825	38.9152
8	13	12	36	2116	32683	-30567	1644	48.23601	793	736	575	-836	41.21438
9	13	9	9	1976	25105	-23129	968	56.81818	550	375	662	-907	45.64545
10	13	10	18	1129	25627	-24498	1066	53.18949	567	442	594	-1014	45.19753
11	11	13	43	226	28106	-27880	1260	42.77778	539	640	1138	-575	52.14471
12	12	14	53	172	27064	-26892	1158	44.21416	512	575	850	-631	52.85938
13	9	9	5	0	0	0	0	0	0	0	0	0	0
14	10	10	15	0	0	0	0	0	0	0	0	0	0
15	11	11	25	0	0	0	0	0	0	0	0	0	0
16	12	12	35	0	0	0	0	0	0	0	0	0	0
17	13	13	45	0	0	0	0	0	0	0	0	0	0
18	13	16	72	-42	23428	-23470	938	42.4307	398	488	756	-600	58.86432
19	13	11	27	-226	27880	-28106	1260	50.79365	640	539	575	-1138	43.5625
20	13	14	54	-494	30391	-30885	1570	44.64968	701	745	785	-756	43.35378
21	13	27	171	-567	15354	-15921	412	41.01942	169	230	1231	-756	90.85207
22	10	25	150	-952	16679	-17631	464	34.69828	161	290	750	-744	103.5963
23	10	24	141	-976	17129	-18105	478	36.19247	173	292	861	-744	99.01156

FIGURE 17.10 Optimization Output File in Excel

definitely more disk space, but I have my reasons. What I don't do is save each and every optimization I've ever run to my hard drive. I save some spreadsheets and throw most of them away.

Here's the important part: If you run an optimization that runs 100,000 tests and have TS set to save the best 900 tests, you will be throwing most of the tests away. If you are saving the best Net Profit, you will have thrown away 99,100 tests which might contain very valuable information. You might determine that you want to know the highest CPC Index for each of your tests, and not necessarily the highest Net Profit. In fact, that is what I *usually* want to know. To calculate CPC, you need to know the Percent Profitable, Profit Factor, and Ratio of Avg Win/Avg Loss (look back at Chapters 2 and 4 where I discussed CPC Index). TradeStation doesn't allow you to sort by more than one parameter, so let's pick Percent Profitable to keep the best 900 trials. Doing so, we may be throwing away some or even many of the Highest Net Profits. That's okay; Net Profit isn't the most important statistic. CPC Index is!

When I said TS's statement in the help files wasn't quite true, here's what I meant. If you are running fewer tests than the maximum number you specified to save, then you will be saving all of your tests. If you are saving all of the tests you run, then you can sort by any one of the 22 criteria your spreadsheet after the fact. If you didn't set TS to save the right ranking criterion before running the tests, it doesn't matter as long as you are saving all of the tests you run.

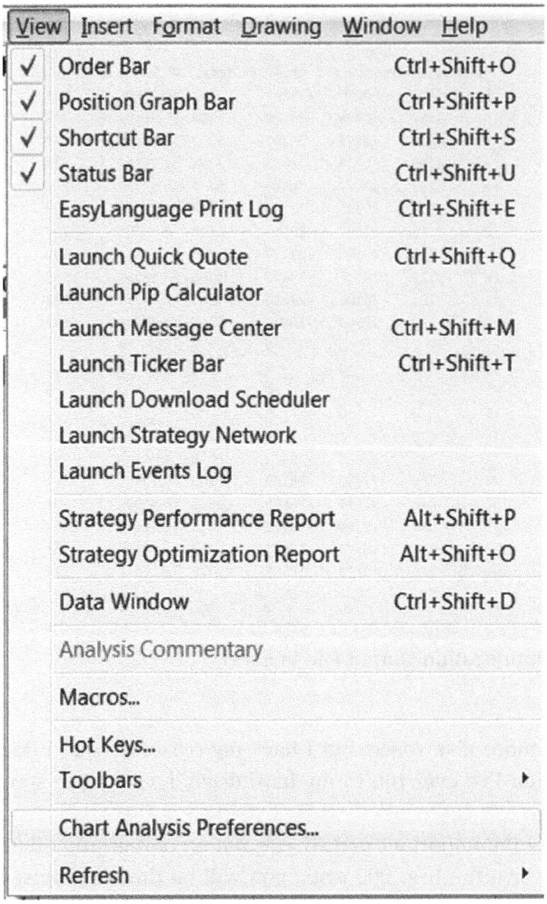

View Insert Format Drawing Window Help

✓	Order Bar	Ctrl+Shift+O
✓	Position Graph Bar	Ctrl+Shift+P
✓	Shortcut Bar	Ctrl+Shift+S
✓	Status Bar	Ctrl+Shift+U
	EasyLanguage Print Log	Ctrl+Shift+E
	Launch Quick Quote	Ctrl+Shift+Q
	Launch Pip Calculator	
	Launch Message Center	Ctrl+Shift+M
	Launch Ticker Bar	Ctrl+Shift+T
	Launch Download Scheduler	
	Launch Strategy Network	
	Launch Events Log	
	Strategy Performance Report	Alt+Shift+P
	Strategy Optimization Report	Alt+Shift+O
	Data Window	Ctrl+Shift+D
	Analysis Commentary	
	Macros...	
	Hot Keys...	
	Toolbars	▸
	Chart Analysis Preferences...	
	Refresh	▸

FIGURE 17.11 View → Chart Analysis Preferences

WORKING WITH THE OPTIMIZATION REPORT

The Strategy Optimization Report lets you look at the results of all your tests, as well as perform more detailed analysis by graphing the results. It provides a spreadsheet-type view of all 22 strategy performance fields for each test and shows the results sorted by the selections you made in Figure 17.12. If you selected highest percent profitable, for instance, the top row of the report will contain the results for the highest percent profitable and they will descend from there.

Each row in Figure 17.10 represents a set of test results. The columns are performance fields, and are the same fields you can choose as the optimization criteria. The row with the best results is marked with a different color than the rest. The first column(s) is/are your

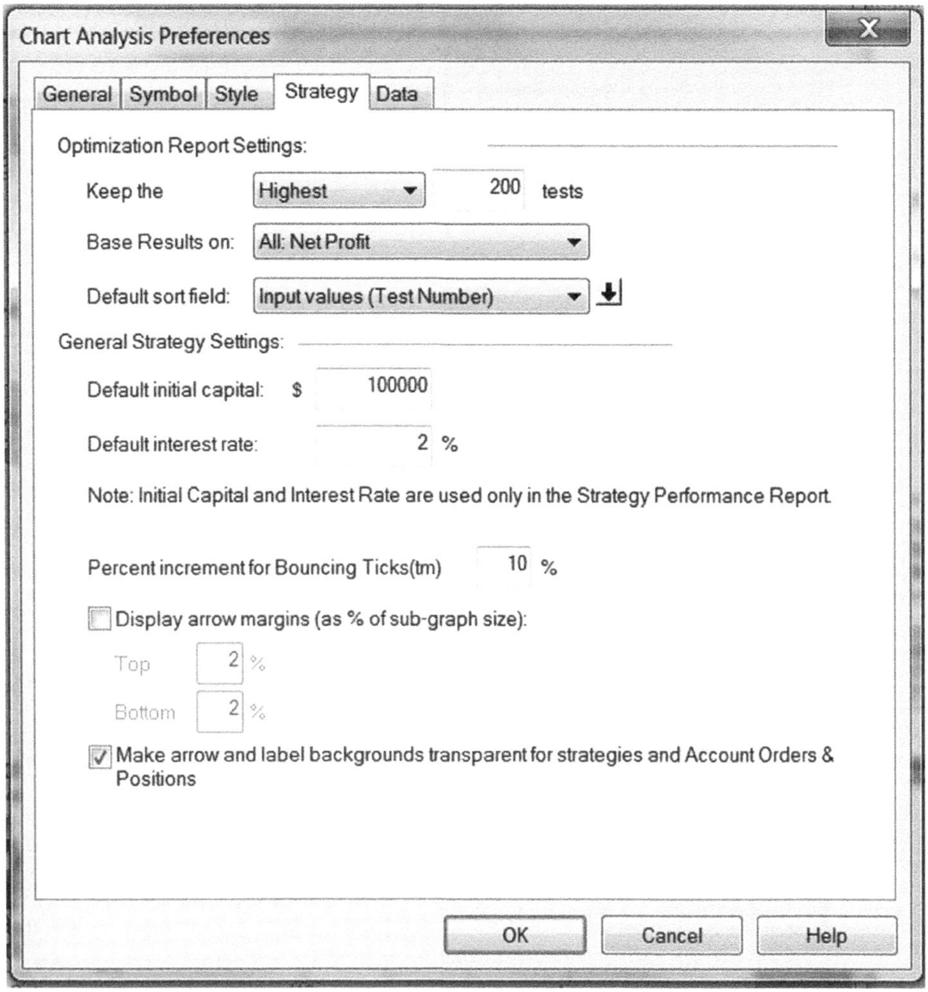

FIGURE 17.12 Strategy Optimization Parameters

input parameters. The next column after the inputs is the test number showing the order in which the tests were run.

If you want to reorder the report by any other criterion, simply double-click on the heading and it will immediately sort by highest first. If you wanted to see lowest first, double-click again and it will resort. If you want the report sorted by the order in which the tests were run, simply double-click on the Tests column.

At the top of the report is a menu bar with several icons. It looks like Figure 17.14. The arrow points to the little menu bar. The first four icons are for saving and printing, adding or removing data fields, and formatting the window. The fifth icon is a tiny spreadsheet with

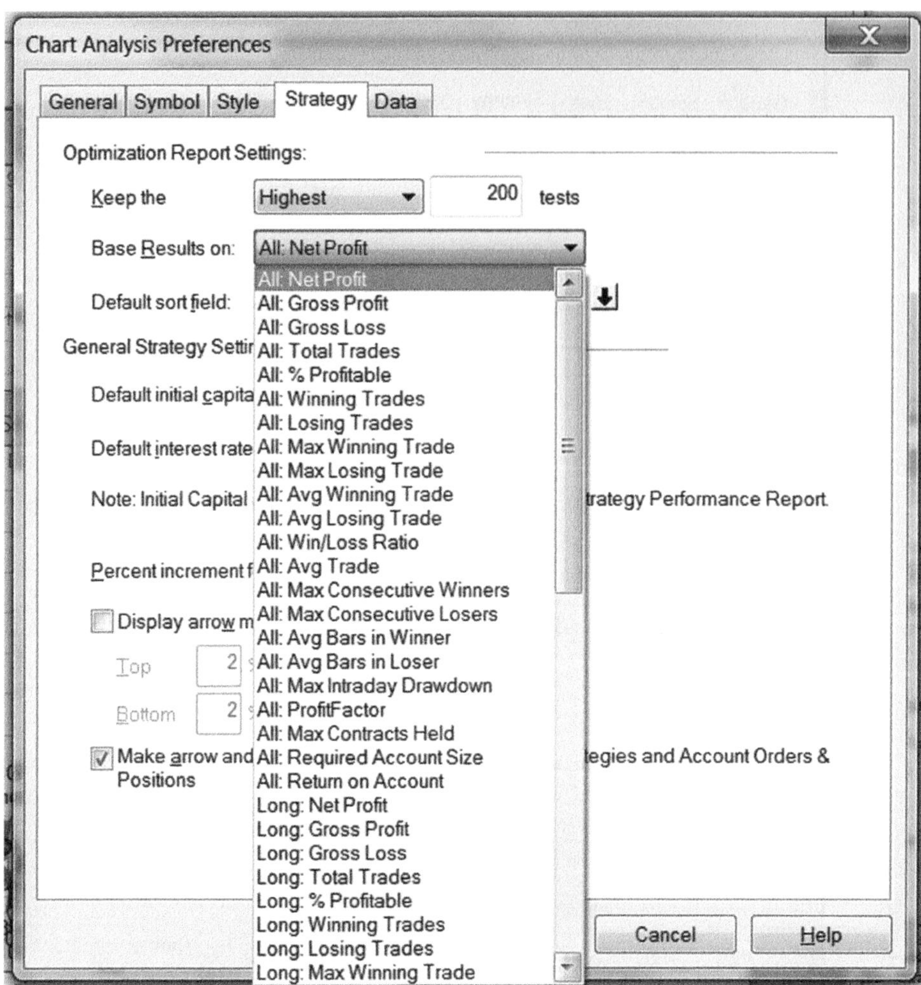

FIGURE 17.13 Sort Criteria for Optimization Report

which you can come back to the spreadsheet view after you have gone on to other views. The next six icons allow you to format your data in various graphical forms. Play with these views by clicking on them. You won't break anything. You can view your data in line charts, bar charts, area charts, and tape charts.

The Optimization Report charts are pretty simplistic, but like all charts (versus lists of numbers), a picture is worth 1,000 words. I find it much easier to read a chart than a long display of tabular numbers. Figure 17.15 shows this simple moving average optimization in graphical format.

TradeStation Strategy Optimization Report - DIS Daily [NYSE] Disney (W

	_2MAVCrc jL1	_2MAVCrc jL2	Test	All: Net Profit	All: Gross Profit	All: Gross Loss	All: Total Trades	All: % Profitab
1	5	9	1	-10,181.00	23,603.00	33,784.00	1,297	34.:
2	6	9	2	-8,775.00	23,592.00	32,367.00	1,373	36.!
3	7	9	3	-6,676.00	26,696.00	33,372.00	1,545	40.!

FIGURE 17.14 Menu Bar

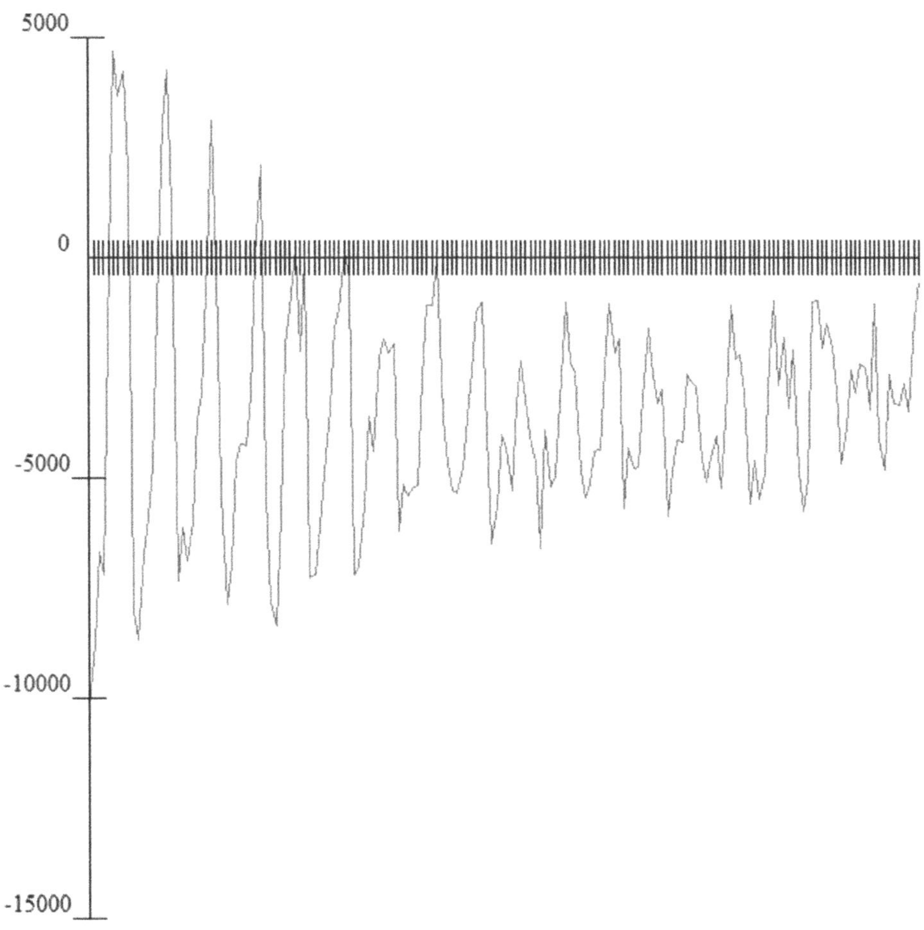

FIGURE 17.15 Optimization Report Graph

The chart in Figure 17.15 was sorted by Test Number. Look how different the information is when sorted by Net Profit, in Figure 17.16. It makes a world of difference to me. Keep in mind that this is a very simple test of two simple moving averages.

NOTE: Save your Optimization Report to a file, if there is any chance you will want to view it again, before doing anything else. As soon as you look at anything else, the Optimization Report will disappear and then you'll have to run that lengthy optimization all over again.

Just so I can show you a more interesting graph than this one, I'm running a huge optimization that would, in Exhaustive mode, have many millions of tests. I've taken the Final Our Strategy from Appendix D and optimized the heck out of each and every input value. Of course, I couldn't run millions of tests because TS doesn't allow it, even if I had gobs of

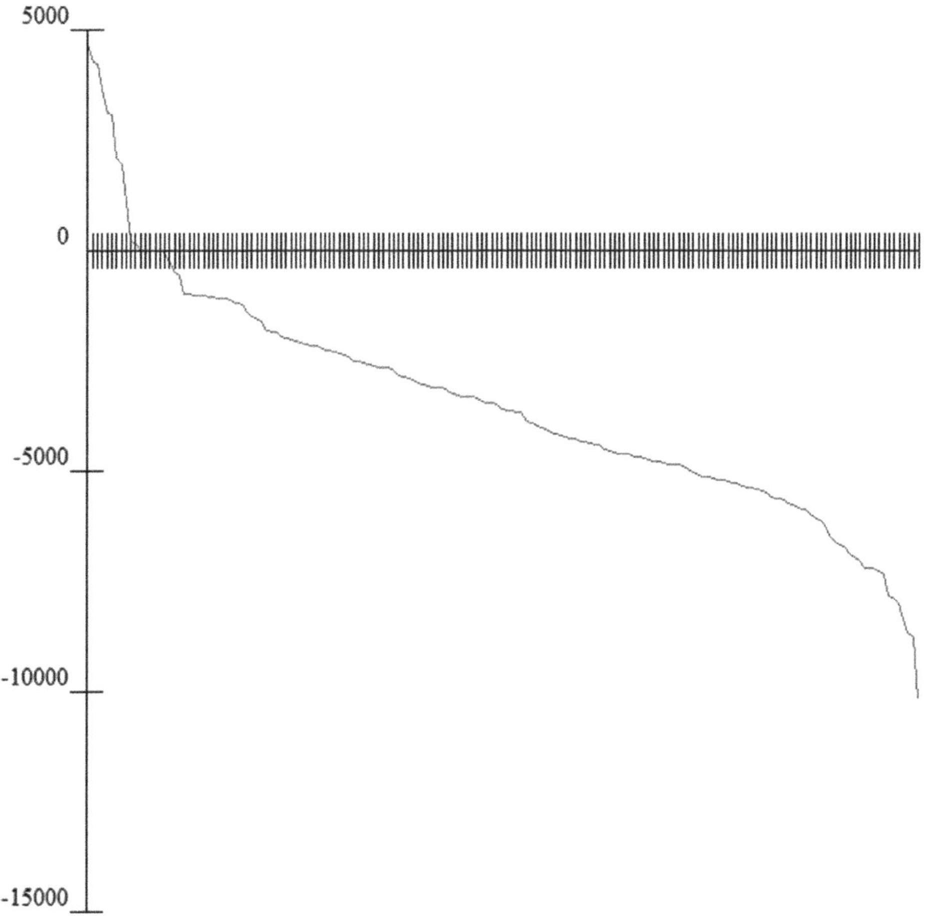

FIGURE 17.16 Sorted by Net Profit

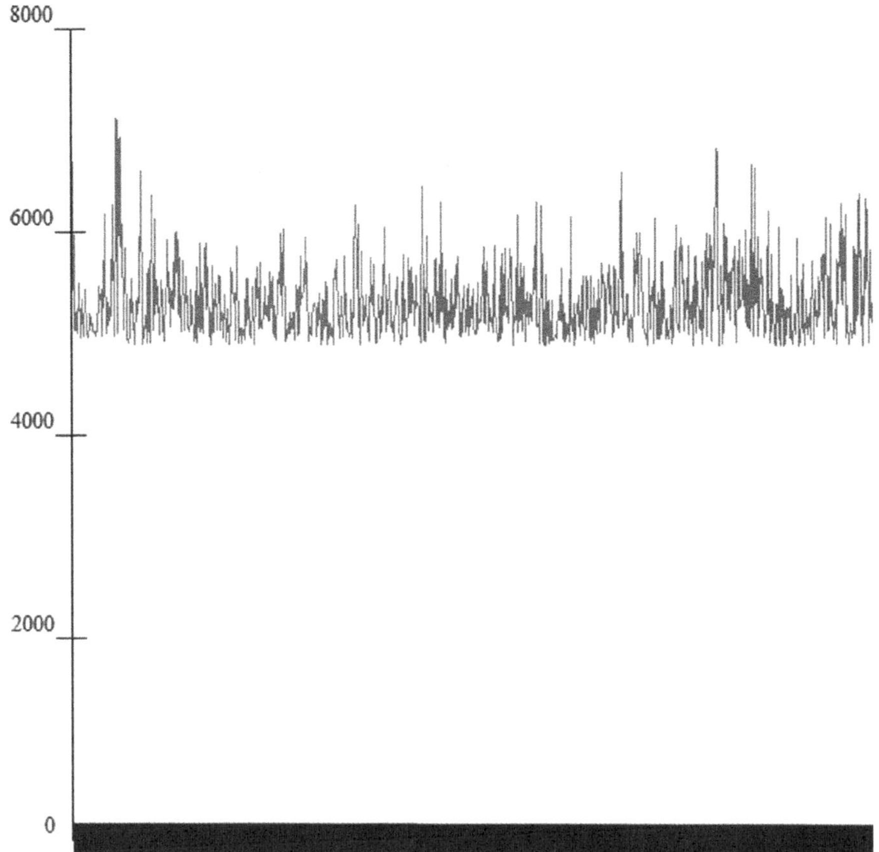

FIGURE 17.17 Genetic Testing of "Our Strategy"

memory, so I selected **Genetic** mode and ran 10,000 tests. It took just over two hours to run the full optimization.

In Figure 17.16 very few of the tests were successful. In Figure 17.17 all of the tests were successful. Remember that in the second test we saved only the best 900 out of 10,000 tests.

Save the Results to a Spreadsheet

If you thought ahead, you will have selected **Save to File** before running the optimization. But if you're like me you forgot to do that and you'll have to save it from the Optimization Report. To do so, click on the little diskette icon and save the report to your hard drive, giving it a name and location that you will remember. Just remember to do it immediately after the test completes or it will disappear into never never land.

The saving will create a file of text separated by commas. It is not of very much use in this format, but it can be imported by just about any spreadsheet program, where you can sort and calculate till your heart's content. From Excel simply navigate to **File** → **Open** and find the location and file name you created earlier. Excel will display the contents of the file, which will look pretty much like gobbledegook until you tell it that the file is comma delimited on the **Next** page. Clicking on **Finish** will bring up a nice, organized spreadsheet.

If you would like to do some calculations and save them for a later time, you will want to change the file extension from **.txt** type to **Excel Workbook** type. To do so just **File** → **Save As** → **Excel Workbook,** as in Figure 17.18. This process will change the file extension

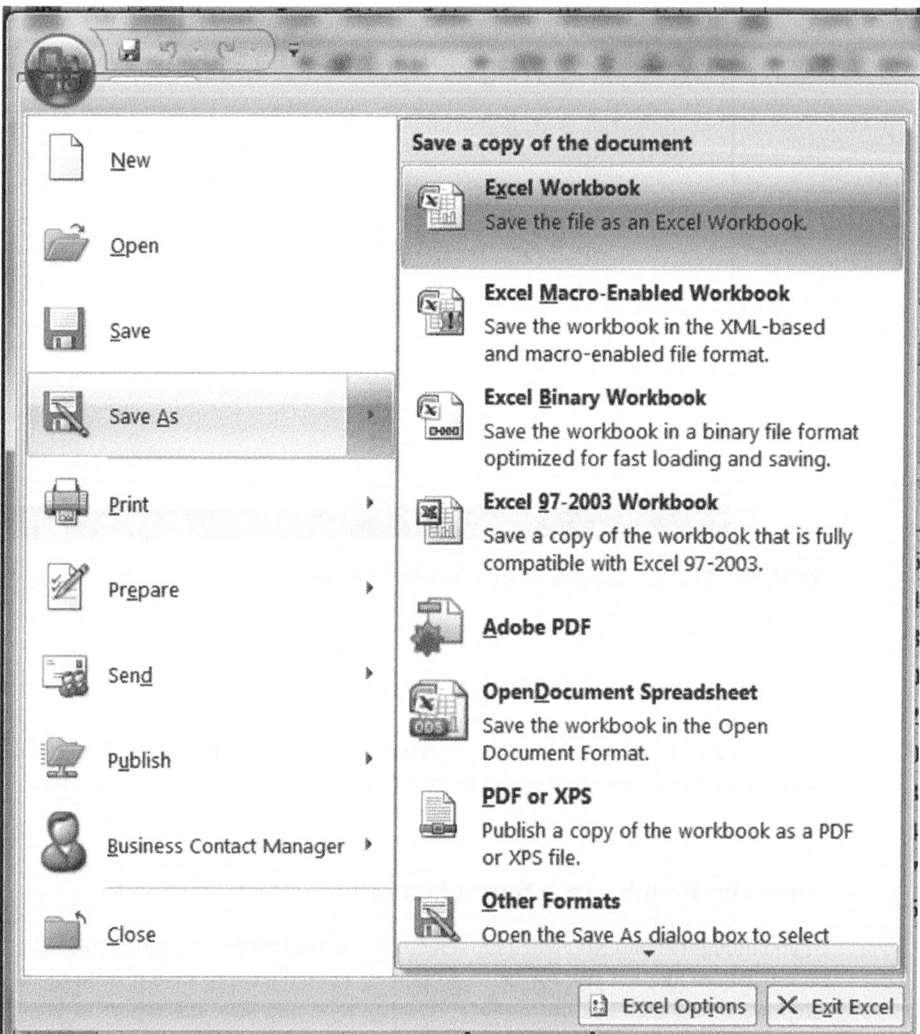

FIGURE 17.18 Save As Excel Workbook

and file type so that it becomes an official spreadsheet. It will readily store calculations and formulae in this format. And that's what we want.

At this juncture, I like to add a column to the spreadsheet for calculating the CPC Index. In case you don't remember how to do it, the formula is:

```
CPC = (Percent Profitable) * (Profit Factor) * (Ratio Avg Win/Avg
Loss)
```

Remember also that we want this number to be 1.2 or greater to signify potentially successful systems.

To create this column in the spreadsheet:

- Insert a new column by highlighting any column and selecting **Insert → Insert Sheet Columns.** This is shown in Figure 17.19, number 2. (Your new column will appear to the left of the column you highlighted. (I like to insert the CPC column just to the left of the **Test** column.)
- Type **CPC Index** in the header cell so you can later identify this column.
- Find the columns that contain the three statistics in the preceding formula. In my spreadsheet they are in columns T, AH, and AA. Note that Percent Profitable is 100 times too large for these calculations, as it is not expressed as a percentage but rather as a whole number.
- In the Formula Bar (labeled "1" in Figure 17.19), you need to type your formula. Begin by typing the equals symbol ("="). As soon as you type = Excel will help you by letting you click on the cell in the column you want. Click on the first statistic and then type "*" to tell Excel to multiply. Then click on the next cell and again type *. Now click on the last statistic and press **Enter.**
- My formula is now: =**T2*AH2*AA2**
- Yours may not be the same as your statistics may be in different columns. Be sure, however, always to stay in the same row as you are clicking the statistics. You don't want to mix and match from different rows.

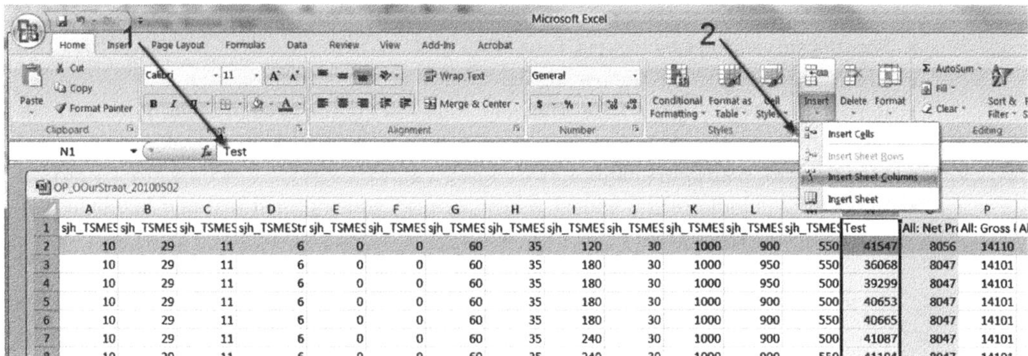

FIGURE 17.19 Insert a New Column

- The formula is not right quite yet, since the **Percent Profitable** was not expressed as a percent. You have to divide the whole thing by 100 to get the right results. Thus, type **"/100"** at the end of the formula you have created. Since division and multiplication are commutative, you don't have to put parentheses around the rest of the formula. Your final formula should be like: =**T2*AH2*AA2/100**
- Last, you need to pull down the formula for the entire column, so that every row has the CPC formula in it. To do this, click on the first cell containing the formula and while still holding the mouse button down, drag all the way down to the bottom of your spreadsheet. When you get to the bottom, let go of the mouse button and type **CTRL + D** (which means **Fill Down**).

After following those steps you will have a spreadsheet that contains the CPC Index formula for every test you ran in the optimization. You can now sort your spreadsheet by the CPC Index column to visualize which tests are the most robust.

Cluster Your Results to Find Alligators and Islands

You cannot just take the highest CPC Index as your answer to the optimization—at least, according to my philosophy of testing. This is not necessarily the **best** test. If, for instance, the highest CPC was an isolated example and the parameters on either side of the test were failures, this would be a bad choice.

In my work I developed the theory of finding clusters of tests where the parameters on either side are also successful. The larger the cluster, the safer you are in choosing these parameters. If, for instance, the combination 11, 15 was profitable and 10, 15 and 12, 15 were also profitable, it would be a safer area to trade than if only 11, 15 was profitable. I call these success clusters "islands" and the bad tests on either side "alligators." It is a good visual reminder that you want to stay as far away as possible from the failed tests on either side of the successful tests.

To generate a spreadsheet that shows alligators and islands, here is what I do:

- Sort the spreadsheet by highest Total Net Profit.
- Highlight the top 10% of the tests in light yellow.
- Resort the spreadsheet by Test Numbers. This will put the tests in order of the parameters tested.
- Find the widest strip of yellow.
- Choose the middle of the widest yellow strip as your optimal test and highlight it in orange. (See Figure 17.20.)

To my mind this is the set of numbers that is the safest to trade. If the market changes or you've made some kind of mistake, then the parameters on either side are still profitable. It gives you the widest berth of successful tests.

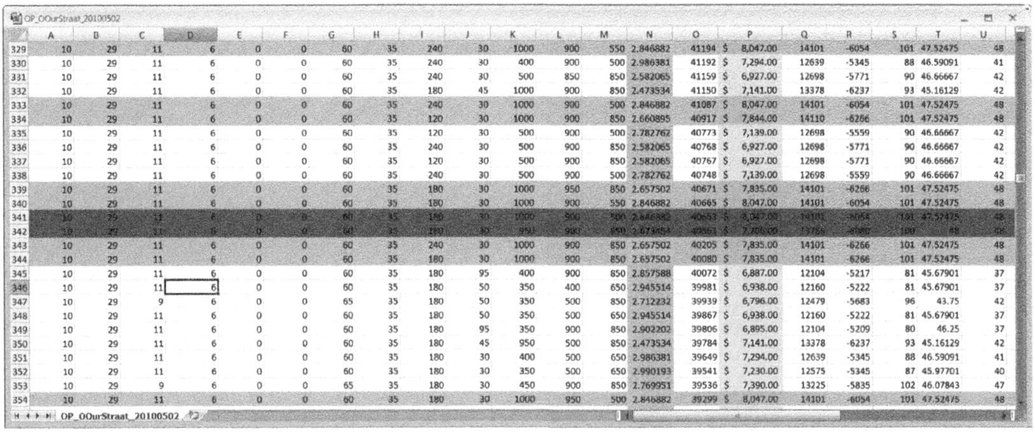

OP_OOurStraat_20100502

	A	B	C	D	E	F	G	H	I	J	K	L	M	N	O	P	Q	R	S	T	U
329	10	29	11	6	0	0	60	35	240	30	1000	900	550	2.846882	41194	$ 8,047.00	14101	-6054	101	47.52475	48
330	10	29	11	6	0	0	60	35	240	30	400	900	500	2.986381	41192	$ 7,294.00	12639	-5345	88	46.59091	41
331	10	29	11	6	0	0	60	35	240	30	500	850	850	2.582065	41159	$ 6,927.00	12698	-5771	90	46.66667	42
332	10	29	11	6	0	0	60	35	180	45	1000	900	850	2.473534	41150	$ 7,141.00	13378	-6237	93	45.16129	42
333	10	29	11	6	0	0	60	35	240	30	1000	900	500	2.846882	41087	$ 8,047.00	14101	-6054	101	47.52475	48
334	10	29	11	6	0	0	60	35	120	30	1000	900	850	2.660895	40917	$ 7,844.00	14110	-6266	101	47.52475	48
335	10	29	11	6	0	0	60	35	120	30	500	900	500	2.782762	40773	$ 7,139.00	12698	-5559	90	46.66667	42
336	10	29	11	6	0	0	60	35	240	30	500	900	850	2.582065	40768	$ 6,927.00	12698	-5771	90	46.66667	42
337	10	29	11	6	0	0	60	35	120	30	500	900	850	2.582065	40767	$ 6,927.00	12698	-5771	90	46.66667	42
338	10	29	11	6	0	0	60	35	240	30	500	900	500	2.782762	40748	$ 7,139.00	12698	-5559	90	46.66667	42
339	10	29	11	6	0	0	60	35	180	30	1000	950	850	2.657502	40671	$ 7,835.00	14101	-6266	101	47.52475	48
340	10	29	11	6	0	0	60	35	180	30	1000	900	550	2.846882	40665	$ 8,047.00	14101	-6054	101	47.52475	48
341	10	29	11	6	0	0	60	35	180	30	1000	900	500	2.846882	40653	$ 8,047.00	14101	-6054	101	47.52475	48
342	10	29	11	6	0	0	60	35	[illegible]	30	950	900	850	[illegible]	40563	$ 7,706.00	[illegible]	[illegible]	100	48	[illegible]
343	10	29	11	6	0	0	60	35	240	30	1000	900	850	2.657502	40205	$ 7,835.00	14101	-6266	101	47.52475	48
344	10	29	11	6	0	0	60	35	180	30	1000	900	850	2.657502	40080	$ 7,835.00	14101	-6266	101	47.52475	48
345	10	29	11	6	0	0	60	35	180	95	400	900	850	2.857588	40072	$ 6,887.00	12104	-5217	81	45.67901	37
346	10	29	11	6	0	0	60	35	180	50	350	400	650	2.945514	39981	$ 6,938.00	12160	-5222	81	45.67901	37
347	10	29	9	6	0	0	65	35	180	50	350	500	850	2.712232	39939	$ 6,796.00	12479	-5683	96	43.75	42
348	10	29	11	6	0	0	60	35	180	50	350	500	650	2.945514	39867	$ 6,938.00	12160	-5222	81	45.67901	37
349	10	29	11	6	0	0	60	35	180	95	350	900	850	2.902202	39806	$ 6,895.00	12104	-5209	80	46.25	37
350	10	29	11	6	0	0	60	35	180	45	950	500	850	2.473534	39784	$ 7,141.00	13378	-6237	93	45.16129	42
351	10	29	11	6	0	0	60	35	180	30	400	500	650	2.986381	39649	$ 7,294.00	12639	-5345	88	46.59091	41
352	10	29	11	6	0	0	60	35	180	30	350	500	650	2.990193	39541	$ 7,230.00	12575	-5345	87	45.97701	40
353	10	29	9	6	0	0	65	35	180	30	450	900	850	2.769951	39536	$ 7,390.00	13225	-5835	102	46.07843	47
354	10	29	11	6	0	0	60	35	180	30	1000	950	500	2.846882	39299	$ 8,047.00	14101	-6054	101	47.52475	48

OP_OOurStraat_20100502

FIGURE 17.20 Islands and Alligators Spreadsheet

Verify Findings on Other Thirds

Now that you have a range of good parameters for the middle third of your data, you want to see if these values are also profitable on the first and last thirds of the data. The code in Appendix D for **Our Strategy** makes this isolating of data thirds easy. I have provided two inputs values called Date1 and Date2 for just this purpose. For the first test you would set the dates to the middle third of your data. For the second test you would set these dates to the first third of your data. And for the last test you would set Date1 and Date2 to the final third of your data. It is very helpful to add these two inputs, and the corresponding True/False code, to any test for which you are running large optimizations. It is easier than specifying the data ranges in TradeStation.

If you wanted to change the dates in TradeStation, rather than using these two inputs, here's how you would do it.

- Using menu sequence **Format** → **Symbol** bring up the window in Figure 17.21.
- Under **Range,** change the **Last Date** and **Years Back** to specify your date range.
- Click **OK** to accept the date range.

Just don't forget to change your dates back to the full range when you are done optimizing.

CURIOUSER AND CURIOUSER

There is a glitch in the optimization feature of TradeStation . . . it seems. At least this feature is not adequately explained in the documentation by the folks in Florida.

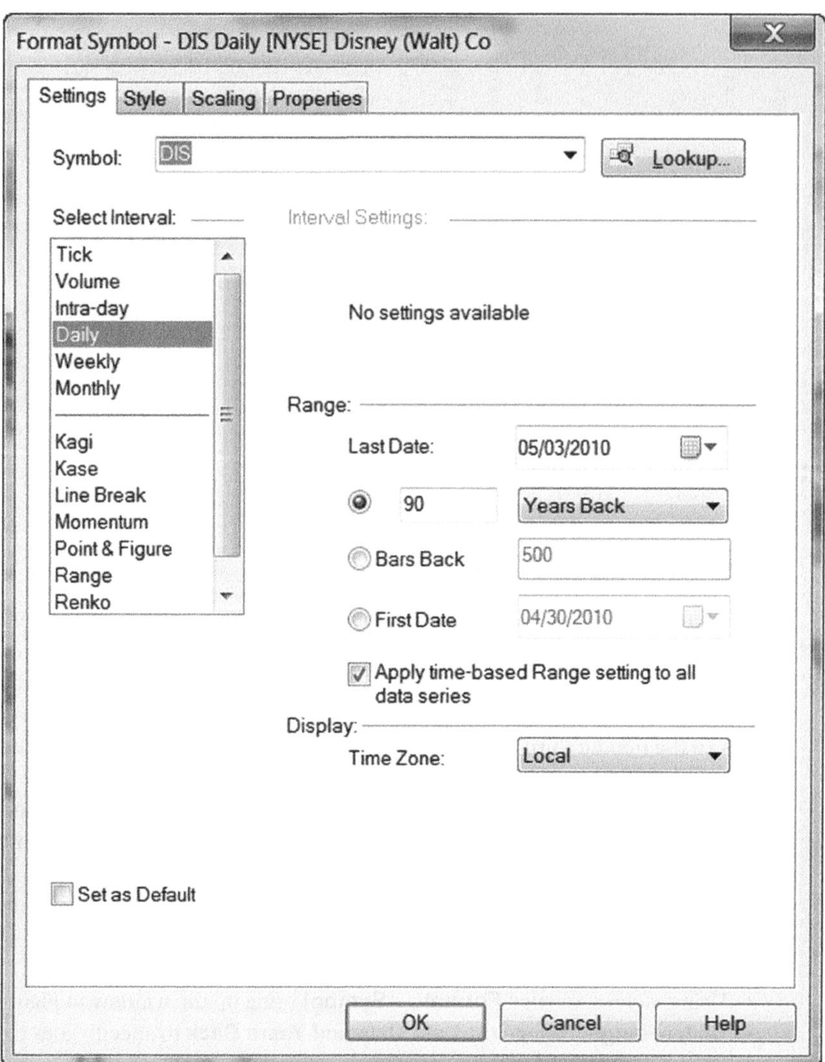

FIGURE 17.21 Specifying Date Ranges

Here's the example. I set my input parameters up in this particular test in this way:

```
INPUTS: jType, jPrice, jValue1, jValue2;
```

and I set up the optimization as shown in Figure 17.22.

So, on running this optimization, TradeStation should run 3 * 4 * 17 * 24 tests, for a total of 4,896. That's all well and good. It does just that. When the optimization completes, I anxiously take a look at the results in the **Strategy Performance Report** window; Figure

Variable	Starting Value	Ending Value	Increment
jType	1	3	1
jPrice	1	4	1
jValue1	4	20	1
jValue2	7	30	1

FIGURE 17.22 Optimizing Example

17.23 shows what I get. That seems just fine until I open up the **Strategy Optimization Report** window and take a look at the same test, the one with the highest **Net Profit.** In Figure 17.24, you can see a snippet of the **Optimization Report**—specifically the portion in question.

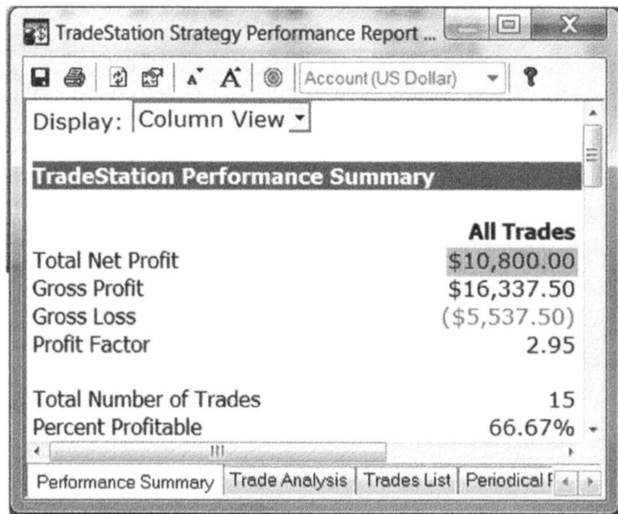

FIGURE 17.23 Strategy Performance Report

What has happened between Figure 17.23 and Figure 17.24 to make the **Total Net Profit** vary from $13,100 to $10,800? I thought it might be the open trade. So I added the open trade amount to the $10,800. Nope, that didn't quite make up the difference.

Well, of course then I called TradeStation up to see what's the matter. The answer is important to those of you who will be using the optimization feature, especially if you are using it to test a strategy you have bought from a vendor or are using on a trial basis. Your vendor will have one set of values for his reported profits and you will come up with a different set of numbers in your testing. Then, of course, you will accuse your vendor of being untruthful in his advertising, when he in fact was not lying at all.

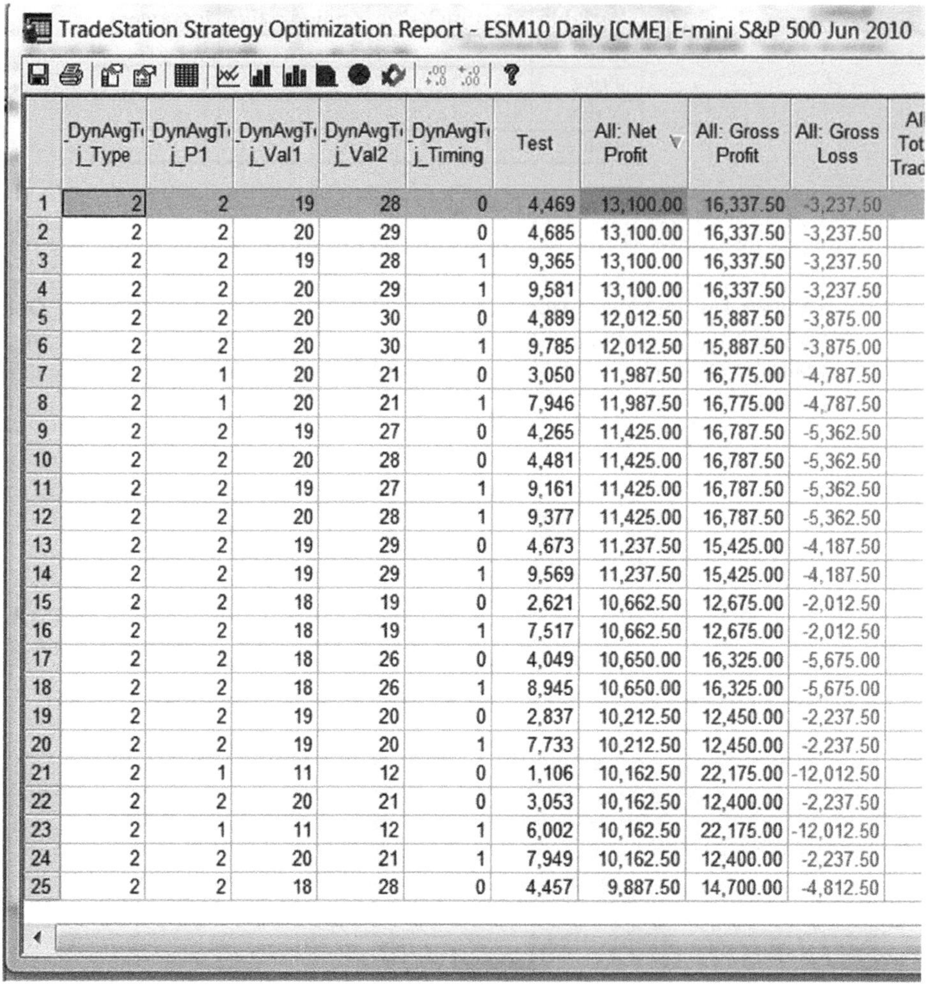

TradeStation Strategy Optimization Report - ESM10 Daily [CME] E-mini S&P 500 Jun 2010

	_DynAvgT i_Type	_DynAvgT i_P1	_DynAvgT i_Val1	_DynAvgT i_Val2	_DynAvgT i_Timing	Test	All: Net Profit	All: Gross Profit	All: Gross Loss	Al Tot Trac
1	2	2	19	28	0	4,469	13,100.00	16,337.50	-3,237.50	
2	2	2	20	29	0	4,685	13,100.00	16,337.50	-3,237.50	
3	2	2	19	28	1	9,365	13,100.00	16,337.50	-3,237.50	
4	2	2	20	29	1	9,581	13,100.00	16,337.50	-3,237.50	
5	2	2	20	30	0	4,889	12,012.50	15,887.50	-3,875.00	
6	2	2	20	30	1	9,785	12,012.50	15,887.50	-3,875.00	
7	2	1	20	21	0	3,050	11,987.50	16,775.00	-4,787.50	
8	2	1	20	21	1	7,946	11,987.50	16,775.00	-4,787.50	
9	2	2	19	27	0	4,265	11,425.00	16,787.50	-5,362.50	
10	2	2	20	28	0	4,481	11,425.00	16,787.50	-5,362.50	
11	2	2	19	27	1	9,161	11,425.00	16,787.50	-5,362.50	
12	2	2	20	28	1	9,377	11,425.00	16,787.50	-5,362.50	
13	2	2	19	29	0	4,673	11,237.50	15,425.00	-4,187.50	
14	2	2	19	29	1	9,569	11,237.50	15,425.00	-4,187.50	
15	2	2	18	19	0	2,621	10,662.50	12,675.00	-2,012.50	
16	2	2	18	19	1	7,517	10,662.50	12,675.00	-2,012.50	
17	2	2	18	26	0	4,049	10,650.00	16,325.00	-5,675.00	
18	2	2	18	26	1	8,945	10,650.00	16,325.00	-5,675.00	
19	2	2	19	20	0	2,837	10,212.50	12,450.00	-2,237.50	
20	2	2	19	20	1	7,733	10,212.50	12,450.00	-2,237.50	
21	2	1	11	12	0	1,106	10,162.50	22,175.00	-12,012.50	
22	2	2	20	21	0	3,053	10,162.50	12,400.00	-2,237.50	
23	2	1	11	12	1	6,002	10,162.50	22,175.00	-12,012.50	
24	2	2	20	21	1	7,949	10,162.50	12,400.00	-2,237.50	
25	2	2	18	28	0	4,457	9,887.50	14,700.00	-4,812.50	

FIGURE 17.24 Optimization Report

The problem lies somewhere between the way TradeStation uses the MaxBarsBack setting and the bar on which it starts its calculations for trades. By default, I have my software set to MaxBarsBack = 50. But when the Optimizer starts running, it apparently looks at every bar and computes the MaxBarsBack setting depending on the parameters it is using in the optimization. For instance, if jValue 1=15 and jValue2=20, then TradeStation needs 20 bars for its MaxBarsBack setting. But when it continues on through the optimization and gets to jValue1=20 and jValue2=30, it now needs 30 bars for MaxBarsBack.

Turns out it's not really a problem, it's a well-designed feature that needs to be kept in mind when you can't figure out how much profit you are supposed to be making. **Your profit numbers will vary greatly, depending on your MaxBarsBack setting!** And don't forget, it will also vary greatly depending on how many days are included in the test. If you include as few as one extra day that was not included on the original test, the results will not match. Consider, for instance, if the one extra day had been October 19, 1987.

CONCLUSION

Optimization is a powerful feature—one that can easily be misused. Left in the hands of novices, it can generate seemingly sophisticated outputs that lead them to believe they have conducted scientifically sound experiments. While the calculations are sound and sophisticated, the proper analysis of the results, and the determination of whether to trade based on the experiments, is precarious at best.

It is very easy to pick up TradeStation, grab a moving average, and optimize the heck out of it. Yes, you get results, but what the results actually mean is learned only after years of working with Optimization Reports or weeks of education by a properly trained and experienced trader who has been doing this for years. The outcome is not obvious—it is elusive.

CHAPTER 18

System Performance

In This Chapter

- Introduction
- Performance Summary
- Trade-by-Trade Reports
- Sunny's Important Numbers
- Sharpe Ratio

INTRODUCTION

Our last subject is about assessing the success of your strategy. Not just how much money does it make, but how robust is it, how will it stand up over time, will you be able to withstand the drawdowns . . . and also how much money does it make. In this chapter we will study the **Strategy Performance Report** and each of its components. We will study some of the important statistics contained in that report. And we will ignore some of the more esoteric numbers, which are better left for advanced study.

To bring up the **Strategy Performance Report** (SPR) from the main TradeStation window, use the menu sequence **View→Strategy Performance Report** or **Alt+Shift+P.** Doing this will bring up a large window with tabs across the bottom (shown in Figure 18.2) and a menu bar at the top (shown in Figure 18.1).

FIGURE 18.1a SPR Menu Bar

Performance Summary | Trade Analysis | Trades List | Periodical Returns | Performance Graphs | Trade Graphs | Settings

FIGURE 18.1b Tabs on the Performance Report

Between the top and the bottom, you will see a report headed "TradeStation Performance Summary" that looks like something you might see in a banker's report or a quarterly stock report. The first line of the report reads "Total Net Profit" and has headers "All Trades", "Long Trades", and "Short Trades". In Figure 18.2 you can see the first page of the Performance Report. A typical Performance Summary is presented in Figure 18.2.

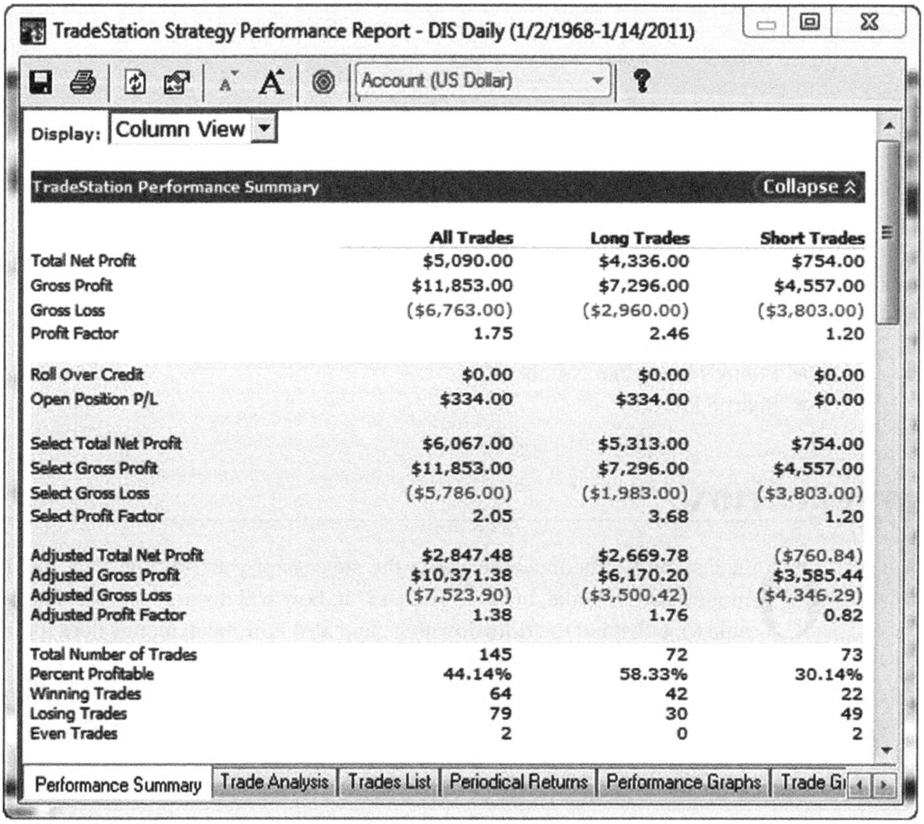

TradeStation Strategy Performance Report - DIS Daily (1/2/1968-1/14/2011)

Account (US Dollar)

Display: Column View

TradeStation Performance Summary — Collapse

	All Trades	Long Trades	Short Trades
Total Net Profit	$5,090.00	$4,336.00	$754.00
Gross Profit	$11,853.00	$7,296.00	$4,557.00
Gross Loss	($6,763.00)	($2,960.00)	($3,803.00)
Profit Factor	1.75	2.46	1.20
Roll Over Credit	$0.00	$0.00	$0.00
Open Position P/L	$334.00	$334.00	$0.00
Select Total Net Profit	$6,067.00	$5,313.00	$754.00
Select Gross Profit	$11,853.00	$7,296.00	$4,557.00
Select Gross Loss	($5,786.00)	($1,983.00)	($3,803.00)
Select Profit Factor	2.05	3.68	1.20
Adjusted Total Net Profit	$2,847.48	$2,669.78	($760.84)
Adjusted Gross Profit	$10,371.38	$6,170.20	$3,585.44
Adjusted Gross Loss	($7,523.90)	($3,500.42)	($4,346.29)
Adjusted Profit Factor	1.38	1.76	0.82
Total Number of Trades	145	72	73
Percent Profitable	44.14%	58.33%	30.14%
Winning Trades	64	42	22
Losing Trades	79	30	49
Even Trades	2	0	2

Performance Summary | Trade Analysis | Trades List | Periodical Returns | Performance Graphs | Trade Gr

FIGURE 18.2 TradeStation Strategy Performance Report

TradeStation separates out the long from the short trades and also gives you the combined total. It makes sense that in a normal market with ups, downs, and sideways periods you should have approximately half your trades long and half short. And you should have about half of your profit coming from long trades and half coming from short trades.

At the top of the report, on the left side of the menu bar, the first icon is a little diskette (see Figure 18.2), for saving your report. When you click the icon it will bring up a **Save As** window where you can specify the location to which you want your report saved and where you can check off which components of the report to save. You may not want to save the entire report. The components are shown in Figure 18.3, which is from the lower portion of the screen. Be sure to click the radio button for **Select pages** if you don't want the **Entire Report.**

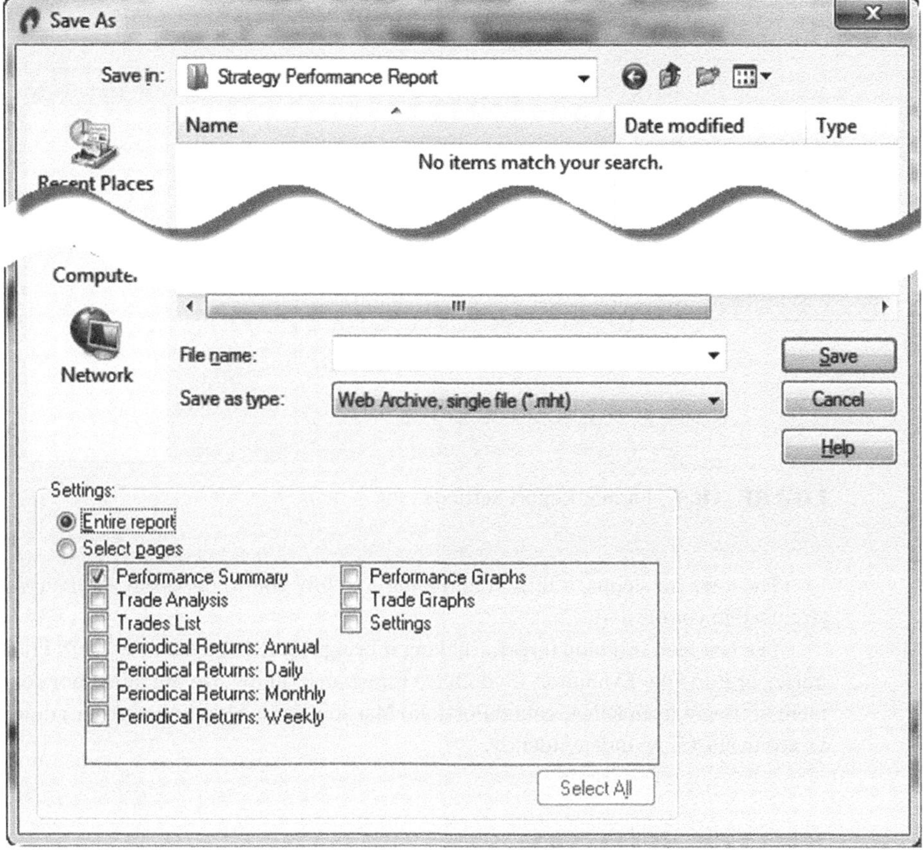

FIGURE 18.3 Saving Your Report

Generally I just save the **Performance Summary,** but on occasion I will also save the **Trades List** so I can review each trade, trade by trade.

The next icon is for printing your report. Again, you may print the entire report or you may select pages and only print the ones you want.

The next button looks like a recycle symbol. That's about what it is. It means refresh. Clicking this button will recalculate your Performance Report based on the currently active chart.

The next icon is a hand holding a buy/sell card. This button lets you **Format the Report Settings.** There's not much to format, but Figure 18.4 shows you the areas you are allowed to format.

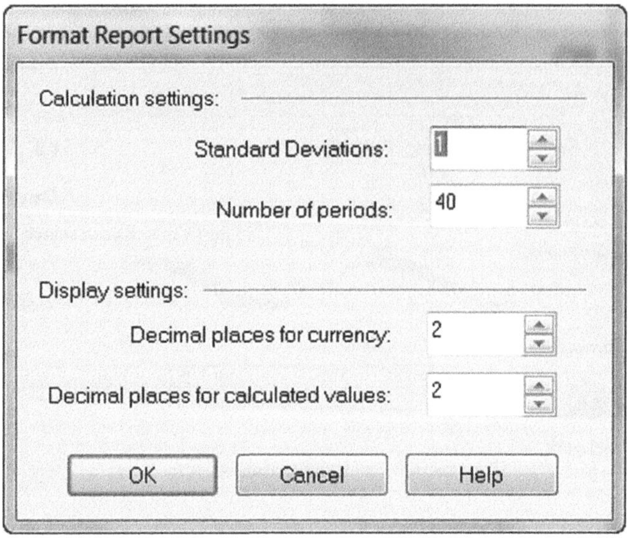

FIGURE 18.4 Format Report Settings

The next two icons, a little A and a big A, allow you to decrease and increase the font size used in your report.

The last icon is a blue target. Clicking it brings up RINA Systems,[1] Inc.'s Portfolio Maximizer or Portfolio Evaluator, if you have it installed. I now use the latest portfolio management software from RINA, called Portfolio Maestro. It isn't yet linked from TradeStation, so I have to start it up independently.

PERFORMANCE SUMMARY

If you will optimize the strategy we have developed over the course of this book (and which is located in Appendix D), you will get a chart something like mine in Figure 18.5. Yours will be different, because you will have data months or years later than mine, depending on when this book is published and when you are reading it. Furthermore, if you run a large genetic

[1]RINA Systems, Inc., by Leo Zamansky. www.rinafinancial.com.

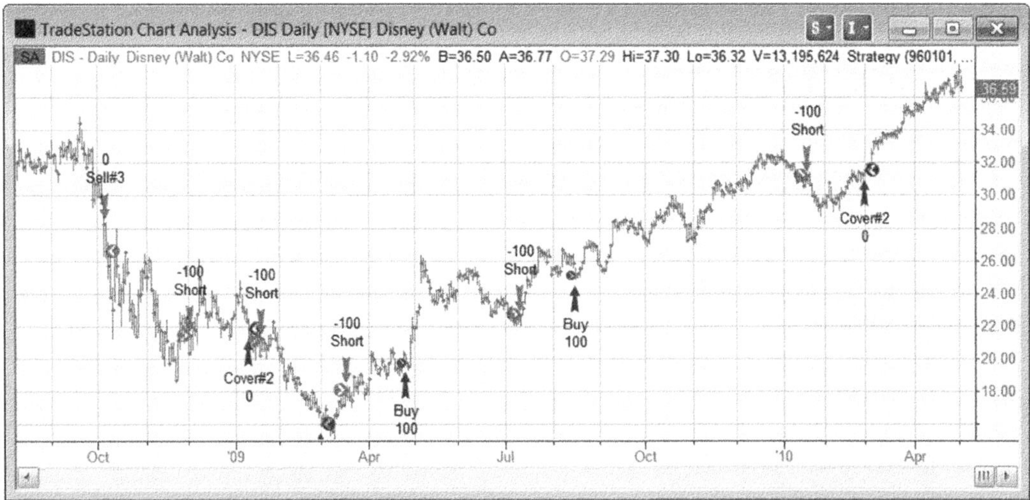

FIGURE 18.5 Our Strategy on DIS

optimization twice, it appears not to produce the same results each time. It looks to me like the genetic algorithms are biological in nature.

Near the top of the Performance Summary Report (see Figure 18.6), there is a menu item labeled "Display:" followed by a pull-down that shows "Column View" by default. By clicking on the down arrow you can change it to "Table View". If I'm not mistaken, "Table View" is the report the way it appeared before there were RINA enhancements. I've gotten accustomed to the "Column View" and never bother changing it.

On the top right of the Performance Summary, in the blue strip, is the word "Collapse". Clicking there does just that.

If you toggle the **Collapse** button you will see "**Expand**" come up. By going back and forth between them you can view the longer and shorter versions of the report.

Statistics on the Performance Summary

Every statistic in the report has values for All Trades, Long Trades, and Short Trades. I'm only going to discuss the numbers for All Trades, and assume you realize that the other two are there as well.

In the TradeStation help files, under Performance Report, there is a full explanation of each value on the report, listed alphabetically. I'm not going to go into them one at a time here. You can read about them in the help files. I do, however, want to point out a few key statistics. I am going to go through them from the top of the report (Figure 18.6) and work down.

Total Net Profit, in the first row, is always important. If this number is positive, your system has potential. If it is negative, don't even think about trading it. No amount of hope will make it better.

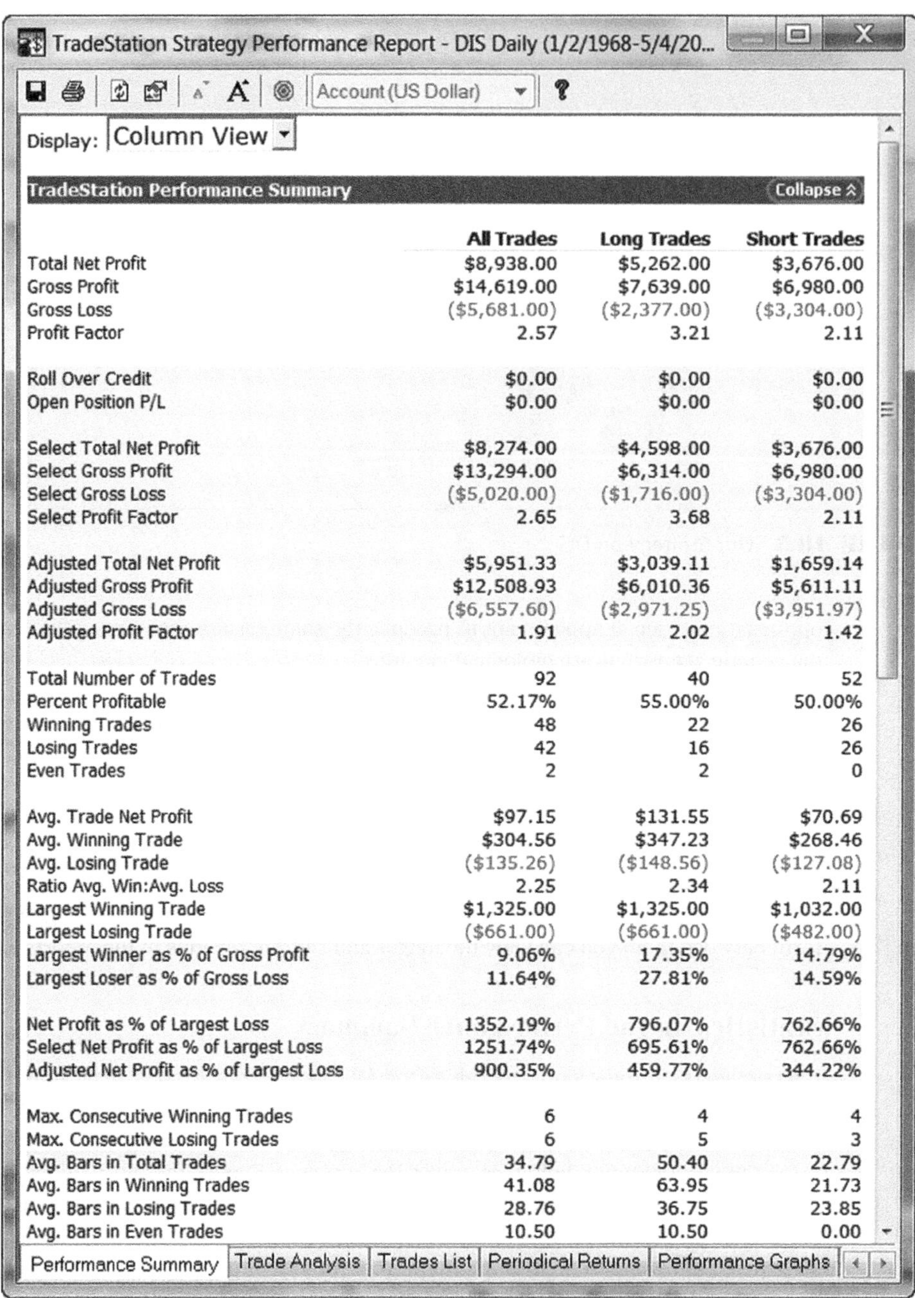

	All Trades	Long Trades	Short Trades
Total Net Profit	$8,938.00	$5,262.00	$3,676.00
Gross Profit	$14,619.00	$7,639.00	$6,980.00
Gross Loss	($5,681.00)	($2,377.00)	($3,304.00)
Profit Factor	2.57	3.21	2.11
Roll Over Credit	$0.00	$0.00	$0.00
Open Position P/L	$0.00	$0.00	$0.00
Select Total Net Profit	$8,274.00	$4,598.00	$3,676.00
Select Gross Profit	$13,294.00	$6,314.00	$6,980.00
Select Gross Loss	($5,020.00)	($1,716.00)	($3,304.00)
Select Profit Factor	2.65	3.68	2.11
Adjusted Total Net Profit	$5,951.33	$3,039.11	$1,659.14
Adjusted Gross Profit	$12,508.93	$6,010.36	$5,611.11
Adjusted Gross Loss	($6,557.60)	($2,971.25)	($3,951.97)
Adjusted Profit Factor	1.91	2.02	1.42
Total Number of Trades	92	40	52
Percent Profitable	52.17%	55.00%	50.00%
Winning Trades	48	22	26
Losing Trades	42	16	26
Even Trades	2	2	0
Avg. Trade Net Profit	$97.15	$131.55	$70.69
Avg. Winning Trade	$304.56	$347.23	$268.46
Avg. Losing Trade	($135.26)	($148.56)	($127.08)
Ratio Avg. Win:Avg. Loss	2.25	2.34	2.11
Largest Winning Trade	$1,325.00	$1,325.00	$1,032.00
Largest Losing Trade	($661.00)	($661.00)	($482.00)
Largest Winner as % of Gross Profit	9.06%	17.35%	14.79%
Largest Loser as % of Gross Loss	11.64%	27.81%	14.59%
Net Profit as % of Largest Loss	1352.19%	796.07%	762.66%
Select Net Profit as % of Largest Loss	1251.74%	695.61%	762.66%
Adjusted Net Profit as % of Largest Loss	900.35%	459.77%	344.22%
Max. Consecutive Winning Trades	6	4	4
Max. Consecutive Losing Trades	6	5	3
Avg. Bars in Total Trades	34.79	50.40	22.79
Avg. Bars in Winning Trades	41.08	63.95	21.73
Avg. Bars in Losing Trades	28.76	36.75	23.85
Avg. Bars in Even Trades	10.50	10.50	0.00

FIGURE 18.6 Performance Summary Report

Gross Profit is the total of all winning trades, while **Gross Loss** is the total of all losing trades.

Profit Factor, in the fourth row, is the ratio of the amount made to the amount lost. It is Gross Profit divided by Gross Loss. By definition a value greater than 1 signifies the trades have a positive net profit. (Used in calculating the **CPC Index.**)

Total Number of Trades tells you how many trades would have been completed by this strategy. Total Number of Trades is equal to the total number of winning trades plus the total number of losing trades. For your system to be statistically significant, this number needs to be largish. What do I mean by that? Well, if the number is small, then you have very little room for error. A system with only one trade, for instance, is likely not to have that one trade in the future. I can't tell you that this number needs to be greater than 30, however, because you might be testing over a one-week period and thus have very few trades. If you look at your chart and count the pivots, that's about how many trades your strategy should have. If this number is too large, then you will be overtrading and the net profit from each trade will be small. You don't want that either.

Percent Profitable is the number of Winning Trades divided by the Total Number of Trades. This is an important measure of the success of your system. Most professional traders work with strategies that are 40% to 50% profitable. Don't expect you can find a strategy that is successful that is 80% or more profitable. Usually a strategy with a large Percent Profitable has only a few trades and thus isn't meaningful. (Used in calculating the CPC Index.)

Avg. Trade Net Profit displays the average amount of money (win or loss) for all completed trades during the specified period. Average Trade Net Profit = Total Net Profit divided by Total Number of Trades. This number should be large enough to cover all slippage and commission and still leave a sizable net profit. A good rule of thumb is for Average Trade Net Profit to be about $200.

Ratio Avg. Win:Avg. Loss is on average how many dollars you win for every dollar you lose. Ratio Average Win/Average Loss = Average Winning Trade divided by Average Losing Trade. (Used in calculating the CPC Index.)

The next two numbers, **Largest Winning Trade** and **Largest Losing Trade,** are self-explanatory. The word on the street is that one should eliminate the largest win from the statistics and double the largest loss. See how your strategy performs under those conditions.

Max. Consecutive Winning Trades displays the longest string of consecutive completed winning trades, looking across all profitable trades. This is also known as the largest winning, or positive, run. Similarly, **Max. Consecutive Losing Trades** displays the longest string of losing trades, or the largest losing, or negative, run. You want your strings of wins to be large and your strings of losses to be small. Psychologically, you won't be able to handle a system with large strings of losses, whether it is ultimately profitable or not.

Avg. Bars in Winning Trades displays the average number of bars included in all completed winning trades, looking across all profitable trades. This is calculated by dividing the cumulative number of bars in all winning trades by the total number of winning trades. Likewise, **Avg. Bars in Losing Trades** tells you, on average, how many bars are in the losing trades. Again, you want the Avg. Bars in Winning Trades to be double (or more) the count of

Avg. Bars in Losing Trades. Psychologically, you need your wins to last for more bars than your losses.

Skipping down a little bit (you would have to scroll down, which we can't do on paper), let's look now at **Account Size Required.** This is the absolute value of the amount of money you must have in your account to trade this strategy. This is calculated as: Account Size Requires = AbsValue of Max. Drawdown. It is not the single worst trade but rather the string of worst trades. A strategy with a large Max. Drawdown, or large Account Size Required, is not tradable if you have a small account.

Return on Initial Capital is the percentage return of the Total Net Profit to the initial starting capital. Clearly, if you have initial starting capital set to $100,000 in the default settings, your Return on Initial Capital will be much smaller than if you have it set to $10,000.

The last statistic we will discuss in this section is called the RINA Index. It was originated by the folks at RINA Systems, who are the same folks who make Portfolio Maestro. The RINA Index is proprietary to them, and combines Select Total Net Profit, time in the market, and drawdown calculations into a single reward/risk ratio that can be used to compare strategies. The larger the number the more efficient/risk averse the strategy. RINA Index = (Select Total Net Profit) / ((Average Drawdown) × (Percent time in the market)). Like my CPC Index, this is a single measure for evaluating systems.

TRADE-BY-TRADE REPORTS

There are two tabs on the lower part of the Strategy Performance Report that deal with individual trades: **Trade Analysis** and **Trades List.** These two reports are shown in Figure 18.7 and Figure 18.8.

I will leave it to RINA Systems and the TradeStation help files to explain each separate entry of these reports. Suffice it to say that there are more statistics here than you will ever use, but you should take a look them at nevertheless. Get to know your trading system inside and out.

SUNNY'S IMPORTANT NUMBERS

CPC Index

As powerful as TradeStation is, its Performance Report is missing at least one critical statistic, at least for my analysis. Mine, of course. Over the years I found it difficult to compare systems to each other. It was rather like squeezing oatmeal. Squeeze one direction and everything squishes out the other side; squeeze another direction and the oatmeal oozes in a different direction. How could I compare apples to oranges and come up with anything meaningful?

The most important number is not necessarily total net profit. What if you have two strategies that each make $10,000, but the first one does it all in one trade while the second

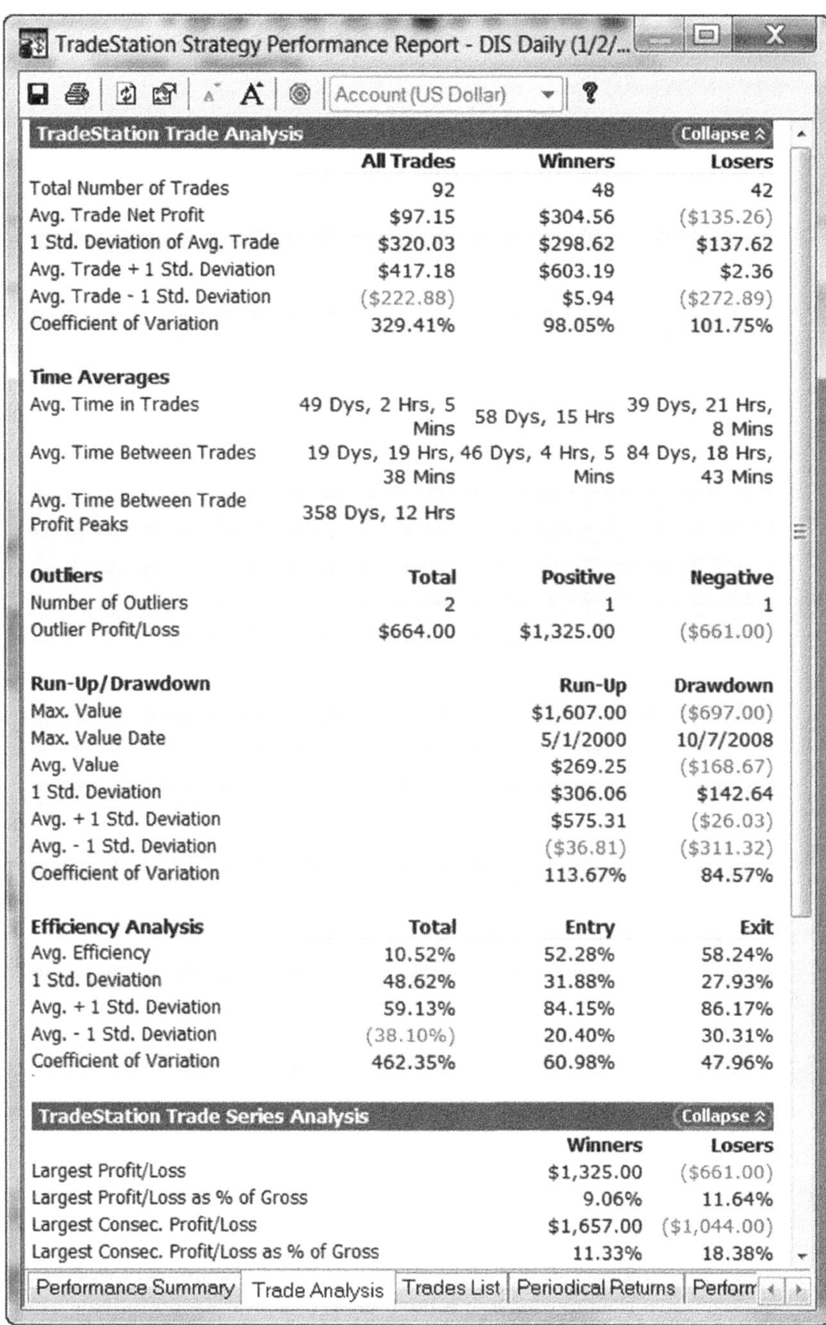

TradeStation Strategy Performance Report - DIS Daily (1/2/...

Account (US Dollar)

TradeStation Trade Analysis Collapse

	All Trades	Winners	Losers
Total Number of Trades	92	48	42
Avg. Trade Net Profit	$97.15	$304.56	($135.26)
1 Std. Deviation of Avg. Trade	$320.03	$298.62	$137.62
Avg. Trade + 1 Std. Deviation	$417.18	$603.19	$2.36
Avg. Trade - 1 Std. Deviation	($222.88)	$5.94	($272.89)
Coefficient of Variation	329.41%	98.05%	101.75%

Time Averages			
Avg. Time in Trades	49 Dys, 2 Hrs, 5 Mins	58 Dys, 15 Hrs	39 Dys, 21 Hrs, 8 Mins
Avg. Time Between Trades	19 Dys, 19 Hrs, 38 Mins	46 Dys, 4 Hrs, 5 Mins	84 Dys, 18 Hrs, 43 Mins
Avg. Time Between Trade Profit Peaks	358 Dys, 12 Hrs		

Outliers	Total	Positive	Negative
Number of Outliers	2	1	1
Outlier Profit/Loss	$664.00	$1,325.00	($661.00)

Run-Up/Drawdown	Run-Up	Drawdown
Max. Value	$1,607.00	($697.00)
Max. Value Date	5/1/2000	10/7/2008
Avg. Value	$269.25	($168.67)
1 Std. Deviation	$306.06	$142.64
Avg. + 1 Std. Deviation	$575.31	($26.03)
Avg. - 1 Std. Deviation	($36.81)	($311.32)
Coefficient of Variation	113.67%	84.57%

Efficiency Analysis	Total	Entry	Exit
Avg. Efficiency	10.52%	52.28%	58.24%
1 Std. Deviation	48.62%	31.88%	27.93%
Avg. + 1 Std. Deviation	59.13%	84.15%	86.17%
Avg. - 1 Std. Deviation	(38.10%)	20.40%	30.31%
Coefficient of Variation	462.35%	60.98%	47.96%

TradeStation Trade Series Analysis Collapse

	Winners	Losers
Largest Profit/Loss	$1,325.00	($661.00)
Largest Profit/Loss as % of Gross	9.06%	11.64%
Largest Consec. Profit/Loss	$1,657.00	($1,044.00)
Largest Consec. Profit/Loss as % of Gross	11.33%	18.38%

Performance Summary | Trade Analysis | Trades List | Periodical Returns | Perform

FIGURE 18.7 Trade Analysis

TradeStation Strategy Performance Report - DIS Daily (1/2/1968-5/4/2010)

Account (US Dollar)

TradeStation Trades List

Page 1 of 1 Find <None>

#	Type	Date/Time	Signal	Price	Roll Over USD/Lot	Shares/Ctrts ProfitCum	Net Profit Net Profit
1	Buy	01/04/96	Buy	$20.17	$0.00	100	$0.00
	Sell	01/23/96	Short	$20.17		$0.00	$0.00
2	Sell Short	01/23/96	Short	$20.17	$0.00	100	($183.00)
	Buy to Cover	03/01/96	Cover#2	$22.00		($183.00)	($183.00)
3	Buy	03/19/96	Buy	$21.67	$0.00	100	($88.00)
	Sell	04/17/96	Short	$20.79		($88.00)	($271.00)
4	Sell Short	04/17/96	Short	$20.79	$0.00	100	($4.00)
	Buy to Cover	05/24/96	Cover#2	$20.83		($4.00)	($275.00)
5	Buy	05/29/96	Buy	$20.17	$0.00	100	$66.00
	Sell	06/06/96	Short	$20.83		$66.00	($209.00)
6	Sell Short	06/06/96	Short	$20.83	$0.00	100	$50.00
	Buy to Cover	07/03/96	Buy	$20.33		$50.00	($159.00)
7	Buy	07/03/96	Buy	$20.33	$0.00	100	$363.00
	Sell	12/05/96	Sell#2	$23.96		$363.00	$204.00
8	Buy	12/12/96	Buy	$23.37	$0.00	100	$438.00
	Sell	05/19/97	Sell#2	$27.75		$438.00	$642.00
9	Buy	05/30/97	Buy	$27.29	$0.00	100	($106.00)
	Sell	08/18/97	Short	$26.23		($106.00)	$536.00
10	Sell Short	08/18/97	Short	$26.23	$0.00	100	($27.00)
	Buy to Cover	09/25/97	Cover#2	$26.50		($27.00)	$509.00
11	Buy	10/27/97	Buy	$25.92	$0.00	100	$154.00
	Sell	10/31/97	Short	$27.46		$154.00	$663.00
12	Sell Short	10/31/97	Short	$27.46	$0.00	100	($23.00)
	Buy to Cover	11/12/97	Buy	$27.69		($23.00)	$640.00
13	Buy	11/12/97	Buy	$27.69	$0.00	100	$898.00
	Sell	03/16/98	Short	$36.67		$898.00	$1,538.00
14	Sell Short	03/16/98	Short	$36.67	$0.00	100	$59.00
	Buy to Cover	04/06/98	Buy	$36.08		$59.00	$1,597.00
15	Buy	04/06/98	Buy	$36.08	$0.00	100	$202.00
	Sell	05/27/98	Short	$38.10		$202.00	$1,799.00
16	Sell Short	05/27/98	Short	$38.10	$0.00	100	$283.00
	Buy to Cover	07/06/98	Cover#2	$35.27		$283.00	$2,082.00
17	Sell Short	07/10/98	Short	$38.31	$0.00	100	$125.00
	Buy to Cover	07/22/98	Buy	$37.06		$125.00	$2,207.00
18	Buy	07/22/98	Buy	$37.06	$0.00	100	($300.00)
	Sell	08/25/98	Short	$34.06		($300.00)	$1,907.00
19	Sell Short	08/25/98	Short	$34.06	$0.00	100	$881.00
	Buy to Cover	10/02/98	Cover#2	$25.25		$881.00	$2,788.00
20	Sell Short	10/20/98	Short	$27.06	$0.00	100	($482.00)
	Buy to Cover	11/27/98	Cover#2	$31.88		($482.00)	$2,306.00
21	Buy	12/03/98	Buy	$30.88	$0.00	100	$456.00
	Sell	04/12/99	Short	$35.44		$456.00	$2,762.00

Performance Summary | Trade Analysis | Trades List | Periodical Returns | Performance Graphs | Trade Graphs | Settings

FIGURE 18.8 Trades List

does it in 10 trades of $1,000 each? Which one would you prefer? I would prefer the 10-trade approach as it is more robust. It is more likely to repeat the performance in the future.

So, if net profit is not the answer, what is? I wanted a single number that would compare all systems. Eventually a light bulb went on, and I realized that there are three numbers in TradeStation's report that measure the robustness of the overall system. They are **Profit**

Factor (PF), Percent Profitable (P), and the **Ratio of Average Win to Average Loss (R).** But even having realized that these three numbers indicate robustness, I was still comparing three different numbers. The light bulb was when I multiplied all three of them together and found a single statistic that measures each system against every other system.

Multiplied by the basic components of each number and factored out, the CPC formula actually comes to:

$$CPC = (GP^2 * (T - N))/(T * GL^2)$$

where GP = Gross profit
T = Total number of trades
N = Number of profitable trades
GL = Gross loss

Expressed as the product of the three numbers mentioned,

$$CPC = P * PF * R$$

where P = Percent profitable
PF = Profit factor
R = Ratio Avg Win/Avg Loss

Because it was such an important discovery, I called the product my Cardinal Profitability Construct, or CPC™. I have used this number ever since in thousands and thousands of trials, and it is continually the single number that lets me know how to rate the performance of any one system against a backdrop of thousands.

It is important to note that there is a threshold below which systems do not consistently make profits. By trial and error I have found that it is imperative that CPC be equal to or greater than 1.2 for a system to be profitable. I am certain that there are other mathematicians who can do some inductive proof and tell me why that is so. But, for me, it is sufficient to know that I won't trade a system whose CPC is less than 1.2. In fact, I prefer systems that have a CPC >= 2.0.

To view what this looks like in real life, let's take the Performance Report from Figure 18.6. The values from it are:

P = 52.17%
R = 2.25
PF = 2.57

Thus, $CPC = P * R * PF = .5217 * 2.25 * 2.57 = 3.01673$.

That is well above 1.2, so theoretically we are safe. The one thing I still don't like about this system is the size of the average trade. It is too low to cover commission and slippage very well.

The data from this example starts in 1968. Comparing $75 per trade profit from 1968 and $75 in today's dollars is not apples and apples. Today $75 hardly buys anything, while in 1968 it bought a week's worth of groceries. Today a week's worth of groceries would be about $300. To my knowledge there is no switch in TradeStation to convert dollars logarithmically over time. I'll make this suggestion to the company and to its competitors and see who comes up with it first.

Mathematical Expectation

To learn just how important mathematical expectation (ME) is to your trading, pick up a copy of Ralph Vince's *Mathematics of Money Management.* He drills it into you in a way that sticks forever. In short, the first thing you need to know about your trading strategy is mathematical expectation. If ME is negative you will not make a profit over time with this strategy. A positive ME is requisite to successful trading. In Vince's words: "In a negative expectation game, there is no money-management scheme that will make you a winner. If you continue to bet, regardless of how you manage your money, it is almost certain that you will be a loser, losing your entire stake no matter how large it was to start."

Mathematic expectation is calculated by multiplying each possible gain or loss by the profitability of that gain or loss and then summing up the products. Here is the formula:

$$ME = (1 + A) * P - 1$$

where A = (amount you can win) / (amount you can lose)
P = probability of winning

In our example, A = (14,619.00)/(5,681.00) = 2.57, while P = 0.5217. Thus, ME = 1.342, definitely a positive number.

You would do well in your trading not only to read Ralph Vince's books but to study them seriously. His work is critical to successful trading and a real breakthrough in money management and portfolio theory.

Dependency

Dependency is another concept I learned at the feet of Ralph Vince. Many traders try to stop trading when their system is losing and start trading again when the system is winning once again. Ralph's books demonstrate mathematically when this tactic will work and when it will not.

Unless dependency is proven, no attempt to improve performance based on the stream of profits and losses alone is of any value. If the calculations in Figure 18.9 show that your strategy has dependent runs, then altering your trading style when you encounter losses is a valid technique. If, however, your strategy is independent, then attempts to change your trading behavior based on changes in the equity curve are futile and may even be harmful.

Speaking of Ralph, if you'll just put his name in Google and do a search, you'll come upon his webpage at **www.parametricplanet.com/rvince.** If you get in contact, tell him I said "hi."

Runs

Another concept garnered from Ralph Vince (who in my book is the master of modern portfolio management theory) is the part runs play in calculating the success or failure of your system. Vince is not only brilliant, he is funny. From his book *The Mathematics of Money Management*, on page 5, here is his discussion of the runs test.

> *When we do sampling without replacement from a deck of cards, we can determine by inspection that there is dependency. For certain events (such as the profit and loss stream of a system's trades) where dependency cannot be determined upon inspection, we have the runs test. The runs test will tell us if our system has more (or fewer) streaks of consecutive wins and losses than a random distribution.*
>
> *The runs test is essentially a matter of obtaining the Z scores for the win and loss streaks of a system's trades. A Z score is how many standard deviations you are away from the mean of a distribution. Thus, a Z score of 2.00 is 2.00 standard deviations away from the mean (the expectation of a random distribution of streaks of wins and losses).*
>
> *The Z score is simply the number of standard deviations the data is from the mean of the Normal Probability Distribution. For example, a Z score of 1.00 would mean that the data you are testing is within 1 standard deviation from the mean. Incidentally, this is perfectly normal.*

The book goes on and on. It goes into great depth explaining all the concepts you need to know to evaluate your system for payoffs and consequences. This work is the only way to obtain the greatest potential investment growth for your strategies.

Now for the formulas:

N = total number of trades
W = number of winning trades
L = number of losing trades
X = 2 * W * L
R = runs in a sequence of trades
Y = N * (R − .5) − X
P = (X * (X − N)) / (N − 1)
S = SQRT(Z)
Z = Y / S
Z score = AbsValue(Z)

FIGURE 18.9 Formulas for Arriving at Your Z-Score

A negative Z implies positive dependency, meaning fewer streaks than the normal probability function would imply. Thus, wins follow wins and losses follow losses. Conversely, a positive Z implies independence, and thus your wins and losses are random in nature. Changing your commitment based on your equity will not improve your results and may even be harmful.

Beyond these equations, which are critical to your ultimate success as a trader, is the concept that any system with a negative ME cannot be improved through portfolio manipulation, while a system with even marginally positive ME can become very successful through portfolio management techniques. Ralph Vince says it best on page 62:

> *I hope you will now begin to see that the computer has been terribly misused by most traders. Optimizing and searching for the systems and parameter values that made the most money over past data is, by and large, a futile process. You only need something that will be marginally profitable in the future. By correct money management you can get an awful lot out of a system that is only marginally profitable. In general, then, the degree of profitability is determined by the money management you apply to the system more than by the system itself.*

SHARPE RATIO

The **Sharpe ratio** (or Sharpe index or Sharpe measure or reward-to-variability ratio) is used frequently in the literature to compare trading systems. It is used widely by professional money managers to compare their trading methodology to that of other managers. The Sharpe ratio is a measure of the excess return (or risk premium) per unit of risk in an investment asset or a trading strategy, named after William Forsyth Sharpe. Since its revision by the original author in 1994, it is defined as:

$$S = \frac{R - R_f}{\sigma} = \frac{E[R - R_f]}{\sqrt{\mathrm{var}[R - R_f]}}$$

where

R = asset return

R_f = return on a benchmark asset, such as the risk-free rate of return

$E[R - R_f]$ = expected value of the excess of the asset return over the benchmark return

σ = standard deviation of the asset

Note, if R_f is a constant risk-free return throughout the period,

$$\sqrt{\mathrm{var}[R - R_f] = \sqrt{\mathrm{var}[R]}}$$

The Sharpe ratio is used to characterize how well the return of an asset compensates the investor for the risk taken, the higher the Sharpe ratio number the better. When comparing two assets, each with the expected return $E[R]$, against the same benchmark with return R_f, the asset with the higher Sharpe ratio gives more return for the same risk. Investors are often advised to pick investments with high Sharpe ratios. However, like any mathematical model, the Sharpe ratio relies on the data being correct. Pyramid schemes with a long duration of operation would typically provide a high Sharpe ratio when derived from reported returns, but the inputs are false. When examining the investment performance of assets with smoothing of returns, the Sharpe ratio should be derived from the performance of the underlying assets rather than the fund returns.

Third-Party Software: Portfolio Maestro

If you want incredible power for portfolio analysis and combinations of portfolios, RINA Systems is the place to get it. RINA traditionally has been linked very closely with TradeStation but recently has developed a stand-alone product—the one I use. It is called Portfolio Maestro, and is available at the RINA Web site: www.rinafinancial.com. RINA was the developer of the "new" TradeStation Strategy Performance Report, way back when. TradeStation worked out some kind of arrangement for RINA to include its statistics in TradeStation. Later, RINA went back out on its own and continued development of portfolio management software, which is what it still does today.

RINA's software is incredibly powerful and can tell you everything you ever wanted to know about your strategy or combination of strategies, and even numbers and facts you never knew existed.

Give RINA a call and ask for a demo. It's well worth your time and energies.

CHAPTER 19

Conclusion

In This Chapter

- Summary: Putting It All Together
- Last Words

Having completed reading this book, it might be a good idea to go back to the beginning and read it again. Programming is not something you master with one read. Almost everyone who has contacted me after reading my other books says that they've read them more than once. And, yes, I do like to be contacted. I like to entertain your questions and comments; I like to help people learn to trade. My greatest reward is to see you successful.

This book is only a beginning. After practicing with the examples I have given you, you should tackle the EasyLanguage manual and the EasyLanguage PowerEditor. You can't break it, so don't be afraid to try things. The best programmers are the ones who have made the most errors. Programming is a trial-and-error profession. Try something; see how it works, then try something else.

For further reading I suggest:

- *Using Easy Language* by Arthur G. Putt
- *New Trading Systems and Methods* by Perry J. Kaufman
- *TS Express* by Bill Brower
- *Trading with the Odds* by Cynthia Kase
- *Street Smarts* by Laurence Connors and Linda Raschke
- *The Trading Systems ToolKit* by Joe Krutsinger
- *Inside Advantage* by Murray Ruggiero
- *Master Trader Series* by Tom DeMark

- *Chuck LeBeau's System Traders Club*
- *TradeStation STAD Club*
- and, of course, the TradeStation documentation

I wish you enormous success in your efforts. I hope you love trading and research as much as I do. If your trading gives you enough positive rewards, you probably will.

When you have questions or want to chat, remember I'm online at www.moneymentor.com, or you can email me at sunny@moneymentor.com. Lately I've begun a new chat/blog space at www.moneymentor.com/ blog.html. Check it out.

SUMMARY: PUTTING IT ALL TOGETHER

Before leaving you to your own devices, I need to address one more really important topic. It is imperative that you have not only a strategy (or system) that you can follow religiously but that you have a business plan for your operation.

Right from the start you need to ask yourself whether you are prepared to work toward achieving a trading plan that will work. If yes, great! **Many people have come before you, and have not succeeded at trading.** You need to separate yourself from all those people and let's face it—this takes work! **Of all beginning traders, 80% to 90% will have lost their capital within the first 12 months.** I talk to wannabe traders every day; without exception they all think they can buy TradeStation, spend a few weeks designing and testing a trading strategy, and start trading successfully.

If it was that easy, we'd all be rich. The truth is, it's next to impossible to find a trading system that works. I spent three solid years in 18-hour-a-day research to come up with mine, and I'm a PhD mathematician. Please don't be fooled by the charlatans who want to sell you their system. If it was so good, why aren't they trading it instead of selling it? That's not to say that all for-sale-strategies are bogus; they're not. But before you buy a strategy, ask for a trial period where you can use it on your own computer for a week or two.

Here are the key points I have uncovered in my 30+ years of trading, which you should keep in mind.

1. Trading has a very high FAILURE rate. What one (or few) thing(s) will separate you from the losers? Why are YOU going to be successful trading?
2. How will you overcome the feelings and EMOTIONS (e.g., fear, greed, worry, excitement, etc.) and their influences on you when you are making your trading decisions?
3. In the interest of having few distractions and clear thought, WHERE are you going to make your trading decisions? Which location provides you the privacy to spend time by yourself and with your own thoughts in peace and quiet? Identify a time in the day when you are likely to have this time to yourself.
4. Write down your own STRENGTHS and WEAKNESSES, considering at least these areas: your self-confidence, patience, discipline, organizational skills, computer proficiency, motivation, tolerance when things don't go your way, and ability to commit.

5. Remember the saying "If you aim at nothing, you are sure to hit!" In line with this, you want to identify your trading goals. Why are you trading and what do you expect to ACHIEVE in the next six months, one year, or five years? All business plans include 30-day, one-year and five-year goals.
6. How much TIME will you have to trade? This is crucial as it will most likely affect the style of trading you adopt. Not much time available? Then short-term trading is probably not for you. Maybe you should be an investor rather than a trader.
7. You must set in stone the most important point regarding MONEY MANAGEMENT—protecting your capital. Even though your primary motivation is to make money and you consider this important, protecting your trading capital is even more important. How can you make money if you don't have any money to trade with? Remember, it takes a lot higher percentage return to recover from losses, because you are doing it with a smaller pile.
8. The most important trading rule is to CUT YOUR LOSSES (and let your winners run). To do this, it is important to use stop losses. A stop loss is a predefined level (price) at which you will exit a trade based on the premise that it is not moving in the direction you had anticipated and therefore you are losing money. How are YOU going to determine your stop losses?
9. One of the best ways to MANAGE YOUR RISK when trading is to limit or set a cap on how much money you put into a single position. This is to guard against the possibility of something adverse occurring. What is the maximum percentage of your trading capital you are prepared to commit to a single trade?
10. Another crucial part of money management is POSITION SIZING. How are you going to size your position? Examples include the equal portion method and the model based on your risk amount and where you position your initial stop loss. Which one are you going to use? What is going to be your maximum risk exposure across your trading portfolio at any one time? Will you limit the number of trades based on how much risk capital you have at risk across all of your open trades? I use an Excel spreadsheet with what I call ultimate F fractional sizing. This scheme is available for purchase. Call me at (760) 908-3070. It's only $995. It is loosely based on the original works of Ralph Vince, but it's considerably improved and it's the only successful way to compound your profits.
11. What happens if you keep LOSING MONEY? This question has little to do with trading but rather your own financial situation. Are you prepared to lose every cent of your allocated trading capital before you are forced to stop, or do you think you would like to hold on to some of the money and commit it somewhere else, with the plan of either not trading again for an extended period of time or giving up altogether?
12. RUNS: Unless your trading strategy is "dependent," it is not likely that a series of losses will be followed by a string of wins. You really can't tell. Psychologically you might be better off decreasing your bet size after a few losses, until your "winning streak" comes back. The only way to assess this is to use Ralph Vince's equations to determine dependence or independence. (You might want to buy a copy of my pamphlet "Ralph Vince at a Glance" or get one of his books on money management.)

13. LIQUIDITY is your ability to trade a stock without adversely affecting the market price due to insufficient buyers and sellers in the market for that stock. **Don't buy something you can't sell.** You never want to be stuck with a stock that you need to exit from just because there are insufficient buyers in the market. How are you going to measure liquidity, and what will be your minimum level you will accept?
14. VOLATILITY is directly linked to risk. But without a degree of volatility, a stock would not be tradable. Would you consider using a minimum or maximum filter for volatility percentage? In trying to avoid speculative stocks, will you enter trades only when the price is above a set amount? If so, what is that amount? I measure sufficient volatility with my PHW Indicator (i.e., is there enough money per hour in the market to make a living?).
15. There are numerous VEHICLES available for trading, including shares, futures contracts, options on futures, as well as options on stock, currencies (foreign exchange or forex), CFDs and more, and they all have different risk profiles. If you are trading multiple products, how are you going to allocate your capital accordingly based on the different levels of risk?
16. What would you describe as an ADVERSE MOVE against you, and what will you do should it happen to you? Under what other circumstances will you consider selling regardless of what exit points you set?
17. Now to some happier money management areas—selling with a PROFIT. How are you going to trail the stock price with your exit once the price moves higher? How are you going to calculate this? Are you going to use the TradeStation built-in trailing stops?
18. Consider PYRAMIDING or COMPOUNDING—adding more money to a profitable trade. Will you consider pyramiding into profitable trades? If so, at what point will you purchase more shares in the company, and how will you determine how much more to buy? Will you add positions to a losing trade in order to average down the entry price?
19. SCALING OUT of a trade is a similar concept. Just as you can add positions on to a profitable trade, you might consider taking positions off of a profitable trade. Make a plan that takes scaling into account.
20. Conceptualize your trading METHODOLOGY. Talk in very general terms about how you are going to approach your trades. For example, are you going to trade a leveraged instrument and trade short-term reversals in medium-term trends? Are you going to trade in only the top 200 stocks from your exchange and look at medium-term trends only with a view to buying stocks as they trade to 12-month highs? Are you going to trade more speculative stocks at the other end of the scale and trade breakouts from trading ranges?
21. If you are going to use TECHNICAL ANALYSIS, what items are of most interest to you? For example, are you interested in trends? If so, over what time frame and how are you going to identify them? Are you interested in reversals of short-term or medium-term trends? If so, how will you identify them, and then what will you do once you identify them? How about technical indicators? Will you use any of them? Consider moving averages and MACD; they are very successful long term. For an even more successful

moving average, ask me about my dynamic moving average, which self-adjusts to the speed of the market and adapts to slow and fast markets.

22. If you are going to use FUNDAMENTAL ANALYSIS, what items are of most interest to you? For example, are you interested in earnings, dividends, growth, acquisitions? If so, how will you use that information?

23. Which VEHICLES (or products) will you trade? Will you trade multiple products? Should you be trading anything other than stocks if you are just starting out?

24. One of the most time-tested and proven strategies is "follow the trend," followed by "the trend is your friend." Consider staying on the right side of the trend. And along with that, determine in what time frame your trend occurs. For instance, are you looking at long-term, medium-term, or short-term trends?

25. Are you going to use TECHNICAL INDICATORS? What tangible value does that indicator(s) provide you, and how are you going to interpret it?

26. Despite the passage of time, human nature and behavior over the years remains constant. All market participants are driven by similar emotions and often react to situations in the same way. Moreover, there is a continual flow of new participants into the market, and they are generally ignorant of the way the market has behaved in the past. For this reason, the same mistakes often are repeated by each new group of market participants—this is why CHART PATTERNS often work. Will you consider a particular chart pattern as a setup (lead into) for a trade entry? Are there any chart patterns that will immediately stop you entering a trade or at least have you waiting until the pattern has completed or dissolved?

27. There is a process that seeks to categorize the industry/economic sectors in an equities market. In most markets, the performance of all industry sectors is reflected in an index for each. Will you use any form of SECTOR ANALYSIS in your method? If so, how will you use it? Will it be the starting point for your trade selection process, or will it be a final filter to ensure that you don't enter stocks that belong to poorly performing sectors?

28. A WATCH LIST is a list of stocks that have met all or most of your selection criteria and are waiting for final approval for a trade entry—it is a list of potential trades. Often watch lists cause people a great deal of frustration because it takes so much effort to monitor all the stocks and then it becomes overwhelming and altogether too hard. It becomes inefficient, and the primary purpose for using the watch list in the first place is forgotten. Will you set up a list containing potential trading opportunities (a watch list), and how will you manage it? How will you set it up? Will it be in a written diary, an Excel spreadsheet, or another format? How often will you analyze the contents of the watch list to ensure it remains accurate? What additional comments will you make for each stock that will help you when you revisit that stock for further analysis in the near future?

29. Your decision to ENTER a trade is one of the first decisions you make when trading. However, it is also one of the least important. There are far more important issues, such as your position size and what your exit plan is. What are the conditions that you look for in all of your trades? What setups may spark your interest and have you closely monitoring the price of a stock? Finally, what triggers will you use? Here's a tip—don't stress over this. Follow the time-tested trading rules and keep it simple. Simple works!

30. Using a WEIGHT OF EVIDENCE approach can add to the effectiveness of your stock selection process. What this means is that you may place greater emphasis on certain conditions over others. You may set up a decision matrix and have a minimum score that a potential trade needs to reach before becoming a genuine trading opportunity. Do you think you may consider using this approach? Does it offer you some ideas for modifying your current approach?

31. A TRADING DIARY should detail all of your trading decisions, including reasons for initiating a trade, your emotions when opening the trade, notes concerning the short- and medium-term trends of the price and relevant economic sector, as well as daily adjustments of exits. A trading diary provides you with a methodical way of maintaining a clear focus. It can also assist you with learning from your mistakes. Will you use one? If so, what information will it contain?

32. It is imperative that you MONITOR YOUR PERFORMANCE for a variety of reasons. The most basic of these is to ensure the you oversee your trading capital. Why? The most important aim in trading is to preserve your capital. Further, monitoring your performance allows you to review your past trades and learn from your mistakes. This is a tactic employed by some of the best traders in the world. They periodically review all of the trades they have conducted, both winners and losers, and learn from them. How will you go about conducting a review of your trading activities, and how often will you do this?

33. Having a STRATEGY (aka plan, routine, recipe, system) (preferably written down) makes it so much easier to follow your plan. Why is this critical? Why do most traders fail? They have no plan, or if they have one, they don't follow it. Simple. What the strategy should do is compile most of the parts of your trading plan so you ensure that for every trading opportunity and subsequent trade, you process it methodically and efficiently. It will also stop you getting distracted by other matters. What will be in your routine? Write it down and make up many copies so you can check it off every day and for every trade.

34. When you place your order, what type of ORDER will you use? How will you place your order? If you use a human broker, this question is of less importance than for those who use a trading platform or web browser and have no human intervention. Will you use the same type of order under all circumstances?

35. With regard to WEB SITES and managing the information flow, it is important to identify what information you need and where you will source it. With RSS feeds now available and people blogging, this is becoming easier and easier. What information do you really need to trade, and what information is for interest only but doesn't impact on your decisions? Keep MoneyMentor.com loaded in your bookmarks, as information here changes rapidly.

36. There are many and varied STOCKBROKERS available to individual traders. With the rapid expansion of the Internet over the last decade, the stockbrokering industry has changed considerably. Which broker accounts do you already have, and what additional

accounts may you establish? What is each of the accounts for? I have my accounts at TradeStation.com, where I also use my technical analysis software.

37. The final step is to document your thoughts and answers into a WRITTEN TRADING PLAN. When you do not have a written plan, even though you have developed a plan, it is too easy to drift away and go back to old habits. Having the written plan provides you with something tangible—something you place your hand on, which will guide you to making the right decisions. Consider the difference between knowing what **has to be done** and what you **want to do.** In trading, what has to be done is always the right choice, yet if you don't have a plan, you can easily decide with what you want to do instead.

LAST WORDS

Many happy returns! As always, feel free to give me a call. Observe Pacific Time Zone business hours, please, and here's my cell: (760) 908-3070. If you want to talk "face-to-face," my Skype number is (760) 444-4174. Actually, now that I think about it, it's probably better to talk first on the cell to alert me that you want to talk on Skype, or I'll probably just refuse the call. Unexpected video calls can be unsettling.

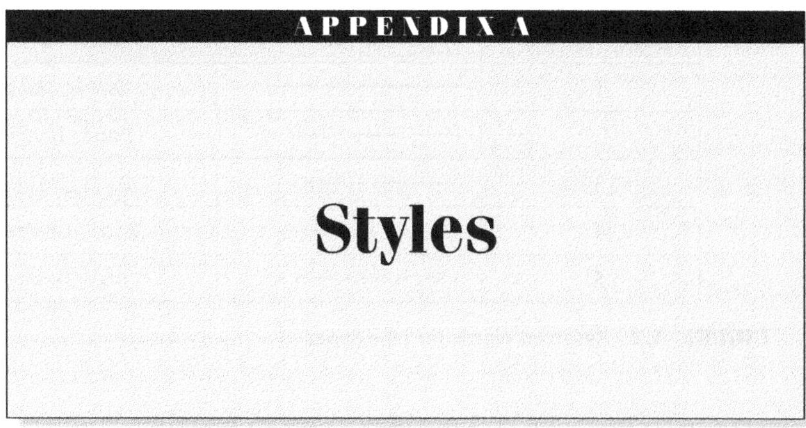

APPENDIX A

Styles

In EasyLanguage you can set colors for tools like Background, Plots, Text, and Trendlines.

LINE STYLE

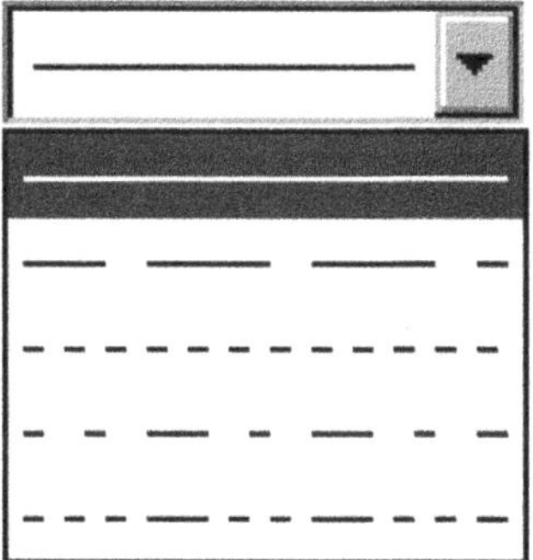

FIGURE A.1 Line Styles

Line Style Value	Sample	Reserved Word
1		Tool_Solid
2		Tool_Dashed
3		Tool_Dotted
4		Tool_Dashed2
5		Tool_Dashed3

FIGURE A.2 Reserved Words for Line Styles

FIGURE A.3 Line Thickness

Thickness Value	Sample
0	no line is drawn; invisible
1	
2	
3	
4	
5	
6	
7	

FIGURE A.4 Thickness Values

The syntax of the command to set the plot's line thickness is:

```
SetPlotWidth(Number, Width);
```

where Number is a number from 1 to 99 representing the number of the plot to modify.
Width is a number from 0 to 6 specifying the width of the line.

EXAMPLE

The next EasyLanguage statements change the width of the plot to a thicker line when the Momentum Indicator is over 0 and to a thinner line when it is under 0:

```
Plot1(Momentum(Close, 10), "Momentum");
If Plot1 > 0 Then
   SetPlotWidth(1, 4);
If Plot1 < 0 Then
   SetPlotWidth(1, 1);
```

This code would generate a plot looking like Figure A.4.1, with the thinner and thicker lines in the subplot area representing the output from the code.

FIGURE A.4.1 Varying Thickness in a Plot

Another way to specify line thickness would be within the plot statement itself, in the width parameter. However, this approach limits you to a single value for width and would not allow you to make value-dependent widths as in the example.

```
PlotN(Expression[,"<PlotName>"[,ForeColor[,Default[,Width]]]]);
```

COLORS

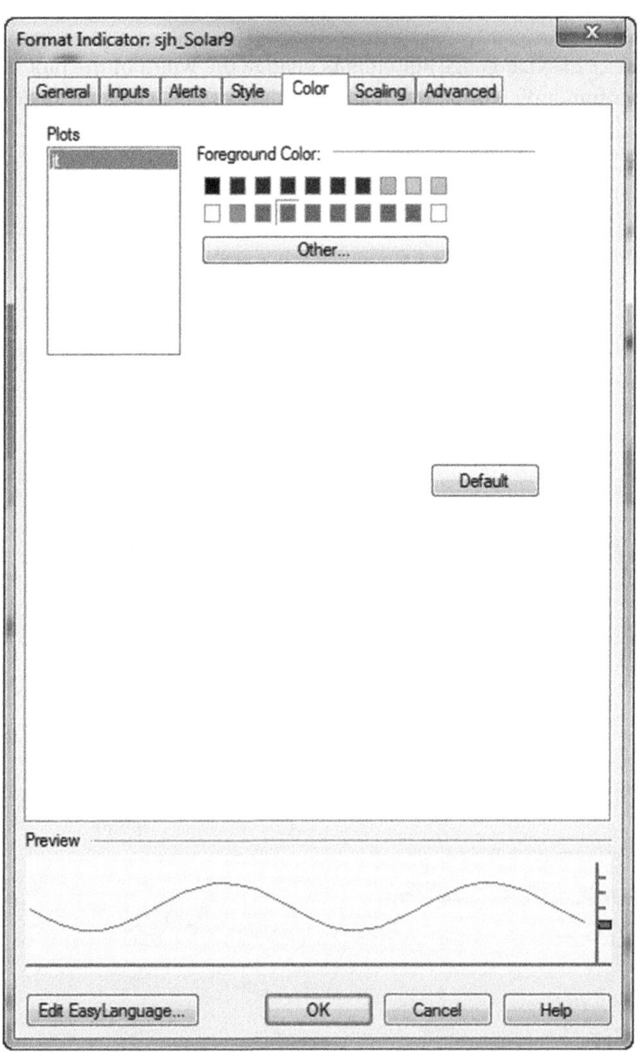

FIGURE A.5 Foreground Colors

EasyLanguage Color Reserved Word	EasyLanguage RGB Value	EasyLanguage Legacy Color Value
Black	0	1
Blue	16711680	2
Cyan	16776960	3
Green	65280	4
Magenta	16711935	5
Red	255	6
Yellow	65535	7
White	16777215	8
DarkBlue	8388608	9
DarkCyan	8421376	10
DarkGreen	32768	11
DarkMagenta	8388736	12
DarkRed	128	13
DarkBrown	32896	14
DarkGray	8421504	15
LightGray	12632256	16

FIGURE A.6 Some Legacy Colors versus RGB Values

In more recent versions of TradeStation, the full facility of RGB color schemes is available. Inside an EasyLanguage document you can set the color of the plot in question by specifying the Red, Green, and Blue (RGB) component values of the color. This allows you 16 million colors to choose from. If you don't know the RGB value of the color you want, simply type "RGB color values" into a Google search, and you'll find lots of references to samples and values for the color possibilities.

To specify values for plots, backgrounds, and the like, use the functions SetPlotColor and SetPlotBGColor. Within the function reference you will need reference to another function to specify the color values, where RGB (RedValue, GreenValue, BlueValue); the call to the function would then look like: SetPlotColor (1, RGB (255,255,0)), where each red, blue, and green color value can be an integer from 0 to 255.

Color	Hex Code	Color	Hex Code	Color	Hex Code
		Antique white	#FAEBD7	Aqua	#00FFFF
Aquamarine	#7FFFD4			Beige	#F5F5DC
Bisque	#FFE4C4	Black	#000000	Blanche dalmond	#FFEBCD
Blue	#0000FF	Blue violet	#8A2BE2	Brown	#A52A2A
Burlywood	#DEB887	Cadet blue	#5F9EA0	Chartreuse	#7FFF00
Chocolate	#D2691E	Coral	#FF7F50	Cornflower blue	#6495ED
Cornsilk	#FFF8DC	Crimson	#DC143C	Cyan	#00FFFF
Dark blue	#00008B	Dark cyan	#008B8B	Dark goldenrod	#B8860B
Dark gray	#A9A9A9	Dark green	#006400	Dark khaki	#BDB76B
Dark magenta	#8B008B	Dark olive green	#556B2F	Dark orange	#FF8C00
Dark orchid	#9932CC	Dark red	#8B0000	Dark salmon	#E9967A
Dark seagreen	#8DBC8F	Dark slate blue	#483D8B	Dark slate gray	#2F4F4F
Dark turquoise	#00DED1	Dark violet	#9400D3	Deep pink	#FF1493
Deep sky blue	#00BFFF	Dim gray	#696969	Dodger blue	#1E90FF
Firebrick	#B22222			Forest green	#228B22
Fuchsia	#FF00FF	Gainsboro	#DCDCDC		
Gold	#FFD700	Goldenrod	#DAA520	Gray	#808080
Green	#008000	Green yellow	#ADFF2F		
Hot pink	#FF69B4	Indian red	#CD5C5C	Indigo	#4B0082
		Khaki	#F0E68C	Lavender	#E6E6FA
		Lawngreen	#7CFC00	Lemon chiffon	#FFFACD
Light blue	#ADD8E6	Light coral	#F08080	Light cyan	#E0FFFF
Light goldenrod yellow	#FAFAD2	Light green	#90EE90	Light grey	#D3D3D3
Light pink	#FFB6C1	Light salmon	#FFA07A	Light seagreen	#20B2AA
Light sky blue	#87CEFA	Light slate gray	#778899	Light steel blue	#B0C4DE
Light yellow	#FFFFE0	Lime	#00FF00	Lime green	#32CD32
Linen	#FAF0E6	Magenta	#FF00FF	Maroon	#800000
Medium aquamarine	#66CDAA	Medium blue	#0000CD	Medium orchid	#BA55D3
Medium purple	#9370DB	Medium sea green	#3CB371	Medium slate blue	#7B68EE
Medium spring green	#00FA9A	Medium turquoise	#48D1CC	Medium violet red	#C71585

FIGURE A.7 Colors and Hex Codes

REMARKS

The value returned is a RGB color number (16 million color) from 0 to 16777215.

EXAMPLE

If you wanted to change the foreground (i.e., the line generated by the Plot command) color of Plot1 to yellow, you could use this syntax:

```
SetPlotColor (1, RGB (255,255,0)); //sets color to yellow
```

EXAMPLE

If you wanted to change the background color of your window to yellow, you could use this syntax:

```
SetPlotBGColor (1, RGB (255,255,0));
```

REMARKS

Another fun facility in later TradeStations is to set gradient colors for plots and backgrounds. For instance, you can fade a colored plot line from white to blue by specifying:

```
SetPlotColor(1, GradientColor(RSIValue, 20, 80, White, Blue));
```

You can also use the RGB values to specify colors by making a call to the function **RGB(k,m,n)** where k, m, and n are the Red, Green and Blue color values, specified by a number from 0 to 255. A variety of colors and their RGB values is shown in Figure A.8.

R - 000 G - 204 B - 000	R - 051 G - 255 B - 051	R - 102 G - 000 B - 102	R - 153 G - 051 B - 153	R - 204 G - 102 B - 204	R - 255 G - 153 B - 255
00FF00 R - 000 G - 255 B - 000	330033 R - 051 G - 000 B - 051	663366 R - 102 G - 051 B - 102	996699 R - 153 G - 102 B - 153	CC99CC R - 204 G - 153 B - 204	FFCCFF R - 255 G - 204 B - 255
00FF33 R - 000 G - 255 B - 051	330066 R - 051 G - 000 B - 102	663399 R - 102 G - 051 B - 153	9966CC R - 153 G - 102 B - 204	CC99FF R - 204 G - 153 B - 255	FFCC00 R - 255 G - 204 B - 000
00FF66 R - 000 G - 255 B - 102	330099 R - 051 G - 000 B - 153	6633CC R - 102 G - 051 B - 204	9966FF R - 153 G - 102 B - 255	CC9900 R - 204 G - 153 B - 000	FFCC33 R - 255 G - 204 B - 051
00FF99 R - 000 G - 255 B - 153	3300CC R - 051 G - 000 B - 204	6633FF R - 102 G - 051 B - 255	996600 R - 153 G - 102 B - 000	CC9933 R - 204 G - 153 B - 051	FFCC66 R - 255 G - 204 B - 102
00FFCC R - 000 G - 255 B - 204	3300FF R - 051 G - 000 B - 255	663300 R - 102 G - 051 B - 000	996633 R - 153 G - 102 B - 051	CC9966 R - 204 G - 153 B - 102	FFCC99 R - 255 G - 204 B - 153

FIGURE A.8 A Few RGB Color Values

To see lots and lots of RGB color values, go to my Web site (www.moneymentor.com) and in the center panel click on TradeStation Made Easy readers' link. It will take you to the page where I'm accumulating links and templates for readers of this book. Another way to get to the color palette is to click on the word "Reference" in the leftmost column of www.MoneyMentor.com

APPENDIX B

Reserved Words

Certain words are set aside (reserved) as part of the syntax of EasyLanguage. These words have special meaning to TradeStation. You may not use these words in your own programming to mean anything other than the meaning reserved to EasyLanguage.

You will probably never use most of these words. EasyLanguage is so complex and full of possibility that your personal programming will more than likely be limited to a vocabulary of 50 or so favorite words. This list serves both as a reminder of the limitless possibilities within EasyLanguage and as a reference for the words that are reserved. The list of words in this appendix is by no means the complete list of reserved words available in EasyLanguage. I have not, for instance, included the words related to ActivityBars, Options nor Arrays. For the complete list of reserved words you can open the help files from within TradeStation or the EasyLanguage Dictionary from within EasyLanguage.

In Figure B.1, the most commonly used Reserved Words are presented. Many of these have not been explained in this book. They are presented here so you can look them up in this appendix and study their meanings. Information in this appendix is copyrighted by ©TradeStation Technologies, Inc. All rights reserved.

This appendix is a nearly complete list of reserved words, taken from the EasyLanguage Help Files. (Thanks to the folks at TradeStation.) At the time of this writing the current version of TradeStation is 8.8; new words added after that time will not be in this appendix.

I would seriously advise you to read this whole appendix once now and once again in a week or two. Only then will you know what reserved words are available to you. You don't have to memorize them, just know they are here so you can look them up later.

above	alert	and	array	bar
barinterval	barssinceentry	begin	below	bigpointvalue
breakpoint	buy	buytocover	c	close
commentary	contracts	cross	crosses	currentbar
currentdate	currenttime	d	data	date
definedllfunc	downto	else	end	entryprice
false	for	from	getsymbolname	h
high	i	if	input	l
limit	low	market	marketposition	maxbarsback
minmove	newline	next	noplot	numeric
numericarray	o	of	on	open
or	over	plot1	plot2	plot3
plot99	plotpb	points	+	pointvalue
pricescale	print	sell	sellshort	setplotcolor
shares	stop	t	than	then
this	ticks	time	true	under
v	variables	volume	while	=

FIGURE B.1 Most Commonly Used Reserved Words

RESERVED WORD AND MEANING

#	Character used to denote compiler directives
(	Open parenthesis, used in formulas
)	Close parenthesis, used in formulas
*	Multiplication sign
+	Addition sign
-	Subtraction sign
/	Division sign
//	Comment
<	Less than sign
>	Greater than sign
<>	Not equal sign
{ }	Comment

#BEGINALERT

A compiler directive including all EasyLanguage instructions between #BeginAlert and #End in the analysis technique's calculation when the Enable Alert check box is selected and the study is evaluating the last bar of a chart. All syntax between #BeginAlert and #End are ignored, including the calculation of MaxBarsBack, unless the Enable Alert check box is selected in charting and the analysis technique is evaluating the last bar of a chart.

EXAMPLE

```
#BeginAlert
If Close[50] > Close and ADX(Length) > ADX(Length)[1] then
        Alert("ADX Alert");
#End;
```

#BEGINCMTRY

A compiler directive that executes the EasyLanguage instructions between #BeginCmtry and #End only when using the Expert Commentary tool to select a bar on a chart or a cell in a grid.

Note that all statements between the #BeginCmtry and #End are ignored, including calculation of MaxBarsBack, unless commentary is generated.

EXAMPLE

```
{Calling Accumulation Swing Index Expert Commentary}
#BeginCmtry
        Commentary(ExpertADX(Plot1));
#End;
```

#BEGINCMTRYORALERT

A compiler directive that executes the EasyLanguage instructions between #BeginCmtryOrAlert and #End only when the Enable Alert check box is selected when using the Expert Commentary tool to select a bar on a chart or a cell in a grid.

Note that all statements between #BeginCmtryOrAlert and #End are ignored, including calculation of MaxBarsBack, unless the Enable Alert check box is selected or commentary is generated.

EXAMPLE

```
{Calling Accumulation Swing Index Expert Commentary}
#BeginCmtryOrAlert
If Close[50] > Close and ADX(Length) > ADX(Length)[1] then
Alert("ADX Alert");
        Commentary(ExpertADX(Plot1));
#End;
```

#END

A compiler directive used in conjunction with #BeginAlert, #BeginCmtry, and #BeginCmtryOrAlert to terminate an alert or commentary statement.

EXAMPLES

```
{Calling Accumulation Swing Index Expert Commentary}
#BeginCmtryOrAlert
      If Close[50] > Close and ADX(Length) > ADX(Length)[1] then
             Alert("ADX Alert");
       Commentary(ExpertADX(Plot1));
#End;
```

A

A

Skip word.

REMARKS

This word is skipped in EasyLanguage and is not necessary. These skipped words, however, do make it easier to understand the purpose of the code.

By default, unnecessary words and sections marked as comments will appear dark green in the EasyLanguage PowerEditor.

EXAMPLE

If a Close is > 100, then the word "a" is not necessary and the code functions the same way regardless of its presence.

Above

This word is used to check for the direction of a cross between values. It is used in conjunction with the reserved word "crosses" to detect when a value crosses above, or becomes greater than, another value. A value (Value1) crosses above another value (Value2) whenever Value1 is greater than Value2 in the current bar, but Value 1 was equal to or less than Value 2 in the previous bar. `Above` is a synonym for the reserved word "Over."

EXAMPLES

```
If Plot1 Crosses Above Plot2 Then Buy;
If Value1 Crosses Above Value2 Then Buy;
```

AbsValue

Returns the absolute value of the input value "num," a numeric expression.

EXAMPLES

```
Value1=AbsValue(-25.543) returns a value of 25.543
Value1=AbsValue(25.778) also returns a value of 25.778
```

Ago

Refers to values from another reference point. `Ago` can also be referred to as an offset and can be represented by using notation consisting of a number in square brackets where x is the number of points offset.

EXAMPLE

```
Value1 = C[1]; //sets Value1 to the Closing price of the previ-
ous bar
Value1 = Close of 1 Bar Ago; //same as above
```

Alert

True/False value will determine whether the study generates an alert condition.

REMARKS
A True value for Alert will generate an alert only when alerts have been enabled for the study in the Properties tab.

Alerts are generated only for the last bar.

EXAMPLE
Alert = True will generate an alert if the Enable Alert check box is enabled under the Properties tab.

ADDITIONAL EXAMPLE
If you wanted an alert to be triggered only under certain conditions, you could use the following syntax:

```
If {Your Alert Criteria} Then
        Alert = True;
```

AlertEnabled

Returns True if alerts have been enabled in the Properties tab of an analysis technique, False is returned if alerts are not enabled.

REMARKS
Alerts are generated only for the last bar.

EXAMPLE
`AlertEnabled` will return True if alerts have been enabled.

ADDITIONAL EXAMPLE
If you wanted code to be evaluated only when the user had set the study to enable alerts, you could use the following syntax:

```
If AlertEnabled Then
        Begin
                {Your Code Here}
        End;
```

All

Used in conjunction with “share(s)” or “contract(s)” in trading strategies specifying that all shares/contracts are to be sold (for long positions) or covered (for short positions) when exiting the current position.

EXAMPLE

```
If Condition1 then
    ExitLong all shares next bar at market;
```

An

Skip word.

REMARKS
This word is skipped in EasyLanguage and is not necessary. These skipped words, however, do make it easier to understand the purpose of the code. By default, unnecessary words and sections marked as comments will appear dark green in the EasyLanguage PowerEditor.

EXAMPLE

```
If an Open is > 100 Then ...
```

The word "an" is not necessary and the code functions the same way regardless of its presence.

And

This boolean operator is used in condition statements to check multiple conditions.

REMARKS

And requires that in order for a condition to be True, all conditions must be True.

EXAMPLES

```
If Plot1 Crosses Above Plot2 And Plot2 > 5 Then ...
```

`And` is used here to determine if the direction of the cross of the values `Plot1` and `Plot2`, and that `Plot2` is greater than `5`, are both True on the bar under consideration. If either is False, the condition returns False.

```
If Value1 Crosses Above Value2 And Value1 > Value1[1] Then
```

`And` is used here to determine if the direction of the cross of the variables `Value1` and `Value2`, and that `Value1` is greater than `Value1` of one bar ago, are both True on the bar under consideration. If either is False, the condition returns False.

Arctangent(num)

Returns the arctangent value of the specified (num) of degrees.

(num) is a numeric expression to be used in the calculation.

REMARKS

The arctangent is the inverse of the tangent function.

(num) should be the number of degrees in the angle.

EXAMPLE

ArcTangent(45) returns a value of 88.7270.

ArcTangent(72) returns a value of 89.2043.

Array

Reserved word used to declare variable names that can contain multiple values.

REMARKS

A variable declared as an array can hold more than one value at the same time.

The number of values that can be held by an Array is determined when the Array name is declared by a number in square brackets, following the variable name.

The initial value of an Array can be determined for all values by one number in parentheses after the declaration.

EXAMPLES

```
Array: AnyName[4](0);
```

declares the variable AnyName that can hold four distinct values and initializes them to zero.

```
Array: NewName[10](5);
```

declares the variable NewName that can hold 10 distinct values and initializes each value to 5.

Arrays

Reserved word used to declare multiple variable names that can contain multiple values.

REMARKS

A variable declared as an array can hold more than one value at the same time.

The number of values that can be held by an Array is determined when the Array name is declared by a number in square brackets, following the variable name.

The initial value of an Array can be determined for all values by one number in parentheses after the declaration.

EXAMPLES

```
Arrays: AnyName[4](0), AnotherName[4](0);
```

declares the variables AnyName and AnotherName that can hold four distinct values each and initializes all of the values to zero.

```
Arrays: OldName[10](5),NewName[10](5);
```

declares the variables OldName and NewName that can hold ten distinct values and initializes each value to 5.

ARRAYSIZE

Reserved for use with custom DLLs designed for EasyLanguage. Refer to the documentation in the TradeStation Developer's Kit for more information about this and the EasyLanguage Tool Kit Library ELKIT32.DLL.

ARRAYSTARTADDR

Reserved for use with custom DLLs designed for EasyLanguage. Refer to the documentation in the TradeStation Developer's Kit for more information about this and the EasyLanguage Tool Kit Library ELKIT32.DLL.

Ask

Returns the ask value of an option or leg calculated by a bid/ask model.

EXAMPLE

```
If Ask of Option - Close of Option < .125 then
      Alert("Very Low Ask");
```

Asset

Refers to an option's underlying asset in OptionStation.

EXAMPLE

Value1 = Volume of Asset;

AssetType

Evaluates a position leg to determine if it is an asset.

EXAMPLE

```
If LegType of Leg(1) = AssetType Then {Your Operation Here}
```

AssetVolatility

Returns the volatility of the underlying asset.

REMARKS

If no value is available for AssetVolatility, then zero is returned.

EXAMPLE

```
If AssetVolatility > 50 Then {Your Operation Here}
```

At

Skip word.

REMARKS

This word is skipped in EasyLanguage and is not necessary. These skipped words, however, do make it easier to understand the purpose of the code. By default, unnecessary words and sections marked as comments will appear dark green in the EasyLanguage PowerEditor.

EXAMPLE

```
Buy 100 Contracts at Market
```

The word "at" is not necessary and the code functions the same way regardless of its presence.

At$

Used in trading strategies to anchor exit prices to the bar where the entry order was placed. **At$** must be used in conjunction with an entry order that has an assigned label.

EXAMPLE

The following strategy buys when the 10-bar moving average crosses over the 20-bar moving average, placing a stop loss order 1 point under the Low of the bar where the crossover occurred by appending **At$** to the Sell statement.

```
If Average(Close, 10) Crosses Over Average(Close,20) then
Buy ("MA Cross Over") next bar at market;
Sell next bar from entry ("MA Cross Over") At$
Low - 1 point stop;
```

AtCommentaryBar

Returns True if the user has selected this bar as the Expert Commentary Bar. False is returned if the bar is not the Expert Commentary bar or if the user has not inserted the Expert Commentary Tool.

EXAMPLE

`AtCommentaryBar` returns True if the bar has been selected with the Expert Commentary Tool.

ADDITIONAL EXAMPLE

If you wanted to begin a commentary section based only on the selected bar, you could use the following syntax:

```
If AtCommentaryBar Then
        Begin
              {Your Commentary Code Here}
        End;
```

AvgBarsLosTrade

Returns the average number of bars that elapsed during losing trades for all closed trades.

EXAMPLES

`AvgBarsLosTrade` returns 3 if the number of bars elapsed during 4 losing trades were 4, 3, 6, and 2.

`AvgBarsLosTrade` returns 5 if the number of bars elapsed during two losing trades were 7 and 3.

AvgBarsWinTrade

Returns the average number of bars that elapsed during winning trades for all closed trades.

EXAMPLES

`AvgBarsWinTrade` returns 3 if the number of bars elapsed during four winning trades were 4, 3, 6 and 2.

`AvgBarsWinTrade` returns 5 if the number of bars elapsed during two winning trades were 7 and 3.

AvgEntryPrice

Returns the average entry price of each open entry in a pyramided position.

REMARKS

AvgEntryPrice returns the average entry price only for open trades.

EXAMPLES

`AvgEntryPrice` returns 150 if three trades are currently open and were entered at a price of 130, 145 and 175.

`AvgEntryPrice` returns 50 if four trades are currently open and were entered at a price of 42, 53, 37 and 68.

AvgList(Num1, Num2, Num3, . . .)

Returns the average value of the inputs.

(Num1) is a numeric expression representing a value to be used in the calculation.

(Num2) is a second numeric expression representing a value to be used in the calculation.

(Num3) is a third numeric expression representing a value to be used in the calculation, and so on.

REMARKS

The AvgList calculates a simple average of all of the values of (NumN). The sum of all values of Num divided by the number of members.

EXAMPLES

`AvgList(45, 72, 86, 125, 47)` returns a value of 75.

`AvgList(18, 67, 98, 24, 65, 19)` returns a value of 48.5.

B

Bar

References the open, high, low, and closing prices for a specific interval. The interval is determined by the data compression of the symbol.

REMARKS

`Bar` is normally used with the reserved word Ago to specify a value or condition (usually 1) "Bar Ago". When the data compression is set to Daily, this and the reserved word Day are identical.

EXAMPLES

`Close of 1 Bar Ago` returns the Close price of the previous bar.

`Sell this bar on close` orders a trading strategy to exit all long positions on the close of the current bar.

ADDITIONAL EXAMPLE

`Buy (''Signal Name'') next bar at open` will buy during the formation of the next bar if a price meets the open price of the bar.

BarInterval

Reserved word that returns the number of minutes used for the time compression that an analysis technique is applied to.

REMARKS

`BarInterval` is valid only when used on minute-based charts.

EXAMPLES

`Condition1 = BarInterval = 5` is a statement that will cause `Condition1` to be true if the analysis technique is applied to a 5-minute chart.

`CalcTime(Sess1StartTime, BarInterval)` will add the time compression of a bar to the start time of the asset trading.

ADDITIONAL EXAMPLE

`CalcTime(Sess1EndTime, -BarInterval)` returns the time of the last bar before the close of the trading session.

Bars

Reserved word used to reference a set of price data based on the compression to which a technique is applied.

REMARKS

`Bars` is normally used with the reserved word Ago to specify a value or condition any number of "Bars Ago".

EXAMPLES

`Close of 5 Bars Ago` returns the Close price of the bar 5 bars previous to the current bar.

`Average(Close, 10) of 5 bars ago` returns the Average of the last 10 Close prices as calculated on the previous bar.

ADDITIONAL EXAMPLE

`Buy (''Signal Name'') next bar at open` will buy when the formation of the current bar is complete, based on the type of compression of the bar.

BarsSinceEntry(Num)

Returns the number of bars since the specified entry.

(Num) is a numeric expression representing the number of positions ago.

REMARKS

This function can be used only in the evaluation of strategies.

EXAMPLE

`BarsSinceEntry(2)` might return a value of 68 if it has been 68 bars since the entry that occurred 2 positions ago.

BarsSinceExit(Num)

Returns the number of bars since the specified exit.

(Num) is a numeric expression representing the number of positions ago.

REMARKS

This function can be used only in the evaluation of strategies.

EXAMPLE

`BarsSinceExit(2)` might return a value of 46 if it has been 46 bars since the exit that occurred 2 positions ago.

BarStatus

Used with multiple data series (same symbol, different data compressions) or ActivityBar studies to determine whether the current tick is the opening or closing tick of a bar in the other data series, or whether it is a trade "inside the bar."

BarStatus (DataNum)

REMARKS

`DataNum` is used to specify the data series to evaluate. 1 refers to Data1, 2 to Data2, and so on. The data series must be applied to the chart. For example, to use `BarStatus (2)`, a second data series must be applied to the chart.

This reserved word is generally used with ActivityBar studies. For example, it is useful to know when the closing tick of the ActivityBar is the last trade of the "big" bar or a tick within the bar:

2 = the closing tick of the bar
1 = a tick within the bar
0 = an opening tick (valid only when referring to the open of the next bar)
−1 = an error in the execution of the reserved word

EXAMPLE

To perform an operation when the ActivityBar is the last trade of the "big" bar, you could write:

```
If BarStatus(1) = 2 Then {Your Operation Here}
```

. . . where Data1 is the price chart, and your analysis technique is an ActivityBar study.

Based

This word is a skip word retained for backward compatibility.

REMARKS

This word is skipped in EasyLanguage and is not necessary. These skipped words, however, do make it easier to understand the purpose of the code. By default, unnecessary words and sections marked as comments will appear dark green in the PowerEditor.

Begin

This word is used to begin a series of code that should be executed on the basis of an `If... Then, If...Then... Else, For, or While` statement.

REMARKS

`Begin` is necessary only if using more than one line of code after an If . . . Then, If . . . Then . . . Else, For, or While statement.

Each `Begin` must have a corresponding `End`.

EXAMPLES

```
If Condition1 Then
      Begin
      {Your Code Line1}
      {Your Code Line2, etc.}
      End;
```

Begin is used here to include the execution of Line1 and Line2 only when Condition1 is True.

```
If Condition1 Then
     Begin
     {Your Code Line1}
     {Your Code Line2, etc.}
     End
     Else
          Begin
          {Your Code Line3}
          {Your Code Line4, etc.}
End;
```

Begin is used here twice to include the execution of Line1 and Line2 only when Condition1 is True and execute Line3 and Line4 only when Condition1 is False.

Below

This word is used to check for the direction of a cross between values.

REMARKS

Used in conjunction with the "crosses" to detect when a value crosses below, or becomes less than another value. A value (Value1) crosses below another value (Value2) whenever Value1 is greater than Value2 in the current bar but Value 1 was equal to or less than Value 2 in the previous bar.

Below is a synonym for Under.

EXAMPLES

```
If Plot1 Crosses Below Plot2 Then ...
```

Below is used here to determine the direction of the cross of the values Plot1 and Plot2.

```
If Value1 Crosses Below Value2 Then ...
```

Below is used here to determine the direction of the cross of the variables Value1 and Value2.

Beta

Returns the Beta value of a stock.

REMARKS

A Beta of 1 means that as the market moves, the stock should follow along.

EXAMPLES

Beta returns 3 if the stock should move up 3% for each 1% move of the market.

Beta returns 0.5 if the stock should move up half as much as the market.

Beta_Down

Returns the `Beta_Down` value of a stock.

REMARKS

A `Beta_Down` is the same as Beta; however, it is used when the market is going down.

EXAMPLES

`Beta_Down` returns 3 if the stock should move 3% for each 1% move of the market.

`Beta_Down` returns .5 if the stock should move half as much as the market.

Beta_Up

Returns the `Beta_Up` value of a stock.

REMARKS

A `Beta_Up` is the same as Beta; however, it is used when the market is going up.

EXAMPLES

`Beta_Up` returns 3 if the stock should move 3% for each 1% move of the market.

`Beta_Up` returns .5 if the stock should move half as much as the market.

Bid

Returns the bid value of an option or leg calculated by a bid/ask model.

EXAMPLE

```
If Close of Option - Bid of Option < .125 then
        Alert(''Very Low Bid'');
```

BigPointValue

Returns the dollar value represented by one full point of a security's price.

REMARKS

`BigPointValue` reads the field Big Point Value specified in the Symbol Dictionary.

EXAMPLES

`Close * BigPointValue` returns the current value of an asset.

`CurrentContracts * BigPointValue` returns the value of a current position.

ADDITIONAL EXAMPLE

The initial amount needed to enter a trade can be given by:

```
Value1 = BigPointValue * EntryPrice;
```

Black

Sets the plot color or background color to Black.

REMARKS

There are 16 colors available in EasyLanguage. For more information, see Appendix A for color values.

EXAMPLES

`Plot1(Value1, ''Test'', Black)` plots Value1 with the name Test and sets the color of Plot1 to Black.

`TL_SetColor(1, Black)` sets the color of a TrendLine with a reference number of 1 to Black.

BlockNumber

Returns the block number of the security block attached to the machine.

REMARKS

The BlockNumber function can be used to check for the presence of a particular security block before ploting an indicator.

EXAMPLES

If you wanted to display an indicator only when the user had block number 55522 attached to the machine, you could use the following syntax:

```
If BlockNumber = 55522 Then
Plot1(Value1, ‘‘Indicator’’);
```

Blue

Sets the plot color or background color to Blue.

REMARKS

There are 16 colors available in EasyLanguage. See Appendix A for color values.

EXAMPLES

`Plot1(Value1, ‘‘Test’’, Blue)` plots Value1 with the name Test and sets the color of Plot1 to Blue.

`TL_SetColor(1, Blue)` sets the color of a TrendLine with a reference number of 1 to Blue.

Book_Val_Per_Share

Returns the book value per share of a stock.

REMARKS

`Book_Val_Per_Share` is calculated by dividing common shareholders' equity by the number of shares outstanding.

BOOL

Reserved for use with custom DLLs designed for EasyLanguage. Refer to the documentation in the TradeStation Developer's Kit for more information about this and the EasyLanguage Tool Kit Library ELKIT32.DLL.

BoxSize

Reserved word used to refer to the minimum change in price that is required for the addition of an X to the top or an O to the bottom of a Point & Figure column.

REMARKS

The `BoxSize` is set when creating a Point & Figure column.

BreakEvenStopFloor

This word is retained for backward compatibility.

REMARKS

This word has been replaced by the Signals Break Even Stop LX and Break Even Stop SX.

BreakPoint ("BreakPointNameID")

Used with the EasyLanguage Debugger. When placed in your EasyLanguage code, it automatically opens the EasyLanguage Debugger window when encountered as the study calculates.

`BreakPoint` is a compiler directive that opens the EasyLanguage Debugger when encountered.

PARAMETERS

`BreakPointNameID` A string expression or string variable. This is a required parameter.

REMARKS

Each occurrence of `BreakPoint` must be named. The name parameter may be specified as a string expression, following the keyword, using the form: `BreakPoint (''MyBreak-Name'')`. A string variable can also be used as the name or in combination with a literal string value such as: `BreakPoint(''Break ID'' + GetSymbolName)`.

IMPORTANT: While the EasyLanguage Debugger is open, activity in all TradeStation windows is halted. No data, alerts, or strategy orders will be generated. Any window, including Chart Analysis, in open workspaces will not update until the EasyLanguage Debugger is closed. The EasyLanguage Debugger is intended for use in a development environment. Debugging should not take place while trading or using strategy automation.

EXAMPLES

Open the EasyLanguage Debugger from within a loop.

```
For Counter = 0 to Length -1 Begin
    Sum = Sum + Close[Counter];
    BreakPoint(''BreakID'');
End;
```

Buy

Used to generate an order for a long entry.

REMARKS

The earliest order entry that can be generated is for the close of the current bar.

Orders can be generated for:

```
this bar on Close
next bar at Market
next bar at PRICE Stop
next bar at PRICE Limit
```

An entry statement consists of: Entry/Exit order, Signal name, number of contracts, timing, Price, Market/ Stop/Limit.

EXAMPLES

```
Buy (``LongEntry'') 5 contracts this bar on close;
```

generates an order to enter a long position of five contracts at the Close of the current bar.

```
Buy (``NextEntry'') next bar at market;
```

generates an order to enter a long position at the first price of next bar.

ADDITIONAL EXAMPLE

`Buy (``MyTrade'') next bar at 75 Stop;` generates an order to enter a long position on the next bar at a price of 75 or higher.

By

Skip word.

REMARKS

This word is skipped in EasyLanguage and is not necessary. These skipped words, however, do make it easier to understand the purpose of the code. By default, unnecessary words and sections marked as comments will appear dark green in the EasyLanguage PowerEditor.

BYTE

Reserved for use with custom DLLs designed for EasyLanguage. Refer to the documentation in the TradeStation Developer's Kit for more information about this and the EasyLanguage Tool Kit Library ELKIT32.DLL.

C

C

Shortcut notation that returns the Close of the bar.

REMARKS

Anytime the Close of a bar is needed, the letter `C` can be used in an equivalent fashion.

EXAMPLES

`C of 1 bar ago` returns the Close price of the previous bar.

`Average(C, 10)` returns the Average of the last 10 Close prices.

ADDITIONAL EXAMPLE

To check that the last two bars have Close prices higher than the previous bar, write:

```
If C > C[1] and C[1] > C[2] then
Plot1(High,"ClosedUp");
```

Cancel

Cancel is used to cancel Alerts that have been previously triggered.

REMARKS

Cancel must always be followed by "Alert" in EasyLanguage code.

Alerts are generated only for the last bar.

EXAMPLE

`Cancel Alert` will cancel any alerts previously enabled.

ADDITIONAL EXAMPLE

If you wanted to cancel any alerts that have previously been enabled within the code based on certain criteria, you could use the following syntax:

```
If {Your Criteria Here} Then Cancel Alert;
```

Ceiling (Num)

Returns the lowest integer greater than the specified (Num).

EXAMPLES

`Ceiling(4.5)` returns a value of 5.

`Ceiling(-1.72)` returns a value of −1.

CHAR

Reserved for use with custom DLLs designed for EasyLanguage. Refer to the documentation in the TradeStation Developer's Kit for more information about this and the EasyLanguage Tool Kit Library ELKIT32.DLL.

CheckAlert

Returns True on only the last bar if alerts have been enabled in the Properties tab of the study. False is returned if alerts are not enabled, and on every bar except the last bar.

REMARKS

`CheckAlert` differs from AlertEnabled by checking only the value in the Properties tab of the study to see if alerts are enabled on the last bar.

Alerts are generated only for the last bar.

EXAMPLE

`CheckAlert` will return True if alerts have been enabled and the bar is the last bar.

ADDITIONAL EXAMPLE

If you wanted code to be evaluated only on the last bar and only when the user had set the study to enable alerts, you could use the following syntax:

```
If CheckAlert Then
        Begin
               {Your Code Here}
End;
```

CheckCommentary

Returns True if the user clicks on a chart with the Expert Commentary pointer on the specified bar. False is returned if the pointer has not been inserted or if the pointer was inserted on a different bar.

EXAMPLE

`CheckCommentary` will return True if the Expert Commentary Tool has been inserted for the specified bar.

ADDITIONAL EXAMPLE

If you wanted code to be evaluated only for the bar where the user had inserted the Expert Commentary Tool, you could use the following syntax:

```
If CheckCommentary Then
        Begin
              {Your Code Here}
        End;
```

Close

Reserved word used to return the last price of the specified time increment or group of ticks.

REMARKS

`Close` is synonymous with `Last`.

EXAMPLES

`Close of 1 bar ago` returns the Close price of the previous bar.

`Average(Close, 10)` returns the Average of the last 10 Close prices.

ADDITIONAL EXAMPLE

To check that the last two bars have Close prices higher than the previous bar, write:

```
If Close > Close[1] and Close[1] > Close[2] then
Plot1(High,"ClosedUp");
```

Commentary

Sends the expression to the commentary window for the bar that is selected by the commentary pointer.

```
Commentary("My Expression");
```

where `MyExpression` is a single or a list of numerical, string, or true/false expressions separated by commas, that are to be sent to the commentary window.

EXAMPLE

The following will result in the string "This is one line of commentary" being sent to the commentary window. Any additional commentary sent will be placed on the same line.

```
Commentary("This is one line of commentary");
```

You can use the Commentary reserved word multiple times, and it will not include a carriage return at the end of each expression (or list of expressions) sent. In order to generate a message that includes carriage returns, you will have to use either the NewLine or CommentaryCL reserved word.

CommentaryCL("MyExpression")

Sends the expression to the commentary window for the bar that is specified by the Analysis Commentary Pointer (AKA the cursor).

```
CommentaryCL("My Expression");
```

where `MyExpression` is a single or a list of numerical, string, or true/false expressions separated by commas, that are to be sent to the commentary window.

EXAMPLE

The following will result in the string "This is one line of commentary" being sent to the commentary window. Any additional commentary sent will be placed on the next line.

```
CommentaryCL("This is one line of commentary");
```

You can use the CommentaryCL reserved word multiple times, and it will include a carriage return at the end of each expression (or list of expressions) sent. In order to generate a message that does not include carriage returns, use the reserved word Commentary.

CommentaryEnabled

Returns True for every bar if the Expert Commentary pointer has been applied to the chart. False is returned if the pointer has not been applied.

EXAMPLE

`CommentaryEnabled` will return True if the Expert Commentary Tool has been applied to the chart.

ADDITIONAL EXAMPLE

If you wanted code to be evaluated only when the user had applied the Expert Commentary Tool to the chart, you could use the following syntax:

```
If CommentaryEnabled Then
    Begin
        {Your Code Here}
    End;
```

Commission

Returns the commission setting in the applied strategy's Costs tab.

REMARKS

This reserved word can be used only in the evaluation of strategies.

EXAMPLE

Commission returns a value of 17.50 if the commission under the strategy's Costs tab has been set to 17.50.

CommodityNumber

Returns the value represented under Symbol Number in the Symbol Dictionary.

REMARKS

CommodityNumber returns the value specified in the Symbol Dictionary. If there is no value specified, CommodityNumber will return 0.

EXAMPLES

If the Symbol Number field is 149 for the S&P and 44 for the 30-year Treasury Bond:

`SymbolNumber` returns 149 when used on an analysis technique applied to S&P future data.

`SymbolNumber` returns 44 when used on an analysis technique applied to 30-year Treasury Bond data.

ADDITIONAL EXAMPLE

To force an analysis technique to run only on S&P future data, block the entire technique with

```
If SymbolNumber = 149 then begin ...
```

Contract

Reserved word used in conjunction with a numeric value specifying the number of units to trade within a trading strategy.

REMARKS

Contract is normally used in a Buy, Sell, or Exit statement.

EXAMPLES

`Buy 1 contract next bar at market` generates an order to buy one contract at the open of the next bar.

`Sell 1 contract next bar at market` generates an order to sell one contract at the open of the next bar.

ADDITIONAL EXAMPLE

To exit from only one contract when you have multiple long positions, write:

```
ExitLong 1 contract total next bar at market;
```

ContractMonth

Refers to the delivery/expiration month of any option, future, or position leg.

EXAMPLE

```
If ContractMonth of option = 10 then Plot("October Expiration",
"Expiration");
```

Contracts

Reserved word used in conjunction with a numeric value specifying the number of units to trade within a trading strategy.

REMARKS

`Contract(s)` is normally used in a Buy, Sell, or Exit statement.

EXAMPLES

`Buy 5 contracts next bar at market` generates an order to buy five contracts at the open of the next bar.

`Sell 3 contracts next bar at market` generates an order to sell three contracts at the open of the next bar.

ADDITIONAL EXAMPLE

To exit from only one contract from multiple long positions, write:

```
ExitLong 1 contract total next bar at market;
```

ContractYear

Refers to the delivery/expiration year of any option, future, or position leg.

EXAMPLE

```
If ContractMonth of option = 10 and ContractYear of option =
99 then Plot("October 99 Expiration", "Expiration");
```

Cosine(Num)

Returns the cosine value of the specified number of degrees in the angle.

(Num) is a numeric expression representing the number of degrees for which you want the cosine value.

REMARKS

The cosine is a trigonometric function that for an acute angle is the ratio between the leg adjacent to the angle when it is considered part of a right triangle and the hypotenuse.

EXAMPLES

`Cosine(45)` returns a value of 0.7071.

`Cosine(72)` returns a value of 0.3090.

Cost

Returns the value of the cost of establishing a leg or position.

EXAMPLE

```
Plot1(Cost of Leg(1), "Cost");
```

Cotangent(Num)

Returns the cotangent value of the specified (Num) of degrees in the angle.

REMARKS

The cotangent is a trigonometric function that is equal to the cosine divided by the sine.

EXAMPLES

`CoTangent(45)` returns a value of 1.0.

`CoTangent(72)` returns a value of 0.3249.

Cross

This word is used to check for the crossover of two values.

REMARKS

`Cross` is always followed by `Above`, `Below`, `Over`, or `Under`.

`Cross` is equivalent to `Crosses`.

EXAMPLES

```
If Plot1 does Cross Above Plot2 Then ...
```

`Cross` is used here to determine whether the value of `Plot1` does cross above the value of `Plot2` on the bar under consideration.

```
If Value1 does Cross Above Value2 Or Value1 does Cross
Below Value2 Then ...
```

`Cross` is used here to determine whether `Value1` does cross above or below `Value2` on the bar under consideration.

Crosses

This word is used to check for the crossover of two values.

REMARKS

`Crosses` is always followed by `Above`, `Below`, `Over`, or `Under`.

`Crosses` is equivalent to `Cross`.

EXAMPLES

```
If Plot1 Crosses Above Plot2 Then ...
```

`Crosses` is used here to determine whether the value of `Plot1` crosses above the value of `Plot2` on the bar under consideration.

```
If Value1 Crosses Above Value2 Or Value1 Crosses Below
Value2 Then ...
```

`Crosses` is used here to determine whether `Value1` crosses above or below `Value2` on the bar under consideration.

Current

Reserved for future use.

Current_Ratio

Returns the current ratio of a stock.

REMARKS

`Current_Ratio` is calculated by dividing Total Current Assets by Total Current Liabilities.

`Current_Ratio` is not available for companies that do not distinguish between current and long-term assets and liabilities.

CurrentBar

Returns the number of the bar currently being evaluated.

Each bar on a chart (after the number of bars specified by the Maximum number of bars referenced by a study, known as MaxBarsBack) is assigned a number, which is incremented by 1 with each successive bar. For example, if your `MaxBarsBack` is set to 10, the 11th bar is `CurrentBar` number 1, the 12th bar is `CurrentBar` number 2, and so on.

REMARKS

`CurrentBar` can be used to return only the number of the current bar; for example, you cannot use:

```
CurrentBar [n]
```

to obtain the bar number of the bar n bars ago. However, you can obtain the number of the bar n bars ago (e.g., 5) by using:

```
CurrentBar - 5
```

Also, the `CurrentBar` reserved word is the same as the user function `BarNumber`. The only difference is that you can use the BarNumber function to reference past bars:

```
BarNumber [5]
```

EXAMPLES

You can use `CurrentBar` to determine how long ago a particular condition occurred:

```
IF Condition1 then
            Value1 = CurrentBar;
IF CurrentBar > Value1 then
            Value2 = CurrentBar — Value1;
```

Value2 would hold the number of bars ago Condition1 occurred.

CurrentContracts

Returns the number of contracts in the current position.

REMARKS

This function can be used only in the evaluation of strategies.

Positive values represent long positions, and negative values represent short positions.

EXAMPLE

`CurrentContracts` returns a value of 1 if the strategy is currently long 1 contract.

CurrentDate

Returns the current date in the format YYMMDD or YYYMMDD.

EXAMPLES

`CurrentDate` returns a value of 991016 on October 16, 1999.

`CurrentDate` returns a value of 1011220 on December 20, 2001.

CurrentEntries

Returns the number of entries currently open.

REMARKS

This function can be used only in the evaluation of strategies.

EXAMPLE

`CurrentEntries` returns a value of 3 if the strategy has made three entries in the current open position.

CurrentTime

Returns the current time in the format HHMM using military representation of hours. (0000 to 2359)

EXAMPLES

`CurrentTime` returns a value of 1718 at 5:18 pm.

`CurrentTime` returns a value of 0930 at 9:30 am.

Cusip

Returns a numeric expression representing the CUSIP number for stocks.

```
Value1 = CUSIP;
```

You must assign the reserved word to a numeric variable in order to obtain the CUSIP number.

NOTE: This word can be referenced only when writing analysis techniques for RadarScreen and OptionStation. This word is not available for use with EasyLanguage for use with charting applications such as TradeStation or SuperCharts.

Cyan

Sets the plot color or background color to Cyan.

REMARKS

There are 16 colors available in EasyLanguage. For more information, see Appendix A for color values.

EXAMPLES

`Plot1(Value1, ''Test'', Cyan)` plots Value1 with the name Test and sets the color of Plot1 to Cyan.

`TL_SetColor(1, Cyan)` sets the color of a TrendLine with a reference number of 1 to Cyan.

D

D

Shortcut notation that returns the Date of the bar.

REMARKS

Anytime the Date of a bar is needed, the letter D can be used in an equivalent fashion.

`D` returns the date in YYMMDD format.

EXAMPLES

`D` returns 990107 if the Date of the bar is January 7, 1999.

`D` returns 990412 if the Date of the bar is April 12, 1999.

ADDITIONAL EXAMPLE

To check the Time of the previous bar, write:

`D of 1 bar ago`

DailyLimit

Returns the value represented under `DailyLimit` in the Symbol Dictionary.

REMARKS

`DailyLimit` represents the largest number of increments of the Price Scale that the price of a security can move before the exchange closes the session.

DarkBlue

Sets the plot color or background color to Dark Blue.

REMARKS

There are 16 colors available in EasyLanguage. For more information, see color values in Appendix A.

EXAMPLES

`Plot1(Value1, ''Test'', Dark Blue)` plots Value1 with the name Test and sets the color of Plot1 to Dark Blue.

`TL_SetColor(1, Dark Blue)` sets the color of a TrendLine with a reference number of 1 to Dark Blue.

DarkBrown

Sets the plot color or background color to Dark Brown.

REMARKS

There are 16 colors available in EasyLanguage. For more information, see color values in Appendix A.

EXAMPLES

`Plot1(Value1, ''Test'', Dark Brown)` plots Value1 with the name Test and sets the color of Plot1 to Dark Brown.

`TL_SetColor(1, Dark Brown)` sets the color of a TrendLine with a reference number of 1 to Dark Brown.

DarkCyan

Sets the plot color or background color to Dark Cyan.

REMARKS

There are 16 colors available in EasyLanguage. For more information, see color values in Appendix A.

EXAMPLES

`Plot1(Value1, ''Test'', Dark Cyan)` plots Value1 with the name Test and sets the color of Plot1 to Dark Cyan.

`TL_SetColor(1, Dark Cyan)` sets the color of a TrendLine with a reference number of 1 to Dark Cyan.

DarkGray

Sets the plot color or background color to Dark Gray.

REMARKS

There are 16 colors available in EasyLanguage. For more information, see color values in Appendix A.

EXAMPLES

`Plot1(Value1, ''Test'', Dark Gray)` plots Value1 with the name Test and sets the color of Plot1 to Dark Gray.

`TL_SetColor(1, Dark Gray)` sets the color of a TrendLine with a reference number of 1 to Dark Gray.

DarkGreen

Sets the plot color or background color to Dark Green.

REMARKS

There are 16 colors available in EasyLanguage. For more information, see color values in Appendix A.

EXAMPLES

`Plot1(Value1, ''Test'', Dark Green)` plots Value1 with the name Test and sets the color of Plot1 to Dark Green.

`TL_SetColor(1, Dark Green)` sets the color of a TrendLine with a reference number of 1 to Dark Green.

DarkMagenta

Sets the plot color or background color to Dark Magenta.

REMARKS

There are 16 colors available in EasyLanguage. For more information, see color values in Appendix A.

EXAMPLES

`Plot1(Value1, ''Test'', Dark Magenta)` plots Value1 with the name Test and sets the color of Plot1 to Dark Magenta.

`TL_SetColor(1, Dark Magenta)` sets the color of a TrendLine with a reference number of 1 to Dark Magenta.

DarkRed

Sets the plot color or background color to Dark Red.

REMARKS

There are 16 colors available in EasyLanguage. For more information, see color values in Appendix A.

EXAMPLES

`Plot1(Value1, ''Test'', Dark Red)` plots Value1 with the name Test and sets the color of Plot1 to Dark Red.

TL_SetColor(1, Dark Red) sets the color of a TrendLine with a reference number of 1 to Dark Red.

Data

Reserved word used to specify a data stream within a multidata chart.

REMARKS

`Data` is normally used with a number between 1 and 50 that allows the specification of which data set is being referred to in terms of price values and functions calculations.

EXAMPLES

`Close of Data3` returns the Close price of Data stream 3.

`Low of Data10` returns the Low price of Data stream 10.

DataCompression

Returns a number indicating the compression setting of the price data an analysis technique is applied to.

REMARKS

The number returned is based on the data compression of the price data. `DataCompression` will return:

0 = TickBar
1 = Intraday
2 = Daily
3 = Weekly
4 = Monthly
5 = Point & Figure

EXAMPLES

`DataCompression` returns 0 when applied to price data based on tick compression.

`DataCompression` returns 2 when applied to price data based on daily compression.

ADDITIONAL EXAMPLE

To ensure that a statement is executed only on a daily chart, we can write:

```
If DataCompression = 2 then ExitLong next bar at market;
```

DataInUnion

Reserved for future use.

Date

Reserved word used to return the Date of the current bar.

REMARKS

`Date` returns a numeric value in YYMMDD format.

EXAMPLES

`Date` returns 990107 if the day is January 7, 1999.

`Date` returns 990412 if the day is April, 12, 1999.

ADDITIONAL EXAMPLE

`Date` can be used to restrict strategies to certain trading days.

```
If Date < 990101 then buy this bar on close;
```

Limits a buy order to take place only on dates before 1999.

DateToJulian(cDate)

Returns the Julian date for the specified calendar date.

`(cDate)` is a numeric expression representing the six- or seven-digit calendar date in the format YYMMDD or YYYMMDD respectively (1999 = 99, 2001 = 101).

REMARKS

If a specific date is entered for the numeric expression, it must be a valid date between January 1, 1901 and February 28, 2150, expressed in YYMMDD or YYYMMDD format.

EXAMPLES

`DateToJulian(980804)` returns a value of 36011 for the date August 4, 1998.

`DateToJulian(991024)` returns a value of 36457 for the date October 24, 1999.

Day

Reserved word used to represent a bar of data.

REMARKS

When your data compression is set to daily, the reserved words Bar and Day are the same.

EXAMPLES

`Close of 1 day Ago` returns the Close price of the previous bar.

`BuyToClose this day on close` orders a trading strategy to exit all long positions on the close of the current bar.

ADDITIONAL EXAMPLE

`Buy (''Signal Name'') next day at open` will buy during the formation of the next bar if a price meets the open price of the bar.

DayOfMonth(cDate)

`(cDate)` is a numeric expression representing the six- or seven-digit calendar date in the format YYMMDD or YYYMMDD respectively (1999 = 99, 2001 = 101).

EXAMPLES

`DayOfMonth(980804)` returns a value of 4 for the date August 4, 1998.

`DayOfMonth(1011024)` returns a value of 24 for the date October 24, 2001.

DayOfWeek

Returns the day of week for the specified calendar date. (0 = Sun, 6 = Sat).

`(cDate)` is a numeric expression representing the six- or seven-digit calendar date in the format YYMMDD or YYYMMDD respectively. (1999 = 99, 2001 = 101)

EXAMPLES

`DayOfWeek(980804)` returns a value of 2 because August 4, 1998 is a Tuesday.

`DayOfWeek(1011024)` returns a value of 3 because October 24, 2001 is a Wednesday.

Days

Reserved word used for backward compatibility.

REMARKS

Days has been replaced with the reserved word Bar.

EXAMPLES

`Close of 5 Days Ago` returns the Close price of the bar five bars previous to the current bar.

`ExitShort this day on close` closes a position at the close of the bar.

ADDITIONAL EXAMPLE

`Buy (''Signal Name'') next bar at open` will buy when the formation of the current bar is complete, based on the type of compression of the bar.

Default

This word is used in plot statements to set one of its styles (e.g., color) to the default value.

EXAMPLE

```
Plot1(Value1, ''Plot1'', Default, Default, 5);
```

`Default` is used here to designate the items as the user set default values.

DefineCustField

This word has been reserved for future use.

DEFINEDLLFUNC

Reserved for use with custom DLLs designed for EasyLanguage. Refer to the documentation in the TradeStation Developer's Kit for more information about this and the EasyLanguage Tool Kit Library ELKIT32.DLL.

DeliveryMonth

Reserved word used for contracts that expire which returns the month of expiration.

REMARKS

The value returned represents any of the 12 calendar months according to this table:

1	January
2	February
3	March
4	April
5	May
6	June
7	July
8	August
9	September
10	October
11	November
12	December

EXAMPLES

`DeliveryMonth` will return 6 if the technique is applied to the S&P June contract.

`DeliveryMonth` will return 12 if the technique is applied to the Treasury Bond December contract.

ADDITIONAL EXAMPLE

You can exit from a trade on the first day of the month prior to expiration using:

```
IF DeliveryMonth = Month(Date) Then
        ExitLong This Bar on Close;
```

DeliveryYear

Reserved word used for contracts that expire which returns the year of expiration.

REMARKS

The value returned by `DeliveryYear` is a four-digit year.

EXAMPLES

`DeliveryYear` will return 1998 if the technique is applied to the S&P June '98 contract.

`DeliveryYear` will return 1999 if the technique is applied to the Treasury Bond March '99 contract.

ADDITIONAL EXAMPLE

You can exit from a trade on the first day of the year prior to expiration using:

```
IF DeliveryYear = Year(Date) Then
        ExitLong This Bar on Close;
```

Delta(Value)

Returns the Delta value of an option, leg, or position. The value of Delta can also be established in a pricing model by using `Delta(Value)`.

REMARKS

Debit positions will return positive numbers and credit positions will return negative numbers.

EXAMPLES

```
If Delta of Option > HighVal Then
      Alert("High Delta");
```

In a pricing model, you can set the value of Delta by using the following syntax:

```
Delta(0);
```

Description

Returns a string containing the description of the symbol if it is available. When any symbol is added to the GlobalServer portfolio, the description is automatically obtained from the Symbol Dictionary. If the symbol has no description, this reserved word will return a blank string ("").

TextString = Description;

You must assign the reserved word to a string variable in order to obtain the description. EasyLanguage does not provide predeclared string variables; you must declare the string variable before you can assign a reserved word to it.

NOTE: This word can be referenced only when writing analysis techniques for RadarScreen and OptionStation. This word is not available for use with EasyLanguage for use with charting applications such as TradeStation or SuperCharts.

Dividend(Num)

Returns the dividend paid any number of periods ago.

REMARKS

`Dividend` does not require an input; it returns the most recently reported dividend amount. However, by using an input, you can obtain the amount for a dividend other than the most recent.

EXAMPLES

`Dividend` returns the last dividend amount paid.

`Dividend(2)` returns the last dividend amount paid two periods ago.

Dividend_Yield

Returns the indicated annual dividend rate.

REMARKS

`Dividend_Yield` is generally calculated by the most recent cash dividend paid or declared multiplied by the dividend payment frequency, plus any regular dividends.

DividendCount

Returns the number of times that dividends have been reported in the time frame considered.

REMARKS

`DividendCount` counts the number of dividends paid during the time frame specified.

DividendDate(Num)

Returns the date on which a stock dividend was paid out.

REMARKS

`DividendDate` does not require an input; it returns the most recently reported dividend date. However, by using an input, you can obtain the date for a dividend other than the most recent.

EXAMPLES

`DividendDate` returns the date of the last reported dividend.

`DividendDate(2)` returns the date of the dividend two periods ago.

DividendTime(Num)

Returns the time at which a stock dividend was paid out.

REMARKS

`DividendTime` does not require an input; it returns the most recently reported dividend time. However, by using an input, you can obtain the time for a dividend other than the most recent.

EXAMPLES

`DividendTime` returns the time of the last reported dividend.

`DividendTime(2)` returns the time of the dividend reported two periods ago.

Does

Skip word.

REMARKS

This word is skipped in EasyLanguage and is not necessary. These skipped words, however, do make it easier to understand the purpose of the code. By default, unnecessary words and sections marked as comments will appear dark green in the EasyLanguage PowerEditor.

EXAMPLE

```
If Plot1 does Cross Over Plot2 Then ...
```

The word "does" is not necessary, and the code functions the same way regardless of its presence.

DOUBLE

Reserved for use with custom DLLs designed for EasyLanguage. Refer to the documentation in the TradeStation Developer's Kit for more information about this and the EasyLanguage Tool Kit Library ELKIT32.DLL.

DownTicks

Returns the number of ticks on a bar whose value is lower than the tick immediately preceding it.

REMARKS

Returns the down volume of a bar when Trade Volume is used for the chart.

EXAMPLES

`DownTicks` returns 5 if there were 5 ticks on a bar whose value was lower than the tick immediately preceding it.

`DownTicks` returns 12 if there were 12 ticks on a bar whose value was lower than the tick immediately preceding it.

ADDITIONAL EXAMPLE

To check if a bar of data appears to reflect a steady downturn, compare `DownTicks` to `UpTicks`:

```
Value1 = DownTicks - Upticks;
```

DownTo

This word is used as a part of a For statement where the execution values will be decreasing to a finishing value.

REMARKS

`Downto` will always be placed between two arithmetic expressions.

EXAMPLES

```
For Value5 = Length Downto 0 Begin
        {Your Code Here}
End;
```

`Downto` is used here to indicate that for each value of Value5 from Length down to zero, the following `Begin... End` loop will be executed.

```
For Value5 = Length Downto 0 Begin
        {Your Code Here}
End;
```

`Downto` is used here to indicate that for each value of Value5 from Length down to zero, the following `Begin... End` loop will be executed.

DWORD

Reserved for use with custom DLLs designed for EasyLanguage. Refer to the documentation in the TradeStation Developer's Kit for more information about this and the EasyLanguage Tool Kit Library ELKIT32.DLL.

E

EasyLanguageVersion

Returns the EasyLanguage version currently installed.

REMARKS

The EasyLanguage version for TradeStation 2000i is 5.1.

EXAMPLE

If you wanted to display an indicator only when the user had EasyLanguage 4.0 or later installed on the machine, you could use the following syntax:

```
If EasyLanguageVersion >= 4.0 Then
      Plot1(Value1, "Indicator");
```

Else

This word is used to execute a series of code based on a condition that has returned a value of False.

REMARKS

`Else` can be used only following an `If ... Then` statement.

EXAMPLES

```
If Condition1 Then
      {Your Code Line1}
      Else
            Begin
            {Your Code Line2}
            End;
```

`Else` is used here to begin the code that will be executed if Condition1 returns a value of False. No semicolon should be used after the single line of code following Then.

```
If Condition1 And Condition2 Then
      Begin
      {Your Code Line1};
      {Your Code Line2, etc.};
End
      Else
            Begin
            {Your Code Line3};
            {Your Code Line4, etc.};
            End;
```

`Else` is used here to begin the code that will be executed if either Condition1 or Condition2 return a value of False. No semicolon should be used after the End preceding the Else statement.

End

This word is used to end a series of code that should be executed on the basis of an If... Then, If... Then... Else, For, or While statement.

REMARKS

Each `Begin` must have a corresponding `End`.

A `Begin... End` statement is necessary only if using more than one line of code after an If... Then, If... Then... Else, For, or While statement.

EXAMPLES

```
If Condition1 Then
      Begin
      {Your Code Line1}
      {Your Code Line2, etc.}
      End;
```

`End` is used here to exclude the execution of code beyond Line1 and Line2 as a part of the If... Then statement.

```
If Condition1 Then
      Begin
      {Your Code Line1}
      {Your Code Line2, etc.}
      End
      Else
            Begin
            {Your Code Line3}
            {Your Code Line4, etc.}
End;
```

`End` is used here twice to limit the execution to the two lines of each section that are intended based on Condition1. No semicolon should be used after the End preceding the Else statement. If... Then... Else is part of a continuous section of code, and only the End that finishes the If... Then... Else statement should be followed by a semicolon.

Entry

Reserved word used to specify the name of a Long or Short entry.

REMARKS

Entry names are not required.

`Entry` is exclusively used in an `Exit` condition to specify the Entry from which to exit.

EXAMPLES

```
ExitLong from entry ("MyTrade") next bar market;
```

generates an order to exit the long position "MyTrade" on the first price of the next bar.

```
BuyToCover from entry ("MyTrade") this bar on close;
```

generates an order to exit the short position "MyTrade" at the close of the current bar.

ADDITIONAL EXAMPLE

```
Sell from entry ("MyTrade") next bar at 75 Stop;
```

generates an order to exit the long position "MyTrade" on the next bar at a price of 75 or lower.

EntryDate(Num)

Returns the entry date for the specified position in the format YYYYMMDD.
`(Num)` is a numeric expression representing the number of positions ago.

REMARKS

This function can be used only in the evaluation of strategies.

EXAMPLES

`EntryDate(2)` would return a value of 981005 if the entry date of two positions ago was October 5, 1998.

EntryPrice(Num)

Returns the entry price for the specified position.
`(Num)` is a numeric expression representing the number of positions ago.

REMARKS

This function can be used only in the evaluation of strategies.

EXAMPLE

`EntryPrice(2)` would return a value of 101.19 as the entry price of two positions ago on a chart of Microsoft stock.

EntryTime(Num)

Returns the entry time for the specified position in military time format HHMM.
`(Num)` is a numeric expression representing the number of positions ago.

REMARKS

This function can be used only in the evaluation of strategies.

EXAMPLE

`EntryTime(2)` might return a value of 1600 as the entry time of two positions ago on a daily chart of Microsoft stock.

EPS(Num)

Returns the reported earnings per share.

REMARKS

EPS does not require an input; it returns the most recently reported earnings per share. However, by using an input `(Num)`, you can obtain the earnings per share other than the most recent.

EXAMPLES

`EPS` returns the last reported earnings per share.

`EPS(2)` returns the earnings per share two periods ago.

EPS_PChng_Y_Ago

Returns the year ago earnings per share percent change value.

EPS_PChng_YTD

Returns the Year to Date Earnings Per Share Percent Change value.

EPSCount

Returns the number of times that earnings per share have been reported in the time frame considered.

REMARKS

EPSCount counts the number of dividends paid during the time frame specified.

EPSDate(Num)

Returns the date on which earnings per share were reported.

REMARKS

`EPSDate` does not require an input; it returns the date on which the current earnings per share were reported. However, by using an input `(Num)`, you can obtain the date of an earnings per share report other than the most recent.

EXAMPLES

`EPSDate` returns the date of the last earnings per share report.

`EPSDate(2)` returns the date of the last earnings per share report two periods ago.

EPSTime(Num)

Returns the time at which the earnings per share were reported.

REMARKS

`EPSTime` does not require an input; it returns the time at which the current earnings per share were reported. However, by using an input (`Num`), you can obtain the time of an earnings per share report other than the most recent.

EXAMPLES

`EPSTime` returns the time of the last earnings per share report.

`EPSTime(2)` returns the time of the last earnings per share report two periods ago.

ExitDate(Num)

Returns the exit date for the specified position.

`(Num)` is a numeric expression representing the number of positions ago.

REMARKS

This function can be used only in the evaluation of strategies, and you can reference up to 10 positions ago.

EXAMPLES

`ExitDate(2)` might return a value of 981022 if the exit date of two positions ago was October 22, 1998.

ExitLong

No longer used to generate an order to close a Long position. `Sell` is used instead.

ExitPrice(Num)

Returns the exit price for the specified position.

`(Num)` is a numeric expression representing the number of positions ago.

REMARKS

This function can be used only in the evaluation of strategies, and you can reference up to 10 positions ago.

EXAMPLE

`ExitPrice(1)` might return a value of 107.750 as the exit price of the last position on a chart of Microsoft stock.

ExitShort

No longer available. Use `BuyToCover` to close short positions.

ExitTime(Num)

Returns the exit time for the specified position in military time format HHMM.

`(Num)` is a numeric expression representing the number of positions ago.

REMARKS

This function can be used only in the evaluation of strategies, and you can reference up to 10 positions ago.

EXAMPLE

`ExitTime(3)` might return a value of 1050 as the exit time of three positions ago on an intraday chart of Microsoft stock.

ExpirationDate

Returns the date of expiration of the asset to which a technique is applied.

REMARKS

`ExpirationDate` returns a four-digit year.

ExpirationMonth

Returns a numeric expression representing the expiration month of the symbol where 1 is January and 12 is December.

NOTE: This word can be referenced only when writing analysis techniques for RadarScreen and OptionStation. This word is not available for use with EasyLanguage for use with charting applications such as TradeStation or SuperCharts.

ExpirationRule

Returns a string containing the description of the expiration rule used for the symbol.

NOTE: This word can be referenced only when writing analysis techniques for RadarScreen and OptionStation. This word is not available for use with EasyLanguage for use with charting applications such as TradeStation or SuperCharts.

ExpirationStyle

Returns a numeric expression representing the expiration style of an option where 0 is American and 1 is European. Debit positions return positive numbers and credit positions return negative numbers.

NOTE: This word can be referenced only when writing analysis techniques for RadarScreen and OptionStation. This word is not available for use with EasyLanguage for use with charting applications such as TradeStation or SuperCharts.

ExpirationYear

Returns a numeric expression representing the four-digit expiration year of the option.

NOTE: This word can be referenced only when writing analysis techniques for RadarScreen and OptionStation. This word is not available for use with EasyLanguage for use with charting applications such as TradeStation or SuperCharts.

Expired

Returns a numeric expression where 0 is the option is expired and 1 is the option is not expired.

NOTE: This word can be referenced only when writing analysis techniques for RadarScreen and OptionStation. This word is not available for use with EasyLanguage for use with charting applications such as TradeStation or SuperCharts.

ExpValue(Num)

Returns the exponential value of the specified (Num).

`(Num)` is a numeric expression to be used in the calculation.

EXAMPLES

`ExpValue(4.5)` returns a value of 90.0171.

`ExpValue(6)` returns a value of 403.4288.

F

False

This word is used as the value for an input or untrue condition.

REMARKS

False can be used only in EasyLanguage as the value for a True/False input.

False is the value returned by an untrue or invalid condtition, such as 1 < 0.

EXAMPLES

```
Input:Test(False);
```

would set the value of an input "Test" to a default value of False.

```
If 50 > 100 Then ...
```

would result in a value of False and the statement following `Then` would not be executed.

File("str_Filename")

Sends information to a specified file from a Print statement.

`(str_Filename)` is a string expression that must be a valid path and file name encompassed in quotes.

REMARKS

The name of the file must be string literal as variables are not permitted as file names.

EXAMPLE

If you wanted to send the date, time, and close information from a chart to a new ASCII file named mydata and located in the data directory by applying an indicator, you could use the following syntax:

```
Print(File("c:\data\mydata.txt"), Date, Time, Close);
```

FileAppend("str_Filename", "str_Text")

Sends information to an existing ASCII file specified by the user and adds the information to the bottom of the file.

where

`str_Filename` is a string expression that is the path and file name for the existing ASCII text file to which you want to append the string of text. The path and file name should be enclosed in quotes.

`str_Text` is the string expression to be appended to the file.

REMARKS

Variables are not permitted as file names.

If the file does not exist, it will be created.

To send numeric expressions to a file, it must first be converted to a string expression using the NumToStr function.

EXAMPLE

To create indicator that would send the date to an ASCII file every time the symbol gapped up 10% on the open, you would write:

```
If Open > High[1] * 1.1 Then
   FileAppend("c:\mydata.txt", "This symbol gapped up on "
+ NumToStr(Date, 0) + NewLine);
```

FileDelete("str_Filename")

Deletes the specified file.

`(str_Filename)` is a string expression that must be a valid path and file name encompassed in quotes.

REMARKS

The name of the file must be string literal as variables are not permitted as file names.

EXAMPLE

If you wanted to delete a file when an analysis technique was initially applied, you could use the following syntax:

```
If BarNumber = 1 Then
FileDelete("c:\mydata.txt");
```

FirstNoticeDate

Returns a numeric expression representing the EasyLanguage date of the first notice of the symbol. The first notice date is defined by the expiration rules.

EXAMPLES

```
If FirstNoticeDate then Alert("First Notice Expiration");
```

NOTE: This word can be referenced only when writing analysis techniques for RadarScreen and OptionStation. This word is not available for use with EasyLanguage for use with charting applications such as TradeStation or SuperCharts.

FirstOption

Returns true/false indicating if an option is the first option initiating an option core calculation event. `FirstOption` is used in conjunction with a global variable to increase the efficiency of OptionStation core calculations.

NOTE: GVvalue0 - 99 are global variables used in Volatility Models, GPvalue0 - 99 are global variables used in Pricing Models, and GBvalue0 - 99 are global variables used in Bid/Ask models.

EXAMPLE

```
If FirstOption then begin
GVvalue1 = .40;
ModelVolatilty(GVValue1);
```

FLOAT

Reserved for use with custom DLLs designed for EasyLanguage. Refer to the documentation in the TradeStation Developer's Kit for more information about this and the EasyLanguage Tool Kit Library ELKIT32.DLL.

Floor(Num)

Returns the highest integer less than the specified (Num).

`(Num)` is a numeric expression to be used in the calculation.

EXAMPLES

`Floor(4.5)` returns a value of 4.

`Floor(-1.72)` returns a value of –2.

For

`For` loops are used to conduct a repeated line or lines of code for a specified number of intervals.

REMARKS

`For` will always be followed by a variable name, the range to be repeated, and finally a `Begin ... End` section containing the code to be executed based on the For expression.

EXAMPLES

```
For Value5 = Length To Length + 10 Begin
       {Your Code Here}
End;
```

`For` is used here to initiate a loop that will be executed for each value of `Value5` from `Length` to `Length` plus 10.

```
Variables: Sum(0), Counter(0);
Sum = 0;
For Counter = 0 To Length - 1 Begin
       Sum = Sum + Price[Counter];
End;
```

`For` is used here to initiate the accumulation of the variable `Sum` for each value of `Counter` from 0 to `Length` minus 1.

FracPortion(Num)

Returns the fractional portion of the specified (Num).

`(Num)` is a numeric expression to be used in the calculation.

EXAMPLES

`FracPortion(4.5)` returns a value of 0.5.

`FracPortion(-1.72)` returns a value of –0.72.

FreeCshFlwPerShare

Returns the free cash flow per share value.

REMARKS

`FreeCshFlwPerShare` is calculated by `Cash From Operations - Capital Expenditures –Dividends Paid.`

Friday

Returns the number 5 as the value for Friday.

REMARKS

The value returned is an integer representing Friday and is the same value returned by using the function `DayOfWeek(Friday)`.

EXAMPLE

`Friday` returns a value of 5 as the value for Friday.

From

Reserved word used in an Exit statement to specify the name of a Long or Short entry.

REMARKS

Entry names are not required.

`From` is exclusively used in an Exit condition along with "entry" to specify the Entry to exit from.

EXAMPLES

```
ExitLong from entry ("MyTrade") next bar market;
```

generates an order to exit the long position "MyTrade" on the first price of the next bar.

```
Exitshort from entry ("MyTrade") this bar on close;
```

generates an order to exit the short position "MyTrade" at the close of the current bar.

ADDITIONAL EXAMPLE

```
ExitLong from entry ("MyTrade") next bar at 75 Stop;
```

generates an order to exit the long position "MyTrade" on the next bar at a price of 75 or lower.

Future

Used to reference the current futures contract in a Position Analysis window.

REMARKS

The current contract can be referenced only for data from the Global Server.

EXAMPLES

```
If High of Future > 1000 then
Alert("High is greater than 1000");
```

FutureType

Evaluates a position leg to determine if it is a future.

EXAMPLE

```
If LegType of Leg(1) = FutureType Then {Your Operation Here}
```

G

G_Rate_EPS_Y

Returns the number of years over which the earnings per share growth rate is calculated.

G_Rate_Nt_In_NY

Returns the number of years over which the net income growth rate is calculated.

G_Rate_P_Net_Inc

Returns the net income growth rate percentage for a stock.

Gamma

Returns the Gamma value of an option, leg, or position. The value of Gamma can also be established in a pricing model by using `Gamma(Value)`.

REMARKS

Debit positions will return positive numbers and credit positions will return negative numbers.

EXAMPLES

```
If Gamma of Option > LowVal Then
      Alert("Low Gamma");
```

In a pricing model, you can set the value of Gamma by using the following syntax:

```
Gamma(0);
```

GetAppInfo(InfoName);

Returns a numeric value based on the keyword used (see below).

aiApplicationType

Identifies the calling application:

- cUnknown = 0
- cChart = 1
- cRadarScreen = 2
- cOptionStation = 3
- cScanner = 4

aiBarSpacing

- Identifies the number of spaces displayed between bars on a chart.
- Returns a positive nonzero value when called from a chart; otherwise returns 0.

aiHighestDispValue

- Identifies highest possible value of the underlying data visible on the screen for which the analysis technique is plotted. Note that this value is useful only if the chart is visible in the active workspace and the value is updated only when a new trade or bar close occurs.
- Returns the highest displayed value when called from a chart; otherwise returns 0.

aiLeftDispDateTime

- Identifies date and time of the first (leftmost) bar displayed on the chart.
- Returns a DateTime(double) value when called from a chart; otherwise returns 0.

aiLowestDispValue

- Identifies lowest possible value of the underlying data visible on the screen for which the analysis technique is plotted. Note that this value is useful only if the chart is visible in the active workspace and the value is only updated when a new trade or bar close occurs.
- Returns the lowest displayed value when called from a chart; otherwise returns 0.

aiMacroEnabled

- Identifies whether the calling application can execute a macro.
- Returns 1 if macros are enabled; otherwise returns 0. Note that if the EasyLanguage code contains no macros, 0 will be returned.

aiMacroConf

- Identifies whether the calling application will display the macro confirmation dialog.
- Returns 1 if macro confirmation is enabled; otherwise returns 0.

aiOptionStationPane
Identifies the OptionStation pane where the analysis technique is called from.

- osInvalidAppType = 0
- osAssetPane= 1
- osOptionPane = 2
- osPositionPane = 3

aiPLofAcctCurrency

- Identifies the state of the strategy properties "Base Currency" setting.
- Returns 1 if the currency setting is Account and 0 if the currency setting is Symbol.

aiRightDispDateTime

- Identifies date and time of the last (rightmost) bar displayed on the chart.
- Returns a `DateTime(double)` value when called from a chart, otherwise returns 0.

aiRow

- Identifies the symbol's row number in RadarScreen.
- Returns a positive nonzero value from a RadarScreen application; else returns 0.

aiSpaceToRight

- Identifies the number of bar spaces inserted to the right of the last bar on a chart.
- Returns a nonzero value when called from a chart; else returns 0.

aiPercentChange

- Identifies whether the chart is displayed as a percent change chart.
- Returns 1 if the chart is displayed using percent change; else returns 0. If not called from a chart, this will return 0.

aiOptimizing

- Identifies whether the calling application is currently performing an optimization.
- Returns 1 if the calling application is currently performing an optimization; otherwise returns 0. This will return 0 when called from RadarScreen or OptionStation since currently these applications do not allow strategy testing.

aiStrategyAuto

- Identifies whether the calling application is automating a strategy. Intended for use within a strategy.
- Returns 1 if the calling application is currently automating a strategy; otherwise returns 0. Note that this will always return 0 when called from any type of analysis technique.

aiStrategyAutoConf

- Identifies whether the calling application is automating a strategy using order confirmation. Intended for use within a strategy.
- Returns 0 if the calling application is currently automating a strategy with order confirmation turned off; otherwise returns 1 (even if no strategy is applied). Note that this will always return 0 when called from any type of analysis technique.

aiIntrabarOrder

- Identifies whether the calling application is running a strategy that generates orders intrabar.
- Returns 1 if the calling application is currently running a strategy that generates orders intrabar, otherwise returns 0. This will return 0 when called from RadarScreen or OptionStation since currently these applications do not allow strategy testing.

aiAppId

- A unique number used to identify the calling application.
- Returns a nonzero integer.

aiRealTimeCalc

- Identifies whether the calling application is calculating as a result of a real-time trades.
- Returns 1 if the calculation results from a real-time trade; otherwise 0 is returned.

REMARKS
The value returned by `GetAppInfo` depends on the keyword specified. `GetAppInfo` can be called multiple times to return different application values.
EXAMPLES
The following EasyLanguage instructions are used to check for RadarScreen as the calling application and then return the row of the calling symbol.

```
Value1 = GetAppInfo(aiApplicationType);      // returns a value
       that identifies the calling window type
if Value1 = 2 then Value2 = GetAppInfo(aiRow); // returns a
positive row value from RadarScreen
```

GetBackgroundColor

Returns the numeric color value for the background color of the chart.
REMARKS
The value returned is a number from 1 to 16 for the 16 possible colors.
EXAMPLE
If you wanted to set a variable, Value1, to the color of the background, you could use the following syntax:

```
Value1 = GetBackgroundColor;
```

GetBotBound

Returns the bottom boundary of a ProbabilityMap array.

EXAMPLE

If you wanted to set the variable, Value1, equal to the bottom boundary of the ProbabilityMap array, you could use the following syntax:

```
Value1 = GetBotBound;
```

GetCDRomDrive

Returns a string expression of the drive letter for the first CD ROM drive detected.

REMARKS

The value returned for a CD ROM drive of D would be "D".

EXAMPLE

The following sets the variable Drive equal to the first CD ROM drive detected.

```
Vars: Drive("D");
Drive = GetCDRomDrive;
```

GetExchangeName

Returns the name of the exchange of the symbol to which the technique is applied.

EXAMPLES

`GetExchangeName` returns NYSE for IBM trading on the New York Stock Exchange.

`GetExchangeName` returns CME for SP trading on the Chicago Mercantile Exchange.

GetPlotBGColor(PlotNum)

Returns the numeric background color of the cell to which a specified analysis technique is applied.

- `(PlotNum)` is a numeric expression representing a plot number.

REMARKS

`GetPlotBGColor` is only valid for indicators applied to grids.

The value returned is an integer that represents the EasyLanguage RGB (16 million) color value from 0 to 16777215.

If `LegacyColorValue=True` then the value returned will be the nearest legacy color from 1 to 16. See `LegacyColorValue` for details.

EXAMPLE

If you wanted to set a variable, Value1, to the color of the Plot1 background, you could use the following syntax:

```
Value1 = GetPlotBGColor(1);
```

GetPlotColor(PlotNum)

Returns the numeric color value of a plot line in a chart or foreground color in a grid.

- (PlotNum) is a numeric expression representing a plot number.

REMARKS

The value returned is an integer that represents the EasyLanguage RGB (16 million) color value from 0 to 16777215.

If `LegacyColorValue=True` then the value returned will be the nearest legacy color from 1 to 16. See LegacyColorValue for details.

EXAMPLE

If you wanted to set a variable, Value1, to the color of the Plot1 foreground, you could use the following syntax:

```
Value1 = GetPlotColor(1);
```

GetPlotWidth(Plot)

Returns the numeric width value of a plot line in a chart.

- (Plot) is a numeric expression representing a plot number.

REMARKS

The value returned is a number representing the assigned width of the specified plot line.

EXAMPLES

If you wanted to set a variable, Value1, to the width of the Plot1 line on a chart, you could use the following syntax:

```
Value1 = GetPlotWidth(1);
```

GetPredictionValue(Column, Price)

Returns the number of columns in a ProbabilityMap array.

`(Column)` is a numeric expression representing the desired column number from which to retrieve the prediction value.

`(Price)` is a numeric expression representing the desired price level from which to retrieve the prediction value.

REMARKS

It may be necessary to use the `GetNumColumns`, `GetBotBound`, and `GetTopBound` reserved words in order to verify that the requested prediction value is a possibility within the array.

EXAMPLES

If you wanted to send the prediction value of the cell in column 5 and price 95.250 in the ProbabilityMap array to the Message Log, you could use the following syntax:

```
Print(GetPredictionValue(5, 99.250)," Predicted value");
```

GetRowIncrement

Returns the row increment value in a ProbabilityMap array.

EXAMPLE

If you wanted to set the variable, Value1, equal to the row increment value in the ProbabilityMap array, you could use the following syntax:

```
Value1 = GetRowIncrement;
```

GetStrategyName

Returns the strategy name as a string value.

REMARKS

This reserved word can be used only in the evaluation of strategies.

EXAMPLE

`GetStrategyName` returns a value of "Moving XAvg Cross" when the Moving XAvg Cross strategy is applied.

GetSymbolName

Returns the `Name` of the symbol to which the technique is applied.

REMARKS

Return value is a string.

Returns the root, year, and contract month for futures symbols.

EXAMPLES

`GetSymbolName` returns IBM for International Business Machines trading on the New York Stock Exchange

GetSystemName

Reserved for backward compatibility. See `GetStrategyName`. Returns the strategy name as a string value.

REMARKS

This reserved word can be used only in the evaluation of strategies.

EXAMPLE

`GetSystemName` returns a value of "Moving XAvg Cross" when the Moving XAvg Cross strategy is applied.

GetTopBound

Returns the top boundry of a ProbabilityMap array.

EXAMPLE

If you wanted to set the variable, Value1, equal to the top boundary of the ProbabilityMap array, you could use the following syntax:

```
Value1 = GetTopBound;
```

Gr_Rate_P_EPS

Returns the earnings per share growth rate for a stock.

Green

Sets the plot color or background color to green.

REMARKS

There are 16 colors available in EasyLanguage. For more information, see color values in Appendix A.

EXAMPLES

`Plot1(Value1, ''Test'', Green)` plots `Value1` with the name `Test` and sets the color of Plot1 to `Green`.

`TL_SetColor(1, Green)` sets the color of a TrendLine with a reference number of 1 to Green.

GrossLoss

Returns the total dollar amount of all closed losing trades.

REMARKS

`GrossLoss` does not include the current open position or the value of winning trades.

EXAMPLES

`GrossLoss` returns −1000 if there are three losing trades of –500, −200, and −300.

`GrossLoss` returns 0 if there are no closed losing trades, even if the current position is losing.

GrossProfit

Returns the total dollar amount of all closed winning trades.

REMARKS

`GrossProfit` does not include the current open position or the value of losing trades.

EXAMPLES

`GrossProfit` returns 1000 if there are three winning trades of 500, 200, and 300.

`GrossProfit` returns 0 if there are no closed winning trades, even if the current position is winning.

H

H

Reserved word used to return the high price of the specified time increment or group of ticks.

REMARKS

Any time the high of a bar is needed, the letter H can be used as an equivalent.

EXAMPLES

`High of 1 bar ago` returns the high price of the previous bar.

`Average(High, 10)` returns the Average of the last 10 high prices.

ADDITIONAL EXAMPLE

To check that the last two bars have high prices higher than the previous bar, write:

```
If High > High[1] and High[1] > High[2] then
Plot1(High,"Rising");
```

High

Reserved word used to return the high price of the specified time increment or group of ticks.

REMARKS

The letter H can be used as an equivalent to high.

EXAMPLES

`High of 1 bar ago` returns the high price of the previous bar.

`Average(High, 10)` returns the average of the last 10 high prices.

ADDITIONAL EXAMPLE

To check that the last two bars have high prices higher than the previous bar, write:

```
If High > High[1] and High[1] > High[2] then
Plot1(High,"Rising");
```

Higher

Synonym for stop or limit orders depending on the context used within a strategy.

`Higher` means `stop` when used in the following context:

```
Buy next bar at MyEntryPrice or Higher;
ExitShort next bar at MyExitPrice or Higher;
```

`Higher` means `limit` when used in the following context:

```
Sell next bar at MyEntryPrice or higher;
ExitLong next bar at MyEntryPrice or higher;
```

EXAMPLE

```
Buy next bar at Average(High,8) or higher;
```

HistFundExists

Returns True if historical fundamental information (EPS, dividends, and stock splits) exists, False if not.

HistorySettings

Returns a string with the description of the available history settings for a symbol.

NOTE: This word can be referenced only when writing analysis techniques for RadarScreen and OptionStation. This word is not available for use with EasyLanguage for use with charting applications such as TradeStation or SuperCharts.

I

I

Shortcut notation that returns the open interest of a bar.

REMARKS

Anytime the open interest of a bar is needed, the letter I can be used in an equivalent fashion.

EXAMPLES

`I of 1 bar ago` returns the open interest of the previous bar.

`Average(I, 10)` returns the average of the last 10 open interest values.

ADDITIONAL EXAMPLE

To check that the last two bars have open interest values higher than the previous bar, write:

```
If I > I[1] and I[1] > I[2] then
Plot1(High,"Rising");
```

I_AvgEntryPrice

Returns the average entry price of each open entry in a pyramided position.

REMARKS

`I_AvgEntryPrice` only returns the average entry price for open trades.

`I_AvgEntryPrice` can be used only in a study.

`I_AvgEntryPrice` will return a value only if a strategy is applied to the same data.

EXAMPLES

`I_AvgEntryPrice` returns 150 if three trades are currently open and were entered at a price of 130, 145, and 175.

`I_AvgEntryPrice` returns 50 if four trades are currently open and were entered at a price of 42, 53, 37, and 68.

I_ClosedEquity

Returns the profit or loss realized when a position has been closed.

REMARKS

- `I_ClosedEquity` returns the profit or loss only for closed trades.
- `I_ClosedEquity` can be used only in a study.
- `I_ClosedEquity` will return a value only if a strategy is applied to the same data.

I_CurrentContracts

Returns the number of contracts held in all open positions.

REMARKS

- `I_CurrentContracts` can be used only in a study.
- `I_CurrentContracts` will return a value only if a strategy is applied to the same data.

EXAMPLES

`I_CurrentContracts` returns 3 if there are three open positions of one contract each.

`I_CurrentContracts` returns 10 if there are three open positions of 3, 4, and 3 contracts respectively.

I_MarketPosition

Returns the current market position.

REMARKS

`I_MarketPosition` returns the following numbers:

1	For a long position
−1	For a short position
0	For a flat position

`I_MarketPosition` can be used only in a study.

`I_MarketPosition` will return a value only if a strategy is applied to the same data.

EXAMPLES

`I_MarketPosition` returns 1 if the current position is a long position.

`I_MarketPosition` returns −1 if the current position is a short position.

I_OpenEquity

Returns the current gain or loss while a position is open.

REMARKS

- `I_OpenEquity` returns the profit or loss only for open positions.
- `I_OpenEquity` can be used only in a study.
- `I_OpenEquity` will return a value only if a strategy is applied to the same data.

If

This word is used to introduce a condition that will be evaluated to determine execution of additional code.

REMARKS

`If` can be used only to begin an `If... Then or If... Then... Else` statement.

In order to use an `If... Then... Else` statement, a `Begin... End` statement must follow `Then` as in the second example below.

EXAMPLES

```
If Condition1 Then
      {Your Code Line1}
```

`If` is used here to start the `If... Then` statement. The Line1 code will be executed if `Condition1` returns a value of True. If `Condition1` is false, the Line1 code will not be executed.

```
If Condition1 And Condition2 Then
      Begin
      {Your Code Line1}
      {Your Code Line2, etc.}
      End
      Else
            Begin
            {Your Code Line3}
            {Your Code Line4, etc.}
            End;
```

`If` is used here to start the `If... Then... Else` statement. The Line1 and Line2 code will be executed if `Condition1` and `Condition2` return a value of True. If `Condition1` or `Condition2` is false, the Line3 and Line4 code will be executed.

IncludeSignal: "SignalName", InputNames, ...

Included for backward compatibility.

This word is used to include a trading signal in another trading signal.

Multiple input names should be separated by commas. The EasyLanguage PowerEditor evaluates the EasyLanguage in the trading signal from the top of the file to the bottom of the file. When the IncludeSignal Reserved Word is reached, the EasyLanguage PowerEditor evaluates the EasyLanguage in the referenced signal from top-to-bottom, then returns to the original signal and continues its top-to-bottom evaluation.

You can include as many signals as you want, although we recommend you create separate signals and mix and match them together in strategies using TradeStation StrategyBuilder. This is a more efficient way of grouping signals together and achieves the same purpose.

REMARKS

The use of signals in TradeStation 2000i eliminates the need for the IncludeSystem statement.

EXAMPLE

```
IncludeSignal:"Consecutive Closes", LEconsec, SEconsec,
```

IncludeSystem

This word is retained for backward compatibility. TradeStation 2000i does not have the 64K limit of its predecessor, and it has adopted modular strategy design where a strategy is made up of one or more trading signals. Therefore, when you create a trading strategy, you no longer use the word `IncludeSystem`.

REMARKS

You can include a signal within another signal using the reserved word `IncludeSignal`.

InitialMargin

Returns the intial margin requirement of a position.

EXAMPLE

```
If InitialMargin of Position > 500 Then {Your Operation Here}
```

Input

Reserved word used to declare an Input name used to represent user-defined values anywhere in a technique.

REMARKS

- An input name can contain up to 20 alphanumeric characters plus the period (.) and the underscore (_).
- An input name cannot start with a number or a period (.).
- Inputs are constants that cannot start a statement.

The default value of an input is declared by a number in parentheses after the input name.

EXAMPLES

`Input: Length (10);` declares the constant Length initializes the value to ten.

`Input: Price(Close);` declares the constant Price initializes the value to the Close of a bar.

Inputs

Reserved word used to declare multiple Input name, used to represent user-defined values anywhere in a technique.

REMARKS

- An input name can contain up to 20 alphanumeric characters plus the period (.) and the underscore (_).
- An input name cannot start with a number or a period (.).
- Inputs are constants that cannot start a statement.
- The default value of an input is declared by a number in parentheses after the input name.

EXAMPLES

```
Input: Price(Close), Length(10);
```

declares the constants Price and Length, initializing the values to the Close of the bar and 10, respectively.

```
Input: SlowMA(9), FastMA(4);
```

declares the constants SlowMA and FastMA, initializing the values to 9 and 4, respectively.

Inst_Percent_Held

Returns the percent of common stock held by all the reporting institutions as a group.

REMARKS

`Inst_Percent_Held` is calculated by dividing total shares held by institutions by total shares outstanding and multiplying the result by 100.

InStr (String1, String2)

Returns the location of String2 within String1.

(`String1`) represents the string that will be evaluated.

(`String2`) represents the string to be located.

REMARKS

Returns the location of `String2` within `String1`, represented as the number of characters from the left side.

If the specified string (`String2`) is found more than once in `String1`, the value returned refers to only the first occurrence.

0 is returned if the specified string (`String2`) does not exist in the evaluated string (`String1`).

EXAMPLES

```
InStr("Net Profit in December", "Profit")
```

returns the value 5, indicating that the string "Profit" begins at position 5 of String1.

```
InStr("Net Profit in December", "January")
```

returns the value 0 since the string "January" does not exist in String1.

INT

Reserved for use with custom DLLs designed for EasyLanguage. Refer to the documentation in the TradeStation Developer's Kit for more information about this and the EasyLanguage Tool Kit Library ELKIT32.DLL.

IntPortion(Num)

Returns the integer portion of the specified number.

(`Num`) is a numeric expression representing the number for which you want the integer portion.

EXAMPLES

`IntPortion(4.5)` returns a value of 4.

`IntPortion(-1.72)` returns a value of –1.

Is

Skip word.

REMARKS

This word is skipped in EasyLanguage and is not necessary. These skipped words, however, do make it easier to understand the purpose of the code. By default, unnecessary words and sections marked as comments will appear dark green in the EasyLanguage PowerEditor.

EXAMPLE

`If an Open is > 100 Then...` The word "is" is not necessary and the code functions the same way regardless of its presence.

J

JulianToDate(jDate)

Returns the calendar date for the specified Julian date.

`(jDate)` is a numeric expression representing the Julian date.

EXAMPLES

`JulianToDate(36011)` returns a value of 980804 for the date August 4, 1998.

`JulianToDate(36457)` returns a value of 991024 for the date October 24, 1999.

L

L

Shortcut notation that returns the low of the bar.

REMARKS

Anytime the Low of a bar is needed, the letter L can be used in an equivalent fashion.

EXAMPLES

`L of 1 bar ago` returns the low price of the previous bar.

`Average(L, 10)` returns the average of the last 10 low prices.

ADDITIONAL EXAMPLE

To check that the last two bars have low prices lower than the previous bar, write:

```
If L < L[1] and L[1] < L[2] then
    Plot1(High,"Falling");
```

LargestLosTrade

Returns the dollar value of the largest closed losing trade.

EXAMPLES

`LargestLosTrade` returns –500 if there are three losing trades of –500, –200 and –300.

`LargestLosTrade` returns 0 if there are no closed losing trades, even if the current position is losing.

LargestWinTrade

Returns the dollar value of the largest closed winning trade.

EXAMPLES

```
Value44 = LargestWinTrade;
    Print(Date:7:0, `` ``, Time:4:0, `` LargestWin= ``, Value44);
```

`LargestWinTrade` returns 500 if there are three winning trades of 500, 200, and 300.

`LargestWinTrade` returns 0 if there are no closed winning trades, even if the current position is winning.

Last_Split_Date

Returns the date on which the last stock split was reported.

Last_Split_Fact

Returns the ratio of the last stock split.

EXAMPLES

`Last_Split_Fact` returns 2 if the last split ratio was 2:1.

`Last_Split_Fact` returns 1.5 if the last split ratio was 3:2.

LastCalcJDate

Returns the Julian date for the last completed bar.

EXAMPLES

`LastCalcJDate` returns a value of 36011 if the last bar was completed on August 4, 1998.

`LastCalcJDate` returns a value of 36173 if the last bar was completed on January 13, 1999.

LastCalcMMTime

Returns the time, in number of minutes since midnight, for the last completed bar.

EXAMPLES

`LastCalcMMTime` returns a value of 540 if the last bar was completed at 9:00 am.

`LastCalcMMTime` returns a value of 835 if the last bar was completed at 1:55 pm.

LastTradingDate

Refers to the last day an option, future, position leg, or asset may be traded.

EXAMPLE

```
If DateToJulian(LastTradingDate) - DateToJulian(Date) < 5
thenAlert(``Less than 5 trading days left'');
```

LeftSide

Used to specify ActivityBar actions on the left side of the bar.

EXAMPLE

`GetCellChar(Close, Leftside, 3)` Leftside is used to specify the left side of the ActivityBar.

LeftStr("Str1", sSize)

Returns a string expression of `(sSize)` characters taken from `(Str1)` beginning with the leftmost character.

`(Str1)` is the string expression to reduce. It must be enclosed in quotation marks.

`(sSize)` is the numeric expression indicating the number of characters that will be retained, counting from the beginning of the string expression.

EXAMPLE

`LeftStr(''Net Profit'', 3)` returns the string expression `''Net''`.

Leg(LegOfPosition)

Returns the requested information for the specified leg.

`(Leg of Position)` is a numeric expression representing a specific position leg.

REMARKS

`Leg (Leg of Position)` references the position leg specified by `(Leg of Position)`. Placing "of Leg(Leg of Position)" after any bar data element (Open, High, Low, Close, Volume, OpenInt, Date, Time, UpTicks, DownTicks, Ticks) or any option-related reserved word (e.g., Strike, ExpirationDate, Delta, Gamma, Theta, etc.) returns the specified value.

EXAMPLES

```
If Volume of Leg(1) > HighVal Then {Your Operation Here}
If Close of Leg(1) = Highest(High of Leg(1),10) Then
      Alert(''Highest High'');
```

LegType

Returns the type of position leg: asset, future, call, or put.

EXAMPLE

```
If LegType of Leg(1) = Call Then
      Plot1(''Call'', ''Leg Type'');
If LegType of Leg(1) = Put Then
      Plot2(''Put'', ''Leg Type'');
```

LightGray

Sets the plot color or background color to Light Gray.

REMARKS

There are 16 colors available in EasyLanguage. For more information, see color values in Appendix A.

EXAMPLES

`Plot1(Value1, ''Test'', Light Gray)` plots Value1 with the name Test and sets the color of Plot1 to Light Gray.

`TL_SetColor(1, Light Gray)` sets the color of a TrendLine with a reference number of 1 to Light Gray.

Limit

Reserved word used in an Entry or Exit statement to specify how to fill an order.

REMARKS

Limit orders can be executed only on the next bar.

Limit can be read as "this price or better," meaning lower for a long entry and short exit, higher for a short entry and long exit.

Limit orders require a reference price.

EXAMPLES

`Buy next bar at 75 Limit;` generates an order to enter a long position on the next bar at a price of 75 or lower.

`Sell next bar at 75 Limit;` generates an order to enter a long position on the next bar at a price of 75 or higher.

ADDITIONAL EXAMPLE

`ExitLong next bar at 75 Limit;` generates an order to enter a long position on the next bar at a price of 75 or higher.

Log(Num)

Returns the logarithm for the specified `(Num)`.

`(Num)` is a numeric expression to be used in the calculation.

REMARKS

A logarithm is the exponent that indicates the power to which a number is raised to produce a given number. This reserved word uses a base e system.

Log can be calculated only for positive numbers.

EXAMPLES

`Log(4.5)` returns a value of 1.5041.

`Log(172)` returns a value of 5.1475.

LONG

Reserved for use with custom DLLs designed for EasyLanguage. Refer to the documentation in the TradeStation Developer's Kit for more information about this and the EasyLanguage Tool Kit Library ELKIT32.DLL.

Low

Represents the low price of the specified time increment or group of ticks.

REMARKS

`L` can be used in place of `Low`.

EXAMPLES

`Low of 1 bar ago` returns the low price of the previous bar.

`Average(Low, 10)` returns the average of the last 10 low prices.

ADDITIONAL EXAMPLE

To check that the last two bars have low prices lower than the previous bar, write:

```
If Low < Low[1] AND Low[1] < Low[2] Then
Plot1(Low, ''Decline'');
```

Lower

Synonym for stop or limit orders depending on context used within a strategy.

`Lower` means limit when used in the following context:

```
Buy next bar at MyEntryPrice or Lower;
ExitShort next bar at MyExitPrice or Lower;
```

`Lower` means stop when used in the following context:

```
Sell next bar at MyEntryPrice or Lower;
ExitLong next bar at MyEntryPrice or Lower;
```

EXAMPLE

```
Buy next bar at the Average(Low,8) or lower;
```

LowerStr

Used to convert a string expression to lowercase letters.

```
LowerStr (''Str1'');
```

`(Str1)` the string expression to change to lowercase letters. Make sure the string expression is enclosed in quotation marks.

EXAMPLE

`LowerStr(''Net Profit'')` returns the string expression “net profit”.

M

Magenta

Sets the plot color or background color to magenta.

REMARKS

There are 16 colors available in EasyLanguage. For more information, see color values in Appendix A.

EXAMPLES

`Plot1(Value1, ''Test'', Magenta)` plots Value1 with the name Test and sets the color of Plot1 to Magenta.

`TL_SetColor(1, Magenta)` sets the color of a TrendLine with a reference number of 1 to Magenta.

MakeNewMovieRef

Creates a new movie chain with the reference number specified.

REMARKS

The reference number should be a whole positive number.

EXAMPLES

`Print(MakeNewMovieRef = 1)` creates a new movie chain with a reference number of 1.

Margin

Returns the margin setting in the applied strategy's Costs tab.

REMARKS

This reserved word can be used only in the evaluation of strategies.

EXAMPLE

`Margin` returns a value of 1500 if the margin under the strategy's Costs tab has been set to 1500.00.

Market

Reserved word used to indicate the next trade or tick, not specific to the price.

REMARKS

`Market` is normally used in trading signals.

EXAMPLE

To enter a trade when the price of entry is not an issue:

```
Buy next bar at market;
```

MarketPosition(Num)

Returns a numeric value for a short or long position for the specified position.

(Num) is a numeric expression representing the number of positions ago.

REMARKS

- −1 is returned for a short position.
- 1 is returned for a long position.
- 0 is returned if the current position is specified, and you are not currently in the market.

This function can be used only in the evaluation of strategies.

EXAMPLE

`MarketPosition(0)` returns a value of 0 if the current position is neutral.

MaxBarsBack

Reserved word used to represent the number of bars of data necessary to calculate the rules in any analysis technique.

REMARKS

The MaxBarsBack setting may prevent values from being displayed when an indicator is first applied. When enough data sets have been acquired to satisfy the MaxBarsBack setting, values will appear.

When analysis techniques are applied to more than one data set at a time (i.e. a multi-data chart), each data set must meet the MaxBarsBack requirement individually before values will be generated.

MaxBarsForward

Represents the number of bars to the right of the last bar on the chart.

REMARKS

MaxBarsForward returns the number of bars used for space to the right.

MaxConsecLosers

Returns the largest number of consecutive closed winning trades.

EXAMPLES

`MaxConsecWinners` returns 5 if the largest number of consecutive closed winning trades is 5.

`MaxConsecWinners` returns 2 if the largest number of consecutive closed winning trades is 2.

MaxConsecWinners

Returns the largest number of consecutive closed losing trades.

EXAMPLES

`MaxConsecLosers` returns 5 if the largest number of consecutive closed losing trades is 5.

`MaxConsecWinners` returns 2 if the largest number of consecutive closed losing trades is 2.

MaxContracts(Num)

Returns the maximum number of contracts held during the specified position.

(Num) is a numeric expression representing the number of positions ago.

REMARKS

This function can be used only in the evaluation of strategies.

EXAMPLE

`MaxEntries(2)` returns a value of 3 if the second most recent position held a maximum of 3 contracts.

MaxContractsHeld

Returns the maximum number of contracts held at any one time.

MaxEntries(Num)

Returns the maximum number of entries of the specified position.

(Num) is a numeric expression representing the number of positions ago.

REMARKS

This function can be used only in the evaluation of strategies.

EXAMPLE

`MaxEntries(2)` returns a value of 3 if the second most recent position had three entry signals.

MaxGain

Returns the maximum gain of the position.

EXAMPLE

```
If MaxGain of Position < HighVal Then {Your Operation Here}
```

MaxIDDrawDown

Returns the largest drop in equity throughout the entire trading period.

REMARKS

`MaxIDDrawDown` returns the true number of dollars needed to sustain the largest equity dip.

EXAMPLES

`MaxIDDrawDown` returns 5000 if the largest equity dip throughout the entire trading period is 5000.

`MaxIDDrawDown` returns 2000 if the largest equity dip throughout the entire trading period is 2000.

MaxList(Num1, Num2, Num3, . . . , NumN)

Returns the highest value of the specified inputs.

(`Num1`) is a numeric expression representing a value to be used in the calculation.

(`Num2`) is a second numeric expression representing a value to be used in the calculation.

(`Num3`) is a third numeric expression representing a value to be used in the calculation, etc.

EXAMPLES

`MaxList(45, 72, 86, 125, 47)` returns a value of 125.

`MaxList(18, 67, 98, 24, 65, 19)` returns a value of 98.

MaxList2(Num1, Num2, Num3, . . . , NumN)

Returns the second highest value of the specified inputs.

(`Num1`) is a numeric expression representing a value to be used in the calculation.

(`Num2`) is a second numeric expression representing a value to be used in the calculation.

(`Num3`) is a third numeric expression representing a value to be used in the calculation, and so on.

EXAMPLES

`MaxList2(45, 72, 86, 125, 47)` returns a value of 86.

`MaxList2(18, 67, 98, 24, 65, 19)` returns a value of 67.

MaxLoss

Returns the maximum loss of the position.

EXAMPLE

```
If MaxLoss of Position > LowVal Then {Your Operation Here}
```

MaxPositionLoss(Num)

Returns the largest loss of the specified position.

`(Num)` is a numeric expression representing the number of positions ago.

REMARKS

This function can be used only in the evaluation of strategies.

EXAMPLE

`MaxPositionLoss(1)` returns a value of –3750.00 if the second most recent position had a maximum loss of 3750.00.

MaxPositionProfit(Num)

Returns the largest gain of the specified position.

`(Num)` is a numeric expression representing the number of positions ago.

REMARKS

This function can be used only in the evaluation of strategies.

EXAMPLE

`MaxPositionProfit(1)` returns a value of 29200.00 if the second most recent position had a maximum profit of 29200.00.

MessageLog(Parameters)

Sends information to the Message Log.

`(Parameters)` may be a single string or numeric expression, or a multiple string or numeric expression, with each expression separated by a comma.

EXAMPLES

To send the date, time, and close information to the Message Log, you would use:

```
MessageLog(Date, Time, Close);
```

MidStr("String", Pos, Siz)

Returns a string expression of `(Siz)` characters taken from `(String)` beginning with the `(Pos)` character measured from the left.

`(String)` is the string expression to reduce. It must be enclosed in quotation marks.

`(Pos)` is the numeric expression indicating how many characters from the beginning of the string expression to remove.

`(Siz)` is the numeric expression indicating the number of characters to be retained. Any additional characters to the right of these are removed.

EXAMPLE

`MidStr("Net Profit in December", 5, 6)` returns the string expression "Profit".

MinList(Num1, Num2, Num3, . . . , NumN)

Returns the lowest value of the specified inputs.

`(Num1)` is a numeric expression representing a value to be used in the calculation.

`(Num2)` is a second numeric expression representing a value to be used in the calculation.

`(Num3)` is a third numeric expression representing a value to be used in the calculation, and so on.

EXAMPLES

`MinList(45, 72, 86, 125, 47)` returns a value of 45.

`MinList(18, 67, 98, 24, 65, 19)` returns a value of 18.

MinList2(Num1, Num2, Num3, . . . , NumN)

Returns the second lowest value of the specified inputs.

`(Num1)` is a numeric expression representing a value to be used in the calculation.

`(Num2)` is a second numeric expression representing a value to be used in the calculation.

`(Num3)` is a third numeric expression representing a value to be used in the calculation, and so on.

EXAMPLES

`MinList2(45, 72, 86, 125, 47)` returns a value of 47.

`MinList2(18, 67, 98, 24, 65, 19)` returns a value of 19.

MinMove

Returns a numeric expression representing the minimum movement allowed for a particular symbol. The minimum movement for a symbol is specified in the GlobalServer settings for each symbol.

NOTE: This word can be referenced only when writing analysis techniques for RadarScreen and OptionStation. This word is not available for use with EasyLanguage for use with charting applications such as TradeStation or SuperCharts.

EXAMPLES

`MinMove * PriceScale` returns the smallest increment between trades.

`MinMove * PriceScale * BigPointValue` returns the dollar value of the smallest change in price.

MIVonAsk

Returns the market implied volatility of an option or position leg based on the ask price defined by a Bid/Ask Model.

EXAMPLE

```
If ModelVolatility of Option > MIVonAsk of Option * 1.2 then
Alert("High Modeled Volatility");
```

MIVonBid

Returns the market implied volatility of an option or position leg based on the bid price defined by a Bid/Ask Model.

EXAMPLE

```
If ModelVolatility of Option > MIVonBid of Option * 1.2 then
Alert("High Modeled Volatility");
```

MIVonClose

Returns the market implied volatility of an option or position leg based on the closing price.

EXAMPLE

```
If ModelVolatility of Option > MIVOnClose of Option * 1.2 then
Alert("High Modeled Volatility");
```

MIVonRawAsk

Returns the market implied volatility of an option or position leg based on the last ask price received from your data feed.

EXAMPLE

```
If ModelVolatility of Option > MIVonRawAsk of Option * 1.2 then
Alert("High Modeled Volatility");
```

MIVonRawBid

Returns the market implied volatility of an option or position leg based on the last bid price received from your data feed.

EXAMPLE

```
If ModelVolatility of Option > MIVonRawBid of Option * 1.2 then
Alert("High Modeled Volatility");
```

Moc

This word has been reserved for future use.

Mod (Num, Divisor)

Returns the remainder for the specified calculation of `(Num)` divided by `(Divisor)`.

`(Num)` is a numeric expression to be used in the calculation.

`(Divisor)` is a numeric expression representing the divisor.

EXAMPLES

`Mod(17, 5)` returns a value of 2.

`Mod(457, 9)` returns a value of 7.

ModelPosition

Used to reference a modeled position in a search strategy.

EXAMPLES

If you wanted to look for a Delta-neutral position, you could use the following syntax:

```
Condition1 = Delta of ModelPosition < .1 And Delta of
ModelPosition > -.1; PositionStatus(Condition1);
```

ModelPrice

Used to reference the underlying price currently used by the Pricing or Volatility Model.

EXAMPLE

If you wanted to calculate the dollar amount of the option being used, you could use the following syntax:

```
Value1 = ModelPrice * BigPointValue of Option;
```

ModelVolatility(Value)

References the volatility calculated by the Volatility Model. The value of `ModelVolatility` can also be established in a Volatility Model by using `ModelVolatility(Value)`.

(`Value`) is a numeric expression representing the volatility, when ModelVolatility is used to set a default value in a Volatility Model.

REMARKS

Debit positions will return positive numbers and credit positions will return negative numbers.

EXAMPLES

```
If ModelVolatility > 75 Then
        Alert("High Modeled Volatility");
```

In a Volatility Model, you can set the value of `ModelVolatility` by using the following syntax:

```
ModelVolatility(30);
```

Monday

Returns the number 1 as the value for Monday.

REMARKS

The value returned is an integer representing `Monday` and is the same value returned by using the function `DayOfWeek(Monday)`.

EXAMPLE

`Monday` returns a value of 1 as the value for Monday.

MoneyMgtStopAmt

This word is retained for backward compatibility.

REMARKS

This word has been replaced by the `Signals Initial $ Risk Stop LX` and `Initial $ Risk Stop SX`.

Month(cDate)

Returns the corresponding month for the specified calendar date (1 = Jan, 12 = Dec).

`(cDate)` is a numeric expression representing the six- or seven-digit calendar date in the format YYMMDD or YYYMMDD respectively (1999 = 99, 2001 = 101).

EXAMPLES

`Month(990613)` returns a value of 6 because 990613 represents June 13, 1999.

`Month(1011220)` returns a value of 12 because 1011220 represents December 20, 2001.

MULTIPLE

Reserved for use with custom DLLs designed for EasyLanguage. Refer to the documentation in the TradeStation Developer's Kit for more information about this and the EasyLanguage Tool Kit Library ELKIT32.DLL.

N

Neg(Num)

Returns the negative value of the number specified.

EXAMPLES

`Neg(17)` returns -17.

`Neg(-9)` returns a value of –9.

Net_Profit_Margin

Returns the net profit margin reported.

REMARKS

`Net_Profit_Margin` is calculated by dividing income after taxes by the total revenue and is expressed as a percentage.

NetProfit

Returns the total dollar amount of all closed trades, both winning and losing.

REMARKS

`NetProfit` can be computed by `GrossProfit – GrossLoss`.

EXAMPLES

`NetProfit` returns 1000 if there are four trades returning –500, 1200, and 300.

`NetProfit` returns 0 if there are no closed trades.

NewLine

Used to start a new line when appending to a file using the `FileAppend` reserved word. Also used to place a carriage return/linefeed command into expert commentary.

REMARKS

Use the + character to add `NewLine` to a string expression.

EXAMPLE

```
FileAppend("c:\mydata.txt", "This symbol gapped up on " +
NumToStr(Date, 0) + NewLine);
```

Next

Reserved word used to reference the upcoming set of price data based on the compression to which a technique is applied.

REMARKS

`Next` is normally used with the reserved word `Bar` to specify an action to take place on the "Next Bar".

EXAMPLES

`Open of next day` returns the Open price of the next bar.

`Date of next bar` returns the Date of the next bar.

ADDITIONAL EXAMPLE

To place an order to execute one bar into the future:

```
Buy next bar at market;
```

NoPlot(Plot)

Removes the plot specified by `(Plot)` from the current bar in a chart or cell in a grid.

`(Plot)` is a numeric expression representing the specified plot number you want to remove from a bar in a chart or cell in a grid.

REMARKS

The value returned is a number representing the assigned width of the specified plot line.

EXAMPLE

If you wanted to mark the high of a bar when the condition Close > Close[1] is true but remove the mark if `Close > Close[1]` is not true for the next bar, you could use the following syntax:

```
If Close > Close[1] Then
      Plot1(High, "CloseUp")
Else
      NoPlot(1);
```

Not

This word has been reserved for future use.

NthMaxList(N, Num1, Num2, Num3, . . . , NumN)

Returns the Nth highest value of the specified inputs.

`(N)` is a numeric expression representing the rank number of the inputs.

(`Num1`) is a numeric expression representing a value to be used in the calculation.

(`Num2`) is a second numeric expression representing a value to be used in the calculation.

(`Num3`) is a third numeric expression representing a value to be used in the calculation, and so on.

REMARKS

A value of 3 for (`N`) would return the third highest value of the specified inputs.

EXAMPLES

`NthMaxList(3, 45, 72, 86, 125, 47)` returns a value of 72.

`NthMaxList(4, 18, 67, 98, 24, 65, 19)` returns a value of 24.

NthMinList(N, Num1, Num2, Num3, . . . , NumN)

Returns the Nth lowest value of the specified inputs.

(`N`) is a numeric expression representing the rank number of the inputs.

(`Num1`) is a numeric expression representing a value to be used in the calculation.

(`Num2`) is a second numeric expression representing a value to be used in the calculation.

(`Num3`) is a third numeric expression representing a value to be used in the calculation, and so on.

REMARKS

A value of 3 for (`N`) would return the third lowest value of the specified inputs.

EXAMPLES

`NthMinList(3, 45, 72, 86, 125, 47)` returns a value of 72.

`NthMinList(4, 18, 67, 98, 24, 65, 19)` returns a value of 65.

Numeric

Reserved word used to define the type of input expected to be passed to a function.

REMARKS

`Numeric` can be used for inputs that can be either NumericSimple or NumericSeries.

EXAMPLES

`Input: Price(Numeric);` declares the constant Price as a numeric value to be used in a function.

`Input: Length(Numeric);` declares the constant Length as a numeric value to be used in a function.

NumericArray

`NumericArray` declares a function input as a numeric array being passed by value.

REMARKS

A function input is declared as a numeric array when it is passing in a numeric array by value.

EXAMPLE

`Input: PassedValues[n](NumericArray)` indicates that a numeric array is being passed into the function by value through the input `PassedValues`.

NumericArrayRef

`NumericArrayRef` declares a function input as a numeric array being passed by reference.

REMARKS

A Function Input is declared as a numeric array reference when it is passing in a numeric array by reference.

EXAMPLE

`PassedValues[n](NumericArrayRef)` indicates that a numeric array is being passed into the function by reference through the input `PassedValues`.

NumericRef

`NumericRef` declares a function input as a numeric value being passed by reference.

REMARKS

A function input is declared as a numeric reference when it is passing in a value by reference.

EXAMPLE

`PassedValue(NumericRef)` indicates that a numeric value is being passed into the function by reference through the input `PassedValue`.

NumericSeries

Reserved word used to define the type of input expected to be passed to a function.

REMARKS

`NumericSeries` is used for inputs whose values can be referred to historically.

EXAMPLES

`Input: Price(NumericSeries);` declares the constant `Price` as a `Numeric` value to be used in a function, where historical values of `Price` are available.

`Input: Length(NumericSeries);` declares the constant `Length` as a `Numeric` value to be used in a function, where historical values of `Length` are available.

NumericSimple

Reserved word used to define the type of input expected to be passed to a function.

REMARKS

`NumericSimple` cannot be used for inputs whose values can be referred to historically.

EXAMPLES

`Input: Price(NumericSimple);` declares the constant `Price` as a `Numeric` value to be used in a function, restricting `Price` to be a value that does not contain historical values.

`Input: Length(NumericSimple);` declares the constant `Length` as a `Numeric` value to be used in a function, restricting `Length` to be a value that does not contain historical values.

NumFutures

Returns the total number of futures contracts associated with a future symbol root or position leg.

EXAMPLES

If you wanted to average the prices of all the futures available for a particular symbol root, you could use the following syntax:

```
Vars: Total(0), Avg(0);
For Value1 = 1 to NumFutures of Asset Begin
        Total = Total + Close of Future(Value1);
End;
```

NumLegs

Returns the total number of position legs associated with any position. A position leg may consist of an asset, a future, or an option.

EXAMPLE

If you wanted to show the total number of legs of a position in an indicator, you could use the following syntax:

```
Plot1(NumLegs of Position, "NumLegs");
```

NumLosTrades

Returns the number of closed losing trades.

EXAMPLES

`NumLosTrades` returns 5 if the number of closed losing trades is 5.

`NumLosTrades` returns 2 if the number of closed losing trades is 2.

NumOptions

Returns the total number of position legs associated with any position. A position leg may consist of an asset.

EXAMPLE

If you wanted to show the total number of options available in an indicator, you could use the following syntax:

```
Plot1(NumOptions of Asset, "NumOptions");
```

NumToStr(Num, Dec)

Converts the specified numeric expression to a string expression.

(`Num`) is the numeric expression that you want converted to a string expression.

(`Dec`) is the numeric expression indicating how many decimal places to retain in the string expression.

EXAMPLE

`NumToStr(1170.5, 2)` returns the string expression "1170.50".

NumWinTrades

Returns the number of closed winning trades.

EXAMPLES

`NumWinTrades` returns 5 if the number of closed winning trades is 5.

`NumWinTrades` returns 2 if the number of closed winning trades is 2.

O

O

Shortcut notation that returns the `Open` of the bar.

REMARKS

Anytime the `Open` of a bar is needed, the letter `O` can be used in an equivalent fashion.

EXAMPLES

`O` of 1 bar ago returns the open price of the previous bar.

`Average(O, 10)` returns the average of the last 10 open prices.

ADDITIONAL EXAMPLE

To check that the last two bars have open prices higher than the previous bar, write:

```
If O > O[1] and O[1] > O[2] then
Plot1(High,"Rising");
```

Of

Skip word.

REMARKS

This word is skipped in EasyLanguage and is not necessary. These skipped words, however, do make it easier to understand the purpose of the code. By default, unnecessary words and sections marked as comments will appear dark green in the EasyLanguage PowerEditor.

EXAMPLE

```
If Close of Data1 = Highest(High, 14) Then...
```

The word "`of`" is not necessary and the code functions the same way regardless of its presence.

On

Skip word.

REMARKS

This word is skipped in EasyLanguage and is not necessary. These skipped words, however, do make it easier to understand the purpose of the code. By default, unnecessary words and sections marked as comments will appear dark green in the EasyLanguage PowerEditor.

EXAMPLE

```
Buy 100 Contracts on Next Bar Open
```

The word "`on`" is not necessary and the code functions the same way regardless of its presence.

Open

Reserved word used to return the first price of the specified time increment or group of ticks.

REMARKS

Anytime the `Open` of a bar is needed, the letter `O` can be used in an equivalent fashion.

EXAMPLES

`Open of 1 bar ago` returns the open price of the previous bar.

`Average(Open, 10)` returns the average of the last 10 open prices.

ADDITIONAL EXAMPLE

To check that the last two bars have open prices higher than the previous bar, write:

```
If Open > Open[1] and Open[1] > Open[2] then
Plot1(High,"Rising");
```

OpenInt

Reserved word used to return the open interest of the specified time increment or group of ticks.

REMARKS

`Open Interest` is the number of contracts/shares outstanding at the close of a bar.

EXAMPLES

`OpenInt of 1 bar ago` returns the open interest of the previous bar.

`Average(OpenInt, 10)` returns the average of the last 10 open interest values.

ADDITIONAL EXAMPLE

To check that the last two bars have open interest values higher than the previous bar, write:

```
If OpenInt > OpenInt[1] and OpenInt[1] > OpenInt[2] then
Plot1(High,"Rising");
```

OpenPositionProfit

Returns the current gain or loss of the current open position.

REMARKS

This function can be used only in the evaluation of strategies.

EXAMPLE

`OpenPositionProfit` returns a value of 86400.00 if the current open position on an S&P Futures chart had an open position profit of 86400.00.

Option(OptionNum)

References the current option contract in a Position Analysis window. Option can also be used as `Option(OptionNum)` to reference a specific option.

`(OptionNum)` is a numeric expression representing a specific option contract.

REMARKS

Used to reference information of a specific option contract. Placing ``` ``of Option(OptionNum)'' ``` after any bar data element (e.g., Open, High, Low, Close, Volume, etc.) or any option-related reserved word (e.g., Strike, ExpirationDate, Delta, etc.) returns the requested information for the option specified by `(OptionNum)`.

When using (`OptionNum`), the total number of options available should be verified before using `Option(OptionNum)` to ensure that (`OptionNum`) is set to a valid option.

EXAMPLES

```
Value1 = Close of Option;
```

You can set `Value1` to the value of a specifc option by using the following syntax:

```
Value1 = Close of Option(5);
```

OptionType

Evaluates an option to determine if it is a call or put.

EXAMPLES

```
If OptionType = Call Then {Your Operation Here}
```

Or

This boolean operator is used in condition statements to check multiple conditions.

REMARKS

`Or` requires that in order for a condition to be true, one or more of multiple conditions must be true.

EXAMPLES

```
If Plot1 Crosses Above Plot2 Or Plot2 > 5 Then ...
```

`Or` is used here to determine if either the direction of the cross of the values Plot1 and Plot2, or that Plot2 is greater than 5, is true on the bar under consideration. If either is true, the condition returns true.

```
If Value1 Crosses Above Value2 Or Value1 > Value1[1] Then ...
```

`Or` is used here to determine if either the direction of the cross of the variables Value1 and Value2, or that Value1 is greater than Value1 of one bar ago is true on the bar under consideration. If either is true, the condition returns true.

Over

This word is used to check for the direction of a cross between values.

REMARKS

Used in conjunction with the "crosses" to detect when a value crosses over, or becomes greater than another value. A value (`Value1`) crosses over another value (`Value2`) whenever `Value1` is greater than `Value2` in the current bar but `Value1` was equal to or less than `Value2` in the previous bar.

`Over` is a synonym for `Above`.

EXAMPLES

```
If Average(Close, 9) Crosses Over the Average(Close, 18) Then ...
```

Over is used here to determine the direction of the cross of the values of two moving averages on the bar under consideration.

```
If Value1 Crosses Over Value2 Then ...
```

Over is used here to determine the direction of the cross of the variables Value1 and Value2 on the bar under consideration.

P

Pager_DefaultName

Returns the string value of the default message recipient as specified in the Messaging tab under the **File → Desktop Options** menu.

REMARKS

The string is returned in the format "Default Name".

EXAMPLE

Pager_DefaultName returns a value of "This is a test message for Default User" if that is the string specified in the Messaging tab under the **Tools → Desktop Options** menu.

Pager_Send("Str_Name", "Str_Msg")

Sends the specified string value to the specified string name.

(str_Name) is a string expression that specifies the recipient of the message.

(str_Msg) is a string expression containing the message that will be sent to the pager.

REMARKS

Paging must be enabled and installed for delivery of the message to be completed.

EXAMPLE

The following sends the message "Buy 200 AMD at Market" to Joe Trader:

```
Pager_Send("Joe Trader", "Buy 200 AMD at Market");
```

PercentProfit

Returns the percentage of all closed trades that were winners.

REMARKS

PercentProfit can be calculated by NumWinTrades/TotalTrades.

EXAMPLES

PercentProfit returns 80 if the 8 winning trades resulted from 10 total trades.

PercentProfit returns 25 if the 4 winning trades resulted from 16 total trades.

Place

This word is a skip word retained for backward compatibility.

REMARKS

This word is skipped in EasyLanguage and is not necessary. These skipped words, however, do make it easier to understand the purpose of the code. By default, unnecessary words and sections marked as comments will appear dark green in the PowerEditor.

PlayMovieChain(Num)

Plays the movie chain with the specified reference number.

REMARKS

The reference number should be a whole positive number.

EXAMPLE

`Print(PlayMovieChain(1))` plays the movie chain with a reference number of 1.

PlaySound

Plays the specified sound file.

REMARKS

The specified file should be a ***.wav** audio file.

EXAMPLE

`Print(PlaySound(''c:\sounds\Thatsabuy.wav''))` plays the sound file `Thatsabuy.wav` that resides in directory `c:\sounds`.

Plot

A reserved word used to obtain the value of the specified plot for the purposes of comparison or calculation.

Plot(n)

EasyLanguage allows four plot statements per analysis technique, Plot1 through Plot4. The parameter `(n)` is a numeric expression 1 to 4 identifying the plot for which to obtain the value.

REMARKS

This reserved word enables you to use an input or a variable to specify dynamically the plot to reference.

You cannot use the reserved word Plot to draw values in a chart or grid; the reserved words Plot1 to Plot4 are used to display values.

EXAMPLE

The following statement uses a variable, Value1, to specify the plot number:

```
If Plot(Value1) crosses under Close then buy next bar on Open;
```

PlotN(Expression,"<PlotName>"[, ForeColor [, Default [, Width]]]])

Used to plot values (numeric, boolean, or string) in a price chart or in a grid-based analysis window. Plotted values can be standard bar values (such as Close or Volume), inputs, or variable values resulting from a calculation or an expression.

`N` is a number between 1 and 99, representing one of the 99 available plots. `Expression` is the value to be plotted, and `<PlotName>` is the name of the plot. `ForeColor` is an Easy Language color used for the plot (also referred to as `PlotColor`), `Default` (reserved for future use), and `Width` is a numeric value representing the width of the plot. The parameters `<PlotName>`, `ForeColor`, `Default`, and `Width` are optional.

NOTES

The parameter `Default` currently has no effect. However, a value for the parameter is required in order to specify a width, as discussed in the example.

REMARKS

The reserved word `Plot` can also be used in an assignment or condition to refer to a plotted value. When used this way, the plot name must appear in parentheses immediately following the reserved word (i.e., `Plot(''PlotName'')`. Refer to Plot (Reserved Word) for more information.

EXAMPLE 1

Any one or more of the optional parameters can be omitted, as long as there are no other parameters to the right. For example, the `Default` and `Width` parameters can be excluded from a statement as follows:

```
Plot1(Volume, ''V'', Red);
```

But the plot name cannot be omitted if you want to specify the plot color and width. For instance, the following example generates a syntax error because the name of the plot statement is expected:

INCORRECT:

```
Plot1(Volume, Black, Default, 2);
```

CORRECT:

```
Plot1(Volume, ''V'', Black, Default, 2);
```

The only required parameter for a valid **Plot** statement is the value to be plotted. The following statement is valid:

```
Plot1(Volume);
```

When no plot name is specified, EasyLanguage uses `Plot1, Plot2...Plot99` as the plot names for each plot. The first plot is named `Plot1`, the second `Plot2`, and so on.

Whenever referring to the plot color or width, you can use the word `Default` in place of the parameter(s) to have the `Plot` statement use the default color and/or width selected in the Properties tab of the Format indicator dialog box.

For example, the following statement will display the volume in the default color but indicates a specific width:

```
Plot1(Volume, "V", Default, Default, 3);
```

Again, you can use the word `Default` for the color parameters or the width parameter.

Also, the same plot (i.e., `Plot1, Plot2`) can be used more than once in an analysis technique; the only requirement is that you use the same plot name in both instances of the Plot statement. If no name is assigned, then the default plot name is used (i.e., `Plot1, Plot2`).

For example, if you want to plot the net change using red when it is negative and green when it is positive, you can use the same plot number (in this case `Plot1`) twice, as long as the name of the plot is the same:

```
Value1 = Close - Close[1];
If Value1 > 0 Then
   Plot1(Value1, "NetChg", Green)
Else
   Plot1(Value1, "NetChg", Red);
```

In this example, the plot name "NetChg" must be the same in both instances of the Plot statement.

EXAMPLE 2

When applying the analysis technique to a chart, you can displace the plot to the right or left. For example:

```
Plot1[3](Value1);
```

This example calculates the plot value using the current bar but draws it on the chart three bars ago. Use a negative number to draw the value three bars ahead of the current bar.

EXAMPLE 3

You can plot a text string (enclosed in double quotes) or a boolean value (true/false) to a cell in a grid-based window or on the status line of a subgraph in a chart. The second parameter label is optional and becomes the column heading when used with a grid-based application. For example:

```
Plot1("Up","Upward Value", Green);
```

In this example, the word "`Up`" is displayed in green within a grid cell or on the subgraph status line.

EXAMPLE 4

Getting Plot Value (Refer to Plot (Reserved Word) for more information)

Once you have defined a plot using the PlotN statement, you can reference the value of the plot simply by using the reserved word Plot in a calculation or condition. In the next example, the Plot1 statement is used to plot the accumulation distribution of the volume. The value of the plot is referenced in the next statement, in order to write the alert criteria:

```
Plot1(AccumDist(Volume), "AccumDist");
If Plot("AccumDist") > Highest(Plot("AccumDist"), 20)
then Alert;
```

PM_GetNumColumns

Returns the number of columns in a ProbabilityMap array.

EXAMPLE

If you wanted to set the variable, Value1, equal to the number of columns in the ProbabilityMap array, you could use the following syntax:

```
Value1 = PM_GetNumColumns;
```

PM_SetNumColumns(num)

Sets the number of columns in a ProbabilityMap array.

`(num)` is a numeric expression representing the desired number of columns for the ProbabilityMap.

EXAMPLE

If you wanted to set the input, BarColumns, as the number of columns in the ProbabilityMap array, you could use the following syntax:

```
SetNumColumns(PM_BarColumns);
```

POB

This word is retained for backward compatibility.

REMARKS

`POB` has been replaced by `Limit`.

`POB` is a synonym for a limit order meaning "or higher" or "or lower", depending on the context used within a strategy.

Point

Reserved word that represents one increment of the price scale.

REMARKS

`Point` reflects a change in the decimal portion of a price.

EXAMPLES

`Close + 1 point` returns one increment of the price scale added to the Close price.

`Low - 1 point` returns the `Low` of the bar minus one increment of the price scale.

ADDITIONAL EXAMPLE

An exit statement can be written to prevent large losses by:

```
Sell This Bar at EntryPrice - 1 point Stop;
```

Pointer

Reserved for use with custom DLLs designed for EasyLanguage. Refer to the documentation in the TradeStation Developer's Kit for more information about this and the EasyLanguage Tool Kit Library ELKIT32.DLL.

Points

Reserved word that represents multiple increments of the price scale.

REMARKS

Similar to the reserved word `Point`.

Represents multiple value change in the decimal portion of a price.

EXAMPLES

`Close + 5 points` returns the close price plus five increments of the price scale added to it.

`Low - 2 points` returns the low of the bar minus two increments of the price scale.

ADDITIONAL EXAMPLE

An exit statement can be written to prevent large losses by:

```
Sell This Bar at EntryPrice - 3 points Stop;
```

PointValue

Returns the dollar value represented by one increment of a security's price scale.

REMARKS

`PointValue` can be calculated as Big Point Value divided by the price scale, as specified in the Symbol Dictionary.

EXAMPLES

`PointValue` returns 2.5 for the S&P 500 Future trading on the Chicago Mercantile Exchange.

`PointValue` returns .001 for IBM trading on the New York Stock Exchange.

ADDITIONAL EXAMPLE

The smallest dollar move of an asset can be calculated by:

```
Value1 = PointValue * MinMove;
```

NOTE: This word can be referenced only when writing analysis techniques for RadarScreen and OptionStation. This word is not available for use with EasyLanguage for use with charting applications such as TradeStation or SuperCharts.

Pos(Num)

`(Num)` is a numeric expression.

Returns the absolute value of num.

EXAMPLES

`Pos(-5)` returns 5.

`Pos(350)` returns 350.

Position

References a position in a Position Search Strategy.

EXAMPLE

If you wanted to search for a Delta neutral position, you could use the following syntax:

```
Condition1 = Delta of Position < .1 And Delta of Position > -.1;
PositionStatus(Condition1);
```

PositionID

References the PositionID of the Position in a Search Strategy.

EXAMPLE

If you wanted to plot the Position ID in an indicator, you could use the following syntax:

```
Plot1(PositionID of Position, "Position ID");
```

PositionProfit (Num)

Returns the current gain or loss of the specified position.

(Num) is a numeric expression representing the number of positions ago.

REMARKS

This function can only be used in the evaluation of strategies. PositionProfit does not require an input, it returns the gain or loss of the current position. However, by using the input Num, you can obtain the gain or loss for a previous position.

EXAMPLES

`PositionProfit(3)` returns a value of -1.00 if the third most recent position on a chart had a loss of 1.00.

PositionStatus (Condition)

Defines the true/false expression that must be true in order to create a position in a Position Search Strategy. (`Condition`) is a true/false expression that determines when to create a position.

EXAMPLE

If you wanted to create Search Strategy that searched for positions of in the money calls, you could use the following syntax:

```
CreateLeg(1, Call);
Condition1 = Close of asset > Strike of Leg(1);
PositionStatus(Condition1);
```

Power(Num, Pow)

Returns the number raised to the specified power.

(`Num`) is the number to raise to the specified power

(`Pow`) is the power by which to raise the number

EXAMPLES

`Pow(2,3)` returns 8

`Pow(4,5)` returns 4096.

Price_To_Book

Returns the primary EPS, excluding extraordinary items and discontinued operations.

REMARKS

`Price_To_Book` is calculated by the adjusted income available to common stockholders divided by the primary average shares outstanding.

PriceScale

Returns the precision to which a security trades.

REMARKS

`PriceScale` reads the field `Price Scale` specified in the Symbol Dictionary.

Returns the lower portion of the price scale fraction.

EXAMPLES

`PriceScale` returns 1/100 for the S&P 500 futures.

`PriceScale` returns 1/4 for corn futures.

Print (Parameters)

Sends information to the Print Log or, if specified, to an output location (a file or the default printer).

`Parameters` is any number of valid string, true/false, numeric series, or numeric expressions, each separated by a comma. To send output to a printer or file instead of the Print Log, you must also specify output location. The maximum number of displayed characters supported for the combined Parameters is 255.

REMARKS

If no output location is specified, the information is sent to the Print Log.

To send information to a specified file instead of the Print Log, specify the file and path as the first parameter. Enclose the file name and path in quotation marks. To send the information to the default printer, include the word `Printer` as the first parameter.

You can format the numeric expressions displayed using the Print reserved word. To do so, use the following syntax:

```
Print(Value1:N:M);
```

`Value1` is any numeric expression, `N` is the minimum number of integers to use, and M is the number of decimals to use. If the numeric expression being sent to the Print Log has more integers than what is specified by `N`, the `Print` statement uses as many digits as necessary, and the decimal values are rounded to the nearest value. For example, assume `Value1` is equal to 3.14159 and we have written the following statement:

```
Print(Value1:0:4);
```

The numeric expression displayed in the Print Log would be 3.1416. As another example, to format the closing prices, you can use the following statement:

```
Print(ELDateToString(Date), Time, Close:0:4);
```

EXAMPLES

The following statement sends the date, time, and closing price of the current bar to the Print Log:

```
Print(Date, Time, Close);
```

The following statement sends the same information to an ASCII file called Mydata.txt:

```
Print(File("c:\data\mydata.txt"), Date, Time, Close);
```

The following statement sends the information to the default printer instead:

```
Print(Printer, Date, Time, Close);
```

Printer

Sends information to the default printer from a Print statement.

REMARKS

The word `Printer` must be the first expression listed in the print statement followed by a comma and then the requested information. Commas must be used to separate multiple expressions in a print statement.

EXAMPLE

If you wanted to send the date, time, and close information to the printer when you applied an analysis technique, you could use the following syntax:

```
Print(Printer, Date, Time, Close);
```

Product

Returns the number representing the product being used.

REMARKS

The Product function returns values based on the following table.

Product Name	Product Number
TradeStation	0
SuperCharts	1

EXAMPLES

If you wanted to display an indicator only when the user applied the indicator to a TradeStation chart, you could use the following syntax:

```
If Product = 0 Then
      Plot1(Value1, "Indicator");
```

Profit

This word has been reserved for future use.

ProfitTargetStop

This word has been replaced by the Reserved Word `SetProfitTarget`.

Protective

This word has been reserved for future use.

Q

NOTE: APPLIES TO ALL FOLLOWING Q_ QUOTE FIELDS. This word can be referenced only when writing analysis techniques for RadarScreen and OptionStation. This word is not available for use with EasyLanguage for use with charting applications such as TradeStation or SuperCharts.

q_7DayYield

Returns a numeric expression representing the net 7-day yield for a mutual fund.

q_Ask

Returns a numeric expression representing the last ASK for a symbol.

q_AskExchange

Returns a string expression representing the exchange the last bid was sent from.

q_AskSize

Returns a numeric expression representing the number of units offered at the best ask price.

q_Bid

Returns a numeric expression representing the last bid price for a symbol.

q_BidExchange

Returns a string expression representing the exchange the last bid was sent from.

q_BidSize

Returns a numeric expression representing the number of units bid at the best bid price.

q_Close

Returns a numeric expression representing the price of the close of the last completed trading session.

q_DatafeedID

Returns a numeric expression representing the data feed ID.

q_Date

Returns a numeric expression representing the EasyLanguage date of the last time any price of field of this symbol was updated.

q_DateLastAsk

Returns a numeric expression representing the EasyLanguage date of the last ask transmitted by the data feed.

q_DateLastBid

Returns a numeric expression representing the EasyLanguage date of the last bid transmitted by the data feed.

q_DateLastTrade

Returns a numeric expression representing the EasyLanguage date of the last trade transmitted by the data feed.

q_DownVolume

Returns a numeric expression representing the down volume for the current trading day.

q_ExchangeListed

Returns a string expression representing the exchange under which the symbol is listed.

q_ExpirationDate

Returns a numeric expression representing the EasyLanguage date of the expiration date for the symbol. The expiration date is defined by the expiration rule chosen for the symbol.

q_Headline

Returns a string expression containing the last headline transmitted by the data feed for this symbol.

q_HeadlineCount

Returns a numeric expression representing the number of headlines transmitted by the data feed on the current day.

q_High

Returns a numeric expression representing the highest price traded during the current trading day.

q_Hour

Returns a numeric expression representing the hour of the last time any price field of this symbol was updated.

q_Last

Returns a numeric expression representing the last traded price of the symbol.

q_LastTradingDate

Returns a numeric expression representing the EasyLanguage date of the last trading date for the symbol. The last trading date is defined by the expiration rule chosen for the symbol.

q_Low

Returns a numeric expression representing the lowest price traded during the current trading session.

q_Margin

Returns a numeric expression representing the margin for a future.

q_Minute

Returns a numeric expression representing the minutes of the last time any price field of this symbol was updated.

q_MinutesDelayed

Returns a numeric expression representing the number of minutes this symbol is delayed.

q_Month

Returns a numeric expression representing the month of the last time any price field of the symbol was updated.

q_NetAssetValue

Returns a numeric expression representing the net asset value for a mutual fund.

q_NetChange

Returns a numeric expression representing the net change for the previous day's close to the current day's last price.

q_NewsCount

Returns a numeric expression representing the number of headlines transmitted by the data feed on the current day.

q_NewsDay

Returns a numeric expression representing the EasyLanguage date of the last headline transmitted by the data feed for the symbol.

q_NewsTime

Returns a numeric expression representing the time of the last headline transmitted by the data feed for the symbol.

q_Open

Returns a numeric expression representing the opening price of the symbol.

q_OptionType

Returns a numeric expression representing the option type.

q_PreviousClose

Returns a numeric expression representing the close of the previous trading session.

q_PreviousDate

Returns a numeric expression representing the EasyLanguage date of the previous trading session.

q_PreviousHigh

Returns a numeric expression representing the highest traded price for the previous trading day.

q_PreviousLow

Returns a numeric expression representing the lowest traded price for the previous trading day.

q_PreviousOpen

Returns a numeric expression representing the opening price of the previous trading day.

q_PreviousOpenInterest

Returns a numeric expression representing the open interest of the previous trading day.

q_PreviousTime

Returns a numeric expression representing the time of the previous trading day.

q_StrikePrice

Returns a numeric expression representing the strike price of the an option.

q_Time

Returns a numeric expression representing the EasyLanguage time of the last time the symbol was updated.

q_TimeLastAsk

Returns a numeric expression representing the time of the last ask price.

q_TimeLastBid

Returns a numeric expression representing the time of the last bid price.

q_TimeLastTrade

Returns a numeric expression representing the time of the last trade price.

q_TotalVolume

Returns a numeric expression representing the total trade volume of the trading day.

q_TradeVolume

Returns a numeric expression representing the trade volume of the last trade.

q_UnchangedVolume

Returns a numeric expression representing the unchanged volume for the current trading day.

q_UpVolume

Returns a numeric expression representing the up volume for the current trading day.

q_Year

Returns a numeric expression representing the year of the last trade.

q_Yield

Returns a numeric expression representing the yield of a bond.

Quick_Ratio

Returns the Quick Ratio value.

REMARKS

`Quick Ratio` is calculated by `(Cash + Short Term Investments + Accounts Receivable) / Total Current Liabilities.`

R

Random(Num)

Returns a random number in the range between `0` and (`Num`).

(`Num`) is a numeric expression to be used in the calculation.

EXAMPLES

`Random(35)` might return a value of 21.26.

`Power(142.56)` might return a value of 136.23.

RawAsk

Returns the raw ask value received from the data provider.

EXAMPLE

```
If RawAsk of Option - Close of Option < .125 then
        Alert(''Very Low Ask'');
```

RawBid

Returns the raw bid value received from the data provider.

EXAMPLE

```
If Close of Option - RawBid of Option < .125 then
        Alert(''Very Low Bid'');
```

Red

Sets the plot color or background color to Red.

REMARKS

There are 16 colors available in EasyLanguage. For more information, see color values in Appendix A.

EXAMPLES

`Plot1(Value1, ''Test'', Red)` plots Value1 with the name Test and sets the color of Plot1 to Red.

`TL_SetColor(1, Red)` sets the color of a TrendLine with a reference number of 1 to Red.

Repeat

Evaluates one or more statements in a loop and exits the loop only when the until condition is true.

```
Repeat
  statement(s);
Until (condition_is_true);
```

REMARKS

There is no need to use the begin/end keywords to group more than one program statement, as all statements between `repeat` and `until` are treated as a block.

The repeat statement is similar to the while loop; however, with the repeat statement, the conditional test occurs after the loop. This means that the program statement(s) that constitute the loop body will be executed at least once.

Ret_On_Avg_Equity

Returns the return on average equity.

REMARKS

`Ret_On_Avg_Equity` is calculated by income available to common stockholders divided by the average common equity and is expressed as a percentage.

RevSize

Returns the reversal size of a Point & Figure chart.

REMARKS

The reversal size of a Point & Figure chart is defined by the user on the **Format Symbol → Settings** tab.

EXAMPLES

`RevSize` returns 3 if the reversal size is set to 3.

`RevSize` returns 1 if the reversal size is set to 1.

Rho

Returns the Rho value of an option, leg, or position. The value of Rho can also be established in a Pricing Model by using `Rho(Value)`.

REMARKS

Debit positions will return positive numbers and credit positions will return negative numbers.

EXAMPLES

```
If Rho of Option > HighVal Then
Alert("High Rho");
```

In a Pricing Model, you can set the value of Rho by using the following syntax:

```
Rho(0);
```

RightSide

Used to specify ActivityBar actions on the right side of the bar.

EXAMPLE

`GetCellChar(Close, Rightside, 3)` Rightside is used to specify the right side of the ActivityBar.

RightStr("Str1", sSize)

Reduces the specified string expression.

(`Str1`) is the string expression that you want to reduce. It must be enclosed in quotation marks.

(`sSize`) is the numeric expression indicating the number of characters, counting from the end of the string expression, that will be retained. Any additional characters are removed.

EXAMPLE

`RightStr(''Net Profit'', 6)` returns the string expression "Profit".

Round(Num, Prec)

Returns (`Num`) rounded to `(Prec)` decimal places.

(`Num`) is a numeric expression to be used in the calculation.

(`Prec`) is a numeric expression representing the number of decimal places to keep.

EXAMPLES

`Round(142.3215, 2)` returns a value of 142.32.

`Round(9.5687, 3)` returns a value of of 9.569.

S

Saturday

Returns the number 6 as the value for Saturday.

REMARKS

The value returned is an integer representing `Saturday` and is the same value returned by using the function `DayOfWeek(Saturday)`.

EXAMPLE

`Saturday` returns a value of 6 as the value for Saturday.

Screen

This word has been reserved for future use.

Sell

Reserved word used to generate an order for a short entry.

REMARKS

The earliest order entry that can be generated is for the close of the current bar.

Orders can be generated for:

- this bar on Close.
- next bar at Market.
- next bar at PRICE Stop.
- next bar at PRICE Limit.

An entry statement consists of: Entry/Exit order, Signal name, number of contracts, timing, Price, Market/Stop/Limit.

EXAMPLES

```
Sell (“ShortEntry”) 5 contracts this bar on close;
```

generates an order to enter a short position of five contracts at the close of the current bar.

```
Sell (“NextEntry”) next bar at market;
```

generates an order to enter a short position at the first price of next bar.

ADDITIONAL EXAMPLE

```
Sell (“MyTrade”) next bar at 75 Stop;
```

generates an order to enter a short position on the next bar at a price of 75 or lower.

SeriesCount

Returns the number of series available in the option chain.

REMARKS

`SeriesCount` is used in navigating the option chain within OptionStation. OptionStation keeps an array of all available options for EasyLanguage calculations, and this reserved word can be used to help determine the makeup of that array.

EXAMPLE

```
Value1 = SeriesCount of Asset;
```

Sess1EndTime

Returns the ending time of the first trading session for the security.

REMARKS

`Sess1EndTime` returns the time in 24-hour format.

EXAMPLES

`Sess1EndTime` returns 1500 when applied to the U.S. Treasury Bonds trading on the Chicago Board of Trade.

`Sess1EndTime` returns 1615 when applied to IBM trading on the New York Stock Exchange.

ADDITIONAL EXAMPLE

You can check the last bar of the day on an intraday chart with:

```
IF Time = Sess1EndTime THEN
   Sell this bar on Close;
```

Sess1FirstBarTime

Returns the time of the first bar generated during the first session of trading of the day.

REMARKS

`Sess1FirstBarTime` returns the time in 24-hour format.

EXAMPLES

`Sess1FirstBarTime` returns 1000 when applied to IBM data with a 30-minute compression.

`Sess1FirstBarTime` returns 0825 when applied to U.S. Treasury Bond data with a 5-minute compression.

Sess1StartTime

Returns the starting time of the first trading session of the security.

REMARKS

`Sess1StartTime` returns the time in 24-hour format.

EXAMPLES

`Sess1StartTime` returns 0820 when applied to the U.S. Treasury Bonds trading on the Chicago Board of Trade.

`Sess1StartTime` returns 0930 when applied to IBM trading on the New York Stock Exchange.

ADDITIONAL EXAMPLE

You can check the first bar of the day on an intraday chart with:

```
IF Time = CalcTime(Sess1StartTime, BarInterval) THEN
    Sell this bar on Close;
```

Sess2EndTime

Returns the ending time of the second trading session for a security.

REMARKS

`Sess2EndTime` returns the time in 24-hour format.

EXAMPLES

`Sess2EndTime` returns 0745 when applied to the U.S. Treasury Bonds trading on the Chicago Board of Trade.

`Sess2EndTime` returns 0915 when applied to the S&P 500 Futures trading on the Chicago Mercantile Exchange.

ADDITIONAL EXAMPLE

You can check the last bar of the session on an intraday chart with:

```
IF Time = Sess2EndTime THEN
Sell this bar on Close;
```

Sess2FirstBarTime

Returns the time of the first bar generated during the second session of trading of the day.

REMARKS

`Sess2FirstBarTime` returns the time in 24-hour format.

EXAMPLES

`Sess2FirstBarTime` returns 1715 when applied to S&P 500 Futures data with a 30-minute compression.

`Sess2FirstBarTime` returns 1535 when applied to U.S. Treasury Bond data with a 5-minute compression.

Sess2StartTime

Returns the starting time of the second trading session of the security.

REMARKS

`Sess2StartTime` returns the time in 24-hour format.

EXAMPLES

`Sess2StartTime` returns 1530 when applied to the U.S. Treasury Bonds trading on the Chicago Board of Trade.

`Sess2StartTime` returns 1645 when applied to the S&P 500 Futures trading on the Chicago Mercantile Exchange.

ADDITIONAL EXAMPLE

You can check the first bar of the second session on an intraday chart with:

```
IF Time = CalcTime(Sess2StartTime, BarInterval) THEN
    Sell this bar on Close;
```

SetBotBound(Price)

Sets the bottom boundary of a ProbabilityMap array.

`(Price)` is a numeric expression representing the desired price level on the chart.

REMARKS

`(Price)` must represent a constant value.

EXAMPLE

If you wanted to set the variable `MapBottom` as the bottom boundry of the ProbabilityMap array, you could use the following syntax:

```
SetBotBound(MapBottom);
```

SetBreakEven(FloorAmnt)

SetBreakEven sets a built-in breakeven stop.

`(FloorAmnt)` is a numeric expression that represents the floor, or minimum, equity needed for the stop to become active.

EXAMPLE

In order to place a breakeven stop once a position has made a $250 profit, you would write:

```
SetStopPosition;
SetBreakEven(250);
```

SetDollarTrailing(DollarValue)

Used to place a dollar risk trailing stop.

(DollarValue) is a numeric expression representing the dollar amount that you are willing to risk per position or per contract/share.

EXAMPLE

To place a dollar risk trailing stop at $500 for the entire position, write:

```
SetStopPosition;
SetDollarTrailing(500);
```

As the price rises, so does the placement of the stop. It is maintained at a dollar value that results in a total of $500 loss for the entire position.

SetExitOnClose

SetExitOnClose exits a position at the last bar of the day for intraday charts.

EXAMPLE

In order to exit all positions at the end of the day, you would write:

```
SetExitOnClose;
```

SetPercentTrailing(FloorAmnt, Percent)

Used to place a percent risk trailing stop.

(FloorAmnt) is a numeric expression representing the floor, or minimum, equity needed to activate the stop. You can use 0, in which case, the stop is activated regardless of equity achieved.

(Percent) is a numeric expression representing the percentage of the maximum equity needed to be lost to close the trade.

EXAMPLE

In order to place a percentage-based trailing stop that exits a position once it has returned 15% of the maximum equity earned after the position has made $500, you would write:

```
SetStopPosition;
SetPercentTrailing(500,15);
```

SetPlotBGColor(PlotNum, BGColor)

Sets the background color of the cell(s) to which a specified analysis technique is applied.

(PlotNum) is a numeric expression representing a plot number.

(BGColor) corresponds to the numeric value or EasyLanguage reserved word corresponding to the background color you want to assign to a plot when applying an indicator to a grid.

REMARKS

SetPlotBGColor is valid only for indicators applied to grids.

EXAMPLE

If you wanted to set the background color of the cell for Plot1 to white, you could use the following syntax:

```
SetPlotBGColor(1, White);
```

SetPlotColor(FGColor)

Sets the plot line color in a chart or the foreground color of the cell(s) in a grid to which a specified analysis technique is applied.

(PlotNum) is a numeric expression representing a plot number.

(FGColor) corresponds to the numeric value or EasyLanguage reserved word corresponding to the plot line in a chart or the foreground color in a grid you want to assign to a plot when applying an indicator.

REMARKS

SetPlotColor is valid for indicators applied to both charts and grids.

EXAMPLE

If you wanted to set the foreground color for Plot1 to blue, you could use the following syntax:

```
SetPlotColor(1, Blue);
```

SetPlotWidth

Sets the width of the specified plot line in a chart.

(PlotNum) is a numeric expression representing a plot number.

(Width) is a numeric expression representing the plot's width.

REMARKS

SetPlotWidth can be used only to change the width of plot lines in charts.

EXAMPLE

If you wanted to set the width of Plot1 to 5, you could use the following syntax:

```
SetPlotWidth(1, 5);
```

SetProfitTarget

SetProfitTarget sets a built-in profit target stop.

(DollarValue) is a numeric expression representing the dollar value of the profit target.

EXAMPLE

In order to exit a position once the price has returned $400, you would write:

```
SetStopContract;
SetProfitTarget(400);
```

SetPredictionValue

Returns the number of columns in a ProbabilityMap array.

(Column) is a numeric expression representing the desired column number for the prediction value.

(Price) is a numeric expression representing the desired price level from the prediction value.

(Value) is a numeric expression representing the value of prediction value from 0 to 100.

EXAMPLE

If you wanted to set the prediction value of the cell in column 5 with a price of 95.250 to 86.53 in the ProbabilityMap array, you could use the following syntax:

```
SetPredictionValue(5, 92.250, 86.53);
```

SetRowIncrement

Sets the row increment value in a ProbabilityMap array.

EXAMPLE

If you wanted to set the variable RowHeight as the row increment value in the ProbabilityMap array, you could use the following syntax:

```
SetRowIncrement(RowHeight);
```

SetStopContract

Instructs TradeStation to evaluate all stop values of a strategy on a per contract basis.

REMARKS

If `SetStopPosition` and/or `SetStopContract` are used multiple times, even in different signals within a strategy, the last instance is used. Therefore, in the next example, `Signal2` is ignored.

Signal1: `SetStopPosition`;
Signal2: `SetStopContract`;
Signal3: `SetStopPosition`;

EXAMPLE

If you want to place a stop loss order of $500 per contract, you would write:

```
SetStopContract;
SetStopLoss(500);
```

SetStopLoss (DollarValue)

Used to place a stop loss order (money management stop).

(`DollarValue`) is a numeric expression representing the dollar amount that must be incurred before the position or contract/share is liquidated.

EXAMPLE

You are long 10 shares and the entry price is 52. To exit your long position when you are down $2/per contract or share, write:

```
SetStopContract;
SetStopLoss (2);
```

ADDITIONAL EXAMPLE

You are long 500 shares, and the entry price is 12. To exit your long position when you are down $1000 for the entire position, write:

```
SetStopPosition;
SetStopLoss(1000);
```

In this case, when the price reaches 10, you are exited from your long position ($500 \times \$2 = 1000$).

SetStopPosition

Instructs TradeStation to evaluate all stop values of a strategy on a per position basis.

REMARKS

If `SetStopPosition` and/or `SetStopContract` are used multiple times, even in different signals within a strategy, the last instance is used. Therefore, in the next example, Signal2 is ignored.

Signal1: `SetStopPosition;`
Signal2: `SetStopContract;`
Signal3: `SetStopPosition;`

EXAMPLE

If you want to place a stop loss order of $1200 for the entire position, you would write:

```
SetStopPosition;
SetStopLoss(1200);
```

SetTopBound(Price)

Sets the top boundary of a ProbabilityMap array.

`(Price)` is a numeric expression representing the desired price level on the chart.

REMARKS

`(Price)` must represent a constant value.

EXAMPLE

If you wanted to set the variable MapTop as the top boundary of the ProbabilityMap array, you could use the following syntax:

```
SetTopBound(MapTop);
```

SGA_Exp_By_NetSales

Returns the total revenue divided by the number of outstanding shares.

Share

Reserved word used to specify the number of units to trade within a trading strategy.

REMARKS

Share is normally used in a Buy, Sell, or Exit statement.

EXAMPLES

`Buy 1 share next bar at market` generates an order to buy one share at the open of the next bar.

`Sell 1 share next bar at market` generates an order to sell one share at the open of the next bar.

ADDITIONAL EXAMPLE

To exit from only one contract from multiple long positions, write:

```
Sell 1 share total next bar at market;
```

Shares

Reserved word used to specify the number of units to trade within a trading strategy.

REMARKS

Shares is normally used in a Buy, Sell or Exit statement.

EXAMPLES

`Buy 5 shares next bar at market` generates an order to buy five shares at the open of the next bar.

`Sell 5 shares next bar at market` generates an order to sell five shares at the open of the next bar.

ADDITIONAL EXAMPLE

To exit from only five contracts from multiple long positions, write:

```
ExitLong 5 shares total next bar at market;
```

Sign (Num)

Returns an integer based on the sign on (`Num`). 1 is returned for a positive value, −1 is returned for a negative value, and 0 is returned for zero.

(`Num`) is a numeric expression to be used in the calculation.

EXAMPLES

`Sign(56.23)` returns a value of 1.

`Sign(-9.5687)` returns a value of −1.

Sine(Num)

Returns the sine value of the specified `(Num)` of degrees.

(`Num`) is a numeric expression to be used in the calculation.

REMARKS

The sine is the trigonometric function that for an acute angle is the ratio between the leg opposite the angle when it is considered part of a right triangle and the hypotenuse.

(`Num`) should be the number of degrees in the angle.

EXAMPLES

`Sine(45)` returns a value of 0.7071.

`Sine(72)` returns a value of 0.9511.

Skip

This word has been reserved for future use.

Slippage

Returns the slippage setting in the applied strategy's Costs tab.

REMARKS

This reserved word can be used only in the evaluation of strategies.

EXAMPLES

Slippage returns a value of .50 if the slippage under the strategy's Costs tab has been set to .5.

SnapFundExists

Returns True if snapshot fundamental data exists in the data stream, False otherwise.

Spaces(Cnt)

Adds the specified number of blank spaces into the line of commentary or text output.

`(Cnt)` is the numeric expression indicating the number of spaces to be inserted.

EXAMPLE

```
Print("Close" + Spaces(5) + NumToStr(Close, 3));
```

This example results in five blank spaces between the string "Close" and the closing price.

Square

Returns the square of the specified `(Num)`.

(`Num`) is a numeric expression to be used in the calculation.

REMARKS

The square is a number raised to the second power.

EXAMPLES

`Square(6.23)` returns a value of 38.8219.

`Square(-9.5687)` returns a value of 91.5600.

SquareRoot(Num)

Returns the square root of the specified `(Num)`.

(`Num`) is a numeric expression to be used in the calculation.

REMARKS

The square root is the number that must be raised to the second power in order to produce a given number, (`Num`).

(`Num`) must be a positive number or zero.

EXAMPLES

`SquareRoot(6.23)` returns a value of 2.4960.

`SquareRoot(121)` returns a value of 11.

StartDate

Reserved word used with GlobalServer Expiration rules.

StockSplit

Returns the ratio of the stock split reported during a certain period.

```
StockSplit (Num);
```

REMARKS

`StockSplit` does not require an input; it returns the most recently reported stock split ratio. However, by using an input, you can obtain the ratio of a stock split report other than the most recent.

EXAMPLES

`StockSplit` returns the last split ratio reported.

`StockSplit(2)` returns the split ratio reported two periods ago.

StockSplitCount

Returns the number of times that stock splits have been reported in the time frame considered.

REMARKS

`StockSplitCount` counts the number of times that stock splits have been reported during the time frame specified.

StockSplitDate (Num)

Returns the date on which a stock split was reported.

REMARKS

`StockSplitDate` does not require an input; it returns the date of the most recently reported stock split. However, by using an input, you can obtain the date of a stock split report other than the most recent.

EXAMPLES

`StockSplitDate` returns the date of the last reported stock split.

`StockSplitDate(2)` returns the date of the last reported stock split two periods ago.

StockSplitTime(Num)

Returns the time of the last stock split report.

REMARKS

`StockSplitTime` does not require an input; it returns the time for the most recently reported stock split. However, by using an input, you can obtain the time of a stock split report other than the most recent.

EXAMPLES

`StockSplitTime` returns the time of the last stock split report.

`StockSplitTime(2)` returns the time of the stock split report two periods ago.

Stop

Used in an entry or exit statement to specify how to fill an order.

REMARKS

Stop orders can be executed only on the next bar.

`Stop` can be read as "this price or worse," meaning higher for a long entry and short exit, lower for a short entry and long exit.

Stop orders require a reference price.

EXAMPLES

```
Buy next bar at 75 Stop;
```

Generates an order to enter a long position on the next bar at a price of 75 or higher.

```
Sell next bar at 75 Stop;
```

Generates an order to enter a short position on the next bar at a price of 75 or lower.

ADDITIONAL EXAMPLE

```
ExitLong next bar at 75 Stop;
```

Generates an order to exit a long position on the next bar at a price of 75 or lower.

Strike

Returns the strike price of an option or position leg.

EXAMPLE

```
If OptionType of Option = Call AND Close of Asset > Strike of Option
then
     Plot1(``Call in-the-money'', ``Option'')
Else
     Plot1(``Call out-of-the-money'',''Option'');
```

StrikeCount

Returns the number of strikes available in the option chain.

REMARKS

`StrikeCount` is used in navigating the option chain within OptionStation. OptionStation keeps an array of all available options for EasyLanguage calculations, and this reserved word can be used to help determine the makeup of that array.

EXAMPLE

```
Value1 = StrikeCount of Asset;
```

StrikeITMCount

This word has been reserved for future use.

StrikeOTMCount

This word has been reserved for future use.

String

Defines an input as a string expression. Reserved word is used to define the data type of an input to a function that accepts a text string value passed by value.

The type of value returned by a function.

EXAMPLES

`Input: MyMessage(String);` declares the constant `MyMessage` as a string value to be used in a function.

`Input: NewMessage(String);` declares the constant `NewMessage` as a string value to be used in a function.

StringArray

`StringArray` declares a function input as a string array being passed by value.

REMARKS

A function input is declared as a string array when it is passing in a string array by value.

EXAMPLE

`Input: PassedValues[n](StringArray)` indicates that a string array is being passed into the function by value through the input `PassedValues`.

StringArrayRef

`StringArrayRef` declares a function input as a string array being passed by reference.

REMARKS

A function input is declared as a string array reference when it is passing in a string array by reference.

EXAMPLE

`Input: PassedValues[n](StringArrayRef)` indicates that a string array is being passed into the function by reference through the input `PassedValues`.

StringRef

`StringRef` declares a function input as a string being passed by reference.

REMARKS

A function input is declared as a string reference when it is passing in a string by reference.

EXAMPLE

`PassedValue(stringRef)` indicates that a string is being passed into the function by reference through the Input PassedValue.

StringSeries

Reserved word used to define the type of input expected to be passed to a function.

REMARKS

`StringSeries` is used for inputs whose values can be referred to historically.

EXAMPLES

`Input: MyMessage(StringSeries);` declares the constant MyMessage as a string value to be used in a function, where historical values of MyMessage are available.

`Input: NewMessage(StringSeries);` declares the constant NewMessage as a string value to be used in a function, where historical values of NewMessage are available.

StringSimple

Reserved word used to define the type of input expected to be passed to a function.

REMARKS

StringSimple cannot be used for inputs whose values can be referred to historically.

EXAMPLES

`Input: MyMessage(StringSimple);` declares the constant MyMessage as a string value to be used in a function, restricting MyMessage to be a value that does not contain historical values.

`Input: NewMessage(StringSimple);` declares the constant NewMessage as a string value to be used in a function, restricting NewMessage to be a value that does not contain historical values.

StrLen

Counts and returns number of characters in the specified string expression.

```
StrLen(Str);
```

(`Str`) is the string expression to count. It must be enclosed in quotation marks.

EXAMPLE

`StrLen(''Net Profit'')` returns the numeric expression 10 for the number of characters in the string.

StrToNum("Str")

Converts the specified string expression to a numeric value.

(`Str`) is the string expression to convert to a numeric expression. It must be enclosed in quotation marks.

REMARKS

If any nonnumeric characters are included in the string expression, zero (0) is returned. The only exception is when nonnumeric characters are located at the end of the string expression, in which case they are dropped from the numeric expression.

EXAMPLE

`StrToNum(''1170.50'')` returns the numeric expression 1170.50.

SumList(Num1, Num2, Num3, . . . , NumN)

Returns the sum of the inputs.

(`Num1`) is a numeric expression representing a value to be used in the calculation.

(`Num2`) is a second numeric expression representing a value to be used in the calculation.

(`Num3`) is a third numeric expression representing a value to be used in the calculation, and so on.

EXAMPLES

`SumList(45, 72, 86, 125, 47)` returns a value of 375.

`SumList(18, 67, 98, 24, 65, 19)` returns a value of 291.

Sunday

Returns the number 0 as the value for `Sunday`.

REMARKS

The value returned is an integer representing `Sunday` and is the same value returned by using the function `DayOfWeek(Sunday)`.

EXAMPLE

`Sunday` returns a value of 0 as the value for `Sunday`.

SymbolName

Returns a string expression representing the symbol name. See also `GetSymbolName`.

NOTE: This word can be referenced only when writing analysis techniques for RadarScreen and OptionStation. This word is not available for use with EasyLanguage for use with charting applications such as TradeStation or SuperCharts.

SymbolNumber

Returns a numeric expression representing the symbol number defined in the GlobalServer symbol portfolio. See also `CommodityNumber` and `Cusip`.

NOTE: This word can be referenced only when writing analysis techniques for RadarScreen and OptionStation. This word is not available for use with EasyLanguage for use with charting applications such as TradeStation or SuperCharts.

SymbolRoot

Returns a string expression representing the root of the symbol (for futures and options only).

NOTE: This word can be referenced only when writing analysis techniques for RadarScreen and OptionStation. This word is not available for use with EasyLanguage for use with charting applications such as TradeStation or SuperCharts.

T

T

Shortcut notation that returns the time of a bar.

REMARKS

Anytime the `Time` of a bar is needed, the letter `T` can be used in an equivalent fashion.

`T` returns the time in 24-hour format.

EXAMPLES

`T` returns 1600 if the time of the bar is 4:00 pm.

`T` returns 0930 if the time of the bar is 9:30 am.

ADDITIONAL EXAMPLE

To check the Time of the previous bar, write:

```
T of 1 bar ago
```

Tangent(Num)

Returns the tangent value of the specified `(Num)` of degrees.

(`Num`) is a numeric expression to be used in the calculation.

REMARKS

The tangent the trigonometric function that for an acute angle is the ratio between the leg opposite to the angle when it is considered part of a right triangle and the leg adjacent, also equal to the sine divided by the cosine.

(`Num`) should be the number of degrees in the angle.

EXAMPLES

`Tangent(45)` returns a value of 1.0.

`Tangent(72)` returns a value of 3.0776.

Target

This word has been reserved for future use.

TargetType

This word has been reserved for future use.

Text

This word is retained for backward compatibility.

Text_Delete

Deletes the specified text object.

```
Text_Delete (TX_Ref);
```

`(TX_Ref)` is the identification number of the text object or a numeric expression representing the identification number.

REMARKS

If the text cannot be deleted, `TX_Delete` returns an error code. When the text is successfully deleted, it returns 0. For a list of error codes, see `Trendline` and `Text Error Codes`.

EXAMPLES

The following deletes the text object with the identification number 3:

```
Text_Delete(3);
```

To obtain the error code (or 0 when no error) returned by the reserved word, you can assign the reserved word to a numeric variable, as follows:

```
Value1 = Text_Delete(3);
```

Text_GetColor (TX_Ref)

Returns the numeric value corresponding to the color of the specified text object.

Where (`TX_Ref`) is the identification number of the text object or a numeric expression representing the identification number.

REMARKS

For a list of possible colors and their corresponding numeric values, see EasyLanguage Colors in Appendix A.

When the reserved word performs its operation successfully, it returns the numeric value corresponding to the color. When a reserved word cannot perform its operation, it returns an error code. For a list of error codes, see Trendline and Text Error Codes.

EXAMPLE

To obtain the numeric color value returned by the reserved word, you need to assign the reserved word to a numeric variable. The text object with the identification number 1 is yellow. Therefore, the following returns the value 7.

```
Value1 = Text_GetColor(1);
```

Text_GetDate(TX_Ref)

Returns the date where the specified text object's left edge begins in YYMMDD or YYYMMDD format (three digits are used to express the year 2000 and higher).

(`TX_Ref`) is the identification number of the text object or a numeric expression representing the identification number.

REMARKS

When the reserved word performs its operation successfully, the date is returned. When a reserved word cannot perform its operation, it returns an error code. For a list of error codes, see Trendline and Text Error Codes.

EXAMPLE

To obtain the date returned by the reserved word, you need to assign the reserved word to a numeric variable. The text object with the identification number 1 begins on February 14, 1999. The following returns the value 990214 in the variable Value1.

```
Value1 = Text_GetDate(1);
```

Text_GetFirst (Pref)

Returns the identification number of the first text object drawn in the chart

where `(Pref)` is a numeric expression representing the origin of the text object for which you want to obtain the identification number:
1 = text created by an analysis technique
2 = text created by the text drawing object only
3 = text created by either the text drawing object or an analysis technique

NOTE: Using a value other than 1, 2, or 3 causes the reserved word to assume a value of 3.

REMARKS

When the reserved word performs its operation successfully, the identification number is returned. When a reserved word cannot perform its operation, it returns an error code. For a list of error codes, see `Trendline` and `Text Error Codes`.

EXAMPLE

You must assign the reserved word to a numeric variable to obtain the identification number (or error code) returned by the reserved word. The following returns the identification number of the first text object drawn on the chart, regardless of how it was drawn.

```
Value1 = Text_GetFirst(3);
Text_GetHStyle
```

Returns the horizontal alignment setting for the specified text object.

Text_GetHStyle (TX_Ref);

`(TX_Ref)` is the identification number of the text object or a numeric expression representing the identification number.

REMARKS

The horizontal alignment settings are 0 for Left, 1 for Right, or 2 for Centered. These correspond to the three selections in the HAlign drop-down list in the Style tab of the Format Text dialog box.

When the reserved word performs its operation successfully, a horizontal alignment setting 0 through 2 is returned. When a reserved word cannot perform its operation, it returns an error code. For a list of error codes, see `Trendline` and `Text Error Codes`.

EXAMPLE

To obtain the horizontal alignment setting returned by the reserved word, you need to assign the reserved word to a numeric variable. When the text object with the identification number 1 is centered, the following returns a value of 2.

```
Value1 = Text_GetHStyle(1);
```

Text_GetNext(TX_Ref, Pref)

Returns the identification number of a text of specified origin created immediately after the specified text.

(`TX_Ref`) is the identification number of the text object or a numeric expression representing the identification number.

(`Pref`) is a numeric expression representing the origin of the text for which you want to obtain the identification number:

1 = text created by an analysis technique

2 = text created by the text drawing object only

3 = text created by either the text drawing object or an analysis technique

NOTE: Using a value other than 1, 2, or 3 causes the reserved word to assume a value of 3.

REMARKS

When the reserved word performs its operation successfully, the identification number for the text is returned. When a reserved word cannot perform its operation, it returns an error code. For a list of error codes, see `Trendline` and `Text Error Codes`.

EXAMPLE

To obtain the identification number returned by the reserved word, you need to assign the reserved word to a numeric variable. The following returns the identification number of the text drawn on the chart after the text with the identification number 0 and by the text drawing object.

```
Value1 = Text_GetNext(0, 2);
```

Text_GetString (TX_Ref)

Returns the string value of the specified text object.

(`TX_Ref`) is the identification number of the text object or a numeric expression representing the identification number.

REMARKS

When the reserved word performs its operation successfully, the text string is returned. When a reserved word cannot perform its operation, it returns an error code. For a list of error codes, see `Trendline` and `Text Error Codes`.

EXAMPLE

The following returns the text string used by the text object with the identification number 1. In order to obtain the text string, you must assign the reserved word to a string variable, as follows:

```
TextString = Text_GetString(1);
```

NOTE: EasyLanguage does not provide predeclared string variables so you will have to declare your own string variable in order to assign the reserved word to it.

Text_GetTime (TX_Ref)

Returns the time at which the specified text object is anchored (based on its horizontal and vertical alignment), in the format HHMM.

(`TX_Ref`) is the identification number of the text object or a numeric expression representing the identification number.

REMARKS

When the reserved word performs its operation successfully, the time at which the text object is anchored is returned. When a reserved word cannot perform its operation, it returns an error code. For a list of error codes, see `Trendline` and `Text Error Codes`.

EXAMPLE

The following returns 1300 when the text object with the identification number 1 is anchored at 1:00 pm. To obtain the time returned by the reserved word, you need to assign the reserved word to a numeric variable.

```
Value1 = Text_GetTime(0);
```

Text_GetValue (TX_Ref)

Returns the vertical axis (price) value at which the text object is anchored (based on its horizontal and vertical alignment).

`(TX_Ref)` is the identification number of the text object or a numeric expression representing the identification number.

REMARKS

When the reserved word performs its operation successfully, the price value at which the text object is anchored is returned. When a reserved word cannot perform its operation, it returns an error code. For a list of error codes, see `Trendline` and `Text Error Codes`.

EXAMPLE

The following returns a value of 41.543 when the text object with the identification number 5 is anchored at a price value of 41.543. To obtain the price value returned by the reserved word, you need to assign the reserved word to a numeric variable.

```
Value1 = Text_GetValue(5);
```

Text_GetVStyle(TX_Ref)

Returns the vertical alignment setting for the specified text object.

Where `(TX_Ref)` is the identification number of the text object or a numeric expression representing the identification number.

REMARKS

The vertical alignment settings are 0 for Top, 1 for Bottom, or 2 for Centered. These correspond to the three selections in the VAlign drop-down list in the Style tab of the Format Text dialog box.

When the reserved word performs its operation successfully, a vertical alignment setting 0 through 2 is returned. When a reserved word cannot perform its operation, it returns an error code. For a list of error codes, see Trendline and Text Error Codes.

EXAMPLE

To obtain the vertical alignment setting returned by the reserved word, you need to assign the reserved word to a numeric variable. When the text object with the identification number 1 is centered, the following returns a value of 2.

```
Value1 = Text_GetVStyle(1);
```

Text_New(cDate, tTime, nPrice, "Str1")

Creates a new text object in the specified location. You specify the location by providing a date, time, and price value as well as the string to add to the chart.

(cDate) is the date at which the text object will start, in YYMMDD or YYYMMDD format (three digits are used to express the year 2000 and later), or a numeric expression representing the start point date.

(tTime) is the time at which the text object will start, in HHMM format, or a numeric expression representing the start point time.

(nPrice) is the value for the start point of the text object or a numeric expression representing the start point value.

(Str1) is the string expression providing the text to write on the chart at the specified location. The text must be enclosed in quotation marks.

REMARKS

Drawing objects are numbered by type in the order they are created, from 0 to n. Therefore, 0 is the identification number of the first drawing object of that type created and n is the last object of the same type created.

When the reserved word performs its operation successfully, the reserved word returns the identification number for the new text object. When the reserved word cannot perform its operation, it returns an error code. For a list of error codes, see Trendline and Text Error Codes.

EXAMPLE

The following would write the text Stock Split on the chart at the current date and time, at the high price plus 20 points. You must assign the reserved word to a numeric variable in order to obtain the identification number for the text object.

```
Value1 = Text_New(Date, Time, High + 20, "Stock Split");
```

NOTE: By default, text objects are anchored using the left horizontal and top vertical alignment settings. You can change this and any other formatting setting using the other Text Drawing reserved words.

Text_SetColor(TX_Ref, Clr)

Sets the color for the specified text object.

(TX_Ref) is the identification number of the text object or a numeric expression representing the identification number.

(Clr) corresponds to the numeric value or EasyLanguage reserved word corresponding to the color of the text object. See EasyLanguage Colors in Appendix A for a list of valid colors.

REMARKS

When the reserved word performs its operation successfully, a 0 is returned. When a reserved word cannot perform its operation, it returns an error code. For a list of error codes, see Trendline and Text Error Codes.

EXAMPLE

To set the text object with the identification number 1 to yellow, you would write either of the following:

```
Text_SetColor(1, 7);
Text_SetColor(1, Yellow);
```

To obtain the error code (or 0 when no error) returned by the reserved word, you need to assign the reserved word to a numeric variable, as follows:

```
Value1 = Text_SetColor(1, 7);
```

Text_SetLocation(TX_Ref, cDate, tTime, nPrice)

Moves the specified text object to the specified location.

(`TX_Ref`) is the identification number of the text object or a numeric expression representing the identification number.

(`cDate`) is the date at which the text object will be anchored, in YYMMDD or YYYMMDD format (three digits are used to express the year 2000 and later), or a numeric expression representing the start point date.

(`tTime`) is the time at which the text object will be anchored, in HHMM format, or a numeric expression representing the start point time.

(`nPrice`) is the vertical axis (price) level at which the text object will be anchored or a numeric expression representing the start point value.

REMARKS

When the reserved word performs its operation successfully, a 0 is returned. When a reserved word cannot perform its operation, it returns an error code. For a list of error codes, see `Trendline` and `Text Error Codes`.

EXAMPLE

The following moves the text object with the identification number 2 to January 14, 1999, 3:00 pm, at 150.

```
Text_SetLocation(2, 990114, 1500, 150.00);
```

To obtain the error code (or 0 when no error) returned by the reserved word, you need to assign the reserved word to a numeric variable, as follows:

Value1 = Text_SetLocation(2, 990114, 1500, 150.00);

Text_SetString(TX_Ref, "Str1")

Specifies the text string to use in the specified text object.

(`TX_Ref`) is the identification number of the text object or a numeric expression representing the identification number.

(`Str1`) is the text string to write on the chart. The text string must be enclosed in quotation marks.

REMARKS

When the reserved word performs its operation successfully, a 0 is returned. When a reserved word cannot perform its operation, it returns an error code. For a list of error codes, see `Trendline` and `Text Error Codes`.

EXAMPLE

The following is used to change the string in the text object with the identification number 1 to New String.

```
Text_SetString(1, "New String");
```

To obtain the error code (or 0 when no error) returned by the reserved word, you need to assign the reserved word to a numeric variable, as follows:

```
Value1 = Text_SetString(1, "New String");
```

Text_SetStyle (TX_Ref, Horiz, Vert)

Specifies the anchor position (horizontal and vertical alignment settings) for the specified text object.

(`TX_Ref`) is the identification number of the text object or a numeric expression representing the identification number.

(`Horiz`) is the horizontal alignment setting for the text object, 0 for Left, 1 for Right, and 2 for Centered, or a numeric expression representing the setting.

(`Vert`) is the vertical alignment setting for the text object, 0 for Top, 1 for Bottom, and 2 for Centered, or a numeric expression representing the setting.

REMARKS

When the reserved word performs its operation successfully, a 0 is returned. When a reserved word cannot perform its operation, it returns an error code. For a list of error codes, see `Trendline` and `Text Error Codes`.

EXAMPLE

The following changes the anchor position (horizontal and vertical alignment settings) of the text object with the identification number 1 to the left center of the text object.

```
Text_SetStyle(1, 0, 2);
```

To obtain the error code (or 0 when no error) returned by the reserved word, you need to assign the reserved word to a numeric variable, as follows:

```
Value1 = Text_SetStyle(1, 0, 2);
```

Than

Skip word.

REMARKS

This word is skipped in EasyLanguage and is not necessary. These skipped words, however, do make it easier to understand the purpose of the code. By default, unnecessary words and sections marked as comments will appear dark green in the EasyLanguage PowerEditor.

EXAMPLE

```
If High > than the Highest(Close, 14) Then ...
```

The word "than" is not necessary and the code functions the same way regardless of its presence.

The

Skip word.

REMARKS

This word is skipped in EasyLanguage and is not necessary. These skipped words, however, do make it easier to understand the purpose of the code. By default, unnecessary words and sections marked as comments will appear dark green in the EasyLanguage PowerEditor.

EXAMPLE

```
If High > than the Highest(Close, 14) Then ...
```

The word "the" is not necessary and the code functions the same way regardless of its presence.

Then

This word is used to introduce a condition that will be evaluated to determine execution of additional code.

REMARKS

The second part of an **If**... **Then** or **If**... **Then**... **Else** statement. **If**... **Then** statements allow you to check a true/false condition and then take a specific action depending on the outcome of the condition. If the condition is true, the action after "Then" is executed.

EXAMPLES

```
If Condition1 Then
   (Your Code Line1}
```

`Then` is used here to designate `Line1` as the code that will be executed based on the outcome of `Condition1`. The `Line1` code will be executed if `Condition1` returns a value of True. If `Condition1` is false, the `Line1` code will not be executed.

```
If Condition1 And Condition2 Then
         Begin
         {Your Code Line1}
         {Your Code Line2, etc.}
         End
Else
                 Begin
                 {Your Code Line3}
                 {Your Code Line4, etc.}
                 End;
```

Then is used here to designate `Line1` as the code that will be executed based on the outcome of `Condition1`. The `Line1` and `Line2` code will be executed if `Condition1` and `Condition2` return a value of True. If `Condition1` or `Condition2` is false, the `Line3` and `Line4` code will be executed.

TheoreticalGrossIn

Returns the amount required (or received) in order to establish a position at its theoretical value.

REMARKS

Debit positions will return positive numbers and credit positions will return negative numbers.

EXAMPLE

```
Plot1(TheoreticalGrossIn of Position, "TGI");
```

TheoreticalGrossOut

Returns the amount required (or received) in order to close a position at its theoretical value.

REMARKS

Positive numbers will represent the amount received when closing the position, and negative numbers will represent the amount that must be paid to close the position.

EXAMPLE

```
Plot1(TheoreticalGrossOut of Position, "TGO");
```

TheoreticalValue

Returns the modeled value of an option or position leg.

EXAMPLE

```
If TheoreticalValue of Option < Close of Option then
   Alert("Over Priced Option");
```

Theta

Returns the Theta value of an option, leg, or position. The value of Theta can also be established in a Pricing Model by using `Theta(Value)`.

REMARKS

Debit positions will return positive numbers and credit positions will return negative numbers.

EXAMPLES

```
If Theta of Option > HighVal Then
      Alert("High Theta");
```

In a Pricing Model, you can set the value of Theta by using the following syntax:

```
Theta(0);
```

This

Reserved word used to refer to the present bar.

REMARKS

`This` is normally used with Bar or Day to specify the current Bar or Day.

EXAMPLES

`Buy This Bar on Close` refers to a long entry placed on the close of the current bar.

`Sell This Bar on Close` refers to a short entry placed on the close of the current bar.

Thursday

Returns the number 4 as the value for Thursday.

REMARKS

The value returned is an integer representing `Thursday` and is the same value returned by using the function `DayOfWeek(Thursday)`.

EXAMPLE

`Thursday` returns a value of 4 as the value for Thursday.

Ticks

Reserved word that represents multiple increments of the Price Scale.

REMARKS

`Ticks` is similar to `Points` and can be used interchangeably.

EXAMPLES

`Close + 5 ticks` returns the close price plus five increments of the Price Scale added to it.

`Low - 2 ticks` returns the low of the bar minus two increments of the Price Scale.

ADDITIONAL EXAMPLE

An exit statement can be written to prevent large losses by:

```
Sell This Bar at EntryPrice - 3 ticks Stop;
```

TickType

What kind of tick triggered the option core event: Asset, Option, Future, or Model.

Time

Reserved word used to return the time of the current bar.

REMARKS

`Time` returns the time in 24-hour format.

EXAMPLES

`Time` returns 1600 if the time of the bar is 4:00 pm.

`Time` returns 0930 if the time of the bar is 9:30 am.

ADDITIONAL EXAMPLE

To check the time of the previous bar write:

```
Time of 1 bar ago
```

TL_Delete (TL_Ref)

Deletes the specified trendline from the chart.

(TL_Ref) is the identification number of the trendline or a numeric expression representing the identification number.

REMARKS

If the trendline cannot be deleted, TL_Delete returns an error code. When the trendline is successfully deleted, it returns 0. For a list of error codes, see Trendline and Text Error Codes.

EXAMPLE

The following deletes the trendline with the identification number 3:

```
TL_Delete(3);
```

To obtain the error code (or 0 when no error) returned by the reserved word, you can assign the reserved word to a numeric variable, as follows:

```
Value1 = TL_Delete(Value1);
```

TL_GetAlert(TL_Ref)

Returns the alert status of the specified trendline object. 0 = no alert, 1 = Breakout Intrabar, 2 = Breakout on Close.

(TL_Ref) is the identification number of the trendline or a numeric expression representing the identification number of the trendline.

REMARKS

When the reserved word performs its operation successfully, it returns a value of 0, 1 or 2, indicating the alert status. When a reserved word cannot perform its operation, it returns an error code. For a list of error codes, see Trendline and Text Error Codes.

EXAMPLE

To obtain the alert status returned by the reserved word, you need to assign the reserved word to a numeric variable.

The following obtains the alert status for the trendline with the identification number 2.

```
Value1 = TL_GetAlert(2);
```

TL_GetBeginDate (TL_Ref)

Returns the date on which the specified trendline begins, in YYMMDD or YYYMMDD format (three digits are used to express the year 2000 and higher).

(TL_Ref) is the identification number of the trendline or a numeric expression representing the identification number.

REMARKS

When the reserved word performs its operation successfully, it returns the date. When a reserved word cannot perform its operation, it returns an error code. For a list of error codes, see Trendline and Text Error Codes.

EXAMPLE

To obtain the date returned by the reserved word, you need to assign the reserved word to a numeric variable. The trendline with the identification number 6 begins on January 14, 1999. The following will return 990114.

```
Value1 = TL_GetBeginDate(6);
```

TL_GetBeginTime(TL_Ref)

Returns the time at which the specified trendline begins (in 24-hour format, HHMM).

(TL_Ref) is the identification number of the trendline or a numeric expression representing the identification number.

REMARKS

When the reserved word performs its operation successfully, it returns the time. When a reserved word cannot perform its operation, it returns an error code. For a list of error codes, see `Trendline` and `Text Error Codes`.

EXAMPLE

To obtain the time returned by the reserved word, you need to assign the reserved word to a numeric variable. The starting point for the trendline with the identification number 2 is at 1:00 pm. The following will return 1300.

```
Value1 = TL_GetBeginTime(2);
```

TL_GetBeginVal(TL_Ref)

Returns the vertical axis (price) value at which the specified trendline begins.

(`TL_Ref`) is the identification number of the trendline or a numeric expression representing the identification number.

REMARKS

When the reserved word performs its operation successfully, it returns the price value. When a reserved word cannot perform its operation, it returns an error code. For a list of error codes, see `Trendline` and `Text Error Codes`.

EXAMPLE

To obtain the price value returned by the reserved word, you need to assign the reserved word to a numeric variable

The trendline with the identification number 5 begins at a price of 41.543. The following will return 41.543.

```
Value1 = TL_GetBeginVal(5);
```

TL_GetColor(TL_Ref)

Returns the numeric value corresponding to the color of the specified trendline.

(`TL_Ref`) is the identification number of the trendline or a numeric expression representing the identification number.

REMARKS

For a list of possible colors and their corresponding numeric values, see EasyLanguage Colors in Appendix A.

When the reserved word performs its operation successfully, it returns the numeric value corresponding to the color. When a reserved word cannot perform its operation, it returns an error code. For a list of error codes, see Trendline and Text Error Codes.

EXAMPLE

To obtain the numeric color value returned by the reserved word, you need to assign the reserved word to a numeric variable. The trendline with the identification number 1 is yellow. Therefore, the following returns the value 7.

```
Value1 = TL_GetColor(1);
```

TL_GetEndDate (TL_Ref)

Returns the date on which the specified trendline ends in YYMMDD or YYYMMDD format (three digits are used to express the year 2000 and higher).

(TL_Ref) is the identification number of the trendline or a numeric expression representing the identification number.

REMARKS

When the reserved word performs its operation successfully, the date is returned. When a reserved word cannot perform its operation, it returns an error code. For a list of error codes, see Trendline and Text Error Codes.

EXAMPLE

To obtain the date returned by the reserved word, you need to assign the reserved word to a numeric variable. The trendline with the identification number 1 ends on February 14, 1999. The following returns 990214.

```
Value1 = TL_GetEndDate(1);
```

TL_GetEndTime (TL_Ref)

Returns the time at which the specified trendline ends (in 24-hour format, HHMM).

(TL_Ref) is the identification number of the trendline or a numeric expression representing the identification number.

REMARKS

When the reserved word performs its operation successfully, the time is returned. When a reserved word cannot perform its operation, it returns an error code. For a list of error codes, see Trendline and Text Error Codes.

EXAMPLE

To obtain the time returned by the reserved word, you need to assign the reserved word to a numeric variable. The trendline with the identification number 3 ends at 10:00 am. The following returns 1000.

```
Value1 = TL_GetEndTime(3);
```

TL_GetEndVal(TL_Ref)

Returns the vertical axis (price) value of the end of the specified trendline object.

(TL_Ref) is the identification number of the trendline or a numeric expression representing the identification number.

REMARKS
When the reserved word performs its operation successfully, the price value is returned. When a reserved word cannot perform its operation, it returns an error code. For a list of error codes, see Trendline and Text Error Codes.
EXAMPLE
To obtain the price value returned by the reserved word, you need to assign the reserved word to a numeric variable

The trendline with the identification number 4 ends at a price of 41.543. The following returns a value of 41.543.

```
Value1 = TL_GetEndVal(4);
```

TL_GetExtLeft(TL_Ref)

Returns a value of true when the specified trendline is extended to the left and a value of false when it is not extended to the left.

(TL_Ref) is the identification number of the trendline or a numeric expression representing the identification number.

REMARKS
When the reserved word performs its operation successfully, the true or false value is returned, indicating whether or not the trendline is extended left. When a reserved word cannot perform its operation, it returns an error code. For a list of error codes, see Trendline and Text Error Codes.
EXAMPLE
To obtain the true/false value returned by the reserved word, you need to assign the reserved word to a true/false variable. The trendline with the identification number 12 is not extended to the left. The following returns the value false.

```
Condition1 = TL_GetExtLeft(12);
```

TL_GetExtRight(TL_Ref)

Returns a value of true when the specified trendline is extended to the right and a value of false when it is not extended to the right.

(TL_Ref) is the identification number of the trendline or a numeric expression representing the identification number.

REMARKS
When the reserved word performs its operation successfully, the true or false value is returned, indicating whether the trendline is extended right or not. When a reserved word cannot perform its operation, it returns an error code. For a list of error codes, see Trendline and Text Error Codes.
EXAMPLE
To obtain the true/false value returned by the reserved word, you need to assign the reserved word to a true/false variable. The trendline with the identification number 12 is extended to the right. The following returns the value true.

```
Condition1 = TL_GetExtRight(12);
```

TL_GetFirst (Pref)

Returns the identification number of the first trendline inserted in a chart.

(Pref) is a numeric expression representing the origin of the trendline for which you want to obtain the identification number:

1 = trendline created by an analysis technique
2 = trendline created by the trendline drawing object only
3 = trendline created by either the trendline drawing object or an analysis technique

NOTE: Using a value other than 1, 2, or 3 causes the reserved word to assume a value of 3.

REMARKS

When the reserved word performs its operation successfully, the identification number is returned. When a reserved word cannot perform its operation, it returns an error code. For a list of error codes, see Trendline and Text Error Codes.

EXAMPLE

You must assign the reserved word to a numeric variable to obtain the identification number (or error code) returned by the reserved word. The following returns the identification number of the first trendline drawn on the chart, regardless of how it was drawn.

```
Value1 = TL_GetFirst(3);
```

TL_GetNext (TL_Ref, Pref)

Returns the identification number of a trendline of specified origin created immediately after the specified trendline.

(`TL_Ref`) is the identification number of the trendline or a numeric expression representing the identification number.

(`Pref`) is a numeric expression representing the origin of the trendline for which you want to obtain the identification number:

1 = trendline created by an analysis technique
2 = trendline created by the trendline drawing object only
3 = trendline created by either the trendline drawing object or an analysis technique

NOTE: Using a value other than 1, 2, or 3 causes the reserved word to assume a value of 3.

REMARKS

When the reserved word performs its operation successfully, the identification number for the trendline is returned. When a reserved word cannot perform its operation, it returns an error code. For a list of error codes, see Trendline and Text Error Codes.

EXAMPLE

To obtain the identification number returned by the reserved word, you need to assign the reserved word to a numeric variable. The following returns the identification number of the trendline drawn on the chart after the trendline with the identification number 0 and by the trendline drawing object.

```
Value1 = TL_GetNext(0, 2);
```

TL_GetSize (TL_Ref)

Returns the line thickness setting (weight) for the specified trendline.

(TL_Ref) is the identification number of the trendline or a numeric expression representing the identification number.

REMARKS

Line thickness ranges from 0 (thinnest) to 6 (thickest). These correspond to the seven selections in the Weight drop-down list in the Style tab of the Format Trendline dialog box.

When the reserved word performs its operation successfully, a line thickness setting 0 through 6 is returned. When a reserved word cannot perform its operation, it returns an error code. For a list of error codes, see Trendline and Text Error Codes.

EXAMPLE

To obtain the line thickness value returned by the reserved word, you need to assign the reserved word to a numeric variable. When the trendline with the identification number 1 is drawn with the third heaviest weight, the following returns a value of 2. The first weight is 0, the second is 1, and the third weight is 2. Thus, Value1 would be equal to 2.

```
Value1 = TL_GetSize(1);
```

TL_GetStyle (TL_Ref)

Returns the line style setting for the specified trendline.

(TL_Ref) is the identification number of the trendline or a numeric expression representing the identification number.

REMARKS

There are five possible line styles:

Style Name	Number
Tool_Solid	1 (solid)
Tool_Dashed	2 (dashed)
Tool_Dotted	3 (dotted)
Tool_Dashed2	4 (dashed pattern)
Tool_Dashed3	5 (dashed pattern)

These correspond to the five selections in the Style drop-down list in the Style tab of the Format Trendline dialog box.

When the reserved word performs its operation successfully, it returns the number corresponding to the line style setting. When a reserved word cannot perform its operation, it returns an error code. For a list of error codes, see Trendline and Text Error Codes.

EXAMPLE

To obtain the line style value returned by the reserved word, you need to assign the reserved word to a numeric variable. The trendline with the identification number 1 is drawn using a solid line style. The following returns 1.

```
Value1 = TL_GetStyle(1);
```

TL_GetValue (TL_Ref, cDate, tTime)

Returns the vertical axis (price) value of the specified trendline at the specific date and time.

(`TL_Ref`) is the identification number of the trendline or a numeric expression representing the identification number.

(`cDate`) is the date for which you want the value of the trendline, in YYMMDD or YYYMMDD format (three digits are used to express the year 2000 and later).

(`tTime`) is the time at which you want the value of the trendline (in 24-hour format, HHMM).

REMARKS

When the reserved word performs its operation successfully, the vertical axis (price) value is returned. When a reserved word cannot perform its operation, it returns an error code. For a list of error codes, see Trendline and Text Error Codes.

EXAMPLE

To obtain the price value returned by the reserved word, you need to assign the reserved word to a numeric variable

On January 7, 1999 at 4:00 pm, the trendline with the identification number 5 intersects the price value of 53.350. The following returns 53.350.

```
Value1 = TL_GetValue(5, 990107, 1600);
```

TL_New(sDate, sTime, sVal, eDate, eTime, eVal)

Creates a new trendline with the specified start and end points. To identify the start and end points, you provide the date, time, and value for both.

(`sDate`) is the date for the start point of the trendline, in YYMMDD or YYYMMDD format (three digits are used to express the year 2000 and later), or a numeric expression representing the start point date.

(`sTime`) is the time for the start point of the trendline (in 24-hour format, HHMM) or a numeric expression representing the start point time.

(`sVal`) is the value for the start point of the trendline or a numeric expression representing the start point value.

(`eDate`) is the date for the end point of the trendline, in YYMMDD or YYYMMDD format (three digits are used to express the year 2000 and later), or a numeric expression representing the end point date.

(`eTime`) is the time for the end point of the trendline (in 24-hour format, HHMM) or a numeric expression representing the end point time.

(`eVal`) is the value of the end point of the trendline or a numeric expression representing the end point value.

REMARKS

Drawing objects are numbered by type in the order they are created, from 0 to n. Therefore, 0 is the identification number of the first drawing object of that type created and n is the last object of the same type created.

When the reserved word performs its operation successfully, the reserved word returns the identification number for the new trendline. When the reserved word cannot perform its operation, it returns an error code. For a list of error codes, see Trendline and Text Error Codes.

EXAMPLE

The following creates a trendline that begins at 9:30 am on January 7, 1999 at a value of 45 and ends at 4:00 pm on January 25, 1999 at a value of 37.250:

```
Value1 = TL_New(990107, 0930, 45, 990125, 1600, 37.250);
```

You must assign the reserved word to a numeric variable in order to obtain the identification number for the trendline.

TL_SetAlert(TL_Ref, alertVal)

Sets the alert status for the specified trendline.

(`TL_Ref`) is the identification number of the trendline or a numeric expression representing the identification number.

(`alertVal`) is the alert setting for the trendline:

0 = no alert

1 = Breakout Intrabar alert

2 = Breakout on Close alert

REMARKS

When the reserved word performs its operation successfully, a 0 is returned. When a reserved word cannot perform its operation, it returns an error code. For a list of error codes, see Trendline and Text Error Codes.

EXAMPLE

The following sets the alert of the trendline with the identification number 1 to Breakout Intrabar:

```
TL_SetAlert(1, 1);
```

To obtain the error code (or 0 when no error) returned by the reserved word, you can assign the reserved word to a numeric variable, as follows:

```
Value1 = TL_SetAlert(1, 1);
```

TL_SetBegin(TL_Ref, sDate, sTime, sVal)

Sets the beginning of the specified trendline.

(`TL_Ref`) is the identification number of the trendline or a numeric expression representing the identification number.

(`sDate`) is the starting date for the trendline (in YYMMDD or YYYMMDD format).

(`sTime`) is the starting time for the trendline (in 24-hour format, HHMM).

(`sVal`) is the starting value for the trendline.

REMARKS

When the reserved word performs its operation successfully, a 0 is returned. When a reserved word cannot perform its operation, it returns an error code. For a list of error codes, see Trendline and Text Error Codes.

EXAMPLE

The following sets the trendline with the identification number 4 to a value of 107.225 on February 21, 1999 at 10 am.

```
TL_SetBegin(4, 990221, 1015, 107.225);
```

To obtain the error code (or 0 when no error) returned by the reserved word, you can assign the reserved word to a numeric variable, as follows:

```
Value1 = TL_SetBegin(4, 990221, 1015, 107.225);
```

TL_SetColor(TL_Ref, Clr)

Sets the color for the specified trendline.

(`TL_Ref`) is the identification number of the trendline or a numeric expression representing the identification number.

(`Clr`) corresponds to the numeric value or EasyLanguage reserved word corresponding to the color of the trendline. See the EasyLanguage colors in Appendix A for a list of valid colors.

REMARKS

When the reserved word performs its operation successfully, a 0 is returned. When a reserved word cannot perform its operation, it returns an error code. For a list of error codes, see Trendline and Text Error Codes.

EXAMPLE

To set the color of the trendline with the identification number 1 to yellow, you would write either of the following:

```
TL_SetColor(1, 7);
TL_SetColor(1, Yellow);
```

To obtain the error code (or 0 when no error) returned by the reserved word, you need to assign the reserved word to a numeric variable, as follows:

```
Value1 = TL_SetColor(1, 7);
```

TL_SetEnd(TL_Ref, eDate, eTime, eVal)

Sets the end point of the specified trendline object based on the specified parameters.

(`TL_Ref`) is the identification number of the trendline or a numeric expression representing the identification number.

(`eDate`) is the ending date of the trendline (in YYMMDD or YYYMMDD format).

(`eTime`) is the ending time of the trendline (in 24-hour format, HHMM).

(`eVal`) is the ending value of the trendline.

REMARKS

When the reserved word performs its operation successfully, a 0 is returned. When a reserved word cannot perform its operation, it returns an error code. For a list of error codes, see Trendline and Text Error Codes.

EXAMPLE

The following sets the end point of the first trendline created in a chart to a value of 207.125 on February 21, 1999 at 3:15 pm.

```
TL_SetEnd(0, 990221, 1515, 207.125);
```

To obtain the error code (or 0 for no error) returned by the reserved word, you need to assign the reserved word to a numeric variable, as follows:

```
Value1 = TL_SetEnd(0, 990221, 1515, 207.125);
```

TL_SetExtLeft (TL_Ref, tfExt)

Specifies whether to extend left the specified trendline.

(`TL_Ref`) is the identification number of the trendline or a numeric expression representing the identification number.

(`tfExt`) specifies the extend status of the trendline:

True = extend left

False = do not extend left

REMARKS

When the reserved word performs its operation successfully, a 0 is returned. When a reserved word cannot perform its operation, it returns an error code. For a list of error codes, see Trendline and Text Error Codes.

EXAMPLE

The following turns off the extend left status of the second trendline created in a chart (i.e., the trendline will not extend left):

```
TL_SetExtLeft(1, False);
```

To obtain the error code (or 0 for no error) returned by the reserved word, you need to assign the reserved word to a numeric variable, as follows:

```
Value1 = TL_SetExtLeft(1, False);
```

TL_SetExtRight (TL_Ref, tfExt)

Specifies whether to extend right the specified trendline.

(`TL_Ref`) is the identification number of the trendline or a numeric expression representing the identification number.

(`tfExt`) specifies the extend status of the trendline:

True = extend right

False = do not extend right

REMARKS

When the reserved word performs its operation successfully, a 0 is returned. When a reserved word cannot perform its operation, it returns an error code. For a list of error codes, see Trendline and Text Error Codes.

EXAMPLE

The following turns on the extend right status of the second trendline created in a chart (i.e., the trendline will extend right):

```
TL_SetExtRight(1, True);
```

To obtain the true/false value returned by the reserved word, you need to assign the reserved word to a numeric variable, as follows:

```
Value1 = TL_SetExtRight(1, True);
```

TL_SetSize(TL_Ref, Size)

Sets the width (line thickness) setting for the specified trendline object.

(`TL_Ref`) is the identification number of the trendline or a numeric expression representing the identification number.

(`Size`) is the thickness value for the trendline.

REMARKS

Thickness widths range from 0 (the thinnest) to 6 (the thickest).

When the reserved word performs its operation successfully, a 0 is returned. When a reserved word cannot perform its operation, it returns an error code. For a list of error codes, see Trendline and Text Error Codes.

EXAMPLE

The following sets the size of the fifth trendline created in a chart to the fourth thickest width:

```
TL_SetSize(4, 3);
```

To obtain the error code (or 0 when no error) returned by the reserved word, you need to assign the reserved word to a numeric variable, as follows:

```
Value1 = TL_SetSize(4, 3);
```

TL_SetStyle (TL_Ref, Style)

Sets the line style setting for the specified trendline.

(`TL_Ref`) is the identification number of the trendline or a numeric expression representing the identification number.

(`Style`) is the line style setting for the trendline.

REMARKS

There are five possible line styles:

Style Name	Number
Tool_Solid	1 (solid)
Tool_Dashed	2 (dashed)
Tool_Dotted	3 (dotted)
Tool_Dashed2	4 (dashed pattern)
Tool_Dashed3	5 (dashed pattern)

When the reserved word performs its operation successfully, a 0 is returned. When a reserved word cannot perform its operation, it returns an error code. For a list of error codes, see `Trendline` and `Text Error Codes`.

EXAMPLE

The following sets the line style of the fifth trendline created in a chart to `Tool_Dotted` (dotted):

```
TL_SetStyle(4, 3);
```

To obtain the error code (or 0 when no error) returned by the reserved word, you need to assign the reserved word to a numeric variable, as follows:

```
Value1 = TL_SetStyle(4, 3);
```

To

This word is used as a part of a For statement where the execution values will be increasing to a finishing value.

REMARKS

`To` will always be placed between two arithmetic expressions.

EXAMPLES

```
For Value5 = Length To Length + 10 Begin
      {Your Code Here}
End;
```

To is used here to indicate that for each value of Value5 from `Length to Length plus 10`, the following `Begin`... `End` loop will be executed.

```
Variables: Sum(0), Counter(0);
Sum = 0;
For Counter = 0 To Length - 1 Begin
      Sum = Sum + Price[Counter];
End;
```

`To` is used here to accumulate the variable `Sum` for each value of `Counter` from 0 to `Length` minus one.

Today

This word is retained for backward compatibility.

REMARKS

`Today` is used to reference the most current bar, even when analyzing intraday bars.

`Today` is no longer necessary as the following are equivalent:

```
Value1 = Close of Today;
Value1 = Close;
```

Tomorrow

This word is retained for backward compatibility. Replaced by Next Bar.

REMARKS

`Tomorrow` references the next bar, even when analyzing intraday bars.

`Tomorrow` is no longer necessary as the following are equivalent:

```
Buy at Open Tomorrow + Range Stop;
Buy at Open Next Bar + Range Stop;
```

Tool_Black

This word has been replaced by the reserved word Black.

Tool_Blue

This word is retained for backward compatibility.

REMARKS

This word has been replaced by the reserved word Blue.

Tool_Cyan

This word is retained for backward compatibility.

REMARKS

This word has been replaced by the reserved word Cyan.

Tool_DarkBlue

This word is retained for backward compatibility.

REMARKS

This word has been replaced by the reserved word DarkBlue.

Tool_DarkBrown

This word is retained for backward compatibility.

REMARKS

This word has been replaced by the reserved word DarkBrown.

Tool_DarkCyan

This word is retained for backward compatibility.

REMARKS

This word has been replaced by the reserved word DarkCyan.

Tool_DarkGray

This word is retained for backward compatibility.

REMARKS

This word has been replaced by the reserved word DarkGray.

Tool_DarkGreen

This word is retained for backward compatibility.

REMARKS

This word has been replaced by the reserved word DarkGreen.

Tool_DarkMagenta

This word is retained for backward compatibility.

REMARKS

This word has been replaced by the reserved word DarkMagenta.

Tool_DarkRed

This word is retained for backward compatibility.

REMARKS

This word has been replaced by the reserved word DarkRed.

Tool_DarkYellow

This word is retained for backward compatibility.

REMARKS

This word has been replaced by the reserved word DarkYellow.

Tool_Dashed

Line style used for trendlines.

REMARKS

There are five line styles available for use in charting:

Style Name	Number
Tool_Solid	1 (solid)
Tool_Dashed	2 (dashed)
Tool_Dotted	3 (dotted)
Tool_Dashed2	4 (dashed pattern)
Tool_Dashed3	5 (dashed pattern)

Tool_Dashed2

Line style used for trendlines.

REMARKS

There are five line styles available for use in charting:

Style Name	Number
Tool_Solid	1 (solid)
Tool_Dashed	2 (dashed)
Tool_Dotted	3 (dotted)
Tool_Dashed2	4 (dashed pattern)
Tool_Dashed3	5 (dashed pattern)

Tool_Dashed3

Line style used for trendlines.

REMARKS

There are five line styles available for use in charting:

Style Name	Number
Tool_Solid	1 (solid)
Tool_Dashed	2 (dashed)
Tool_Dotted	3 (dotted)
Tool_Dashed2	4 (dashed pattern)
Tool_Dashed3	5 (dashed pattern)

Tool_Dotted

Line style used for trendlines.

REMARKS

There are five line styles available for use in charting:

Style Name	Number
Tool_Solid	1 (solid)
Tool_Dashed	2 (dashed)
Tool_Dotted	3 (dotted)
Tool_Dashed2	4 (dashed pattern)
Tool_Dashed3	5 (dashed pattern)

Tool_Green

This word is retained for backward compatibility.

REMARKS

This word has been replaced by the reserved word Green.

Tool_LightGray

This word is retained for backward compatibility.

REMARKS

This word has been replaced by the reserved word LightGray.

Tool_Magenta

This word is retained for backward compatibility.

REMARKS

This word has been replaced by the reserved word Magenta.

Tool_Red

This word is retained for backward compatibility.

REMARKS

This word has been replaced by the reserved word Red.

Tool_Solid

Line style used for trendlines.

REMARKS

There are five line styles available for use in charting:

Style Name	Number
Tool_Solid	1 (solid)
Tool_Dashed	2 (dashed)
Tool_Dotted	3 (dotted)
Tool_Dashed2	4 (dashed pattern)
Tool_Dashed3	5 (dashed pattern)

Tool_White

This word is retained for backward compatibility.

REMARKS

This word has been replaced by the reserved word White.

Tool_Yellow

This word is retained for backward compatibility.

REMARKS

This word has been replaced by the reserved word Yellow.

Total

Reserved word used in an Exit statement to specify the number of contracts to exit from a long or short entry.

REMARKS

Specifying the number of contracts to exit from a position is not required in an Exit statement.

`Total` is exclusively used in an Exit condition to specify the number of contracts to exit.

EXAMPLES

`Sell 1 contract total next bar at market;` generates an order to exit only one contract from a short position on the first price of the next bar.

`Sell 1 contract total next bar at market;` generates an order to exit only one contract from a long position on the first price of the next bar.

ADDITIONAL EXAMPLE

`Sell 5 contracts total next bar at market;` generates an order to exit only five contracts from a long position on the first price of the next bar.

TotalBarsLosTrade

Returns the total number of bars that elapsed during losing trades for all closed trades.

EXAMPLES

`TotalBarsLosTrade` returns 73 if the number of bars elapsed during four losing trades were 40, 23, 6, and 4.

`TotalBarsLosTrade` returns 10 if the number of bars elapsed during two losing trades were 7 and 3.

TotalBarsWinTrade

Returns the total number of bars that elapsed during winning trades for all closed trades.

EXAMPLES

`TotalBarsWinTrade` returns 73 if the number of bars elapsed during four winning trades were 40, 23, 6, and 4.

`TotalBarsWinTrade` returns 10 if the number of bars elapsed during two winning trades were 7 and 3.

TotalTrade

Returns the total number of closed trades.

EXAMPLES

`TotalTrades` returns 7 if the number of closed trades is 7.

`TotalTrades` returns 5 if the number of closed trades is 5.

TrailingStopAmt

This word is retained for backward compatibility.

REMARKS

This word has been replaced by the signals TrailingStopLX and TrailingStopSX.

TrailingStopFloor

This word is retained for backward compatibility.

REMARKS

This word has been replaced by the signals TrailingStopLX and TrailingStopSX.

TrailingStopPct

This word is retained for backward compatibility.

REMARKS

This word has been replaced by the signals TrailingStopLX and TrailingStopSX.

True

This word is used as the value for an input or valid condition.

REMARKS

`True` can be used only in EasyLanguage as the value for a true/false input.

`True` is the value returned by a correct or valid condtition such as, 0 > 1.

EXAMPLES

`Input:Test(True);` would set the value of an input "Test" to a default value of `True`.

`If 50 < 100 Then`... would result in a value of `True` and the statement following `Then` would be executed.

TrueFalse

Reserved word used to define an input that expects a true-false expression passed by a value.

REMARKS

`TrueFalse` can be used for inputs that can be either TrueFalseSimple or TrueFalseSeries.

EXAMPLES

`Input: Switch(TrueFalse);` declares the constant Switch as a TrueFalse value to be used in a function.

`Input: Flag(TrueFalse);` declares the constant Flag as a TrueFalse value to be used in a function.

TrueFalseArray

`TrueFalseArray` declares a function input as a true/false array being passed by value.

REMARKS

A Function input is declared as a TrueFalse array when it is passing in a TrueFalse array by value.

EXAMPLE

`Input: PassedValues[n](TrueFalseArray)` indicates that a TrueFalse array is being passed into the function by value through the input `PassedValues`.

TrueFalseArrayRef

`TrueFalseArrayRef` declares a function input as a true/false array being passed by reference.

REMARKS

A function input is declared as a TrueFalse array reference when it is passing in a TrueFalse array by reference.

EXAMPLES

`PassedValues[n](TrueFalseArrayRef)` indicates that a TrueFalse array is being passed into the function by reference through the input `PassedValues`.

TrueFalseRef

`TrueFalseRef` declares a function input as a TrueFalse value being passed by reference.

REMARKS

A function Input is declared as a TrueFalse reference when it is passing in a value by reference.

EXAMPLES

`PassedValue(TrueFalseRef)` indicates that a TrueFalse value is being passed into the function by reference through the input `PassedValue`.

TrueFalseSeries

Reserved word used to define the type of input expected to be passed to a function.

REMARKS

`TrueFalseSeries` is used for inputs whose values can be referred to historically.

EXAMPLES

`Input: Switch(TrueFalseSeries);` declares the constant Switch as a TrueFalse value to be used in a function, where historical values of Switch are available.

`Input: Flag(TrueFalseSeries);` declares the constant Flag as a TrueFalse value to be used in a function, where historical values of Flag are available.

TrueFalseSimple

Reserved word used to define the type of input expected to be passed to a function.

REMARKS

`TrueFalseSimple` cannot be used for inputs whose values can be referred to historically.

EXAMPLES

`Input: Switch(TrueFalseSimple);` declares the constant Switch as a TrueFalse value to be used in a function, restricting Switch to be a value that does not contain historical values.

`Input: Flag(TrueFalseSimple);` declares the constant Flag as a TrueFalse value to be used in a function, restricting Flag to be a value that does not contain historical values.

TtlDbt_By_NetAssts

Returns the total debt divided by total assets.

Tuesday

Returns the number 2 as the value for Tuesday.

REMARKS

The value returned is an integer representing `Tuesday` and is the same value returned by using the function `DayOfWeek(Tuesday)`.

EXAMPLE

`Tuesday` returns a value of 2 as the value for Tuesday.

U

Under

This word is used to check for the direction of a cross between values.

REMARKS

Used in conjunction with the "crosses" to detect when a value crosses under, or becomes less than, another value. A value (`Value1`) crosses under another value (`Value2`) whenever `Value1` is less than `Value2` in the current bar but `Value1` was equal to or greater than `Value2` in the previous bar.

`Under` is a synonym for `Below`.

EXAMPLES

```
If Average(Close, 9) Crosses Under the Average(Close, 18) Then...
```

`Under` is used here to determine the direction of the cross of the values of two moving averages on the bar under consideration.

```
If Value1 Crosses Under Value2 Then ...
```

`Under` is used here to determine the direction of the cross of the variables Value1 and Value2 on the bar under consideration.

UnionSess1EndTime

Returns the latest time of all the first session end times when a technique is applied to more than one data set.

REMARKS

`UnionSess1EndTime` returns the time in 24-hour format.

`UnionSess1EndTime` is normally used when a technique is applied to more than one data set (i.e., multidata chart).

EXAMPLES

`UnionSess1EndTime` returns 1500 when applied to the U.S. Treasury Bonds trading on the Chicago Board of Trade.

`UnionSess1EndTime` returns 1615 when applied to IBM trading on the New York Stock Exchange.

UnionSess1FirstBar

Returns the time of the earliest First bar generated during the first session of trading of the day.

REMARKS

`UnionSess1FirstBarTime` returns the time in 24-hour format.

`UnionSess1FirstBarTime` is normally used when a technique is applied to more than one data set (i.e., multidata chart).

EXAMPLES

`UnionSess1FirstBarTime` returns 1000 when applied to IBM data with a 30-minute compression.

`UnionSess1FirstBarTime` returns 0825 when applied to U.S. Treasury Bond data with a 5-minute compression.

UnionSess1StartTime

Returns the earliest starting time of the first trading session when a technique is applied to more than one data set.

REMARKS

`UnionSess1StartTime` returns the time in 24-hour format.

`UnionSess1StartTime` is normally used when a technique is applied to more than one data set (i.e., multidata chart).

EXAMPLES

`UnionSess1StartTime` returns 0820 when applied to the U.S. Treasury Bonds trading on the Chicago Board of Trade.

`UnionSess1StartTime` returns 0930 when applied to IBM trading on the New York Stock Exchange.

UnionSess2EndTime

Returns the latest time of all the second session end times when a technique is applied to more than one data set.

REMARKS

`UnionSess2EndTime` returns the time in 24-hour format.

`UnionSess2EndTime` is normally used when a technique is applied to more than one data set (i.e. multidata chart).

EXAMPLES

`UnionSess2EndTime` returns 0745 when applied to the U.S. Treasury Bonds trading on the Chicago Board of Trade.

`UnionSess2EndTime` returns 0915 when applied to the S&P 500 Futures trading on the Chicago Mercantile Exchange.

UnionSess2FirstBar

Returns the time of the earliest First bar generated during the first session of trading of the day.

REMARKS

`UnionSess2FirstBar` returns the time in 24-hour format.

`UnionSess2FirstBar` is normally used when a technique is applied to more than one data set (i.e., multidata chart).

EXAMPLES

`UnionSess2FirstBar` returns 1715 when applied to S&P 500 Futures data with a 30-minute compression.

`UnionSess2FirstBar` returns 1535 when applied to US Treasury Bond Data with a 5-minute compression.

UnionSess2StartTime

Returns the earliest starting time of the first trading session when a technique is applied to more than one data set.

REMARKS

`UnionSess2StartTime` returns the time in 24-hour format.

`UnionSess2StartTime` is normally used when a technique is applied to more than one data set (i.e., multidata chart).

EXAMPLES

`UnionSess2StartTime` returns 1530 when applied to the U.S. Treasury Bonds trading on the Chicago Board of Trade.

`UnionSess2StartTime` returns 1645 when applied to the S&P 500 Futures trading on the Chicago Mercantile Exchange.

Units

This word is retained for backward compatibility.

Unsigned

Reserved for use with custom DLLs designed for EasyLanguage. Refer to the documentation in the TradeStation Developer's Kit for more information about this and the EasyLanguage Tool Kit Library ELKIT32.DLL.

Until

Evaluates one or more statements in a loop and exits the loop only when the until condition is true.

```
Repeat
  statement(s);
Until (condition_is_true);
```

REMARKS

There is no need to use the begin/end keywords to group more than one program statement, as all statements between `Repeat` and `Until` are treated as a block.

The repeat statement is similar to the while loop; however, with the repeat statement, the conditional test occurs after the loop. This means that the program statement(s) that constitute the loop body will be executed at least once.

UpperStr

Used to convert a string expression to uppercase letters.

```
UpperStr (''Str'');
```

(`Str`) is the string expression to change to uppercase letters. Make sure the string expression is enclosed in quotation marks.

EXAMPLE

`UpperStr(''omga'')` returns the string expression "OMGA".

UpTicks

Returns the number of ticks on a bar whose value is higher than the tick immediately preceding it.

REMARKS

Returns the Up volume of a bar when trade volume is used for the chart.

EXAMPLES

`UpTicks` returns 5 if there were 5 ticks on a bar whose value was higher than the tick immediately preceding it.

`UpTicks` returns 12 if there were 12 ticks on a bar whose value was higher than the tick immediately preceding it.

ADDITIONAL EXAMPLE

To check if a bar of data appears to reflect a steady upturn, compare `UpTicks` to `DownTicks`:

```
Value1 = Upticks - DownTicks;
```

V

V

Shortcut notation that returns the volume of a bar.

REMARKS

Anytime the volume of a bar is needed, the letter V can be used in an equivalent fashion.

EXAMPLES

`V of 1 bar ago` returns the volume of the previous bar.

`Average(V, 10)` returns the average of the last 10 volume prices.

ADDITIONAL EXAMPLE

To check that the last two bars have volume prices lower than the previous bar, write:

```
If V < V[1] and V[1] < V[2] then
Plot1(High,"Falling");
```

Var

Shorthand for variable, a reserved word used to declare a variable name to be used in a technique.

REMARKS

A variable name can contain up to 20 alphanumeric characters plus the period (.) and the underscore (_).

A variable name cannot start with a number or a period (.).

The default value of a variable is declared by a number in parentheses after the input name.

EXAMPLES

`Var: Count(10);` declares the variable Count and initializes the value to 10.

`Var: MADiff(0);` declares the variable MADiff and initializes the value to zero.

Variable

Reserved word used to declare a variable name to be used in a technique.

REMARKS

A variable name can contain up to 20 alphanumeric characters plus the period (.) and the underscore (_).

A variable name cannot start with a number or a period (.).

The default value of a variable is declared by a number in parentheses after the input name.

EXAMPLES

`Variable: Count(10);` declares the variable Count and initializes the value to 10.

`Variable: MADiff(0);` declares the variable MADiff and initializes the value to zero.

Variables

Reserved word used to declare multiple variable names to be used in a technique.

REMARKS

A variable name can contain up to 20 alphanumeric characters plus the period (.) and the underscore (_).

A variable name cannot start with a number or a period (.).

The default value of a variable is declared by a number in parenthesis after the input name.

EXAMPLES

`Variables: Countup(0), Countdown(10);` declares the variables Countup and Countdown and initializes their values to zero and 10, respectively.

`Variables: MADiff(0), XMADiff(0);` declares the variables MADiff and XMADiff, initializing the values of both to zero.

Vars

Shorthand for Variables, a reserved word used to declare a variable name to be used in a technique.

VARSIZE

Reserved for use with custom DLLs designed for EasyLanguage. Refer to the documentation in the TradeStation Developer's Kit for more information about this and the EasyLanguage Tool Kit Library ELKIT32.DLL.

VARSTARTADDR

Reserved for use with custom DLLs designed for EasyLanguage. Refer to the documentation in the TradeStation Developer's Kit for more information about this and the EasyLanguage Tool Kit Library ELKIT32.DLL.

VOID

Reserved for use with custom DLLs designed for EasyLanguage. Refer to the documentation in the TradeStation Developer's Kit for more information about this and the EasyLanguage Tool Kit Library ELKIT32.DLL.

Volume

Reserved word used to return the volume of the specified time increment or group of ticks.

REMARKS

`V` can be used in place of `Volume`.

EXAMPLES

`Volume` of 1 bar ago returns the volume of the previous bar.

`Average(Volume, 10)` returns the average of the last 10 volume prices.

ADDITIONAL EXAMPLE

To check that the last two bars have volume prices lower than the previous bar, write:

```
If Volume < Volume[1] and Volume[1] < Volume[2] then
Plot1(High,"Falling");
```

W

Was

Skip word.

REMARKS

This word is skipped in EasyLanguage and is not necessary. These skipped words, however, do make it easier to understand the purpose of the code. By default, unnecessary words and sections marked as comments will appear dark green in the EasyLanguage PowerEditor.

EXAMPLE

```
If Close was < than the Lowest(Close, 14) Then...
```

The word "was" is not necessary and the code functions the same way regardless of its presence.

Wednesday

Returns the number 3 as the value for Wednesday.

REMARKS

The value returned is an integer representing Wednesday and is the same value returned by using the function `DayOfWeek(Wednesday)`.

EXAMPLE

```
Wednesday
```

Returns a value of 3 as the value for Wednesday.

While

This word initiates a `While` loop statement.

REMARKS

A `While` loop statement defines a set of instructions that are executed until a true/false expression returns false. The number of iterations the `While` loop performs depends on the value returned by the true/false expression following While.

EXAMPLE

```
While Condition1 Begin
        {Your Code Here};
End;
```

`While` is used here to initiate the code contained in the `Begin... End` section until `Condition1` returns a value of False. If `Condition1` is false, the `While` loop is not executed.

White

Sets the plot color or background color to White.

REMARKS

There are 16 colors available in EasyLanguage. For more information, see the color values in Appendix A.

EXAMPLES

`Plot1(Value1, ''Test'', White)` plots `Value1` with the name `Test` and sets the color of `Plot1` to `White`.

`TL_SetColor(1, White)` sets the color of a trendline with a reference number of 1 to White.

WORD

Reserved for use with custom DLLs designed for EasyLanguage. Refer to the documentation in the TradeStation Developer's Kit for more information about this and the EasyLanguage Tool Kit Library ELKIT32.DLL.

Y

Year(cDate)

Returns the corresponding year for the specified calendar date (1998 = 98, 2001 = 101).

`(cDate)` is a numeric expression representing the six- or seven-digit calendar date in the format YYMMDD or YYYMMDD respectively (1999 = 99, 2001 = 101).

EXAMPLES

`Year(990613)` returns a value of 99 because 990613 represents June 13, 1999.

`Year(1011220)` returns a value of 101 because 1011220 represents December 20, 2001.

Yellow

Sets the plot color or background color to Yellow.

REMARKS

There are 16 legacy colors available in EasyLanguage. For more information, see color values in Appendix A.

EXAMPLES

`Plot1(Value1, ''Test'', Yellow)` plots `Value1` with the name `Test` and sets the color of `Plot1` to `Yellow`.

`TL_SetColor(1, Yellow)` sets the color of a trendline with a reference number of 1 to `Yellow`.

Yesterday

This word is retained for backward compatibility.

REMARKS

`Yesterday` references the previous bar, even when analyzing intraday bars.

`Yesterday` is no longer necessary as the following are equivalent:

```
Value1 = Close of Yesterday;
Value1 = Close of 1 Bar Ago;
Value1 = Close[1];
```

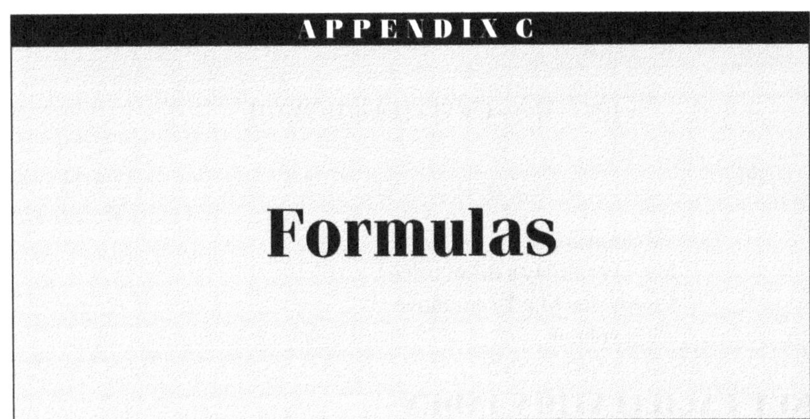

ASYMMETRICAL LEVERAGE

The amount required to recoup a loss increases geometrically with the loss. The percentage gain to recoup a loss is:

$$\text{Required Gain} = (1/(1 - \text{loss in percent})) - 1$$

Thus, a 20% loss requires a 25% gain afterward to recoup. A 30% loss requires a 42% gain afterward to recoup!

CPC™ (CARDINAL PROFITABILITY CONSTRUCTS)

$$\text{CPC} = \text{P} * \text{PF} * \text{R}$$

where P = percent profitable
R = ratio avg win/avg loss
PF = profit factor

EXPONENTIAL MOVING AVERAGE

$$A_i = \alpha P_i + (1 - \alpha)A_i - 1$$

HERICKPAYOFF INDEX

$$\text{HPI} = \text{Ky} + (\text{K'} - \text{Ky})$$

where Ky = yesterday's HPI

$$= [(M - My) * C * V] * [1 \pm \{(I * 2)/G\}]$$

and

M = mean price
My = yesterday's mean price
C = value of a 1-cent move
V = volume

MARKET FACILITATION INDEX

$$MFI = (High - Low) / Volume$$

MATHEMATICAL EXPECTATION (ME)

$$ME = [(1 + A) * P] - 1$$

where P = probability of winning
A = (Amount you can win)/(Amount you can lose)

MOVING AVERAGE (MAV)

$$MAV = (P1 + P2 + P3 + \cdots P(n - 1) + Pn) / n$$

MARKET FACILITATION INDEX

$$MFI = (High - Low) / Volume$$

OPTIMAL-F

Optimal-f is the fixed fraction of your total equity to bet that will maximize your compounded returns. The better a system, the higher the optimal-f. The higher the optimal-f, the higher the drawdown.

Being at the right value for optimal-f is more important than how good your trading system is, as long as the system's mathematical expectation is positive.

Consult Ralph Vince's books for the theory behind optimal-f and for the formulas. To find the optimal-f of your system iteratively, use my optimal-f worksheet, which is available at www.moneymentor.com/TSME.html and which I teach in my seminars and mentoring.

PERCENT PROFITABILITY

This one's simple. If we have 100 trades total in our database, and of those 40 are winners, then we figure the percent profitability thus:

P = [number of profitable trades] / [total number of trades]

So, P = 40 / 100 = 40%. It is how many times we expect to be profitable out of the total number of trades.

PESSIMISTIC RETURN RATIO (PRR)

The PRR is the profit factor (PF) weighted down inversely by the number of trades. PRR values greater than 2.00 are indicative of a very good system. Over 2.50 is excellent. This number is perhaps the single best measure of a system's performance.

The PRR is the PF measure adjusted to give greater weight to passes with more trades.

$$PRR = (((W - (W)) / T) * AW) / (((L + (L)) / T) * AL$$

where W = number of winning trades
L = number of losing trades
T = total number of trades
AW = average winning trade amount
AL = average losing trade amount

PHW™ (POTENTIAL HOURLY WAGE)

40% of the Ideal Possible Profit

PROFIT FACTOR

$$PF = (W\% * AW) / (L\% * AL)$$

where W% = percentage of winning trades
L% = percentage of losing trades (or 1 − W%)
AW = amount of the average winning trade
AL = amount of the average losing trade

Thus, PF = (Total dollars won) / (Total dollars lost)

RATIO OF THE AVERAGE PROFITABLE TRADE TO THE AVERAGE LOSING TRADE (P/L RATIO)

Sometimes referred to as the profit to loss ratio, for this calculation we simply divide the average winner by the average loser. Thus, where

AW = dollar value of the average winning trade (the average of all your wins),
AL = dollar value of the average losing trade (the average of all your losses), then
P/L Ratio = AW / AL.

WILDER'S RSI

$$RSI = 100 - (100 / (1 + RS))$$

where RS = (MAV of x days up closes)/(MAV of x days down closes)

RUNS

N	total number of trades
W	number of winning trades
L	number of losing trades
X	$= 2 * W * L$
R	runs in a sequence of trades
Y	$N * (R - .5) - X$
P	$(X * (X - N)) / (N - 1)$
S	SQRT(Z)
Z	Y / S
Z score	ABS(Z)

A negative Z implies positive dependency, meaning fewer streaks than the normal probability function would imply. Thus, wins follow wins and losses follow losses.

Unless dependency is proven, all attempts to change your trading behavior based on changes in the equity curve are futile, and may even be harmful.

STOCHASTICS

Fast %K = (latest price – lowest low for n periods) / (n period highest high – lowest low)
Fast %D = 3-day average of fast %K
Slow %K = Fast %D
Slow %D = 3-day average of fast %D

APPENDIX D

Full Code for the Systems and Studies in This Book

SIGNAL TO CLOSE THE OPEN TRADE

```
IF LastBarOnChart THEN BEGIN
IF MarketPositon = 1 THEN Sell;
IF MarketPosition = -1 THEN BuyToCover;
END;
```

INDICATOR FOR 200-DAY MOVING AVERAGE

```
PLOT1(Average(C,200),"200MAV");
```

(See Figure D.1.)

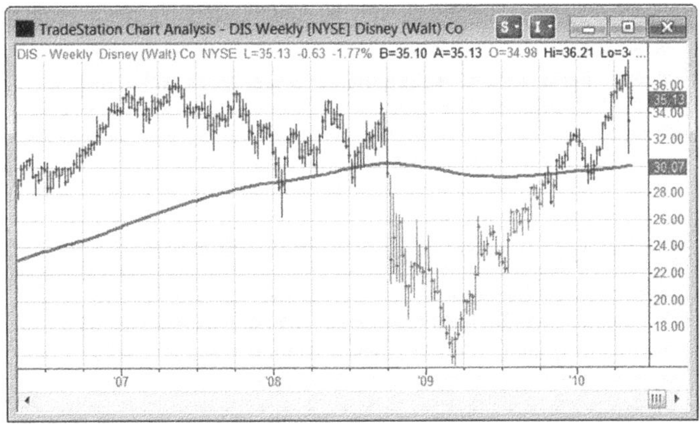

FIGURE D.1 Indicator: 200-Day Moving Average

PAINTBAR FOR 200-DAY MOVING AVERAGE

```
Value91=Average(C,200);
Condition1=H>Value91;
Condition2=L<Value91;
IF Condition1 OR Condition2 THEN BEGIN
PlotPaintBar(L,H,"PB200");
If Condition1 THEN SetPlotColor(1,DarkGreen)
ELSE IF Condition2 THEN SetPlotColor(1,Red);
END;
```

(See Figure D.2.)

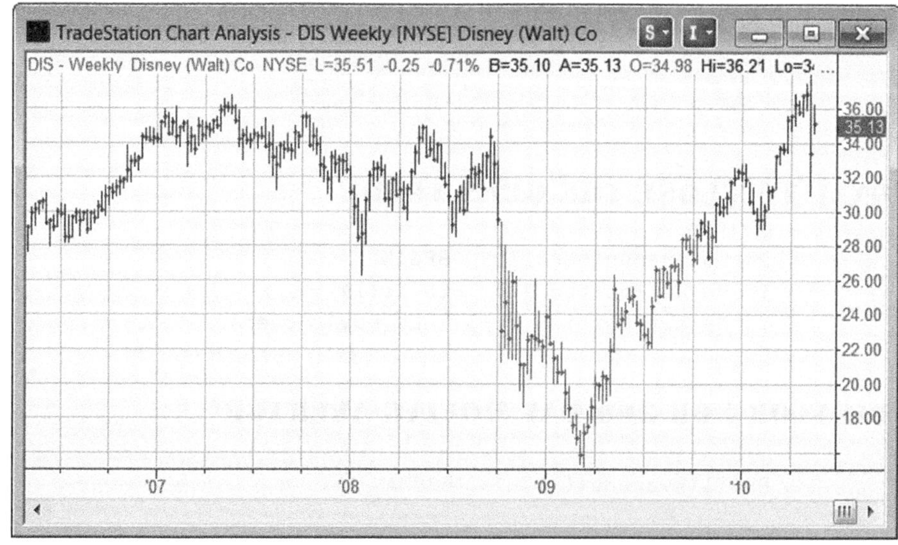

FIGURE D.2 PaintBar for 200-Day Moving Average

SHOWME FOR 200-DAY MOVING AVERAGE

```
Value91=Average(C,200);
Condition1=H>Value91;
Condition2=L<Value91;
IF Condition1 OR Condition2 THEN BEGIN
Plot1(C,"PB200");
If Condition1 THEN SetPlotColor(1,DarkGreen)
ELSE IF Condition2 THEN SetPlotColor(1,Red);
END;
```

(See Figure D.3.)

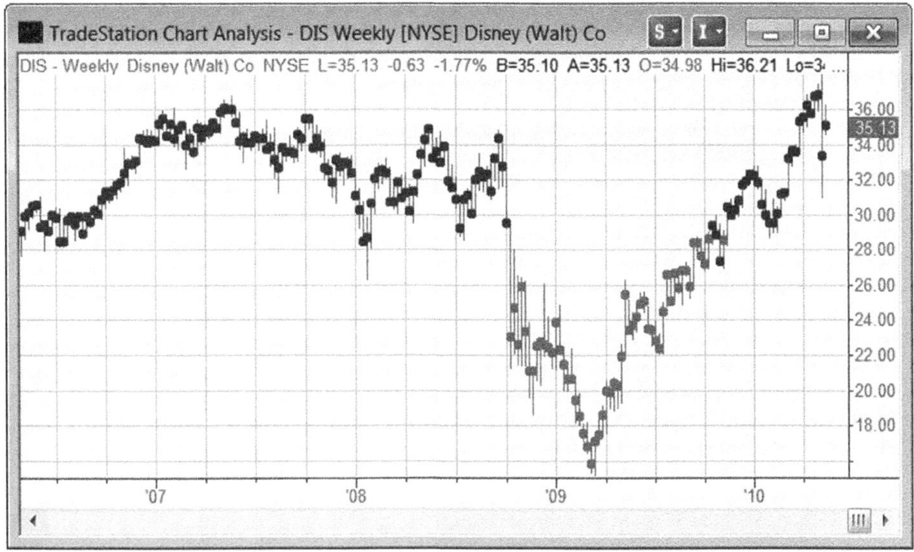

FIGURE D.3 ShowMe for 200-Day Moving Average

FILTER FOR 200-DAY MOVING AVERAGE

```
INPUTS: UpColor(Green), DnColor(Red), L1(200);
VARS: jtext("");
Value1 = sjh_DynamicAvg$$_f(Close,L1,.25,2,31);
IF C > Value1 THEN BEGIN
        jtext = "Long";
       Plot1(jtext, "MA", white); SetPlotBGColor(1,UpColor);
        END;
IF C < Value1 THEN BEGIN
        jtext = "Short";
        Plot1(jtext, "MA",white); SetPlotBGColor(1,DnColor);
        END;
```

(See Figure D.4.)

You may have difficulty getting this one to work at first. The trick to making RadarScreen work is to go into the Format screen and change the value in "Load additional data for accumulative calculation" to a number that is greater than the length of the maximum calculation of the indicator. So, for the 200-day moving average, this value needs to be set to 201.

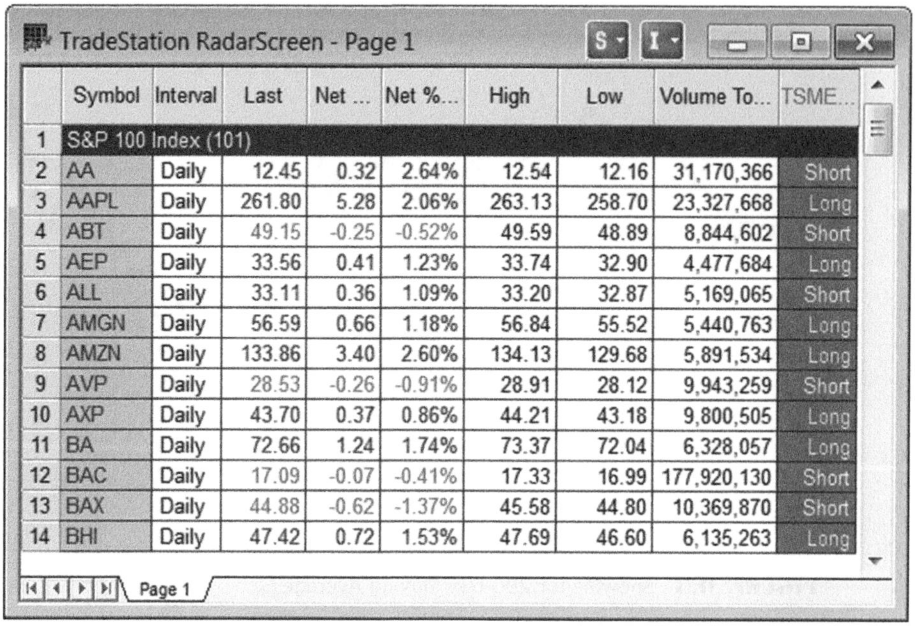

TradeStation RadarScreen - Page 1

	Symbol	Interval	Last	Net ...	Net %...	High	Low	Volume To...	TSME...
1	S&P 100 Index (101)								
2	AA	Daily	12.45	0.32	2.64%	12.54	12.16	31,170,366	Short
3	AAPL	Daily	261.80	5.28	2.06%	263.13	258.70	23,327,668	Long
4	ABT	Daily	49.15	-0.25	-0.52%	49.59	48.89	8,844,602	Short
5	AEP	Daily	33.56	0.41	1.23%	33.74	32.90	4,477,684	Long
6	ALL	Daily	33.11	0.36	1.09%	33.20	32.87	5,169,065	Short
7	AMGN	Daily	56.59	0.66	1.18%	56.84	55.52	5,440,763	Long
8	AMZN	Daily	133.86	3.40	2.60%	134.13	129.68	5,891,534	Long
9	AVP	Daily	28.53	-0.26	-0.91%	28.91	28.12	9,943,259	Short
10	AXP	Daily	43.70	0.37	0.86%	44.21	43.18	9,800,505	Long
11	BA	Daily	72.66	1.24	1.74%	73.37	72.04	6,328,057	Long
12	BAC	Daily	17.09	-0.07	-0.41%	17.33	16.99	177,920,130	Short
13	BAX	Daily	44.88	-0.62	-1.37%	45.58	44.80	10,369,870	Short
14	BHI	Daily	47.42	0.72	1.53%	47.69	46.60	6,135,263	Long

Page 1

FIGURE D.4 Filter for 200-Day MAV

OUR STRATEGY

```
INPUTS: DATE1(960101),DATE2(1101231),Length1(3),Length2(13),Leng(9),
        RSIleng(9),ADXswt(0), RSIswt(0),jRSIOB(75), jRSIOS(25),
        xHR(180), yHR(60),
      Dollars(100),LossL(100),LossS(100);
IF LENGTH1<LENGTH2 THEN BEGIN
IF Date >= Date1 AND DATE<=DATE2 THEN BEGIN
Value1=xHR;
Value2=yHR;
Condition1=ADX(Leng)>ADX(Leng)[1];
Condition2=RSI(C,RSIleng)<jRSIOB;
Condition3=RSI(C,RSIleng)>jRSIOS;
IF ADXswt=1 THEN Condition1=true;
IF RSIswt=1 THEN Condition2=true;
IF RSIswt=1 THEN Condition3=true;
IF CurrentBar > 1
AND XAverage(Close,Length1) > XAverage(Close,Length2)
```

```
AND Condition1 AND Condition2
      THEN BUY This Bar on Close;
IF CurrentBar > 1
       AND XAverage(Close,Length1) < XAverage(Close,Length2)
       AND Condition1 AND Condition3
       THEN SELL SHORT This Bar on Close;
IF date>DATE2 THEN BEGIN
       IF MarketPosition=+1 THEN SELL This Bar on Close;
       IF MarketPosition=-1 THEN BUYTOCOVER This Bar on Close;
END;
IF BarsSinceEntry=xHR AND PositionProfit<Dollars
    THEN Sell This Bar;
IF BarsSinceEntry=yHR AND PositionProfit<Dollars THEN
    BuyToCover This Bar;
IF PositionProfit < -LossL THEN SELL This Bar;
IF PositionProfit < -LossS THEN BUYTOCOVER This Bar;
IF Date>=LastCalcDate THEN BEGIN
SELL This Bar; BUYTOCOVER This Bar;
END;
END;
END;
```

(See Figures D.5 and D.6.)

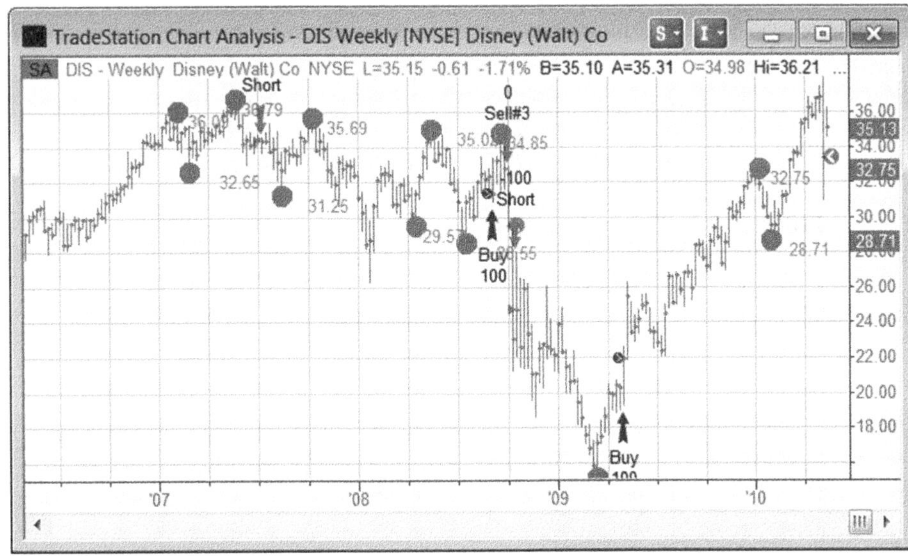

FIGURE D.5 Our Strategy

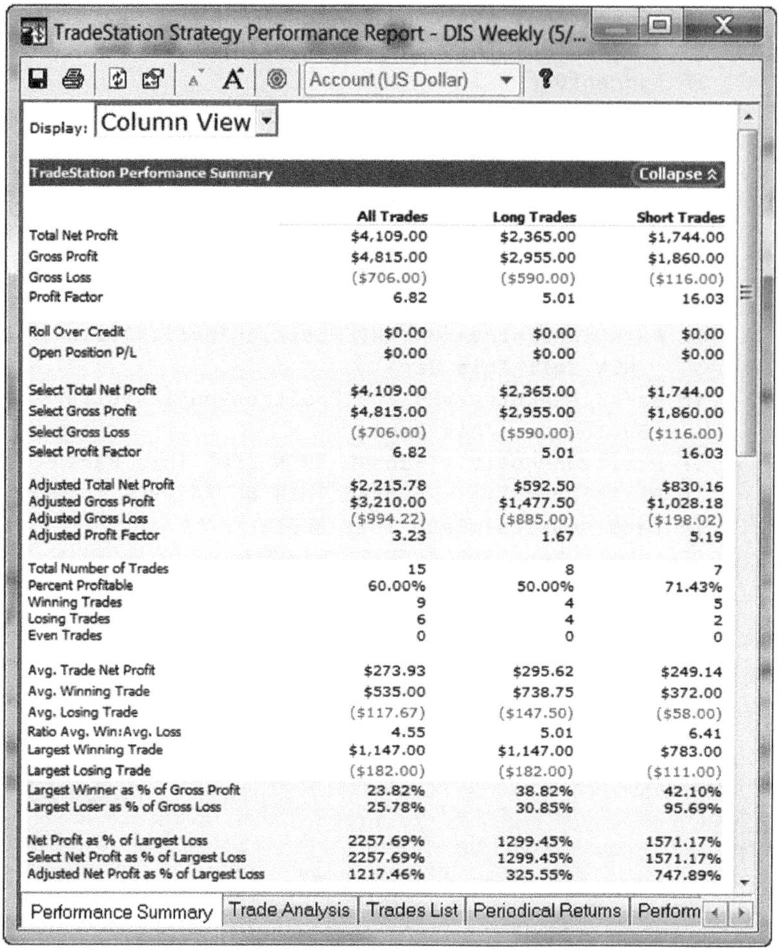

TradeStation Strategy Performance Report - DIS Weekly (5/...

Account (US Dollar)

Display: Column View

TradeStation Performance Summary Collapse

	All Trades	Long Trades	Short Trades
Total Net Profit	$4,109.00	$2,365.00	$1,744.00
Gross Profit	$4,815.00	$2,955.00	$1,860.00
Gross Loss	($706.00)	($590.00)	($116.00)
Profit Factor	6.82	5.01	16.03
Roll Over Credit	$0.00	$0.00	$0.00
Open Position P/L	$0.00	$0.00	$0.00
Select Total Net Profit	$4,109.00	$2,365.00	$1,744.00
Select Gross Profit	$4,815.00	$2,955.00	$1,860.00
Select Gross Loss	($706.00)	($590.00)	($116.00)
Select Profit Factor	6.82	5.01	16.03
Adjusted Total Net Profit	$2,215.78	$592.50	$830.16
Adjusted Gross Profit	$3,210.00	$1,477.50	$1,028.18
Adjusted Gross Loss	($994.22)	($885.00)	($198.02)
Adjusted Profit Factor	3.23	1.67	5.19
Total Number of Trades	15	8	7
Percent Profitable	60.00%	50.00%	71.43%
Winning Trades	9	4	5
Losing Trades	6	4	2
Even Trades	0	0	0
Avg. Trade Net Profit	$273.93	$295.62	$249.14
Avg. Winning Trade	$535.00	$738.75	$372.00
Avg. Losing Trade	($117.67)	($147.50)	($58.00)
Ratio Avg. Win:Avg. Loss	4.55	5.01	6.41
Largest Winning Trade	$1,147.00	$1,147.00	$783.00
Largest Losing Trade	($182.00)	($182.00)	($111.00)
Largest Winner as % of Gross Profit	23.82%	38.82%	42.10%
Largest Loser as % of Gross Loss	25.78%	30.85%	95.69%
Net Profit as % of Largest Loss	2257.69%	1299.45%	1571.17%
Select Net Profit as % of Largest Loss	2257.69%	1299.45%	1571.17%
Adjusted Net Profit as % of Largest Loss	1217.46%	325.55%	747.89%

Performance Summary | Trade Analysis | Trades List | Periodical Returns | Perform

FIGURE D.6 Our Strategy Performance Report

APPENDIX E

Baskets

Dow Jones 30 Industrials (as of May 6, 2010)

3M	MMM
Alcoa Inc.	AA
American Express	AXP
AT&T Inc.	T
Bank of America Corp.	BAC
Boeing Co.	BA
Caterpillar Inc.	CAT
Chevron Corp.	CVX
Cisco Systems	CSCO
Coca-Cola Co.	KO
Disney (Walt) Co.	DIS
E.I. Du Pont De Nemours	DD
ExxonMobil	XOM
General Electric	GE
Hewlett-Packard	HPQ
The Home Depot Inc.	HD
International Business Machines Corp.	IBM
Intel Corp.	INTC
Johnson & Johnson	JNJ
JP Morgan Chase & Co.	JPM
Kraft Foods "A"	KFT
McDonald's Corp.	MCD
Merck & Co.	MRK
Microsoft Corp.	MSFT
Pfizer, Inc.	PFE

Procter & Gamble	PG
The Travelers Companies Inc.	TRV
United Technologies	UTX
Verizon Communications	VZ
Wal-Mart Stores	WMT

FOREX Pairs (Dollar-Based Only)

AUDUSD	Australian Dollar v US Dollar
USDCAD	US Dollar v Canadian Dollar
GBPUSD	Great Britain Pound v US Dollar
EURUSD	EURO v US Dollar
USDJPY	US Dollar v Japanese Yen
NZDUSD	New Zealand $ v US Dollar
USDCAD	US Dollar v Canadian Dollar
USDDKK	US Dollar v Danish Krone
USDHKD	US Dollar v Hong Kong Dollar
USDJPY	US Dollar v Japanese Yen
USDNOK	US Dollar v Norwegian Krone
USDSGD	US Dollar v Singapore Dollar
USDSEK	US Dollar v Swedish Krona
USDCHF	US Dollar v Swiss Franc

Internet HOLDRS

AOL, Inc.	AOL
Amazon.com Inc.	AMZN
Earthlink Inc.	ELNK
eBay Inc.	EBAY
E*Trade Financial Corp.	ETFC
McAfee Inc.	MFE
ModusLink Global Solutions Inc.	MLNK
Priceline.com Inc.	PCLN
RealNetworks Inc.	RNWK
TD Ameritrade Holding Corp.	AMTD
Time Warner	TWX
Time Warner Cable Inc.	TWC
Yahoo Inc.	YHOO

CBOE Internet Index

Akamai Technologies	AKAM
Amazon.com Inc.	AMZN
Check Point Software Tech	CHKP
Cisco Systems	CSCO

Earthlink Inc.	ELNK
eBay Inc.	EBAY
Google Inc. Cl A	GOOG
InfoSpace Inc.	INSP
Juniper Networks	JNPR
Monster Worldwide Inc.	MWW
RealNetworks Inc.	RNWK
Verisign Inc.	VRSN
Yahoo Inc.	YHOO

Internet and Technology Stocks

AT Home Corp. Sr A	ATHM
Amazon.Com Inc.	AMZN
America Online Inc.	AOL
Axent Technologies Inc.	AXNT
Broadband Technologies	BBTK
Broadvision Inc.	BVSN
Cdnow Inc.	CDNW
Checkfree Hldgs Corp.	CKFR
Check Point Software Tech Ltd	CHKPF
CKS Group Inc.	CKSG
CMG Information Svcs Inc.	CMGI
Cnet Inc.	CNWK
Concentric Network Corp.	CNCX
Cybercash Inc.	CYCH
Cyberguard Corp.	CYBG
Cylink Corporation	CYLK
Doubleclick Inc.	DCLK
E*Trade Group Inc.	EGRP
Earthlink Network Inc.	ELNK
Egghead.Com Inc.	EGGS
Excite Inc.	XCIT
IDT Corporation	IDTC
Infoseek Corporation	SEEK
Intuit Inc.	INTU
Lycos Inc.	LCOS
Mecklermedia Corporation	MECK
Metricom Inc.	MCOM
Mindspring Enterprises Inc.	MSPG
N2k Inc.	NTKI
Netscape Communications Corp.	NSCP
Network Solutions Inc. Cl A	NSOL
Networks Associates Inc.	NETA
Newsedge Corp.	NEWZ
Onsale Inc.	ONSL
Open Market Inc.	OMKT

Open Text Corporation	OTEXF
Pairgain Technologies	PAIR
Psinet Inc.	PSIX
Realnetworks Inc.	RNWK
Secure Computing Corporation	SCUR
Security Dynamics Technologies	SDTI
Security First Network Bank	SFNB
Sportsline USA Inc.	SPLN
Spyglass Inc.	SPYG
Usweb Corporation	USWB
Verisign Inc.	VRSN
Versant Corp.	VSNT
Vocaltec Communications Ltd.	VOCLF
Wavephore Inc.	WAVO
Yahoo! Inc.	YHOO

APPENDIX F

Where's the Command?

Often it seems that I remember the name of a command but cannot find it by clicking on the menu items. I click and click and click until I find the command hidden in some obscure pull-down menu. This is especially true as I migrate from older versions to newer versions of TradeStation. If you have that problem too, you've come to the right appendix. Here I've listed common TradeStation commands and the menu sequences under which they reside.

About TradeStation	Help → About TradeStation
Account No.	Format → Account Orders & Positions → Data → Account No
Account Orders/Positions	Format → Account Orders & Positions . . .
Account Services	Help → Account Services
Activity Bar	Insert → ActivityBar . . .
Activity Bar	Insert → Indicator → Analysis Techniques → ActivityBar
Advanced Chart Types	View → Chart Analysis Preferences → Symbol → Chart Types → Advanced (Kagi, Kase, Line Break, Momentum)
Advanced Techniques	Format → Analysis Techniques → Analysis Techniques → Advanced
Alert, Status Line	Format → Window → Status Line → Alert
Alerts	Format → Analysis Techniques → Analysis Techniques → Alerts
Analysis Group	Insert → Analysis Group . . .
Analysis Group	Format → Save Analysis Group
Analysis Group	Format → Manage Analysis Groups
Analysis Technique	Format → Analysis Technique
Analysis Technique Settings	Format → Page → General → Analysis Technique Settings
Analysis Techniques	Format → Analysis Techniques . . .
Analysis Techniques	Help → Analysis Techniques & Strategies
Andrew's Pitchfork	Drawing → Andrew's Pitchfork
Arcs, Resistance	Drawing → Arc
Arcs, Resistance	Drawing → Fibonacci Tools → Speed/Resistance Arcs
Arrange Window	Window → Arrange All

Arrange Window	Window → Arrange Horizontally
Arrange Window	Window → Arrange Vertically
Arrange Windows	Window → Arrange
Arrow Down	Drawing → Arrow Down
Arrow Up	Drawing → Arrow Up
Auto Remove Open Tick	View → Chart Analysis Preferences → General → Bar Spacing: Auto remove open tick
Auto Size Bars	View → Chart Analysis Preferences → General → Bar Spacing: Auto-size bar and drawing object weight...
Auto Space Bars	View → Chart Analysis Preferences → General → Bar Spacing: Auto space bars when chart resizes
Auto. Insert Chart Window	Insert → Analysis Group → Automatically insert into new Chart Analysis windows
Automate Execution	Format → Analysis Techniques → Strategies → Automate execution using ...
Automatic Sorting	Format → Page → Sort → Automatic Sorting Options
Backup	File → Backup/Restore TradeStation → Backup TradeStation
Bar Components	View → Chart Analysis Preferences → Style → Bar components
Bar Spacing	Format → Window → General → Chart Properties → Bar Spacing
Bar Type	Format → Bar Type
Bar Type	View → Chart Analysis Preferences → Style → Bar type
Bars Back	Format → Symbol → Range → < > Bars Back
Base Results on <Net Profit>	View → Chart Analysis Preferences → Strategy → Base Results on → <Net Profit>
Big Point Value	Format → Symbol → Scaling → Properties → Big Point Value
Blank Row	Format → Page → General → Blank Row
Bouncing Ticks	View → Chart Analysis Preferences → Strategy → Percent increment for Bouncing Ticks
Cancelled	Format → Account Orders & Positions → Settings → Cancelled
Cascade Windows	Window → Cascade
Category	Format → Symbol → Scaling → Properties → Category
Center Last Price	Format → Center Last Price
Center Last Price	Format → Symbol → Scaling → Range → Center Last Price
Chart Analysis	View → Toolbars → Chart Analysis
Chart Properties	Format → Window → General → Chart Properties
Circle, Ellipse	Drawing → Ellipse
Close Desktop	File → Close Desktop
Close Window	File → Close Window
Close Workspace	File → Close Workspace
Color	Format → Analysis Techniques → Analysis Techniques → Color
Color	Format → Page → Color
Commentary	View → Analysis Commentary
Copy Window	Edit → Copy Window
Correction	Format → Window → Status Line → Correction
Country	Format → Symbol → Scaling → Properties → Country
Crosshairs	Drawing → Crosshairs Pointer
Currency	Format → Symbol → Scaling → Properties → Currency

Custom Decimal Places	Format → Symbol → Scaling → Display → Custom Decimal Places
Custom Axis Increment	Format → Symbol → Scaling → Display → Custom Axis Increment
Custom Symbol List	Format → Append <x> to Custom Symbol List . . .
Custom Symbol List	Format → Manage Custom Symbol Lists . . .
Custom Symbol List	Format → Append "ALL" to Custom Symbol List
Custom Symbol List	Format → Manage Custom Symbol Lists
Customize	View → Toolbars → Customize . . .
Cycle, Time	Drawing → Time Cycle
Cycles	Drawing → Fibonacci Tools → Cycles
Data Corrections	Format → Data Corrections
Data Range on Screen	Format → Symbol → Scaling → Range → Data Range on Screen
Data Series	View → Chart Analysis Preferences → Style → Data series
Data Window	View → Data Window
Default Initial Capital	View → Chart Analysis Preferences → Strategy → Default initial capital
Default Interest Rate	View → Chart Analysis Preferences → Strategy → Default interest rate
Default Range Above	View → Chart Analysis Preferences → Symbol → Default range setting for interval above → Time or Bars
Desktop	File → New → Desktop
Desktop	File → Open Desktop
Desktop	File → Preferences → TradeStation Desktop . . .
Display Arrow Margins	View → Chart Analysis Preferences → Strategy → Display arrow margins as % of subgraphs size
Display Empty Rows	View → Chart Analysis Preferences → General → Data Tips → Display empty rows for plots w no value
Display Warnings	View → Chart Analysis Preferences → General → Axis: Display warnings for automatic changes . . .
Divide Axis Labels	Format → Symbol → Scaling → Display → Divide Axis Labels by . . .
Download Scheduler	View → Launch Download Scheduler
Download Scheduler Req.	View → Chart Analysis Preferences → Data → Show Download Scheduler Request
Drawing	View → Toolbars → Drawing
Drawing Object, Remove	Drawing → Remove Drawing Objects
Ellipse, Circle	Drawing → Ellipse
Email Update	Format → Page → Messaging → Email Update
Empty Intraday Periods	View → Chart Analysis Preferences → Symbol → Show empty intraday session periods
Events Log	View → Launch Events Log
Exit	File → Exit
Expand Range . . . Analysis	Format → Symbol → Scaling → Range → Expand Range to include Analysis Techniques
Expand Range . . . Open Order	Format → Symbol → Scaling → Range → Expand Range to include Account Open Order Lines
Expired	Format → Account Orders & Positions → Settings → Expired
Extension Lines	Drawing → Fibonacci Tools → Price Extension Lines

Extension Lines	Drawing → Fibonacci Tools → Time Extension Lines
Fan, Resistance	Drawing → Fibonacci Tools → Speed/Resistance Fan
Fibonacci	Drawing → Fibonacci Tools
Fields, Status Line	Format → Window → Status Line → Fields
Filled	Format → Account Orders & Positions → Settings → Filled
First Date	Format → Symbol → Range → First Date
Fixed Range	Format → Symbol → Scaling → Range → Fixed
For Bars Use . . .	View → Chart Analysis Preferences → Symbol → For Bars use . . .
Fractions Stacked	Format → Page → General → Fractions Stacked
Gann Fan	Drawing → Gann Fan
General	View → Chart Analysis Preferences → General
General Analy. Techn.	Format → Analysis Techniques → Analysis Techniques → General
General Strategy Settings	View → Chart Analysis Preferences → Strategy → General Strategy Settings
Gridline Style	Format → Page → Grid → Gridline Style
Gridlines, Horizontal	Format → Page → Grid → Show Horizontal Gridlines
Gridlines, Vertical	Format → Page → Grid → Show Vertical Gridlines
Grid Values Font	Format → Page → Font → Grid Values
Headings Font	Format → Page → Font → Headings
Horizontal Line	Drawing → Horizontal Line
Hot Key	View → Hot Keys . . .
Import	Insert → Indicator → Analysis Techniques → Import
Import/Export	File → Import/Export EasyLanguage . . .
Indicator	Insert → Indicator → Analysis Techniques → Indicator
Indicator	Insert → Indicator . . .
Indicator Axis Scaling	View → Chart Analysis Preferences → General → Axis: Prompt for Indicator Axis Scaling
Inputs	Format → Analysis Techniques → Analysis Techniques → Inputs
Kagi	View → Chart Analysis Preferences → Symbol → Chart Types → Advanced (Kagi, Kase, Line Break, Momentum)
Kase	View → Chart Analysis Preferences → Symbol → Chart Types → Advanced (Kagi, Kase, Line Break, Momentum)
Keep Best <n> Tests	View → Chart Analysis Preferences → Strategy → Keep the best <n> tests
Last Date	Format → Symbol → Range → Last Date < >
Learning Center	Help → Learning Center
Line Break	View → Chart Analysis Preferences → Symbol → Chart Types → Advanced (Kagi, Kase, Line Break, Momentum)
Linear/Semi-log	Format → Symbol → Scaling → Type → Linear or Semi-log
Macros	View → Macros . . .
Main	View → Toolbars → Main
Manage Analysis Groups	Format → Manage Analysis Groups . . .
Max Columns to Display	View → Chart Analysis Preferences → General → Data Tips → Maximum number of columns to display
Message Center	View → Launch Message Center
Min Move	Format → Symbol → Scaling → Properties → Min Move
Momentum	View → Chart Analysis Preferences → Symbol → Chart Types → Advanced (Kagi, Kase, Line Break, Momentum)

Months as Digits	View → Chart Analysis Preferences → General → Axis: Show months as digits
Move Workspace	File → Move Workspace
Movement Size	Format → Symbol → Scaling → Range → Movement Size
Network	File → Preferences → TradeStation Network . . .
Network Subscription	Insert → Strategies → My Strategy Network Subscriptions
Open	Format → Account Orders & Positions → Settings → Open
Opened Workspaces	File → Opened Workspaces
Optimization Report Settings	View → Chart Analysis Preferences → Strategy → Optimization Report Settings
Optimization Report	View → Strategy Optimization Report
Order Bar	View → Order Bar
Order Entry	File → Preferences → TradeStation Order Entry . . .
Order Lines	Format → Account Orders & Positions → Settings → Display Order Lines
Order Settings	Format → Account Orders & Positions → Settings
Outside Regular Session	View → Chart Analysis Preferences → Style → Outside Regular Session → Color & Weight
Page	Format → Page
PaintBar	Insert → Indicator → Analysis Techniques → PaintBar
PaintBar	Insert → PaintBar . . .
Painting Candlestick	View → Chart Analysis Preferences → General → When a study paints a candlestick . . .
Parallel, New	Drawing → New Parallel
Paste Window	Edit → Paste Window
Pending Data	Format → Window → Status Line → Pending Data
Percent Change	Format → Window → General → Percent Change Chart
Percent Change Chart	Format → Percent Change Chart
Pip Calculator	View → Launch Pip Calculator
Pointer, Large	Drawing → Large Pointer
Pointer, Small	Drawing → Small Pointer
Pointer Tracking	Drawing → Pointer Tracking
Position Arrows	Format → Account Orders & Positions → Settings → Display Position Arrows
Position Graph Bar	View → Position Graph Bar
Preferences	File → Backup/Restore TradeStation → Preferences . . .
Preferences	File → Preferences
Price Axis Display	Format → Window → General → Price Axis Display
Price Scale	Format → Symbol → Scaling → Properties → Price Scale
Print	File → Print . . .
Print Log	View → EasyLanguage Print Log
Print Preview	File → Print Preview
Print Setup	File → Print Setup . . .
Probability Map	Insert → Indicator → Analysis Techniques → ProbabilityMap
Probability Map	Insert → ProbabilityMap . . .
Prompt for Format	View → Chart Analysis Preferences → General → Prompt for format
Properties	Format → Symbol → Properties
Queue	Format → Account Orders & Positions → Settings → Queued

Quick Quote	View → Launch Quick Quote
Range Automatic	Format → Symbol → Scaling → Range → Automatic
Range Settings	View → Chart Analysis Preferences → Symbol → Range Settings
Range Values	View → Chart Analysis Preferences → Symbol → Range values to use for the interrval
Recalculate Chart	View → Chart Analysis Preferences → Data → Do not automatically recalculate Chart Analysis ... Strategy applied
Recalculate Chart	View → Chart Analysis Preferences → Data → Do not automatically recalculate Chart Analysis ... alert enabled
Recent Workspaces	File → Recent Workspaces
Rectangle	Drawing → Rectangle
Reference Rows	Format → Page → General → Reference Rows
Refresh	View → Refresh
Regular Session Color/Weight	View → Chart Analysis Preferences → Style → Regular Session → Color & Weight
Regression Channel	Drawing → Regression Channel
Remove Trailing Zeros	View → Chart Analysis Preferences → General → Axis: Remove trailing zeros
Restore	File → Backup/Restore TradeStation → Restore TradeStation Archive...
Restore Prior Scale Range	View → Chart Analysis Preferences → General → Restore prior Scale Range
Retracement Calculator	Drawing → Fibonacci Tools → Price Retracement Calculator
Retracement Lines	Drawing → Fibonacci Tools → Price Retracement Lines
Right-button Double Click	View → Chart Analysis Preferences → General → Enable right-button double click
Same Color/Weight All	View → Chart Analysis Preferences → Style → Use same color/weight for all components
Save All Desktops	File → Save All Desktops
Save Analysis Group	Format → Analysis Techniques → Analysis Techniques → Save Analysis Group
Save Analysis Group	Format → Analysis Techniques → Strategies → Save Analysis Group
Save Analysis Group	Format → Save Analysis Group...
Save as Picture	File → Save as Picture
Save Desktop	File → Save Desktop
Save Desktop as	File → Save Desktop As...
Save Workspace	File → Save Workspace
Scale on <R/L>	Format → Symbol → Scaling → Axis: Scale On <Right> Axis → Sub-graph <1>
Scaling	Format → Analysis Techniques → Analysis Techniques → Scaling
Scaling	Format → Symbol → Scaling
Scroll Bar	Format → Window → General → Scroll Bar
Select Interval	Format → Symbol → Select Interval
Semi-log Scaling	Format → Semi-log Scaling
Session	Format → Symbol → Scaling → Properties → Session
Settings	Format → Symbol → Settings

Shortcut Bar	View → Shortcut Bar
Show Axis	Format → Window → Style → Show Axis
Show Data Tips	View → Chart Analysis Preferences → General → Data Tips → Show Data Tips . . . of the mouse prointer
Show Empty Daily Trading . . .	View → Chart Analysis Preferences → Symbol → Show empty daily trading periods
Show Grid	Format → Window → Style → Show Grid
Show Pointer Update	View → Chart Analysis Preferences → General → Axis: Show Pointer Update
Show Session Break	Format → Window → Style → Show Session Breaks
ShowMe	Insert → Indicator → Analysis Techniques → ShowMe
ShowMe	Insert → ShowMe . . .
Simulated Accounts	File → Manage Simulated Accounts . . .
Snap Mode	Drawing → Snap Mode
Sort	Format → Sort
Sort Keys	Format → Page → Sort → Sort Keys
Space to Right	Format → Space to the Right . . .
Space to the Right	Format → Window → General → Chart Properties → Space to the Right
Status Bar	View → Status Bar
Status Line	Format → Window → Status Line → Show Status Line
Strartegy Automation	Format → Window → Status Line → Indications → Strategy Automation
Strategy Performance Report	View → Strategy Performance Report
Strategies	Format → Strategies . . .
Strategy	Insert → Strategy . . .
Strategy Components	Insert → Strategies → Strategy Components
Strategy Network	Format → Window → Status Line → Strategy Network
Strategy Network	View → Launch Strategy Network
Strategy Orders tab	Format → Analysis Techniques → Strategies → Generate strategy orders in TradeManager
Style	Format → Analysis Techniques → Analysis Techniques → Style
Style	Format → Symbol → Style
Subgraph Divider	Format → Window → Style → Show Subgraph Dividers
Sub-graph Margins	Format → Symbol → Scaling → Range → Sub-graph Margins
Support Forums	Help → Support Forums
Symbol	Format → Symbol . . .
Symbol	Insert → Symbol . . .
Symbol Axis Scaling	View → Chart Analysis Preferences → General → Axis: Prompt for symbol Axis Scaling
Symbol Interval	View → Chart Analysis Preferences → Symbol → Interval
Symbol Properties	Format → Symbol → Scaling → Properties → Symbol
Symbols	Format → Symbols → Selected Symbols
Symbols	Format → Symbols → All Symbols
Symbols to Send	Format → Page → Messaging → Symbols to Send
Template	Format → Apply Template
Template	Format → Save Template

Text	Drawing → Text
Ticker Bar	View → Launch Ticker Bar
Time-based Range	Format → Symbol → Range → Apply time-based Range setting
Time Zone	Format → Symbol → Display → Time Zone
Time Zone	Format → Symbol → Scaling → Properties → Time Zone
Toolbars	View → Toolbars
Tools	View → Toolbars → Tools
Trader Wiki	Help → Trader Wiki
TradeStation Platform	Help → TradeStation Platform Help
Traditional Chart Types	View → Chart Analysis Preferences → Symbol → Chart Types → Traditional
Training	Help → TradeStation Training
Transparent Arrow/Label	View → Chart Analysis Preferences → Strategy → Make arrow and label backgrounds transparent
Trendline	Drawing → Trendline
Update Indication	Format → Page → General → Update Indication
Update Manager	Help → TradeStation Update Manager
Uppercase Conversion	Format → Page → General → Uppercase Conversion
Use 1000's Separator	Format → Symbol → Scaling → Display → Use 1000's separator
Use Days Back	View → Chart Analysis Preferences → Symbol → For Time Use . . . Days Back
Vertical Line	Drawing → Vertical Line
What's New	Help → What's New in TradeStation
Window	File → New → Window
Window	Format → Window . . .
Window Caption	Format → Window Caption
Window Caption	Format → Page → Window Caption
Windows System Colors	View → Chart Analysis Preferences → General → Data Tips → Use Windows system colors
Work Online	File → Work Online
Workspace	File → New → Workspace
Workspace	File → Open Workspace
Year w Months	View → Chart Analysis Preferences → General → Axis: Show year with months
Years Back	Format → Symbol → Range → < > Years Back

APPENDIX G.1

Built-in Functions and Indicators (Alphabetical Listing)

This is an alphabetical listing of the full list of built-in functions and indicators at the time of this writing, and TradeStation version 8.8, build 5808. No explanation of these commands is offered in this section. The commands are listed here so you might peruse them and become familiar with the names of routines available to you. In the next section we will select out the most commonly used functions and indicators and give examples and explanations.

AB_AddCellRange
AB_AverageCells
AB_AveragePrice
AB_CellCount
AB_ColorIntervals
AB_LetterIntervals
AB_Median
AB_ModeCount
AB_ModePrice
AB_RowCalc
AB_StdDev
AbsoluteBreadth
AccumDist
AccumSwingIndex
AdvanceDeclineDiff
AdvanceDeclineRatio
ADX
ADXClassic
ADXCustom
ADXCustomClassic
ADXR
ADXRClassic
ADXRCustom
ADXRCustomClassic
ArmsIndex
Average
Average_a
AverageFC
AverageDnMove
AverageUpMove
AvgDeviation
AvgDeviation_a
AvgPrice
AvgTrueRange
BarAnnualization
BarNumber
BarQuality
BearishDivergence
BearishEngulfing
BlackModel
BlackScholes
BollingerBand
BullishDivergence
BullishEngulfing
BusinessDays
CalcTime
CCI
CCIClassic
ChaikinOsc
CloseD
CloseM
CloseW
CloseY
CoeffR
CoeffR_a
Combination
ContractProfit
Correlation
Correlation_a
CountIF(Criteria,N)
CounterTrendStocks
Covariance
Covariance_a
CSI
CSIClassic
Cum

DailyLosers
DailyWinners
DarkCloud
DayofWeekFix
DaysToExpiration
Delta
Detrend
DevSqrd
DevSqrd_a
DMICustom
DMIMinus
DMIMinusCustom
DMIPlus
DMIPlusCustom
Doji
EaseOfMovement
ELDate
ELDateToString
EntriesToday
EveningStar
ExitsToday
ExtremePrice
Factorial
FastD
FastDClassic
FastDCustom
FastHighestBar
FastK
FastKCustom
FastLowestBar
FindBar
FirstOfMonthJul
FirstOfNextMonthJul
FirstofPrevMonthJul
Fisher
FisherINV
Gamma
GenerateStrike
Hammer
HangingMan
HarmonicMean
HarmonicMean_a
HighD
Highest
Highest_a
HighestBar
HighestFC
HighM
HighW
HighY
HPI
IFF
ImpliedVolatility
Intrinsic
IsWorkDay
KeltnerChannel
Kurtosis
Kurtosis_a
KurtosisOpt
LastBarOnChart
LastCalcDate
LastCalcTime
LastDayOfMonth
LastHour
Leader
LinearRegAngle
LinearRegAngleFC
LinearRegLine
LinearRegSlope
LinearRegSlopeFC
LinearRegValue
LinearRegValueFC
LinRegForecast_a
LinRegIntercept_a
LinRegSlope_a
LowD
Lowest
Lowest_a
LowestBar
LowestFC
LowM
LowW
LowY
LRO
LWAccDis
MACD
MassIndex
MaxContractProfit
McClellanOsc
Median
Median_a
MedianPrice
MFI
MidPoint
MinutesToTime
Mode
Mode_a
Momentum
MoneyFlow
MorningStar
MRO
MyPrice
Next3rdFriday
NormalCumDensity
NormalCumDensity_a
NormalDensity
NormalDensity_a
NormalSCDensity
NthDayOfMonth
NthHighest
NthHighest_a
NthHighestBar
NthLowest
NthLowest_a
NthLowestBar
NumUnits
OBV
OpenD
OpenM
OpenW
OpenY
OS_AnnualDividend
OS_BlackModel
OS_BlackScholes
OS_CheckProx
OS_DaysToExp
OS_DaysToFarExp
OS_DaysToNearExp
OS_DivsBetweenDates
OS_ERT
OS_FindCall
OS_FindPut
OS_FindSeries
OS_FracDaysToExp
OS_GrossIn
OS_GrossOut
OS_Intrinsic
OS_MaxNumStrike
Parabolic
ParabolicCustom
PercentChange

Percentile
Percentile_a
PercentR
PercentRank
PercentRank_a
Permutation
PivotHighVS
PivotHighVSBar
PivotLowVS
PivotLowVSBar
PositionProfitCustom
PriceVolTrend
ProbAbove
ProbBelow
ProbBetween
QualityBar
Quartile
Quartile_a
Range
RangeLeader
Rank
Rank_a
RateOfChange
Ring
Round2Fraction
RSI
RSIClassic
Rsquared
SerialHighsLows
SetPlotColor
ShootingStar
ShowLongStop
ShowShortStop
Skew
Skew_a
SkewOpt
SlowD
SlowDClassic
SlowDCustom
SlowK
SlowKClassic
SlowKCustom
SmoothedAverage
SnapFundValid
SortDown_a
SortUp_a
StandardError
StandardError_a
Standardize
Standardize_a
StdDev
StdDevPAnnualized
StdDevS
StdDevS_a
StdDevSAnnualized
Stochastics
StrColorToNum
Summation
Summation_a
SummationFC
SummationIF
SwingHigh
SwingHighBar
SwingIndex
SwingLow
SwingLowBar
TDC.Channel2.Hi
TDC.Channel2.Lo
TDC.REI
TDC.SEQ.SetUp
TDirec
Theta
TimeSeriesForecast
TimeToMinutes
TL_Exist
TLAngle
TLAngleEasy
TLSlope
TLSlopeEasy
TLValue
TLValueEasy
TrendingStocks
TRIAverage
TrimMean
TRIX
TrueHigh
TrueLow
TrueRange
TrueRangeCustom
TypicalPrice
UlcerIndex
UltimateOsc
Variance
VarianceP
VarianceP_a
VarianceS_a
Vega
Volatility
VolatilityClassic
VolatilityExVal
VolatilityStdDev
VolatilityStocks
VolumeOsc
VolumeROC
WAverage
WeightedClose

APPENDIX G.2

Built-in Functions and Indicators (Functional Listing)

This is a partial list of indicators and functions that come with the vanilla, out-of-the-box version of TradeStation, nothing special added. Only select functions and indicators are included, for beginning users of TradeStation. There are at least 10 times this many in TS. Nevertheless, there are more here than you will ever need, more than a normal person could ever get around to testing. But, I admonish you, don't trade anything until you have thoroughly tested it. I have not included the more esoteric functions and indicators, nor anything pertaining to options or activity bars, just the ones for basic EasyLanguage. To view the entire set of indicators and functions, take a look at the TradeStation Help files or at a pdf book called *EasyLanguage Functions and Reserved Words Reference.* It is available on the TradeStation Web site.

FUNCTIONS AND INDICATORS

AccumDist (AnyVol)

The **AccumDist** series function calculates the accumulation distribution of a security by adding the day's volume (or ticks) to a cumulative total when the price closes up and subtracting the day's volume from the cumulative total when the price closes down.

Returns: A positive or negative number for the current bar representing the accumulation of up versus down volume (ticks). (See Figure G.2.1.)

PARAMETER

Name	Type	Description
`AnyVol`	Numeric	Specifies the volume (or ticks) for one of the symbols in the chart.

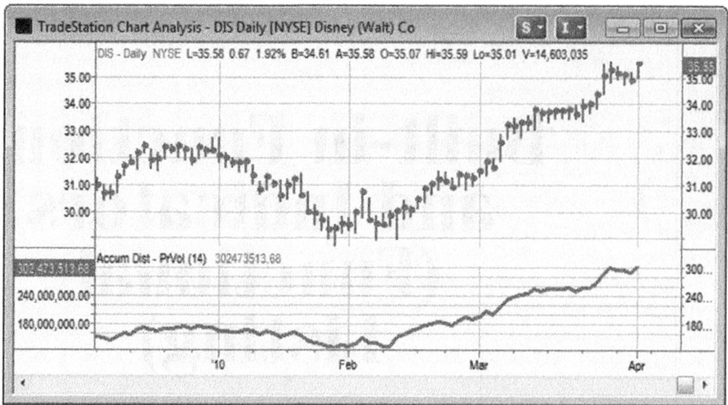

FIGURE G.2.1 AccumDist

REMARKS

Traditionally, this calculation attempts to show if volume is flowing into or out of a security. When the security closes higher than the open, all of the day's volume is considered up volume. When the security closes lower than the open, all of the day's volume is considered down volume.

The use of Trade Volume or Tick Count depends on the For Volume → Use setting for the specified symbol.

This is a cumulative calculation type function, meaning that the current bar's value for this function is based on the values of all previous bars.

EXAMPLE

Assigns the accumulation distribution value to Value1, using the Volume of Data1; then plots Value1:

```
Value1 = AccumDist(Volume);
Plot1(Value1, "AccDist");
```

AdaptiveMovAvg (Price, EffRatioLength, FastAvgLength, SlowAvgLength)

The **AdaptiveMovAvg** series function calculates an adaptive moving average based on a variable speed exponential moving average. The number of bars used in the average is reduced as the price action becomes steadier with lower volatility. The number of bars used increases when the price action becomes more volatile.

This function is used to smooth the values of other functions or values. It calculates an efficiency ratio based on the trending tendency of prices; then a smoothing factor is calculated and applied to the calculation. (See Figure G.2.2.)

RETURNS: A numeric value containing a variable speed exponential moving average.

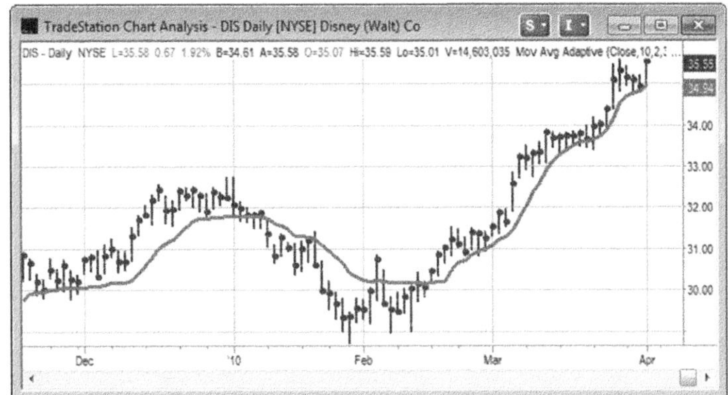

FIGURE G.2.2 Adaptive Moving Average

PARAMETERS

Name	Type	Description
Price	Numeric	Specifies which bar value (price, function, or formula) to consider.
EffRatioLength	Numeric	Sets the number of bars used to calculate an efficiency ratio.
FastAvgLength	Numeric	Sets the number of bars used to calculate a fast smoothing factor.
SlowAvgLength	Numeric	Sets the number of bars used to calculate a slow smoothing factor.

REMARKS

The input parameter Price can be a bar value, such as Close, High, Low, Open, or Volume. It can also be any mathematical calculation, such as (High + Low)/2, or a numeric function, such as RSI, Stochastic, or ADX. The value for the Length input parameter should always be a whole number greater than 0.

EXAMPLE

Assigns the AdaptiveMovAvg value of the bar Close to Value1, then plots Value1:

```
Value1 = AdaptiveMovAvg(Close, 10, 2, 30);
Plot1(Value1, "ADPMA");
```

Assigns the AdaptiveMovAvg value for the RSI function to Value1, then plots Value1:

```
Value1 = AdaptiveMovAvg(RSI(Close,14), 10, 2, 30);
Plot1(Value1, "ADPRSI");
```

ADX (Length)

The **ADX** series function returns the average directional movement index (DMI) for a security. (See Figure G.2.3.)

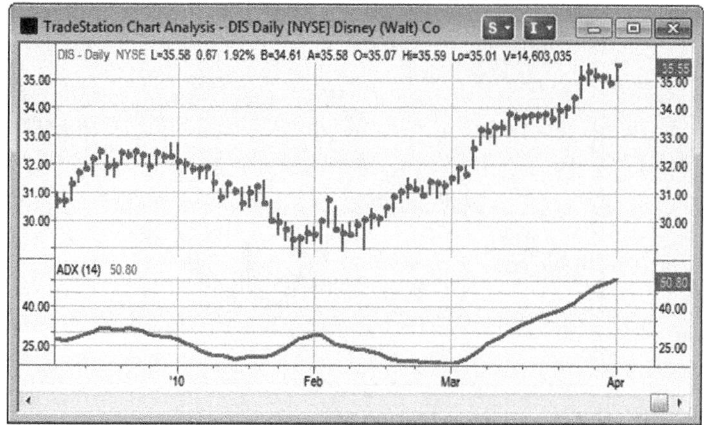

FIGURE G.2.3 ADX

RETURNS: A positive numeric value for the current bar.

PARAMETER

Name	Type	Description
Length	Numeric	Sets the number of bars to consider for the average directional movement index calculation.

REMARKS

ADX attempts to measure the trending quality of a security independent of direction. The greater the ADX value, the stronger a security is trending.

The DirMovement function calculates the DMI and ADX values.

The value for the Length input parameter should always be a whole number.

EXAMPLE

Assigns the ADX value to Value1, where the ADX length is 14 bars, then plots Value1:

```
Value1 = ADX(14);
Plot1(Value1, "ADX");
```

REFERENCE

Wilder, J. Welles. *New Concepts in Technical Trading Systems.* Greensboro, NC: Trend Research, 1978.

See also DirMovement

Average (Price, Length)

The **Average** function calculates the standard arithmetic mean of prices or values over a range of bars. It may also be called a moving average, since the values are recalculated for every bar. (See Figure G.2.4.)

RETURNS: A numeric value for the current bar.

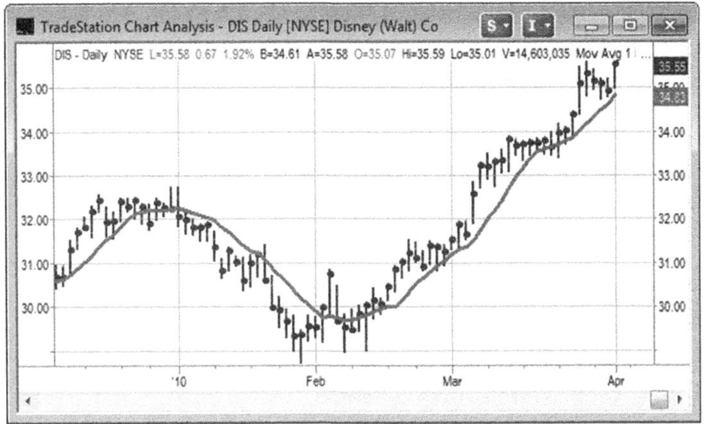

FIGURE G.2.4 Average

PARAMETERS

Name	**Type**	**Description**
Price	Numeric	Specifies which bar value (price, function, or formula) to use.
Length	Numeric	Sets the number of bars to consider.

REMARKS

The Average function is often used to smooth the values of functions or indicators.

Average (arithmetic mean) is the sum of n numbers divided by n.

Average $= (1 + 3 + 5)/3 = 3$

The input parameter Price can be a bar value, such as Close, High, Low, Open, or Volume. It can also be any mathematical calculation, such as (High + Low)/2, or a numeric function, such as RSI, Stochastic, or ADX.

The value for the Length input parameter should always be a positive whole number.

EXAMPLES

Assigns the 9-bar moving average of the Close to Value1, then plots Value1:

```
Value1 = Average(Close,9);
Plot1(Value1, "AvgClose");
```

Assigns the 15-bar moving average of the range; (High + Low)/2 to Value1, then plots Value1:

```
Value1 = Average((High + Low)/2,15);
Plot1(Value1, "AvgRng");
```

Assigns the 10-bar moving average of the RSI function to Value1, then plots Value1:

```
Value1 = Average(RSI(Close,14),10);
Plot1(Value1, "AvgRSI");
```

Assigns the 20-bar moving average of the custom variable myRange to Value1, then plots Value1:

```
Vars: myRange(0);
MyRange = ((High[1]-Low[1]) + (High - Low))/2;
Value1 = Average(myRange, 20);
Plot1(Value1, "AvgRng");
```

AvgPrice

The **AvgPrice** function calculates the average price of a bar by averaging the four bar points: High, Low, Open, and Close. (See Figure G.2.5.)

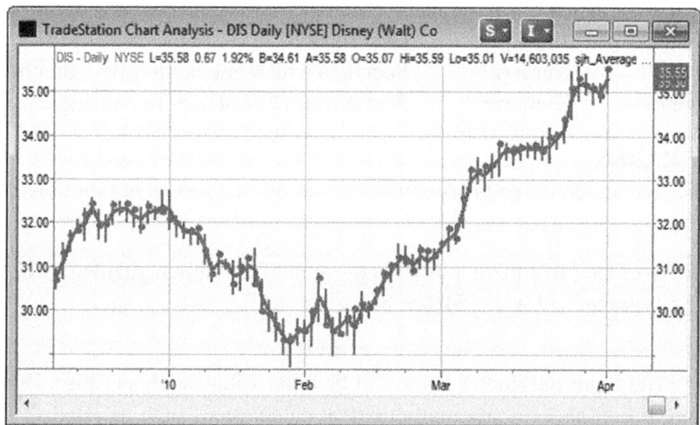

FIGURE G.2.5 Average Price

RETURNS: A positive numeric value for the current bar.

PARAMETERS

None

REMARKS

The **AvgPrice** function is provided as a convenient way to integrate the average bar price into your analysis.

AvgPrice offers a smoothing effect of extreme price points on a bar.

AvgPrice = (Open + High + Low + Close)/4, or (High + Low + Close)/3, (if Open is not applicable).

EXAMPLES

Assigns the average price on a bar to Value1, then plots Value1:

```
Value1 = AvgPrice;
Plot1(Value1, "AvgPrc");
```

Assigns the 10-bar average of the average price on a bar to Value1, then plots Value1:

```
Value1 = Average(AvgPrice, 10);
Plot1(Value1, "AvgAvgPrc");
```

AvgTrueRange (Length)

The **AvgTrueRange** function calculates the average of the TrueRange for some number of bars. (See Figure G.2.6.)

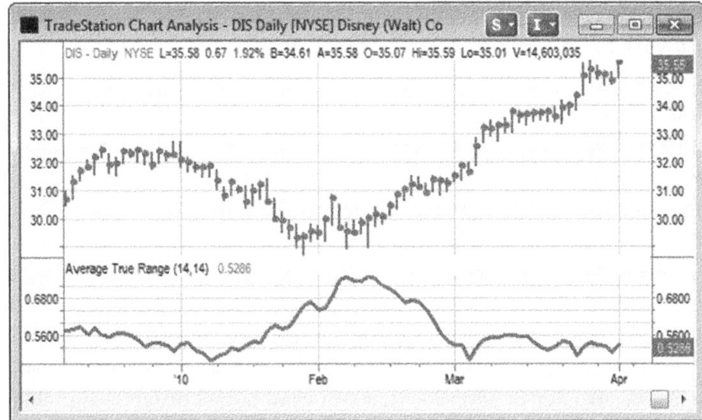

FIGURE G.2.6 Average True Range

RETURNS: A numeric value containing the average TrueRange over some number of bars.

PARAMETER

Name	Type	Description
Length	Numeric	Sets the number of bars to consider for the average true range.

REMARKS

AvgTrueRange is used to smooth out price bars with volatility that is higher or lower than normal.

TrueRange is defined as the larger:

- The distance between today's High and today's Low.
- The distance between today's High and yesterday's Close.
- The distance between today's Low and yesterday's Close.

The value for the Length input parameter should always be a positive whole number greater than 0.

EXAMPLE

Assigns to Value1 the 10-bar average of the TrueRange for each bar, then plots the result:

```
Value1 = AvgTrueRange(10);
Plot1(Value1, "AvgTRng");
```

REFERENCE

Wilder, J. Welles. *New Concepts in Technical Trading Systems.* Greensboro, NC: Trend Research, 1978.

BarNumber

The **BarNumber** series function assigns a reference number to each bar after MaxBarsBack is satisfied.

RETURNS (Integer): A positive numeric reference value for each bar on the chart.

PARAMETERS

None

REMARKS

MaxBarsBack is the minimum number of referenced historical bars required at the beginning of a chart to begin calculating trading strategies, analysis techniques, and functions. For example, a 10-bar moving average would require a MaxBarsBack setting of 9 to calculate, which is 9 historical bars and the current bar.

Since BarNumber is based on MaxBarsBack, if there are 500 bars in a chart, with a MaxBarsBack setting of 50, the next bar after the 50th bar on the chart, moving left to right, will be BarNumber = 1. The last bar on the chart (most recent) will be BarNumber = 451.

BarNumber is often used to identify a particular bar or number of bars because of some special occurrence or situation that you want to test or factor into your analysis.

The BarNumber function is similar to the reserved word CurrentBar. However, CurrentBar does not allow previous bar references: BarNumber[5](of five bars ago) is correct; however, Currentbar[5] is incorrect and does not work.

EXAMPLES

Assigns the BarNumber for each bar to Value1, then plots Value1:

```
Value1 = BarNumber;
Plot1(Value1, "BarNum");
```

Assigns the BarNumber to Value1 when Condition1 is true, and assigns the number of bars since Condition1 occurred to Value2:

```
if Condition1 then
   Value1 = BarNumber;
if BarNumber > Value1 then
   Value2 = CurrentBar - Value1;
```

BollingerBand (Price, Length, NumDevs)

The **BollingerBand** function calculates an n standard deviation (StdDev) line (usually two StdDevs) above or below a center-line simple moving average. (See Figure G.2.7.)

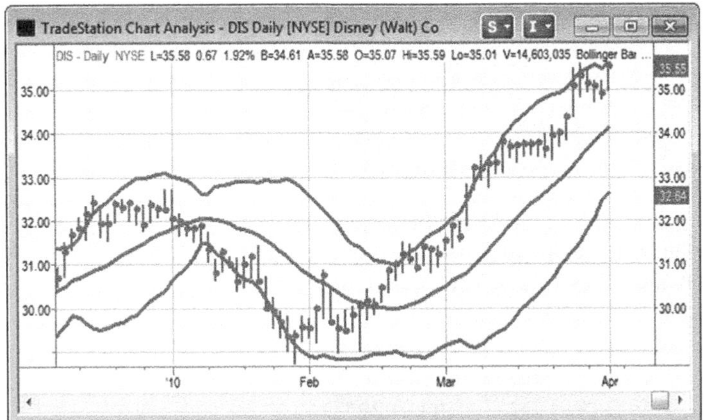

FIGURE G.2.7 Bollinger Bands

RETURNS (Double): A numeric value for the current bar.

PARAMETERS

Name	Type	Description
Price	Numeric	Specifies which bar value (price, function, or formula) to be considered for the center-line average.
Length	Numeric	Sets the number of bars to consider for the center-line average.
NumDevs	Numeric	Sets the number of standard deviations above (positive) or below (negative) the center-line average.

REMARKS

Normally BollingerBands are used with price data, but they can also be used with indicators and other calculated values.

The BollingerBand function can be interpreted in many ways and can be used in multiple time frames. The traditional interpretation would look for a bar to cross over one on the bands and then cross back over, signaling a potential market reversal.

The value for the Length input parameter should always be a positive whole number greater than 0.

The number of standard deviations represents the percentage of values that lie within the normal distribution range of values. At 2 standard deviations, over 95 percent of all values lie within the normal distribution of values. At 3 standard deviations, over 99 percent of all values lie within the normal distribution of values.

By using a number of standard deviations within the normal distribution range of values, the BollingerBand adjusts for price volatility.

The input parameter NumDevs can be any decimal value ranging from −3 to +3 (−3, −2.5, −1.5, 1.5, 2.5, 3).

EXAMPLES

Assigns to Value1 the upper BollingerBand and assigns to Value2 and plots the lower BollingerBand, for each bar based on 2 standard deviations of a simple 20-bar average of the Close, then plots Value1 and Value2:

```
Value1 = BollingerBand(Close,20,2);
Value2 = BollingerBand(Close,20,-2);
Plot1(Value1, "UpperBB");
Plot2(Value2, "LowerBB");
```

Assigns to Value1 the upper BollingerBand, and assigns to Value2 and plots the lower BollingerBand, for each bar based on 2 standard deviations of a simple 5-bar average of the RSI, then plots Value1, Value2, and the RSI value:

```
Value1 = BollingerBand(RSI (Close,14),5,2);
Value2 = BollingerBand(RSI (Close,14),5,-2);
Plot1(Value1, "UpperBB");
Plot2(Value2, "LowerBB");
Plot3(RSI(Close,14, "RSI");
```

REFERENCE

John Bollinger, CFA, President, Bollinger Capital Management, Inc. P.O. Box 3358, Manhattan Beach, CA 90266.

CalcDate (RefDate, DaysChange)

The **CalcDate** function adds and subtracts days from a reference date. The reference date is a numeric value in the EasyLanguage date format: YYYMMDD (Year Month Day).

For example, 1030101 = January 1, 2003 or 9906015 = June 15, 1999.

Since EasyLanguage and Chart Analysis use this special date format, it is sometimes difficult to add or subtract some number of days from the EasyLanguage date. For example, if you wanted to subtract 15 days from January 1, 2003, you might try 1030101 – 15, which would result in an invalid date. CalcDate solves this by returning the correct and valid date of 1021216.

RETURNS (Integer): A numeric value that represents the date in EasyLanguage format for the current bar.

PARAMETERS

Name	Type	Description
RefDate	Numeric	Specifies a chart date in EasyLanguage date format to use as the reference date for the calculation, entered in YYYMMDD format. (Examples: 1030415, 991015, 1000505)
DaysChange	Numeric	Sets the days to be added (positive value) or subtracted (negative value).

REMARKS

EasyLanguage does not see time and date as unique data formats but sees them and treats them as normal numeric values.

The reserved words Date and CurrentDate return numeric date values in an EasyLanguage format (YYYMMDD).

EXAMPLE

Assigns to Value1 the calculated date 14 days prior to the current bar date to value1:

```
Value1 = CalcDate(Date,-14);
```

See also CalcTime

CalcTime (RefTime, MinuteChange)

The **CalcTime** function adds and subtracts minutes from a reference time. The reference time is a numeric value in 24-hour military time format: HHMM (Hour Hour Minute Minute).

For example, 10:15 am = 1015, or 1345 = 1:45 pm.

When working with hour and minutes, it is sometimes difficult to add or subtract some number of minutes with an HHMM time. For example, if you wanted to subtract 15 minutes from noon, you might try 1200 – 15, which would result in an answer of 1185, which is not a valid time. CalcTime solves this by returning the correct and valid time of 1145.

RETURNS (Integer): A numeric value that represents the time in 24-hour format for the current bar.

PARAMETERS

Name	Type	Description
RefTime	Numeric	Specifies the chart time in 24-hour time format to use as the reference time for the calculation, entered in HHMM format. (Examples: 0930, 1245, 1600)
MinuteChange	Numeric	Sets the minutes to be added (positive value) or subtracted (negative value).

REMARKS

EasyLanguage does not see time and date as unique data formats but sees and treats them as normal numeric values.

EXAMPLE

Assigns to Value1 the calculated time 15 minutes from market close and then plots a PaintBar on every bar after that time:

```
Value1 = CalcTime(1600,-15);
if Time >= Value1 then
   PlotPB(High,Low, "CalcTime");
```

See also CalcDate

CCI (Length)

The **CCI** function, (Commodity Channel Index) returns the Commodity Channel Index. (See Figure G.2.8.)

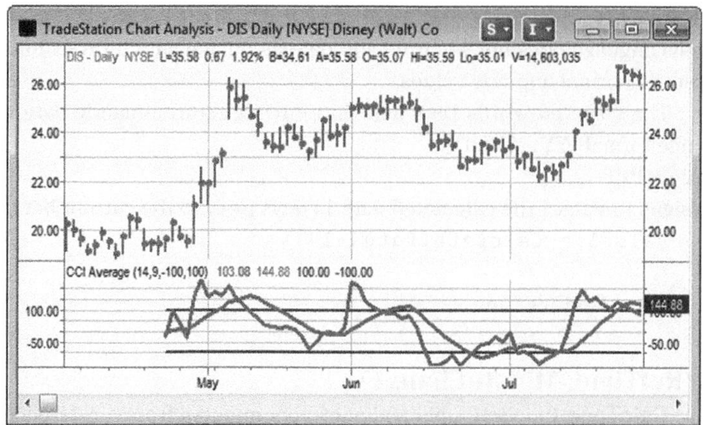

FIGURE G.2.8 CCI Average

RETURNS (Double): A numeric value for the current bar.

PARAMETER

Name	Type	Description
Length	Numeric	Sets the number of trailing bars for the CCI to analyze at a time.

REMARKS

The CCI value usually does not fall outside the −300 to 300 range and is normally in the −100 to 100 range.

The value for the Length input parameter should always be a whole number greater than 0.

The CCI is calculated by determining the difference between the average price of a commodity and the average of the average prices over some number of bars.

This difference is then compared to the average difference over the same time period, to factor in the commodity's volatility. The result is then multiplied by a constant that is designed to adjust the CCI so that it fits into a normalized range of about +/−100.

Traditionally there are two basic methods of interpreting the CCI: looking for divergences or treating it as an overbought/oversold oscillator.

EXAMPLE

Assigns to Value1 and plots a 20-bar CCI value for each bar, then plots Value1:

```
Value1 = CCI(20);
Plot1(Value1, "CCI");
```

REFERENCE

Lamber, Donald R. "Commodity Channel Index," *Commodities Magazine* (October 1980): 40–41.

ChaikinOsc (AnyVol, ShortLength, LongLength)

The **ChaikinOsc** series function calculates an oscillator between the fast and slow exponential moving averages of the Accumulated Distribution (AccumDist). (See Figure G.2.9.)

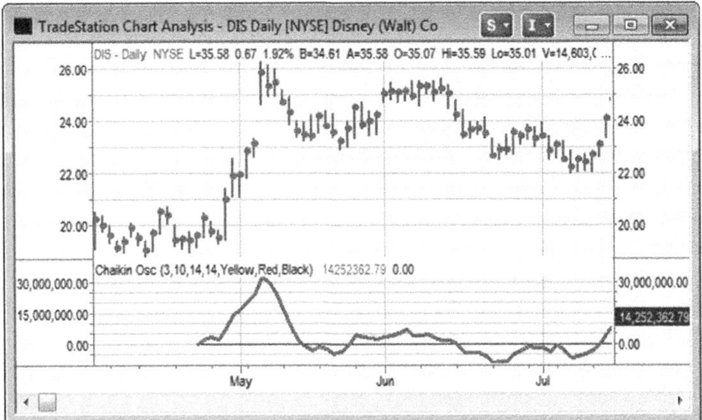

FIGURE G.2.9 Chaikin Oscillator

RETURNS (Double): A numeric value for the current bar.

PARAMETERS

Name	Type	Description
AnyVol	Numeric	Sets the volume (Volume or Ticks) for one of the symbols in the chart.
ShortLength	Numeric	Sets the number of bars for the short/fast exponential average.
LongLength	Numeric	Sets the number of bars for the long/slow exponential average.

REMARKS

The AnyVol input parameter should be set to Volume when referencing daily data and to Ticks when referencing tick/minute data.

The value for the ShortLength and LongLength input parameters should always be a whole number greater than 0.

EXAMPLE

Assigns a ChaikinOsc value based on the daily Volume to Value1, with a short length of 3 and a long length of 10; then plots Value1.

```
Value1 = ChaikinOsc (Volume, 3,10);
Plot1(Value1, "ChaikinOsc");
```

REFERENCE

Colby, Robert W., and Thomas A. Meyers. *The Encyclopedia of Technical Market Indicators.* Homewood, IL: Dow Jones Irwin, 1988.

CloseD (PeriodsAgo)

The **CloseD** function allows you to reference the daily Close of previous days in an intraday chart (minute or tick based) or a daily chart.

CloseD is a function in a family of functions that allows historical daily, weekly, monthly, and yearly references in intraday charts. (See Figure G.2.10.)

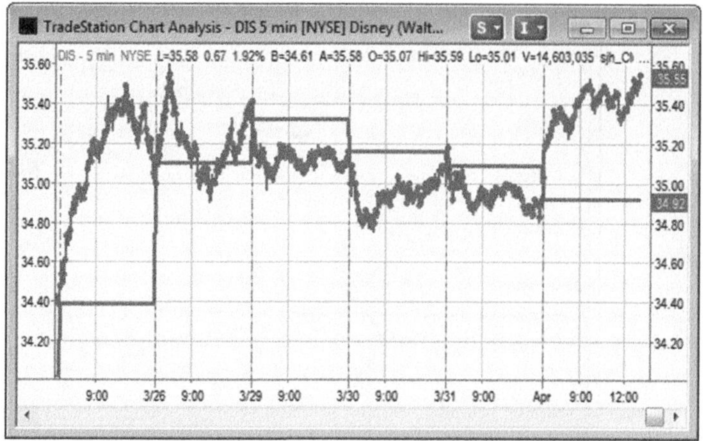

FIGURE G.2.10 CloseD of Yesterday

RETURNS (Double): A numeric value for the current bar. If the PeriodsAgo parameter is out of range (> 50) or there is not enough data, the function will return –1.

PARAMETER

Name	Type	Description
PeriodsAgo	Numeric	The number of days/periods back to reference a previous day's closing price. (50 days back maximum) (0 = Today's current Close)

REMARKS

You must have enough intraday data in the chart in order to look back and reference any previous close. For example, if you want to look back at the close of 25 days ago on a 5-minute chart, you must have 25 days of 5-minute bars in the chart.

The value for the PeriodsAgo input parameter should always be a whole number greater than or equal to 0 but less than 51. Setting PeriodsAgo to 0 equals today's current Close.

EXAMPLE

Assigns the Close of the previous day on an intraday chart to Value1, then plots Value1:

```
Value1 = CloseD(1);
Plot1(Value1, "PrevClose");
```

See also HighD

CloseM (PeriodsAgo)

See **HighD**

CloseW (PeriodsAgo)

See **HighD**

CloseY (PeriodsAgo)

The **CloseY** function allows you to reference the yearly Close of previous years in an intraday chart (minute or tick based) or a daily, weekly, or monthly chart.

CloseY is a function in a family of functions that allows historical daily, weekly, monthly, and yearly references in intraday charts.

RETURNS (Double): A numeric value for the current bar. If the PeriodsAgo parameter is out of range (> 50) or there is not enough data, the function will return –1.

PARAMETER

Name	**Type**	**Description**
PeriodsAgo	Numeric	The number of years/periods back to reference a previous year's closing price. (50 years back maximum) (0 = This year's current Close)

REMARKS

With intraday charts, you must have enough intraday data in the chart in order to look back and reference any previous close. For example, if you want to look back at the close of one year ago on a 5-minute chart, you must have one year of 5-minute bars in the chart.

The value for the PeriodsAgo input parameter should always be a whole number greater than or equal to 0 but less than 51. Setting PeriodsAgo to 0 equals today's current Close.

EXAMPLE

Assigns the Close of the previous year on an intraday chart to Value1, then plots Value1:

```
Value1 = CloseY(1);
Plot1(Value1, "PrevYClose");
```

See also HighY, LowY, OpenY, CloseD, CloseW, and CloseM

Combination (Num, NumChosen)

The **Combination** function calculates the number of unique combination groups for a given set of numbers.

Consider this set of numbers: (1,2,3,4). There are six combinations of unique two-number groups in the four number set; (1,2), (1,3), (1,4), (2,3), (2,4), and (3,4). So, Combination(4, 2) = 6.

RETURNS (Integer): A positive numeric value containing the total number of combination groups for a set of numbers for the current bar.

PARAMETERS

Name	**Type**	**Description**
Num	Numeric	The total number of items in the set to consider.
NumChosen	Numeric	The number of unique items in each group.

REMARKS

The value for Num and NumChosen input parameters should be a positive whole number greater than 0.

EXAMPLE

Assigns the number of unique three-number groups in a set of 10 numbers to Value1:

```
Value1 = Combination(10,3);
```

CountIF (Test, Length) (Function)

The **CountIF** function counts the number of true custom test condition occurrences over some number of bars.

The CountIF function can be used for data mining and testing historical statistical market action. For example, you can ask questions such as "How many days over the last month have been up days with falling volume, and on the following day how many days were up or down?"

RETURNS (Integer): The number of true test condition occurrences.

PARAMETERS

Name	Type	Description
Test	TrueFalse	Specifies a bar or indicator condition (True/False expression) that must be TRUE.
Length	Numeric	Sets the number of bars to consider for testing the condition.

REMARKS

The input parameters Test can be any bar or multidata Condition, such as Close > Open, High[1] < High[2], Close of Data1 – Close of Data2 > 0, or Volume >= 100000. They can also be any mathematical calculation, such as (High + Low)/2 > Average(TrueRange,10), or a numeric indicator function, such as RSI(C,14) < 30, or ADX(C,14) > 25. They can also be another True/False function.

True/False conditions must contain one of these operators: =, >=, <=, >, <, <>, crosses above, or crosses below. You can also test multiple conditions in one expression using OR and AND. Use parentheses (( )) to group conditions logically.

The value for the Length input parameter should always be a positive whole number greater than 0.

EXAMPLES

Assigns the number of bars where the close is greater than open for the last 12 bars to Value1, then plots Value1:

```
Value1 = CountIF(Close > Open, 12);
Plot1(Value1, "C > O");
```

Assigns to Value1 the number of bars where the close is greater than the close of one bar ago, and the volume is greater than the volume of one bar ago, for the last 24 bars, then plots Value1:

```
Value1 = CountIF(Close > Close[1] AND Volume > Volume[1], 24);
Plot1(Value1, "C+V+");
```

Detrend (Price, Length)

The **Detrend** function calculates the detrended value of a price from an offset average of the price. (See Figure G.2.11.)

RETURNS (Double): The numeric detrend value for the current bar.

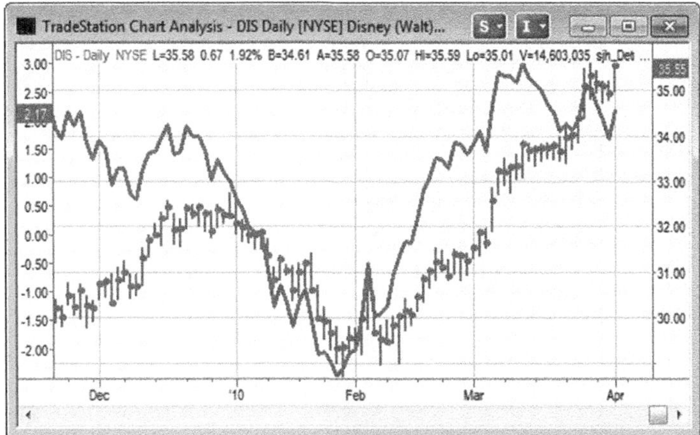

FIGURE G.2.11 Detrend

PARAMETERS

Name	Type	Description
Price	Numeric	Specifies which bar value (price, function, or formula) to consider for the detrended average.
Length	Numeric	Sets the number of bars to consider for the detrended average calculation.

REMARKS

The detrend average offset is half of the average length plus one.

The input parameter Price can be a bar value, such as Close, High, Low, Open, or Volume. It can also be any mathematical calculation, such as (High + Low)/2, or a numeric function, such as RSI, Stochastic, or ADX.

The value for the Length input parameter should always be a whole number greater than 0.

EXAMPLE

Assigns to Value1 the detrended price value for the Close from the 14 bar average of the Close, then plots Value1:

```
Value1 = Detrend(Close, 14);
Plot1(Value1, "Detrend");
```

DevSqrd (Price, Length)

The **DevSqrd** function calculates the sum of squares of deviations of a price from the average.

The calculation of this formula is similar to the classic statistical volatility (Statistical Standard Deviation), the difference being that peaks (higher values) are accentuated because the values are squared. (See Figure G.2.12.)

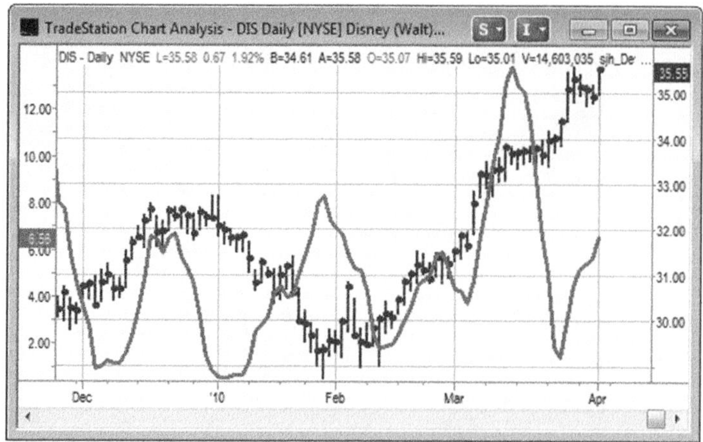

FIGURE G.2.12 DevSqrd

RETURNS (Double): A numeric value for the current bar.

PARAMETERS

Name	Type	Description
Price	Numeric	Specifies which bar value (price, function, or formula) to use.
Length	Numeric	Sets the number of trailing bars to consider for the calculation.

REMARKS

The input parameter Price can be a bar value, such as Close, High, Low, Open, or Volume. It can also be any mathematical calculation, such as (High + Low)/2, or a numeric function, such as RSI, Stochastic, or ADX.

The value for the Length input parameter should always be a whole number greater than 0.

EXAMPLE

Assigns to Value1 the DevSqrd value for the Close looking at the 14 bar average of the Close, then plots Value1:

```
Value1 = DevSqrd(Close, 14);
Plot1(Value1, "DevSqrd");
```

DirMovement (PriceH, PriceL, PriceC, Length, oDMIPlus, oDMIMinus, oDMI, oADX, oADXR, oVolatility)

The **DirMovement** series function calculates the Directional Movement values described by J. Welles Wilder.

The DirMovement function is a multiple-output function that consolidates the calculations of several related functions: ADX, ADXCustom, ADXR, ADXRCustom, DMI, DMICustom, DMIMinus, DMIMinusCustom, DMIPlus, and DMIPlusCustom. (See Figure G.2.13.)

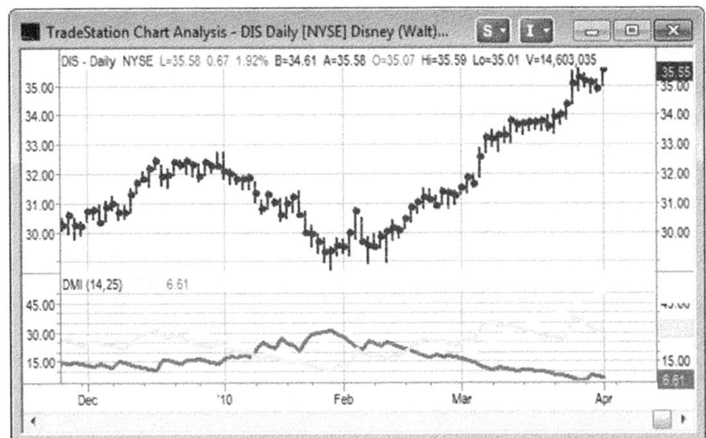

FIGURE G.2.13 Directional Movement Index

RETURNS (Integer): The oDMIPlus, oDMIMinus, oDMI, oADX, oADXR, and oVolty output parameters return the related directional movement values. The DirMovement function itself returns a value of 1.

PARAMETERS

Name	Type	Description
PriceH	Numeric	Specifies which bar value (price, function, or formula) to use for the directional movement high price.
PriceL	Numeric	Specifies which bar value (price, function, or formula) to use for the directional movement low price.
PriceC	Numeric	Specifies which bar value (price, function, or formula) to use for the directional movement close price.
Length	Numeric	Sets the number of bars to consider for the average directional movement index rating calculation.
oDMIPlus	Numeric	Outputs the DMIPlus value.
oDMIMinus	Numeric	Outputs the DMIMinus value.
oDMI	Numeric	Outputs the DMI value.
oADX	Numeric	Outputs the ADX value.
oADXR	Numeric	Outputs the ADXR value.
oVolty	Numeric	Outputs the volatility value.

REMARKS

The PriceH, PriceL, and PriceC input parameters will need to reference some High, Low, and Close values based on the symbol(s) in your chart.

The value for the Length input parameter should always be a positive whole number.

See Multiple Output Function for more information on using output parameters to return values

EXAMPLE

Assigns to Value2 the calculated 14-bar ADX value passed by reference to the oADX parameter and assigns to Value3 the calculated 14-bar ADXR value passed by reference to the oADXR. Value1 is assigned the value of 1:

```
Value1 = DirMovement (High, Low, Close, 14,
oDMIPlus, oDMIMinus, oDMI, oADX, oADXR, oVolatility);
Value2 = oADX;
Value3 = oADXR;
```

NOTE: This example only uses two of the six output parameters, although the other output values are still valid.

REFERENCE

Colby, Robert F., and Thomas. A. Myers. *The Encyclopedia of Technical Market Indicators.* Homewood, IL: Dow Jones – Irwin, 1988.

Murphy, John J. *The Visual Investor.* New York: John Wiley & Sons, 1996.

Wilder, J. Welles. *New Concepts in Technical Trading Systems.* Greensboro, NC: Trend Research, 1978.

Divergence (Price1, Price2, Strength, Length, HiLo)

The **Divergence** function identifies occurrences of divergences in two Pivot high or low conditions for the BullishDivergence and the BearishDivergence functions.

A BullishDivergence is normally identified when a price (Low) makes a Pivot low that is lower than the previous.

Pivot low and an oscillator (Stochastic, RSI, BollingerBands) makes a Pivot low that is higher than the previous Pivot low.

A BearishDivergence is normally identified when a price (High) makes a Pivot high that is higher than the previous Pivot high, and an oscillator (Stochastic, RSI, BollingerBands) makes a Pivot high that is lower than the previous Pivot high. (See Figure G.2.14.)

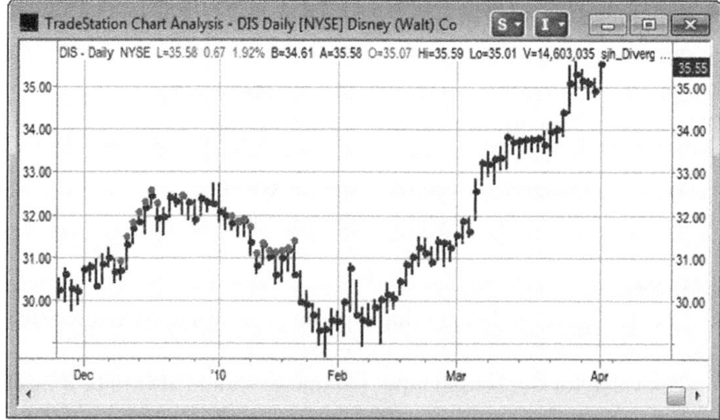

FIGURE G.2.14 Divergence

RETURNS (Integer): The function returns a positive one (1) if the divergence condition is found true for the current bar and returns a zero (0) if the divergence condition is not found for the current bar.

PARAMETERS

Name	Type	Description
Price1	Numeric	Specifies which bar value (price, function, or formula) to use for the first pivot point.
Price2	Numeric	Specifies which bar value (price, function, or formula) to use for the second pivot point.
Strength	Numeric	Sets the number of bars on either side of the pivot high point.
Length	Numeric	Sets the maximum number of trailing bars between pivot high points.
HiLo	Numeric	Set the type of divergence to calculate. −1 = bullish divergence, 1 = bearish divergence.

REMARKS

The input parameters Price1 and Price2 can be a bar value, such as Close, High, Low, Open, or Volume.

They can also be any mathematical calculation, such as (High + Low)/2, or a numeric function, such as RSI, Stochastic, or ADX.

Increasing the Strength input parameter will normally decrease the number of True occurrences.

Increasing the Length input parameter will normally increase the number of True occurrences.

The value for the Length and Strength input parameters should always be a whole number greater than 0.

The HiLo input parameter is a switch: when HiLo = −1, the bullish divergence is identified, when HiLo = 1, the bearish divergence is identified.

EXAMPLE

Plots a ShowMe on the High when a bearish divergence occurs between a Pivot high and the Pivot high of the RSI oscillator on any bar, where the Pivot Strength is 2 and the Pivot Length is 20:

```
if Divergence(High, RSI(Close,14), 2, 20, 1) = 1 then
Plot1(High, "BearDvrg");
```

REFERENCE

Wilder, J. Welles. *New Concepts in Technical Trading Systems.* Greensboro, NC: Trend Research, 1978.

See also BearishDivergence, BullishDivergence

DMI (Length)

The **DMI** series function returns the directional movement index (DMI) for a security.

RETURNS (Double): A positive numeric value for the current bar.

PARAMETER

Name	Type	Description
Length	Numeric	Sets the number of bars to consider for the directional movement index calculation.

REMARKS

DMI attempts to measure the trending quality of a security independent of direction. The greater the DMI value, the stronger a security is trending. DMI does not indicate direction.

The DirMovement function calculates the DMI value.

The value for the Length input parameter should always be a whole number greater than zero.

EXAMPLE

Assigns to Value1 the DMI value where the DMI length is 14 bars, then plots Value1:

```
Value1 = DMI(14);
Plot1(Value1, "DMI");
```

REFERENCE

Wilder, J. Welles. *New Concepts in Technical Trading Systems.* Greensboro, NC: Trend Research, 1978.

See also DMICustom, DMIMinus, DMIPlus, DirMovement

DMIMinus (Length)

The **DMIMinus** series function returns the directional movement index minus value for a security. (See Figure G.2.15.)

RETURNS (Double): A positive numeric value for the current bar.

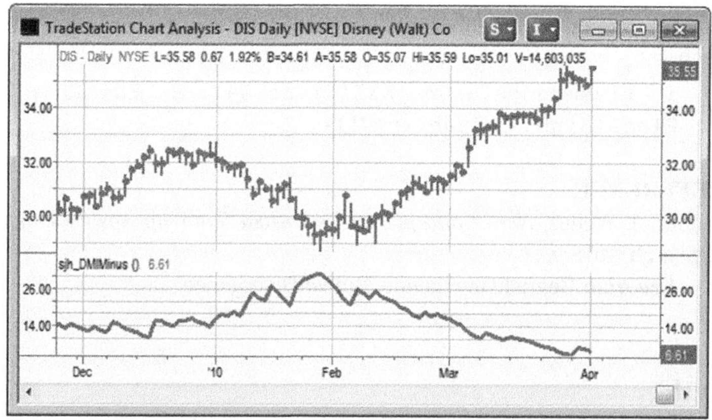

FIGURE G.2.15 DMIMinus

PARAMETER

Name	Type	Description
Length	Numeric	Sets the number of bars to consider for the directional movement index plus calculation.

REMARKS

DMIMinus measures downward movement strength.

DMIMinus is the one of the core components to the directional movement calculations. It is derived by comparing the Low of the current bar to the Low of the previous bar. If the Low of the current bar is less than the Low of the previous bar, then the DMIMinus value is that difference for the current bar.

The DirMovement function calculates the DMIMinus value.

The value for the Length input parameter should always be a whole number.

EXAMPLE

Assigns to Value1 the DMIMinus value where the DMI length is 14 bars, then plots Value1:

```
Value1 = DMIMinus(14);
Plot1(Value1, "DMIMinus");
```

REFERENCE

Wilder, J. Welles. *New Concepts in Technical Trading Systems*. Greensboro, NC: Trend Research, 1978.

See also DMIPlusCustom, DMIPlus, DMI, DirMovement

DMIPlus(Length)

The **DMIPlus** series function returns the directional movement index plus value for a security. (See Figure G.2.16.)

RETURNS (Double): A positive numeric value for the current bar.

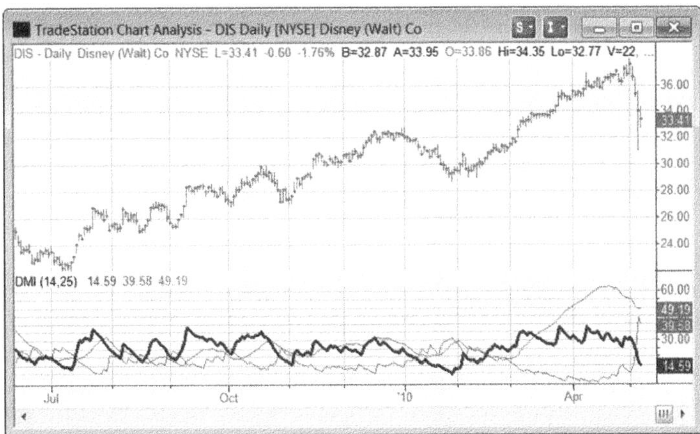

FIGURE G.2.16 DMIPlus

PARAMETER

Name	Type	Description
Length	Numeric	Sets the number of bars to consider for the directional movement index plus calculation.

REMARKS

The value for the `Length` input parameter should always be a whole number greater than zero.

`DMIPlus` measures upward movement strength.

`DMIPlus` is the one of the core components to the directional movement calculations. It is derived by comparing the High of the current bar to the High of the previous bar. If the High of the current bar is greater than the High of the previous bar, than `DMIPlus` value is that difference for the current bar.

The DirMovement function calculates the `DMIPlus` value.

EXAMPLE

Assigns to Value1 the DMIPlus value where the DMI length is 14 bars, then plots Value1:

```
Value1 = DMIPlus(14);
Plot1(Value1, "DMIPlus");
```

REFERENCE

Wilder, J. Welles. *New Concepts in Technical Trading Systems.* Greensboro, NC: Trend Research, 1978.

Doji(Percent)

The **C_Doji** function identifies the occurrence of a Doji Japanese candlestick pattern. (See Figure G.2.17.)

FIGURE G.2.17 ShowMe Doji

`Doji` is defined as:

The body of the candle is very small; the close is equal or almost equal to the open by some percent of the range of the bar. Seen as a cross on the chart.

RETURNS (Integer): The function returns a positive one (1) when the matching candlestick pattern is found on the current bar or returns a zero (0) if the pattern is not found.
PARAMETER

Name	Type	Description
Percent	Numeric	Doji threshold for the (open – close) as a percent of the range of the bar.

EXAMPLE
Plots a ShowMe on the Close of the current bar when a Doji candlestick pattern is found on the current bar based on a Percent of 5:

```
if C_Doji(5) = 1 then
Plot1(Close, "Doji");
```

EaseOfMovement

The **EaseOfMovement** function calculates the relationship between volume and price change using the Market Facilitation Index (MFI) function. (See Figure G.2.18.)
RETURNS (Double): A positive or negative number for the current bar.
REMARKS
The EaseOfMovement function tries to gauge how easily prices are moving up or down and is usually smoothed with a moving average.

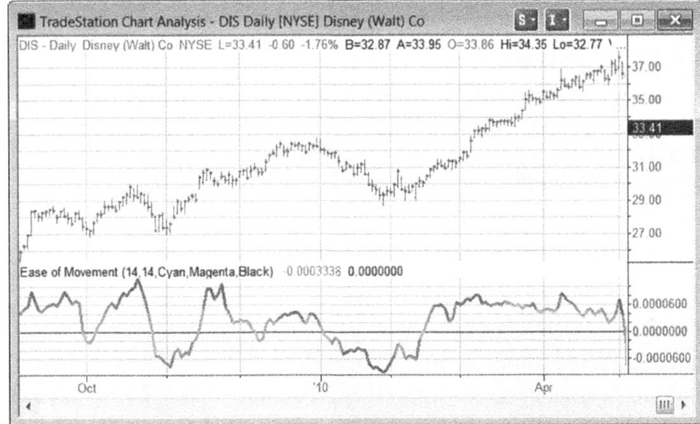

FIGURE G.2.18 Ease of Movement

High positive `EaseOfMovement` values occur when prices are moving upward on light volume. Low negative `EaseOfMovement` values occur when prices are moving downward on light volume. If prices are not moving, or if heavy volume is required to move prices, then the indicator will be near zero.

EXAMPLE

Assigns to `Value1` and plots the 10-bar average of the `EaseOfMovement` value:

```
Value1 = Average(EaseOfMovement, 10);
Plot1(Value1, "EOM");
```

REFERENCE

Richard W. Arms Jr. developed the Ease of Movement concept.

Colby, Robert W., and Thomas A. Meyers. *The Encyclopedia of Technical Market Indicators.* Homewood, IL: Dow Jones Irwin, 1988.

ELDate (MM, DD, YYYY)

The **ELDate** function returns a date in EasyLanguage format (YYYMMDD) based on a specified month, date, and year.

RETURNS (Integer): A numeric value that represents the date in EasyLanguage format for the current bar.

PARAMETERS

Name	Type	Description
MM	Numeric	Sets the two-digit month code: 01 = January, 12 = December, and so on.
DD	Numeric	Sets the two-digit date code: 01 = 1st of the month, 30 = the 30th of the month, and so on.
YYYY	Numeric	Sets the four-digit year code: 1998, 2002, 2006, and so on.

REMARKS

The values for MM, DD, or YYYY input parameters should always be whole numbers representing valid calendar dates.

For example, in EasyLanguage format, 1020704 = July 4, 2002, or 991225 = December 25, 1999, where the year is represented as 103 for 2003, 102 for 2002, 101 for 2001, 100 for 2000, 99 for 1999, and so on.

The reserved words Date and CurrentDate return numeric date values in this same EasyLanguage format (YYYMMDD).

EXAMPLE

Assigns to Value1 the numeric EasyLanguage date of 1020704, for the input parameters of; 07,04,2002, (July 4, 2002):

```
Value1 = ELDate(07, 04, 2002);
```

ELDateToString(DateSelect)

The **ELDateToString** function returns a 10-character date string in MM/DD/YYYY format from the EasyLanguage date specified. Example: 1020704 = "07/04/2002"

RETURNS (String): A text string containing a 10-character date in MM/DD/YYYY format for the current bar.

PARAMETER

Name	Type	Description
`DateSelect`	Numeric	Sets the target date, entered in the EL format "YYYMMDD" or a numeric date related function or calculation.

REMARKS

The value for the `DateSelect` input parameter can be any valid date (past or future) in EasyLanguage format.

For example, in EasyLanguage format, 1020704 = July 4, 2002, or 991225 = December 25, 1999, where the year is represented as 103 for 2003, 102 for 2002, 101 for 2001, 100 for 2000, 99 for 1999, and so on.

The reserved words Date and CurrentDate return numeric date values in EasyLanguage format (YYYMMDD).

EXAMPLES

Assigns to Value1 the text string for the numeric EasyLanguage date of 1020704 (July 4, 2002):

```
Value1 = ELDateToString(1020704);
```

Assigns to Value1 the text string for the current data feed time:

```
Value1 = ELDateToString(CurrentDate);
```

Assigns to Value1 the text string for the current bar date:

```
Value1 = ELDateToString(Date);
```

EntriesToday(TargetDate_YYYMMDD)

The **EntriesToday** function returns the number of strategy position entries that were taken throughout the specified date.

RETURNS (Integer): The number of strategy position entries on a date.

PARAMETER

Name	Type	Description
`TargetDate_YYYMMDD`	Date	Sets the Target date, entered in the format "YYYMMDD", or a date-related function or calculation.

REMARKS

The `EntriesToday` function works only in Strategies and will not work in any other indicator or analysis technique study type. The function is limited to looking back 10 positions, so the maximum number of `EntriesToday` that could be reported is 10, if there were 10 entries today.

The input parameter can be a constant value, such as 1020601 (6-1-2002), where 102 = 2002, 103 = 2003, 99 = 1999, and so on. It can also reference date-related keywords like Date (which returns the current bar date) and CurrentDate (which returns the datafeed date).

EXAMPLES

Assigns to Value1 the number of entries throughout each day on the chart:

```
Value1 = EntriesToday(Date);
```

Assigns to Value1 the number of entries throughout the current day only and then checks for three entries:

```
Value1 = EntriesToday(CurrentDate);
if Value1 = 3 then ...
```

See also `ExitsToday`

EveningStar

The **C_MornStar_EveStar** function identifies occurrences of two Japanese candlestick patterns; Morning Star and Evening Star.

Morning Star is defined as:

A three-candlestick pattern, the first is a long red candle, followed by a small body candle that gaps lower to form the star, the third is a green candle that closes into the first candle's real body.

The first candle body needs to be larger than the average body.

Evening Star is defined as:

A three-candlestick pattern, the first is a long green candle, followed by a small body candle that gaps lower to form the star, the third is a red candle that closes into the first candle's real body.

The first candle body needs to be larger than the average body.

SYNTAX

C_MornStar_EveStar(Length, oMorningStar, oEveningStar)

RETURNS (Integer): Each pattern is represented by an output parameter (oMorningStar or oEveningStar) that returns a positive one (1) when the matching candlestick pattern is found on the current bar or returns a zero (0) if the pattern is not found. The C_MornStar_EveStar function itself returns a value of 1.

PARAMETERS

Length	Numeric	Length used to calculate the average body.
oMorningStar	Numeric	Output variable returns a 1 if the Morning Star candlestick pattern exists on the current bar or 0 if the pattern does not exist.
oEveningStar	Numeric	Output variable returns a 1 if the Evening Star candlestick pattern exists on the current bar or 0 if the pattern does not exist.

EXAMPLE

Plots a ShowMe on the High of the current bar when a Morning Star candlestick pattern is found on the current bar based on a Length of 14:

```
Value1 = C_MornStar_EveStar(14, oMorningStar, oEveningStar)
if oMorningStar = 1 then
   Plot1(Low, "MorningStar");
```

ExitsToday(TargetDate_YYYMMDD)

The **ExitsToday** function returns the number of strategy position exits that occurred throughout the date specified by the input parameter Date0.

RETURNS (Integer): The number of strategy position exits on a date.

PARAMETER

Name	Type	Description
TargetDate_YYYMMDD	Date	Sets the target date, entered in the format "YYYMMDD", or a date-related function or calculation.

REMARKS

The `ExitsToday` function works only in Strategies and will not work in any other indicator or analysis technique study type. The function is limited to looking back 10 positions, so the maximum number of ExitsToday that could be reported is 10, if there were 10 entries today.

The input parameter can be a constant value, such as 1020601 (6-1-2002), where 102 = 2002, 103 = 2003, 99 = 1999, and so on. It can also reference date-related keywords, like Date (which returns the current bar date) and CurrentDate (which returns the datafeed date).

EXAMPLES

Assigns to `Value1` the number of exits throughout each day on the chart:

```
Value1 = ExitsToday (Date);
```

Assigns to `Value1` the number of exits throughout the current day only and then checks for three exits:

```
Value1 = ExitsToday (CurrentDate);
if Value1 = 3 then ...
```

See also EntriesToday

ExtremePriceRatio(Length, UseLog)

The **ExtremePriceRatio** function calculates the ratio of the extreme prices for a specified number of trailing bars. The extreme prices used are the Highest High and Lowest Low over a specified number of bars. (See Figure G.2.19.)

Ratio = x/y, where x is the Highest High and y is the Lowest Low in the range of bars.

RETURNS (Double): A numeric value for the current bar.

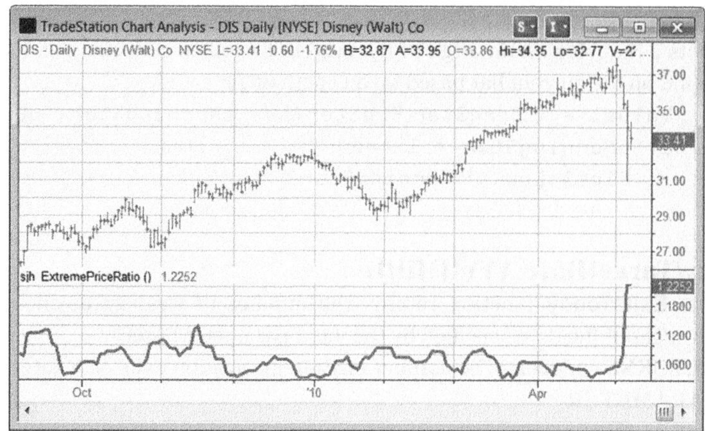

FIGURE G.2.19 Extreme Price Ratio

PARAMETERS

Name	Type	Description
Length	Number	A numeric value. The number of trailing bars to consider for the calculation range.
UseLog	Boolean	True/false expression. TRUE = Use a Log of the ratio calculation, FALSE = Use a simple ratio calculation.

REMARKS

If the input parameter `Length` were set to 1, the ratio of the current bar's High and Low would be returned.

The value for the `Length` should always be a whole number greater than 0.

The input parameter `UseLog` is a switch; it allows you to select the type of calculation to be performed. When TRUE, a Log of the ratio of extreme prices is calculated. When FALSE, a simple ratio of the extreme prices is calculated.

EXAMPLES

Assigns to Value1 and plots the simple ratio of extreme prices for the trailing 10 bars:

```
Value1 = ExtremePriceRatio(10, FALSE);
Plot1(Value1, "EPR");
```

Assigns to Value1 and plots the logarithmic ratio of extreme prices for the trailing 10 bars:

```
Value1 = ExtremePriceRatio(10, TRUE);
Plot1(Value1, "LogEPR");
```

Extremes(Price, Length, HiLo, oExtremeVal, oExtremeBar)

The **Extremes** function returns the extreme highest or lowest value over a range of bars and how many bars ago the extreme value occurred. There may be times when two or more bars have the exact same extreme highest or lowest value; when this happens, the function identifies the most recent occurrence.

RETURNS (Integer): The `oExtremeVal` and `oExtremeBar` output parameters return the extreme value and the number of bars ago it occurred. The Extremes function itself returns a value of 1.

PARAMETERS

Name	Type	Description
Price	Numeric	Specifies which bar value (price, function, or formula) to compare for highest and lowest extremes.
Length	Numeric	Sets the number of bars to consider for extremes.
HiLo	Numeric	Sets whether the function will return the highest or lowest extreme value. 1 = Highest, −1 = Lowest.
oExtremeVal	Numeric	Outputs the highest or lowest extreme value found for the range of bars based on the HiLo setting.
oExtremeBar	Numeric	Outputs the number of bars ago the extreme value occurred.

REMARKS

The input parameter `Price` can be a bar value such as `Close`, `High`, `Low`, `Open`, or `Volume`. It can also be any mathematical calculation such as: `(High + Low)/2`, or a numeric function such as RSI, Stochastic, or ADX.

See Multiple Output Function for more information on using output parameters to return values

EXAMPLE

Assigns to `Value2` the highest High of the last 20 bars using the `oExtremeVal` output parameter, and assigns to `Value3` the number of bars ago the highest `High` occurred using `oExtremeBar` output parameter. `Value1` is assigned a value of 1:

```
vars: oExtremeVal(0), oExtremeBar(0);
Value1 = Extremes(High, 20, 1, oExtremeVal, oExtremeBar);
Value2 = oExtremeVal;
Value3 = oExtremeBar;
```

FastD

The **Stochastic** series function returns the four core values (FastK, FastD, SlowK and SlowD) associated with the Stochastic oscillator. (See Figure G.2.20.)

SYNTAX

Stochastic(PriceH, PriceL, PriceC, StochLength, Length1, Length2, SmoothingType, oFastK, oFastD, oSlowK, oSlowD)

RETURNS (Integer): The oFastK, oFastD, oSlowK, and oSlowD output parameters return the fast and slow averages for the K and D lines. The Stochastic function itself returns 1 if successful, otherwise −1 if both FastK = 0 and SlowK = 0.

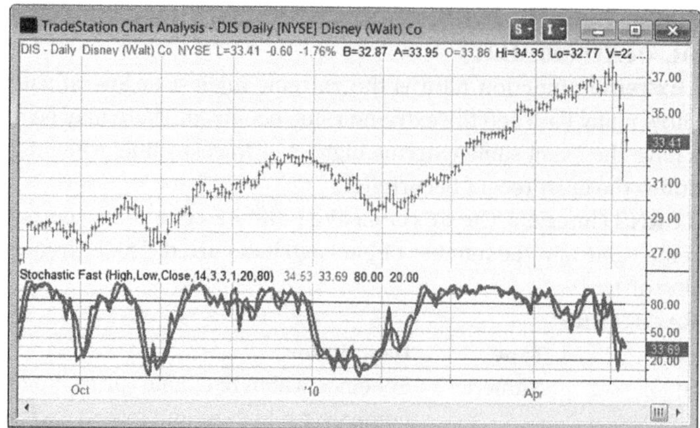

FIGURE G.2.20 Stochastics with FastK & FastD

PARAMETERS

Name	Type	Description
PriceH	Numeric	Specifies which bar value (price, function, or formula) to use for the high in stochastic calculations.
PriceL	Numeric	Specifies which bar value (price, function, or formula) to use for the low in stochastic calculations.
PriceC	Numeric	Specifies which bar value (price, function, or formula) to use for the close in stochastic calculations.
StochLength	Numeric	Sets the number of bars to consider.
Length1	Numeric	Sets the constant for smoothing the fast K line.
Length2	Numeric	Sets the constant for smoothing the fast D line.
SmoothingType	Numeric	Sets the calculation method for smoothing: 1 for calculations based on the original formula. 2 to conform to legacy TradeStation calculations.
oFastK	Numeric	Outputs the value for the fast K line.
oFastD	Numeric	Outputs the value for the fast D line.
oSlowK	Numeric	Outputs the value for the slow K line.
oSlowD	Numeric	Outputs the value for the slow D line.

REMARKS

The Stochastic oscillators indicate overbought and oversold areas in the market, based upon momentum or price velocity.

Stochastics are made up of four individual calculations: FastK, FastD, SlowK, SlowD. The core of the calculations is based upon the FastK value that is calculated in the following manner.

```
FastK = (C - L)/(H - L)*100... where
    L = Lowest Low of a specified period
    H = Highest High of a specified period
    C = Current bar Close
```

`FastD` is a smoothed average of `FastK`, `SlowK` is equal to `FastD`, and `SlowD` is a further smoothed `SlowK`.

See Multiple Output Function for more information on using output parameters to return values

EXAMPLE

Outputs the FastK, FastD, SlowK, and SlowD stochastic values to the declared variables over 14 bars.

```
Vars: oFastK(0), oFastD(0), oSlowK(0), oSlowD(0);
Value1 = Stochastic(H, L, C, 14, 3, 3, 1, oFastK, oFastD, oSlowK, oSlowD);
```

REFERENCE

Stein, John. "The Traders' Guide to Technical Indicators," *Futures Magazine.* (August 1990).

Takano, Mike. "Stochastic Oscillator," *Technical Analysis of Stocks and Commodities.* (April 1991).

FindBar(TargetDate, TargetTime)

The **FindBar** function searches back in time for the first bar matching the date and time specified through the inputs TargetDate and TargetTime.

RETURNS (Integer): The number of bars ago on which the target time and date occurs.

PARAMETERS

Name	Type	Description
TargetDate	Numeric	Sets the date of the bar to find, entered in YYYMMDD format. Enter 1060115 for January 15, 2006.
TargetTime	Numeric	Sets the time of the bar to find, entered in 24-hour military format. Enter 1300 for 1:00 pm.

REMARKS

It searches back through the full range of bars specified in the Maximum number of bars referenced by a study setting (known as MaxBarsBack). By default, FindBar requests 50 bars of data. If additional bars are needed to perform a calculation, the MaxBarsBack setting must be increased manually. If the target bar time and date cannot be found, the function returns a −1 (e.g., if the bar time has not yet occurred).

EXAMPLE

Sets `Value1` to the number of bars ago that the bar with the date of 5/10/2005 and time of 10:30 am occurred.

```
Value1 = FindBar(1050510, 1030);
```

Hammer and Hanging Man

The **C_Hammer_HangingMan** function identifies occurrences of two Japanese candlestick patterns: Hammer and Hanging Man. (See Figure G.2.21.)

Hammer is defined as:

The body of the candle is in the upper half of the bar, and the tail is usually twice as long as the body.

The price trend is declining.

It can be a red or green candle but not a Doji.

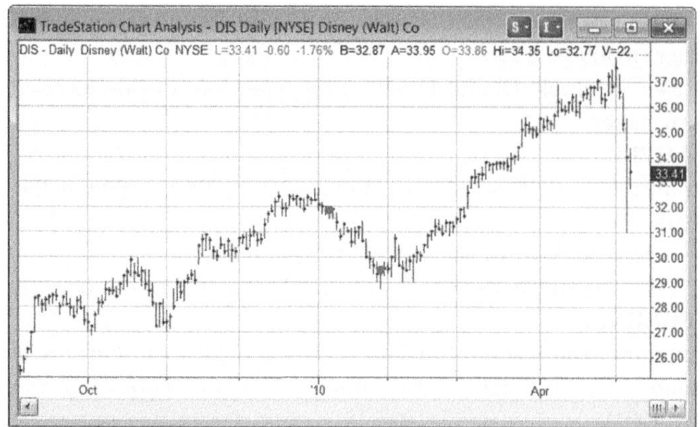

FIGURE G.2.21 ShowMe Hammer

Hanging Man is defined as:

The body of the candle is in the upper half of the bar, and the tail is usually twice as long as the body.

The price trend is advancing.

It can be a red or green candle but not a Doji.

SYNTAX

C_Hammer_HangingMan(Length, Factor, oHammer, oHangingMan)

RETURNS (Integer): Each pattern is represented by an output parameter (oHammer or oHangingMan) that returns a positive one (1) when the matching candlestick pattern is found on the current bar or returns a zero (0) if the pattern is not found. The C_Hammer_HangingMan function itself returns a value of 1.

PARAMETERS

Parameter	Type	Description
Length	Numeric	Length used to calculate the average body.
Factor	Numeric	Threshold factor for the size of body in relation to the range of the bar (2 = Tail must be two times larger than body).
oHammer	Numeric	Output variable returns a 1 if the Hammer candlestick pattern exists on the current bar or 0 if the pattern does not exist.
oHangingMan	Numeric	Output variable returns a 1 if the Hanging Man candlestick pattern exists on the current bar or 0 if the pattern does not exist.

EXAMPLE

Plots a ShowMe on the High of the current bar when a Hammer candlestick pattern is found on the current bar based on a Length of 14 and a Factor of 2:

```
VARS: oHammer(0), oHangingMan(0);
Value1 = C_Hammer_HangingMan(14, 2, oHammer, oHangingMan)
if oHammer = 1 then
   Plot1(High, “Hammer”);
```

HangingMan

See **Hammer**

HarmonicMean (Price, Length)

The **HarmonicMean** function calculates the harmonic mean of prices over a range of bars. (See Figure G.2.22.)

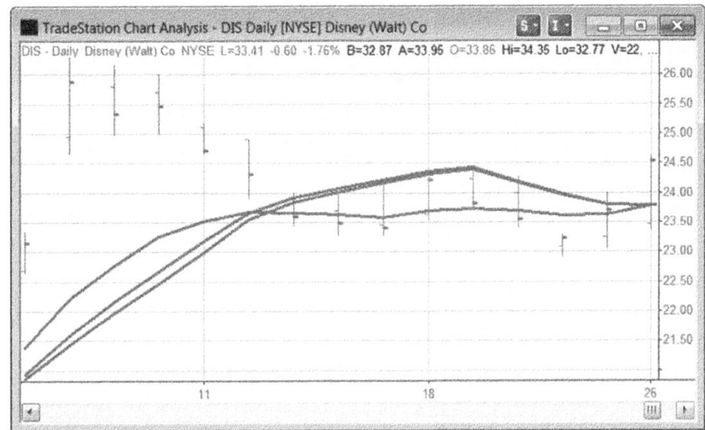

FIGURE G.2.22 Harmonic Mean

RETURNS (Double): A numeric value containing the HarmonicMean of a data set.

PARAMETERS

Name	Type	Description
Price	Numeric	Specifies which bar value (price, function, or formula) to use.
Length	Numeric	Sets the number of bars to consider.

REMARKS

The harmonic mean is the reciprocal of the arithmetic mean of reciprocals. The harmonic mean is always less than the geometric mean, which is always less than the arithmetic mean.

EXAMPLE

This EasyLanguage code plots the harmonic mean, a simple moving average, and an exponential moving average. Look closely, it is very difficult to distinguish between the simple moving average and the harmonic mean.

```
Value1 = HarmonicMean(Close, 10);
Value2 = Average(Close, 10);
Value3 = XAverage(Close, 10);
Plot1(Value1, "HM");
Plot2(Value2, "Avg");
Plot3(Value3, "XAv");
```

HighD(PeriodsAgo)

The **HighD** series function allows you to reference the daily high of a previous day in an intraday chart (minute or tick based) or a daily chart. HighD is one of a family of functions that allows historical references across various data intervals. These functions will not be discussed separately, as they are all similar except for whether you are finding the O, H, L, or C of Daily, Weekly, or Monthly data. (See Figure G.2.23.)

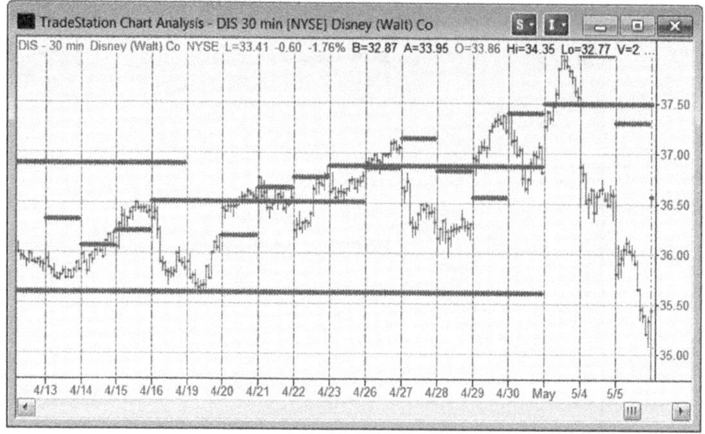

FIGURE G.2.23 HighD, HighW, HighM

RETURNS (Double): The daily high price from a specified number of days ago. If the PeriodsAgo parameter is out of range (>50) or there is not enough data, the function will return –1.

PARAMETER

Name	Type	Description
PeriodsAgo	Numeric	Sets the number of days/periods back to reference a previous day's high price. (50 days back maximum) (0 = Today's current high)

REMARKS

You must have enough intraday data in the chart in order to look back and reference any previous daily high. For example, if you want to look back at the high of 25 days ago on a 5-minute chart, you must have at least 26 full days of 5-minute bars in the chart.

The value for the `PeriodsAgo` input parameter should always be a whole number greater than or equal to 0 but less than 51. Setting `PeriodsAgo` to 0 returns today's current high.

EXAMPLE

In order to show the highs of the previous day, week, and month on an intraday chart, you would write a ShowMe like this:

```
INPUTS: jD(1), jW(1), jM(1);
Value1 = HighD(jD);
Plot1(Value1, "HighD", Green, default, 3);
```

```
Value2 = HighW(jW);
Plot2(Value2, "HighW", Red, default, 3);
Value3 = HighM(jM);
Plot3(Value3, "HighM", Blue, default, 3);
```

See also LowD, CloseD, OpenD, HighW, HighM, and HighY

Highest(Price, Length)

The **Highest** function returns the highest price over a range of bars. (See Figure G.2.24.)

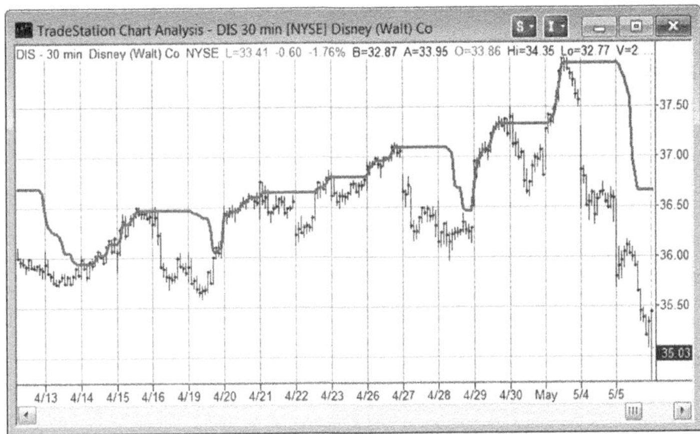

FIGURE G.2.24 Highest Typical Price

RETURNS (Double): The highest price found over a range of Length bars.

PARAMETERS

Name	Type	Description
Price	Numeric	Specifies which bar value (price, function, or formula) to evaluate.
Length	Numeric	Sets the number of bars to consider.

REMARKS

The input parameter `Price` can be a bar value, such as `Close`, `High`, `Low`, `Open`, or `Volume`. It can also be any mathematical calculation, such as `(High + Low)/2`, or a numeric function, such as RSI, Stochastic, or ADX.

EXAMPLE

The following assigns the highest calculated TypicalPrice value over the last 20 bars to `Value1`:

```
Value1 = Highest((Close + Open + High + Low)/4, 20);
Plot1(Value1, "TypicalPrice");
```

See also HighestFC, HighestArray, Lowest, Extremes, HighestBar

HighestBar(Price, Length)

The **HighestBar** function returns the number of bars ago the highest price occurred. There may be times when two or more bars have exactly the same highest value; when this happens the function identifies the most recent occurrence.

RETURNS (Integer): The number of bars ago the highest Price occurred.

PARAMETERS

Name	Type	Description
Price	Numeric	Specifies which bar value (price, function, or formula) to evaluate.
Length	Numeric	Sets the number of bars to consider.

REMARKS

The input parameter Price can be a bar value such as Close, High, Low, Open, or Volume. It can also be any mathematical calculation such as: (High + Low) / 2, or a numeric function such as RSI, Stochastic, or ADX.

EXAMPLE

The following assigns the number of bars ago the highest value of the last 14 bars occurred to Value1:

```
Value1 = HighestBar(High, 14);>:
```

See also Highest, LowestBar, Extremes

HighM

See **HighD**

HighW

See **HighD**

HighY

See **HighD**

HPI(OneCent, SmFactor)

The **HPI** series function returns the Herrick Payoff Index that is used to analyze futures and options. It is a measure of the money flow in and out of the market to which it is applied. (See Figure G.2.25.)

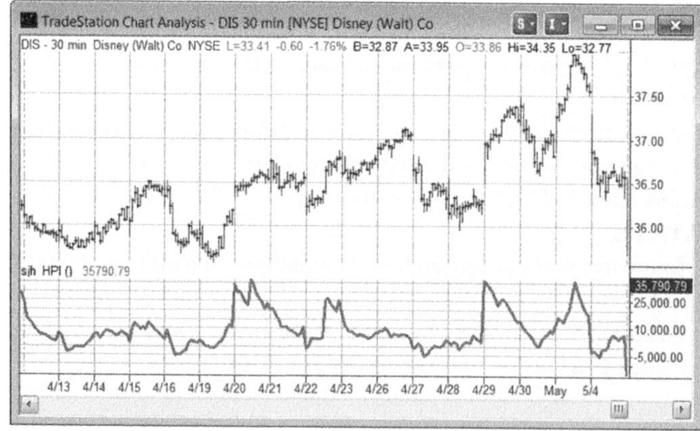

FIGURE G.2.25 HPI: Herrick Payoff Index

RETURNS (Double): A numeric value containing HPI for the current bar.

PARAMETERS

Name	Type	Description
OneCent	Numeric	Sets the contract value of a 1-cent move in the underlying asset.
SmFactor	Numeric	Sets a user-defined smoothing constant, typically a decimal value between 0 and 1.

REMARKS

Open Interest is a requirement in the Herrick Payoff Index; therefore, this study is applicable only to daily data for futures data. The formula applied is:

$$HPI = \frac{\left(Ky + \left(CV(M - My)\left[1 \pm \frac{2I}{G}\right] - Ky\right) S\right)}{100{,}000}$$

where Ky = yesterday's HPI
S = user-entered smoothing factor
C = value of a 1-cent move
V = volume
I = absolute value of today's open interest or yesterday's open interest, whichever is greater
G = greater of today's or yesterday's open interest
M = High minus Low and the difference is divided by 2
My = yesterday's High minus yesterday's Low and the difference is divided by 2

The formula has a minus sign below a plus sign. If M > My, the plus sign is used; however, if M < My, the minus sign is used.

When the Herrick Payoff Index function is called by any analysis technique, it will require two parameters from the user. The first parameter, OneCent, is the value of a 1-cent move, the letter C in the equation. This value will depend on the security that is loaded. For example, if the security being loaded was cattle, this value would be $400. If the security being loaded was soybeans, this value would be $50.

The second parameter, SmFactor, is the user-entered smoothing factor, the letter S in the equation. The SmFactor more or less corresponds to a moving-average time span. Higher values used for the smoothing factor tend to give more reliable results.

EXAMPLE

```
Plot1(HPI(.25, .133));
```

IFF(Test, TrueVal, FalseVal)

The **IFF** function is used to conditionally return one of two specified numeric values. Do not mistake it with the mathematical meaning of IFF, which is "if and only if." This TradeStation function is akin to the Excel function If in its usage.

RETURNS (Double): The numeric value of TrueVal if Test is true and the numeric value of FalseVal if Test is false.

PARAMETERS

Name	Description
Test	Specifies a conditional expression to check (such as Close > Open).
TrueVal	Sets a numeric value to return if Test expression is true.
FalseVal	Sets a numeric value to return if Test expression is false.

REMARKS

By using the IFF function, you are able to evaluate one or more conditions in the Test input expression, returning one numeric value if Test is true and returning another numeric value if Test is false.

EXAMPLE

Assigns to Value1 the number 1 if Close>Open is true or the number −1 if Close>Open is false.

```
Value1 = IFF(Close>Open,1,-1);
```

KeltnerChannel (Price, Length, NumATRs)

The **KeltnerChannel** function calculates the Keltner Channel value. (See Figure G.2.26.)

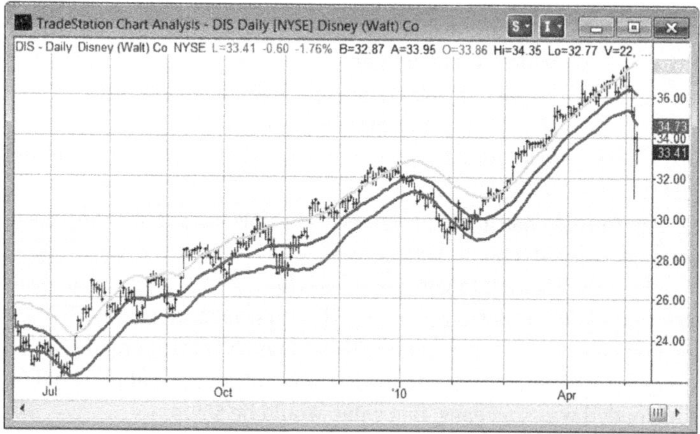

FIGURE G.2.26 Keltner Channel

RETURNS (Double): A numeric value containing the Keltner Channel value for a specified bar.

PARAMETERS

Name	Type	Description
Price	Numeric	Specifies which bar value (price, function, or formula) to average.
Length	Numeric	Sets the period of time (in bars) over which an average will be taken.
NumATRs	Numeric	Sets a multiplier to be used in the calculation. Enter a positive value for the upper band and a negative value for the lower band.

USAGE

Keltner Channel is a channel that is based on a multiple (NumATRs) of average true ranges above and below a moving average. KeltnerChannel is most commonly used with studies or strategies that measure or take advantage of market volatility. It is similar in concept to the BollingerBand function.

EXAMPLES

Assigns to Value1 the upper band of a Keltner Channel that is based on the Close, a 10-bar average, and a factor of 2.5.

```
Value1 = KeltnerChannel(Close, 10, 2.5)
```

Assigns to Value2 the lower band of a Keltner Channel that is based on the Close, a 20-bar average, and a factor of 1.5.

```
Value2 = KeltnerChannel(Low, 20, -1.5)
```

ADDITIONAL EXAMPLE

If you wanted to create an analysis technique that would alert you when the Close of a bar is higher than the value of the upper Keltner Channel using the closing prices over the last 14 bars and NumATRs of 2.5, you could use this syntax:

```
Plot1(KeltnerChannel(Close, 14, 2.5), "KChannel");
If Close > Plot1 Then
Alert("Close is above the upper Keltner Band");
```

Kurtosis(Price, Length)

The **Kurtosis** function calculates the Kurtosis of a data set, which is based on the size of the tails of a distribution curve. (See Figure G.2.27.)

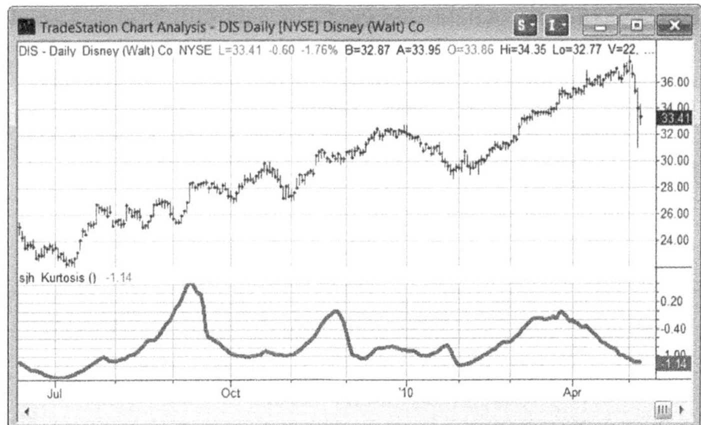

FIGURE G.2.27 Kurtosis

RETURNS (Double): A numeric value containing the Kurtosis of the specified data set. If Length is less than 3, the function returns zero.

PARAMETERS

Name	Type	Description
Price	Numeric	Specifies which bar value (price, function, or formula) to use for the distribution.
Length	Numeric	Sets the number of bars used to build the distribution.

REMARKS

Kurtosis characterizes the relative peakedness or flatness of a distribution compared with the normal distribution. Positive Kurtosis indicates a relatively peaked distribution. Negative Kurtosis indicates a relatively flat distribution.

EXAMPLE

Assigns to Values1 the Kurtosis of the distribution of the closing prices during the last 100 periods:

```
Value1 = Kurtosis(Close, 100);
```

LastBarOnChart

The **LastBarOnChart** function is used to determine if the current bar being evaluated is the last bar on the chart. The Last Bar is the one on the farthest right.

RETURNS (Boolean): True if LastBarOnChart is the last charted bar; False if not.

EXAMPLE

In order to close any open trades at the end of the analysis:

```
If LastBarOnChart Then Begin
   If MarketPosition = 1 Then Sell This Bar;
   If MarketPosition = -1 Then BuyToCover This Bar;
End;
```

LastCalcDate

The **LastCalcDate** function returns the date for the last completed bar.

RETURNS (Integer): A numeric value containing the date of the last completed bar in YYYMMDD format.

REMARKS

For example, if the function returns 960203, it means the last bar was completed on 02/03/96, or February 3, 1996.

EXAMPLE

```
Value1 = LastCalcDate;
```

See also LastCalcTime

From *Using EasyLanguage 2000* by Arthur G. Putt we have this example:

```
If Date = LastCalcDate and Time = LastCalcTime then begin
      Print(Spaces(15), "Date: ", Date:8:0);
      Print(Spaces(5a), "Symbol: ", Sym);
      Print(Spaces(5), "Length of Symbol String:
      ", StrLen(Sym):2:0);
End;
```

LastCalcTime

The **LastCalcTime** function returns the time of completion (Close) of the last bar, in 24-hour military format (HHMM).

RETURNS (Integer): A numeric value containing the time of the last completed bar in 24-hour (HHMM) format.

REMARKS

For example, if the function returns 1700, the last bar was completed, or closed, at 5:00 pm.

EXAMPLES

Value1 = LastCalcTime;

See example in LastCalcDate, above.

See also LastCalcDate

LastDayOfMonth(TargetMonth)

The **LastDayOfMonth** function returns the last calendar day of a month.

RETURNS (Integer): A numeric value representing the last calendar day of the specified month.

PARAMETER

Name	Type	Description
TargetMonth	Numeric	Sets the number of the month to be evaluated.

REMARKS

Returns 28, 30, or 31, depending on the month being evaluated. No consideration is given for leap years.

EXAMPLES

`LastDayOfMonth(03)` returns 31, indicating that the 31st is the last calendar day in March.

`LastDayOfMonth(Month(Date))` returns the last calendar day of the month using the Month function to get the month number from the Date reserved word.

LastHour

The **LastHour** function determines if the current time is within the last hour of the first trading session. (See Figure G.2.28.)

RETURNS (boolean): True if the current time is within the last hour of the first trading session. False if the time is not within the last hour of the trading session.

REMARKS

`LastHour` returns True if referring to an S&P futures data stream and the time is 3:30 pm EST:

```
Condition1 = LastHour;
```

`LastHour` returns False if referring to Intel (INTC) and the time is 12:34 pm EST:

```
Condition2 = LastHour;
```

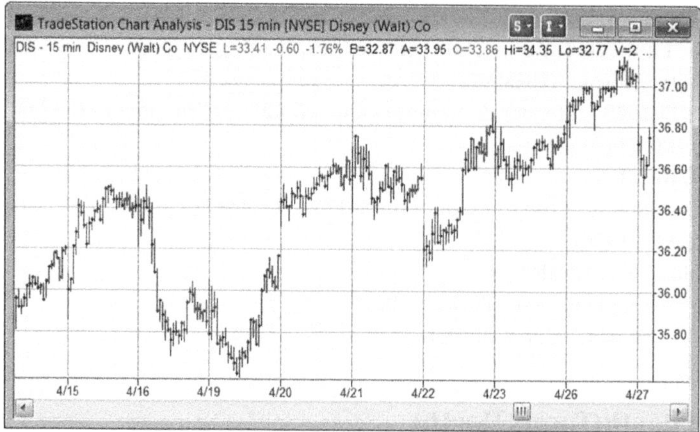

FIGURE G.2.28 Last Hour

EXAMPLE

The following PaintBar study paints any bar within the last hour of the first session:

```
If LastHour Then Begin
   Plot1(Low, "PBLow");
   Plot2(High, "PBHi");
End;
```

Leader

The **Leader** function compares the current and previous bars to determine if the midpoint of the current bar is greater than the previous High or less than the previous Low. (See Figure G.2.29.)

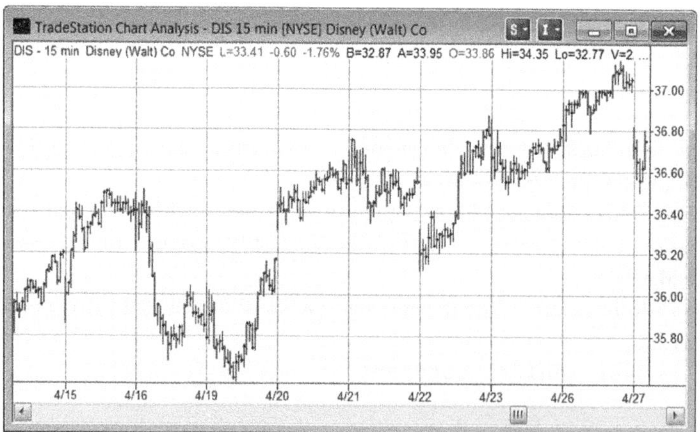

FIGURE G.2.29 Leader

RETURNS (Integer): The function returns one (1) if the midpoint of the current bar is greater than the previous High or less than the previous Low; otherwise it returns zero (0).

EXAMPLE

This PaintBar study paints any bar for which the Leader function equals 1.

```
If Leader=1 Then Begin
   Plot1(Low, "PBLow");
   Plot2(High, "PBHi");
End;
```

LinearRegAngle(Price, Length)

Linear regression is a concept also known as the least squares method or best fit. Linear regression attempts to fit a straight line between several data points in such a way that distance between each data point and the line is minimized. Having found the least squares line of best fit, this function then finds the angle of that line. Angle is expressed in degrees with whole numbers and decimals. A positive angle is rising; a negative angle is falling. A line that rises one unit of price for every one unit of time would be 45 degrees. (See Figure G.2.30.)

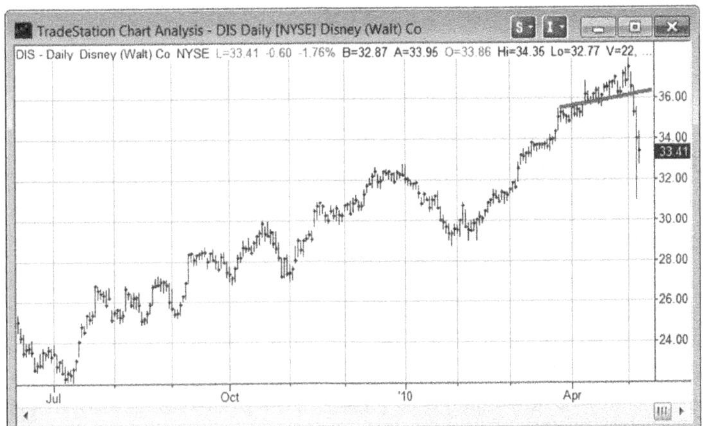

FIGURE G.2.30 Linear Regression Line

PARAMETERS

Name	Type	Description
Price	Numeric	Specifies the value of interest to be used.
Length	Numeric	Specifies the number of bars to consider in the regression calculation.

RETURNS: A numeric value containing the angle of the current regression line.

USAGE

The input Price can be hard coded with a bar attribute such as Close, Open, High, Low, and Volume or a numeric series type input. It can also be replaced with a valid EasyLanguage expression. For example: Close + Open, or Average(RSI(Close,14),14).

The input Length can be hard coded replaced with a numeric simple type input.

REFERENCE

Linear regression is a principle found in most statistical publications.

1100507 1300 Angle = −18.36 Slope = −0.331879 Value = 32.91

LinearRegLine(Price, Length, N)

This indicator draws a **least squares line** of best fit on Price, over the last N bars. N can be a negative number, which causes TS to draw the line into the future. (See Figure G.2.31.)

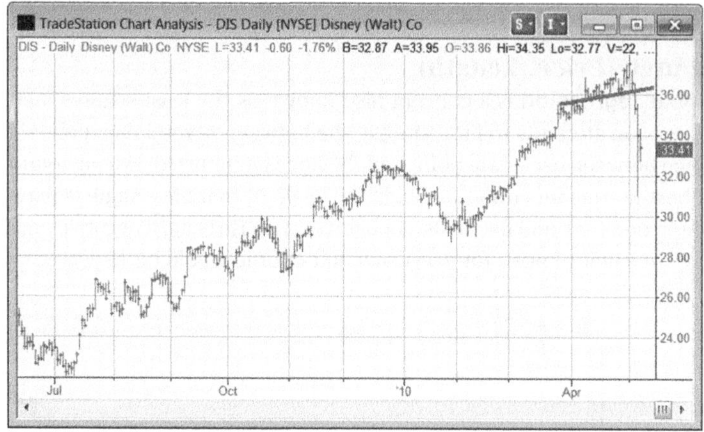

FIGURE G.2.31 Linear Regression Line

LinearRegSlope(Price, Length)

Linear regression is a concept also known as the least squares method or best fit. Linear regression attempts to fit a straight line between several data points in such a way that distance between each data point and the line is minimized. Having found the least squares line of best fit, this function then finds the slope of that line. Slope is calculated as Rise/Run, (Price/Time), or how much time passes in the price change. Slope is expressed as a fraction or a decimal number.

PARAMETERS

Name	Description
Price	Specifies the value of interest to be used.
Length	Specifies the number of bars to consider in the regression calculation.

RETURNS: A numeric value containing the slope of the current regression line.

USAGE

The input Price can be hard coded with a bar attribute such as Close, Open, High, Low, and Volume or a numeric series type input. It can also be replaced with a valid EasyLanguage expression. For example:

```
Close + Open, or Average(RSI(Close,14),14).
```

The input `Length` can be hard coded replaced with a numeric simple type input.

REFERENCE

Linear regression is a principle found in most statistical publications.

LinearRegValue(Price, Length, TgtBar)

Linear regression is a concept also known as the least squares method or best fit. Linear regression attempts to fit a straight line between several data points in such a way that distance between each data point and the line is minimized.

The `LinearRegValue` function **projects,** based on the current regression line, the regression values for x number of bars **out into the future** or x number of bars back in the past, and returns the projected value of Price at that bar.

PARAMETERS

Name	Type	Description
Price	Numeric	Specifies the value of interest to be used.
Length	Numeric	Specifies the number of bars to consider in the regression calculation.
TgtBar	Numeric	Represents the number of bars into the future or back into the past, zero for the current bar.

RETURNS: A numeric value containing the current value of the specified regression line at TgtBar.

USAGE

The input `Price` can be hard coded with a bar attribute such as Close, Open, High, Low, and Volume or a numeric series type input. It can also be replaced with a valid EasyLanguage expression. For example: Close + Open, or Average(RSI(Close,14),14).

The input Length can be hard coded replaced with a numeric simple type input.

TgtBar represents the number of bars into the future or back into the past. If TgtBar is a positive number, LinearRegValue will be for a bar in the past. If TgtBar is negative, the LinearRegValue will be for a bar in the future. TgtBar can be replaced with a numeric simple input.

EXAMPLE

The projected value five bars in the future for the line in Figure G.2.31 is 32.91.

LowD

See **HighD**

Lowest(Price, Length)

The **Lowest** function returns the lowest price over a range of bars. (See Figure G.2.32.)

RETURNS (Double): The lowest Price found over the past Length bars.

PARAMETERS

Name	Type	Description
Price	Numeric	Specifies which bar value (price, function, or formula) to evaluate.
Length	Numeric	Sets the number of bars to consider.

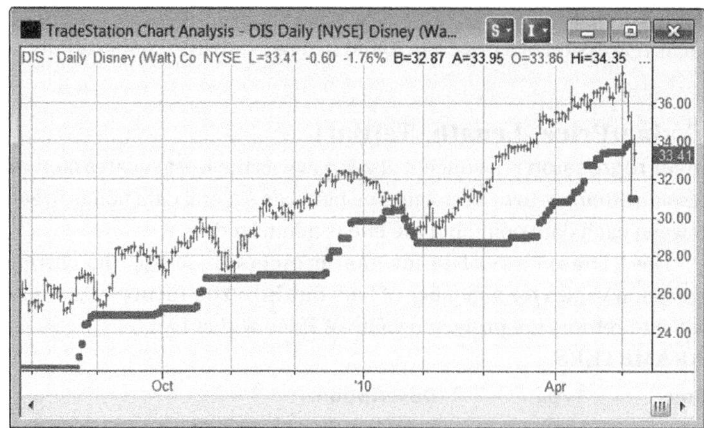

FIGURE G.2.32 Lowest

REMARKS

The input parameter Price can be a bar value such as Close, High, Low, Open, or Volume. It can also be any mathematical calculation such as: `(High + Low)/2`, or a numeric function such as RSI, Stochastic, or ADX.

EXAMPLE

The next code assigns the lowest `Close` value for the last 20 bars to `Value1`:

```
INPUTS: jLen(20);
Value1 = Lowest(Low, jLen);
Plot1(Value1, "Low");
```

See also LowestFC, LowestBar, LowestArray, Highest, Extremes

LowestBar(Price, Length)

The **LowestBar** function returns the number of bars ago the lowest price occurred. There may be times when two or more bars have exactly the same lowest value; when this happens, the function identifies the most recent occurrence. (See Figure G.2.33.)

RETURNS (Integer): The number of bars ago the lowest `Price` occurred.

PARAMETERS

Name	Type	Description
Price	Numeric	Specifies which bar value (price, function, or formula) to evaluate.
Length	Numeric	Sets the number of bars to consider.

REMARKS

The input parameter `Price` can be a bar value, such as `Close`, `High`, `Low`, `Open`, or `Volume`. It can also be any mathematical calculation, such as `(High + Low)/2`, or a numeric function, such as RSI, Stochastic, or ADX.

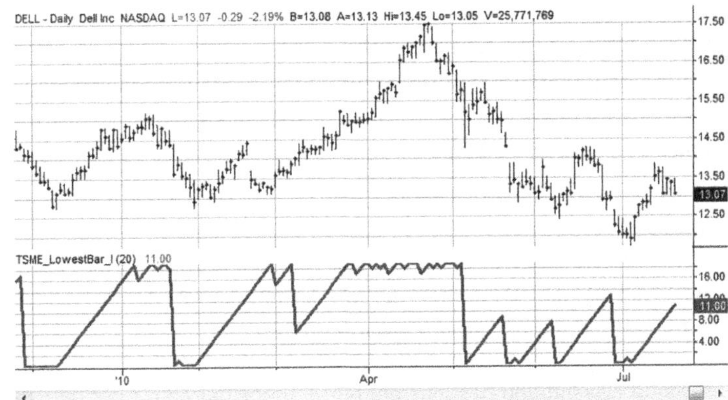

FIGURE G.2.33 Lowest Bar

EXAMPLE

The next code assigns the number of bars ago the lowest value of the last 14 bars occurred to `Value1`:

```
Value1 = LowestBar(Low, 14);
```

See also Lowest, HighestBar, Extremes

LowM

See **HighD**

LowW

See **HighD**

LowY

See **HighD**

LRO(Test, Length, Instance)

The **LRO** (Least Recent Occurrence) function returns the number of bars ago the specified expression was True. Or, if the specified expression did not occur within the last x number of bars, the function informs you of such.

RETURNS (Integer): A numeric value containing the number of bars ago that the specified Test was True.

PARAMETERS

Name	Type	Description
Test	TrueFalse	Sets the true/false expression to check for (i.e., Close > Open).
Length	Numeric	Sets the number of bars to check.
Instance	Numeric	Sets which occurrence: for example, 1 = most recent, 2 = 2nd most recent, and so on.

REMARKS

The LRO function is specifically designed to identify when a certain condition occurred. *It checks from the bar farthest away and works toward the current bar.* The MRO checks from the current bar and works away from it.

The function always returns a number representing how many bars ago the true/false expression was fulfilled (0 = current bar, 1 = one bar ago, 2 = 2 bars ago . . .). If the function does not find a bar within the specified `Length` that meets the criteria, it will return a −1.

NOTE: When using the `LRO` function in an analysis technique, always check the result of the `LRO` function before using the value in another calculation or function. If the condition occurred over `Length` number of bars, a −1 value will be returned.

EXAMPLE

```
Value1 = LRO(Close>Open, 5, 1);
```

See also MRO

LWAccDis

The **LWAccDis** series function accumulates price differences based on a method described by renowned trader and author Larry Williams. (See Figure G.2.34.)

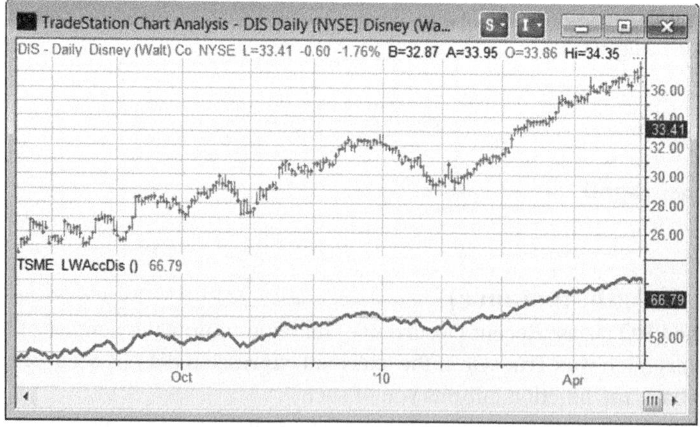

FIGURE G.2.34 Larry Williams Accumulation Distribution

RETURNS (Double): A numeric value containing the accumulation distribution for the current bar.

EXAMPLE

```
Plot1(LWAccDis);
```

REFERENCE

Williams, Larry. *Secret of Selecting Stocks*. New York: Windsor Books.

MACD(Price, FastLength, SlowLength)

The **MACD** (Moving Average Convergence Divergence) series function returns the difference between a fast and slow exponential moving average based on the same Price. (See Figure G.2.35.)

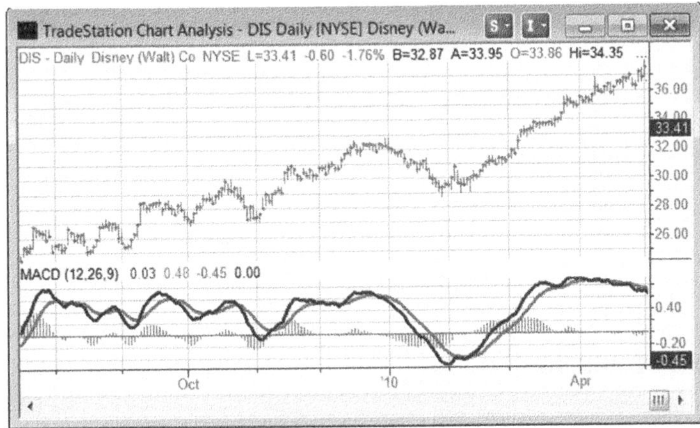

FIGURE G.2.35 Moving Average Convergence Divergence

RETURNS (Double)

A numeric value containing `MACD` for the current bar.

PARAMETERS

Name	Type	Description
Price	Numeric	Specifies which bar value (price, function, or formula) to be considered.
FastLength	Numeric	Sets the number of bars to consider for the fast average.
SlowLength	Numeric	Sets the number of bars to consider for the slow average

REMARKS

FastLength and SlowLength refer to the number of bars used in the moving averages. This should be a whole number that cannot change on a bar-by-bar basis. FastLength, by definition, should be less than SlowLength. If the specified length of FastLength is greater than that of the SlowLength, the oscillator will invert.

EXAMPLE

```
Plot1(MACD(Close,16,26));
```

REFERENCE

Gerald Appel, Signalert Corporation, 150 Great Neck Road, Great Neck, NY 11021.

MassIndex(SmoothingLength, SummationLength)

The **MassIndex** series function returns a value that is used to warn of an impending direction change. (See Figure G.2.36.)

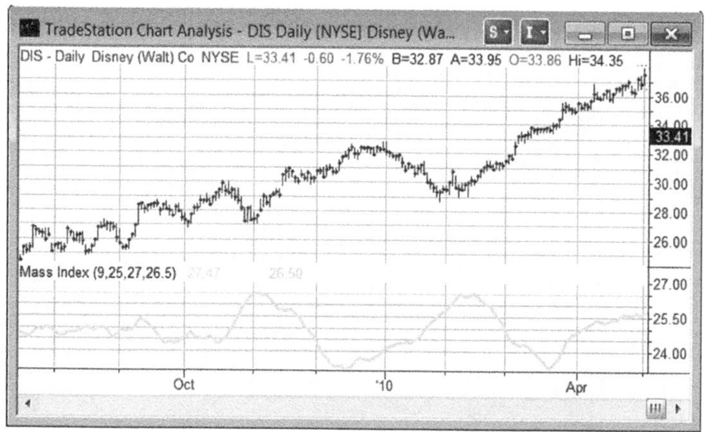

FIGURE G.2.36 Mass Index

RETURNS (Double): A numeric value containing `MassIndex` for the current bar.

PARAMETERS

Name	Type	Description
SmoothingLength	Numeric	Sets the number of periods for the exponential moving average.
SummationLength	Numeric	Sets the number of periods for the summation and second exponential moving average.

REMARKS

The formula for the function is:

```
MassIndex = Numerator/Denominator
```

where Numerator = Summation(XAverage(High-Low, Smoothing), Summation)
Denominator = XAverage(XAverage(High-Low, Smoothing), Summation)

EXAMPLE

```
Plot1(MassIndex(9,25));
```

REFERENCE

Dorsey, Donald. "The Mass Index." *Technical Analysis of Stocks and Commodities.* (June 1992): 67–69.

MaxContractProfit

Calculates the **maximum position profit** per contract or share. `MaxContractProfit` will divide the complete position profit by the number of contracts/shares for the maximum position profit for a single share/contract

REMARKS

The reserved words `ContractProfit` and `MaxContractProfit` include both closed profits and losses and open profits and losses in their calculations. The sum of open and closed P&L is then divided by only the number of shares in the open position to obtain the value returned by `ContractProfit` or `MaxContractProfit`. For this reason, when scaling out of a position using exits that do not exit the entire position all at once, the values returned by these reserved words will not be the profit or maximum profit per open contract or share. Instead, the value returned is the result of this calculation:

```
ContractProfit = ( Closed P&L + Open P&L ) / Number of Open
Shares (or contracts)
```

If it is desired to calculate the profit per open share or contract, the next formula may be implemented in your EasyLanguage strategy:

```
Variables: PerSharePL( 0 ) ;
If CurrentShares <> 0 then
PerSharePL = OpenPositionProfit / CurrentShares ;
```

The same value can be calculated by the next formula, since `CurrentContracts` and `CurrentShares` are synonymous and do not depend on the type of security traded:

```
If CurrentContracts <> 0 then
PerSharePL = OpenPositionProfit / CurrentContracts;
```

EXAMPLE

Value1 will hold the maximum position profit for the current position.

```
Value1 = MaxContractProfit;
```

ADDITIONAL EXAMPLE

If you wanted to exit a long position after the profit per share reached $25, you could use the next syntax: This command is handy because it is often easier to think of your profit in a per share valuation.

```
If MaxContractProfit >= 25 Then
   Sell This Bar on Close;
```

McClellanOsc(AdvIssues, DecIssues, FastLength, SlowLength)

The **McClellanOsc** series function was originated by Sherman McClellan and his wife, Marian. She, in fact, was the mathematician, while he is the theorist. The McClellan Oscillator calculates the smoothed difference between the New York Stock Exchange Advancing and the Declining Issues, which is a measure of market breadth. They have special theories of how to interpret the oscillator readings, one of which is that small moves in the oscillator foretell large moves in the market. Kennedy Gammage, of La Jolla, CA, is the "keeper" of the official oscillator values. (See Figure G.2.37.)

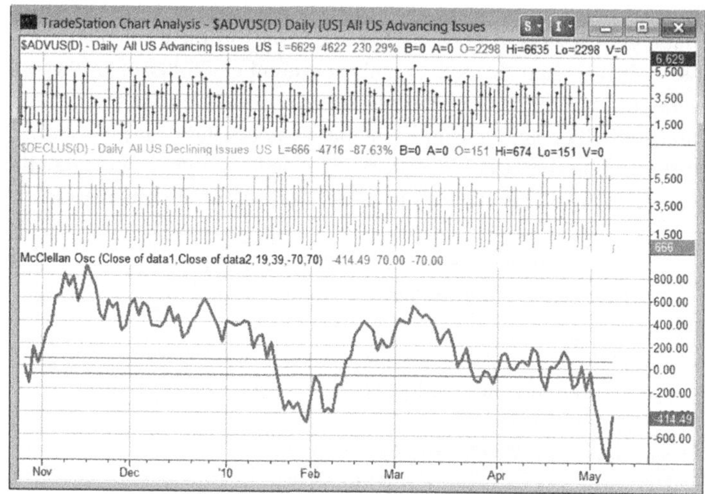

FIGURE G.2.37 McClellan Oscillator

This indicator is not plotted on our symbol DIS but rather on two data streams, ADV and DECL. For this example I am using AllUSAdvancing Index and ALLUSDeclining Index, symbols $ADVUS and $DECUS.

RETURNS (Double): A numeric value containing the McClellan Oscillator for the current bar.

PARAMETERS

Name	Type	Description
AdvIssues	Numeric	Specifies which bar value (price, function, or formula) to be considered for the numeric series representing advancing issues.
DecIssues	Numeric	Specifies which bar value (price, function, or formula) to be considered for the numeric series representing declining issues.
FastLength	Numeric	Sets the number of bars used to calculate the exponentially smoothed average of the declining issues.
SlowLength	Numeric	Sets the number of bars used to calculate the exponentially smoothed average of the advancing issues.

REMARKS

McClellan Oscillator formations help to identify changes in market direction.

EXAMPLES

The McClellan Oscillator calculation is based on the advancing issues (plotted in Data1) and the declining issues (plotted in Data2). The advancing issues (Data1) are smoothed by a 39-bar exponential average, while the declining issues (Data2) are smoothed by a 19-bar exponential average.

```
Value1 = McClellanOsc(Close of Data1, Close of Data2, 19, 39);
```

If you wanted a mark on the High of a bar if the McClellan Oscillator became overbought (greater than 100), you could use the following syntax:

```
If McClellanOsc(Close of Data1, Close of Data2, 19, 39) > 100 Then
Plot1(High, "OverBght");
```

Median(Price, Length)

The **Median** function returns the middle value after sorting numbers over a specified range of bars. It is not the average or the mean; it is the middle-most value. (See Figure G.2.38.)

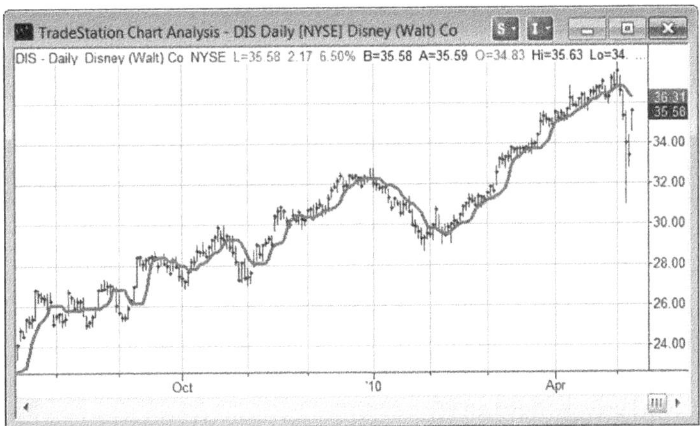

FIGURE G.2.38 Median

RETURNS (Double): A numeric value containing the median value of a specified number of sorted values.

PARAMETERS

Name	Type	Description
Price	Numeric	Specifies which bar value (price, function, or formula) to use.
Length	Numeric	Sets the number of bars to consider.

REMARKS

The input `Price` tells the function what values to look at, while the `Length` input tells the function how many bars to include in the calculations. The function will sort `Length` number of `Price` elements in ascending order and return the middle element. If `Length` is an even number, it will choose the two values that fall at the middle of the sort and average them. See Table A. If `Length` is an odd number the function will return the middle value. See Table B.

Table A

BarNumber	Price	Rank (1 = smallest)	Median
Close[0]	3646.6	2	
Close[1]	3625.0	1	
Close[2]	3667.1	3	
Close[3]	3669.6	4	3656.8

Table B

Bar Number	Price	Rank	Median
Close[0]	3646.6	2	
Close[1]	3625.0	1	
Close[2]	3667.1	3	
Close[3]	3669.6	4	
Close[4]	3670.0	5	3667.1

`Price` is a numeric series type input. The input `Length` must be a whole number as it represents the number of bars, and it cannot change on a bar-to-bar basis.

EXAMPLE

```
INPUTS: jLen(10);
Value1 = Median(C, jLen);
Plot1(Value1, "Median");
```

MedianPrice

The **MedianPrice** function returns the median (mid) price of a bar. Again, this is not the mean, or the average; it is the middle-most price. In the Figure below, the example shows a plot of the Median Price and another plot of the Typical Price. The code is included. Notice the slight difference between the red line (Median Price) and the green line (Typical Price). (See Figure G.2.39.)

RETURNS (Double): A numeric value containing the median bar price.

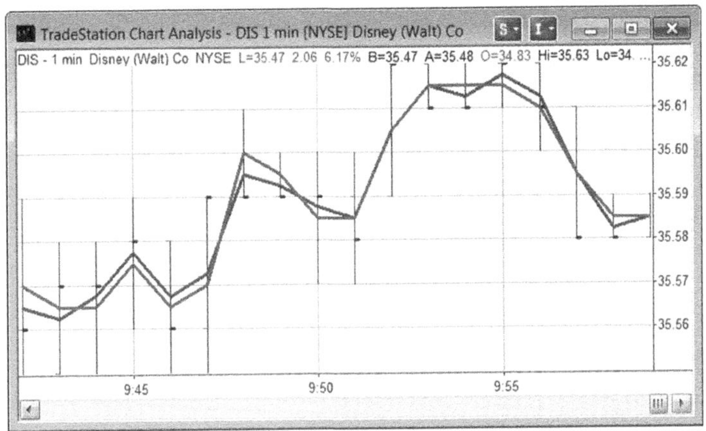

FIGURE G.2.39 Median Price

REMARKS

The median price is the sum of the High and Low of a bar divided by 2 or (H+L)/2.

EXAMPLE

Assigns to Value1 the median price of five bars ago.

```
Value1 = MedianPrice;
Plot1(Value1, "MP");
Value2 = (O+H+L+C)/4; //Typical Price
Plot2(Value2, "TP");
```

MFI(AnyVol)

The **MFI** function returns the Market Facilitation Index value. (See Figure G.2.40.)

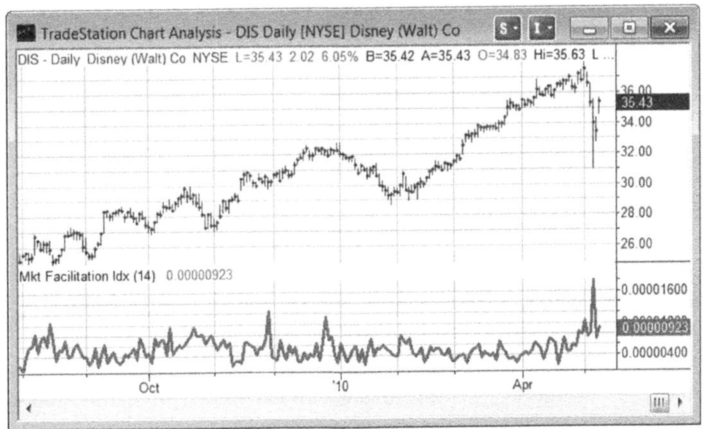

FIGURE G.2.40 Market Facilitation Index

RETURNS (Double): A numeric value containing MFI for the current bar.

PARAMETER

Name	Type	Description
AnyVol	Numeric	Sets the volume value (Volume or Ticks) to use

REMARKS

The `AnyVol` input parameter should be set to `Volume` when referencing daily data and to `Ticks` when referencing tick/minute data.

The formula for `MFI` is:

```
MFI = Range / AnyVol
```

Please refer to the discussion on Range.

EXAMPLE

Plots MFI for intraday or tick data.

```
Plot1(MFI(Ticks),"MFI");
```

MidPoint(Price, Length)

The **MidPoint** function finds the highest and lowest value of a Price over a given Length and returns the average of the two. (See Figure G.2.41.)

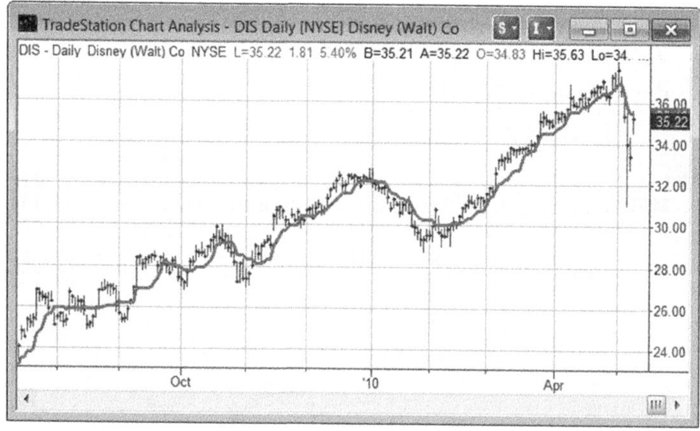

FIGURE G.2.41 MidPoint

RETURNS (Double): The MidPoint price of the period specified.

PARAMETERS

Name	Type	Description
Price	Numeric	Specifies which bar value (price, function, or formula) to be used for the calculation.
Length	Numeric	Sets the number of bars to consider.

REMARKS

The input parameter Price can be a bar value, such as Close, High, Low, Open, or Volume. It can also be any mathematical calculation, such as (High + Low)/2, or a numeric function such as RSI, Stochastic, or ADX.

EXAMPLE

```
Plot1(MidPoint(C,10));
```

MinutesIntoWeek(XDay, XTime)

The **MinutesIntoWeek** function returns the number of minutes since 12 am Sunday.

RETURNS (Integer): The total minutes from 12 am Sunday to the specified `XDay` and `XTime`.

PARAMETERS

Name	Type	Description
XDay	Numeric	Sets an integer value for the day of the week. Enter 0 for Sunday, 1 for Monday, through 6 for Saturday.
XTime	Numeric	Specifies the time in 24-hour HHMM format. For example, enter 2150 for 9:50 pm.

EXAMPLE

Assigns to Value1 the number of minutes between Sunday at 12:00 am and Monday at 10:20 am, which is 2060 minutes.

```
Value1 = MinutesIntoWeek(1, 1020);
```

MinutesToTime(Minutes)

The **MinutesToTime** function converts a number of minutes from midnight to a 24-hour military time format (HHMM).

RETURNS (Integer): A numeric value containing the time in military format (e.g., 1530 = 3:30 pm).

PARAMETER

Name	Type	Description
Minutes	Numeric	Specifies the number of minutes since midnight

EXAMPLE

Assigns to `Value1` the 24-hour military time value of 0130 based on an input of 90 minutes.

```
Value1 = MinutesToTime(90);
```

Using this statement and issuing a `Print` statement so I can see the result, when I put the indicator on a chart, I get 130.00 for the output of `Value1`. Clearly that would need a little massaging before using the value in a pretty report. To pretty up the output we would need to get rid of the zeros and the decimal point, using the `INTPORTION` function, or by specifying number of decimals in the `Print` statement. Then, to really make it look good, we would need to convert it to text and concatenate a leading zero on the front to get the output to be `0130`. Then it would be pretty.

Mode(Price, Length, Type)

The **Mode** function returns the most frequently occurring or repetitive value over a specified range of bars.

RETURNS (Double): A numeric value containing the most frequently occurring or repetitive value in a specified period. If there is no repetition in the range of data, the Function will return a −1.

PARAMETERS

Name	Type	Description
Price	Numeric	Specifies which bar value (price, function, or formula) to use.
Length	Numeric	Sets the number of bars to consider.
Type	Numeric	A numeric value that determines if the higher (1) or lower (−1) of the values will be displayed in the event that there are multiple repetitious values in the data series.

EXAMPLES

Assigns to `Value1` the most frequently occurring `Close` value in the last 21 bars. If there happens to be multiple sets of frequently occurring `Close` values, the higher value of the `Close` sets will be returned.

```
Value1 = Mode(Close, 21, 1);
```

Assigns to `Value2` the most frequently occurring `Range` value in the last 30 bars. If there happens to be multiple sets of frequently occurring `Range` values, the lower value of the `Range` sets will be returned.

```
Value2 = Mode(Range, 30, -1);
```

Momentum(Price, Length)

The **Momentum** function calculates the change in momentum on the current bar relative to a specified number of bars ago. (See Figure G.2.42.)

RETURNS (Double): A numeric value containing `Momentum` for the current bar.

PARAMETERS

Name	Type	Description
Price	Numeric	Specifies which bar value (price, function, or formula) to use.
Length	Numeric	Sets the number of bars to consider.

REMARKS

`Momentum` is an oscillator calculated by subtracting the `Price` value for the bar occurring `Length` bars ago from the `Price` value for the current bar. Therefore, if the value for the current bar exceeds that of the bar in the past, the result will be positive. If the value for the current bar is less than that of the bar in the past, the result will be negative. Values returned by the `Momentum` function oscillate above and below zero. Trading strategies are built around the momentum crossing over or under the zero line.

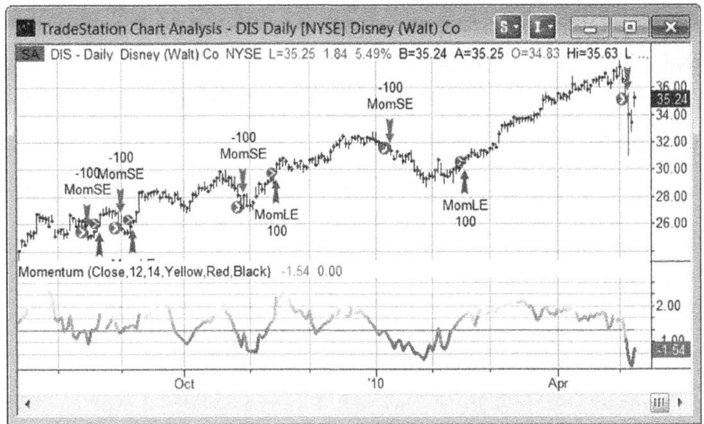

FIGURE G.2.42 Momentum

EXAMPLE

Assigns to `Value1` the momentum difference of the Close from 10 bars ago.

```
Value1 = Momentum(Close,10);
```

MoneyFlow(Length)

The **MoneyFlow** function is an index based on the ratio between positive money flows and all money flows over a specified number of bars. (See Figure G.2.43.)

RETURNS (Double): A numeric value containing `MoneyFlow` for the current bar.

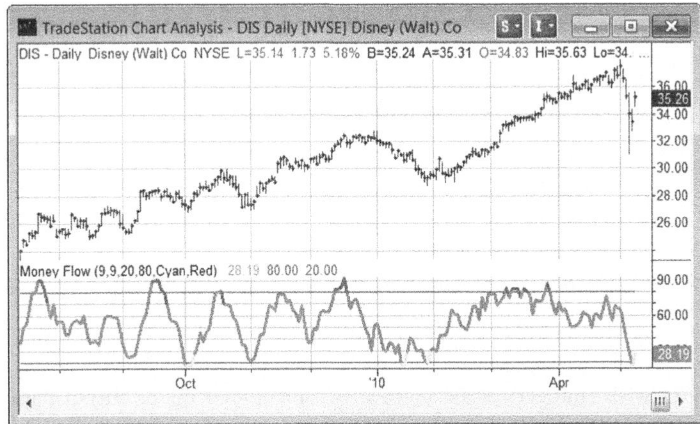

FIGURE G.2.43 Money Flow

PARAMETER

Name	Type	Description
Length	Numeric	Sets the number of bars used in calculation.

REMARKS

AvgPrice is calculated by taking the average of the Open (if available), Close, High, and Low of a bar. Positive money flow occurs when the current bar's AvgPrice exceeds the previous bar's AvgPrice and is calculated by multiplying the current bar's Volume and its AvgPrice. The positive money flows are then summed over the number of bars specified in Length and divided by the sum of all the money flows specified in Length.

The formula for money flow is:

```
MoneyFlow = 100 * Sum of Positive MF / Sum of All MF
```

EXAMPLE

```
Plot1(MoneyFlow(10), "M");
```

MorningStar

SYNTAX

```
C_MornStar_EveStar(Length, oMorningStar, oEveningStar)
```

The **C_MornStar_EveStar** function identifies occurrences of two Japanese candlestick patterns, Morning Star and Evening Star.

`Morning Star` is defined as:

A three-candlestick pattern, the first is a long red candle, followed by a small body candle that gaps lower to form the star, the third is a green candle that closes well into the first candle's real body.

The first candle body needs to be larger than the average body.

`Evening Star` is defined as:

A three-candlestick pattern, the first is a long green candle, followed by a small body candle that gaps lower to form the star, the third is a red candle that closes well into the first candle's real body.

The first candle body needs to be larger than the average body.

(See Figure G.2.44.)

RETURNS (Integer): Each pattern is represented by an output parameter (oMorningStar or oEveningStar) that returns a positive one (1) when the matching candlestick pattern is found on the current bar or returns a zero (0) if the pattern is not found. The `C_MornStar_EveStar` function itself returns a value of 1.

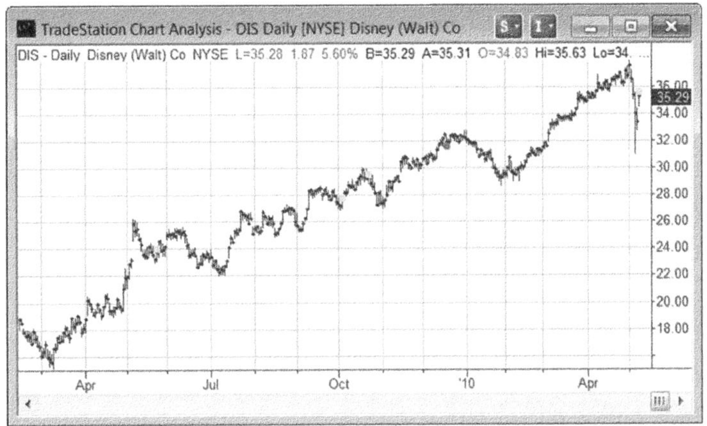

FIGURE G.2.44 Morning Stars and Evening Stars

PARAMETERS

Name	Type	Description
Length	Numeric	Length used to calculate the average body.
oMorningStar	Numeric	Output variable returns a 1 if the Morning Star candlestick pattern exists on the current bar or 0 if the pattern does not exist.
oEveningStar	Numeric	Output variable returns a 1 if the Evening Star candlestick pattern exists on the current bar or 0 if the pattern does not exist.

EXAMPLE

Plots a ShowMe on the High of the current bar when a Morning Star candlestick pattern is found on the current bar based on a Length of 14:

```
Value1 = C_MornStar_EveStar(14, oMorningStar, oEveningStar)
if oMorningStar = 1 then
    Plot1(Low, "MorningStar");
```

MRO(Test, Length, Instance)

The **MRO** (most recent occurrence) function returns the number of bars ago the specified expression was True. Or, if the specified expression did not occur within the last x number of bars, the function informs you of such by returning a −1. (See Figure G.2.45.)

RETURNS (Integer): A numeric value containing the number of bars ago that the specified Expression was True; −1 if Expression was not found to be True within the last Length bars.

PARAMETERS

Name	Type	Description
Test	TrueFalse	Sets the true/false expression to check for (i.e., Close > Open).
Length	Numeric	Sets the number of bars to check.
Instance	Numeric	Sets which occurrence (e.g., 1 = most recent, 2 = 2nd most recent, etc.).

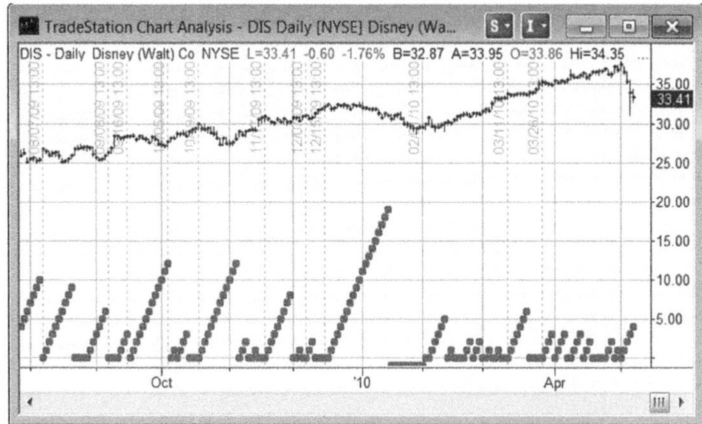

FIGURE G.2.45 Most Recent Occurrence

REMARKS

The `MRO` function is specifically designed to identify when a certain condition occurred. It checks from the current bar and works away from it. The `LRO` function checks from the bar farthest away and works toward the current bar.

The function returns a number representing how many bars ago the true/false expression was fulfilled (0 = current bar, 1 = one bar ago, 2 = 2 bars ago . . .). If the function does not find a bar within the specified Length that meets the criteria, it will return a −1.

NOTE: When using the MRO function in an analysis technique, always check the result of the function before using the value in another calculation or function. If the condition occurred over Length number of bars, a −1 value will be returned.

EXAMPLE

```
INPUTS: jLen(20), jLen2(5), jInst(1);
Condition1 = Close > Highest(Close, jLen2)[1];
Value1 = MRO(Condition1, jLen, jInst);
Plot1(Value1, "MRO");
```

See also LRO

MyPrice

The **MyPrice** function returns the average price of the `High`, `Low`, and `Close` prices of the bar. Some use this as the definition of TypicalPrice, and some also factor in the `Open` price. In the TS function `TypicalPrice`, you can see that TS has `TypicalPrice` and `MyPrice` defined as identical, using the three price components. (See Figure G.2.46.)

RETURNS (Double): A numeric value containing the average price of the bar.

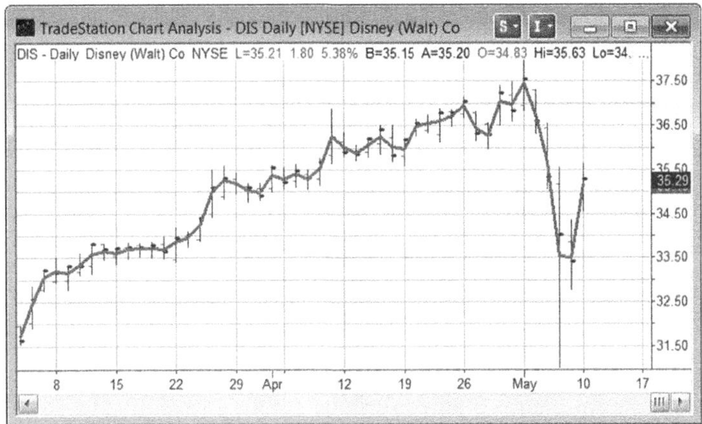

FIGURE G.2.46 My Price

EXAMPLE

Assigns to Value1 the average bar price of five bars ago.

```
Value1 = MyPrice[5];
```

Next3rdFriday(Series)

Futures and options contracts expire on third Fridays. For that reason, there is a function already built in to TS that makes it easy for the user to identify these expiration days. Often the expiration day will cause heavier volume and/or erratic trading patterns. At the very least, traders want to know when to switch over to the next "front month" contract.

The **Next3rdFriday** function calculates the number of calendar days to the next third Friday of a month.

RETURNS (Integer): A numeric value containing the number of calendar days to the third Friday of the Nth month ahead.

PARAMETER

Name	Type	Description
Series	Numeric	Sets the months (ahead) to get the next third Friday. 0 = current month, 1 = next month, and so on.

REMARKS

For the current month, Next3rdFriday(0) will return a negative number of days if the current day of the current month is past the third Friday. In a similar manner, Next3rdFriday(1) returns the number of days to the next third Friday even if it is in the same month as the current day.

EXAMPLE

If you want to exit out of long positions eight days before the third Friday of the coming month, you can write

```
If Next3rdFriday(1) <= 8 Then
   Sell Next Bar at Market;
```

This snippet of code is useful for closing out expiring contracts on the Thursday of the week before the expiration Friday. That is usually the all the pros switch over to the new front month.

ANOTHER EXAMPLE

The following code puts a ShowMe dot on every third Friday of the month. The chart is in Figure G.2.47.

FIGURE G.2.47 Next Third Friday

```
INPUTS: jLen(1);
If Next3rdFriday(jLen) <= 1
THEN BEGIN
Value1 = Next3rdFriday(1);
Plot1(Close, "3rdFriday");
END
ELSE
        NoPlot( 1 ) ;
```

NormCumDensity(Price, Length)

The **NormCumDensity** function calculates the normal density (also called distribution) for the specified mean and standard deviation. (See Figure G.2.48.)

RETURNS (Double): A numeric value containing the normal cumulative density for the specified mean and standard deviation.

PARAMETERS

Name	Type	Description
Price	Numeric	Specifies which bar value (price, function, or formula) to be considered.
Length	Numeric	Sets the number of bars to be considered.

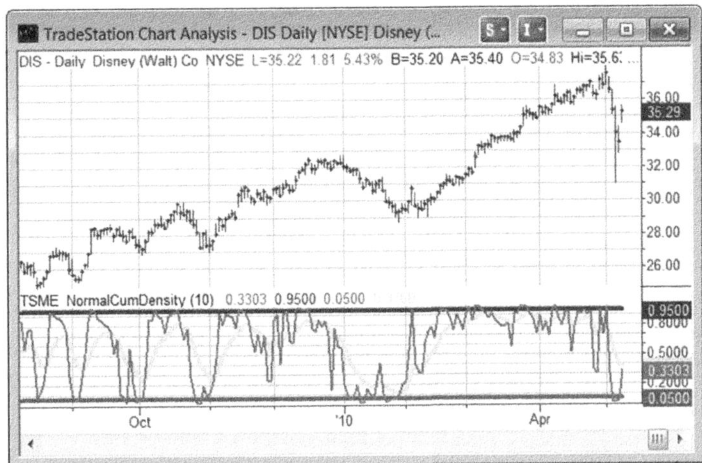

FIGURE G.2.48 Normal Cumulative Density

REMARKS
This function has a very wide range of applications in statistics, including hypothesis testing.
EXAMPLE
Assigns to `Value1` the normal cumulative density of the current `Close` based on the last 20 bars.

```
Value1 = NormalCumDensity(Close, 20);
```

NormDensity(Price, Length)

The normal distributions are an important class of statistical distributions. All normal distributions are symmetric and have bell-shaped density curves with a single peak. To speak specifically of any normal distribution, two quantities have to be specified: the mean μ, where the peak of the density occurs, and the standard deviation σ, which indicates the spread or girth of the bell curve. Different values of and yield different normal density curves and hence different normal distributions. (See Figure G.2.49.)

The height of the normal density can be calculated as:

$$\frac{1}{\sigma\sqrt{2\pi}}e^{-\frac{1}{2}\left(\frac{x-\mu}{\sigma}\right)^2}$$

The **NormDensity** function calculates the normal density (also called distribution) for a specific value.

RETURNS (Double): A numeric value containing the normal density (also called distribution) for a specific value.

PARAMETERS

Name	**Type**	**Description**
Price	Numeric	Specifies which bar value (price, function, or formula) to be considered.
Length	Numeric	Sets the number of bars to be considered.

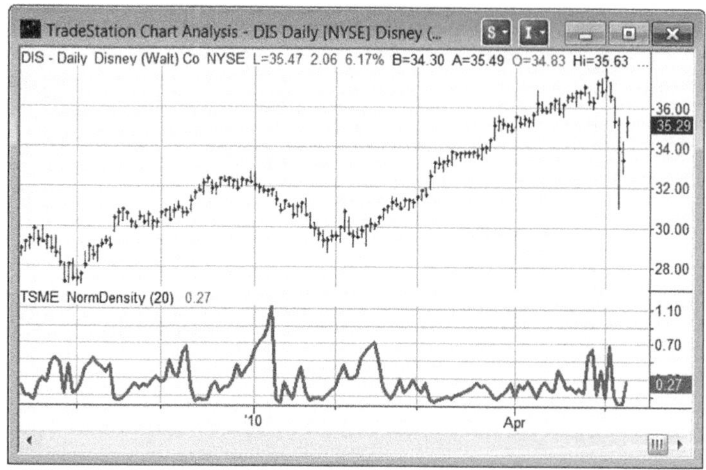

FIGURE G.2.49 Normal Density

REMARKS

This function has a very wide range of applications in statistics, including hypothesis testing.

EXAMPLE

Assigns to `Value1` the normal density of the current `Close` based on the last 20 bars.

```
Value1 = NormDensity(Close, 20);
```

NthHighest(N, Price, Length)

The **NthHighest** function will return the highest, second highest, third highest (and so on) price over a specified number of bars. It is similar to NthLowest, except it returns the lowest price. (See Figure G.2.50.)

RETURNS (Double): A numeric value containing the Nth highest occurrence of `Price` over the last `Length` bars.

PARAMETERS

Name	Type	Description
N	Numeric	The occurrence to return. 1 = lowest, 2 = 2nd lowest, and so on.
Price	Numeric	Specifies which bar value (price, function, or formula) to compare for the lowest occurrence.
Length	Numeric	The number of trailing bars to consider.

REMARKS

Just like the `Highest` function, `NthHighest` has the inputs `Price` and `Length`. It also has the input N that allows you to specify if it is the second, third, and so on highest value desired.

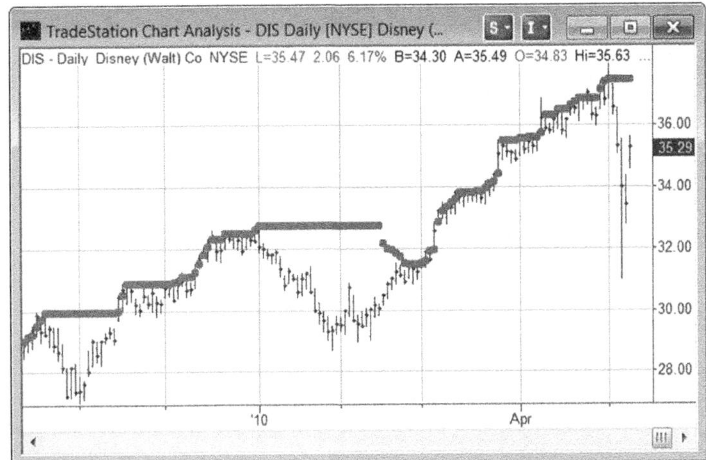

FIGURE G.2.50 Nth Highest

NOTE: The `Length` input in the `NthHighest` function can be replaced only with a value equal to or less than 100. The value for `N` should not be greater than the value for the input `Length`.

EXAMPLE

Returns the value of second highest `Close` that occurred during the past 30 bars.

```
Value1 = NthHighest(2, Close, 30);
```

NthHighestBar(N, Price, Length)

The **NthHighestBar** function will return the number of bars ago the highest, second highest, third highest (and so on) price occurred. It is similar to NthLowestBar, except it finds the lowest price. (See Figure G.2.51.)

RETURNS (Integer): A numeric value containing the number of bars ago the NthHighest occurrence of Price occurred.

PARAMETERS

Name	Type	Description
N	Numeric	The occurrence to return. 1 = highest, 2 = 2nd highest, and so on.
Price	Numeric	Specifies which bar value (price, function, or formula) to compare for the highest occurrence.
Length	Numeric	The number of trailing bars to consider.

REMARKS

Just like the HighestBar function, NthHighestBar has the inputs Price and Length. It also has the input N that allows you to specify if it is the second, third, and so on highest value desired.

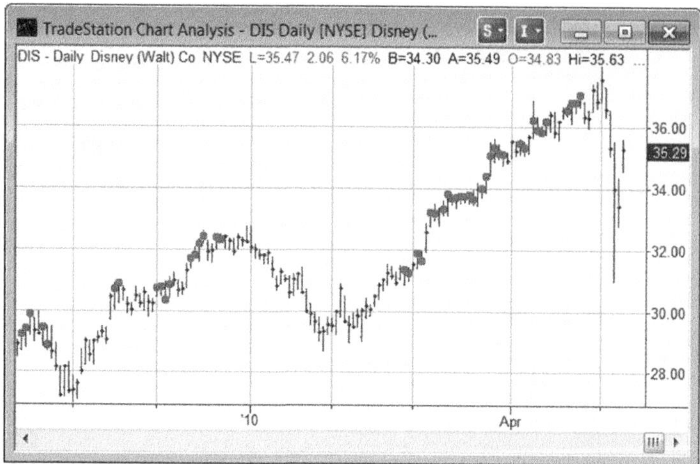

FIGURE G.2.51 Nth Highest Bar

NOTE: The Length input in the NthHighestBar function can be replaced only with a value equal to or less than 100. The value for N should not be greater than the value for the input Length.

EXAMPLE

Returns the number of bars ago that the second-highest Close occurred during the past 25 bars.

```
INPUTS: jLen(1);
If NthHighestBar(2,Close,25) <= 1
THEN BEGIN
        Value1 = NthHighestBar(2, Close, 25);
        Plot1(Close, "NH");
END
ELSE
        NoPlot( 1 ) ;
```

NthLowest

See **NthHighest**

NthLowestBar

See **NthHighestBar**

NumUnits(Amnt, MinLot)

The **NumUnits** function returns the number of units/shares/contracts for a dollar investment. This allows users to determine how many shares/contracts can be traded with a set amount of dollars. (See Figure G.2.52.)

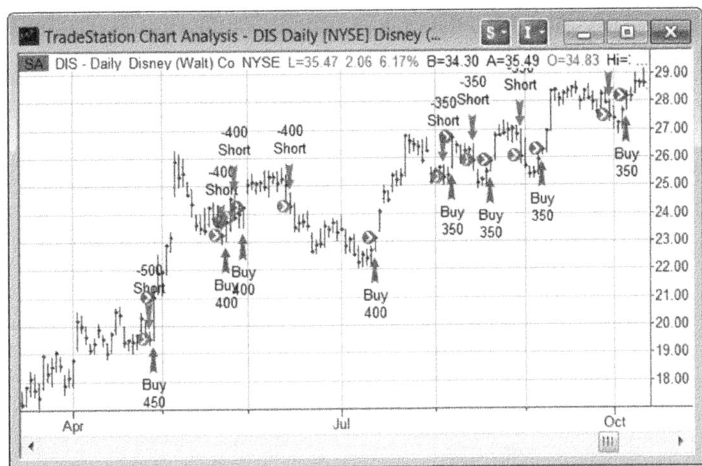

FIGURE G.2.52 NumUnits

RETURNS (Integer): A number of shares/contracts based on the `Amnt` and `MinLot` values specified.

PARAMETERS

Name	**Type**	**Description**
Amnt	Numeric	Sets the investment amount, in dollars, per trade.
MinLot	Numeric	Sets the minimum lot size desired per transaction.

REMARKS

`NumUnits` determines the equivalent number of shares/contracts represented by the dollar amount and current price, given a minimum lot size.

EXAMPLE

Assuming that your active stock is currently trading for $65 per share, if you wanted to invest $15,500 in 100 share lots, you would be able to trade 200 shares:

```
Value1 = NumUnits(15500, 100);
```

`Value1` then contains the return value of 200.

ADDITIONAL EXAMPLE

In order to base the number of shares purchased on a dollar/lot amount entered as an Input in a Moving Average Crossover entry, you could use this syntax:

```
Inputs: Amnt(10000), MinLot(50);
Value1 = NumUnits(Amnt, MinLot);
If Close Crosses Above Average(Close, 18) Then
   Buy Value1 Shares This Bar on Close
```

Notice in Figure G.2.51 that the number of shares for each trade, shown at each buy and sell arrow, changes based on the price of the stock. At the left of the chart the trades have a quantity of 500 and 450, while at the right, when the stock is more expensive, the trades are quantity 350. Notice also that this code does not take into account the change in equity due to profits and losses, but rather uses only the price of the stock itself.

OBV

The **OBV** function calculates "On Balance Volume". (See Figure G.2.53.)

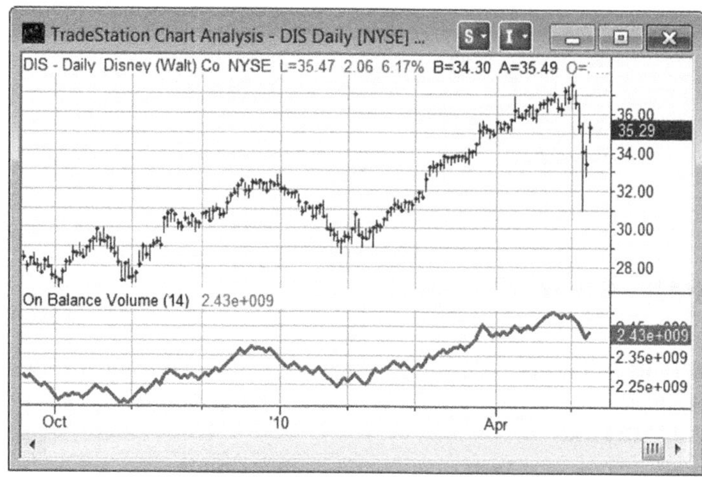

FIGURE G.2.53 On Balance Volume

RETURNS (Double): A numeric value containing OBV for the current bar.

REMARKS

Mathematically, the cumulative OBV formula is represented as:

```
OBV = Σ [(C - Cp / |C - Cp|)*V]
```

where C = current period's closing price.
Cp = previous period's closing price.
|C – Cp| = absolute value of the difference between the two closing prices.

Since any number divided by itself is equal to one (1), the only bearing the expression in parentheses has is on the sign. If the previous Close is greater than the current Close, the sign will be negative. If the previous Close is less than the current Close, the sign will be positive.

Therefore, the function either subtracts the current volume from the running total of the OBV line or adds current volume to the running total of the OBV line.

EXAMPLE

```
Value1 = OBV;
```

REFERENCE

Granville, Joseph E. *Granville's New Strategy of Daily Stock Market Timing for Maximum Profit*. Englewood Cliffs, NJ: Prentice-Hall.

OpenD

See **HighD**

OpenM

See **HighD**

OpenW

See **HighD**

OpenY

See **HighD**

Parabolic(AfStep)

The **Parabolic** series function returns the parabolic stop/reversal for the current bar. (See Figure G.2.54.)

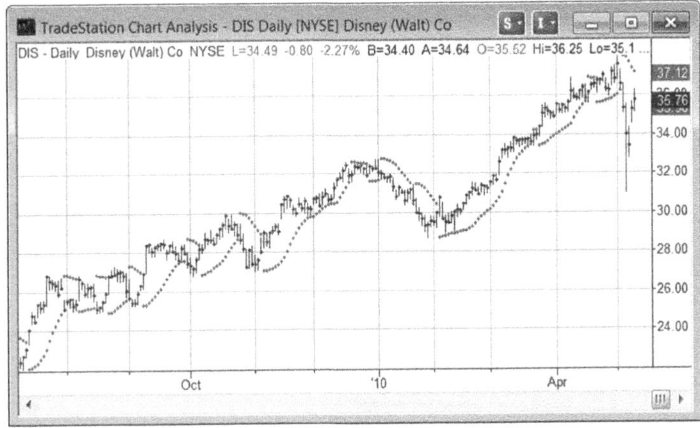

FIGURE G.2.54 Parabolic Stop and Reverse

RETURNS (Double): A numeric value containing the parabolic stop/reversal for the current bar.

PARAMETER

Name	Type	Description
AfStep	Numeric	Sets the acceleration factor increment, generally set to 0.02.

REMARKS

This function is based on a relationship between time and price. Based on the first bar of a chart, the function first calculates a value at an extreme reference point above a bar, and as each bar progresses, the value calculated will approach each bar progressively. Once a calculated value falls within the High-Low range of a bar, the next value will be calculated at an extreme reference point below the next bar. Again, the incremental approach will resume from the bottom up, alternating again when the calculated value falls within the High-Low range of a bar.

The expression "parabolic" derives from the shape of the curve the values create as the results of this function are plotted on a chart.

This function provides the calculations necessary to generate order(s) for the Parabolic trading strategy described in J. Welles Wilder's book *New Concepts in Technical Trading Systems*.

The value returned by this function is the `Parabolic` stop value on the current bar.

EXAMPLE

Plots the parabolic close value based on a .02 increment:

```
Plot1(Parabolic(.02));
```

REFERENCE

Wilder, J. Welles. *New Concepts in Technical Trading Systems*. Greensboro, NC: Trend Research, 1978.

PercentChange(Price, Length)

The **PercentChange** function calculates the percent change in price of the current bar over the price length bars ago. (See Figure G.2.55.)

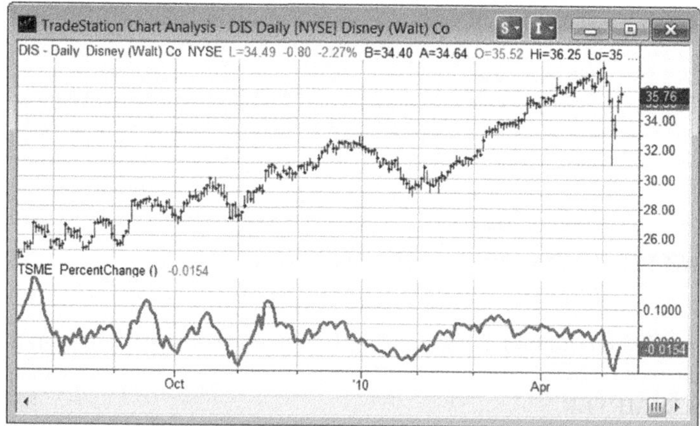

FIGURE G.2.55 Percent Change

RETURNS (Double): A numeric value containing the percent change in price of the current bar over the price length bars ago.

PARAMETERS

Name	Type	Description
Price	Numeric	Specifies which bar value (price, function, or formula) to be considered.
Length	Numeric	Sets the number of bars to be considered.

REMARKS

`PercentChange` takes the difference in between the current value of Price and the Price specified by Length bars ago, and then divides the result by the Price of Length bars ago.

EXAMPLE

```
PercentChange(Close, 14)
```

If the equation returns a value of 0.35, there was a 35% increase in the closing price of the current bar compared to the closing price of 14 bars ago.

```
PercentChange(High, 25);
```

returns a value of −0.15 indicating that there was a 15% decrease in the High price of the current bar compared to the High price of 25 bars ago.

ADDITIONAL EXAMPLE

You could use the PercentChange function to alert you when the closing price has increased 10% from the closing price of 10 bars ago by using this syntax:

```
Value1 = PercentChange(Close, 10);
Plot1(Value1, "PrctChange");
If Value1 >= .10 Then
Alert;
```

Percentile(PcntRank, Price, Length)

The **Percentile** function returns a price value at the boundary of the specified percentile level. (See Figure G.2.56.)

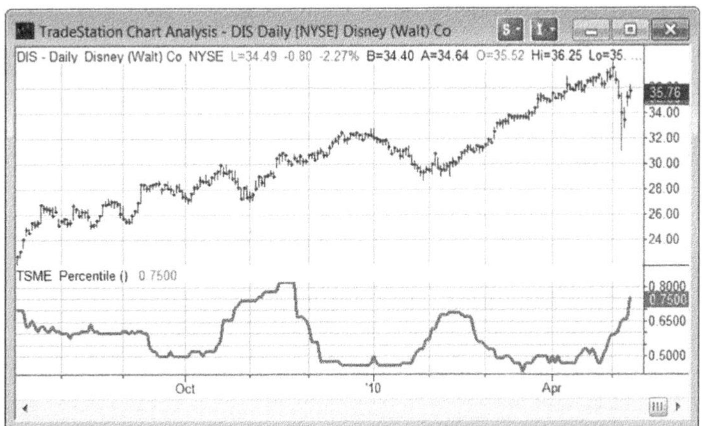

FIGURE G.2.56 Percentile

RETURNS (Double): A numeric value containing the percentile (kth value) of a specified period, as defined by Price and Length.

PARAMETERS

Name	Type	Description
PcntRank	Numeric	Sets the percentile to be considered using a decimal value between 0 and 1. Enter .25 for 25%.
Price	Numeric	Specifies which bar value (price, function, or formula) to be considered.
Length	Numeric	Sets the number of bars to be considered.

REMARKS

The `Percentile` value that is returned is at the point in the `Price` data series where a specified percentage of the prices are below the `PcntRank` level.

EXAMPLES

Assigns to `Value1` the value of the 25th percentile, based on the Closing prices of the last 10 bars:

```
Value1 = Percentile(.25, Close, 10);
```

Assigns to `Value2` the value of the 50th percentile, based on the `Range` of the last 21 bars:

```
Value2 = Percentile(.5, Range, 21);
```

PercentR

The **PercentR** function evaluates the price range over Length number of bars. It then returns a percentage of where the current price lies, related to the evaluated trading range. (See Figure G.2.57.)

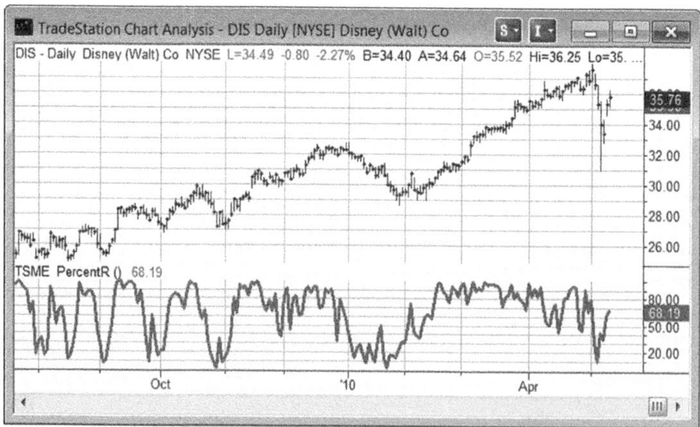

FIGURE G.2.57 PercentR

Syntax
PercentR(Length)
Returns (Double)
A numeric value containing the current %R value.
Parameters
Name
Type
Description
Length
Numeric
Sets the number of bars to consider in the calculation of PercentR.

REMARKS
The formula used to calculate the Percentage Range follows:

$$\%R = 100 * ((Hr - C) / (Hr - Lr))$$

where r = Time period selected
Hr = Highest High of that period
Lr = Lowest Low of that period
C = Today's Close

The input `Length` can be hard coded with a whole number or can be replaced by a numeric simple input whose default value is a whole number.

EXAMPLE
Plots the PercentR over a length of 10 bars.

```
Plot1(PercentR(10));
```

REFERENCE
Williams, Larry. *How I Made One Million Dollars Last Year Trading Commodities*, 2nd ed. Monterey, CA: Conceptual Management, 1973.

To be consistent with other oscillators, `PercentR` takes Williams's value and subtracts it from 100. For example, if Williams's Percent Range returns 80, PercentR will return 20.

PercentRank(PriceToRank, Price, Length)

The **PercentRank** function calculates the percentile rank of a bar value in a data set. It basically asks the question "Where is this value in my data?" (See Figure G.2.58.)

RETURNS (Integer): The percentile rank of a value in a data set. The function returns −1 if PriceToRank is outside the range of the data set or if there is a Length error.

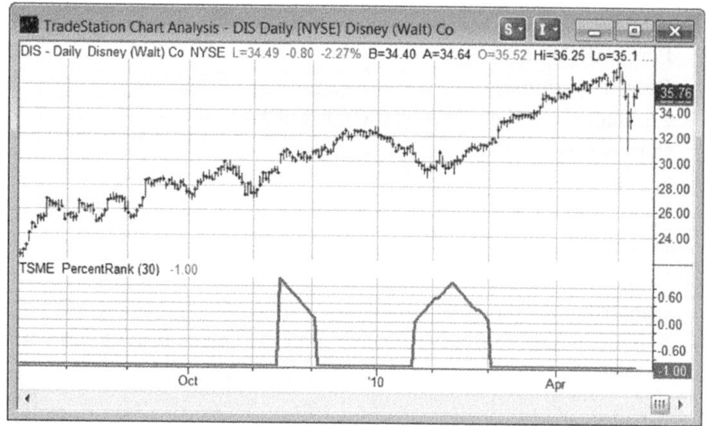

FIGURE G.2.58 Percentage Rank

PARAMETERS

Name	Type	Description
PriceToRank	Numeric	Sets the value to be ranked within the Price data series.
Price	Numeric	Specifies which bar value (price, function, or formula) to be considered.
Length	Numeric	Sets the number of bars to be considered.

REMARKS

This function can be used to evaluate the relative standing of a value within a data set, as specified by the Price and Length inputs. If PriceToRank < the lowest price in the data series, PriceToRank > the highest price in the data series or the Length <= 0 the function will return −1.

EXAMPLES

Assigns to `Value1` the percentage rank of the value 260 within the data set defined by the `Closes` of the last 21 bars:

```
Value1 = PercentRank(260, Close, 21);
```

Assigns to `Value2` the percentage rank of the value 3 within the data set defined by the `Closes` of the last 14 bars:

```
Value2 = PercentRank(3, Close, 14);
```

Permutation(Num, NumChosen)

Permutation is a mathematical function which calculates the number of different choices for a given number of objects that can be selected from a range of objects.

For instance, suppose we want to find the number of ways to arrange the three letters in the word CAT in different two-letter groups where CA is different from AC and there are no repeated letters. That is three things taken two at a time.

Because order matters, we are finding the number of permutations of size 2 that can be taken from a set of size 3. This is often written **3_P_2.** We can list them as: CA CT AC AT TC TA.

RETURNS (Double): A numeric value containing the number of permutations for a given number (`NumChosen`) of objects that can be selected from number objects (`Num`).

PARAMETERS

Name	Type	Description
Num	Numeric	Sets the number of bars to be considered.
NumChosen	Numeric	Sets the number of objects within the range (Num) that can be selected.

USAGE

A permutation is any set or subset of objects or events where internal order is significant. If `Num` <= 0, `NumChosen` < 0, or `Num` < `NumChosen`, the Function will return a −1. −1 will also be returned if there is a divisor of zero within the calculation.

EXAMPLE

Assigns to `Value1` the number of permutations for a range of 50, containing permutations with three elements:

```
Value1 = Permutation(50, 3);
```

Pivot(Price, Length, LeftStrength, RightStrength, Instance, HiLo, oPivotPrice, oPivotBar)

The **Pivot** function returns the value of a pivot point and the number of bars ago the pivot occurred. (See Figure G.2.59.)

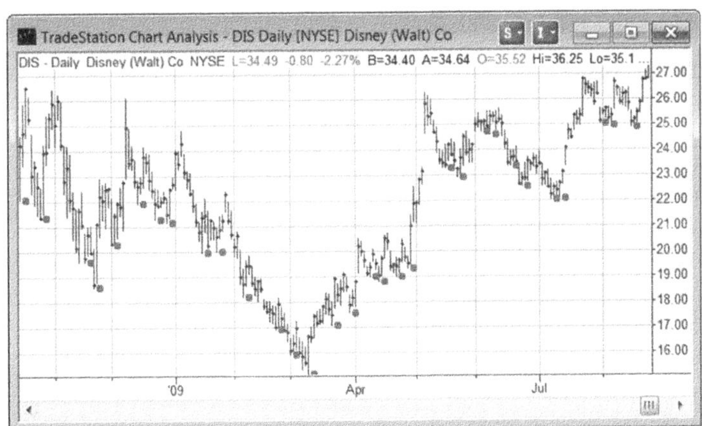

FIGURE G.2.59 Pivot

RETURNS (Integer): The `oPivotPrice` and `oPivotBar` output parameters return the price value of the pivot point and the number of bars ago it occurred. The `Pivot` function itself returns a value of 1 if a pivot is found, and −1 if not found.

PARAMETERS

Name	Type	Description
Price	Numeric	Specifies which bar value (price, function, or formula) to be considered.
Length	Numeric	Sets the number of bars to consider for the pivot.
LeftStrength	Numeric	Sets the required number of bars on the left side of the pivot bar.
RightStrength	Numeric	Sets the required number of bars on the right side of the pivot bar.
Instance	Numeric	Sets which occurrence (i.e., 1 = most recent, 2 = second most recent, etc.) to return.
HiLo	Numeric	Sets which pivot values to return, 1 = High, −1 = Low.
oPivotPrice	Numeric	Outputs the specified bar value at the pivot point.
oPivotBar	Numeric	Outputs the number of bars ago the pivot point occurred.

REMARKS

This function is used to find pivot or swing points. This function allows you to specify variable strength sides as well as whether the pivot point should be a high or low pivot.

EXAMPLE

Assigns to `Value2` the most recent pivot low price over the last 21 bars and to `Value3` the number of bars ago the pivot low occurred using a left strength of 4 and a right strength of 2.

```
Vars: oPivotPrice(0), oPivotBar(0);
Value1 = Pivot(Low,21,4,2,1,-1,oPivotPrice,oPivotBar);
Value2 = oPivotPrice;
Value3 = oPivotbar;
```

PositionProfit(Num)

Returns the current gain or loss of the specified position.

`Num` is a numeric expression representing the number of positions ago (up to a maximum of 10).

REMARKS

This function can be used only in the evaluation of strategies. It does not require an input; however, by using the input Num, you can obtain the specified value from a previous position, up to 10 positions ago.

EXAMPLE

`PositionProfit(3)` returns a value of −1.00 if the third most recent position on a chart had a loss of 1.00.

PriceOscillator(Price, FastLength, SlowLength)

The **PriceOscillator** series function calculates the difference between the Slow Moving Average and the Fast Moving Average. (See Figure G.2.60.)

RETURNS (Double): The difference between the fast moving average and the slow moving average.

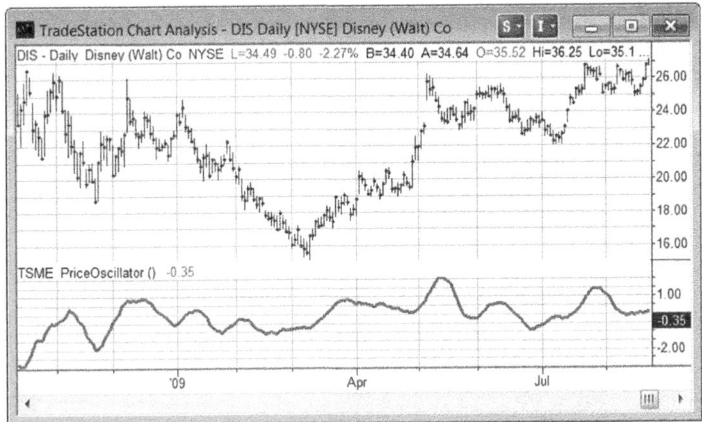

FIGURE G.2.60 Price Oscillator

PARAMETERS

Name	**Type**	**Description**
Price	Numeric	Specifies which bar value (price, function, or formula) to consider.
FastLength	Numeric	Sets the number of bars over which the fast average will be calculated.
SlowLength	Numeric	Sets the number of bars over which the slow average will be calculated.

EXAMPLES

Assigns to Value1 the difference between the 9-bar moving average and the 18-bar moving average, both based on the Close:

```
Value1 = PriceOscillator(Close, 9, 18);
```

Assigns to `Value2` the difference between the 3-bar moving average and the 5-bar moving average, both based on the `Close`:

```
Value2 = PriceOscillator(Close, 3, 5);
```

ADDITIONAL EXAMPLE

If you wanted an Alert when the PriceOscillator, based on 10- and 20-bar moving averages, crosses above zero, indicating that the fast average has crossed above the slow average, you could use this syntax:

```
If PriceOscillator(Close, 10, 20) Crosses Above 0 Then
    Alert("The Price Oscillator has crosses above zero");
```

PriceVolTrend

The **PriceVolTrend** (`PVT`) function calculates the price volume trend for the current bar. (See Figure G.2.61.)

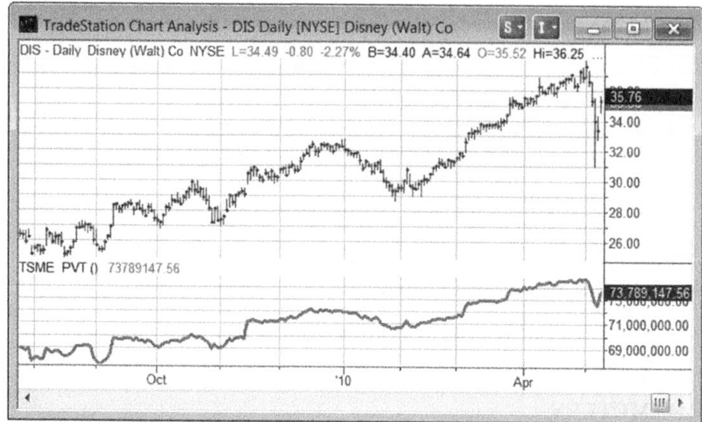

FIGURE G.2.61 Price Volume Trend

RETURNS (Double): A numeric value containing PVT for the current bar.
REMARKS
`PriceVolTrend` multiplies the day's trade volume by the percentage difference between today's `Close` and yesterday's `Close`. It accumulates the resulting value for each day, either up or down.

The function is calculated as:

```
PriceVolTrend = (((C - C[1]) / C[1]) * V)
```

for the first day and for subsequent days as:

```
PriceVolTrend = (((C - C[1]) / C[1]) * V) + PriceVolTrend[1];
```

EXAMPLE

```
Plot1(PriceVolTrend);
```

Range

The **Range** function subtracts the Low of a bar from the High to determine the range of the bar. (See Figure G.2.62.)
RETURNS (Double): A numeric value containing the current range (High minus Low) value.

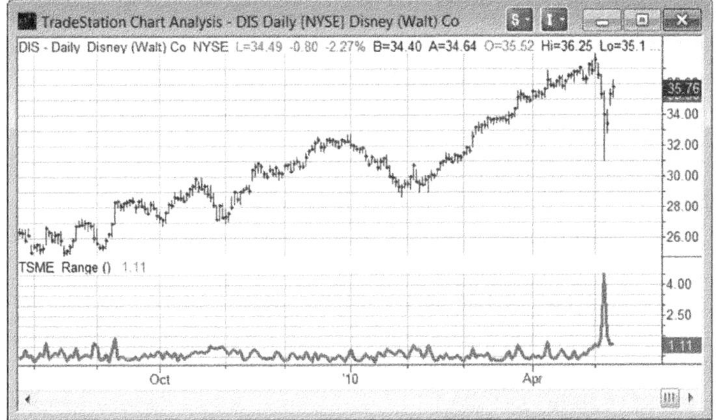

FIGURE G.2.62 Range

EXAMPLE

```
Plot1(Range);
```

RangeLeader

The **RangeLeader** function checks to see if the current bar is a range leader.

RETURNS (Integer): A value of 1 is returned if the current bar is considered a range leader based on a pair of conditions (see Remarks); 0 if it is not.

REMARKS

This function compares the current and previous bar and looks at two conditions:

1. Whether the midpoint of the current bar is greater than the previous High or less than the previous Low.
2. Whether the Range of the current bar is greater than the Range of the previous bar. If both conditions are met, the function returns 1; if one or neither is met, the function returns 0.

EXAMPLE

```
Value1 = RangeLeader;
```

RateOfChange(Price, Length)

The **RateOfChange** function returns the Rate of Change calculation for the current bar.

RETURNS (Double): A numeric value containing `ROC` for the current bar.

PARAMETERS

Name	Type	Description
Price	Numeric	Specifies which bar value (price, function, or formula) to be considered.
Length	Numeric	Sets the number of bars to be considered.

REMARKS

`RateOfChange` is calculated using the division method. The equivalent of the subtraction method is found in the function Momentum.

$$ROC = ((Price/Pricep) - 1) * 100$$

where Price = Current value (i.e., Close, High, Low, etc.)
Pricep = Previous value (determined by the value returned for the input Length)

The input `Price` usually is hard coded with some bar attribute, such as Close, Open, High, Low, and Volume, or is replaced with a numeric series type input. However, it can be replaced with a valid EasyLanguage expression. For example: `Close + Open`, or `Average(RSI(Close,14),14)`.

EXAMPLE

```
Value1 = RateOfChange(Close,20);
```

REFERENCE

Kaufman, Perry J. *The New Commodity Trading Systems and Methods*. Hoboken, NJ: John Wiley & Sons, 2005.

Round2Fraction (DecAmt)

The **Round2Fraction** function calculates a value rounded to the nearest minmove fraction.

PARAMETER

Name	Type	Description
DecAmt	Numeric	Sets a decimal value to be rounded to the nearest fractional price scale.

RETURNS (Double): A numeric value containing the nearest fractional value for a decimal variable.

REMARKS

The nearest fraction is based on the price scale for the symbol type being evaluated. You can determine the price scale for any symbol by looking at the symbol properties.

EXAMPLE

Assigns to `Value1` the number 100.375 as the nearest fractional value for a stock with a price scale of 1/8th.

```
Value1 = RoundToFraction(100.3732);
```

RSI(Price, Length)

The **RSI** (Relative Strength Index) series function returns a value between zero and 100, regardless of the asset it is applied to. It is easy to calculate and keep track of. After calculating the initial RSI, only the previous day's data is required for the next calculation. (See Figure G.2.63.)

RETURNS: A numeric value containing RSI for the current bar.

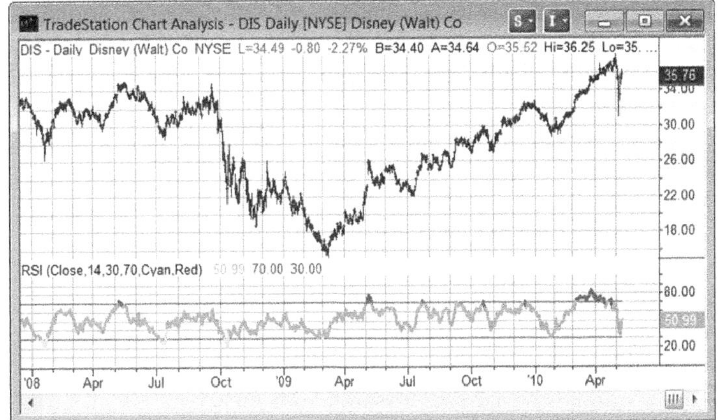

FIGURE G.2.63 Relative Strength Index

PARAMETERS

Name	Type	Description
Price	Numeric	Specifies which bar value (price, function, or formula) to be considered.
Length	Numeric	Sets the number of bars to consider.

REMARKS

The equation for the Relative Strength Index (`RSI`) is:

$$RSI = 100 - (100/(1 + RS))$$

where RS = Average of 14 day's closes UP/Average of 14 day's closes DOWN

To calculate the first `RSI` value:

Calculate the sum of the UP closes for the previous 14 days and divide this sum by 14. This is the average UP Close.

Calculate the sum of the DOWN closes for the previous 14 days and divide by 14. This is the average DOWN Close.

Divide the average UP Close by the average DOWN Close. This is the Relative Strength (RS).

Add 1.00 to the RS.

Divide the result obtained in Step 4 into 100.

Subtract the result obtained in Step 5 from 100. This is the first RSI.

To calculate the RSI each time following the first RSI value.

To obtain the next average UP Close: Multiply the previous average UP Close by 13, add to this amount today's UP Close (if any), and divide the total by 14.

To obtain the next average DOWN: Multiply the previous average DOWN Close by 13, add to this amount today's DOWN Close (if any), and divide the total by 14.

Steps 3, 4, 5, and 6 are the same as for the initial RSI.

The input `Price` is usually hard coded with some bar attribute, such as Close, Open, High, Low, and Volume, or is replaced with a numeric series type input. However, it can be replaced with a valid EasyLanguage expression. For example: Close + Open, or Average(RSI(Close,14),14).

The input `Length`, just like `Price`, can be hard coded or replaced with a numeric simple type input.

EXAMPLE

```
Plot1(RSI(Close,14));
```

REFERENCE

Wilder, J. Welles. *New Concepts in Technical Trading Systems.* Greensboro, NC: Trend Research, 1978.

SetPlotColor(Number, Color)

This reserved word is used to change the color of a particular plot in a price chart or grid.

`Number` is a number from 1 to 99 representing the number of the plot to modify. `Color` is the EasyLanguage color to be used for the plot. (See Figure G.2.64.)

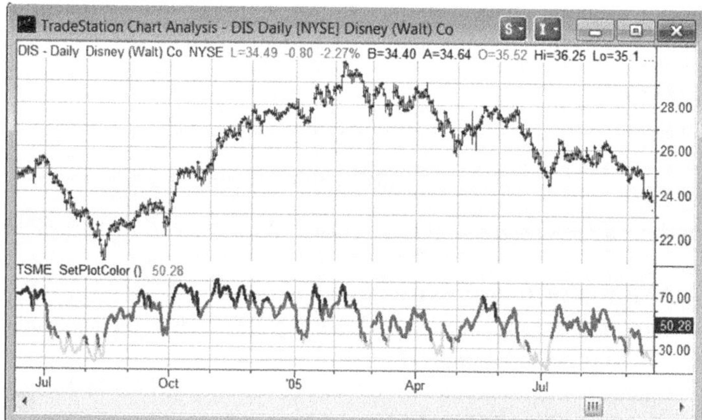

FIGURE G.2.64 SetPlotColor

EXAMPLE

The next EasyLanguage statements change the color of the plot to Blue when the RSI Indicator is over 75 and Green when it is under 25.

```
Plot1(RSI(Close, 9), "RSI");
If Plot1 > 75 Then
   SetPlotColor(1, Blue);
If Plot1 < 25 Then
   SetPlotColor(1, Green);
```

Notice that the initial `Plot1` statement resets the plot color to the indicator's default color setting each time the EasyLanguage code is run on each bar. This means that the indicator plots the default color unless the `RSI` value is greater than 75 or less than 25.

ShootingStar(Percent)

The **C ShootingStar** function identifies the occurrence of a Shooting Star candlestick pattern. Shooting Star is defined as:

The body of the candle is small but not a Doji. Near the low of the bar, the tail is usually twice as long as the body.
The price trend is rising.
The body gaps up from the body on the previous bar.
The previous body is green and larger than the average body.

(See Figure G.2.65.)

FIGURE G.2.65 Shooting Star

RETURNS (Integer): The function returns a positive one (1) when the matching candlestick pattern is found on the current bar or returns a zero (0) if the pattern is not found.

PARAMETERS

Name	Type	Description
Length	NumericSimple	Length used to calculate the average body.
Factor	NumericSimple	Threshold factor for the size of body in relation to the range of the bar (2 = Tail must be two times larger than body).

EXAMPLE

Plots a ShowMe on the `Close` of the current bar when a Shooting Star candlestick pattern is found on the current bar based on a Length of 14 and a Factor of 2:

```
if C_ShootingStar(14, 2) = 1 then
   Plot1(Close, "ShootingStar");
```

ShowLongStop(StopVal)

The **ShowLongStop** function adds text to a chart that displays the stop level on the chart for a long-side stop. This function is designed for use only with strategies. (See Figure G.2.66.)

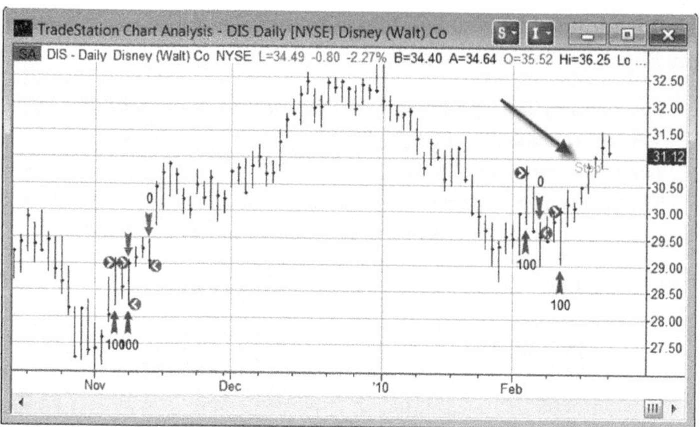

FIGURE G.2.66 ShowLongStop

RETURNS (Integer): In addition to displaying "Stop–", the function itself returns a numeric value representing the current market position (−1 for short, 1 for long, and 0 for no position).

PARAMETER

Name	Type	Description
StopVal	Numeric	Sets the stop value where the text will be displayed.

REMARKS

The function adds the text "Stop–" in the default text color and style. If the stop value is beyond the upper/lower limit of the chart, the text will not appear unless the chart scaling is adjusted to include that area. In addition, the function returns the current market position that is assigned to a variable.

EXAMPLE

This code will display the "Stop–" at the lowest Low of the last two bars while the market position is long:

```
Value1 = ShowLongStop(Lowest(Low, 2));
```

ADDITIONAL EXAMPLE

If you want to show the stop text for a long trailing stop, you could use this code:

```
Variables: StopValue(0);
If Close Crosses Above Average(Close, 18) Then
 Buy This Bar on Close;
StopValue = Lowest(Low, 2);
```

```
If MarketPosition = 1 Then
 Sell Next Bar at StopValue Stop;
Value1 = ShowLongStop(StopValue);
```

ShowShortStop

Same as **ShowLongStop** except that it adds text for the stop level on a short-side stop.

Skew(Price, Length)

The **Skew** function calculates the skewness of a distribution for a set of values. (See Figure G.2.67.)

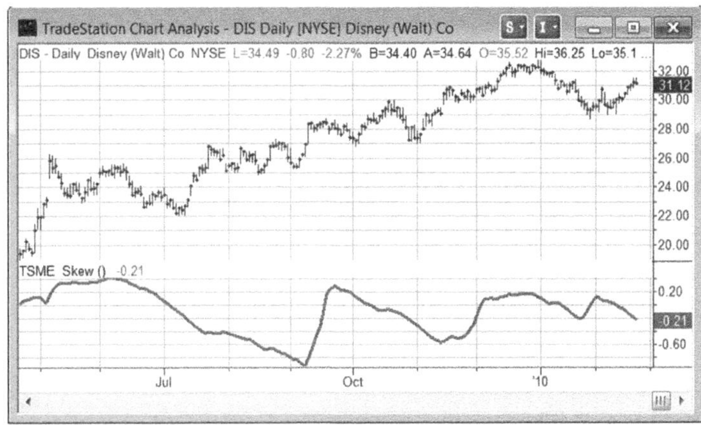

FIGURE G.2.67 Skew

RETURNS (Double): A numeric value containing the skewness of a distribution.

PARAMETERS

Name	Type	Description
Price	Numeric	Specifies which bar value (price, function, or formula) the skew will be based on.
Length	Numeric	Sets the number of bars to use to build the distribution.

REMARKS

Skewness characterizes the degree of asymmetry of a distribution around its mean. Positive skewness indicates a distribution with an asymmetric tail extending toward more positive values. Negative skewness indicates a distribution with an asymmetric tail extending toward more negative values.

EXAMPLE

Assigns to `Value1` the skew of the distribution of the closes of the last 100 bars:

```
Value1 = Skew(Close, 100);
```

SlowD

See **Stochastics** and FastD

SlowK

See **Stochastics** and FastD

SmoothedAverage(Price, Length)

The **SmoothedAverage** series function further smooths an average of the last x bars. It does this by using the previous value of itself. This function is used in the same way as the Average function. (See Figure G.2.68.)

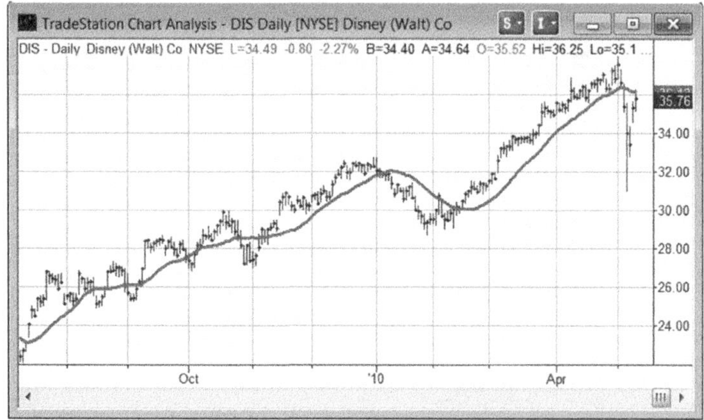

FIGURE G.2.68 Smoothed Average

RETURNS (Double): A numeric value containing the Smoothed Average of values over a specified number of bars.

PARAMETERS

Name	Type	Description
Price	Numeric	Specifies which bar value (price, function, or formula) to use.
Length	Numeric	Sets the number of bars to consider.

REMARKS

On the first bar, this function adds together all the values returned by the input Price for the specified Length, divides the sum by the Length, then stores the value in a variable called SUM. Only on the first bar is the SmoothedAverage function equal to the value stored in SUM.

```
SUM = Summation(Price, Length)
```

On each bar thereafter, the function uses a different equation.

```
SmoothedAverage = (Sum[1] - SmoothedAverage[1] + Price)/Length
```

EXAMPLE

```
Plot1(SmoothedAverage(C,20));
```

Standardize(Price, Length, NumDevs)

The **Standardize** function returns a normalized value from a distribution characterized by the mean based on the Price for Length bars and standard deviation. (See Figure G.2.69.)

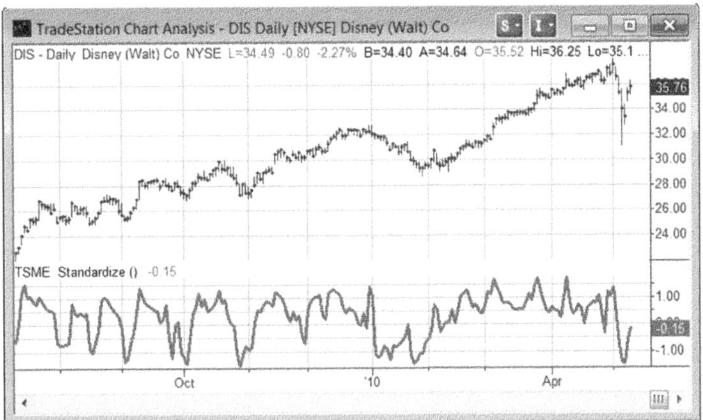

FIGURE G.2.69 Standardize

PARAMETERS

Name	Type	Description
Price	Numeric	Specifies which bar value (price, function, or formula) to use.
Length	Numeric	Sets the number of bars to be considered.
NumDevs	Numeric	Sets the number of standard deviations to consider in the standardization.

RETURNS (Double): A numeric value containing the normalized value from a distribution characterized by the mean based on the Price for Length bars and standard deviation (NumDevs).

REMARKS

The normalized value is based on a distribution with a mean of 0 and a standard deviation of 1.

EXAMPLES

Assigns to `Value1` the standardization of the Close over the last 14 bars, using two standard deviations.

```
Value1 = Standardize(Close, 14, 2);
```

Assigns to `Value2` the standardization of the High over the last 10 bars, using 1.5 standard deviations:

```
Value2 = Standardize(High, 10, 1.5);
```

StdDev(Price, Length)

The **StdDev** function calculates a standard deviation of a population of values. (See Figure G.2.70.)

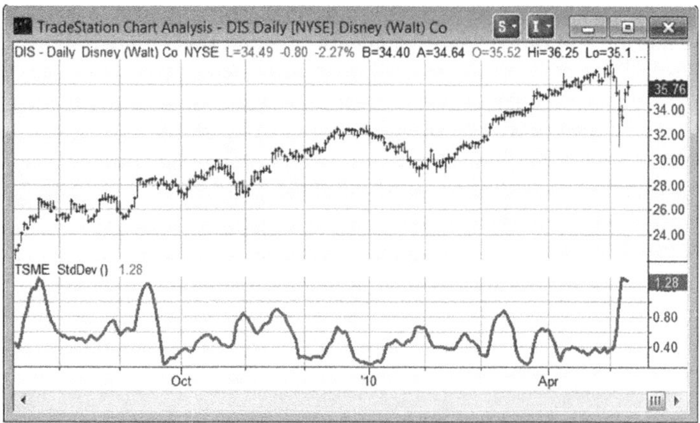

FIGURE G.2.70 Standard Deviation

RETURNS (Double): A numeric value containing the current standard deviation.

PARAMETERS

Name	Type	Description
Price	Numeric	Specifies which bar value (price, function, or formula) to be considered.
Length	Numeric	Sets the number of bars to be considered.

REMARKS

To find the standard deviation, first find the variance and then take its square root:

$$\text{StdDev} = \sqrt{\frac{1}{N}\sum_{i=1}^{N}(D_i - M)^2}$$

where N = Number of elements
D = Individual elements in the sample
M = Sample mean

EXAMPLE

Assigns to `Value1` the standard deviation of Close over 10 bars.

```
Value1 = StdDev(Close, 10);
```

Stochastics(PriceH, PriceL, PriceC, StochLength, Length1, Length2, SmoothingTpe, oFastK, oFastD, oSlowK, oSlowD)

The **Stochastic** series function returns the four core values (FastK, FastD, SlowK and SlowD) associated with the Stochastic oscillator. (See Figure G.2.71.)

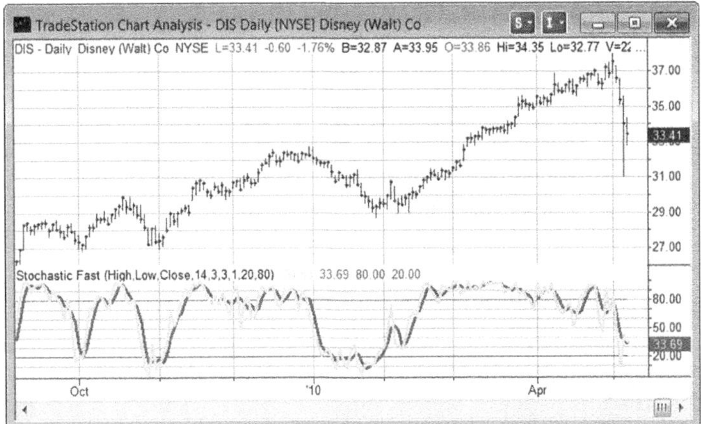

FIGURE G.2.71 Stochastics

RETURNS (Integer): The oFastK, oFastD, oSlowK, and oSlowD output parameters return the fast and slow averages for the K and D lines. The Stochastic function itself returns 1 if successful, otherwise −1 if both FastK = 0 and SlowK = 0.

PARAMETERS

Name	**Type**	**Description**
PriceH	Numeric	Specifies which bar value (price, function, or formula) to use for the high in stochastic calculations.
PriceL	Numeric	Specifies which bar value (price, function, or formula) to use for the low in stochastic calculations.
PriceC	Numeric	Specifies which bar value (price, function, or formula) to use for the close in stochastic calculations.
StochLength	Numeric	Sets the number of bars to consider.
Length1	Numeric	Sets the constant for smoothing the fast K line.
Length2	Numeric	Sets the constant for smoothing the fast D line.
SmoothingType	Numeric	Sets the calculation method for smoothing: 1 for calculations based on the original formula. 2 to conform to legacy TradeStation calculations.
oFastK	Numeric	Outputs the value for the fast K line.
oFastD	Numeric	Outputs the value for the fast D line.
oSlowK	Numeric	Outputs the value for the slow K line.
oSlowD	Numeric	Outputs the value for the slow D line.

REMARKS

The Stochastic oscillators indicate overbought and oversold areas in the market, based on momentum or price velocity.

Stochastics are made up of four individual calculations: FastK, FastD, SlowK, SlowD. The core of the calculations is based on the FastK value that is calculated in this manner:

```
FastK = (C - L)/(H - L)*100
```

where L = Lowest Low of a specified period
H = Highest High of a specified period
C = Current bar Close

FastD is a smoothed average of FastK; SlowK is equal to FastD; and SlowD is a further smoothed SlowK.

See Multiple Output Function for more information on using output parameters to return values

EXAMPLE

Outputs the FastK, FastD, SlowK, and SlowD stochastic values to the declared variables over 14 bars.

Vars: oFastK(0), oFastD(0), oSlowK(0), oSlowD(0);

Value1 = Stochastic(H, L, C, 14, 3, 3, 1, oFastK, oFastD, oSlowK, oSlowD);

REFERENCE

Stein, John. "The Traders' Guide to Technical Indicators," *Futures Magazine* (August 1990).
Takano, Mike. "Stochastic Oscillator," *Technical Analysis of Stocks and Commodities* (April 1991).

StrColorToNum(Color)

The **StrColorToNum** function returns the color number for a specific color name.

RETURNS: A numeric value containing the color number of a color name.

PARAMETER

Name	**Type**	**Description**
Color	Numeric	Sets a text string containing a color name.

REMARKS

A numeric value containing the color number of a color name.

EXAMPLE

Assigns to `Value1` the color number 6 for the color name "`Red`".

```
Value1 = StrColorToNum("Red");
```

Summation(Price, Length)

The **Summation** function adds a series of numbers together over a specified number of bars.

PARAMETERS

Name	**Type**	**Description**
Price	Numeric	Specifies which bar value (price, function, or formula) to sum.
Length	Numeric	Sets the number of bars to consider.

RETURNS (Double): A numeric value containing the sum of the last `Length` occurrences of `Price`.

REMARKS

The number of values in the series is determined by the input `Length`. The values added together are determined by the input `Price`. For example, if the inputs `Price` and `Length` were replaced by `Close` and `14`, respectively, the function would add together the last 14 closes.

NOTE: The current bar's `Price` is included in the calculation, unless the function is offset.

EXAMPLE

```
Plot1(Average(Close,9));
```

SummationIF(Test, Price, Length)

The **SummationIf** function performs a summation of price when a condition is true.

RETURNS (Double): A numeric value containing the sum of the last Length occurrences of Price if Test is True.

PARAMETERS

Name	Type	Description
Test	Numeric	Specifies the criteria that must be true for summation to occur.
Price	Numeric	Specifies which bar value (price, function, or formula) to sum.
Length	Numeric	Sets the number of bars used in the calculation.

REMARKS

The number of values in the series is determined by the input Length. The values added together are determined by the input Price. For example, if the inputs `Price` and `Length` were replaced by `Close` and `14`, respectively, the function would add together the last 14 closes.

NOTE: The current bar's `Price` is included in the calculation, unless the function is offset.

EXAMPLE

```
Value1 = SummationIf(High>Close[1], High-Close, 14);
```

SwingHigh(Instance, Price, Strength, Length)

The **SwingHigh** function returns the high pivot price where a Swing High occurred. (See Figure G.2.72.)

RETURNS (Integer): A numeric value containing the high pivot price where the specified Swing High occurred, or −1 if not found.

PARAMETERS

Name	Type	Description
Instance	Numeric	Sets which occurrence (i.e., 1 = most recent, 2 = second most recent, etc.) to return.
Price	Numeric	Specifies which bar value (price, function, or formula) to use.
Strength	Numeric	Sets the required number of bars on either side of the swing bar.
Length	Numeric	Sets the number of bars to be considered.

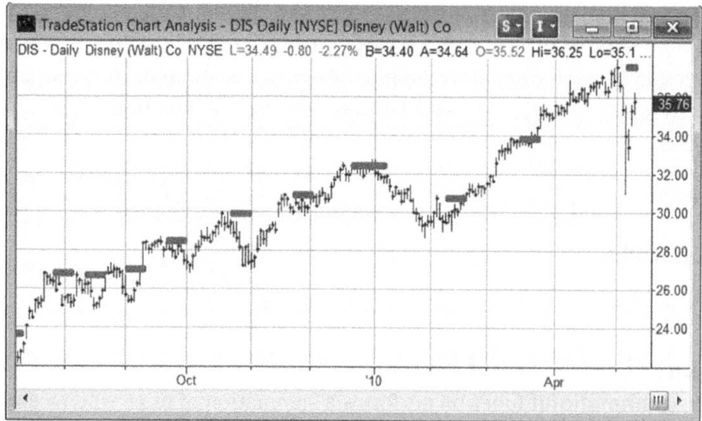

FIGURE G.2.72 SwingHigh

REMARKS

A `SwingHigh` occurs when the `Price` of a bar is at least as high as the same `Price` on the preceding bar(s) and higher than the same `Price` on the bar(s) that follow it.

The input `Strength` is the number of bars on each side of the `SwingHigh`. A strength of 1 indicates that the value returned by the input `Price` must be greater than or equal to the same value returned for the bar on its left and greater than the bar on its right.

The input `Length` refers to the number of bars being examined for the `SwingHigh`.

The input `Instance` refers to which `SwingHigh` you want to use. For example, if in a 21-bar period three swing highs were found, it becomes necessary to specify which SwingHigh is desired. If the most recent SwingHigh is desired, a one (1) would be substituted for the input `Instance`.

NOTE: If no `SwingHigh` is found in the period (`Length`) specified, the function will return a minus one (−1). The value of the input `Length` must exceed `Strength` by at least 1. In addition, the Maximum number of bars referenced by a study (known as MaxBarsBack) must be greater than the sum of the values of `Strength` and `Length`.

EXAMPLE

Assigns to `Value1` the most recently occurring `High` over the last 10 bars that has a strength of 4 on both the left and right sides of the swing bar.

```
Value1 = SwingHigh(1,Close,4,10);
```

SwingHighBar(Instance, Price, Strength, Length)

The **SwingHighBar** function returns the number of bars ago a Swing High bar occurred. (See Figure G.2.73.)

RETURNS (Integer): A numeric value containing the number of bars ago the specified Swing High occurred, or −1 if not found.

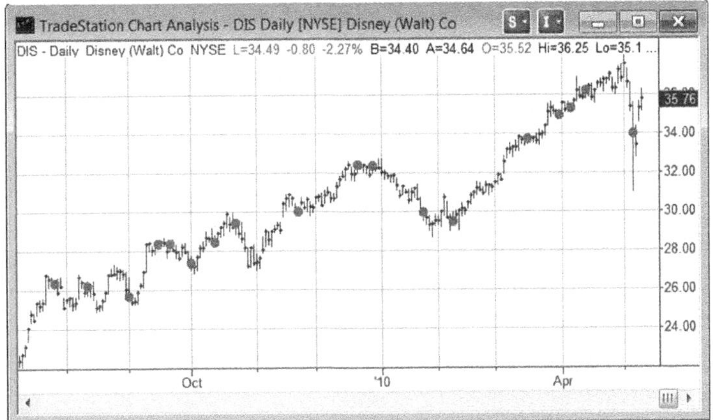

FIGURE G.2.73 SwingHighBar

PARAMETERS

Name	Type	Description
Instance	Numeric	Sets which occurrence (i.e., 1 = most recent, 2 = second most recent, etc.) to return.
Price	Numeric	Specifies which bar value (price, function, or formula) to use.
Strength	Numeric	Sets the required number of bars on either side of the swing bar.
Length	Numeric	Sets the number of trailing bars to consider.

REMARKS

A Swing High occurs when the Price of a bar is at least as high as the same Price on the preceding bar(s) and higher than the same Price on the bar(s) that follow it.

The input Strength is the number of bars on each side of the SwingHighBar. A strength of 1 indicates that the value returned by the input Price must be greater than or equal to the same value returned for the bar on its left and greater than the bar on its right.

The input Length refers to the number of bars being examined for the SwingHighBar.

The input Instance refers to which SwingHighBar you want to use. For example, if in a 21-bar period three swing highs were found, it becomes necessary to specify which SwingHighBar is desired. If the most recent SwingHighBar is desired, a one (1) would be substituted for the input Instance.

NOTE: If no SwingHighBar is found in the period (Length) specified, the function will return a minus one (−1). The value of the input Length must exceed Strength by at least 1. In addition, the Maximum number of bars referenced by a study (known as MaxBarsBack) must be greater than the sum of the values of Strength and Length.

EXAMPLE

Plots the number of bars ago that the most recent swing bar high occurred based on the `Close` with 3 bars on either side of the swing within 10 trailing bars.

```
Value1 = SwingHigh(1,Close,4,10);
Value2 = SwingHighBar(1,Close,3,10);
If Value2=3 THEN Begin
Plot1(close);
end
```

SwingIndex

The **SwingIndex** function returns a positive or negative value that represents the comparative up or down swing strength between two bar periods. (See Figure G.2.74.)

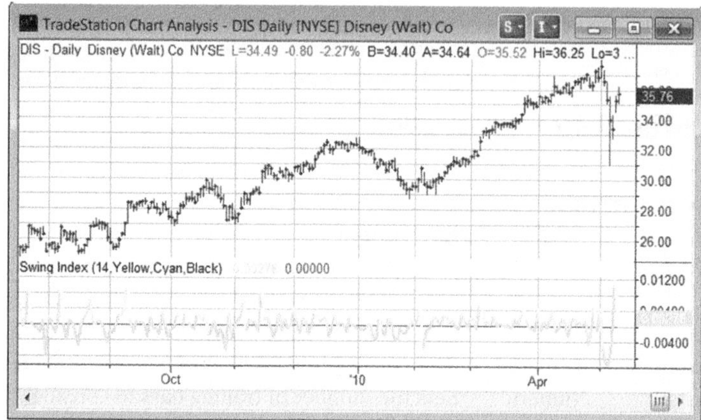

FIGURE G.2.74 Swing Index

RETURNS (Double): A numeric value containing the current Swing Index.

REMARKS

The SwingIndex function examines the next four cross-bar comparisons and one intra-bar comparison that are strong indicators of an up day or a down day:

- Close today above or below previous Close.
- Close today above or below Open today.
- High today above or below previous Close.
- Low today above or below previous Close.
- Previous Close minus previous Open.

If the factors pointed toward an up day, the SwingIndex would be a positive value from zero to 100. If the factors pointed toward a down day, the function would return a value between zero and −100.

where K = The larger of
H2–C1
L2–C1
L = Value of a limit move in one direction.

To obtain R, first determine the largest of:

H2–C1 – If the largest, R = (H2-C1) – .5(L2-C1) + .25(C3-O1)
L2–C1 – If the largest, R = (L2-C1) – .5(H2-C1) + .25(C3-O1)
H2–L2 – If the largest, R = (H2-L2) + .25(C3-O1)

NOTE: Since only futures have a relative daily limit value, this function makes sense only if it is applied to a futures contract. If you use the Swing Index Indicator or Accumulation Swing Index Indicator and it plots a zero flat line, check the Daily Limit value.

EXAMPLE

```
Plot1(SwingIndex);
```

REFERENCE

Wilder, J. Welles. *New Concepts in Technical Trading Systems*. Greensboro, NC: Trend Research, 1978.

SwingLow

See **SwingHigh**

SwingLowBar

See **SwingHigh**

TimeSeriesForecast(Length, TgtBar)

The **TimeSeriesForecast** function returns the value where a linear regression line of the Close is projected to be relative to a future (or past) bar position. (See Figure G.2.75.)

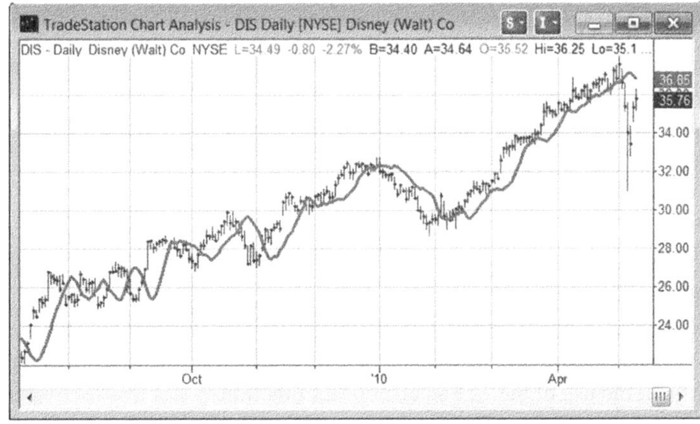

FIGURE G.2.75 Time Series Forecast

RETURNS (Integer): A numeric value of a future (or past) bar position.

PARAMETERS

Name	Type	Description
Length	Numeric	Sets the bars to consider.
TgtBar	Numeric	Sets the point in the past or future to use for projecting a regression value. Use a positive integer for a previous point and a negative integer for a future point.

REMARKS

Linear regression is a concept also known as the least squares method or best fit. Linear regression attempts to fit a straight line between several data points in such a way that distance between each data point and the line is minimized.

The equation of any line resembles:

$$y = mx + b$$

where m = Slope of the regression line
b = Constant intercept of the y-axis
x = Independent variable
y = Dependent variable

This function returns all values.

EXAMPLE

Assigns to `Value1` the projected value five bars in the future of a linear regression line over the past 20 bars.

```
Value1 = TimeSeriesForecast (20, -5);
```

REFERENCE

Linear regression is a principle found in most statistical publications.

TimeToMinutes (XTime)

The **TimeToMinutes** function calculates the number of minutes from midnight for any 24-hour (HHMM) time value.

RETURNS (Integer): A numeric value containing the number of minutes between midnight and XTime.

PARAMETERS

Name	Type	Description
XTime	Numeric	Specifies a time in 24-hour format.

REMARKS

This function allows for the proper addition and subtraction of time. The first step when adding or subtracting a number of minutes from time is to convert the time to minutes through the use of the `TimeToMinutes` function.

Then, add or subtract the number of minutes, and, finally convert the number of minutes back to time using the MinutesToTime function.

`XTime` is a numeric simple type input and can be hard coded with a number or can be replaced by a numeric simple input.

EXAMPLE

Assigns to `Value1` the number of minutes since midnight, 150 in this case, based on a 24-hour time input equivalent to 2:30am.

```
Value1 = TimeToMintues(0230);
```

ANOTHER EXAMPLE

```
Value1 = SwingHighBar(Instance, Price, Strength, Length);
Value2 = Time[Value1];
Value3 = TimeToMinutes(Value2);
Value4 = Value3 + 30;
```

This example allows you to find the time 30 minutes after a swing high occurred.

TL_Exist(TrendLineID)

The **TL_Exist** function returns true if a trendline exists.

RETURNS (Boolean): True if the specified trendline (using TrendLineID) exists in the current chart, False if not.

PARAMETER

Name	Type	Description
TrendLineID	Numeric	Sets the identification number of the trendline.

EXAMPLE

If you want to place a buy order to buy at the trendline number 1, only if the trendline exits, you can write:

```
If TL_Exist(1) Then
   Buy Next Bar at TL_GetValue(1, Date, Time) Stop;
```

TL_GetEndTime

This reserved word returns the time of the ending point of the trendline. The ending point of the trendline is the one with the later time; if the trendline is vertical, the higher of the two points is considered to be the ending point.

```
Value1 = TL_ GetEndTime(Tl_ID)
```

`Tl_ID` is a numeric expression representing the ID number of the trendline whose ending time you want to obtain.

`Value1` is any numeric variable or array, and holds the time of the starting point.

REMARKS

When the reserved word performs its operation successfully, the time is returned. When a reserved word cannot perform its operation, it returns an error code. For a list of error codes, see EasyLanguage Drawing Object Error Codes.

It is important to remember that if an invalid ID number is used, the reserved word will return a value of −2 and no additional operations will be performed on any trendlines by the trading strategy, analysis technique, or function that generated the error.

EXAMPLE

The next statement assigns the EasyLanguage time of the bar used as the end point for the trendline referenced by Value99 to the variable Value1:

```
Value1 = TL_GetEndTime(Value99);
```

TL_GetValue

This reserved word returns a numeric expression corresponding to the value of a trendline at a specific bar. It is important to remember that this reserved word returns a value even if the trendline is not shown on or projected through the bar specified. For example, if a trendline is drawn from December 1 to January 5, and the following statement is used:

```
Value1 = TL_GetValue(10, 990203, 1400);
```

Even though the date specified is in February, the TL_GetValue reserved word will return the trendline value as if the trendline were extended to that particular bar (along the same slope).

```
Value1 = TL_GetValue(Tl_ID, TLDate, TLTime)
```

`Tl_ID` is a numeric expression representing the ID number of the trendline whose price value you want to obtain. `TLDate` and `TLTime` are the date and time, respectively, of the bar for which you want to obtain the trendline's value.

`Value1` is any numeric variable or array. You must assign the trendline reserved word to a numeric variable or array so that you can determine whether the reserved word performed its operation successfully.

REMARKS

When the reserved word performs its operation successfully, the vertical axis (price) value is returned. When a reserved word cannot perform its operation, it returns an error code. For a list of error codes, see EasyLanguage Error Codes.

It is important to remember that if an invalid ID number is used, the reserved word will return a value of −2 and no additional operations will be performed on any trendlines by the trading strategy, analysis technique, or function that generated the error.

EXAMPLE

To obtain the price value returned by the reserved word, you need to assign the reserved word to a numeric variable. On January 7, 1999 at 4:00 pm, the trendline referenced by Value99 intersects the price value of 53.350. The next statement returns 53.350.

```
Value1 = TL_GetValue(Value99, 990107, 1600);
```

ADDITIONAL EXAMPLE

The next statement triggers an alert when the close crosses over the trendline referenced by Value99:

```
If Close Crosses Over TL_GetValue(Value99, Date, Time) Then
Alert("Trendline is broken");
```

TLAngle(StartPrice, StartBar, EndPrice, EndBar)

The **TLAngle** function returns the angle of a trendline. (See Figure G.2.76.)

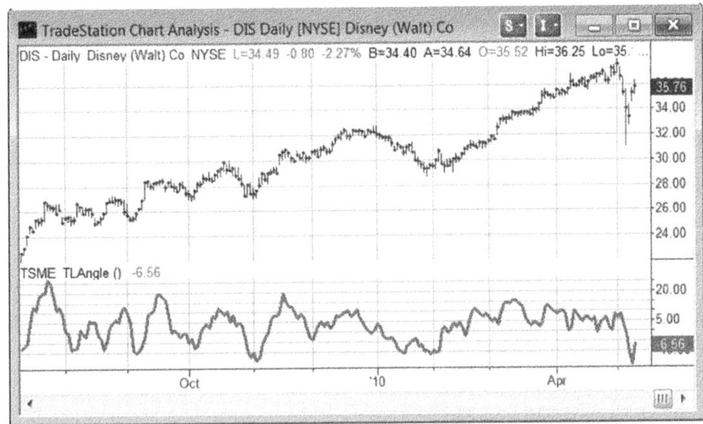

FIGURE G.2.76 TLAngle

PARAMETERS

Name	**Type**	**Description**
StartPrice	Numeric	Sets the price of the trendline start point.
StartBar	Numeric	Sets the bar number of the trendline start point.
EndPrice	Numeric	Sets the price of the trendline end point.
EndBar	Numeric	Sets the bar number of the trendline end point.

RETURNS (Double): A numeric value representing the angle of the specified trendline.

REMARKS

To calculate the angle, the function requires that you specify the start and end bars for the trendline as well as the start and end prices. The inputs `StartPrice` and `EndPrice` are the start price and end price, respectively, of the trendline. They are usually replaced by values such as Close, High, Low, and so on, or are replaced with numeric series type inputs.

Also, you must offset the `Price` by its corresponding bar number. For example, if you want the trendline angle for a line drawn from the `Close` of 10 bars ago to the `Close` of the current bar, replace the inputs `StartPrice, StartBar, EndPrice`, and `EndBar` with the values `Close[10], 10, Close[0]`, and `0` respectively.

The inputs `StartBar` and `EndBar` refer to the bar numbers of the starting and ending points of the trendline. These inputs must be replaced by positive whole numbers or numeric simple type inputs.

The formula used is a simple rise over run calculation to obtain the slope; the formula then takes the arctangent of that slope. In fact, you can obtain the same value as the TLAngle function by taking the ArcTangent of the TLSlope function.

EXAMPLE

```
Plot1(TLAngle(High[1],1,High[9],9));
```

TLAngleEasy(Price, StartBar, EndBar)

The **TLAngleEasy** function returns the angle of a trendline with one price input.

RETURNS (Double): A numeric value containing the angle of a trendline.

PARAMETERS

Name	Type	Description
Price	Numeric	Specifies which bar value (price, function, or formula) to use.
StartBar	Numeric	Sets the bar number of the trendline start point.
EndBar	Numeric	Sets the bar number of the trendline end point.

REMARKS

This function is similar to `TLAngle`, except that you cannot specify different prices for the start and end points. This function uses the same price on the start and end bars.

The formula used is a simple rise over run calculation to obtain the slope; the formula then takes the cotangent of that slope. In fact, you can obtain the same value as the `TLAngleEasy` function by taking the ArcTangent of the TLSlope function.

EXAMPLE

```
Plot1(TLAngleEasy(High,1,9);
```

TLSlope (StartPrice, StartBar, EndPrice, EndBar)

The **TLSlope** function returns the slope of a trendline. (See Figure G.2.77.)

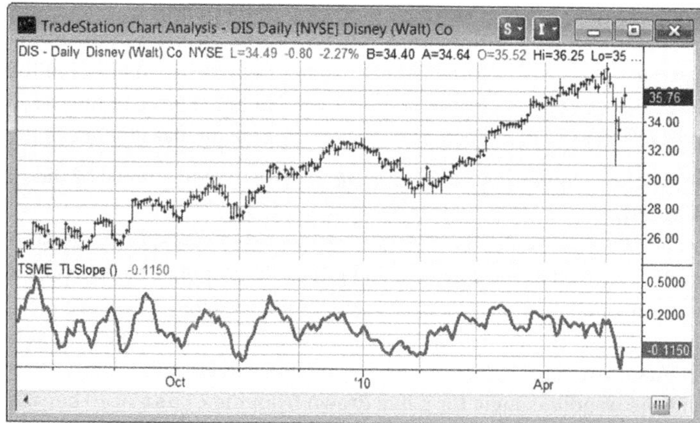

FIGURE G.2.77 TLSlope

RETURNS (Double): A numeric value containing the slope of the specified trendline.

PARAMETERS

Name	Type	Description
StartPrice	Numeric	Sets the price of the trendline start point.
StartBar	Numeric	Sets the bar number of the trendline start point.
EndPrice	Numeric	Sets the price of the trendline end point.
EndBar	Numeric	Sets the bar number of the trendline end point.

REMARKS

To calculate the angle, the function will need the bar numbers and prices for the two endpoints of the trendline. The inputs EndPrice and StartPrice are the starting point and ending points of the trendline, respectively. They are usually replaced by values such as Close, High, Low, and so on or can be replaced with numeric series inputs.

NOTE: You must offset the price by its corresponding bar number. For example, if you wanted the trendline angle for a line drawn from the Close of 10 bars ago to the Close of the current bar, replace the inputs StartPrice, StartBar, EndPrice, and EndBar would be replaced with the values Close[10], 10, Close[0], and 0 respectively.

The inputs EndBar and StartBar refer to the bar numbers of the starting and ending points of the trendline. These inputs can be replaced by whole numbers or with numeric simple type inputs that return positive whole numbers when using their default values. The formula used is a simple rise over run calculation.

EXAMPLE

```
Plot1(TLSlope(High[1],1,High[9],9));
```

See also TLSlopeEasy

TLSlopeEasy(Price, StartBar, EndBar)

The **TLSlopeEasy** function returns the slope of a trendline, if that trendline were to be drawn between two data points on your chart.

RETURNS (Double): A numeric value containing the slope of a trendline.

PARAMETERS

Name	Type	Description
Price	Numeric	Specifies which bar value (price, function, or formula) to use.
StartBar	Numeric	Sets the bar number of the trendline start point.
EndBar	Numeric	Sets the bar number of the trendline end point.

REMARKS

This function is similar to TLSlope, except that you cannot specify different prices for the start and end points. This function uses the same price for both the start and end bars.

EXAMPLE

```
Plot1(TLSlopeEasy(High,1,9));
```

TLValue (StartPrice, StartBar, EndPrice, EndBar, TgtBar)

The **TLValue** function returns the value of a trendline at specified point. (See Figure G.2.78.)

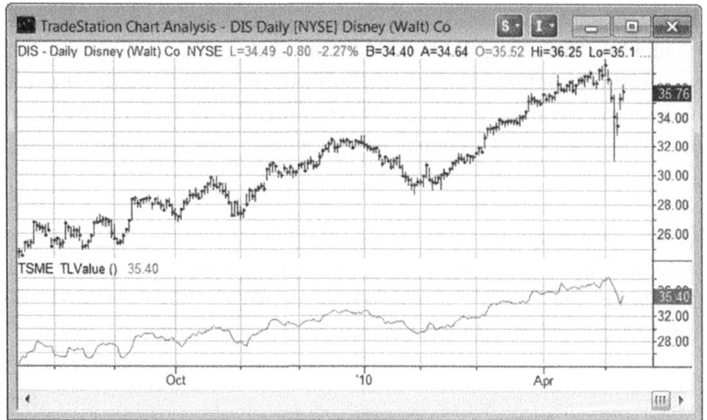

FIGURE G.2.78 TLValue

PARAMETERS

Name	Type	Description
StartPrice	Numeric	Sets the price of the trendline start point.
StartBar	Numeric	Sets the bar number of the trendline start point.
EndPrice	Numeric	Sets the price of the trendline end point.
EndBar	Numeric	Sets the bar number of the trendline end point.
TgtBar	Numeric	Set the number of bars to extend trendline (positive number = backward in time and negative number = forward in time).

RETURNS (Double): A numeric value containing the specified trendline at point `TgtBar`.

REMARKS

The two points allow us to calculate the slope of the line; by extending that line, the `TLValue` function is able to calculate the Price of the target bar in the future.

To calculate the value, the function will need the bar numbers and prices for the two endpoints of the trendline as well as the target bar out in the future or back in the past. The input `StartPrice` and `EndPrice` are the starting point and ending points of the trendline respectively. They are usually replaced by values such as Close, High, Low, and so on or with numeric series type inputs.

The inputs `StartBar` and `EndBar` refer to the bar numbers of the starting and ending points of the trendline. These inputs must be replaced by valid numbers or with numeric simple type inputs.

NOTE: You must offset the price by its corresponding bar number. For example, if you wanted the trendline angle for a line drawn from the `Close` of 10 bars ago to the `Close` of the current bar, replace the inputs StartPrice, StartBar, EndPrice, and EndBar with the values Close[0], 0, Close[10], and 10 respectively.

The input `TgtBar` must be replaced by either a positive or negative number that represents the number of bars back in the past or out in the future that the trendline is to be extended. Negative values of `TgtBar` project the trendline into the future while positive values of `TgtBar` project the trendline back into the past.

The formula used to calculate the slope is a simple rise over run calculation.

EXAMPLE

```
Plot1(TLValue(High[1],1,High[9],9,1));
```

TLValueEasy(Price, StartBar, EndBar, TgtBar)

The **TLValueEasy** function returns the value of a trendline. (See Figure G.2.79.)

FIGURE G.2.79 TLValueEasy

RETURNS (Double): A numeric value containing the specified trendline.

PARAMETERS

Name	Type	Description
Price	Numeric	Specifies which bar value (price, function, or formula) to use.
StartBar	Numeric	Sets the bar number of the trendline start point.
EndBar	Numeric	Sets the bar number of the trendline end point.
TgtBar	Numeric	Set the number of bars to extend trendline (positive number = backward in time & negative number = forward in time).

REMARKS

This function is similar to `TLValue`, except that you cannot specify different prices for the start and end prices. This function uses the same price on the start and end bar.

The inputs `StartBar` and `EndBar` refer to the bar numbers of the starting and ending points of the trendline. These inputs must be replaced by valid numbers or replaced with numeric simple type inputs.

The input `TgtBar` must be replaced by either a positive or negative number that represents the number of bars back in the past or out in the future that the trendline is to be extended. Negative values of TgtBar project the trendline into the future while positive values of TgtBar project the trendline back into the past.

EXAMPLE

```
Plot1(TLValueEasy(High,1,9,1));
```

TriAverage(Price, Length)

The **TriAverage** series function places the majority of the weighting on the middle portion of the specified length. (See Figure G.2.80.)

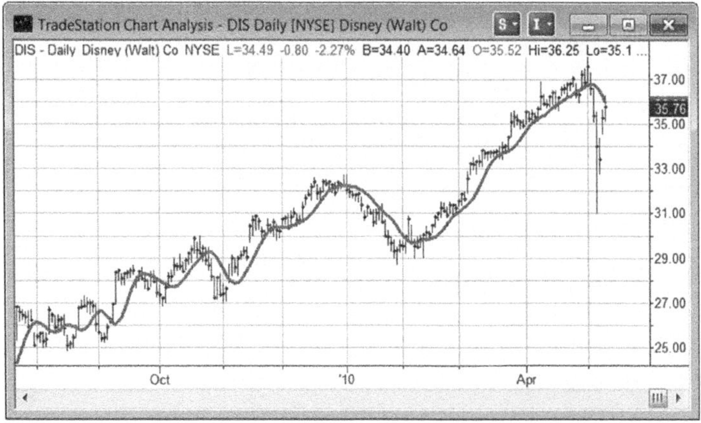

FIGURE G.2.80 TriAverage

RETURNS (Double): A numeric value containing the Triangular Moving Average for the current bar.

PARAMETERS

Name	Type	Description
Price	Numeric	Specifies which bar value (price, function, or formula) to use.
Length	Numeric	Sets the number of bars to consider.

REMARKS

In calculating the Triangular Average, the Average is inherently double-smoothed.

EXAMPLES

Assigns to Value1 the Triangular Moving Average based on the Close of the last 14 bars:

```
Value1 = TriAverage(Close, 14);
```

Assigns to Value2 the Triangular Moving Average based on the High of the last 21 bars:

```
Value2 = TriAverage(High, 21);
```

ADDITIONAL EXAMPLE

If you wanted to place a Buy on Close order when the `Close` crossed above the Triangular Moving Average, you could use this syntax:

```
If Close Crosses Above TriAverage(Close, 18) Then
   Buy This Bar on Close;
```

See also Average, WAverage, and XAverage

TrimMean(Price, Length, TrimPct)

The **TrimMean** function calculates the Interior Mean value of the specified bar after trimming extremes. (See Figure G.2.81.)

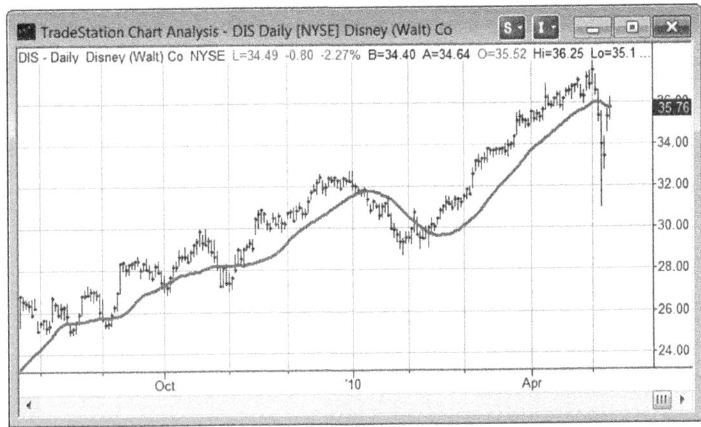

FIGURE G.2.81 TrimMean

RETURNS (Double): A numeric value containing the mean of a range of bars. If `TrimPct` is less than 0 or greater than 1, then the Function will return a −1.

PARAMETERS

Name	**Type**	**Description**
Price	Numeric	Specifies which bar value (price, function, or formula) to use.
Length	Numeric	Sets the number of bars used in the calculation.
TrimPct	Numeric	Sets the percentage of data to exclude from calculation. Enter 0.20 for 20%, which will exclude 10% of the data values from each end of the number of bars selected.

REMARKS

`TrimMean` calculates the mean taken by excluding a percentage (`TrimPct`) of data points from the top and bottom tails of a data set. This function can be used to exclude outlying data from your analysis.

If `TrimPct` is less than 0 or if `TrimPct` is greater than 1, the function will return −1.

EXAMPLES

Assigns to `Value1` the TrimMean value calculated over the past 14 closing prices with a TrimPct of .25 or 25%:

```
Value1 = TrimMean(Close, 14, .25);
```

Assigns to `Value2` the TrimMean value calculated over the past 14 High prices with a TrimPct of .10 or 10%:

```
Value2 = TrimMean(High, 21, .1);
```

TRIX(Price, Length)

The **TRIX** function calculates the percent rate of change of a triple exponentially smoothed moving average of the security's closing price. (See Figure G.2.82.)

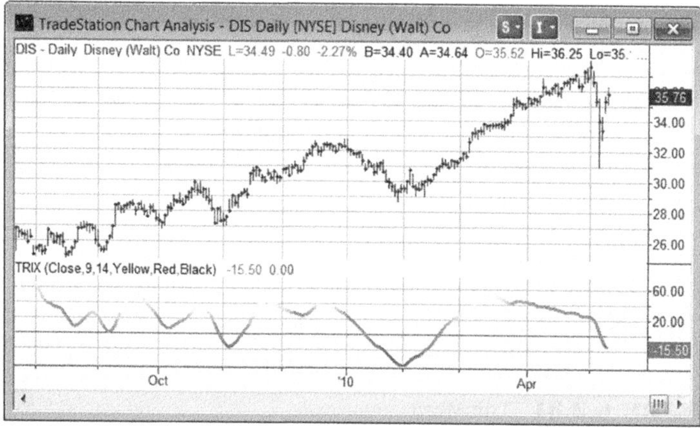

FIGURE G.2.82 TRIX

RETURNS (Double): A numeric value containing TRIX for the current bar.

PARAMETERS

Name	Type	Description
Price	Numeric	Specifies which bar value (price, function, or formula) to use.
Length	Numeric	Sets the number of bars to consider.

REMARKS

`TRIX` is a momentum indicator that displays the percent rate of change of a triple exponentially smoothed moving average of the security's closing price. The TRIX indicator oscillates around a zero line. Its triple exponential smoothing is designed to filter out noise.

EXAMPLE

If you want to initiate a short position when TRIX crosses under zero, you can write:

```
If TRIX(Close, 10) Crosses Under 0 Then
   SellShort Next Bar at Market;
```

TrueHigh

The **TrueHigh** function returns either the `High` of the current bar or the `Close` of the previous bar if its value is higher. (See Figure G.2.83.)

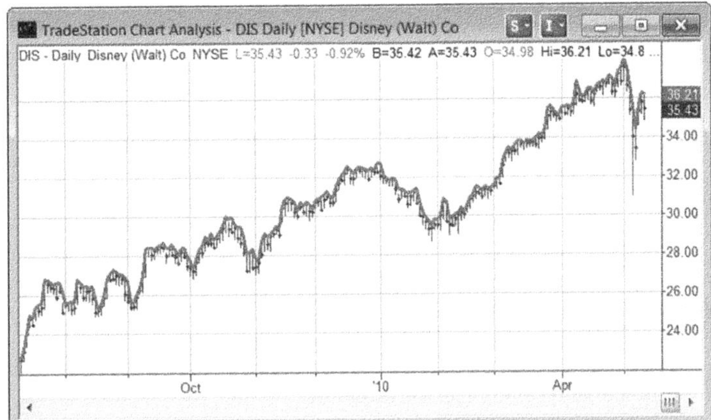

FIGURE G.2.83 TrueHigh

RETURNS (Double): A numeric value containing the greater of the current bar `High` or previous bar `Close`.

REMARKS

The `TrueHigh` function is most commonly used in finding Gap Open bars. A Gap Open bar is when the Open is greater than the previous bar's High.

EXAMPLE

```
Plot1(TrueHigh, "TrueHi");
```

See also TrueLow, TrueRange

TrueLow

See **TrueHigh**

TrueRange

The **TrueRange** function returns the difference between the `TrueHigh` and `TrueLow` values. (See Figure G.2.84.)

RETURNS (Double): A numeric value containing the difference between the `TrueHigh` and `TrueLow` for the current bar.

REMARKS

This function is similar to `Range` except that it uses the `TrueHigh` and `TrueLow` values that take into account the previous bar close in addition to the current bar `High` and `Low`.

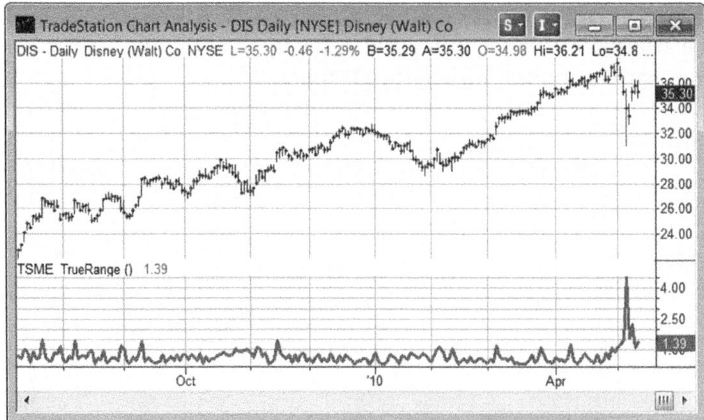

FIGURE G.2.84 True Range

TrueRange is defined as the larger of:

- The distance between today's High and today's Low.
- The distance between today's High and yesterday's Close.
- The distance between today's Low and yesterday's Close.

EXAMPLE

```
Plot1(TrueRange, "TRange");
```

TypicalPrice

The **TypicalPrice** function returns average of the `High`, `Low`, and `Close` prices of a bar. (See Figure G.2.85.)

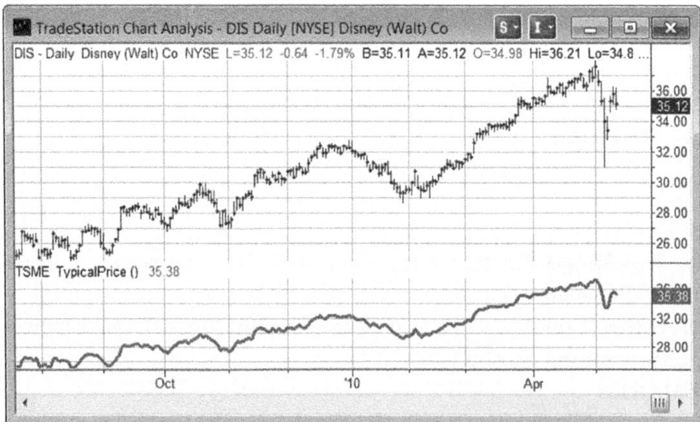

FIGURE G.2.85 TypicalPrice

RETURNS (Double): A numeric value containing the typical average price for the current bar.

EXAMPLE

Assigns to Value1 the typical average price on a bar, then plots Value1.

```
Value1 = TypicalPrice;
Plot1(Value1, "AvgPrc");
```

UlcerIndex(Price, Length)

The **UlcerIndex** function is a measure of the stress level related to market conditions. (See Figure G.2.86.)

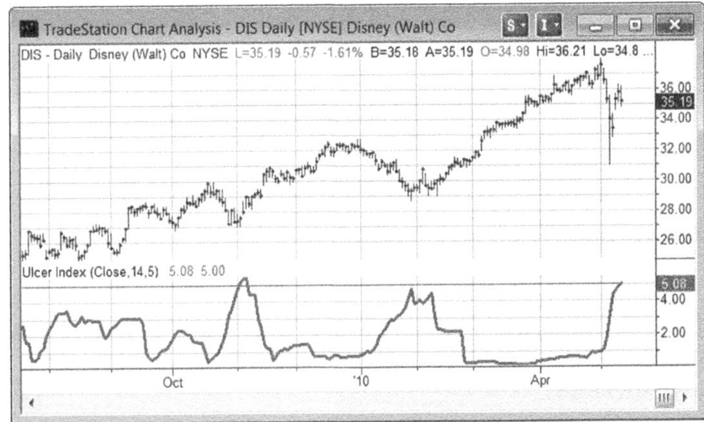

FIGURE G.2.86 Ulcer Index

RETURNS (Double): A numeric value containing the Ulcer Index for the current bar.

PARAMETERS

Name	Type	Description
Price	Numeric	Specifies which bar value (price, function, or formula) to be considered.
Length	Numeric	Sets the number of bars to consider.

REMARKS

The Ulcer Index uses retracements to measure the "stressfulness" associated with the instrument at the current time. As stated by Peter Martin and Byron McCann, "the higher an investment's UI, the more likely investing in it will cause ulcers or sleepless nights."

EXAMPLES

Assigns to `Value1` the Ulcer Index calculated over the past 14 closing prices:

```
Value1 = UlcerIndex(Close, 14);
```

Assigns to `Value2` the Ulcer Index calculated over the past 21 High prices:

```
Value2 = UlcerIndex(High, 21);
```

UltimateOsc(ShortLength, MiddlLength, LongLength)

The **UltimateOscillator** function returns the Ultimate Oscillator value developed by Larry Williams. (See Figure G.2.87.)

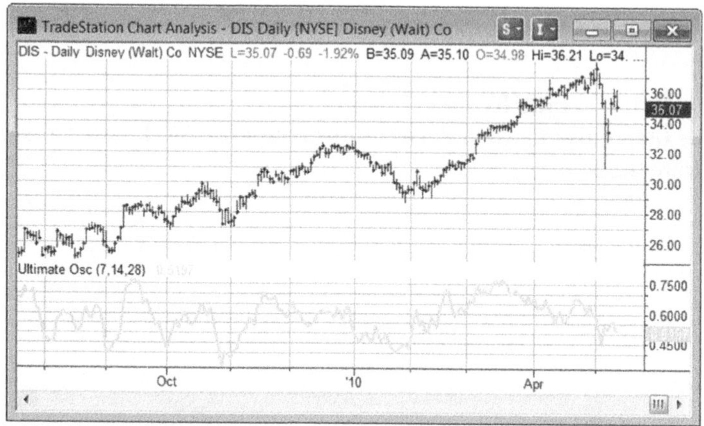

FIGURE G.2.87 Ultimate Oscillator

RETURNS (Double): A numeric value containing the current value of the Ultimate Oscillator.

PARAMETERS

Name	Type	Description
ShortLength	Numeric	Sets the number of bars in short-term average.
MiddlLength	Numeric	Sets the number of bars in intermediate-term average.
LongLength	Numeric	Sets the number of bars in long-term average.

REMARKS

Larry Williams contends that an oscillator based on one time span is subject to a number of false alerts. To combat this problem, he combines three such oscillators, each based on different time frames. Williams states that oscillators with shorter time frames tend to peak well ahead of price, usually causing several divergences prior to the ultimate peak. Indicators based on longer time spans do not tend to reverse direction until after market turning points.

EXAMPLE

Assigns to `Value1` and plots the `UltimateOscillator` based on the specified short-, medium-, and long-term averages.

```
Value1 = UltimateOscillator(7,14,28);
Plot1(Value1, "UltOsc");
```

REFERENCE

Larry Williams.

Volatility(Length)

The **Volatility** series function measures the market volatility by plotting a smoothed average of the `TrueRange`. It returns an average of the `TrueRange` over a specific number of bars, giving higher weight to the `TrueRange` of the most recent bar. (See Figure G.2.88.)

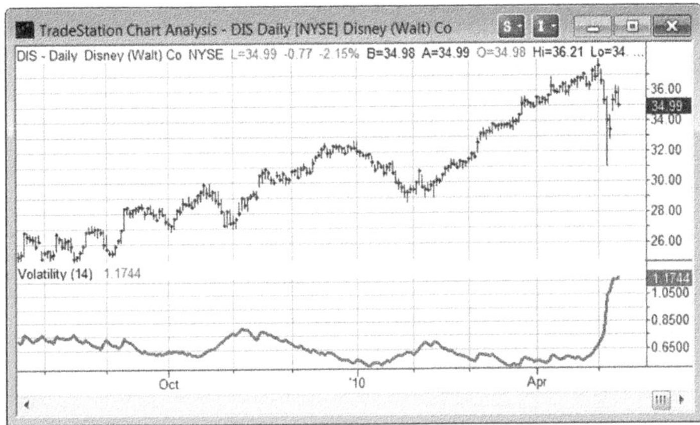

FIGURE G.2.88 Volatility

RETURNS (Double): A numeric value containing the market volatility. As the number increases, the market is more volatile.

PARAMETER

Name	Type	Description
Length	Numeric	Sets the number of bars to include in the volatility calculation.

REMARKS

Volatility is the variation in price over a specific interval (the difference between the highest and lowest prices). As the time interval being studied increases, volatility also increases to a maximum before leveling off. As prices increase, the volatility tolerance also increases.

NOTE: The Volatility function uses a slightly different set of calculations from the original formula. The Volatility variation tends to smooth recent activity, which means that it will take more time (bars) to "normalize." The original formula is provided in the VolatilityClassic function.

EXAMPLE

Plots the volatility over the last 20 bars.

```
Plot1(Volatility(20);
```

Assigns to `Value1` the volatility of the last 15 bars.

```
Value1 = Volatility(15):
```

REFERENCE

Kaufman, P. J. *The New Commodity Trading Systems and Methods.* New York: John Wiley & Sons, 1980, pp. 99–101.

VolumeOsc

The **VolumeOsc** function calculates the difference between a slow and fast period moving average in terms of points. (See Figure G.2.89.)

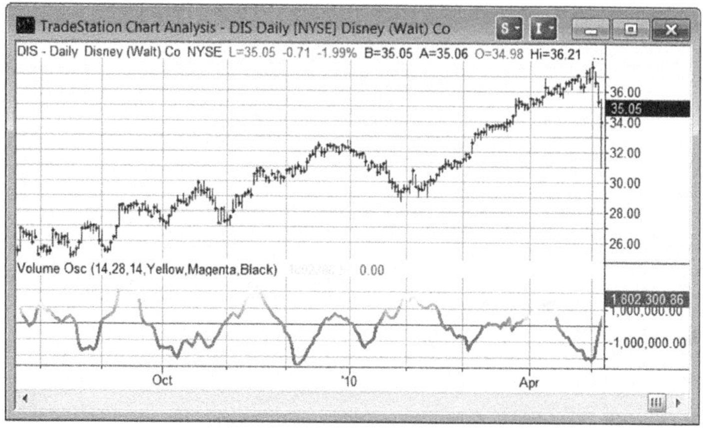

FIGURE G.2.89 Volume Oscillator

RETURNS (Double): A numeric value containing a positive or negative value of `VolumeOsc` for the current bar.

PARAMETERS

Name	Type	Description
FastLength	Numeric	Sets the time period of the slow moving average.
SlowLength	Numeric	Sets the time period of the fast moving average.

EXAMPLE

```
Value1 = VolumeOsc(9,18);
```

VolumeROC(Length)

The **VolumeROC** function returns the volume rate of change based on a range of bars. (See Figure G.2.90.)

RETURNS (Double): A numeric value containing a positive or negative value of VolumeROC for the current bar.

PARAMETER

Name	Type	Description
Length	Numeric	Sets the number of bars to consider.

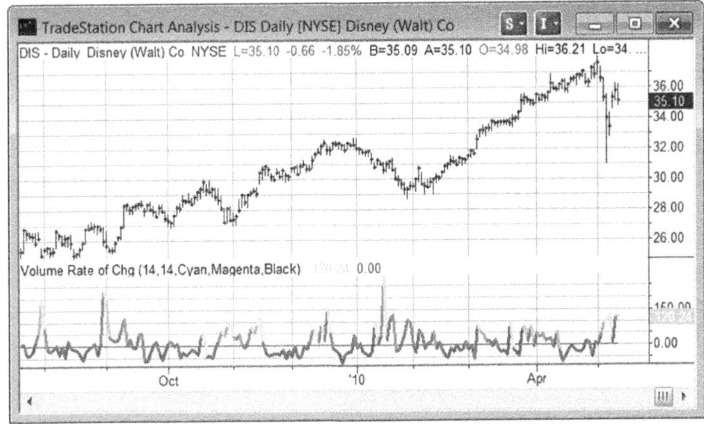

FIGURE G.2.90 VolumeROC

REMARKS

The most common use of this function is to determine the likelihood of a continuation in the current move.

EXAMPLE

```
Value1 = VolumeROC(20);
```

WAverage(Price, Length)

The **WAverage** is a weighted moving average of the `Price` over the `Length` specified. It is calculated by giving the more current data a heavier weight and the oldest data less weight. (See Figure G.2.91.)

RETURNS (Double): A numeric value containing the weighted moving average over a specified number of bars.

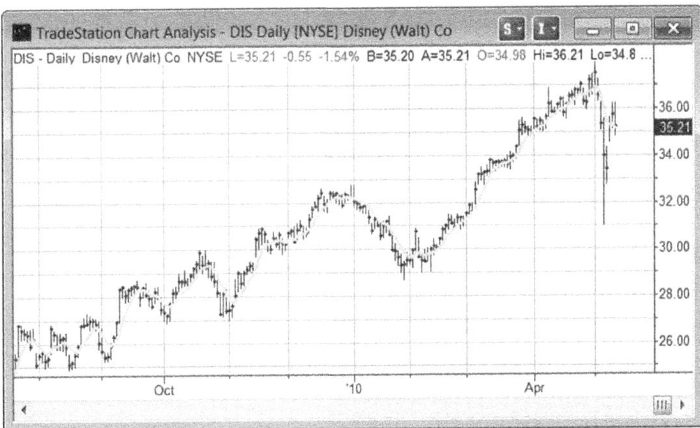

FIGURE G.2.91 Weighted Average

PARAMETERS

Name	Type	Description
Price	Numeric	Specifies which bar value (price, function, or formula) to use.
Length	Numeric	Sets the number of bars to consider.

REMARKS

Just as the Average function needs a Price and Length to calculate, the WAverage function also needs the Price and Length inputs. The Price is the unit you want to average, and the Length is the number of units you are averaging. The WAverage is used in the same way as the average function and can give stronger and earlier indications to trend direction as it follows the most recent data more closely.

EXAMPLE

```
Plot1(WAverage(Close,20));
```

See also Average, TriAverage, and XAverage.

At my Web site (www.moneymentor.com), look under TradeStation Made Easy for a system with all the different average types. It's free to download and is nice for optimizing on each of the moving averages.

WeightedClose

The **WeightedClose** function returns an average price that gives more precedence to the Close than the High or Low. (See Figure G.2.92.)

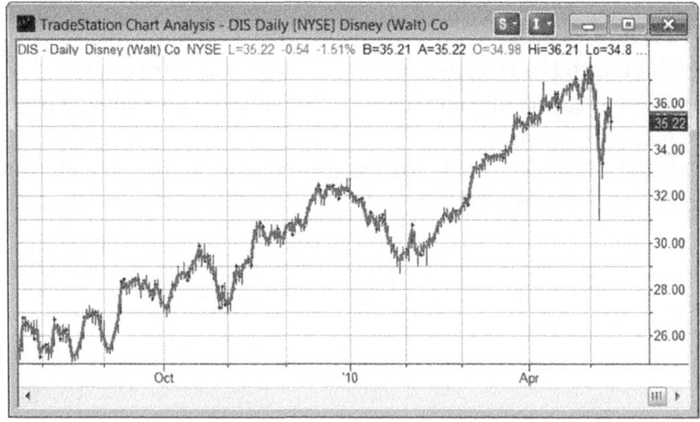

FIGURE G.2.92 Weighted Close

RETURNS (Double): A numeric value containing the weighted close.

REMARKS

The `WeightedClose` function calculates the average price of the bar by taking the `High` and `Low` and adding it to two `Closes` and dividing by four.

EXAMPLE

```
Value1 = WeightedClose;
Plot1(Value1);
```

APPENDIX H

TradeStation Add-on Products and Services

TRADER'S CATALOG & RESOURCE GUIDE(TM): THE FINANCIAL YELLOW PAGES

Prior to version 6, also known as TradeStation Pro, the company itself was known as Omega Research. As such, it helped promote a special group of users known as Omega Solution Providers. The solution providers had products or services of their own for sale, which work alongside or on top of TradeStation. With the advent of version 6, the company became an IB (Introducing Broker) offering brokerage services and no longer promotes Solution Providers. Now known as TradeStation, the company is entirely separate from the solution providers, although there is a somewhat up-to-date list of them on the TradeStation Web site. And they are no longer called solution providers, they are add-on products.

In memory of my erstwhile publication, *Traders' Catalog & Resource Guide*, I am presenting the solution providers here in Yellow Pages format. I loved publishing *TC&RG*, but it was ahead of its time, as are many of the things I do. It was terribly expensive to produce and, while everyone seemed to love it, they didn't want to pay for it. So I stopped publishing it in 1998, after eight years of being supported mainly by my trading profits.

If you want more details on any of these solution providers, visit www.moneymentor.com.

!QCL Solutions
David O'Dell
P.O. Box 2304
Palm City, FL 34990
Phone: 347-682-2377
Email: DODell@QCLsolutions.com
http://qclsolutions.com/

1st Trading Tools
Steven Guiot
1449 N. Burns Street
Wichita, KS 67203
Phone: 316-265-8996
Email: guiot@cox.net

A

Accurate Trading Systems
Brett Beshey
1201 S. Alma School #11550
Mesa, AZ 85210
Phone: 310-601-7263
Email: accuratetrading@aol.com

Acme Trader
Mark Conway
237 Moody Street, Suite 565
Waltham, MA 02453
Phone: 781-209-1910
sales@acmetrader.com

Advanz Companies, LLC
Joe Garcia-Rios
7301SW 57th Ct, suite 525
Miami, FL 33143
Phone: 305-573-1110
Fax: 305-573-3223
Email: prophetsoft@advanzteam.com
www.advanzteam.com/

AIM Trading Systems
Bill Sadek
37 La Gaviota
Pismo Beach, CA 93449
Phone: 805-556-0801
Fax: 805-556-0891
Email: sales@AimTradingSystems.com

Alchemy Trading Technologies
Joe Jogerst
P.O. Box 7506
Boulder, CO 80306
Phone: 303-258-9786
Email: info@tradingalchemy.com
www.tradingalchemy.com/

All Pro Trader
Chuck Ramus
15834 Dawson Ridge Drive
Tampa, FL 33647
Phone: 813- 977-5978
Fax: 813-978-8998
Email: Sales@AllProtrader.com

ALVentures
Al Gietzen
2140 Alessandro Trail
Vista, CA 92084
Phone: 760-630-5555
Fax: 760-630-5665
Email: ALVentures@cox.net

AmCanTrading
Bertrand Wibbing
Email: amcantrading@hotmail.de
www.amcantrading.net/

AmNet Enterprises, Inc.
Dean Lyon
5821 Town Bay Drive Apt. 5-16
Boca Raton, FL 33486
Phone: 561-362-9795
Email: ceecoast@bellsouth.net

ARC Systems Inc.
Roy Kelly
2533 N. Carson Street Suite P-361
Carson City, NV 89706
Phone: 775-443-7677
Fax: 775-627-9999
Email: support@trendpro.com
www.trendpro.com/

Arman Glen Allen
Arman Glen Allen
215 Walnut Hill Street
Lone Grove, OK 73443
Email: bill@endoftrendtrading.com

Aster Investor Resources, LLC
Warren Rosenfeld
660 Preston Forest, Suite 383
Dallas, TX 75230
Phone: 214-265-1632
Email: wrosenfeld@tradersreports.com

ATCM
Vaughn Townsend
17857 Maple Lane
Rogers, AR 72756
Phone: 417-766-8921
Email: vaughn@atcmfx.com

August Trade Consulting, Inc.
Robert Goold
338 Harvard Street
Cambridge, MA 02139
Phone: 617-402-0004
Email: 0004rrgoold@augusttrade.com

Austin Trading Tools
Richard Jennings
Austin, TX 78750
Phone: 512-258-0403
Email: rcjaustin@yahoo.com

Avicom, Inc.
Brian Massey
3642 248th Avenue SE
Issaquah, WA 98029
Email: sales@avicominc.com

AvSoft Consulting, Inc.
Jim Alger
1702 Vestment Court
Severn, MD 21144
Phone: 410-519-0740
Fax: 410-551-6254
Email: elassist@avsoftinc.com
www.avsoftinc.com/

B

BackTesting Report
Jackie Ann Patterson
P.O. Box 620427
Woodside, CA 94062-0427
Phone: 650-752-4921
Email: support@backtestingreport.com
http://home.backtestingreport.com/

Bahati Holding, LLC
Ronald Berry
5201 Commonwealth Unit 14
Detroit, MI 48208
Phone: 313-432-7859
Email: bahatihldgs@cs.com

Barry Taylor International Pty Ltd.
Barry Taylor
16/32 Bonner Avenue
Manly, NSW Australia 2095
Phone: [011] 0414303524
Email: barry@taylorintl.com.au
http://emini-watch.com/

Bloomfield, Grant
Grant Bloomfield
227A-1255 Commissioners Road West
London, ON N6K 3N5

Phone: 519-668-6133
Email: trader@ody.ca

BlueWaveTrading
Randy Sarrow
44 Laenui Place
Paia, HI 96779
Phone: 808-579-6294
Email: systems@bluewavetrading.com
www.bluewavetrading.com/

Breakout Futures
Michael Bryant
1116-A 8th Street #168
Manhattan Beach, CA 90266
Phone: 951-302-1624
Fax: 208-977-1111

C

CAP Portfolios
Steve Freundlich
Phone: [44] 02078706619
Email: info@cap-protection.com
www.cap-protection.com/

Cash Cow Trading Strategies
Bob Bilyea
264 Chambers Court
London, ON N5X 4H5
Phone: 519-663-0015
Email: rbilyea@ody.ca
www.cashcow-windicator.com/

CFRN
DeWayne Reeves
911 W Woodland Avenue
Phoenix, AZ 85007
Phone: 602-743-3695
Email: ct@cfrn.net
www.cfrn.net/

Clayburg, John
John Clayburg
29568 Highway 141
Coon Rapids, IA 50058-7178
Phone: 712-830-5062
Fax: 712-684-5239
Email: clayburg@pionet.net
www.clayburg.com/

Cooper Advanced Technologies, Inc.
Terry Cooper
P.O. Box 560634
Montverde, FL 34756
Phone: 877-468-6228
Fax: 407-469-4894
Email: cat@catech.com
www.neuralscope.com/

Critical Mass Enterprises LLC
James P. McGrew
5756 NW 120th Terrace
Coral Springs, FL 33076
Phone: 954-344-8180
Email: pmcgrew@myacc.net

Currenzo
Charles Villeneuve
7A Camborne Road
Singapore, Singapore 299859
Phone: [65] 91187064
Email: charles@villeneuve.net
www.currenzo.com/

Custom Trading Solutions, Inc.
Brian R. Bell
5930 Logan Street
Littleton, CO 80121
Phone: 303-730-3388
Fax: 303-730-3389
Email: bbell@customtradingsolutions.com
www.customtradingsolutions.com/

D

Day Trader Wanna Be
Michael Taivalmaa
932 E. Evergreen Drive
Kaukauna, WI 54130
Phone: 920-450-6961
Email: mike.taivalmaa@daytraderwannabe.com

DBTrader Services
Sean Beebe
4676 Commercial Street SE
#98
Salem, OR 97302
Phone: 503-569-0457
Email: sean@dbtrader.com
www.dbtrader.com/

DEL Associates Ltd.
Dale Glaspie
4342 NW Claymont Drive
Kansas City, MO 64116-1675
Phone: 800-453-9080
Email: dglaspie@kc.rr.com
http://cupwatch.com/

Derivalores, S.A.
10000 NW 25th Street
Suite 1-L
Miami, FL 33172
Phone: 419-793-7350
www.derivalorex.webs.com/

Derivative Concepts Inc.
Matthew Reynolds
7635 Avila Drive
Sparks, NY 89436
Phone: 626-808-7546
Email: derivativeconceptsinc@gmail.com

Dimension Trader, Inc.
Michael Green
11270 Terwilligers Valley
Suite 101
Cincinnati, OH 45249
Phone: 513-277-0305
Fax: 877-485-7687
Email: fibbal@confluencezones.com
http://traderusa.net/trader/

Dynamic Trading Bars
Robert Cherry
3068 Crown Heron Point
Venice, FL 34293
Phone: 941-323-4389
EMail: robottrader@comcast.net
www.dynamictradingbars.com/

E

E.I.I Capital Group
Trupti Patel
4480-H South Cobb Drive #230

Smyrna, GA 30082
Phone: 678-389-9053
Email: mpatel@eiicapital.com
www.eiicapital.com/

ECF Company
Stan Ehrlich
111 Pine Street Suite 1300
San Francisco, CA 94111
Phone: 415-433-8888
Fax: 415-433-8880
Email: stan@stanehrlich.com
www.stanehrlich.com/

EdgePlayerTrading
James Carlson
61 Maxwelton Road
Piedmont, CA 946108
Phone: 510-658-9107
Email: edgeplayer@edgeplayertrading.com
www.edgeplayertrading.com/

Elite E Services
Joseph James Gelet
2620 Regatta Drives Suite 102
Las Vegas, NV 89128
Phone: 646-837-0059
Email: info@ees.net.nz

ETA, LLC
Dale Kazdan
3317 N Claremont Avenue
Suite 2
Chicago, IL 60618
Phone: 586-323-9941
Email: motowndale@hotmail.com

EXC Global
Doug Goeckel
1912 Cherry Road
Oswego, IL 60543
Phone: 630-554-6212
Email: doug@excglobal.com

F

Financial Software Systems, Inc.
Duane Davis
987 Howard Moore Road
Hot Springs, NC 28743
Phone: 828-622-7717
Fax: 828-622-9558
Email: duanedavis@starband.net
www.marketstudies.com/

Financial Trading, Inc.
Dr. Alexander Elder
Phone: 718-507-1033
Email: info@elder.com
www.elder.com/

Fitzgerald Enterprises Inc.
Michael Fitzgerald
12004 Cottonwood Creek Blvd
Kennewick, WA 99338
Phone: 509-628-1511
Email: mpfitz@charter.net

Futures Group, Inc. (The)
Scott Krieger
P.O. Box 131
Leeds, MA 01053
Email: support@about-online-trading.com
www.about-online-trading.com/

G

GannStation
Christopher Cheetham
6541 Winton Street
Dallas, TX 75214
Email: info@GannStation.com

Gladiator Trading Systems
Ghulam Raza Manekia
6590 Valinda Avenue
Alta Loma, CA 91737
Phone: 909-228-1991
Fax: 877-902-9761
Email: grmanekia@msn.com

Good Faith, LLC
Dwain Sachs
HC 1 Box 312
Silva, MO 63964
Phone: 573-224-3366
Fax: 573-224-3367
Email: dsachs@direcway.com
www.thesystemtrader.com/

GridTrader
Alfred Morrissette
17 Alvina Avenue
San Raphael, CA 94901-4926
Phone: 707-938-9164
Email: grid22@gridtrader.com

H

Harrington Trading Company
Neil Harrington
558 E. 3125 North
Provo, UT 84604-4244
Phone: 801-369-6133
Fax: 801-373-4946
Email: njh@iname.com

Harvest Investor
Terry Nash
2076 Valley View Road
Joelton, TN 37080
Phone: 615-876-6634
Email: goforut@yahoo.com

Hawkeye Trading Company UK
Bob Saeger
9 Old Park Avenue
London, United Kingdom SW12 8rh
Phone: [44] 2086758082
Email: bobsaeger@btinternet.com

HeartBeat International Enterprise Corporation
Rolf Pilz
430 Clifton Road
N-Box 1086 St A
Kelowna, BC V1Y 7P8
Phone: 250-862-1915
Fax: 250-862-1915
Email: Info@HeartBeatTrading.com
www.heartbeattrading.com/

Hencorp Becstone Financial Services, L.C.
Victor Henriquez
777 Brickell Avenue Suite 1010
Miami, FL 33131

Phone: 305-373-9000
Email: vhenriquez@hencorp.com
www.hencorp.com/

I

Impressive Publishing
Louis Wayne Delph
1400 E. Shipley Ferry Road
Kingsport, TN 37663
Phone: 800-208-1977
Fax: 423-239-3090
Email: wd@imppub.com
www.formsboss.com/

Inside Edge Systems Inc.
William Brower
200 Broad Street
#2350
Stamford, CT 06901
Phone: 203-454-2754
Fax: 203-286-1321
Email: 1000mileman@mindspring.net
www.insideedge.net/

Inspired Trading Systems
Paul Sigalos
421 67th Avenue
Laval, PQ H7V 2M2
Phone: 450-687-9787
Email: info@inspiredtradingsystems.com
www.inspiredtradingsystems.com/

IsoSoft Solutions LLC
Carl Mohrbacher
79 W. Monroe
Chicago, IL 60603
Phone: 847-679-0427 x105
Email: carlm@isosoftsol.com
www.isosoftsol.com

J

JAM Strategy Trading
Martin Millar
12 Derby Road
Maidstone, United Kingdom ME15 7JB
Phone: US 845-704-7179
UK: (0207) 193-6073
Fax: 845-704-7179
Email: support@jamstrategytrading.com
www.jamstrategytrading.com/

Jan Arps' Traders' Toolbox
Jan Louis Arps
534 Lindley Road
Greensboro, NC 27410
Phone: 336-282-1237
Fax: 336-282-7213
Email: jarps@triad.rr.com
www.janarps.com/main/

Joe Krutsinger, CTA
Joe Krutsinger
PO Box 4223
Kansas City, KS 66104
Phone: 913-334-2002
Fax: 888-455-4612
Email: joekrut@aol.com
http://etrackrecords.com/

Jurik Research Software
Mark Jurik
686 S. Arroyo Parkway
Suite 237
Pasadena, CA 91105
Phone: 323-258-4860
Fax: 323-258-0598
Email: mark_omega@jurikres.com
www.jurikres.com/

JW Associates
John Waugh
631 Mt. Lebanon Road
Wilmington, DE 19803-1707
Phone: 302-479-5860
Fax: 302-478-9942
Email: jbsw7@comcast.net

K

Kase & Company
Cynthia Kase
3920 Snyder Avenue
Cheyenne, WY 82001
Phone: 505-237-1600
Fax: 505-237-1659
Email: kase@kaseco.com
www.kaseco.com/

Keener Capital Management, LLC
Robert F Keener III
294 N Hillside Road
Hendersonville, NC 28791
Phone: 828-692-4230
Fax: 828-692-7375
Email: rob@keenercapital.com

Keypoint Market Analytics, Inc
Joe Duffy
1514 Skyline Drive
Mississauga, Canada L5E2W5
Phone: 905-278-4048
Email: keypoint@sympatico.ca
www.keypointtrading.com/

Knight Research
Kirk Robichaux
131 Mockingbird Lane
Sunset, LA 70584
Phone: 337-662-6352
Email: krobichaux@centurytel.net

L

Linetrol Development
Lukasz Kozuch
Email: linetrol@gmail.com
www.linetrol.com/

LongTermTrading.com
Alan Pryor
2736 Brentwood Place
Davis, CA 95616
Phone: 530-758-6969
Email: ozone21@att.net
www.longtermtrading.com/

M

Marshall Sass Software
Marshall Sass
9417 Great Hills Trail #3036

Austin, TX 78759
Phone: 512-338-4791
Email: msass@austin.rr.com

Mathematicus Laboratories, LLC
Tim Hatamian
P.O. Box 1296
Sound Beach, NY 11789-0972
Phone: 718-832-6348
Fax: 810-583-6318
Email: mlTrade@mathematicuslabs.com
www.mathematicuslabs.com/OmegaLib.html

MESA Software
John Frederick Ehlers
6595 Buckley Drive
Cambria, CA 93428
Phone: 800-633-6372
Fax: 805-969-1358
Email: ehlers@mesasoftware.com
www.mesasoftware.com/

Micro-Labs, Inc.
Ted Carter
204 Lost Canyon Court
Richardson, TX 75080
Phone: 972-234-5842
Fax: 972-234-5896
Email: sales@microlabs.com
www.microlabs.com/trade.html

MoneyMentor.com
Sunny J. Harris
1547 Mission Meadows Drive
Oceanside, CA 92057
Phone: (760) 908-3070
Skype: (760) 444-4174
Fax: (760) 859-3057
Email: sunny@moneymentor.com
www.moneymentor.com

MPHoldings Corp.
Michael Bourque
36 Buckingham Road
Norwood, MA 02062
Phone: 617-685-9126
Email: Eminidaytrading@aol.com
www.stacktrade.com/

N

Neal Goldstein
659 Tennyson Avenue
Palo Alto, CA 94301
Phone: 650-327-4565
Email: neal@nealgolstein.com

Newport Coast Capital Corp.
Tim Cho
620 Newport Center Drive
Suite 1100
Newport Beach, CA 92660
Phone: 800.883.9621
Email: info@nccptl.com

Nexgen Software Services Inc.
John Novak
3400 Research Forest Drive
Suite B-9
The Woodlands, TX 77381
Phone: 281-298-9918
Fax: 281-298-9533
Email: johnnovak@nexgent3.com
www.nss-t3.com/

North Dallas Asset Management
David Bean
Preston Oaks, Suite 624
Dallas, TX 75254
Phone: 214-498-5029
Fax: 866-702-8489
Email: david@sp-trader.com
www.sp-trader.com/

Northington Trading
Kirk Northington
9538 Alice McGinn Drive
Charlotte, NC 28277
Phone: 704-542-0156
Email: admin@metaswing.com
www.metaswing.com/

NPA Futures Inc.
John Bonin
1440 Camper View G-72
San Dimas, CA 91773
Phone: 909-630-3368
Fax: 413-674-6154
Email: talkingtools@verizon.net
www.talkingtools.com/

O

Okorofsky, Stuart
Stuart Okorofsky
P.O. Box 23 Old Country Road #1
Rosendale, NY 12472
Phone: 845-658-9706
Fax: 845-658-9853
Email: krofs@aol.com
www.okor.com/

P

Petros Development Corporation
Peter B. Waite
9450 SW 77 Avenue #Q4
Miami, FL 33156
Phone: 305-270-9767
Fax: 305-574-7817
Email: petros1000@msn.com
www.andromedafutures.com/

Pivot Research & Trading Company
Jim White
3203 Provence Place
Thousand Oaks, CA 91362
Phone: 805-493-4221
Fax: 806-493-4349
Email: pivottrader@pivottrader.com
www.pivottrader.com/

PMKing Trading, LLC
Paul King
10 Seymour Street, Suite B
Middlebury, VT 05753
Phone: 802-349-9501
Email: public@pmkingtrading.com
www.pmkingtrading.com/

Pounds, Jonathan
Jonathan Pounds
2917 Lake Drive
Lake Stevens, WA 98258
Phone: 425-397-7828
Email: JonPounds@comcast.net

PowerSwings
Teresa Lo
227 Bellevue Way NE #211
Bellevue, WA 98004
Phone: 206-331-4451
Email: tlo@powerswings.com
http://invivoanalytics.com/

PowerZone Trading
Lee Leibfarth
250 High Valley Road
Bryson City, NC 28713
Phone: 828-488-5604
Email: info@powerzonetrading.com
www.powerzonetrading.com/

Professional Software Solutions
Burkhard Eichberger
301 Malley Drive #321
North Glen, CO 80233-2045
Email: pss@pobox.com
www.profsoftware.com/

Programmers Plus, Inc.
Glenn Canavan
19700 Belmont Drive
Miami, FL 33157
Phone: 305-216-4028
Email: glenn@programmersplus.com
www.programmersplus.com/

Progster's Purple Unity
Steve Johns
21 Lakeside Drive
Greenbelt, MD 20770-1973
Phone: 301-345-1548
Email: steve.johns@verizon.net

PsyTrade
Carlos Correia
5/9 Wilson's Ramp
Prince Edwards Road
Gibraltar
Phone: [00] 35020072021
Email: psytrade@gibtelecom.net

Q

Quantum Trading Analytics
Claude Chauveau
P.O. Box 1836
Beaverton, OR 97075
Phone: 503-690-8106
Fax: 503-690-8253
Email: cjc@teleport.com

R

Rick Saidenberg
35 Tamarack Way
Pleasantville, NY 10570
Phone: 914-925-0200
Fax: 914-925-0202
Email: ricksaidenberg@spitfire.net

RSKsys International
Roderic Kuusinen
9393 E. Atlantic Place
Denver, CO 80231
Phone: 303-750-8234
Email: spooman@comcast.net
www.rsksys.com/

Ruggiero Press
Murray Ruggiero
18 Oregon Ave., East Haven, CT 06512
(203) 564-1956

S

S&P Scalper Software
Gregory Richards
1510 Ventana Drive
Escondido, CA 92029
Phone: 760-739-5526
Email: sales@ScalperSoftware.com
www.scalpersoftware.com/

Sacred Chao
Marc Aniballi
66 rue des Hortensias
Salon de Provence
Bouches du Rhone 13300
Phone: [33] 617791586
FRANCE
Email: max@sacred-chao.net

Saks, Philip
Philip Saks
Vitus Berings Alle 6
Klampenborg, DK 2930
Phone: [45] 26139078
Email: philipsaks@email.dk

Scalper Ltd.
Franco Dimuccio
14 Victoria Mews
Keighley, W. York BD212SF
Phone: [44] 1535669338
Email: franco@scalper.co.uk

Scientific Software Inc.
Philip Baulch
218 Main Street
Nettleton, MI 38858
Phone: 662-963-2854
Email: info@sssi2000.com

SignalExpress.com
Rob Mitchell
6631 Fiona Place
Carlsbad, CA 92009
Phone: 760-476-9301
Email: Support@SignalExpress.com

SirTrade International
Pierre Orphelin
110 avenue du President Wilson
Montreuil, FR 93100
Phone: [33] 142874074
Fax: [33] 142873081
Email: sales@sirtrade.com
www.sirtrade.com/default0.htm

Smartetrades.com
David Nelson
2745 Whittleby Court

Westchester, PA 19382
Phone: 877-467-6278
Email: dnelson@smartetrades.com
www.smartetrades.com/

Software Engineering
Frank H. Ritz
Wolkerweg 4
Munich, Bavaria, Germany 81375
Phone: [49] 1792292658
Email: ritz@info-d.com
www.info-d.com/

SR Enterprises
Steve Richards
1872 N. Clybourn Suite 101
Chicago, IL 60614
Phone: 773-918-2274
Email: srdiamond@yahoo.com

StratOpt, Inc
Greg Ballard
3204 Old Excelsior Road
Greenwood, AR 72936
Phone: 479-461-3798
Email: easylanguage@stratopt.com
www.stratopt.com/

Sunny Harris Enterprises, Inc.
Sunny J. Harris
1547 Mission Meadows Drive
Oceanside, CA 92057
Phone: 760-908-3070
Fax: 760-859-3057
Email: sunny@moneymentor.com
www.moneymentor.com

SystemFrame.com, LLC
Festus Redelinghuys
9417 Great Hills Trail
Apt 1074
Austin, TX 78759
Phone: 512-345-7896
Email: email@systemframe.com

T

Tandy, Robert
Robert Tandy
50 Old Country Road
Elmsford, NY 10523-2056
Phone: 914-329-3430
Email: btandy@optonline.net

TCI Corporation
Tim Cho
5267 Warner Avenue Suite 107
Huntington Beach, CA 92649
Phone: 800-883-9621
Fax: 714-845-1920
Email: info@nccptl.com

Ted Hearne Associates, Inc.
Ted Hearne
4509 North Dover Street
Chicago, IL 60640
Phone: 800-552-2317
Email: Ted@Tedtick.com
www.tedtick.com/

Telephone Support Services
Bill Soloman
2076 Valley View Road
Joelton, TN 37080
Phone: 615-876-6634
Email: bill@billsoloman.com

The Lloyd/Harvey Corporation
Harvey Gand
75-5591 Hienaloli Road #9
Kailua-Kona, HI 96740
Phone: 808-331-8655
Email: customerservice@islandbounty.com

The Pattern Trapper
Robert M. Hunt
16445 Linch Avenue
Lakeville, MN 55044
Phone: 952-892-5550
Email: rhunt@patterntrapper.com
www.patterntrapper.com/#

The Penmacsar Group
Maceo Jourdan
5501 N. 7th Avenue #732
Phoenix, AZ 85013
Phone: 602-510-9800
Fax: 530-688-8792
Email: mjourdan@cox.net

The Roy Funds
Jeffrey Roy
822 West Washington Blvd.
Chicago, IL 60607
Phone: 800-929-5600
Fax: 312-563-8140
Email: jeff.roy@royfunds.com

The Trading Room
Ricardo Lazoff
20201 E Country Club Edr Apt 1710
Aventura, FL 33180
Phone: 787-424-5007
Email: rlazoff@gmail.com

The Trading Tutor, LLC
Michael Charness
10027 Shadow Wood Drive
Huntsville, AL 35803
Phone: 256-882-7117
Email: info@tradetutor.com
www.tradetutor.com/

Tigga Trading
Nils Kahle
Hornschuchpromenade 16a
Fuerth, 90762
Germany
Email: tigga@tigga-trading.com

Tom Batchelor
Tom Batchelor
2601 Midway Branch Drive #201
Odenton, MD 21113
Phone: 410-305-8419
Email: tom_batchelor@hotmail.com

Tomato Springs Software
Bill Conley
28 Bloomdale, Suite 100
Irvine, CA 92614
Phone: 949-679-7842
Fax: 309-437-7099

Email: bill.conley@tomatosprings.com
www.slebaron.typepad.com/

Trade Robot Ltd.
Josip Papic
Smrecnikova 19
Novo Mesto, Slovenia 8000
Phone: [1] 38641714511
Email: josip@traderobot.com

Trade Smart Research Ltd.
Vladislav Gorbunov
5 Noliktavas Str.
Riga LV 1010
Phone: 371-968-2700
Fax: 371-732-4544
Email: info@tsresearchgroup.com
www.tsresearchgroup.com/

Trader4X, LLC
Robert Mackovski
100 West Beaver Road, Suite 200
Troy, MI 48084
Phone: 734-676-8234
Email: Info@Trader4X.com
www.trader4x.com/

Traders Software
Michael Mermer
Parkland, FL 33076
Phone: 954-753-0199
Email: support@traderssoftware.com
www.traderssoftware.com/

Trading System Lab
Mike Barna
140 Old Orchard Drive
Los Gatos, CA 95032
Phone: 408-356-1800
Email: tsda@comcast.net
www.tradingsystemlab.com/

Trading Systems Club
Richard Aubin
625 Atwater S-6
Montreal, PQ H3J 2T8
Phone: 514-567-8678
Email: richard@trading-systems-club.com

TradingMagic
Stanley Moore
34 Avenida Fiori
Henderson, NV 89011
Phone: 800-686-0833
Fax: 775-851-7182
Email: Easyryhthm@aol.com
www.rhythmofthemarkets.com/

TradingMentors.com
Dan Wurl
2020 Bloomsbury Run
Heathrow, FL 32746
Phone: 877-687-3704
Email: danwrl@prodigy.net
www.tradingmentors.com/

TradingVisions
Lincoln Fiske
7321 N. Altamont Street
Spokane, WA 99217-7737
Phone: 509-466-8435
Email: systems@tradingvisions.com
www.tradingvisions.com/

Tradology
Robert Mackovski
100 West Beaver Road, Suite 200
Troy, MI 48084
Phone: 734-676-8234
Email: info@tradology.com
www.tradology.com/

TrendAdvisor
Chuck Dukas
8 Beach Street
Westboro, MA 01581
Phone: 508-841-4195
Email: info@trendadvisor.com
www.trendadvisor.com/

TrendMedium
Eugene Labunsky
Katukove 22/1 248
Moscow, Russian Federation 123183
Phone: [49] 8324 933977
Email: elabunsky@trendmedium.com
www.trendmedium.com/

Triage Corporation Ltd.
Amy Huang
15B Granville House, 41C Granville Road
Tsim Sha Tsui, Kowloon, Hong Kong
Phone: 415-671-6286
Fax: 415-520-1469
Email: support@triagetrading.com
http://triagetrading.com/

Triangle Trading
Peter Schmid
Altgasse 9
Wien, AU 1130
Phone: [44] 7092805099
Email: support@triagetrading.com
http://triagetrading.com/

TS Leasing Group Inc.
Wayne Harrison
2524 N.E. 48th Court
Lighthouse Point, FL 33064
Phone: 561-963-8155
Email: kwikpop@kwikpop.com
www.kwikpop.com/

Turning Point Research Corp.
Dave Poxon
840 Sundance Circle
Oshawa, ON Canada L1J 8B4
Phone: 905-436-0441
Email: dpoxon@turningpointresearch.com
www.turningpointresearch.com/

TurnSignal
Jim Shane
2840 Highway
Alt S #7
Silver Springs, NV 89429
Phone: 678-560-5980
Email: jim@turnsignal.biz
http://www.turnsignal.biz/

Turtle Trader
Russell Sands
17927 Foxborough Lane

Boca Raton, FL 33496
Phone: 561-477-6259
Fax: 561-477-6260
Email: turtltalk@aol.com
www.turtletrading.com/

U

UEB.Trading
Robert Uberbacher
Haussnummer 20
Unterperfuss, A6175
Austria
Phone: [43] 52322560
Fax: [43] 523220015
Email: ru@uebtrading.com

V

Volume Hunter
Nigel Hawkes
Clematis Cottage St. James St.
Yarmouth, PO41 ONU, UK
Email: team1@hawkeyetraders.com
www.hawkeyetraders.com/

W

Walter Bressert, Inc.
William Bressert
Vero Beach, FL
Phone: 520-777-0012
Email: teresa@walterbressert.com

Wright, David
David Wright
33 Fourwinds Road
London, ON N6K 3L1
Phone: 519-668-2220
Email: dwright@ody.ca

X

XY Financial Group, LLC
Lisa Xu
130 S. Canal Street, Suite 820
Chicago, IL 60606
Phone: 312-906-8556
Email: info@bestesignal.com

APPENDIX I

TradeStation User Groups

There is no longer such a thing as a true TradeStation User Group, where users are supported in their activities by Omega Research, which no longer exists. Still, there are traders' groups that meet regularly and gather to exchange ideas and information and to enhance their trading skills and abilities. They often discuss many other trading programs, and few are dedicated strictly to TradeStation. But, still, they are a great way to meet other traders and exchange thoughts and questions.

Most user groups complement their meetings with guest speakers and informative presentations. Membership standards and requirements are determined by the individual groups.

For the convenience of users of TradeStation products and readers of this book, this appendix lists the active user groups at the time of this printing. If you are looking for a user group in your area and one is not listed herein, please contact me at 1.760.908.3070.

The information in this appendix was made available by RINA's Web site, www.tradestationzone.com. Please check there for updates.

CITY	LEADER	PHONE	EMAIL	WEB SITE

CALIFORNIA

Active Traders Users Group

Los Angeles	Fari Hamzei	(310) 306-1200	Fari@ActiveTraders.org	www.ActiveTraders.org

Active Traders Users Group meets every third Saturday of the month at the Brentwood-Bel Air Holiday Inn Hotel, centrally located at 170 North Church Lane in West Los Angeles. Tel: (310) 476-6411 (310) 476-6411

Palm Springs

Palm Springs, Coachella Vly		(760) 772-0446	plperk@msn.com	

79325 Camino Rosada, La Quinte, CA 92253

San Diego Trader Group

San Diego	Greg Meyer	(619) 449-3957	futures@home.com	

The San Diego Trader Group meets first Saturday of every month from 9 am to 12 pm at the Tierrasanta Recreation Center, 11220 Clairemont Mesa Blvd. 92124. The group has speakers or members presenting. We use a large screen and are set up for presentations. There is $25 initiation fee and $5/meeting. Speakers are encouraged to submit their agenda in advance. There about 50 members with an average attendance of 20.

Santa Clarita Valley

Santa Clarita Vly	Bob Copeland	(661) 288-2029	racope320@aol.com	

The Santa Clarita Valley User Group holds meetings on the first Saturday of the month. The meetings are held at 10:00 am. This group is nonprofit; there are no membership fees or dues.

Southern California Traders Association

Walnut	Bruce Arnheim	(310) 416-7293	bruce.arnheim@aero.org	

Meetings are held on the first Saturday morning of each month at Mt. San Antonio College in Walnut Ca. Bldg 11, Room 6. Our meetings typically feature guest lecturers and members talking about various trading techniques and methods. The focus of our group is on trading and technical analysis of the markets. Meetings start at 8:30 am and end around 11:30 am.

The first meeting is held on the First Saturday of each month. This meeting typically features guest lecturers and members talking about different trading techniques and methods. Meeting time is 8:30 am until about 11:30 am and breakfast can be ordered from the menu.

The second meeting is held on the third Thursday of each month. This meeting focuses on using technical analysis tools and techniques. Ideally, we try to apply and test the concepts that were discussed at the Saturday meeting. The format is intended to be less formal and more interactive. Meeting time is 6:30 pm until about 9 pm and dinner can be ordered from the menu, gratuity is included.

CANADA

Alberta Canada Group

Canmore	Cliff Atkinson	(403) 678-2093	catkins@telusplanet.net	

405 Canyon Close, Canmore, AB T1W144

FLORIDA

Gainsville User Group

Ray Haufler (352) 376-3336 cash@starban.net
Route 3 Box 24, Hawthorne, FL 32640

Key West Omega User Group

Larry Johnson (305) 443-0377 ljohn@spreenet.com
21052 6th Ave, Kudjoe Key, FL 33042

Miami User Group

Miami Robert Valdes trade00@bellsouth.net
2310 S West 26th St, Miami, FL 33133

The Miami User group holds meetings once a month with an average attendance of 25 members. The group is nonprofit; there are no membership fees or dues.

Sarasota S&C Trading Group

Sarasota Sunny Decker (941) 747-5858 sunnydecker@juno.com
2112 39th West St, Bradenton, FL

The Sarasota S&C Trading Group meets regularly on Saturdays at 10:00 am at the Selby Library in Sarasota. Your first visit is free; there is a $25 per year membership fee if you would like to join. We have members and speakers presenting and encourage people who are interested in speaking at the meeting to submit agendas in advance. There are about 400 members with an average attendance of 75 to 80.

South Florida User Group

Ft Lauderdale Leonard Steinman (800) 858-2340 leonard@angusjackson.com

Join our trading and investing strategies club with monthly meetings in Ft. Lauderdale, Florida. This is a volunteer organization and is dedicated to providing its members with current information on a wide variety of investment subjects. We strive to present knowledgeable, national and local speakers who present interesting and informed discussions on their specific areas of expertise. You can find the postings of FTL-CIN meetings on the calendar as well as several other local investment clubs meetings (Metastock Usergroup, TradeStation Usergroup, VectorVest, AAII, US Investors Club, TC2000 Usergroup, and others).

GERMANY

Germany Omega User Group

Jo Haas +49 7138 94110-39 omegagroup@tradernet.de
Frankenstrasse 14, Schwaigern, D-74193, Germany

The Omega User Group Germany consists of five regional groups located in Frankfurt, Berlin, Munich, Duesseldorf, and Hamburg. Each group has its own specific schedule but commonly meets every four to six weeks. You can find specifics and meeting times and dates on the groups' Web site. There are speakers and members presenting, and we encourage people who are interested in speaking at the meeting to submit agendas in advance. The group is nonprofit; there are no membership fees or dues.

ILLINOIS

Chicago

Striker TradeStation User Group Chicago

Chicago William Gallwas (312) 987-0043 william@striker.com

Chigago Board of Trade Bldg, 37th Flr, 141 W Jackson #3706, Chicago, IL 60604

Striker Securities, Inc.—"Striker"—was established 1991. It has been hosting a Chicago-based user group on TradeStation software since 1994. Striker principal William Gallwas, a former member of the Chicago Board of Trade, organzies these meetings about once a month in and around the Chicago area. William is a former featured speaker at Omega World in Las Vegas and New York on behalf of TradeStation. Within Striker's offices are about a half-dozen TradeStations running. As Striker is located in the Chicago Board of Trade Building, world's oldest and largest Exchange, people interested in learning more about TradeStation and seeing the software live often visit Striker's offices. In addition to learning about TradeStation, visitors can also enjoy a floor tour conducted by William, thanks to his Exchange membership. Contact Striker (www.striker.com) for more information. Striker is a proud user of TradeStation technology and software and has a lot of respect for TradeStation as a company and its people.

Wizards of the Roundtable

Chicago William Gallwas (312) 987-0043 william@striker.com

Wizards of the Roundtable is the largest user group in the Midwest and perhaps in the country. The user group has a mailing list of 425 persons and a Yahoo club site membership of about 145 persons. The group is nonprofit, there are no membership fees or dues. We meet about once a month in a library, coffee shop, bar or brewery. About 80% of the members use the trading software Omega's TradeStation. The group is open to the public—anyone can join! To find out more, join the Yahoo club site. Wizards is now live online via a yahoo study group. For information e-mail william@striker.com.

INDIANA

Noblesville Bill Werier (317) 877-7753 bwerler@home.com

844 Dorchester Dr., Noblesville, IN 46060

The Indy TradeStation User Group meets twice a month for lunch. There is an initial membership fee of $29. There are about 20 members with an average attendance of 6.

MASSACHUSETTS

Boston User Group

Westboro Chuck Dukas (508) 366-6102 chuck@trendadvisor.com

8 Beach St, Westboro, MA 01581

The Boston TradeStation User Group meets on the second Tuesday of every month at 6:30 pm to 8:30 pm at the MIT Sloan Building, Cambridge MA. The group regularly has speakers. There is no initial membership fee but there is a $15 charge per meeting. There are about 250 members with an average attendance of at least 60.

MICHIGAN

Detroit User Group

Detroit Al Stalter (248) 362-2650 astalter@maximumfinancial.com

The Detroit User Group holds monthly meetings on either a Tuesday or Thursday of ever month at 7:00 pm. The group is a nonprofit organization; there are no membership fees or dues. There are about 100 members with an average attendance of 25.

West Michigan User Group

Don Eerdmans (616) 534-0494 deerdmans@aol.com

MISSOURI

San Antonio User Group

San Antonio Don Schnyder (210) 223-5807 dschnyder@satx.rr.com

The San Antonio User Group meets on the third Wednesday of every month around 7:00 pm. We have speakers and members presenting and encourage people who are interested in speaking at the meeting to submit agendas in advance. The group is nonprofit; there are no membership fees or dues. There are about 20 members with an average attendance of 15.

St. Louis Omega User Group

Maryland Hts Al Perkins (314) 894-4847 APerk75329@aol.com

3004 Autumn Lakes Ct, Maryland Heights, MO 63043

The St. Louis Omega User Group meets on the second Saturday of every month. The group meets from 9:00 am to 10:00 am to discuss EasyLanguage; a general meeting runs from and 10:00 am to 12:00 noon. The group meets at Lindenwood University and regularly has speakers. There is a membership fee of $29 per year. There are about 38 members with an average attendance of at least 9.

NEBRASKA

Nebraska User Group

Lincoln Mike Berger (402) 488-5133 mlbne@cs.com

Lincoln, NB

NORTH CAROLINA

Carolinas Omega User Group

Hendersonville Rob Keener (828) 692-4230 keener@mezzaluna.net

815 Hillside Rd, Hendersonville, NC 28791

OHIO

Cincinnati Omega Research User Group

Mason Ronald M. Brandt (513) 459-4740 traderon@aol.com

400 W Main St, Mason, OH 45040

The Cincinnati Omega Research User Group meets on the second Thursday of each month at the New Horizons Computer Learning Center in Blue Ash. There is a membership fee of $100 per year if paid in advance or $10 per meeting. No meeting charge. There are no fees for the first six months. Members regularly give presentations and we bring in outside speakers two to three times per year. There are about 40 members with an average attendance of 40%.

OKLAHOMA

Tulsa Oklahoma User Group

Tulsa Lee Ray Smith (918) 252-4362 L.Smith7@gte.net
9019 S 73rd East Av, Tulsa, OK 74133

PENNSLYANIA

South Central Pennsylvania Omega User Group

York Ivan Fillmore (717) 792-9278 fillmores@cyberia.com
3985 W Market Av, York, PA 17404

The South Central Pennsylvania Omega User Group meets on third Thursday of each month around 7:00 pm. This is nonprofit organization; there are no membership fees or dues. We have members presenting and encourage people who are interested in speaking at the meeting to submit agendas in advance. There are about 20 members with an average attendance of 6.

Philadelphia

Omega Research User Group Mid-Atlantic

Philadelphia David Groom (215) 289-2028 yankee93@bellatlantic.net

VIRGINIA

Richmond Virginia Beach User Group

Richmond David Worstine (804) 359-9671 worstine@aol.com
2200 Stuart Ave, Richmond, VA 23220

The Richmond Virginia Beach User Group holds monthly meeting where both speakers and members present. The group is nonprofit; there are no membership fees or dues. There are 18 members with an average attendance of 10.

WASHINGTON D.C.

Washington DC TradeStation Users Group (WTSUG)

Bruce DeVault (301) 739-1701 bdevault@quantevo.com

The Washington DC TradeStation Users Group (WTSUG) generally meets on the third Wednesday of each month at Potomac Community Library. It has a website at www.wtsug.org.

WISCONSIN

Wisconsin User Group

Gerald Bodway (608) 833-4040 ggeorgeb@aol.com
Madison, WI

APPENDIX J

Error Messages

As a quick reference, I have included EasyLanguage's syntax errors here. You can find detailed explanations, with examples, in the EasyLanguage dictionary, (upper right menu bar in the EasyLanguage PowerEditor) under Error. This list is just that, a list. The details are not included here, just the cryptic messages.

61 "Word not recognized by EasyLanguage."
62 "Invalid number."
63 "Number out of range."
65 "Invalid variable name."
66 "Invalid input name."
70 "Array size cannot exceed 2 billion elements."
74 "Invalid array name."
90 "The first jump command must be a begin: (\\hb,\\pb,\\wb)"
91 "You cannot nest jump commands within other jump commands."
92 "You must terminate all jump commands with ends (\\he,\\pe,\\we)"
151 "This word has already been defined."
154 "=, <>, >, >=, <, <= expected here."
155 " '(' expected here."
157 "Arithmetic (numeric) expression expected here."
158 "An equal sign '=' expected here."
159 "This word cannot start a statement."
160 "Semicolon (;) expected here."
161 "The word THEN must follow an If condition."
162 "STOP, LIMIT, CONTRACTS, SHARES expected here."
163 "The word TO or DOWNTO was expected here."
165 "The word BAR or BARS expected here."
166 "The word AGO expected here."
167 " '}' was expected before end of file."

168 " '[' was expected here."
169 "']' was expected here."
170 "Assignment to a function not allowed."
171 "'A value was never assigned to user function."
172 "Either NUMERIC, TRUEFALSE, STRING, NUMERICSIMPLE, NUMERICSERIES, TRUEFALSESIMPLE, TRUEFALSESERIES, STRINGSIMPLE, or STRINGSERIES expected."
174 "Function not verified."
175 " ',' or ')' expected here."
176 "More inputs expected here."
177 "Too many inputs supplied."
180 "The word #END was expected before end of file."
181 "There can only be 10 dimensions in an array."
183 "More than 100 errors. Verify termination."
185 "Either HIGHER or LOWER expected here."
186 "Input name too long."
187 "Variable name too long."
188 "The word BEGIN expected here."
189 "This word not allowed in a strategy."
190 "This word not allowed in a function."
191 "This word not allowed in a study."
192 "This word not allowed in an ActivityBar."
193 "Comma (,) expected here."
195 "Matching quote is missing."
197 "Strategy not verified."
200 "Error found in function."
201 "User function cannot refer to current cell of itself."
204 "Orders cannot be inside a loop."
205 "Statement does not return a value."
208 "CONTRACTS, SHARES expected here."
209 "Signal name expected within quotes."
211 "Signal cannot call itself."
213 "Error found in strategy."
214 "Colon (:) expected here."
215 "Cannot use next bar's price and close order in the same strategy."
217 "Function circular reference found."
220 "Cannot anchor a global exit."
223 "A simple function cannot call itself."
224 "Signal name already used."
226 "Next bar's prices can only be used in a strategy."
227 "Default expected here."
229 "Invalid initial value."
230 "Initial value expected here."
231 "Function has no inputs. Parenthesis not needed."
232 "Matching left comment brace '{' is missing."
233 "Extra right parenthesis."
234 "END found without matching BEGIN."
237 "Position Information function not allowed in a study."

238 "Performance Information function not allowed in a study."

239 "Array name too long."

240 "This signal name does not exist."

241 "Cannot exit from an exit signal."

242 "Cannot exitshort from a buy signal."

243 "Cannot exitlong from a sell signal."

244 "At$ cannot be used after the word TOTAL."

247 "References to previous values are not allowed in simple functions."

248 "Either PUT, CALL, ASSETTYPE, or FUTURETYPE expected here."

250 "Cannot reference a previous value of a simple input."

251 "Variables and arrays not allowed here."

253 "Cannot reference a previous value of this input."

258 "Variables, arrays and inputs not allowed here."

260 " 'Next Bar' can only be applied to 'OPEN', 'DATE' and 'TIME'."

261 "The word 'BAR' expected here."

262 "At market order can only be placed for the next bar."

263 "Stop and limit orders can only be placed for the next bar."

264 "On close order must be placed for this bar."

265 "Cannot mix next bar prices with data streams other than data 1."

266 "Library name within double quotes expected here."

267 "DLL function name within double quotes expected here."

274 " Return type of this DLL function must be specified."

276 "DLL name cannot be longer than 60 characters."

277 "DLL function name cannot be longer than 65 characters."

278 "A variable expected here."

279 "An array expected here."

280 "TrueFalse expression expected here."

283 "Signal has no inputs. Comma not needed."

284 "There is no such strategy."

285 "Strategy circular reference found."

286 "Cannot divide by zero."

287 "File name expected here."

288 "A file or directory name must be <260 characters and may not contain "/ : * ? < > |"."

291 "The word 'OVER' or 'UNDER' expected here."

292 "Two constants cannot cross over each other."

293 "This plot has been defined using a different name."

296 "This plot has never been assigned a value."

297 "Server field name too long; cannot be more than 30 characters."

298 "Strategy Information (for plots) function not allowed in a strategy."

299 "Strategy Information function not allowed in a study."

300 "This plot has been defined with a different type."

302 "Different number of dimensions specified in the array than the parameter."

303 "Extraneous text is not allowed after the array-type parameter"

304 "Numeric-Array Parameter expected here."

305 "TrueFalse-Array Parameter expected here."

306 "String Array Parameter expected here."

307 "The word 'Cancel' must be followed by 'Alert'."

323 "'Value-type inputs' may not be passed into 'reference-type inputs'."
325 "Only an array, variable, or reference-input is allowed here"
340 "This word is only allowed when defining array-type inputs."
341 "An array input word (NUMERICARRAY, STRINGARRAY, TRUEFALSEARRAY, NUMERICARRAYREF, STRINGARRAYREF, TRUEFALSEARRAYREF) was expected here."
342 "This word can only be used in a PaintBar study."
396 "This statement cannot specify an odd number of plots."
403 "Cannot implicitly convert String to Numerical"
404 "Cannot implicitly convert String to TrueFalse"
405 "Cannot implicitly convert TrueFalse to String"
406 "Cannot implicitly convert Numerical to String"
407 "Cannot implicitly convert TrueFalse to Numerical"
408 "Cannot implicitly convert Numerical to TrueFalse"
409 "String expression expected here"
569 "Buy or Sell name within double quotes expected here."

APPENDIX K

What's Wrong with This Code?

The EasyLanguage code in each of the next problems will not verify. Why not? Cover up the answer while you study the code to see if you can find the error(s) on your own. This will be a very, very valuable exercise if you allow yourself the time to learn how to debug.

PROBLEM:

```
INPUTS: jLen1(2), jLen2(30);
Value1 = NthHighest(jLen, Close, jLen2);
Plot1(Value1);
```

ERROR MESSAGE(S):

Description	Line
',' or ')' expected here	2
unknown identifier	2

ANSWER:

In line 2, inside the first parenthesis, jLen should read jLen1.

PROBLEM:

```
Value1 = MinutesToTime(90);
Print(``MinutesToTime =``. Value1);
```

ERROR MESSAGE(S):

Description	Line
Semicolon (;) expected here	2
',' or ')' expected here.	2
value1 is not a member of class elsystem	2

ANSWER:
In line 2, right before Value1, there is a period where it should be a comma.

PROBLEM:

```
INPUTS: jLen(1);
If NthHighestBar(2,Close,25) <= 1
THEN BEGIN
      Value1 = NthHighestBar(2, Close, 25);
      Plot1(Close, 'NH');
END
ELSE
      NoPlot(1);
```

ERROR MESSAGE(S):

Description	Line
Semicolon (;) expected here.	5
The word END was expected before end. . .	5
Semicolon (;) expected here.	5
Plot name expected here.	5

ANSWER:
In line 4, the quotation marks are single quotes(') where they should be double quotes (").

PROBLEM:

```
//Pivot(Price, Length, LeftStrength, RightStrength, Instance,
       HiLo, oPivotPrice, oPivotBar)

Vars: oPivotPrice(0), oPivotBar(0);
Value1 = Pivot(Low,21,2,2,1,-1,oPivotPrice,oPivotBar);
Value2 = oPivotPrice;
Value3 = oPivotbar;

Print(D:8:0,," ", T:4:0, " PivotPrice= ",Value2,
" PivotBar= ", Value3);
If Value1 = 1
THEN BEGIN
Plot1(Value2);
END
ELSE
       NoPlot(1);
```

ERROR MESSAGE(S):

Description	Line
This plot has never been assigned a value	12
Semicolon (;) expected here.	8
',' or ')' expected here.	8
Arithmetic (numeric) expression expect. . .	8

ANSWER:
In line 8, the print statement, there are two commas after the Date designation, where there should only be one comma.

PROBLEM:

```
if C ShootingStar(14, 2) = 1 then
   Plot1(Close, "ShootingStar");
```

ERROR MESSAGE(S):

Description	Line
This plot has never been assigned a value	2
Semicolon (;) expected here.	1
The word THEN must follow an if condit. . .	1
Cannot implocitly convert Numerical to . . .	1

ANSWER:
In line 1, the underscore character is missing between the C and the S in C_ShootingStar, the function name.

PROBLEM:

```
Value1 = Skew(Close, 100);
Plot(Value1);
```

ERROR MESSAGE(S):

Description	Line
This plot name has never been defined	2
Semicolon (;) expected here.	1
This word cannot start a statement.	2

ANSWER:
The plot statement needs a number after the word plot. Line 2 should read Plot1(Value1);

PROBLEM:

```
Value1 = TypicalPrice;
Plot1(Value1, "AvgPrc");
Error Message(s):
```

ERROR MESSAGE(S):

Description	Line
Semicolon (;) expected here.	2
Plot name expected here.	2

ANSWER:

The quotes in line 2 are what is gotten from a cut-and-paste from the manuscript. The quotes are not acceptable to TradeStation. You must replace them with double quotes from your keyboard.

PROBLEM:

```
Print(FILE("C:\temp\profit.txt", Date:9:0, " ", Time:4:0,
NetProfit);
```

ERROR MESSAGE(S):

Description	Line
")" expected here.	1
Semicolon (;) expected here.	1

ANSWER:

The right paren is missing at the end of the FILE command. The single line of code should look like this:

```
Print(FILE("C:\temp\profit.txt"), Date:9:0, " ", Time:4:0,
NetProfit);
```

PROBLEM:

```
If MarketPosition = 1 Then Begin
      Sell next bar ("Long profit") at 1.038 * EntryPrice limit;
        Sell next bar ("Long loss") at 0.99 * EntryPrice stop;
        If Close > 1.014 * EntryPrice Then
           Sell ("Long prot") next bar at 1.014 * EntryPrice stop;
End;
```

ERROR MESSAGE(S):

Description	Line
unknown identifier	2
")" expected here	2
STOP, LIMIT, CONTRACTS, SHARES expected here.	2
Semicolon (;) expected here.	2
The word END was expected before end of file.	2
Semicolor (;) expected here.	2

ANSWER:

Look at this one very carefully. It took me a long time to find the problem. And, of course, once you see it, it is a simple solution.

The order statements are not in the correct sequence. The Sell Name needs to come before the "next bar" part of the order. The code should look like this:

```
If MarketPosition = 1 Then Begin
      Sell (''Long profit'') next bar at 1.038 * EntryPrice limit;
        Sell (''Long loss'') next bar at 0.99 * EntryPrice stop;
        If Close > 1.014 * EntryPrice Then
          Sell (''Long prot'') next bar at 1.014 * EntryPrice stop;
End;
```

It is a subtle, but critical, difference.

Bibliography

Achelis, Steven B. *Technical Analysis from A to Z*. New York: McGraw-Hill, 2001.

Bollinger, John. *Bollinger on Bollinger Bands*. New York: McGraw-Hill, 2001.

Brower, William. *TS Express™*. Westport, CT: Inside Edge Systems, 1999.

Brower, William. *EasyLanguage Programming, Learning by Example*. Westport, CT: Inside Edge Systems, 2010.

DeMark Tom *DeMark Indicators*. Bloomberg Press, 2008, New York.

Kase, Cynthia. *Trading with the Odds*. Irwin Professional, 1996.

Kaufman, Perry J. *New Trading Systems and Methods*. Hoboken, NJ: John Wiley & Sons, 2005.

LeBeau, Chuck. *Day Trading Systems and Methods*. Marketplace Books, 1999, Glenelg, MD.

Murphy, John J. *Technical Analysis of the Financial Markets*. New York: New York Institute of Finance, 1999.

Pring, Martin. *Technical Analysis Explained*. New York: McGraw-Hill, 2002.

Putt, Arthur G. *Using EasyLanguage*. East Haven, CT: Ruggiero Press, 2000.

Raschke, Linda, and Laurence A. Connors. *Street Smarts*. Marlton, NJ, M. Gordon Publishing Group, 1995.

Stridsman, Thomas. *Trading Systems That Work*. New York: McGraw-Hill, 2001.

Wilder, J. Welles, Jr. *New Concepts in Technical Trading Systems*. Trend Reseach, 1978, McLeansville, NC.

Williams, Larry. *The Definitive Guide to Futures Trading*. Solana Beach, CA: Windsor Books, 1988.

Index

T

Printed and bound by CPI Group (UK) Ltd, Croydon, CR0 4YY

16/04/2025

14658467-0002